HUMAN DEVELOPMENT
Across the Lifespan

SEVENTH EDITION

John S. Dacey
Boston College

John F. Travers
Boston College

Lisa Fiore
Lesley College

McGraw-Hill
Higher Education

Boston   Burr Ridge, IL   Dubuque, IA   New York   San Francisco   St. Louis
Bangkok   Bogotá   Caracas   Kuala Lumpur   Lisbon   London   Madrid   Mexico City
Milan   Montreal   New ~~Delhi~~   ~~Singapo~~re   Sydney   Taipei   Toronto

McGraw-Hill Higher Education

HUMAN DEVELOPMENT: ACROSS THE LIFESPAN

Published by McGraw-Hill, an imprint of The McGraw-Hill Companies, Inc., 1221 Avenue of the Americas, New York, NY 10020. Copyright © 2009 by The McGraw Hill Companies, Inc. All rights reserved. No part of this publication may be reproduced or distributed in any form or by any means, or stored in a database or retrieval system, without the prior written consent of The McGraw-Hill Companies, Inc., including, but not limited to, in any network or other electronic storage or transmission, or broadcast for distance learning.

Some ancillaries, including electronic and print components, may not be available to customers outside the United States.

This book is printed on acid-free paper.

2 3 4 5 6 7 8 9 0 QPD/QPD 0 9

ISBN: 0-07-128398-6

From John Dacey and John Travers: This book is dedicated with deep affection to the two people who have helped us the most

—Linda Dacey and Barbara Travers, our wives. From Lisa Fiore: To the people who have helped me develop the most

—Steve, Matthew, and Talia.

About the Authors

John S. Dacey, Ph.D., is professor at Boston College in the Department of Counseling, Developmental Psychology, and Research Methods. He began his career as a junior high social studies teacher. Now a college teacher and a researcher in adolescent and adult development, he is the author of 12 books and nearly 30 articles on parenting, creativity, and general human development. His most recently published book is entitled *Your Anxious Child*. He is currently finishing a book on parental techniques for promoting family cohesion.

John Travers has worked with young people all his professional life, beginning with his own four children. He has taught in elementary and high school and now teaches undergraduate and graduate students at Boston College, where, among a faculty of 1,000, he was recognized as one of eight outstanding teachers in the university. He has also been honored as Teacher of the Year. His undergraduate and graduate teaching has been in the field of developmental psychology. Teaching, counseling, and writing have been constant themes in his professional life. He has written 17 books and approximately 30 professional articles.

Lisa B. Fiore, Ph.D. is an Associate Professor and Director of Early Childhood Education at Lesley University. She primarily teaches graduate students preparing to be early childhood and elementary educators, but also enjoys working with in-service teachers around professional development. Recent interests include the use of documentation to extend and enhance learning environments (inspired by the Reggio Emilia approach to early childhood education), and the use of rich media in classroom teaching. The mother of two young children, she is reminded daily of the competence and curiosity of young people, and how much grown-ups have to learn about the way things work. She has written several books, the most recent *The Safe Child Handbook* with co-author John Dacey.

Brief Contents

part **8** Middle Adulthood

part **9** Late Adulthood

Table of Contents

Part 3 Infancy

Part 4 Early Childhood

**part 5 Middle
         Childhood**

part 6 Adolescence

part **7** Early Adulthood

part **8** Middle Adulthood

Preface

Two roads diverged in a wood, and I—
I took the one less traveled by,
And that has made all the difference.

These lines from a famous poem by Robert Frost express so well one of the main tasks of a lifetime: should we choose the safe, pragmatic path, or should we stick our necks out and go the unpopular way? Should we be a leader or a follower? Should we couch our opinions in ways calculated to appease authority figures in our lives, or should we speak our minds?

Why do people choose as they do? What are the biological, psychological, and social factors involved? Answering these questions is the task of the lifespan psychologist. And the ideas of psychologists, philosophers, and scientists must undergo scrupulous testing before we can accept them as the reality that leads us to a greater understanding of human development. Since we wrote the previous edition of this book, stunning changes have taken place that help to dispel the shadows. New research into brain development, insights into the complex labyrinth of genetic interaction, the ever-expanding world of cognitive development, and technological products and processes are only a few of the changes that literally demand inclusion in any discussion of the lifespan.

And so, the goal for the lifespan psychologist is clearly identified: to present the most trustworthy, the most recent, the most pertinent, the most helpful facts and interpretations that will help readers comprehend the intricacies and subtleties of the journey through the lifespan. To achieve this goal, we followed these paths:

- We have expanded our coverage of those topics that promised insightful views of lifespan development and that were supported by careful and verified research, such as brain development and various aspects of marital satisfaction.

- We have intensified our efforts to highlight the practical and helpful implications of lifespan research and theory. For example, both theory and research have

contributed significantly to the greater survival rate of premature infants. Another example is new information on how hormones, and medicines related to them, can influence well-being.

- We have expanded our discussion of the role that culture plays in the development of all human beings, from birth to the later years.

- Finally, we have done our best to make this seventh edition of *Human Development Across the Lifespan* as reader-friendly as possible. By the examples that follow from the data, with the range of boxes, with the exercises provided, and with chapter introductions and conclusions, we hope that we have encouraged our readers to share in the excitement and satisfaction that accompanies our journey through the lifespan.

BASIC THEMES OF HUMAN DEVELOPMENT ACROSS THE LIFESPAN

Reflecting the exciting changes that are taking place in our knowledge of human development, we have woven our narrative around several integrating themes: the biopsychosocial model, the cultural context of development, the roles of age and gender, and applications to daily living. We return to these themes in each chapter as a means of making more meaningful the basic knowledge of human development.

The Biopsychosocial Approach

The *biopsychosocial approach* will help you to integrate the wealth of information that you will find in the pages to come. By thinking of lifespan development as the product of the interaction of biological, psychological, and social forces, you will better appreciate the complexity of development. For example, biological influences on development range from the role of genes in development to adult health concerns; psychological influences include all aspects of cognitive and personality development; social influences refer to such powerful forces as family, school, peers, and the media. The biopsychosocial approach helps to explain how the interaction of these forces is key to understanding human development.

Contextual Influences on Development

Our goal in urging you to adopt a sociocultural perspective is to help you develop a greater understanding of those who seem "different." If you adopt this perspective, you will come to realize that different people have different worldviews that decisively influence their thinking. People from different cultures do not always think like one another and, as we will stress, these multiple perspectives are assets. Recognizing how diverse people are in their thinking and behavior will help you to identify and to comprehend variations in how individuals are raised, how they think, and how they become functioning members of their culture.

In various places throughout the book, we discuss the four major tenets of the contextual model: the relative plasticity of life; the historical embeddedness of all development; the diversity of development; and the bidirectionality of the causes of all human behavior. Since we feel so strongly about the importance of these factors, we discuss sociocultural issues in each chapter. We also open several sections of the book with a sociocultural perspective on the issues to be discussed.

The Roles of Age and Gender

Inasmuch as this book is organized chronologically, we explain the influence of age in every chapter. In some ways, the effects of age are quite apparent, and in other ways the effects are subtle and complex. As concerns about gender equity have received more publicity, the stereotypes about males and females have slowly eroded. If people are treated according to stereotypic characteristics, then their potential is immediately limited. Although gender stereotyping is only one part of the gender story, it illustrates the importance of the relationship between gender and development. For example, children at an early age construct social categories from the world around them, attach certain characteristics to these categories, and label the categories. This process may be positive because it helps to organize the world; it may also be negative if the characteristics associated with the category are limiting—"girls just can't do math." We'll examine how this theme plays out, both positively and negatively, throughout the lifespan.

Applications to Daily Living

The study of lifespan development is an exciting, rapidly changing, and highly relevant subject that can shed light on the developmental changes that you witness in yourself and see in your friends and family members of all ages. To help you put the theories and research of this book into a meaningful framework, we have written several **An Applied View** boxes for each chapter. Their topics range from the appeal of street gangs for some children, to the role of television in a child's life, to an adolescent's search for identity, to problems that the adult children of alcoholics encounter.

We have also included boxes that ask you to interact with the text. Called **An Informed View,** these boxes are intended to help you think about and act on topics we have just discussed in the chapter. In these activities, you are invited to reflect on what your knowledge and your experience tell you about these matters. We do not present answers in these boxes. Rather, we hope you apply your best judgment to the issues we raise.

MAJOR CHANGES IN THE SEVENTH EDITION

As a dynamic and challenging field that sheds new light and hope for a better and deeper understanding of human development, lifespan psychology demands constant reassessment to incorporate biopsychosocial changes that enrich and expand our discussion. Guided by our readers' comments, we have explored and evaluated the research that has appeared since our last edition and included hundreds of new findings. We have also thought carefully about the possible use of the ideas and facts that we discuss and have attempted to broaden their application to appropriate developmental epochs. With this in mind, here are samples of the key changes we have made.

Chapter One

1. We have significantly rearranged the historical material of Chapter One to provide our readers with more in-depth discussion of the importance of biopsychosocial interactions, particularly the role that culture plays in development.
2. We have expanded our analysis of the major issues in lifespan psychology.

Chapter Two

1. We have increased our examination of current developmental theory and introduced an important theme that highlights how lifespan psychology can—and should—be applied to development. Improving children's literacy has become a major concern in our

nation; we have presented Maslow's Hierarchy of Needs coupled with examples from children's literature to illustrate one means of improving children's literacy.

Chapter Three

1. We reworked our analysis of the fertilization process and present the latest research on ART procedures.

2. Coverage of the Human Genome Project has been enlarged and updated to broaden our discussion of susceptibility, identification, and treatment.

Chapter Four

1. We have continued to update our analysis of nervous system development and have included *An Applied View* box relating to stem-cell research that incorporates pro and con reactions.

2. The section on maternal nutrition has been enlarged to include the recommendations of the 2005 *USDA Dietary Guidelines for Americans.*

3. We have continued to update our discussion of changes in the world of prematurity.

Chapter Five

1. The material on nutrition has been expanded to broaden our discussion of breast feeding.

2. The analysis of motor skills has been significantly expanded.

3. Both the perceptual and language development sections have been reworked.

Chapter Six

1. We have reworked our discussion of relationships and broadened the input of culture.

2. We have significantly updated the analysis of attachment and introduced findings from children's literature to illustrate the concepts discussed.

3. A new topic, the dimensions of temperament, has been added to our work on temperament and relationships.

4. We have completely reworked our presentation of emotional development and related it to continued brain development.

Chapter Seven

1. Once more, our discussion of the brain has been expanded to include new developmental data.

2. The section on Piaget's work has been rewritten to make its contents more accessible to readers.

3. Additional theoretical explanations have been added with the inclusion of concepts from information processing.

4. We have revised our work on early childhood education by introducing the latest data on Project Head Start and describing the Reggio Emilia approach.

5. The discussion of bilingualism has been completely redone with a more detailed presentation of the various techniques and a discussion of such organizations as TESOL.

Chapter Eight

1. The section on family was rewritten to include the latest research on family relationships.

2. Discussion of sibling relationships and the quality of day care centers was revised to reflect the latest available data.

3. We have completely revised our work on play to emphasize its critical role in development, using illustrations taken from the outstanding children's literature, both fiction and nonfiction.

Chapter Nine

1. An entirely new section on continued brain development was incorporated into the physical development discussion to reflect the ongoing brain discoveries.

2. We revised the work on nutrition to incorporate the *Dietary Guidelines for Americans* as applied to middle-childhood children.

3. We have greatly expanded our work on literacy and introduced the concept of dialogic reading coupled with a broader view of the role that children's literature can play in language development.

Chapter Ten

1. The work on self-development has been expanded to reflect current theory and research.

2. A new section on self-regulation tracing the transition from outer control to inner self-regulation has been added.

3. We have widened our discussion of bullying to include such new forms as racial bullying and cyberbullying.

4. The role of schools in middle childhood has been totally revamped to emphasize the vital role of education in a child's life. The complexity of teaching was stressed by combining it with the themes that run through the teaching-learning process.

5. Television's role in a child's development was reworked, again reflecting ongoing developmental research.

Chapter Eleven

1. Information on physiological changes has been completely updated to include recent findings.

2. The work on body image has been revised to reflect current understandings and biopsychosocial influences.

3. We have improved the presentation of research to incorporate critical elements of Piaget's theory and other psychological influences.

4. Information on Internet bullying and harm has been expanded to include blogs and other websites.

Chapter Twelve

1. The influence and the importance of families have been underscored with recent research findings. Parents' roles are stressed.

2. Sections on sexual behavior, including homosexuality, have been revamped to incorporate new perspectives. Homosexual marriage and divorce are covered.

3. Data to support information presented throughout the chapter has been updated to provide the most current statistics available.

4. The text has been revised to reflect theory and general opinion with respect to illegal behaviors.

Chapter Thirteen

1. Explicit connections between rites of passage and modern adolescent transitions into adulthood in the United States are presented.

2. To present the most accurate picture of young adults, physical development is accentuated by updated research and anecdotes.

3. Effects of lifestyle on health have been thoroughly revised to reflect current trends and facts (for example, hookahs, binge-drinking statistics).

4. The roles of the working woman, wife, and mother are examined through the lens of theory and recent research findings.

Chapter Fourteen

1. More detailed discussion and updates have been included in sections relating to homosexual marriage, including divorce and family initiatives.

2. Interpersonal relations, including sexuality and love, have been infused with research that brings contemporary issues into view alongside situated theory.

3. Stressors, such as fertility challenges (for example, conception, financial implications) are examined.

Chapter Fifteen

1. The sections that focus on physical health and sensory abilities have been completely revamped to incorporate new data and to eliminate extraneous findings.

2. Text discussing the climacteric (for both males and females) has been revised and shortened.

3. Information about memory has been relocated to different chapters in the text accordingly, as it relates to specific developmental stages and current research. This material is extremely important, as reflected in the media and quantity of research attention in this area.

4. New information about lifelong learning has been incorporated into sections on creativity, patterns of work, and midlife crisis.

Chapter Sixteen

1. The sections on marriage have been revised to include current research and opinions.

2. Recent studies have been inserted throughout the chapter in an attempt to balance the formal theory with more contemporary viewpoints.

Chapter Seventeen

1. Findings from current brain research have been added to the chapter, with implications for social and overall development.

2. *Sociocultural View* boxes have been revised, and new material that reflects diverse populations and perspectives has been inserted throughout the chapter.

3. The sections on physical development have undergone major updating and revision.

Chapter Eighteen

1. Research on love has been updated to feature ongoing developmental research.

2. A section on elder abuse, including the impact on families, has been added.

3. Attention to the pharmaceutical industry has been paid with respect to the aging population in the United States and worldwide.

Chapter Nineteen

1. Statistics relating to death and dying have been updated to reflect current findings from multiple sources.

2. Material on mourning practices and funeral rites has been revised and reduced through a multicultural lens.

3. Information about suicide has been given attention in order to include current research.

SUPPLEMENTARY MATERIALS

The supplements listed here may accompany Dacey and Traver's Human Development Across the Lifespan, seventh edition. Please contact your local McGraw-Hill representative for details concerning policies, prices, and availability, as some restrictions may apply.

For The Instructor

The instructor side of the Online Learning Center at www.mhhe.com/dacey7 contains the Instructor's Manual, Test Bank files, PowerPoint slides, CPS Questions, Guides to Lifespan Development for Future Educators and Futures Nurses, and other valuable material to help you design and enhance your course. Ask your local McGraw-Hill representative for your password.

Instructor's Manual by Teresa Hutchens, University of Tennessee

The Instructor's Manual to accompany the seventh edition of *Human Development Across the Lifespan* includes new teaching ideas for each chapter, as well as a summary outline, learning objectives, key terms, lecture suggestions, classroom or student activities, and questions for review and discussion. The summary outline and learning objectives closely follow the text and highlight important concepts and topics from each chapter. The lecture suggestions give entertaining, yet educational, ideas on how to enliven classroom discussion of the text material. Classroom activities provide hands-on suggestions for applying course material to students' everyday lives in and out of the classroom. The questions for review and discussion aid instructors in promoting class participation and can serve as essay question assignments. In addition, each chapter includes supplementary resources lists of both video/film and Internet resources for the human development instructor.

Test Bank and Computerized Test Bank by Rebecca Fraser-Thill, Bates College

This comprehensive Test Bank includes more than 1,500 factual, conceptual, and applied questions specifically related to the main text. Every question indicates the correct answer, is identified by type of question (conceptual, applied, or factual), and indicates the page number in the text where the corresponding material can be found. All test questions are compatible with EZ Test, McGraw-Hill's Computerized Test Bank program.

Powerpoint Slides by Gary Popoli, University of Hartford

These presentations cover the key points of each chapter. They can be used as is, or you may modify them to meet your specific needs.

CPS Questions by Gail Edmunds

These questions, formatted for use with the interactive Classroom Performance System, are organized by chapter and designed to test factual, applied, and conceptual understanding. These test questions are also compatible with EZTest, McGraw-Hill's Computerized Test Bank program.

Guide To Lifespan Development For Future Educators And Guide To Lifespan Development For Future Nurses

These course supplements help students apply the concepts of human development to education and to nursing. Each set of resources contains information, exercises, and sample tests designed to help students prepare for certification and understand human development from a professional perspective.

Mcgraw-Hill's Visual Asset Database For Lifespan Development ("VAD")

McGraw-Hill's Visual Assets Database for Lifespan Development (VAD 2.0) (www.mhhe.com/vad) is an online database of videos for use in the developmental psychology classroom, created specifically for instructors. You can customize classroom presentations by downloading the videos to your computer and showing the videos on their own or insert them into your course cartridge or PowerPoint presentations. All the videos are available with or without captions. Ask your McGraw-Hill representative for access information.

Mcgraw-Hill Contemporary Learning Series Annual Editions: Human Development

This reader is a collection of articles on topics related to the latest research and thinking in human development. Annual Editions are updated regularly and include useful features such as a topic guide, an annotated table of contents, unit overviews, and a topical index.

Taking Sides: Clashing Views on Controversial Issues in Life-Span Development

Current controversial issues are presented in a debate-style format designed to stimulate student interest and develop critical thinking skills. Each issue is thoughtfully framed with an issue summary, an issue introduction, and a postscript.

For The Student

Online Learning Center (OLC)

This companion website, at www.mhhe.com/dacey7, offers a wide variety of student resources. **Multiple Choice and True/False Tests** for each chapter reinforce key principles, terms, and ideas and cover all the major concepts discussed throughout the text. Entirely different from the test items in the Test Bank, the questions have been written to quiz students but also to help them learn. Key terms from the text are reproduced in a **Glossary** where they can be accessed in alphabetical order for easy reference and review. Relevant **web links** introduce Internet resources providing further information on chapter content.

Acknowledgments

We would like to thank the following reviewers for their excellent advice and suggestions for revision:

Maureen C. Cochran,
Potomac State College

Linda E. Flickinger,
St. Clair County Community College

Jeannette W. Murphey,
Meridian Community College

Gary Popoli,
Harford Community College

Todd J. Smith,
Lake Superior State University

Maureen Vandermaas-Peeler,
Elon University

Nancy Wedeen,
Los Angeles Valley College

LIFESPAN PSYCHOLOGY:
An Introduction

1
chapter

Chapter Objectives

After you read this chapter, you should be able to answer the following questions.

- How would you define and describe lifespan development?

- What are the different views of lifespan development?

- What role do biopsychosocial interactions play in lifespan development?

- What are the major issues in lifespan development?

- What is the role of research in studying lifespan development?

The year was 1955. Through those 365 days, psychologists Emmy Werner and Ruth Smith (1992, 1995, 2001) began to collect data on every child born on the island of Kauai, a part of the Hawaiian chain. That year a total of 837 children were born.

Amazingly, Werner and Smith studied 505 of these children from their prenatal days until they were in their early 30s. (The drop in the number of children studied was due to some of the children dying, some moving to other islands, and some moving to the U.S. mainland.)

Of the 505 children in the group, one in three was born with the threat of serious developmental difficulties, such as the effects of a difficult birth or an environment that triggered formidable challenges. Some faced the prospect of a life of grinding poverty. Throughout their lives, others experienced divorce, desertion, alcoholism, or mental illness.

Two out of three people in this vulnerable group were born exposed to four or more formidable risk factors. And yet, one in three of these high-risk children developed into confident, competent young adults.

How can we explain this phenomenon? What developmental forces were at work that enabled certain people to overcome dramatically difficult obstacles and yet permitted others to succumb? In a sense, the children of Kauai provide us with a window through which we can view the events that shape the lifespan, the biological, psychological, and environmental interactions that make us what we are.

Emmy Werner's studies have provided invaluable insights into the characteristics of resilient children.

The encouraging story of the children of Kauai testifies to the remarkable changes that occur in the course of the lifespan. But much more is hidden in the chronicle of these lives. What combination of biological, psychological, and environmental forces interacted at what levels to produce these differences? What were the processes at work that *explain* what happened? These are the questions that will guide our work together as we explore the mysteries of the lifespan.

With these ideas in mind, then, we'll first explore the meaning of lifespan development and follow the developmental path of one distinguished individual. We'll then attempt to indicate its importance to you by illustrating how peaks and valleys come into all our lives. Although we all chart an individual course, we can still identify many similarities in our lives. We walk, we talk, we attend school, and we search for a satisfying career. Yet within this sameness, we all have and choose different experiences that shine a unique light on our journey through the lifespan. To aid in this analysis of lifespan development, we'll introduce the notion of biopsychosocial interactions, those forces that act together to shape the path of development. Such biopsychosocial interaction in turn leads to a consideration of several issues that must be addressed in any scrutiny of lifespan development. Finally, we'll complete this introduction by analyzing pertinent research techniques used in studies of human development.

AN EXAMPLE OF DEVELOPMENT THROUGH THE LIFESPAN

Another book was opened, which is the book of life.

—REVELATIONS

If you think about your own life—starting school, perhaps going off to college, beginning a job, getting married, having a child—you begin to appreciate the complexity of development. Since it's usually difficult to look at ourselves objectively, let's examine the life of an outstanding individual—Barack Obama—whose rise to fame and power with all its accompanying triumphs and tragedies offers an insightful view into what is meant by lifespan development.

Barack Obama—The Promise of Development

Tonight is a particular honor for me because—let's face it—my presence on this stage is pretty unlikely. My father was a foreign student, born and raised in a small village in Kenya. He grew up herding goats, went to school in a tin-roof shack. His father—my grandfather—was a cook, a domestic servant to the British.

I stand here today, grateful for the diversity of my heritage, aware that my parents' dreams live on in my two precious daughters. I stand here knowing that my story is part of the larger American story, that I owe a debt to all of those who came before me, and that in no other country on earth is my story even possible.

These words, spoken on July 27, 2004, to a tumultuous gathering at Boston Garden were part of Barack Obama's keynote address to the Democratic National Convention. The remarkable story of this young United States senator from Illinois is a great example of the potential inherent in human development. Tracing the path that Obama followed in his lifespan dramatically illustrates the trials and tribulations and the success and joys of human development.

Born in 1961 in Honolulu, Hawaii, Obama is the son of Barack Obama (Sr.) and Ann Dunham of Wichita, Kansas. At the time of his birth, Obama's parents were both students at the East-West Center of the University of Hawaii. Following the divorce of his parents, his mother later married Lolo Soetoro from Indonesia, where the family then lived for several years. Obama returned to Hawaii to finish his early education and later graduated from Columbia. He spent three years at Harvard, received his law degree, and joined a corporate law firm. During these years he met and married Michelle Robinson. He and his wife returned to Chicago, where he became active in community affairs and joined a Chicago civil rights law firm. He also lectured on constitutional law at the University of Chicago.

In 1996, he took the first step in a political career when he was elected to the Illinois State Senate. After an unsuccessful campaign for Congress in 2000, an overwhelming majority elected Obama to the United States Senate in 2004. As a United States senator, he has demonstrated an ability to work well with both Democrats and Republicans while furthering his efforts to improve education at all levels. Gradually extending his interest and growing influence to national and international affairs, Obama has become a powerful figure in helping to shape United States policy. In 2006, he led a Congressional delegation to several African countries and made international headlines as he traced his family's origins in Kenya. As one prominent Kenyan noted, "He's a role model for all of Africa." And as of this printing he's a candidate for President of the United States. In 2005, *Time Magazine* selected Obama as one of the "100 most influential people in the world."

Barack Obama with his family.

How did this individual from a modest background achieve such a lofty position? One path leads to the conclusion that Obama's family—parents, wife, children—are of paramount importance to him. Another path identifies those personal concerns that shaped his thinking. His decision to follow a political career provided opportunities for him to influence legislation affecting education, the poor, minorities, and international affairs. Barack Obama is an excellent example of an individual proceeding through his lifespan by remaining faithful to his beliefs, recognizing opportunities, and making the most of his unique abilities. The story of Obama's interactions with his environment is a story of human development.

THINKING ABOUT LIFESPAN DEVELOPMENT

When you pick up this book and open to Chapter 1, you have every right to expect some clues about what lifespan psychology is, this subject that will demand your attention for the next 14 or 15 weeks. So first let's be technically accurate about what you'll be studying. **Lifespan psychology** studies human development from conception to death. In our work, we'll adopt a *normative* approach to development—studying the typical or average developmental path that people follow—but also point out individual variations where necessary.

lifespan psychology
Study of human development from conception to death.

Why Study the Lifespan?

As a discipline, lifespan psychology gathered momentum when developmental psychologists began to realize that development didn't cease when human beings passed from adolescence to adulthood. A developmental view originally inferred a focus on the early years and their experiences, but gradually a lifespan perspective took psychologists into a wider field. The range of explanations included study of the brain, analysis of the development of the mind, and research into the ways developmental levels influence individuals' responses to their experiences

(Rutter, 2006). So today we see development as a lifelong process. But there also can be no argument with the idea that each age (infancy, adolescence, and so on.) has its own developmental agenda and contributes to the entire lifespan.

Consequently, lifespan psychology has several objectives.

- To offer an organized account of development across the lifespan.
- To identify the interconnections between earlier and later events.
- To account for the mechanisms responsible for lifespan development.
- To specify the biological, psychological, and environmental factors that shape an individual's development (Baltes, Lindenberger, & Staudinger, 1998, 2006).

Once these objectives are identified, Baltes and his colleagues believe, developmental psychologists can attempt to trace the range of individual development, encourage individuals to live their lives as positively as possible, and help them avoid negative outcomes (Baltes, Lindenberger, & Staudinger, 2006, p. 570).

What Is Development?

Few readers would argue with the belief that individuals respond to the events of their lives in a manner consistent with their age at that time. But is age alone the cause of their varied responses? Age, as Rutter (2006) points out, is an ambiguous explanation for behavior because:

1. Age tells us about biological maturity and little else.
2. Different elements of biological growth proceed at different rates.
3. Age reflects past experiences that may influence current behavior.
4. Age reflects current social situations.
5. Age tells us little about the underlying causal mechanisms (Rutter, 2006, p. 314).

For example, consider hospital admission at various ages. In the early days of infancy, separation from parents does not seem to cause unusual psychological effects, unlike what happens in the toddler years (one to two years) when a child's upset is much more intense. In the school years, upset occurs, but again is less intense. Age alone doesn't inform us of the psychological mechanism at work here. What seems to happen is that the attachment of toddlers to their parents has developed to the extent that separation causes a severe upset. Although older children also have formed a firm attachment to their parents, their increased cognitive ability allows them to realize that separation does not destroy their parental relationship. Consequently, what appear to be solely age-related changes are due to social relationships and cognitive development. (For an excellent discussion of age, development, and psychopathology see Rutter, 2006.)

Development also implies change, but the two terms are not equivalent. For change to be used in a developmental sense, it must possess a systematic, organized structure that contains a successive theme; that is, it should be clear that the changes that occurred at a later time were influenced by earlier changes. Thus the concept of development signifies systematic and successive changes over time (Lerner, 2002, p. 16). (Even this definition may vary according to the orientation of the psychologists involved—biological, philosophical, and so on.) Consequently, our focus should be on *how* changes come about, *how* they are maintained or lost, and *how* the course of development varies from individual to individual (Rutter & Rutter, 1993).

For purposes of research and analysis we've divided the lifespan into the segments and presented these in Table 1.1. We urge you to remember that each segment is part of a whole.

TABLE 1.1	Developmental Periods of the Lifespan
Period	*Characteristics*
Prenatal (conception to birth)	Nine months of rapid growth in which organs and systems appear; extreme sensitivity to negative influences.
Infancy (birth to 2 years)	Continued rapid growth; brain development provides the basis for the emergence of motor, cognitive, and psychosocial accomplishments.
Early childhood (2 to 6 years)	Physical growth slows somewhat; substantial gains in cognitive and language development; the interplay between socialization and individuation shapes personality and influences adjustment.
Middle childhood (7 to 11 years)	School becomes a major force in development; physical, cognitive, and psychosocial abilities become apparent.
Adolescence (12 to 18 years)	The changes of puberty affect all aspects of development; thought becomes more abstract, academic achievement begins to shape the future; the search for identity continues unabated.
Early adulthood (19 to 34 years)	Higher education or the beginning of work beckons; relationships are a major focus of these years; marriage and children become central concerns of the lifespan.
Middle adulthood (35 to 64 years)	Heightened responsibility; may include care of children and aging parents; growing community involvement; peak period for leadership and influence; a time of physical change (for example, menopause).
Later adulthood (65+)	Retirement; declining health and strength; adjusting to death of loved ones; facing one's own mortality; changing lifestyle to enhance "successful aging"; enjoying greater wisdom.

With these ideas in mind, it's interesting to follow the varied interpretations that society has given lifespan development—childhood, adolescence, and adulthood—over the years.

Guided Review

1. Lifespan psychology studies human development from _____ to _____.
2. Development is about _____.
3. Development cannot be explained by _____ alone.
4. Lifespan psychology attempts to specify the _____ responsible for human development.

CHANGING VIEWS OF THE LIFESPAN

If, as we insist throughout our work, that development is change, then interpretations of the lifespan over the years should also reflect the notion of change. And, not too surprisingly, they do. As we trace the differing images of children, adolescents, and

Answers   1. conception, death 2. change 3. age 4. mechanisms

In earlier times, children were often viewed—and treated—as mature adults.

adults through time, we must remember that these snapshots of development were powerfully influenced by cultural forces reflecting the ideas and values of a particular era.

Childhood

Childhood, according to the seventeenth-century French cleric Pierre de Berulle, "is the most vile and abject state of human nature, after that of death." It is tempting to agree—not least as an antidote to all the sentimental nonsense surrounding the supposedly pure and innocent child of the Victorian era. Such extremes serve to remind us that childhood is a social construct, which changes over time and, no less importantly, varies between social and ethnic groups within any society. (Heywood, 2001, p. 9)

Heywood's somewhat sarcastic words highlight a major obstacle in our attempt to understand children: Without understanding the context of the times how can we interpret children's growth, development, and behavior? How does any society define "child"? Are children seen as miniature adults or youths with potential? What is appropriate for children?

As you follow these paths, you'll come to one inescapable conclusion that will guide your reading and understanding of the history of childhood: *Any interpretation of childhood is a product of the prevailing view of children at any particular time.* As Heywood (2001) notes in his history of childhood, if historians wish to understand children of the past, they must first discover how adults have viewed the young. Peter Hunt (1995, p. ix) also emphasizes this theme when he states that the concept of childhood changes constantly from period to period, place to place to place, culture to culture—perhaps even from child to child. Viewing children as miniature adults (and treating them this way) is quite different from recognizing the significance of the interactions of heredity and environment in a child's development.

We begin to observe a difference in the manner in which societies viewed children when Greek and Roman scholars came to realize that ideal human development involved the cultivation of body and mind. With the gradual spread of

Early societies such as the Greeks and Romans, although viewing children as small adults, nevertheless saw them as cheerful and playful.

Christianity, a small number of schools began to appear. But it wasn't until the invention of the printing press that a changing concept of childhood emerged and children entered the symbolic world of the written word. Children were slowly becoming objects of concern.

Great philosophers such as Locke and Rousseau, for example, presented challenging, often contradictory, ideas of child rearing. As the concept of childhood became more accepted and subject to various interpretations, an important article by Charles Darwin that appeared in 1877 heralded a new and innovative analysis of childhood. Entitled *Biographical Sketch of an Infant,* it provided a scientific basis for studying children.

When this was followed in 1882 by William Preyer's *The Mind of the Child,* childhood was firmly entrenched as a separate subject deserving of study to answer growing questions about human development. The 19th century was to prove remarkably fertile in studies of child development, particularly with Alfred Binet's study of intelligence and G. Stanley's Hall's writings on childhood and adolescence. As the notion of childhood acquired more credit, no one assumed greater importance than did Sigmund Freud, who was among the first to emphasize the importance of the early years. Today children are viewed as the product of genetic, biological, behavioral, and contextual forces constantly interacting. And we see the same level of sophistication applied to the adolescent years.

Adolescence: A Time of Storm, Stress, or Calm?

"Boy!" I said. I also say "Boy!" quite a lot. Partly because I have a lousy vocabulary and partly because I act quite young for my age sometimes. I was 16 then and I'm 17 now, and sometimes I act like I'm about 13. It's really ironical, because I'm six feet two and a half and I have gray hair. I really do. The one side of my head—the right side—is full of millions of gray hairs. I've had them ever since I was a kid. And yet I still act sometimes like I was only about 12. Everybody says that, especially my father. It's partly true, too, but it isn't all true. (Salinger, 1945, p. 7)

Here, in *The Catcher in the Rye,* Holden Caulfield provides a taste of adolescent thought. Storm and stress? Yes, some. Turbulence and uncertainty? Yes, some. But he also offers a thoughtful analysis of his own behavior. Perhaps the best way of

Sigmund Freud with daughter Anna.

thinking about adolescence is to realize that it begins in biology and ends in culture (Petersen, 1988). In other words, the physical maturation of human development initiates the process, but adolescent experiences strongly shape the nature and direction of behavior. Lerner and Galambos (1998, p. 414) nicely summarize the nuances of adolescence when they state that adolescence is that time when a person's biological, cognitive, psychological, and social characteristics are changing from what is considered childlike to what is considered adultlike.

As with childhood, the concept of adolescence has changed remarkably through the years. Adolescents were seen as simply younger adults who were subject to strict rules and harsh discipline. Not until the Industrial Revolution in Western societies was the need for better education seen, and with the passage of child labor laws and a demand for universal school attendance came a separation of adolescents from children and adults (Grotevant, 1998). With the advent of the 20th century, adolescence, as a separate phase of development, was popularized by the writings and teachings of G. Stanley Hall. In his two-volume text *Adolescence* (1904), he popularized a label of adolescence that is still with us today—a time of "storm and stress." But as the days of the 20th century dwindled and with the coming of the 21st century, continued speculation and research has changed the picture of adolescence again. Today most psychologists agree that the majority of adolescents have accepted the values and standards of their parents and that friction between the generations is only slightly higher than that of childhood (Dacey, Kenny, & Margolis, 2002).

Musing about the internal and external changes of adolescence, Lerner and Galambos (1998) have identified a cluster of adolescent risk behaviors, certainly not the storm and stress of earlier interpretations of adolescence but more in the nature of modern challenges facing young adults. These include:

- *Substance Abuse.* There is little doubt that adolescents drink, some heavily, and engage in widespread drug abuse.
- *Sexual Behavior.* It certainly comes as no surprise that young adults frequently engage in sex that produces sexually transmitted diseases and unwanted pregnancies, given the highly erotic nature of modern society.

The many faces of adolescence.

- *School Underachievement, Failure, and Dropout.* About 25% of all elementary and secondary school students in the United States are at risk for school failure. Estimates are that the high school dropout rate has remained fairly consistent at 10%.
- *Delinquency, Crime, and Violence.* Youth gangs, youth unrest, youth violence are all familiar terms with which the public is too familiar and reflect both personal (personality) and societal conditions (poverty, environmental models).

Yet, in spite of these risk factors—the temptations, the dangers, and the seductiveness—most of our young adults accept the challenges of their environment, adjust to the demands made on them, and, with adult patience and understanding, achieve their goals. Finally, we turn our attention to adulthood.

Adulthood

One life stage is not better or more virtuous than another. Adult development is neither a footrace nor a moral imperative. It is a road map to help us make sense of where we and where our neighbors might be located. It also contributes to our "wholeness" from which our word health is derived. In old age there are many losses and these may overwhelm us if we have not continued to grow beyond ourselves. (Vaillant, 2002, p. 50)

Today we realize that lifespan development involves change throughout the lifespan, *adulthood as well as infancy.* As Baltes and his colleagues (2006) state, development is not complete at adulthood (maturity). Rather, development (change) reaches across the entire life course, and developmental changes involve lifelong adaptive processes unique for each phase of the life course, including adulthood.

Changing Perspectives on Aging

As an example of the changed view of aging, consider the results of the Seattle Longitudinal Study of Adult Intelligence (Schaie, 1994). Research suggests that as people age, their physical stamina, memory, and cognitive processing don't decline as much as previously thought. Although some aspects of cognitive functioning lose a degree of efficiency (speed of processing for example), such losses in a healthy 60-, 70-, or 80-year-old is more than offset by gains in knowledge and skill due to experience.

Analyzing the cause of an apparent decline in intelligence (as measured by intelligence tests), leads to several conclusions.

- When *physical health* remains good, cognitive performance suffers only a slight decline. Sight, hearing, and motor coordination play key roles in maintaining the link between health and intellectual performance.

- *Speed of response* is the time taken to perform any task that involves the central nervous system such as perception, memory reasoning, and motor movement. It is the basis for efficient cognitive functioning, especially memory. Much of the decline in memory performance in the later years can be attributed to a decline in verbal speed. If nervous system involvement is slowed, cognitive performance declines because information may be lost during the required cognitive processing (Birren & Fisher, 1992).

- *Attitude,* especially in a testing situation, affects cognitive performance. Test anxiety lowers test scores when older adults find themselves in strange settings. They may fear that their memory will fail them; they may be uncomfortable with the test's problems; they may simply have an expectation of failure because of all they've heard and read about the declining mental abilities of older adults.

As research continues to add to our knowledge of development, the concept of aging itself has also changed. Today's focus is on "successful aging."

These and similar reasons, either singly or in combination, have often led to an underestimation of older people's intelligence. For example, reasoning, problem solving, and wisdom hold up well with age and may even improve. The Seattle Study showed that people with the higher scores, as you would expect, tended to be healthier and better educated, had higher incomes and stable marriages, and were still leading active, stimulating lives (Papalia & Olds, 2004).

To conclude this discussion of aging, we turn once again to Vaillant's study of aging.

> [W]isdom involves the toleration of ambiguity and paradox. To be wise about wisdom we need to accept that wisdom does—and wisdom does not—increase with age. Age facilitates a widening social radius and more balanced ways of coping with adversity, but thus far no one can prove that wisdom is greater in old age. (Vaillant, 2002, p. 256)

Thus we end this section as we began it: Different eras have conceived different views of the various developmental epochs. Consequently, these differences clearly call for us to appraise the meaning of development more closely.

AN APPLIED VIEW

Chart Your Own Lifespan

Endeavoring to illustrate how important knowledge of the lifespan is to each of us, Sugarman (1986) has devised a simple exercise that you can do quickly. Using a blank sheet of paper, assume that the left edge of the page represents the beginning of your life and the right edge where you are today. Now draw a line across the page that indicates the peaks and valleys that you have experienced so far.

For example, the chart for one of the authors of this book (JFT) is shown below.

In this chart, the first valley was a financial reversal for the author's parents. The first peak represents happy and productive high school years, followed by entry into teaching, and then marriage a few years later. The deep valley was a serious accident followed by years of recuperation and then the birth of children and the publication of a first book. You can see that it looks like a temperature chart. Try it for yourself.

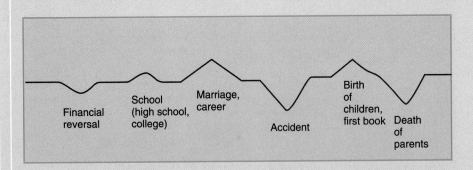

Sugarman (1986) suggested that when you finish, sit back and ask yourself these questions:

- Are there more peaks than valleys?
- Is there a definite shape to my chart?
- Would I identify my peaks and valleys as major or minor?
- What caused the peaks and valleys?
- Could I have done anything to make the peaks higher and the valleys more shallow?

- What happened during the plateaus?
- What's my view of these highs and lows in my life?

You have drawn a picture of your lifespan, and the questions that you have just answered are the subject matter of lifespan development.

Guided Review

5. The infancy period extends from _____ to _____ years.
6. Later adulthood includes the years over _____.
7. Interpretations of the lifespan should reflect the reality of _____.
8. Questions persist as to whether adolescence is a time of storm and _____.
9. _____ wrote an important analysis of childhood that appeared in 1877.
10. One of the great fictional classics of adolescence is _____.
11. Any view of childhood is shaped by how _____ viewed children.

THE IMPORTANCE OF BIOPSYCHOSOCIAL INTERACTIONS

biopsychosocial interactions
The idea that development proceeds by the interaction of biological, psychological, and social forces.

To aid our understanding of human development, we have turned to an examination of **biopsychosocial interactions,** that is, the influence of genetic, biological, environmental, and social forces on development. In this model, development is considered to result from the interaction of genetic, environmental, social, and biological processes. Thinking of lifespan development as the product of the interaction of biological, environmental, as well as psychological forces, helps us to better understand and appreciate the complexity of development. Consequently, the goal of lifespan psychology is to probe the multiple and integrated layers (genetic, physical, behavioral, environmental) that drive development.

Understanding Children's Cultures

culture
The values, beliefs, and behaviors characteristic of a large group of people—for example, those of Hispanic origin.

We think it's important to recognize the contributions that a particular culture makes to the development of its children. Think of **culture** as the customs, values, and traditions inherent in one's environment, that is, the features that define values and styles of life (Rutter & Nikapota, 2006). Different cultures have different developmental expectations for their children. Asian children, for example, are encouraged to avoid emotional displays, a characteristic that does not necessarily apply to Asian-American

We pride ourselves on being a nation of immigrants, a country that welcomes newcomers with the promise of unrestricted opportunity. To achieve this objective during a time of increasing immigration demands consideration and tolerance for those of different color, nationality, and beliefs. Can you make several suggestions for achieving this objective?

A SOCIOCULTURAL VIEW

The Impact of the Cultural Climate

We are a country of Muslims, atheists, Jews, Christians, Hindus, and devout spiritualists without a specific religious affiliation. We celebrate the winter solstice, Hanukkah, Christmas, Kwanza, and Ramadan. We brought longstanding cultural traditions and rites of passage from Haiti, Laos, Ghana, El Salvador, France, Germany, England, and Samoa, among countless others. Many of our children are taken through rites of passage that include bar mitzvahs, inceneros, debutante balls, and gang initiation.
(Muse, 1997, p. 285)

Perhaps nowhere are these words brought to life more dramatically than in the American classroom. A good example of this kind of endeavor can be seen in Kim's (1990) description of Hawaiian children's school experiences. Many Hawaiian children achieve at the lowest academic level and are labeled as lazy and disruptive by some teachers. Yet these same children are remarkably responsible at home—cooking, cleaning, and taking care of their brothers and sisters. They demonstrate considerable initiative and a high performance level. When something needs to be done, they get together and make a group effort to do whatever is necessary. When they find themselves in an individualistic, competitive classroom, however, their performance suffers.

In a series of experiments, teachers were encouraged to model desired behaviors and not assign specific tasks to students. By the end of the academic year, the students would begin the day by examining the schedules of their learning centers and then divide themselves into groups that assigned tasks to individual members, obtained materials, and used worksheets. Although their achievement scores improved significantly, once the students were returned to regular classrooms for the fourth grade, a familiar pattern of problems appeared (Kim, 1990).

The classroom is not the only location in which cultures merge. In the business world, people of various cultures work side by side; those designated as minorities may have leadership positions in which members of the dominant culture report to them. As companies become more global and as the number of international markets increases steadily, the workplace is beginning to resemble the classroom as a meeting place of cultures.

Our goal in urging you to adopt a multicultural perspective is to help you reach a level of significant understanding of people who seem different. If you adopt this perspective, you will come to realize that different people have different worldviews that decisively influence their thinking. People from different cultures do not all think alike. Recognizing how diverse people are in their thinking and behavior will help you to identify and comprehend variations in people's backgrounds and how they become functioning members of their culture. In this way, you will work, play, and study more congenially with others, thus fostering more positive relations in our society.

Finally, cultural awareness should also make us aware that we are all alike in important ways. It's mainly in our behavior, the manner in which we deal with the demands of our environments, that we differ.

children. We also urge you to remember that the equation *biology plus environment equals development* plays out within the confines of a particular culture.

To help you grasp the significance of culture in development, remember that there are three answers to the question: How well do you understand the cultures of your friends, workmates, and your neighbors?

1. You may understand at a *superficial* level; that is, you know only the facts that make up a person's cultural history.

2. You may understand at an *intermediate* level; that is, you understand the central behaviors that are at the core of a person's social life. Language usage is a good example here. Does a child's culture tolerate, even encourage, calling out in class, for example, which could be a major problem for teachers not familiar with the acceptable behaviors of this child's culture?

3. You may understand at a *significant* level; that is, you grasp the values, beliefs, and norms that structure a person's view of the world and how to behave in that world. In other words, you change psychologically as a result of your interactions with a different culture (Casas & Pytluk, 1995).

Consequently, as we begin our work of studying lifespan development we want to impress on you the need to be aware that "different does not mean deficient."

We have integrated examples of the cultural influence on development in a dual manner: through *A Sociocultural View* boxes and by age-specific examples. In this way we hope to accomplish several objectives:

- To understand the relationship between culture and development.
- To identify the values and attitudes that promote healthy development.
- To trace the impact of cultural transmission, such as parenting practices and the influence of peers, schools, and media.
- To assess current cultural change initiatives, such as intervention programs in the United States, and program development in other countries, such as Peru's Human Development Institute, which encourages development through the schools (Harrison, 2000).

Contributors to Biopsychosocial Interactions

If you examine Table 1.2 carefully, you'll note several characteristics listed for the biological, psychological, and social aspects of interactions. These certainly aren't exhaustive but indicate several developmental features that affect growth during the lifespan. More importantly, however, we would like you to think about the interactions that occur among the three categories and how these interactions affect development, which is known as the *epigenetic* view of development. A leading proponent of this view, Gilbert Gottlieb, has defined *epigenesis* as an increase in novelty and complexity of organization over time (Gottlieb, Wahlsten, & Lickliter, 2006). These changes in process and function occur as the result of interactions between the organism and the environment at four levels: genetic, neural, behavioral, and environmental. To give a simple example, genetic damage (biological) may negatively affect cognitive development (psychological), and lead to poor peer relationships (social).

We believe that by recognizing the significance of biopsychosocial interactions, you'll better understand and remember the material of any chapter. This perspective also helps to emphasize those social-cultural features that so powerfully influence development through the lifespan.

TABLE 1.2	Elements of Biopsychosocial Interactions	
Bio	*Psycho*	*Social*
Genetics	Cognitive Development	Attachment
Fertilization	Information Processing	Relationships
Pregnancy	Problem Solving	Reciprocal Interactions
Birth	Perceptual Development	School
Physical Development	Language Development	Peers
Motor Development	Moral Development	Television
Puberty	Self-Efficacy	Stress
Menstruation	Personality	Marriage
Disease	Body Image	Family

Guided Review

12. The biopsychosocial model illustrates the interaction of _____ and _____ in development.

13. The values, beliefs, and behaviors that characterize a large group of people refer to that group's _____.

14. You react to a culture at the _____, _____, or _____ level of understanding.

ISSUES IN LIFESPAN DEVELOPMENT

In lifespan psychology, as in any discipline, several issues or themes appear with sufficient frequency to warrant special mention. Here we'll discuss two issues that affect your understanding of development and that appear repeatedly throughout the book.

Continuity versus Discontinuity

In 1980 Orville Brim and Jerome Kagan published *Constancy and Change in Human Development,* which highlighted a long-simmering controversy among developmental psychologists. Arguing that humans have a capacity for change across the lifespan, Brim and Kagan brought new life to the question "*How* do these changes occur?" Does each new stage of development contain most of the structures that appeared in an earlier stage (Kagan, 1998)? Do you think you are basically the same person you were when you were 3 years old? 12 years old? 20 years old? Or do you feel quite different? How would you explain your answer? These questions introduce the issue of continuity versus discontinuity; that is, do developmental changes appear as the result of a slow but steady progression (**continuity**) or as the result of abrupt changes and stages (**discontinuity**)?

As a rather dramatic illustration, consider the phenomenon known as *attachment* in infancy. Sometime after 6 months of age, babies begin to show a decided preference for a particular adult, usually the mother. We then say that the infant has attached to the mother. During any time of stress—anxiety, illness, appearance of strangers—the baby will move to the preferred adult. With regard to continuity or discontinuity, does attachment appear suddenly as completely new and different behavior, or do subtle clues signal its arrival? (For an excellent summary of current research, see Thompson, 2000.)

Continuities and discontinuities appear in all our lives because the term **development** implies change. Puberty, leaving home, marriage, and career all serve to shape psychological functioning. Continuities occur, however, because our initial experiences, our early learning, and our temperaments remain with us. The form of the behavior may change over the years, but the underlying processes remain the same. For example, the conduct disorders of childhood (stealing, fighting, truancy) may become the violence of adulthood (theft, spousal abuse, child abuse, murder, personality disorders). Surface dissimilarities may be evident in the types of behavior, but the processes that cause both kinds of behavior may be identical, thus arguing for continuity in development (Rutter & Rutter, 1993).

continuity
The lasting quality of experiences; development proceeds steadily and sequentially.

discontinuity
Behaviors that are apparently unrelated to earlier aspects of development.

development
The changes that occur in the lifespan.

Answers   12. heredity, environment 13. culture 14. superficial, intermediate, significant

Other behaviors in our lives, however, seem to be quite different from those that preceded them; for example, walking and talking. We also negotiate transitions at appropriate times in our lives, such as leaving home, beginning a career, getting married, adjusting to the birth of children. Events such as these have caused some developmental psychologists, such as Michael Lewis (1997), to note that accidents, wars, famines, disease, and chance encounters have always been our bedfellows. Consequently, Lewis believes that the study of developmental change is actually the study of complex, often random, and certainly unpredictable conditions.

Most developmental psychologists now believe that both continuity and discontinuity characterize development. As Lerner notes (2002, p. 118), any developmental change may be characterized as being either continuous or discontinuous and either stable or unstable.

Nature versus Nurture

An enduring issue in developmental psychology has been the question of which exercises a greater influence on development, our inborn tendencies (nature) or our surrounding world (nurture)? Again, most developmental psychologists lean toward an interplay between these two forces in shaping development. We (the authors) would argue strongly that the *interaction* between genes and environment explains the individual developmental path each of us follows through our lifespan. Lerner (2002, p. 89) has neatly summarized this argument as follows.

1. Nature and nurture are both involved in the production of behavior.
2. Consequently, they cannot function in isolation from each other but must interact.
3. The resulting interaction implies that both nature and nurture are completely intertwined.

Perhaps Bjorklund (2005, p. 7) summarized this issue as well as anyone can when he stated that, for developmental psychologists, there is no nature-nurture controversy because biological factors are inseparable from experiential factors, with the two constantly interacting. It is *how* they interact that produces a particular pattern of development.

These issues help to identify lifespan psychology as a dynamic discipline, one with great theoretical and practical implications. But, as fascinating as these issues are, we can't forget the integrated nature of development. With these ideas in mind to use as we interpret developmental data, we turn now to those research techniques that developmental psychologists use in resolving questions about the lifespan.

Guided Review

15. Developmental psychologists are mainly interested in _____ change occurs.
16. Those who believe that developmental change occurs because of a slow and steady progression believe in _____.
17. Today's developmental psychologists interpret the influence of nature and nurture as one of an _____ between the two.

Answers

15. how 16. continuity 17. interaction

DEVELOPMENTAL RESEARCH

Having identified several key developmental issues and theoretical viewpoints, it is time to ask: How can we obtain reliable data about these topics so that we may better understand them? Today we use many approaches to understanding human behavior. Each has its strengths and weaknesses; none is completely reliable. Most developmental psychologists employ one of three data collection methods: (1) descriptive studies, (2) manipulative experiments, and (3) naturalistic experiments. In the first type, information is gathered on subjects without manipulating them in any way. In the second two, an experiment is performed before the information is gathered.

Developmental psychologists also use one of four time-variable designs: one-time, one-group studies; longitudinal studies; cross-sectional studies; and a combination of the last two, called sequential studies. Each type of study varies according to the effect of time on the results.

Data Collection Techniques

The three data collection techniques are described and explained in the following sections.

Descriptive Studies

descriptive studies
Gather information on subjects without manipulating them in any way.

Descriptive studies are quite common. Most are numerically descriptive; for example, how many 12-year-olds versus 17-year-olds think the government is doing a good job? How much money does the average 40-year-old woman have to spend

---

AN APPLIED VIEW

When Are Research References Too Old?

Probably for the rest of your career, you will be reading research—articles, chapters in books, monographs, and so on. When should you decide that a reference is too old to be credible any longer? As with so many aspects of social science, the answer is "it all depends." Guidelines exist, however, so let's try to understand them by looking at several references. Before reading our decision, you might try to guess what a good judgment would be.

As many as one-third of adolescents receive less than 70% of their minimum daily requirement for the most common minerals, such as calcium and iron *(U.S. Department of Health, Education, and Welfare, 1972).*

Since eating habits of adolescents are likely to change with the times (depending, among other things, on the economic condition of the country), this statistic is unreliable, because about 30 years have passed since the data were collected.

Although the average number of homosexuals who are contracting AIDS each year is decreasing, homosexuals are still the most vulnerable group *(U.S. National Center for Health Statistics, 1990).*

This study is much more recent, but it too is suspect because we know that the AIDS epidemic is changing very rapidly. In fact, heterosexual females are now experiencing the greatest rate of increase per capita.

Noise-induced hearing loss is recognized as the second most common cause of irreversible hearing loss in older persons *(Surjan et al., 1973).*

Here is another study that is quite dated, but because there is no known reason to believe that aging factors have changed much over the years, if the study was well designed, we may still accept the results.

The major crisis in the first year and one-half of human life is the establishment of basic trust *(Erikson, 1963).*

This statement is not a research finding but rather represents Erikson's belief as reflected in his psychosocial theory of human development. As such, it is accurate because that is exactly what Erikson said.

Can you think of other factors that influence the timeliness of research references? Can you think of other criteria for judging them?

per week? How many pregnant teenage girls were or were not using birth control? How happily or unhappily does the average 66-year-old man view his sex life? Some studies (called self-report studies) ask people their opinions about themselves or other people. These studies may use interviews or questionnaires. Other studies (called *observational studies*) describe people simply by counting the number and the types of their behaviors. A third type of study, the case study, presents data on an individual or individuals in great detail, in order to make generalizations about a particular age group.

An example of the case-study approach is Mack and Hickler's *Vivienne: The Life and Suicide of an Adolescent Girl* (1982). After Vivienne's death, the researchers obtained the family's permission to read her diary, poems, and letters. They also interviewed her relatives, friends, and teachers to shed light on her thinking as she came closer and closer to committing this tragic act. Although their findings may explain the suicide of only this one person, the researchers' hope was to discover the variables that caused such a decision. A more recent case-study approach is of the biographical type. For example, Gardner (1997) closely examined the biographies of four eminent persons: Wolfgang Mozart, Sigmund Freud, Virginia Woolf, and Mahatma Gandhi. From these four cases, he built a new theory about creative innovation.

Descriptive studies have the advantage of generating a great deal of data. Because the sequence of events is not under the observer's control, however, causes and effects cannot be determined; that is, just because two variables are associated does not mean that one causes the other.

Typically, the association between variables is established through a statistical technique known as *correlation.* This technique provides a numerical evaluation of how great the degree of association is between any two variables. For instance, height and weight are associated with each other, but not perfectly. The taller people are, the more they weigh, but this is not always true; the correlation between height and weight for a typical sample of people is moderately high. Although there is a definite association, we would not say the height causes weight, or vice versa— they are simply correlated. We examine the correlation between variables to see how high they are. If high, we may want to set up experiments to further examine the relationship.

Manipulative Experiments

manipulative experiments
The experimenter attempts to keep all variables (all the factors that can affect a particular outcome) constant except one, which is carefully manipulated.

treatment
The variable that the experimenter manipulates.

In the quest for the causes of behavior, psychologists have designed many **manipulative experiments.** In these, the investigators attempt to keep all variables (all the factors that can affect a particular outcome) constant except one, which they carefully manipulate; this is called a **treatment.** If differences occur in the results of the experiment, they can be attributed to the variable that was manipulated in the treatment. The experimental subjects must respond to some test the investigator selects to determine the effect of the treatment. Figure 1.1 illustrates this procedure.

In the figure, E is the experimental group and C is the control group, which receives no special treatment; *x* stands for the treatment; and the lowercase *b* and *a* refer to measurements done before and after the experiment. The two groups must have no differences between them, either before or during the experiment (except the treatment). Otherwise, the results remain questionable.

An example would be a study in which 6th- and 7th-grade inner-city students were taught relaxation techniques as part of a conflict prevention program (Dacey,

FIGURE 1.1

The classic experiment

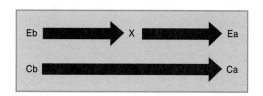

deSalvatore, & Robinson, 1997). Most students benefited from the instruction, but boys were much more apt to use the physiological relaxation technique taught in the program, whereas girls were more likely to employ the cognitive method that was taught.

Though manipulative experiments often can lead us to discover what causes what in life, they have some problems. How do you know your results are reliable? Was the treatment similar to normal conditions? Do subjects see themselves as special because you picked them and thus react atypically? For these reasons, researchers may turn to naturalistic experiments.

Naturalistic Experiments

naturalistic experiments
The researcher acts solely as an observer and does as little as possible to disturb the environment. "Nature" performs the experiment, and the researcher acts as a recorder of the results.

In **naturalistic experiments,** the researcher acts solely as an observer and does as little as possible to disturb the environment. "Nature" performs the experiment, and the researcher acts as a recorder of the results. (Note: Do not confuse these experiments with descriptive studies that are done in a natural setting, such as a park; those are not experiments.) An example is the study of the effects of the Northeast blizzard of 1978 by Nuttall and Nuttall (1980). These researchers compared the reactions of those people whose homes were destroyed with the reactions of people whose homes suffered only minor damage.

Only with a naturalistic experiment do we have any chance of discovering causes and effects in real-life settings. The main challenges with this technique are that it requires great patience and objectivity, and it is impossible to meet the strict requirements of a true scientific experiment.

Time-Variable Designs

In the following sections, we'll describe the four time-variable designs.

One-Time, One-Group Studies

one-time, one-group studies
Studies carried out only once on one group of studies.

As the name implies, **one-time, one-group studies** are those that are carried out only once on one group of subjects. Thus investigating causes and effects is impossible because the sequence of events cannot be known.

Longitudinal Studies

longitudinal studies
The experimenter makes several observations of the same individuals at two or more times in their lives. Examples are determining the long-term effects of learning on behavior; the stability of habits and intelligence; and the factors involved in memory.

The **longitudinal study,** which makes several observations of the same individuals at two or more times in their lives, can answer important questions. Examples are determining the long-term effects of learning on behavior; the stability of habits and intelligence; and the factors involved in memory.

A good example of a longitudinal growth study is that of Werner and Smith (1992), who investigated the long-term effects of birth problems. They found that, even when the problems were of a serious nature, some children proved to be remarkably resilient.

The chief advantage of the longitudinal method is that it permits the discovery of lasting habits and of the periods in which they appear. A second advantage is the possibility of tracing those adult behaviors that have changed since early childhood. Longitudinal research, however, has many problems. It is expensive and often hard to maintain because of changes in availability of researchers and subjects. Changes in the environment can also distort the results. For example, if you began in 1960 to study changes in political attitudes of youths from 10 to 20 years of age, you would probably have concluded that adolescents become more and more radical as they grow older. But the war in Vietnam would surely have had much to do with this finding. The results of the same study done between 1970 and 1980 would probably not show this trend toward the left. And today the data would show something else again.

FIGURE 1.2

Comparison of the longitudinal and cross-sectional approaches

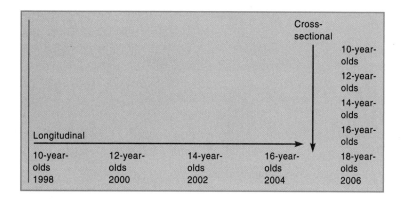

Cross-Sectional Studies

cross-sectional studies
Compare groups of individuals of various ages at the same time in order to investigate the effects of aging.

Cross-sectional studies compare groups of individuals of various ages at the same time to investigate the effects of aging. For example, if you want to know how creative thinking changes or grows during adolescence, you could administer creativity tests to groups of 10-, 12-, 14-, 16-, and 18-year-olds and check on the differences of the average scores of the five groups. Jaquish and Ripple (1980) did this, but their subjects ranged in age from 10 to 84!

As with each of the other research designs, a problem occurs with this method. Although careful selection can minimize the effects of cultural change, it is possible that the differences you may find may be due to differences in age cohort, rather than maturation. Age cohorts are groups of people born at about the same time. Each cohort has had different experiences throughout its history, and this fact can affect the results as well as the actual differences in age. Figure 1.2 compares the longitudinal and cross-sectional approaches.

Sequential (Longitudinal/Cross-Sectional) Studies

sequential (longitudinal/ cross-sectional) studies
A cross-sectional study done at several times with the same groups of individuals.

When a cross-sectional study is done at several times with the same groups of individuals (such as administering creativity tests to the same five groups of youth, but at three different points in their lives), the problems mentioned before can be alleviated. Table 1.3 illustrates such a study. Although **sequential** research is complicated and expensive, it may be the only type that is capable of answering important questions in the complex and fast-changing times in which we live.

TABLE 1.3	Illustration of a Sequential (Longitudinal/ Cross-Sectional) Study		
CREATIVITY TEST			
Test 1 March 4, 1999	*Test 2 March 4, 2001*	*Test 3 March 4, 2003*	
GROUP A (12 years old)	GROUP A (14 years old)	GROUP A (16 years old)	Mean Score Group A
GROUP B (14 years old)	GROUP B (16 years old)	GROUP B (18 years old)	Mean Score Group B
GROUP C (16 years old)	GROUP C (18 years old)	GROUP C (20 years old)	Mean Score Group C
MEAN SCORE 1999	MEAN SCORE 2001	MEAN SCORE 2003	

TABLE 1.4	Relationships of Data Collection Techniques and Time-Variable Designs

	DATA COLLECTION TECHNIQUES		
Time-Variable Designs	*Descriptive*	*Manipulated*	*Naturalistic*
One-time, one-group			
Longitudinal			
Cross-sectional			
Sequential			

Table 1.4 shows how each of the data collection methods may be combined with each of the time-variable designs. For each of the cells in this table, a number of actual studies could serve as examples. Can you see where each study mentioned in this section would go?

AN APPLIED VIEW

Understanding the Research Article

As you continue your reading and work in lifespan development, your instructor will undoubtedly ask you to review pertinent articles that shed light on the topic you're studying. Many of these articles present the results of an experiment that reflects the scientific method.

The typical research article contains four sections: the *Introduction,* the *Method* section, the *Results* section, and *Discussion* (Moore, 1983). We'll review each of these sections using a well-designed study—*The Effects of Early Education on Children's Competence in Elementary School,* published in *Evaluation Review* (Bronson, Pierson, & Tivnan, 1984)—to illustrate each of the four sections.

1. The Introduction

The introductory section states the purpose of the article (usually as an attempt to solve a problem) and predicts the outcome of the study (usually in the form of hypotheses). The introduction section also contains a review of the literature. In the introductory section of the article by Bronson and associates, the researchers state that their intent is to coordinate the effects of early education programs on the performance of pupils in elementary school. They concisely review the pertinent research and suggest a means of evaluating competence.

2. The Method Section

The method section informs the reader about the subjects in the experiment (Who were they? How many? How were they chosen?), describes any tests that were used, and summarizes the steps taken to carry out the study. In the study by Bronson and associates, the subjects were 169 2nd-grade children who had been in an early education program and 169 other children who had not been in the preschool program. The outcome measure was a classroom observation instrument. The authors then explained in considerable detail how they observed the pupils.

3. The Results Section

In the results section, the results gathered on the subjects is presented, together with the statistics that help us to interpret the data. In the article we are using, the authors present their data in several clear tables and show differences between the two groups using appropriate statistics.

4. Discussion

Finally, the authors of any research article will discuss the importance of what they found (or did not find) and relate their findings to theory and previous research. In the Bronson article, the authors report that the pupils who had experienced any early education program showed significantly greater competence in the second grade. The authors conclude by noting the value of these programs in reducing classroom behavior problems and improving pupils' competence.

Don't be intimidated by research articles. Look for the important features and determine how the results could help you to understand people's behavior at a particular age.

FIGURE 1.3

A comparison of research techniques

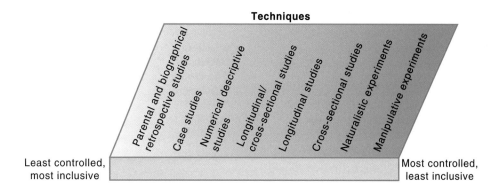

Techniques

Parental and biographical retrospective studies · Case studies · Numerical descriptive studies · Longitudinal/cross-sectional studies · Longitudinal studies · Cross-sectional studies · Naturalistic experiments · Manipulative experiments

Least controlled, most inclusive

Most controlled, least inclusive

To conclude this section, Figure 1.3 compares the various research techniques. By controlled, we mean the degree to which the investigator can control the relevant variables. By inclusive, we mean the degree to which all relevant information is included in the data.

Guided Review

18. In a manipulative experiment, the experimenter attempts to keep all the variables constant except one, which is called the _____.

19. A study that observes the same individuals two or more times in their lives is known as a _____ study.

20. Comparing groups of individuals of various ages at the same time is an example of _____ research.

Answers

18. treatment 19. longitudinal 20. cross-sectional

CONCLUSION & SUMMARY

In this chapter we urged you to think about lifespan development as a rich, multilayered complex of interactions. We presented a model of development—the biopsychosocial model—that forms the structure of this book. We urge you to use this model to help you grasp and retain the material and meaning of the various chapters. We have also identified the age groups that constitute the lifespan and that are the focus of this book. As a result of reading about the strengths and weaknesses of different research methods, you should be more analytical and critical of the studies that are presented.

Lifespan study can aid us in adjusting to a society in which rapid change seems to be an inevitable process. By acquiring insights into your own development and recognizing the developmental characteristics of people of differing ages, you can hope to have more harmonious relationships with others.

How would you define and describe lifespan development?

• As psychologists realized that development did not cease at adolescence but continued into adulthood and old age, lifespan psychology assumed an important place in developmental psychology.

• To understand development is to accept the positive and negative features of change.

• The timing of experiences as well as the transitions during the lifespan help us to gain insights into developmental processes.

• Development cannot be explained by age alone.

How have views of lifespan development changed over the years?

• Children today are seen as complex individuals who develop subject to the interaction of many external and internal factors.

• Conflicting interpretations of adolescence (storm, stress, or calm) continue to rage today.

- The adult years are no longer seen as a time devoid of change until decline sets in.

What are the different views of lifespan development?

- A biological interpretation of development emphasizes the powerful impact the genes have on development.
- The bioecological model recognizes the importance of proximal processes in development.
- The need for more sophisticated perspectives on development has highlighted the place of reciprocal interactions in development.

What role do biopsychosocial interactions play in lifespan development?

- Biopsychosocial interactions in human development refer to the interactions of biological, psychological, and social forces.
- Biopsychosocial interactions occur at multiple levels of the developing person, from the genetic to the environmental levels.
- Analyzing development from a biopsychosocial perspective helps to identify the complexities of human development.

What are the major issues in lifespan development?

- If it is to present a complete picture of development, any analysis of lifespan development must address key developmental issues, such as the importance of culture and development.
- Many psychologists believe that development occurs as a steady progression of small accomplishments (for example, most infants begin to move on the floor by pulling themselves on their stomachs; they then move to a position on their hands and knees and move much more quickly, which is an example of continuous development); other psychologists believe that development occurs in spurts or stages, such as the marked difference between crawling and walking, which is an example of discontinuity.

- The controversy over stability versus change continues to divide developmental psychologists.
- Resiliency is a fact of human development that requires cautious interpretation.

What is the role of research in studying lifespan development?

- To explain the various ages and stages of development, we must use the best data available to enrich our insights and to provide a thoughtful perspective on the lifespan.
- Good data demand careful research methods; otherwise, we would be constantly suspicious of our conclusions.
- The most widely used research techniques include descriptive studies, manipulative experiments, and naturalistic experiments.
- Developmental psychologists also use four time-variable designs: one-time, one-group; longitudinal studies; cross-sectional studies; and sequential studies.

 KEY TERMS

biopsychosocial interactions
continuity
cross-sectional studies
culture
descriptive studies

discontinuity
lifespan psychology
longitudinal studies
manipulative experiments
naturalistic experiments

One-time, one-group studies
sequential studies
time-variable designs
treatment

 WHAT DO YOU THINK?

1. We urged you to refer to the biopsychosocial model as you continue your reading of the text. Can you explain its potential value? Now think of an example in your own life, or in the life of a family member, and describe how biological, psychological, and social factors interacted to produce a particular effect. Do you think the model helped you to explain that person's behavior?

2. We presented several issues that thread their way through lifespan studies; for example, culture and development and continuity versus discontinuity. Why do you think these are issues? Examine each one separately and defend your reasons for stating that each has strong developmental implications.

3. Throughout the chapter, we have stressed the important role that the environment or context plays in development. What do you think of this emphasis? Think about your own life and the influences (both positive and negative) that those around you have had. Cite these personal experiences in your answer.

CHAPTER REVIEW TEST

1. **Development is about**
   a. change.
   b. age.
   c. gender.
   d. genes.

2. **Development is**
   a. a lifelong process.
   b. age focused.
   c. topically restricted.
   d. circular in nature.

3. **Lifespan psychology assumes that development is**
   a. unidimensional.
   b. chronologically explained.
   c. multidimensional.
   d. age limited.

4. **Understanding childhood at any historical period depends on what _____ think of children.**
   a. peers
   b. scientists
   c. siblings
   d. adults

5. **A model that uses the interaction of biological, psychological, and social influences to explain development is the**
   a. psychoanalytic.
   b. cognitive.
   c. biopsychosocial.
   d. behavioral.

6. **One of the first outstanding theorists to recognize the importance of the early years was**
   a. Skinner.
   b. Freud.
   c. Bandura.
   d. Hebb.

7. **Lifespan psychologists cannot focus solely on _____ for explanation.**
   a. maturation
   b. genes
   c. schooling
   d. age

8. **When we refer to the values, beliefs, and characteristics of a people, we are referring to**
   a. culture.
   b. race.
   c. ethnicity.
   d. customs.

9. **Adolescence begins in _____ and ends in _____ .**
   a. biology, culture
   b. school, marriage
   c. structures, schema
   d. ego, superego

10. **Descriptive studies**
    a. determine cause and effect.
    b. manipulate variables.
    c. require experimenter control.
    d. generate considerable data.

11. **When an experimenter keeps all variables constant but one, that one is called**
    a. determined.
    b. predicted.
    c. descriptive.
    d. treatment.

12. **An example of a cross-sectional study is**
    a. comparing individuals of various ages at the same time.
    b. continued observations of the same individuals.
    c. careful description by the researcher.
    d. one that requires no manipulation.

13. **The typical research article contains four sections. Which item is not included in a research article?**
    a. introduction
    b. method
    c. results
    d. author biography

Answers

1.a 2.a 3.c 4.d 5.c 6.b 7.d 8.a 9.a 10.d 11.d 12.a 13.d

2 chapter

THEORIES OF DEVELOPMENT: Interpreting the Lifespan

Chapter Outline

Chapter Objectives

After you read this chapter, you should be able to answer the following questions.

- How does psychoanalytic theory explain development across the lifespan?

- What is the relationship between psychosocial crises and lifespan development?

- How did Piaget explain cognitive development?

- What impact does culture have on lifespan development?

- What is the behavioral perspective on development?

- What is the status of current developmental theory?

n this chapter, you'll read about several of the leading developmental theories. After you have finished your reading, we would like you to analyze the information in the following case study and interpret it according to a theory (or theories) you have just studied. For example, let's assume you use Skinner's ideas on reinforcement. You would want to mention the need for positive reinforcement: Was Thomas receiving needed reinforcements at home and school? If not, could anything be done about it? Do you think proper reinforcement would improve Thomas' behavior? Another of your classmates may believe that Erikson's work is more applicable. Or is the answer to be found in some unique combination of theories? There are no right or wrong answers; rather we would like you and your classmates to discuss your various interpretations and see how theory guides your analysis of behavior.

I. Background Information

A.   Thomas: 8 years old
White
Public school
First grade (not promoted)
Sixth of six children

B.   Home Conditions
The mother is 42 years old, separated from her husband, and almost totally blind. Four of the six children live with her in a low-income section of the city. The oldest son and a married daughter do not reside in the home.

II. The Problem

Thomas, bothered by asthma, exhibits frequent temper tantrums and is failing the first grade for the second time.

III. History

Thomas is the youngest of six children; his birth was accompanied by marital and family problems. The pregnancy was unplanned and unwanted, and the father left home before the child was born. Thomas was born prematurely, had immediate difficulty with breathing, and was put in a respirator for 20 days before coming home.

Feeding, motor development, and verbal development were all normal, but he manifested considerable separation anxiety; that is, he cried excessively when his mother left him alone. He still shows signs of this behavior at 8 years of age, although less frequently. The mother states that he is "fidgety" (cannot remain still) and that he worries about his small size.

IV. Impressions

After several interviews with both the boy and his mother, the caseworker commented that both mother and child display clear signs of anxiety. A definite theme of aggression and violence runs through Thomas's conversation. Teachers report that he exhibits little motivation and bothers other children in class. He has a very short attention span and shows increasing aggressiveness.

The interviewer reported that the mother seeks constant reassurance and experiences great difficulty with the disciplining of her children. The interviewer stated that the combination of an insecure mother and an unhappy, aggressive son whom she is finding difficult to control points to serious developmental problems for Thomas.

V. Summary

Thomas continues to do very poorly in school. He wants love from and dependence on his mother yet simultaneously seeks independence and escape from his mother's control. This conflict produces ambivalent feelings toward his mother; that is, he displays considerable anger toward his mother for trying to control him. Also, he bitterly resents his father's absence.

Instead of expressing his anger, he remains passive, especially in school, which is the primary cause of his poor scholastic performance. Thomas's behavior resolves his conflict, however, since he can remain with his mother but also strike back at her with his school failure.

In an age devoted to scientific fact, why should we bother with theories in our quest to unlock the mysteries of development? The answer is as simple as it is logical. We believe that theories are essential for understanding facts for several reasons. Good theories:

- Help to organize a huge body of information. The published studies on human development number in the tens of thousands, and their conclusions would be incomprehensible unless they were organized in some meaningful manner. A theory provides a way of examining facts and also supplies "pegs" on which we can hang similar types of research findings. In this way we construct a lens through which to view development.

- Help to focus our search for new understandings. Theories offer guideposts in our quest for insights into the enigma of human development.

- Help to explain how findings may be interpreted. They offer a detailed guide that leads us to decide *which* facts are important and *what* conclusions we can draw.

- Help to identify major disagreements among scholars. By focusing on these disagreements, they offer testable ideas that can be confirmed or refuted by research.

As you read the theories summarized in this chapter, we urge you to recognize the increasing sophistication that the theorists bring to their speculations. Lerner (2006) notes that today's developmental psychologists analyze development from the perspective of biopsychosocial interactions while recognizing that the roots of contemporary theories may well be linked to developmental ideas that first appeared in the early days of the 20th century. Finally, remember that the ultimate goal of any theory is to provide a framework for the study of human development that furthers scientific vision and stimulates application of that science for public policy and social programs (Lerner, 2002, p. xvii).

In this chapter, we'll first turn to the major theorists who for many years have guided our thinking about development: Sigmund Freud, Erik Erikson, Jean Piaget, Lev Vygotsky, B. F. Skinner, Albert Bandura, and Uri Bronfenbrenner. Next we'll discuss the present status of developmental theory and several issues related to the direction of developmental theory. Finally, we'll use Richard Lerner's notion of developmental systems theory to reflect recent thinking regarding new directions in developmental analysis, which we hinted at in Chapter 1.

THE PSYCHOANALYTIC APPROACH

There is nothing as practical as good theory.

—KURT LEWIN

On a beautiful spring day in 1885, Sigmund Freud sat down and wrote a startling letter to his fiancée. He told her that he had just about completed a massive task— destroying his notes, letters, and manuscripts of the past 14 years, a destructive act that he would repeat several times in his lifetime—Freud revealed his mistrust of future biographers. Yet, in spite of his efforts, the autobiographical nature of much of his published works and his vast correspondence left a lasting legacy. Freud's ideas (called **psychoanalytic theory**) no longer dominate developmental psychology as they did in the early part of the 20th century, but his insistence on the early years as decisive in development has remained a potent and controversial concept (Cairns, 1998; Crain, 2005).

psychoanalytic theory
Freud's theory of the development of personality.

Dr. Sigmund Freud was a medical doctor who proposed the psychoanalytic theory of development. What do you think was Freud's greatest contribution to developmental psychology?

id
One of the three structures of the psyche according to Freud; the source of our instinctive desires.

ego
One of the three structures of the psyche according to Freud; mediates between the id and the superego.

superego
One of the three structures of the psyche according to Freud; acts as a conscience.

In more than 100 years of psychological research, no one has played a larger role than did Sigmund Freud. Even his most severe critics admit that his theory on the development of personality is a milestone in the social sciences (Ferrris, 1997). For example, his ideas on the unconscious have become almost a given in any psychological discussion—that is, a belief that we possess powerful ideas and impulses of which we're unaware but that exert a strong influence on our behavior (Kahn, 2002).

Let's begin by examining Freud's ideas about the structure of the mind.

Structures of the Mind

Freud divided the mind into three structures: the **id,** the **ego,** and the **superego,** which appear at different stages of a child's development. They are empowered by the *libido,* Freud's term for psychic energy, which is similar to the physical energy that fuels bodily functions. The characteristics of the three structures of the mind are as follows:

- *The id.* This structure, the only one present at birth, contains all our basic instincts, such as the need for food, drink, dry clothes, and nurturance. The simplest of the structures, it strives only to secure pleasure.
- *The ego.* The ego is the central part of our personality, the (usually) rational part that does all the planning and keeps us in touch with reality. It begins to develop from the moment of birth. Freud believed that the stronger the ego becomes, the more realistic, and usually the more successful, a person is likely to be (Lerner, 2002).
- *The superego.* The superego is our conscience. Throughout infancy, we gain an increasingly clearer conception of what the world is like. Toward the end of the first year our parents and others begin to teach us what they believe is right and wrong and expect us to begin to behave according to the principles they espouse.

Now starts the never-ending battle between the desires of the id and the demands of the superego, with the ego struggling unceasingly for compromises between these two powerful forces.

The Developing Personality

For Freud, personality development means moving through five stages, each of which he assigns to a specific age range. Each stage is discrete from the others and has a major function based on a pleasure center. Unless this pleasure center is

Sigmund Freud suggested that babies react to needful feelings such as hunger in several steps. First they become aware of the need; then they cry; next they imagine that the need has been met; and then they fall back to sleep. Slowly they learn that imagination is no substitute for real satisfaction of a need.

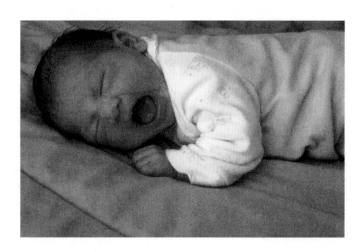

TABLE 2.1	Freudian Stages of Development

- **The oral stage** (0 to 1 1/2 years old). The oral cavity (mouth, lips, tongue, gums) is the pleasure center. Its function is to obtain an appropriate amount of sucking, eating, biting, and talking.

- **The anal stage** (1 1/2 to 3 years old). The anus is the pleasure center. The function here is successful toilet training.

- **The phallic stage** (3 to 5 years old). The glans of the penis and the clitoris are the pleasure centers in this stage and in the two remaining stages. The major function of this stage is the healthy development of sexual interest, which is achieved through masturbation and unconscious sexual desire for the parent of the opposite sex. Resolution of the conflicts caused by this desire (called the *Oedipus conflict* in males and the *Electra conflict* in females) is the goal.

- **The latency stage** (5 to 12 years old). During this stage, sexual desire becomes dormant, which is especially true for boys who may refuse to kiss or hug their mothers and treat female age-mates with disdain. Because our society is more tolerant of the daughter's attraction to her father, the Electra complex is less resolved and girls' sexual feelings may be less repressed during this stage.

- **The genital stage** (12 years old and older). At this stage a surge of sexual hormones occurs in both genders, which brings about an unconscious recurrence of the phallic stage. Normally, however, youths have learned that desire for one's parents is taboo, and so they set about establishing relationships with members of the opposite sex who are their own age. If fixation occurs at any stage, anxiety results, and defense mechanisms will be used to deal with it.

stimulated appropriately (not too much, not too little), the person becomes fixated (remains at that stage) and is unable to become a fully mature person (Kahn, 2002). The five stages are summarized in Table 2.1.

Psychoanalytic theory has undergone many changes since Freud first proposed it, and as the significance of culture's role in development has become increasingly apparent, social influences on development have assumed an ever greater importance in psychoanalytic theory (Eagle, 2000; Westin, 2000). In spite of the diminished acceptance of Freud's ideas, psychoanalytic theory has retained a solid core of support through the years. Recently, neuropsychologist Mark Solm (2004) argued strongly that although Freud's views seemed hopelessly outdated given the findings of the neuroscientists in the 1980s, more current research has drawn renewed interest in the concepts of psychoanalysis.

For example, the 2000 Nobel Laureate, Eric Kandel, stated that psychoanalysis is still the most coherent and intellectually satisfying view of the mind. With this statement, Kandel reflected the belief of several modern neuroscientists that some of Freud's conclusions matched the research results of current experiments. Cognitive neuroscientists, for example, identify different memory systems as *explicit* or *implicit,* which complement Freud's notion of *conscious* and *unconscious* memory.

As you can well imagine, these ideas have not gone unchallenge. J. Allan Hobson, a professor of psychiatry at Harvard Medical School, argued just as forcefully that scientific investigations of Freud's concepts reveal errors in major parts of his theory. For example, most neuroscientists agree that the ego-id struggle does *not* control brain chemistry. To illustrate the wide gulf separating believers from nonbelievers, Hobson (2004, p. 89) states that psychoanalytic theory is indeed comprehensive, but if it is terribly in error, then its comprehensiveness is hardly a virtue. And so the struggle continues!

Maturity is a high price to pay for growing up.

—Tom Stoppard

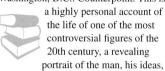

Paul Ferris (1998). *Dr. Freud: A life.* Washington, D.C.: Counterpoint. This is a highly personal account of the life of one of the most controversial figures of the 20th century, a revealing portrait of the man, his ideas, and his technique.

PSYCHOSOCIAL CRISES AND DEVELOPMENT

Influenced by Freud, but searching for a different perspective, Erik Erikson was the chief proponent of a psychosocial theory of development (as opposed to Freud's psychosexual). His seminal work is *Childhood and Society* (1963), a perceptive and at times poetic description of human life.

Erik Erikson's View

Psychologist Erik Erikson is best known for his theory of psychosocial crises. How would you contrast Erikson's work with Freud's?

Erikson's view of human development flowed from his extensive study of people living in an impressive variety of cultures: Germans, East Indians, the Sioux of South Dakota, the Yuroks of California, and wealthy adolescents in the northeastern United States (Erikson, 1959, 1968). His ideas also stem from intensive studies of historical figures such as Martin Luther (Erikson, 1958) and Mahatma Gandhi (Erikson, 1969). Finally, as Lerner (2002) notes, Erikson's theory continues to attract considerable attention and thus remains a vital, living interpretation of human development.

According to Erikson, human life progresses through a series of eight stages. Each of these stages is marked by a crisis that needs to be resolved so that the individual can move on. Erikson (1968) used the term *crisis* as a developmental term—that is, a time of increased vulnerability and heightened potential. Table 2.2 gives an overview of his psychosocial theory.

Erikson's Eight Psychosocial Stages

Let us look at each stage more closely, keeping in mind Erikson's *epigenetic principle,* according to which anything that grows has a ground plan from which the various parts arise at specific times to form a functioning whole (Lerner, 2002).

1. *Basic trust versus mistrust* (birth to 1 1/2 years old). In the first stage, which is by far the most important, infants should develop a sense of basic trust. For Erikson, trust has an unusually broad meaning. To the trusting infant, it is not so much that the world is a safe and happy place but rather that it is an orderly, predictable place; that is, infants learn about causes and effects. Trust flourishes with warmth, care, and also discipline.

2. *Autonomy versus shame and doubt* (2 to 3 years old). When children are about 2 years old, they should move into the second stage, characterized by the crisis of autonomy versus shame and doubt. Children begin to feed and dress themselves, and toilet training usually begins during these years. Erikson agreed with other psychoanalysts about the importance of toilet training and believed

Answers   1. early years 2. three 3. libido 4. id 5. superego 6. oral

TABLE 2.2	Erik Erikson's Psychosocial Theory of Development			
Age (Years)	Stage	Psychosocial Crisis	Psychosocial Strength	Environmental Influence
1	Infancy	Trust vs. mistrust	Hope	Maternal
2–3	Early Childhood	Autonomy vs. shame, doubt	Willpower	Both parents or adult substitutes
4–5	Preschool, nursery school	Initiative vs. guilt	Purpose	Parents, family, friends
6–11	Middle childhood	Industry vs. inferiority	Competence	School
12–18	Adolescence	Identity vs. identity confusion	Fidelity	Peers
18–35	Young Adulthood	Intimacy vs. isolation	Love	Partners: spouse/lover, friends
35–65	Middle age	Generativity vs. stagnation	Care	Family, society
Over 65	Old age	Integrity vs. despair	Wisdom	All humans

Adapted from *Childhood and Society* by Erik H. Erikson. Copyright © 1950, 1963 by W.W. Norton & Company, Inc., renewed © 1978, 1991 by Erik H. Erikson. Used by permission of W.W. Norton & Company, Inc. Published in the UK by Hogarth Press. Reprinted by permission of The Random House Group Ltd.

that the sources of generosity and creativity lie in this experience. Toilet training is not the only accomplishment of the period; children of this age usually start acquiring self-control.

3. *Initiative versus guilt* (3 to 5 years old). The third crisis, initiative versus guilt, begins when children are about 4 years old. Building on the ability to control themselves, children now acquire some influence over others in the family and begin to successfully manipulate their surroundings. They don't merely react, they also initiate. If parents and others make children feel incompetent, however, the children develop a generalized feeling of guilt about themselves. Erikson believed that play was particularly important during these years, both as an aid to a child's identity and as a safe way to reduce tension by dealing with problems in a symbolic way (Csikszentmihalyi & Rathunde, 1998).

4. *Industry versus inferiority* (5 to 12 years old). The fourth stage corresponds closely to the child's elementary school years. Now the task is to go beyond imitating ideal models and acquire the needed information and skills of their culture. Children expand their horizons beyond the family and begin to explore the neighborhood. Their play becomes more purposeful, and they seek knowledge to complete the tasks that they set for themselves. A sense of accomplishment in making and building should prevail, otherwise children may develop a lasting sense of inferiority.

5. *Identity versus identity confusion* (12 to 18 years old). The main task of the adolescent is to achieve a state of identity. Erikson, who originated the term **identity crisis,** used the word in a special way. In addition to thinking of identity as the general picture one has of oneself, Erikson referred to it as a state toward which one strives. If you are in a state of identity, the various aspects of your self-image would be in agreement with one another; they would be identical.

identity crisis
Erikson's term for those situations, usually in adolescence, that cause us to make major decisions about our identity.

According to Erikson, a sense of intimacy with another person of the opposite gender should develop between the ages of 18 and 35. If it does not, a sense of isolation results. How does the concept of biopsychosocial interactions help to explain this behavior?

Live so that when your children think of fairness and integrity, they think of you.
—H. J. BROWN

Erik Erikson (1958). *Young Man Luther.* New York: Norton. Martin Luther was the main force behind the Protestant Reformation. In Erikson's penetrating analysis of the causes behind Luther's actions, we have a wonderfully clear example of Erikson's ideas about adolescence in general and negative identity in particular.

6. *Intimacy versus isolation* (18 to 25 years old). In the sixth stage, intimacy with others should develop. Erikson is speaking here of far more than sexual intimacy. He is talking about the essential ability to relate one's deepest hopes and fears to another person and to accept in turn another person's need for intimacy.

7. *Generativity versus stagnation* (25 to 65 years old). Generativity means the ability to be useful to ourselves and to society. As in the industry stage, the goal here is to be productive and creative, thus leading to a sense of personal fulfillment. Furthermore, a sense of trying to make the world a better place for the young in general, and for one's own children in particular, emerges. In this stage many people become mentors to younger individuals, sharing their knowledge and philosophy of life. When people fail in generativity, they begin to stagnate, to become bored and self-indulgent, unable to contribute to society's welfare. Such adults often act as if they are their own child.

8. *Integrity versus despair* (65 years old and older). To the extent that individuals have been successful in resolving the first seven crises, they achieve a sense of personal integrity. Adults who have a sense of integrity accept their lives as having been well spent. They feel a kinship with people of other cultures and of previous and future generations. They have a sense of having helped to create a more dignified life for humankind. They have gained wisdom.

If, however, people look back over their lives and feel they have made the wrong decisions or, more commonly, that they have too frequently failed to make any decision at all, they see life as lacking integration. They feel despair at the impossibility of "having just one more chance to make things right." They often hide their terror of death by appearing contemptuous of humanity in general, and of those of their own religion or race in particular. They feel disgust for themselves.

THE COGNITIVE DEVELOPMENTAL APPROACH

Imagine for a moment that your name is Jean Piaget. You were born in Neuchatel, Switzerland, in 1896 and are now 15 years old. You began your scholarly career at the age of 10 (!) and published numerous papers on birds, shellfish, and other topics of natural history. Based on these publications, you have just been offered the curator's position at the prestigious Geneva Natural History Museum. What would you do? Realizing that the museum officials didn't know his age, Piaget rejected the offer and went on to finish secondary school, complete his Ph.D. in biology, and write more than 50 influential books during his lifetime.

Piaget's training as a biologist had a major impact on his thinking about cognitive development. His fascination with the processes that led children to make incorrect answers in reasoning tests caused him to turn his attention to the analysis of children's developing intelligence. As Rutter and Rutter (1993) noted, one of Piaget's great legacies is the attention he focused on the role that cognitive mechanisms play in development.

Key Concepts in Jean Piaget's Theory

Have you ever been in a restaurant and wondered why some babies try to find the toy they knocked off their tray, while others make no attempt to retrieve it or even look for it? This apparently simple behavior and other things that babies say and do fascinated the Swiss psychologist, Jean Piaget (1896–1980), who sought to understand the *cognitive structures* of the intellect (1966; Flavell, 1963). How did Piaget explain cognitive development?

Stages

Piaget believed that intelligence matures as we develop increasingly effective **cognitive structures.** (Think of these structures as the blueprints that enable us to organize and adapt to our world.) Piaget believed that cognitive development means that we form more sophisticated cognitive structures as we pass through four stages: the *sensorimotor stage* (birth to 2 years old); the *preoperational stage* (2 to 7 years old); the *concrete operational stage* (7 to 11 years old); and the *formal operational stage* (11 years old and up). Thus, Piaget believed that cognitive functioning begins as responses to concrete phenomena—babies know only what they can touch, taste, or see. Our ability to use symbols and to think abstractly increases with each subsequent stage until we are able to manipulate

Jean Piaget was among the first researchers to study normal intellectual development. How does Piaget's theory reflect his training as a biologist?

cognitive structures
Piaget's term to describe the basic tools of cognitive development.

TABLE 2.3	Piaget's Stages of Cognitive Development

Stage	Age	Major Feature
Sensorimotor	Birth to 2 years	Infants use their bodies to form cognitive structures
Preoperational	2 to 7 years	Use of symbols; rapid language growth
Concrete operational	7 to 11 years	Can reason about physical objects
Formal operational	11+ years	Abstract thinking leads to reasoning with more complex symbols

abstract concepts and consider hypothetical alternatives. Piaget's stages of cognitive development are illustrated in Table 2.3.

Functional Invariants

Piaget stated that we can form cognitive structures because we have inherited a method of intellectual functioning that enables us to respond to our environment. At the heart of this method are two psychological mechanisms, **adaptation** and **organization.** Because we use these two mechanisms constantly throughout our lives from birth through adulthood, Piaget named them **functional invariants** (Lerner, 2002).

Piaget believed that adaptation consists of **assimilation** and **accommodation.** When we assimilate something we incorporate it; we take it in. Think of eating; we take food into the structure of our mouths and change it to fit the shape of our mouths, throats, and digestive tract. We take objects, concepts, and events into our minds similarly: We incorporate them into our mental structures, changing them to fit the structures as we change the food to fit our physical structures. For example, you are now studying Piaget's views on cognitive development. These ideas are unique and will require effort to understand them. You are attempting to comprehend them by using the cognitive structures you now possess. You are assimilating Piaget's ideas; that is, you are mentally taking them in and shaping them to fit your cognitive structures.

But we also change as a result of *assimilation;* that is, we accommodate to what we have taken in. The food we eat produces biochemical changes; the stimuli we incorporate into our minds produce mental changes. *We change what we take in; we are also changed by it.* For example, not only are you taking in and slightly changing Piaget's ideas, but they are also changing your views on intelligence and cognitive development. The change in your cognitive structures will produce corresponding behavioral changes; this is the process of *accommodation.*

Thus, the adaptive process is the heart of Piaget's explanation of learning. As we try to "fit" new material into existing cognitive structures, we try to strike a balance between assimilation and accommodation, a process that is called **equilibration.** For example, we all make mistakes but by continued interaction with the environment, we correct these mistakes and change our cognitive structures (we have accommodated).

But our mental life doesn't consist of random activities; it is organized. The cognitive structures that we form enable us to engage in ever more complex thinking. Physical structures can again provide an analogy for Piaget's ideas on organization. To read this text you are balancing it, turning the pages, and moving your eyes. All these physical structures are organized so that you can read. Likewise,

adaptation
One of the two functional invariants in Piaget's theory.

organization
One of the two functional invariants in Piaget's theory.

functional invariants
In Piaget's theory, the psychological mechanisms of adaptation and organization.

assimilation
Piaget's term to describe the manner in which we incorporate data into our cognitive structures.

accommodation
Piaget's term to describe the manner by which cognitive structures change.

equilibration
Piaget's term to describe the balance between assimilation and accommodation.

for you to understand this material, your appropriate cognitive structures are organized so that they can assimilate and accommodate.

How Does the Theory Actually Work?

Try thinking of Piaget's theory in the following way: Stimuli come from the environment and are filtered through the functional invariants. The functional invariants, adaptation and organization, use the stimuli to form new structures or change existing structures. For example, you may have had your own idea of what intelligence is, but now you change your structures relating to intelligence because of your new knowledge about Piaget. Your content or behavior now changes because of the changes in your cognitive structures. The process is as follows.

Environment
(filtered through)

Functional Invariants
(produce)

Cognitive Structures
(which combine with behavior to form)

Schemes
(organized patterns of thought and action)

Although Piaget's ideas have held the interest of developmental psychologist for more than seven decades, recent research has frequently been critical because he underestimated the cognitive abilities of children (Bjorklund, 2005). Still, as Siegeler and Alibali argue (2005), with all its weaknesses Piaget's theory gives us good ideas about how children think. (Piaget's theory is also discussed in Chapters 5, 7, 9, and 11.) Another theorist, however, who put culture at the center of his work, was Lev Vygotsky.

THE CULTURAL FRAMEWORK APPROACH

A telling example of culture's importance occurred when several American psychologists went to Rwanda to help with the massive psychological problems caused by the savagery and violence the people had experienced (Seppa, 1996). They found that traditional Western therapeutic methods, such as individualized therapy, were useless. Cultural values change, but slowly (Harrison, 2000). Successful programs in Africa demand programs that help restore social supports and relationships. They also discovered that urging patients to "talk it out" simply did not work. Using song, dance, and storytelling, which their patients found natural and comforting, proved to be more successful.

Experiences such as this one testify to the value of the work of the Russian psychologist Lev Vygotsky (1896–1934), who has attracted considerable attention because of his emphasis on social processes. Born in Russia in 1896, Vygotsky was educated at Moscow University and quickly turned his attention to educational psychology, developmental psychology, and psychopathology. For Vygotsky, the clues to understanding mental development are in children's social processes; that is, cognitive growth depends on children's interactions with those around them. The adults around children interact with them in a way that emphasizes those things that a culture values.

Tragically, tuberculosis claimed Vygotsky in 1934. His work today, because of its cultural emphasis, is more popular than it was when he died. In contrast to Piaget who, as we have seen, believed that children function as "little scientists," Vygotsky turned to social interactions to explain children's cognitive development.

Lev Vygotsky's Theory

Lev Vygotsky placed great emphasis on the role of social processes in intellectual development. Explain how Vygotsky's theory helped to emphasize the role of culture in development.

If you understand Vygotsky's basic ideas, you'll be able to grasp how his theory works. For example, Vygotsky identified dual paths of cognitive development—*elementary processes,* which are basically biological, and *psychological processes,* which are essentially sociocultural (Vygotsky, 1978). Children's behaviors emerge from the intertwining of these two paths. For example, brain development provides the physiological basis for the appearance of external or egocentric speech, which gradually becomes the inner speech children use to guide their behavior.

Three fundamental themes run through Vygotsky's work: the unique manner in which he identified and used the concept of development; the social origin of mind; and the role of speech in cognitive development.

1. Vygotsky's *concept of development* is at the heart of his theory. He thought that elementary biological processes are qualitatively transformed into higher psychological functioning by developmental processes. In other words, such behaviors as speech, thought, and learning are all explained by development

2. To understand cognitive development, we must examine *the social and cultural processes* shaping children (Wertsch & Tulviste, 1992). But how do these processes affect cognitive development? Vygotsky argued (1978) that any function in a child's cultural development appears twice, on two planes: first, in an interpsychological category (social exchanges with others), and, second, within the child as an intrapsychological category (using inner speech to guide behavior).

   What happens to transform external activity (interpsychological) to internal activity (intrapsychological)? For Vygotsky, the answer is to be found in the process of *internalization,* about which he believed we still know little.

3. Although Vygotsky lacked hard data to explain it, he believed that *speech* is one of the most powerful tools humans use to progress developmentally.

   . . . the most significant moment in the course of intellectual development, which gives birth to the purely human forms of practical and abstract intelligence, occurs when speech and practical activity, two previously completely independent lines of development, converge. (Vygotsky, 1978, p. 24)

Table 2.4 identifies the most significant differences between Vygotsky and Piaget. (See Chapters 5 and 10 for additional discussion of Vygotsky's work.)

Guided Review

11. Piaget's major concern was with the development of _____ _____.
12. Piaget believed that cognitive development occurred by passage through cognitive _____.
13. _____ are mental, internalized actions.
14. Vygotsky differed from Piaget in that he was more interested in the role that _____ _____ played in cognitive development.
15. Vygotsky also placed greater emphasis on _____ than did Piaget.
16. Vygotsky believed in two processes that lead to cognitive development: elementary and _____.

Answers

11. cognitive structures 12. stages 13. operations 14. social interactions 15. culture 16. psychological

	Piaget	Vygotsky
TABLE 2.4	**Key Differences between Piaget and Vygotsky**	
Perspective	Individual child constructs view of world by forming cognitive structures—"the little scientist"	Child's cognitive development progresses by social interactions with others ("social origins of mind")
Basic psychological mechanism	Equilibration—child acts to regain equilibrium between current level of cognitive structures and external stimuli	Social interaction—encourages development through the guidance of skillful adults
Language	Emerges as cognitive structures develop	Begins as preintellectual speech and gradually develops into a sophisticated form of inner speech; one of the main forces responsible for cognitive development
Learning	Assimilation and accommodation lead to equilibrium	Results from the interaction of two processes: biological elementary processes (such as brain development) and sociocultural interactions
Problem solving	Child independently searches for data needed to change cognitive structures, thus enabling child to reach solution	Two aspects of problem solving: (1) key role of speech to guide "planful" behavior; (2) joint efforts with others

reinforcement
Usually refers to an increase in the frequency of a response when certain pleasant consequences immediately follow it.

Harvard psychologist B. F. Skinner is identified with operant conditioning. How does reinforcement influence development?

THE BEHAVIORAL APPROACH

A strictly behavioral explanation of human development takes us into the world of learning and learning theory. Two of its best-known proponents are B. F. Skinner, famous for his insights into the role of **reinforcement,** and Albert Bandura, who called our attention to the power of modeling in development.

Skinner and Operant Conditioning

About three years before Skinner died, the wife of one of the authors (JFT) called Skinner's office at Harvard to request any available photos of his early work. To her surprise, Skinner himself answered the phone. Slightly nonplussed, she identified herself and told him what she wanted. Sensing her nervousness, Skinner told her a funny story about the rats in one of his early experiments and said he would be delighted to send along some copies. In a very real sense, Skinner demonstrated the proper use of positive reinforcement.

B. F. Skinner (1904–1990) received his doctorate from Harvard and, after teaching for several years at the Universities of Minnesota and Indiana, he returned to Harvard. Convinced of the importance of reinforcement, he developed an explanation of learning that stressed the consequences of behavior. What happens after we do something is all-important. Reinforcement has proven to be a powerful tool in the developing, shaping, and control of behavior, both in and out of the classroom. Prominent in American psychology for over 60 years, Skinner inspired and stimulated research and theory. As Lattal (1992) noted, when Skinner spoke, psychologists listened.

Skinner has been in the forefront of psychological and educational endeavors for the past several decades. Innovative, practical, tellingly prophetic, and witty, Skinner's work has had a lasting effect. In several major publications—*Science and Human Behavior* (1953), *Verbal Behavior* (1957), *The Technology of Teaching* (1968), *Beyond Freedom and Dignity* (1971)—and in a steady flow of articles, Skinner reported his experiments and developed and clarified his theory. In his theory, called **operant conditioning** (also known as **instrumental conditioning**), he demonstrated that the environment has a much greater influence on learning and behavior than previously realized. Skinner argued that the environment (parents, teachers, peers) reacts to our behavior and either reinforces or eliminates that behavior. Consequently, the environment holds the key to understanding behavior.

Skinner argued that if the environment reinforces a certain behavior, it's more likely to result the next time that stimulus occurs. Thus, if the teacher asks a particular question again, the student is more likely to give the right answer, because that response was reinforced. If the response is punished, the response is less likely in the future. If the response is simply ignored, it also becomes less likely in the future. Each of these three concepts—**reinforcement, punishment,** and no response (which Skinner calls **extinction**)—needs further explanation.

Skinner preferred the term *reinforcement* to *reward*. Defining reinforcement as anything that makes a response more likely to happen in the future, Skinner identified two kinds of reinforcement. **Positive reinforcement** refers to any event that, when it occurs after a response, makes that response more likely to happen in the future. **Negative reinforcement** is any event that, when it ceases to occur after a response, makes that response more likely to happen in the future. Note that both types of reinforcement make a response more likely to happen. Giving your daughter candy for doing the right thing would be positive reinforcement. Ceasing to twist your brother's arm when he gives you back your pen would be negative reinforcement. Thus human development is the result of the continuous flow of learning that comes about from the operant conditioning we receive from the environment every day.

Arguing for the importance of the nature-nurture interaction in a biological age, Michael Rutter (2002) has presented a three-fold argument stressing that, although genes are at the heart of all psychological traits, it is the interaction of biological, psychological, and social influences that explain behavior.

1. Given today's remarkable scientific advances, there is little disagreement about the genetic effect on all behavior (Rutter, 2002, p.3). But even from a biological perspective, the real challenge is to discover how genetic influences and brain functions, for example, are altered by experience.

2. Emerging genetic evidence clearly illustrates the significance of *nongenetic* influences. As Rutter notes, even with those traits that are most powerfully influenced by genetic forces, environmental effects are far from trivial (Rutter, 2002, p. 3).

3. Finally, the same genetic factors may be involved in different types of childhood psychopathology, for example, anxiety and depression.

With its curt dismissal of the role of the biological in the nature-nurture interaction, operant conditioning lost its appeal to developmental biologists and disappeared from the mainstream of modern science (Cairns & Cairns, 2006).

These ideas about change in human behavior have been enhanced by the ideas of Albert Bandura and his associates. They extend the behaviorist view to cover social behavior.

---

operant conditioning
Skinner's form of conditioning, in which a reinforcement follows the desired response; also known as *instrumental conditioning.*

instrumental conditioning
Skinner's form of conditioning, in which a reinforcement follows the desired response; also known as *operant conditioning.*

punishment
Usually refers to a decrease in the frequency of a response when certain unpleasant consequences immediately follow it.

extinction
Refers to the process by which conditioned responses are lost.

positive reinforcement
Process whereby stimuli whose presentation as a consequence of a response strengthens or increases the rate of the response.

negative reinforcement
Refers to stimuli whose withdrawal strengthens behavior.

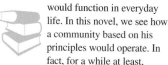

B. F. Skinner (1948). *Walden Two.* New York: Macmillan. Many students find it hard to see how Skinner's behaviorism would function in everyday life. In this novel, we see how a community based on his principles would operate. In fact, for a while at least, several such communities really existed. Reading *Walden Two* will provide you practical insights into Skinner's work.

Bandura and Social Cognitive Learning

modeling
Bandura's term for observational learning.

observational learning
Bandura's term to explain the information we obtain from observing other people, things, and events.

social (cognitive) learning theory
Bandura's theory that refers to the process whereby the information we glean from observing others influences our behavior.

Albert Bandura, one of the chief architects of social learning theory, has stressed the potent influence of **modeling** on personality development (Bandura, 1997). He called this **observational learning.** In a famous statement on **social (cognitive) learning theory,** Bandura and Walters (1963) cited evidence to show that learning occurs through observing others, even when the observers do not imitate the model's responses at that time and get no reinforcement. For Bandura, observational learning means that the information we get from observing other people, things, and events influences the way we act (Bjorklund, 2005).

Social learning theory has particular relevance for development. As Bandura and Walters noted, children often do not do what adults tell them to do but rather what they see adults do. If Bandura's assumptions are correct, adults can be a potent force in shaping the behavior of children because of what they do.

The importance of models is seen in Bandura's interpretation of what happens as a result of observing others:

- By observing others, children may acquire new responses, including socially appropriate behaviors.
- Observation of models may strengthen or weaken existing responses.
- Observation of a model may cause the reappearance of responses that were apparently forgotten.
- If children witness undesirable behavior that is either rewarded or goes unpunished, undesirable behavior may result. The reverse is also true.

Bandura, Ross, and Ross (1963) studied the relative effects of live models, filmed human aggression, and filmed cartoon aggression on preschool children's aggressive behavior. The filmed human adult models displayed aggression toward an inflated doll; in the filmed cartoon aggression, a cartoon character displayed the same aggression. Later, all the children who observed the aggression were more aggressive than were youngsters in a control group. You can see, then, how modeling can be a powerful force in development. (For a more detailed account of how recent research supports these conclusions, see Chapter 10.)

Another example of the power of Bandura's ideas is seen in the concept of self-efficacy. Bandura and colleagues (2001) believe that a child's sense of self-efficacy helps him to produce desired outcomes that might otherwise elude him. Unless children—and adults—believe that their actions will attain desired goals, they have little incentive to act and certainly will not persist in the face of difficulty. Bjorklund (2005) believes that Bandura's ideas testify to the significance of the interaction between a child's cognitive and social world.

Guided Review

17. Skinner's view of learning is referred to as _____ or _____ conditioning.
18. This explanation of learning depends heavily on the role of the _____.
19. When a response is _____, it is more likely to reoccur.
20. Bandura's social learning theory, also called observational learning, stresses the role of _____ in learning.
21. Observation of models may _____ or _____ existing responses.

Answers

17. operant, instrumental 18. environment 19. reinforced 20. modeling
21. strengthen, weaken

A BIOECOLOGICAL MODEL

The environment acts in ways that we are only beginning to comprehend. For example, psychologists have for some time recognized the importance of *reciprocal interactions* in development. Reciprocal interactions mean that we respond to those around us in a way that causes them to change; their responses to us then change, which in turn produces new changes in us. These *bidirectional interactions* are an unending process that doesn't rely exclusively on either heredity or environment. Rather it uses the interactions between the two to describe and explain developmental changes that occur from birth, if not sooner.

Thanks to the systems analysis of Uri Bronfenbrenner (Bronfenbrenner, 1978, 1989; Bronfenbrenner & Morris, 1998, 2006), we now realize that there are many environments acting on us. Bronfenbrenner's perspective is called the **bioecological model,** defined as the continuity and change in the biopsychosocial characteristics of human beings, both as individuals and as groups (Bronfenbrenner & Morris, 2006, p. 793). The bioecological model contains four major components. The first component, *proximal processes,* refers to the reciprocal interactions between a person and the environment (often called the *context* of development). Feeding and playing with a child, peer play, and school learning with teachers are all examples of proximal processes. Bronfenbrenner & Morris (1998, 2006) refer to proximal processes as the primary engines of development.

The second component is the *person* involved, especially an individual's temperament or disposition that activates the proximal processes. Third is the person's *context,* those environmental features that either foster or interfere with development. Finally, developmental changes occur over *time,* the fourth component of the bioecological model.

Bronfenbrenner visualized the environment as a set of nested structures, each inside the next. He identified the deepest level of the environment that affects development as the **microsystem** (for example, the home or school). Next is the **mesosystem,** which refers to the relationship among microsystems. A good example is seen in a child's school achievement. Those children who are fortunate enough to be in a family that maintains close and warm relationships with the school can be expected to do well in their classroom work.

The **exosystem,** Bronfenbrenner's next level, is an environment in which the developing person is not actually present, but which nevertheless affects development. For example, an adolescent has a friend whose parents, unlike her own parents, are relaxed about late hours, exert no pressure to complete assignments, and so on. These different parenting practices may eventually cause conflict with her own parents. The **macrosystem,** Bronfenbrenner's final level, is the blueprint of any society, a kind of master plan for human development within that society. Think for a moment about the differences that people in the mainland Chinese society have encountered when compared to the experiences of American citizens.

But these systems also interact over time (sometimes called the *chronosystem*); they don't remain isolated from one another. Consider the youngster whose father has just lost his job (changes in the exosystem), which then causes the family to move to another location with different friends and schools for the child (changes in the micro- and mesosystems). These examples illustrate how a bioecological analysis emphasizes the significance of context in development.

Let's conclude our discussion of developmental theory by turning to new ideas and new controversies.

DEVELOPMENTAL THEORY: CURRENT STATUS, FUTURE DIRECTION

The world of developmental theory is changing as you read these words, and we want you to be aware of the latest thinking of today's theorists.

bioecological model
The continuity and change in the biopsychosocial characteristics of human beings, both as individuals and as groups.

microsystem
The home or school.

mesosystem
The relationship among microsystems.

exosystem
Environment in which the developing person is not present but that never the less affects development.

macrosystem
The blueprint of any society.

Change in the Field

A persistent criticism of such traditional theorists such as Piaget and Freud is that they were simply too unidimensional to explain the complexity of development. That is, they focused on only one aspect of development. For example, Piaget was consumed by the lure of cognitive development, and Freud spent his lifetime delving into the secrets of personality development. But as Lerner noted (1998), in current developmental theories, the person is not simply "biologized, psychologized, or sociologized."

And yet, we should continue to turn to these theorists for guidance along particular developmental paths. For example, Piaget remains a trusted guide for unlocking many of the enigmas of cognitive development. Erikson's sensitive understanding of psychosocial crises provides cogent clues to the identity problems many adolescents face. We can integrate the knowledge these great theorists have generated to further our vision of the lifespan. With gratitude, then, we'll use their insights throughout our work in this book.

Such restricted viewpoints, however much they have helped us to understand the processes involved in development, present an inadequate portrayal of the richness and dynamism of the lifespan. The nuances of human development can't be captured by theories limited to one facet of development motor, cognitive, or language. Rather, a developmental systems perspective is needed, one that encompasses previously hard-won knowledge and now searches for explanations in the relationships among the multiple levels that contribute to development (Lewis, 2000). As Lerner (2002, p. 134) noted, to describe and understand the changes that take place over the lifespan, *we must pay attention to all the levels at which change can occur and the interactions among these changes.* This important concept, frequently referred to as *epigenesis,* is further developed in Lerner (1998, 2006) and Gottlieb, Wahlsten, and Lickliter, 2006.

Interactions among Levels of Development

As noted in Chapter 1, today's developmental psychologists are analyzing activity at four levels: genetic, neural, behavioral, and environmental (Gottlieb, 1997; Gottlieb, Wahlsten, & Lickliter, 2006). *But more significantly, with this epigenetic analysis, researchers and theorists are scrutinizing the interactions among these levels,* which is the meaning of the multidirectional nature of development mentioned in Chapter 1. Figure 2.1 illustrates interactions of the multiple levels of development.

The genes act to produce a particular physical constitution, which contributes to an individual's behavior, helping that individual to select a particular environment (peers, activities, and so on). But the environment also acts to influence behavior, physical status, and even genetic activity; in other words, each level interacts with all other levels. An attempt to capture this type of analysis is seen in the work of Richard Lerner and in developmental systems theory (1991, 1998, 2002, 2006).

FIGURE 2.1

Interactions of multiple levels of development

Source: Gottlieb, 1997; Gottlieb, Wahlsten, & Lickliter, 2006; Lerner, 1998, 2006.

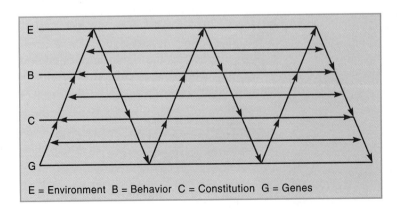

E = Environment B = Behavior C = Constitution G = Genes

Developmental Systems Theory

We know today that heredity and environment produce their results in a complex, interactive manner that reflects the role of reciprocal interactions. By stressing the complexity of developmental analysis, those adhering to a reciprocal interaction perspective have made it clear that there are no simple cause-and-effect explanations of development. All of us, children, adolescents, and adults, experience a constant state of reorganization as we move through the life cycle (Lerner, Fisher, & Weinberg, 2000).

Also known as *developmental contextualism,* **developmental systems theory** was popularized by Richard Lerner (1991, 1998, 2002, 2006) and Gottlieb (1997). The current version attributed to Gottlieb, Wahlstem, and Lickliter (2006) takes a perspective that begins with the idea that all of our characteristics, psychological as well as biological, function by reciprocal interactions with the environment (often referred to as the *context*). In this way, developmental systems theory leads to the belief that we *construct* our view of the surrounding world.

Lerner (2002, p. 222) has emphasized that developmental systems theory requires three levels of analysis.

1. The first demands a knowledge of the characteristics of those being studied.
2. Second is the need to have an understanding of a person's context and a justification for why this portion of the context is significant for the analysis.
3. Third, there must be a conceptualization of the relationship between the individual characteristics and the contextual feature.

These forces are illustrated in Figure 2.2.

Exchanges between individuals and the multiple levels of their contexts are the basic change processes in development (Horowitz, 2000; Lerner, 2006). Consequently,

developmental systems theory
Set of beliefs leading to the conclusion that we construct our own views of the world

FIGURE 2.2

Developmental contextual model of person-context interaction

From R. Lerner, *Developmental Psychology,* Vol. 27, 1991, pp. 27–32, Figure 1, p. 30. Copyright © 1991 by the American Psychological Association. Reprinted with permission.

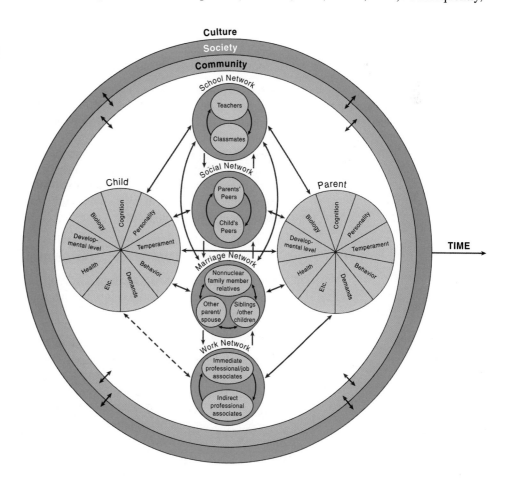

the crucial element in our development is the changing relationship between our complexity and a multilayered context. If you think about this deceptively simple statement, you can appreciate the need to study development, not from any single perspective such as biology or environment but from a more sophisticated analytical appraisal. *No single level of organization is seen as the primary or the ultimate causal influence on behavior and development* (Dixon & Lerner, 1999).

For example, consider what happens when you interact with your environment. Your genes provide a blueprint that is passed on to the cells, tissues, and organs of your body, influencing the growth of such widely divergent features as your brain and your temperament (to name only two). However, the intricate and involved layers of the context, ranging from your family to your peers to your wider social sphere, simultaneously weave their networks of influence. Simple explanations? Hardly. What is needed is a developmental perspective equally as intricate as the behavior it attempts to clarify. As Bjorklund (2005) notes, developmental systems theory was designed to explain *how nature and nurture interact to produce a particular pattern of development.*

Final Theoretical Notes

Although we have used developmental systems theory as an example of the changes taking place in the search for developmental explanations, other ideas continue to emerge. **Life Course Theory,** proposed by Glen Elder, refers to a sequence of socially defined, age-graded events and roles that individuals enact over time. Studying individuals from childhood to old age meant that researchers had to:

- Change from studying children alone to a strategy that focused on aging over the entire life course.

- Rethink how human lives are organized and evolve over time, while searching for patterns of constancy and change.

- Relate individuals' life course to an ever-changing society, stressing the developmental changes brought about by this interaction (Elder & Shanahan, 2006).

Evolutionary developmental psychology is an explanation of development that assumes our physiological and psychological systems resulted from evolution by selection. In 1859, Charles Darwin published *On the Origin of Species,* in which he concluded that natural selection was the basic principle of change. Evolutionary theory suggests that psychological mechanisms evolved to bring about specific adaptive functions (Bjorklund, 2005). It's the study of how our genes are expressed during development and how the context of development influences the expression of genetic action (Geary & Bjorklund, 2000; Gottlieb, 2002). Defining evolutionary developmental psychology as

> *the application of the basic principles of Darwinian evolution, particularly natural selection, to explain contemporary human development,*

Bjorklund and Pellegrini (2002, p. 4) go on to say that it involves the genetic and environmental mechanisms that underlie universal development. These authors believe that evolutionary developmental psychology is not merely evolutionary psychology applied in a general way to human development. Rather, it demands the search for those mechanisms that explain behavior from the viewpoint of natural selection and a recognition that higher level cognitive processes must be examined from an evolutionary perspective.

Evolutionary developmental psychology has also received support from an unrelated and unexpected source: the cognitive revolution. Widely and wildly popular with psychologists, studies of cognition provided respectability to explanations of behavior that were not immediately visible (Geary & Bjorklund, 2000). In tracing the roots of evolutionary psychology, Pinker (1997) stated that evolutionary psychology brings together two scientific revolutions. One is the cognitive revolution that began in the

Life Course Theory
Theory referring to a sequence of socially defined, age-graded events and roles that individuals enact over time.

evolutionary psychology
Explanation of development that rests on the assumption that our physiological and psychological systems resulted from evolution by selection.

1950s and 1960s, which helped us to understand why we have the kind of mind we do. The other is the change in evolutionary biology that explained the ability of living things to adapt by selection. Thus the physiological and psychological mechanisms needed for healthy development are those that survive the process of natural selection. Conversely, developmental psychologists have expressed reservations, lest the notion that "biology is destiny" becomes too easily accepted, thus diminishing the environmental input into development (Geary & Bjorklund, 2000; Gottlieb, 2002).

Finally, the theories we've discussed thus far fall neatly into the realm of developmental psychology. Other theories, however, not as easily classified as developmental, nevertheless have made significant contributions to understanding development. For example, Abraham Maslow (1987), a humanistic psychologist at Brandeis, proposed a theory of human needs that has remained with us to this day. According to Maslow, there are five types of needs: physiological (hunger and sleep), safety (security, protection, stability, and freedom from fear and anxiety), love and belonging (need for family and friends), esteem (positive opinion of self and also by others), and self-actualization (feelings of restlessness unless we are doing what we think we are capable of doing).

Table 2.5 summarizes several features of the theories discussed in this chapter.

TABLE 2.5 Comparing Theories of Development

	Psychoanalytic	*Psychosocial*	*Cognitive*	*Cultural*	*Behavioral*	*Contextual*
Major Figures	Freud	Erikson	Piaget	Vygotsky	Skinner Bandura	Lerner
Major Ideas	Passage through the psychosexual stages	Passage through the psychosocial stages	Development of cognitive structures through stages of cognitive development	Social processes embedded within a culture influence development	Power of operant conditioning; role of modeling in development	Development occurs as an individual's characteristics interact with that person's context
Essential Features	Id, ego, superego; psychosexual stages	Psychosocial crises; psychosocial stages	Formation of cognitive structures; stages of cognitive development	Social processes	Reinforcement of responses; observational learning modeling	Interaction among multiple levels of development
Source of developmental problems	Conflict during development leads to fixation, regression, and personality problems	Inadequate resolution of psychosocial crises	Weak formation of cognitive structures	Environmental support lacking or insufficient	Lack of reinforcement, incorrect pairing of stimuli and responses	Faulty exchanges between the individual and the multiple levels of the context
Goal	Sexually mature individual	A sense of personal integrity	Satisfactory formation and use of cognitive structures	Recognition and use of social processes to guide development	The acquisition of conditioned acts to fulfill needs	Satisfactory relationships between the individual and a multilayered context

AN INFORMED VIEW

Children's Literature and Maslow's Hierarchy of Needs

As we look at each of these needs in turn, beginning with physiological needs, we see the appeal of Maslow's hierarchy. In Katherine Paterson's popular novel *The Same Stuff As Stars,* 11-year-old Angel and her little brother Bernie vividly demonstrate not only the significance of stars and the night sky but also how Maslow's needs reach into the lives of children.

1. Physiological Needs. Physiological needs, such as hunger and sleep, when they are unsatisfied, dominate children's lives. Unless they are satisfied, everything else recedes. Children who frequently do not eat breakfast or suffer from poor nutrition, or adolescents who are extremely sensitive about their weight and diet endlessly, experience a sharp drop in their energy levels and are less likely to be motivated. In the *Same Stuff As Stars,* when Bernie and Angel live with their mother, they are always hungry. Bernie cries: "I didn't have no lunch," and his mother, Verna replies, carelessly, "I never thought of it."

2. Safety Needs. Children need to be free from fear and anxiety to perform and achieve to their potential. Other children who are subject to daily abuse of whatever kind—neglect, a home atmosphere marked by the uncertainties of excessive drug or alcohol use, physical trauma, or psychological sarcasm and ridicule—are constantly anxious. Initially safety and security and freedom from fear and anxiety were not options for Bernie and Angel, since their father was in jail and their mother had abandoned them. Again, when Angel finally goes to middle school and is faced with ridicule and labeled "pond scum" because of her father's misdeeds, she continues to be insecure. Only when she is living with her great-grandmother and makes friends with the librarian and the man who knows the stars does she gradually become comfortable and free from fear.

3. Love and Belongingness Needs. Feelings of being alone, not part of the group, or not having any sense of belongingness raise genuine threats to a child's self-esteem. Children

need to feel they are wanted and accepted. If these needs remain unsatisfied, children may go to great lengths in their efforts to be accepted. Angel tries to justify her mother's cruelty when Bernie cries, "I hate her. She's mean." She knows she should stick up for her mother, but she doesn't know what to say. When her mother later kidnaps Bernie from school, however, Angel is desolate. "Why just Bernie? Why did she take Bernie and leave me behind? Doesn't she love me too? Oh, Momma, I need you, too."

4. Esteem Needs. The opinions of others and a child's own self-judgment act to produce a sense of self-esteem, which if positive leads to a continuous desire to excel. Deserved reinforcement (praise, rewards, and so on) goes a long way to stimulating and maintaining motivation. If children lack self-esteem, their motivation also is lacking. In the beginning, Angel's self-esteem is zero. Her mother constantly called her "Miss Know It All" and frequently complained, "I don't know what I'm going to do with you kids." As the story progresses, and Angel and Bernie find a home with their great-grandma and make new friends, Angel's self-esteem improves.

5. Need for Self-Actualization. As Maslow stated (1987, p. 22), even if all needs are satisfied, there is a tendency to feel restless unless we are doing what we think we are capable of doing. Angel is moving toward self-actualization. Her basic needs are gradually being satisfied. "If it hadn't been for the stars she might have given up trying" is not only the theme of the book but also describes Angel's determination and thoughtfulness.

As children move toward self-actualization, they satisfy their basic needs and continue to progress toward physical and psychological health. If you convince children, by encouragement and the examples of appropriate literature, that they should—and can—fulfill their promise, they will have started on the path to self-actualization.

Guided Review

22. A major criticism of Freud and Piaget is that their theories are too _____.

23. Modern developmental theorists have turned their attention to the _____ among multiple levels of development.

24. Lerner's work is referred to as _____ _____.

25. A term used to describe the influence of environmental complexity on development is _____.

CONCLUSION & SUMMARY

In this chapter, we introduced you to several interpretations of development that will help you to understand and integrate developmental data. Although we might have chosen many theories to include in this chapter (some of which we'll discuss later), the ones we have presented here have played or are playing major roles in our understanding of human development. You have a lot to remember, but we'll be coming back again and again to these seminal ideas to help you to gain a firm understanding of them.

How does psychoanalytic theory explain development across the lifespan?

- Freud considered the unconscious mind to be the key to understanding human beings.
- Important information in the unconscious mind is kept hidden through an array of defense mechanisms.
- The mind is divided into three constructs: the id, the ego, and the superego, each of which appears at different stages of a child's development.
- Personality development is divided into five instinctive stages of life—oral, anal, phallic, latency, and genital—each stage serving a major function.
- Failure to pass through a stage of development results in fixation, which halts a person from becoming fully mature.

What is the relationship between psychosocial crises and lifespan development?

- Erikson believed that human life progresses through eight "psychosocial" stages, each one marked by a crisis and its resolution.
- Although the ages at which one goes through each stage vary, the sequence of stages is fixed. Stages may overlap, however.
- A human being must experience each crisis before proceeding to the next stage. Inadequate resolution of the crisis at any stage hinders development.

How did Piaget explain cognitive development?

- Piaget focused on the development of the cognitive structures of the intellect during childhood and adolescence.
- Organization and adaptation play key roles in the formation of structures.
- Piaget believed that cognitive growth occurred in four discrete stages: sensorimotor, preoperational, concrete operational, and formal operational.

What impact does culture have on lifespan development?

- Lev Vygotsky, a leading commentator on the role of culture in development, emphasized the significance of social processes to bring about satisfactory growth.

- Vygotsky believed that the capacity to learn depends on abilities of the child's teachers as well as on the child's abilities.
- The difference between the child's ability to learn independently and to learn with help is called the zone of proximal development.

What is the behavioral perspective on development?

- Skinner believed that the consequences of behavior are critical.
- Skinner's paradigm involves three steps: a stimulus occurs in the environment; a response is made in the presence of that stimulus; and the response is reinforced, punished, or extinguished.
- Bandura has extended Skinner's work to the area of social learning, which he calls observational learning.

What is the current status of developmental theory?

- Interactions among the various levels of development are the focus of current developmental research.
- Lerner's developmental contextualism concentrates on the exchanges between an individual's levels of developmental and the context to explain developmental processes.

KEY TERMS

accommodation
adaptation
assimilation
bioecological model
cognitive structures
developmental systems theory
ego
equilibration
evolutionary developmental psychology
exosystem

extinction
functional invariants.
id
identity crisis.
instrumental conditioning
Life Course Theory
macrosystem
mesosystem
microsystem
modeling

negative reinforcement
observational learning
operant conditioning
organization
positive reinforcement
psychoanalytic theory
punishment
reinforcement
social (cognitive) learning theory
superego

chapter 2 Review

WHAT DO YOU THINK?

1. What is your reaction to the statement, "The truth or falseness of a theory has little to do with its usefulness"?

2. Some people say that, in his concept of human development, Freud emphasized sexuality too much. What do you think?

3. If Piaget were alive today, what would his reaction be to developmental contextualism?

4. Skinner criticized the other theorists in this chapter for believing they can describe what goes on in the human mind. After all, he said,

no one has ever looked inside one. What's your position?

5. Is it possible for a person to be deeply intimate with another person and still be in a state of identity confusion?

CHAPTER REVIEW TEST

1. **Freud's structure of the mind included**
   a. cognitive structures.
   b. safety needs.
   c. ego.
   d. reinforcing elements.

2. **The id is the structure of the mind that is present**
   a. at birth.
   b. through experience.
   c. by internal representations.
   d. through crisis resolution.

3. **Freud believed that development entailed moving through psychosexual stages. Difficulty at any stage can cause a person to become**
   a. fixated.
   b. operational.
   c. negatively reinforced.
   d. displaced.

4. **According to Freud, sexual desire becomes dormant during the**
   a. oral stage.
   b. anal stage.
   c. phallic stage.
   d. latency stage.

5. **Bronfenbrenner's theory of development is called**
   a. the environmental search model.
   b. the generic trace model.
   c. the bioecological model.
   d. the reinforcement model.

6. **One-year-old Jane has already learned that her mother will be there when Jane needs her. This predictable world helps a child to develop**
   a. creativity.
   b. intimacy.

   c. generativity.
   d. trust.

7. **The psychosocial crisis of industry versus inferiority must be resolved during**
   a. the school years.
   b. early childhood.
   c. adolescence.
   d. adulthood.

8. **Piaget's theory of cognitive development focused on the formation and development of**
   a. zones of proximal development.
   b. reinforcement schedules.
   c. cognitive structures.
   d. modeling strategies.

9. **Piaget placed considerable emphasis on operations, which he viewed as**
   a. reflexes.
   b. age-appropriate responses.
   c. internalized actions.
   d. interactions.

10. **Although both Piaget and Vygotsky devoted their lives to studying cognitive development, Vygotsky placed greater emphasis on**
    a. cognitive structures.
    b. social interactions.
    c. sensitive periods.
    d. observational learning.

11. **Skinner carefully analyzed the role of reinforcement in development and distinguished it from**
    a. cognitive structures.
    b. reward.
    c. operations.
    d. needs.

12. **In operant conditioning, the environment acts as the major source of**
    a. operations.
    b. cognitive structures.
    c. defense mechanisms.
    d. reinforcement.

13. **The great value of observational learning is that a person need not overtly react to learn**
    a. mental operations.
    b. new responses.
    c. ego identity.
    d. schedule of reinforcements.

14. **Today's developmental psychologists consider theories such as those of Freud and Piaget as too**
    a. insensitive.
    b. biologically focused.
    c. cultural oriented.
    d. unidimensional.

15. **Lerner's analysis of development depends on analyzing**
    a. multiple levels of development.
    b. schedules of reinforcement.
    c. identity stages.
    d. cognitive stages.

16. **The resurgence of interest in biological explanations of development is due to**
    a. government subsidies.
    b. the influence of learning theorists.
    c. recent genetic research.
    d. studies of prenatal development.

17. **More complex explanations of development depend on the idea of**
    a. genes.
    b. reciprocal interactions.
    c. naturalistic research.
    d. stimulus-response experiments.

Answers

1. c, 2. a, 3. a, 4. d, 5. c, 6. d, 7. a, 8. c, 9. c, 10. b, 11. b, 12. d, 13. b, 14. d, 15. a, 16. c, 17. b

THE BIOLOGICAL BASIS OF DEVELOPMENT

3
chapter

Chapter Outline

Chapter Objectives

After you read this chapter, you should be able to answer the following questions.

- How does fertilization, both natural and assisted, occur?

- What are the mechanisms of heredity, and what could go wrong?

- What are the major features and anticipated uses of the Human Genome Project?

49

As the sun began to rise on June 26, 2000, the weather gave every indication of becoming hot and humid, a Washington day that seemed ideal for a ceremony in the Rose Garden of the White House. Later, as a crowd gathered to celebrate one of the most remarkable feats in the history of biology—the unveiling of the first rough draft of the human genome—tension in the air seemed to grip everyone.

Some of the great names in American biology were there. James Watson, codiscoverer of DNA and the first director of the Human Genome Project (HGP) in 1988, stood uneasily with others. Inside the White House, Francis Collins, current director of HGP, who had shepherded the federally funded public project to a positive conclusion, chatted with President Bill Clinton, as did Craig Venter, the president of Celera Genomics, who had led the private sector in its race with Collins and the federal project in their efforts to win biology's ultimate prize.

Behind the formality of what appeared to be a festive occasion lay years of bitter infighting between the scientists with the federally funded projects and those with the privately held Celera, a story that included dramatic public battles, private scheming, and feuding, all with one goal in mind—recognition and riches. (We'll return to this fascinating story later in the chapter.)

The Human Genome Project has been nothing less than an attempt to identify and map the 25,000 to 30,000 genes that constitute our genetic makeup. Thanks to recent genetic research, the promise for the future for all human endeavors is staggering. Once specific genes are identified and located, efforts can be made to combat thousands of genetic diseases! Perhaps equally as exciting is the attempt to identify "susceptibility" genes, which do not of themselves cause disease but make certain people susceptible to such diseases as breast cancer, colon cancer, and Alzheimer's. All the principal players—James Watson, Francis Collins, Craig Venter—agreed that we have now entered a time of an astounding new array of biological studies.

Think of Chapter 3 as a guide to studying a map. In this case, however, you'll be studying your own inherited human map, now being traced in exquisite detail in the *Human Genome Project* (HGP). But you may ask: What value is a map of our genes? Some practical contributions of DNA research include its use in paternity identification and criminal investigations. But aside from the contribution it is making to human knowledge, DNA research offers a great potential for identifying and curing disease.

In this chapter, you'll read about the fertilization process, during which the sperm and the egg unite. Today, however, we can no longer refer to simply "the union of sperm and egg." We must ask additional questions: Whose sperm? Whose egg? Where did the union occur? Was it in the woman's body? Which woman will carry the fertilized egg? You can see, then, that fertilization is a process filled with the potential for conflict and controversy because of new techniques that assist fertilization and enable it to occur outside a woman's body.

Also, our characteristics don't just appear; they're passed on genetically from generation to generation. Following our discussion of genes, we'll trace the manner in which hereditary traits are transmitted. And, because occasionally the transmission of traits produces abnormalities, we will discuss them as well. Finally, no discussion of human heredity is complete without acknowledging the ethical issues that have arisen because of new developments. Answers still elude us, but at least we can ask several critical questions: Should scientists be allowed to transfer specific genes to satisfy a couple's preferences? Should society determine that certain types of genes be chosen to ensure "desirable products"? No easy questions, these, but you can be sure that they will arise in the future.

THE FERTILIZATION PROCESS

My mother groan'd!
My father wept.
Into the dangerous world I leapt.

—WILLIAM BLAKE

The fusion of two specialized cells, the sperm and the egg (or ovum), mark the beginning of development, and the zygote (the fertilized ovum) immediately begins to divide. This fertilized ovum contains all the genetic material that the organism will ever possess.

TABLE 3.1	A Genetic Glossary

acrosome: Area at the tip of the sperm that contains the chemicals enabling the sperm to penetrate the egg's surface.

allele: Alternate forms of a specific gene; for example, there are genes for blue eyes and brown eyes.

autosomes: Chromosomes other than the sex chromosomes.

chromosomes: Stringlike bodies that carry the genes; they are present in all of the body's cells.

DNA: Deoxyribonucleic acid, the chemical structure of the gene.

dominance: Tendency of a gene to be expressed in a trait, even when joined with a gene whose expression differs; for example, brown eyes will appear when genes for blue and brown eyes are paired.

fertilization: Union of sperm and egg to form the fertilized ovum or zygote.

gametes: Mature sex cells, either sperm or eggs.

genes: Ultimate hereditary determiners; they are composed of the chemical molecule deoxyribonucleic acid (DNA).

gene locus: Specific location of a gene on the chromosome.

genotype: Genetic composition of a person.

heterozygous: The gene pairs for a trait differ; for example, a person who is heterozygous for eye color has a gene for brown eyes and one for blue eyes.

homozygous: The gene pairs for a trait are similar; for instance, the eye color genes are the same.

meiosis: Cell division in which each daughter cell receives one-half of the chromosomes of the parent cell. For humans, this maintains the number of chromosomes (46) at fertilization.

mitosis: Cell division in which each daughter cell receives the same number of chromosomes as the parent cell.

mutation: Change in the structure of a gene.

phenotype: Observable expression of a gene.

recessive: Gene whose trait is not expressed unless paired with another recessive gene; for example, both parents contribute genes for blue eyes.

sex chromosome: Chromosomes that determine sex; in humans they are the 23rd pair, with an XX combination producing a female and an XY combination producing a male.

sex-linkage: Genes on the sex chromosome that produce traits other than sex.

trisomy: Three chromosomes are present rather than the customary pair; Down syndrome is caused by three chromosomes at the 21st pairing.

zygote: Fertilized egg.

Beginnings

Any discussion of fertilization today must account for the advances that both research and technology have made available. Consequently, our discussion includes *assisted fertilization techniques,* such as *in vitro fertilization* (producing the famous "test-tube" babies). As you read, be sure to refer to the marginal definitions when you meet an unfamiliar term. Otherwise, the amazing richness of the genetic world might escape you.

In our analysis of genetic material and its impact on our lives, we'll attempt to follow the manner in which we receive genes from our parents, so our story begins with the male's sperm and the female's egg.

Sperm

The major purpose of a male's reproductive organs is to manufacture, store, and deliver sperm, which then has as its sole objective the delivery of its DNA to the egg. Males, at birth, have in their testes the cells that will eventually produce sperm. At puberty, the number of chromosomes is halved, and actual sperm are formed.

Sperm, the male germ cells, are produced in the testes and contain one-half the number of chromosomes (23) found in body cells (46). The chief characteristics of the sperm are its tightly packed tip (the *acrosome*) containing the 23 chromosomes plus enzymes that will help the sperm penetrate an egg (Campbell & Reece, 2005). Sperm have short neck regions and tails to propel them in searching for the egg.

Sperm remain capable of fertilizing an egg for about 24 to 48 hours after ejaculation (Moore & Persaud, 2003). Of the more than 200 million sperm that enter the vagina, only about 200 survive the journey to the woman's fallopian tubes, where fertilization occurs. A normal male ejaculation typically results in anywhere from 100 to 650 million sperm (Campbell & Reece, 2005, p. 972). Males whose ejaculations consist of 10 million sperm or less are usually infertile. Male infertility is the estimated cause of one-third to one-half of childless unions.

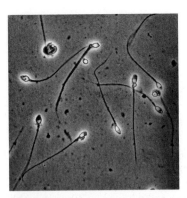

(a)

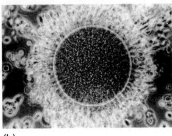

(b)

The sperm (a), in its search for the egg (b), carries the 23 chromosomes from the male.

Ovum (Egg)

The egg, also called the *oocyte,* is the female germ cell that is produced in the ovaries (Moore & Persaud, 2003, p. 2). Larger than the sperm, about the size of the period at the end of this sentence, the egg is round and its surface is about the consistency of stiff jelly. You may find it hard to believe, but a whale and a mouse come from eggs of about the same size. In fact, the eggs of all mammals are about the same size and appearance. When females are born, they already have primal eggs that have begun the maturation process, which will be completed after puberty. Estimates are that about 2 million eggs will be available during the reproductive years, and of these only about 400 will be released (Leifer, 2003). Since only one mature egg is required each month for about 35 years, the number present far exceeds the need.

Eggs are usually fertilized about 12 hours after they are discharged from the surface of the ovary, or they die within 12 to 24 hours (Moore & Persaud, 2003). From this brief discussion, you can identify the major differences between eggs and sperm. Eggs are massive compared to sperm; eggs are well equipped with cytoplasm (contents of cell, exclusive of nucleus), whereas sperm have very little; eggs are immobile while sperm are mobile. There are two types of sperm: X and Y, while there is only the X-type of egg.

Menstrual Cycle

Beginning at puberty and typically continuing throughout the reproductive years, females experience monthly sexual cycles, involving activity of the brain's

FIGURE 3.1

The relationship of ovary, egg, fallopian tube, and uterus.

From John F. Travers, *The Growing Child,* Scott, Foresman and Company, Glenview, Illlinois, 1982. Reprinted by permission of the author.

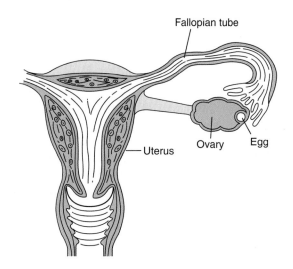

hypothalamus, the pituitary gland, ovaries, uterus, vagina, and mammary glands (Moore & Persaud, 2003). (Figure 3.1 illustrates the relationship of the ovum to the ovary, the fallopian tubes, and the uterus.) This process, called *ovulation,* triggers a chemical reaction that inhibits the ripening of further eggs. It also prepares the uterine lining for a potential fertilized ovum.

If fertilization does not occur, the prepared uterine lining is shed in menstruation, and the entire process begins again. As a woman approaches the end of her egg-producing years, these last ova have been present for as many as 40 years. This may explain why the children of older women are more susceptible to genetic defects. The eggs have been exposed to environmental hazards (such as radiation) too long to escape damage (Jones, 1993, Moore & Persaud, 1998).

Implantation

When the egg is discharged from the ovary's surface (a process called **ovulation**), it is enveloped by one of the **fallopian tubes.** The diameter of each fallopian tube is about that of a human hair, but it almost unfailingly ensnares the egg and provides a passageway to the uterus. If fertilization occurs, it takes place soon after the egg enters the fallopian tube. Figure 3.2 illustrates the fertilization process.

Fusion of the two cells is quickly followed by the first cell division. As the fertilized egg, now called the **zygote,** travels toward **implantation** within the uterus, cell division continues. Implantation usually occurs in the endometrium (lining) of the uterus. The cells multiply rapidly and after about seven days reach the uterine wall. The fertilized egg is now called a **blastocyst.** The journey is pictured in Figure 3.3.

Although individuals may change in the course of their lives, their hereditary properties do not change. The zygote (the fertilized egg), containing all 46 chromosomes, represents the "blueprint" for each person's physical and mental makeup. Under ordinary circumstances, environmental conditions leave the 46 chromosomes unaltered. (We now know that environmental agents such as drugs, viruses, and radiation may cause genetic damage.)

ovulation
Egg bursts from the surface of the ovary.

fallopian tubes
Passageway for the egg once it is discharged from the ovary's surface.

zygote
Fertilized egg.

implantation
Fertilized egg attaches and secures itself to uterine wall.

blastocyst
Name of the fertilized egg after initial divisions.

FIGURE 3.2

Fertilization of the egg. The sperm, carrying its 23 chromosomes, penetrates the egg, with its 23 chromosomes. The nuclei of the sperm and egg fuse, resulting in 46 chromosomes.

From John F. Travers, *The Growing Child,* Scott, Foresman and Company, Glenview, Illlinois, 1982. Reprinted by permission of the author.

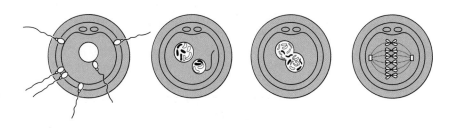

FIGURE 3.3

From ovulation to implantation.

From John F. Travers, *The Growing Child,* Scott, Foresman and Company, Glenview, Illinois, 1982. Reprinted by permission of the author.

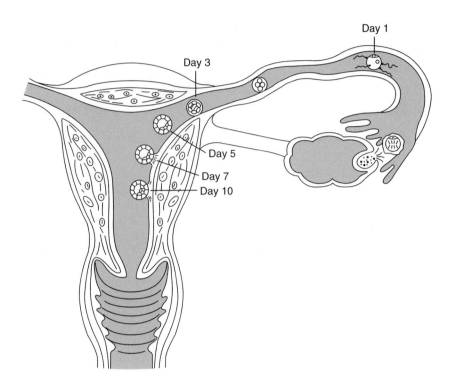

Once fertilization occurs, the zygote is not yet free from risk. Let's use a figure easy to work with and assume that 100 eggs are exposed to sperm. Here is the estimated mortality rate from fertilization to birth:

84 are fertilized

69 are implanted

42 survive one week

37 survive seven weeks

31 survive to birth

Thus, nature's toll results in about a 70% mortality rate.

Twins

Occasionally, and for reasons that still elude us, twins are born. Most twins occur when a woman's ovaries release two ripened eggs (rather than one) and both are fertilized by separate sperm. These twins are called **nonidentical,** or **dizygotic,** and their genes are no more alike than those of siblings born of the same parents but at different times. About two-thirds of all twins are dizygotic. In the United States, twins occur once in every 85 pregnancies, and recent figures show that in 2003 128,665 twins were born. The rate of nonidentical (dizygotic) twin births, however, varies considerably from country to country. For example, the rate of dizygotic twins is 1 in 500 in Asia but 1 in 20 in certain African countries (Moore & Persaud, 2003).

Less frequently, twins develop from a single fertilized egg that divided after conception. Interestingly, identical twins usually do not result when the fertilized egg initially divides into two cells; separation typically occurs at the end of the first week (Moore & Persaud, 2003). Two embryos, each in its own amniotic sac develop within one chorionic sac (fluid-filled sac containing the embryo). This process leads to **identical,** or **monozygotic,** twins whose genes are identical; that is, they share the same genotype. The rate of monozygotic twins is about the same for all populations.

dizygotic twin
Nonidentical twin.

monozygotic twin
Identical twin.

The term *identical* should be used cautiously. Although the interactions with parents supposedly help to account for any differences in the behavior of identical twins, many other influences are also at work (Lytton & Gallagher, 2002). For example, note that monozygotic twins were implanted in different places in the uterus, have different access to food, different exposure to harmful agents (infections, and so on), and different genetic action (genes being turned on and off at different times) (Willmut and Highfield, 2006). Identical twins certainly are more alike than you and I are, but they're really not identical at all (Willmut & Highfield, 2006, p. 42).

INFERTILITY

infertility
Inability to achieve pregnancy after one year.

Although the fertilization process just described is the normal process for most women, there are exceptions. **Infertility,** the inability to conceive when desired (Leifer, 2003), is a serious problem, and today hundreds of thousands of childless couples desperately desire children. Many couples, attempting to overcome this problem, turn to biological and/or adoption procedures. First, however, let's turn our attention to the causes of infertility.

Causes of Infertility

Infertility refers to those couples who have regular, unprotected sexual intercourse for one year and cannot conceive. The American Society for Reproductive Medicine estimates that infertility affects about 6.1 million people, about 10% of the reproductive population. Several reasons have been offered for this increased rate. In males, the number and quality of sperm are often suspected because of the challenges sperm face. Males must deposit a sufficient number of normal sperm near a woman's cervix that can survive the acidic vaginal environment and swim toward the egg (Leifer, 2003, pp. 269–272).

sexually transmitted diseases (STDs)
Class of diseases that may cause infertility.

Females must regularly produce normal eggs and possess a uterine environment that will sustain a pregnancy. **Sexually transmitted diseases** such as *chlamydia,* (usually a silent infection that may lurk in a woman's pelvic organs) and *gonorrhea* may cause infertility. These, in turn, can lead to *pelvic inflammatory disease* (PID), which then can also produce infertility. Also, a growing number of women are delaying child bearing, and older women are more likely to become infertile if they have had abdominal surgery or if they experienced *endometriosis,* a condition that increases with age. (Endometrial tissue is typically found in the lining of the uterus; edometriosis is the growth of endometrial tissue outside the uterus.)

With approximately more than 6 million individuals in the United States who are thought to be infertile, many couples consult fertility specialists. Can you name the most common causes of infertility?

Even if a couple finds that they are indeed infertile, they needn't abandon their hopes of parenthood since many assisted reproductive techniques are available today. The new technologies we are about to discuss offer couples new hope. Hundreds of in vitro fertilization centers and sperm banks now exist around the country.

Assisted Reproduction Technologies

Many forms of **assisted reproduction technologies (ART)** are now available (Gardner & others, 2004; Leifer, 2003; Marrs, Block, & Silverman, 1997).

- Although **in vitro fertilization** is probably the best-known ART procedure, another process, **artificial insemination by donor (AID),** is by far the most widely used one. (This technique is often referred to as *therapeutic insemination*.) Potential users of AID can be encouraged by the positive results of recent research that studied the quality of parenting and the psychological adjustment of AID children in two-parent heterosexual families.

- **Gamete intrafallopian transfer (GIFT),** in which sperm and egg are placed in the fallopian tube with the intent of achieving fertilization in a more natural environment (also known as *embryo transfer*).

- **Zygote intrafallopian transfer (ZIFT),** in which the fertilized egg is transferred to the fallopian tube.

- **Sperm donation** and **egg donation,** in which males and females either donate or sell their sperm and eggs. Today hundreds of sperm banks operate in the United States. Sixteen cryobanks store and sell frozen sperm, which are frozen in liquid nitrogen at $-190°$ C and remain potent for years. Women who will offer their eggs are in great demand. For example, a childless couple placed the following ad in the monthly magazine of a prestigious Eastern university:

    $50,000 to an intelligent, athletic egg donor who must be at least 5' 10",
    have a 1400+ SAT score, and possess no major family medical issues.
    (Sege, 1999)

- **Cryopreservation,** which refers to freezing embryos for future use.

- **Intracytoplasmic sperm injection (ICSI),** in which a sperm is injected directly into an egg, a procedure particularly helpful when a man has a low sperm count.

- **Surrogate motherhood,** in which one woman carries another woman's embryo for nine months.

- Finally, we return to in vitro fertilization, in which fertilization of egg with sperm occurs in a dish, which is probably the technique with which you are most familiar. The procedure is as follows.

    1. The woman is usually treated with hormones to stimulate maturation of eggs in the ovary, and she is observed closely to determine the timing of ovulation (that is, the time at which the egg leaves the surface of the ovary).

    2. The physician uses a laparoscope (a very thin tubular lens through which the physician can see the ovary) to remove mature eggs.

    3. The egg is placed in a solution containing blood serum and nutrients.

    4. **Capacitation** takes place—this is a process in which a layer surrounding the sperm is removed so that it may penetrate the egg, a process that takes about 7 hours (Curtis & Barnes, 1998).

assisted reproduction technologies (ART)
External fertilization procedures. Fertilization occurs with help and outside of the woman's body.

in vitro fertilization
Fertilization that occurs "in the dish;" an assisted fertilization technique.

artificial insemination by donor (AID)
Injection of sperm into woman.

gamete intrafallopian transfer (GIFT)
Sperm and egg are placed in fallopian tube.

zygote intrafallopian transfer (ZIFT)
Fertilized egg (zygote) is transferred to the fallopian tube.

sperm donor
Male either donates or sells sperm.

egg donation
Woman either donates or sells eggs.

cryopreservation
Freezing embryos for future use.

intracytoplasmic sperm injection (ICSI)
Sperm is injected directly into egg.

surrogate motherhood
One woman carries another woman's embryo.

capacitation
Removal of layer surrounding sperm.

AN INFORMED VIEW

To Clone or Not to Clone

Few celebrities have so besotted the world's media as she did. Her arrival caused a sensation, triggering an orgy of speculation, gossip, and hype. She posed for People magazine, and even caught the eye of Bill Clinton. *(Willmut & Highfield, 2006, p. 11)*

Dolly, the most famous lamb in history, was born at 5:00 P.M. on a warm summer's day, July 5, 1996. It was a remarkably quiet introduction to one of the most controversial events of the 20th century. Dolly was a clone; that is, she was not the product of the union of a sperm and egg. Ian Wilmut, a quiet, unassuming embryologist, combined the udder cell of a 6-year-old sheep with the egg of another sheep, after first removing the genetic material from the egg. The udder cell's genes now assumed command of the growth and the development of the newly fertilized egg. The researchers next transferred it to a third sheep, which acted as a surrogate mother (Purves et al., 2004). The result 21 weeks later: Dolly, an identical twin of the original sheep that supplied the udder cell. *But the identical twin was born six years later!* (Kolata, 1998). (Alas, in spite of fame and fortune, Dolly died in 2003 of lung disease.)

You have probably anticipated the next stage in the chronology of cloning: Is it possible to clone a human? This is no longer a question that is the "stuff of science fiction." As you can imagine, this question has ignited a firestorm of controversy. Do the benefits of cloning (replicating perfect farm animals, adding genes so that a cow might have valuable drugs in its milk, allowing childless couples to have children, developing organs to use in transplants) suggest that cloning humans is a necessary next step? Or do the negative features of cloning, which include sacrificing embryos to obtain one healthy clone

(it required 277 attempts to produce Dolly), the possibility of gross genetic defects, and the real likelihood of an accelerated aging process raise prohibitive barriers against human cloning (Krogh, 2002)?

Considering the inevitable collision between available technology and the forces arrayed against cloning, do you think the cloning of humans will ever occur? If you would like to have a more informed view on this issue, you may want to read one or more of the references in this chapter. For example, Gina Kolata (1998) has written a fascinating account of the background and techniques of this process. You may also wish to learn more about it by going to our website at www. mhhe.com/dacey7.

Dolly as a lamb.

For an excellent summary of the cloning process, see Ian Willmut and Roger Highfield, *After Dolly: The Uses and Misuses of Human Cloning,* published by W.W Norton Co. in 2006.

5. Sperm are added to the solution; fertilization occurs.

6. The fertilized egg is transferred to a fresh supporting solution.

7. Fertilized eggs (the number varies) are guided into the uterus.

8. The fertilized egg is transferred to the uterine lining.

During this period, the woman is being treated to prepare her body to receive the fertilized egg. For example, the lining of the uterus must be spongy or porous enough to hold the zygote. The fertilized egg must be inserted at the time it would normally reach the uterine cavity. In the United States, there were 35,025 live-birth in vitro deliveries in 2002 (CDC, 2003).

Adoption

adoption
To take a child of other parents voluntarily as one's own.

For many couples who remain childless in spite of several attempts at assisted fertilization, **adoption** (to take a child of other biological parents voluntarily as one's own) offers a viable option. Middle- to upper-middle class couples of all races and ethnicities who decide to adopt face competition from single adults, older adults, and gay adults. Because single parenthood is widely accepted today, more single women are keeping their children. The increasing use of contraception and the legality of abortion have also caused a sharp reduction in the number of available children, leading to heightened interest in adopting children from other nations. Nevertheless, more children are available for adoption than is commonly thought: older children, minority children, and special-needs children. Although these children are available for immediate adoption, the waiting period for healthy white infants may run into years.

closed adoption
Natural parents know nothing about the adopting parents.

Adoption procedures were formerly closed (**closed adoption**), and the biological parents were completely removed from the life of their child once the child was surrendered for adoption. The bonds between birth parent(s) and child were legally and permanently severed; the child's history was sealed by the court. These procedures were done with good intentions, but it was as if the child had no genetic past. Supposedly, the natural parents and the adoptive couple were saved from emotional upset. Many biological mothers, however, reported in later interviews that they never recovered from the grieving process.

Today, however, when a pregnant woman approaches an adoption agency, she gets what she wants. She can insist that her child be raised by a couple with specific characteristics: nationality, religion, income, number in family. She can ask to see her child several times a year, perhaps take the youngster on a vacation and telephone the child frequently. The adoption agency will try to meet these demands. This process is called **open adoption,** and although many adoptive couples dislike the arrangement, they really have no choice. Thus we see a new definition of adoption: the process of accepting the responsibility of raising an individual who has two sets of parents. Open adoption may also help a child to overcome the sense of loss that can accompany adoption (Leon, 2002).

open adoption
Natural parents have considerable input into the adoption process.

When couples choose to adopt, they should carefully consider the age of the child. They may find one age group more appealing than others. Each developmental period—infancy, early childhood, middle childhood, adolescence—has its own strengths and weaknesses that one should consider as a potential adoptive parent. Adoptive parents should also realize that once children know they are adopted and understand what that means, the relationship with their adoptive parents inevitably changes. This "moment of truth" affects both parents and children. For example, children must cope with the idea of being relinquished, which is not an easy task. Parents must accept the idea that their children will want to know more about their biological parents, which is a natural concern (Brodzinsky & Pinderhughes, 2002).

Finally, a troubling new development has entered the adoption scene. If you recall, in the in vitro process only a few embryos out of about a dozen are transferred to the woman. What happens to the rest? Estimates are that the roughly 300–400 in vitro clinics in the United States now have at least 400,000 embryos stored. Of these, thousands have been donated to infertile couples, thus creating a new avenue toward adoption. What is of concern about this new procedure is the lack of any significant regulations to date to deal with critical issues: screening for disease, donor rights and responsibilities, donor identification (similar to the process for open adoption). This new technique promises to raise controversial legal and ethical issues.

Today in the United States more would-be parents are turning to transracial and international adoption. Census figures indicate that about 25,000 children were obtained through international adoption last year. The majority of these children come from China (about 7,500) and Russia (about 6,000).

A SOCIOCULTURAL VIEW | Foreign Adoption—An Odyssey

Recently, friends of ours, Steve and Nancy, decided to adopt a Romanian infant girl of 15 months. Their story is both touching and moving, as well as a detailed chronicle of what's involved in the process.

The young couple examined the pros and cons of both domestic and foreign adoptions and ultimately decided on a foreign adoption. They felt there were too many complications with most domestic adoptions, less certain outcomes, and often very lengthy waits. The downside of an international adoption is that generally the children are older and often have spent a year or more in an orphanage.

The adoption agency they worked with was certified by the Romanian government. The agency had a Romanian husband-and-wife team working to identify adoptable children and assist with negotiating the process in Romania and also helping the adoptive parents once in Romania. The son of this couple works for the agency in the United States and communicates regularly with his parents.

Steve and Nancy were told they must use one of the certified agencies in order to adopt. They also needed to follow Massachusetts laws for a detailed home study, including criminal background checks. In addition, they had to apply to the Immigration and Naturalization Services (INS) for approval. They were also checked by the FBI. The only input they had to the adoption process was to specify a child as young as possible; the agency matches children and parents. On a second adoption, however, prospective parents are allowed to specify the sex.

They found going through the Romanian system a difficult process. They were told about Katie in June 1996 and anticipated going to Romania the following September to get her. Katie is from Iasi, near the Ukrainian border. The home study done on Steve and Nancy plus their INS paperwork were submitted to the Romanian Adoption Review Committee, which approved them as adoptive parents. (The birth parent(s) must also give their permission for the child to be adopted.)

Once the adoption committee approves both parents and children, the paperwork goes back to the local courts for finalization. Next, a hearing is held followed by an appeal period. Ultimately the adoption paperwork was completed in early January. They had to wait three weeks for Katie's passport and then went back to Romania to bring her home.

At the orphanage, Steve and Nancy were able to see only the main entry way and a small room off to the side. They were told that this orphanage was the best in the country. Supposedly, the director was well educated, with degrees in early childhood education. The orphanage seemed bright and clean, and the children are taken outside to play, which is very unusual in Romania. There were Disney characters on the wall and Polaroid pictures of the children visiting with their version of Santa Claus. Steve and Nancy couldn't learn much about the children's diet or stimulation other than Katie had oranges and in all likelihood bananas. They also learned little about staffing conditions (ratio of staff to children, education of staff, and so on).

When they brought Katie home in late January, she was almost 15 months old. She was slightly anemic when she arrived, but an iron-based formula quickly corrected the problem. Today Katie is an excellent eater and enjoys almost everything except fruit juices. She adjusted quickly to her new parents and their home. She had no difficulty with eating or sleeping, nor was she irritable. The only problem was a viral infection that lasted for about 5 weeks. The social worker visited about 3 weeks after they arrived home and again at the 2+ month mark. In that time she noticed how much more interactive Katie had become. They recently had their final home study visit, and the social worker was very pleased with Katie's development.

Katie will be 22 months old on September 4 and is a normal toddler. She's very active, has good motor skills, is beginning to exhibit a temper when she does not get her own way, and she tests Steve and Nancy to see how much she can get away with—very normal reactions for an almost 2-year-old. The only problem seems to be a language delay, but comprehension seems to be normal. A speech pathologist has recommended a reevaluation in 4 months, with the belief that her language skills will explode before then. She is now mimicking much of what Steve and Nancy say to her; thus it would appear that she will swiftly overcome this language delay.

In summary, Katie came into a warm, loving environment, has adjusted well, and seems on the way to a normal and happy childhood.

Although the process remains complicated, the number of international adoptions is increasing.

Guided Review

1. __________ is the process uniting sperm and egg.
2. A fertilized egg is known as a __________.
3. The __________ ripen and release an egg each month.
4. The most well-known example of an assisted fertilization technique is __________ fertilization.
5. The most widely used assisted fertilization technique is __________.
6. Estimates are that at least ________ % of the reproductive population is infertile.
7. A form of adoption that today is becoming more popular is __________ adoption.

HEREDITY AT WORK

The original cell, the possessor of 46 chromosomes, begins to divide rapidly after fertilization, until the infant has billions of cells at birth. The cells soon begin to specialize: some become muscle, some bone, some skin, some blood, and some nerve cells. These are the *somatic,* or body, cells. The process of division by which these cells multiply is called **mitosis** (see Figure 3.4). In a mitotic division, the number of chromosomes in each cell remains the same. Mitosis is basically a division of cells in which each chromosome is duplicated so that each cell receives a copy of each chromosome of the parent cell. What is doubled in mitotic division is the amount of deoxyribonucleic acid (DNA), the chief component of the genes.

A second type of cell is also differentiated: the germ, or sex, cell that ultimately becomes either sperm or egg. These reproductive cells likewise divide by the process of mitosis until the age of puberty. But then a remarkable phenomenon occurs—another type of division called **meiosis,** or reduction division (see Figure 3.5). Each sex cell, instead of receiving 46 chromosomes upon division, now receives 23.

Meiosis, which occurs only in germ cell reproduction, is responsible both for the shuffling of hereditary characteristics received from each parent and for their random appearance in offspring. During the reduction division, the chromosomes separate longitudinally so that 23 go to one cell and 23 to another (Nusslein-Volhard, 2006).

For the male, reduction division begins to occur just before puberty. For the female, the process differs slightly. Since she is required to produce only one mature egg a month, there is no provision for an indefinitely large number of eggs, as there is for sperm. A woman normally sheds only 300 to 400 mature ova in her lifetime, whereas the normal male in a single ejaculation emits hundreds of millions of sperm.

At birth, the female's ovaries contain tiny clusters of all the eggs that will mature in later years. Just before puberty, the final phases of the reduction division occur, and mature eggs are formed. It is as if there is a lengthy waiting period, from birth until about the age of 12 or 13, before the process is finally completed. The 23 chromosomes with their hereditary content are present at birth but must await the passage of time before biological maturity occurs in the female.

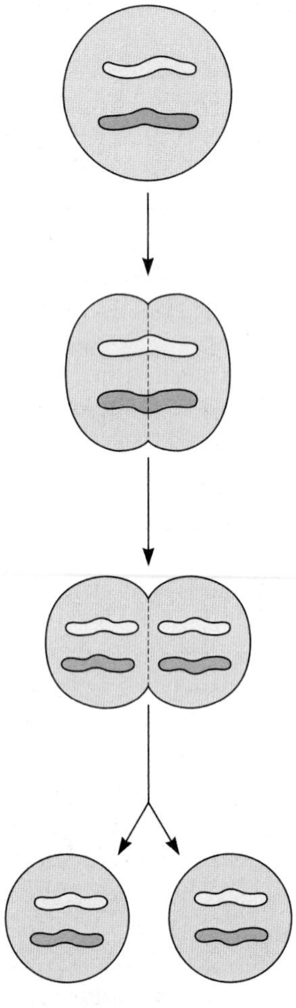

FIGURE 3.4

A mitotic division is a cell division in which each daughter cell receives the same number of chromosomes as a parent cell—46.

mitosis
Cell division in which the number of chromosomes remains the same.

meiosis
Cell division in which the number of chromosomes is halved.

Answers 1. Fertilization 2. zygote 3. ovaries 4. in vitro 5. AID 6. 10 7. open

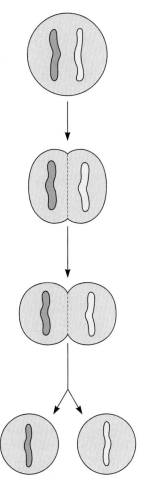

FIGURE 3.5

A meiotic division is a cell division in which each daughter cell receives one half of the chromosomes of the parent cell—23.

chromosomes
Stringlike bodies that carry the genes; they are present in all body cells.

gene
Inherited trait determined by the elements of heredity that are transmitted from parents to offspring in reproduction.

A
adenine

T
thymine

C
cytosine

G
guanine

genotype
Individual's genetic composition.

phenotype
The observable expression of gene action.

Now that we have traced the process by which fertilization occurs and discovered what is passed from parents to child, we still need to know "why I am who I am." This leads us to a discussion of chromosomes and genes.

Chromosomes and Genes

After the sperm and egg unite, the new cell (the potential person) possesses 23 pairs of **chromosomes,** or 46 chromosomes, which represents our total biological heritage. The sperm determines sex, since it alone can carry a Y chromosome. Thus there are two kinds of sperm: the X chromosome carrier and the Y chromosome carrier. The Y carrier is smaller than the X, which contains more genetic material. The Y carrier is also lighter and speedier and can reach the egg more quickly. But it is also more vulnerable.

One member of each pair of chromosomes has been contributed by the father and one by the mother. Each pair, except the 23rd, is remarkably alike. The 23d pair defines the individual's sex: an XX combination indicates a female; XY indicates a male. The male, from conception, is the more fragile of the two sexes. Estimates are that 160 males are conceived for every 100 females. However, so many males are spontaneously aborted that only 105 males are born for every 100 females. A similar pattern appears in neonatal life and continues throughout development, until women finally outnumber men, reversing the original ratio. Consequently, certain conclusions follow:

- Structurally and functionally, females resist disease better than males do.
- The male is more subject to hereditary disease and defect.
- Environmental elements expose the male to greater hazards.
- Females are born with and retain a biological superiority over males.

The significance of the chromosomes lies in the material they contain—the **genes.** Each gene is located at a particular spot on the chromosome, called the *gene locus.* DNA, the chemical structure of genes, was not known until 1944, when Oswald Avery and his colleagues proved that genetic material consisted of deoxyribonucleic acid. Since genes consist of only four building blocks, all genes are almost chemically alike. To determine the specific function of any gene, researchers must identify the exact order of the four chemical bases—**A T C G**—that constitute DNA. As the Nobel prize winner, Christiane Nusslein-Volhard (2006, p. 32) has noted, this seeming simplicity—a language of four letters—permits an exact reading of its structure.

Genes account for all inherited characteristics, from hair and eye color to skin shade, even the tendency toward baldness. Thus our **genotype** (our genetic heritage) is expressed as a **phenotype** (our observable characteristics). Genes always function in an environment, and environmental circumstances affect the way that the genes express themselves.

As critical as genes are to life itself, who owns them? As Stix (2006) notes, there's a gene in your body that is crucial for early spinal cord development. *It belongs to Harvard University!* Incyte Corporation of Delaware has the patent for a gene of a receptor for histamine. Good luck with your hay fever. Nearly half the genes involved in cancer are patented. The United States Supreme Court held that living things are patentable as long as they incorporate human intervention—in other words, as long as they are made by humans (Stix, 2006, p. 78). As of today, universities, corporations, government agencies, and nonprofit organizations have patents for about 20% of the human genome, which has led to intense debate among ethicists, judges, and scientists and which promises only to intensify in the coming years.

FIGURE 3.6

The DNA double helix. (a) The overall structure that gave DNA its famous name. (b) A closer examination reveals that the sides of the spiral are connected by chemicals similar to the rungs of a ladder.

From John F. Travers, *The Growing Child,* Scott, Foresman and Company, Glenview, Illinois, 1982. Reprinted by permission of the author.

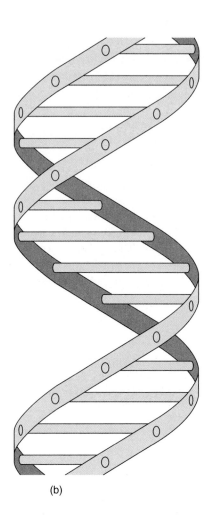

(a)   (b)

Our discussion now brings us to the discovery of DNA, one of the great achievements of the 20th century.

DNA: Structure and Function

I got hooked on the gene during my third year at the University of Chicago. Until then, I had planned to be a naturalist and looked forward to a career far removed from the urban bustle of Chicago's South Side. The notion that life might be perpetuated by means of an instruction book inscribed in a secret code appealed to me. What sort of molecular code could be so elaborate as to convey all the multitudinous wonder of the living world? And what sort of molecular trick could ensure that the code is exactly copied every time a chromosome duplicates? (Watson, 2003, pp. 35–36)

Today we know that each chromosome contains thousands of genes, which are small sections of **DNA (deoxyribonucleic acid).** The amazing chemical compound DNA is the chemical key to life in humans, animals, and plants, and is the molecular basis of the genes. Each gene follows the instructions encoded in its DNA and sends these instructions, as chemical messages called **RNA (ribonucleic acid),** into the surrounding cell. (See Figure 3.6.)

The RNA acts swiftly, forming a particular protein at the staggering rate of 100 molecules per second! These new products then interact with the genes to form new substances, a process that continues to build the millions of cells needed

DNA
Deoxyribonucleic acid; the chemical structure of the gene that accounts for our inherited characteristics.

RNA (ribonucleic acid)
Nucleic acid similar to DNA.

AN INFORMED VIEW

Discovering the Double Helix

At first glance James Watson and Francis Crick looked like any other young instructors at England's Cambridge University. But there was soon to be something quite different about them. On a winter's day in 1953, they shocked the biological world and took the first step toward their future Nobel Prizes when they burst into a pub near their laboratory and announced to their astonished colleagues that "they had discovered the secret of life." Just hours before, they had finally determined the exact model of DNA. In a spirited race with some of the greatest minds in biology—Linus Pauling, Maurice Wilkins, Rosalind Franklin—after years of theory building, testing, failure, and theory revision, Watson and Crick persevered and triumphed. The significance of their discovery can't be overlooked.

> Extraordinary new scientific vistas opened up: We would at last come to grips with genetic diseases from cystic fibrosis to cancer, we would revolutionize criminal justice through genetic finger printing methods; we would profoundly revise ideas about human origins—about who we are and where we came from—by using DNA-based approaches to prehistory; and we would improve agriculturally important species with an effectiveness we had previously only dreamed of. *(Watson, 2003, p. xiiii)*

But the chase had only begun. Although the structure of DNA was now known and provided clues as to function, the question remained: "How does this structure actually work?" Francis Crick initially charted the course when he speculated that genetic information stored in DNA flows through RNA (ribonucleic acid) to proteins (Micklos & Freyer, 2003). Information in DNA is stored as a code (as we'll see in this chapter) and is then translated into the language of RNA, which eventually directs the formation of proteins. And now the race began in earnest. After the discovery of the double helix model in 1953, intense interest mounted as efforts to probe more deeply into genetic action and application.

Francis Crick and James Watson with their model of DNA, which won them the Nobel Prize in 1962.

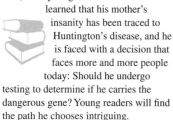

Young adult readers would enjoy reading Nancy Werlin's *Double Helix* (2004, NY: Dial). The young adult narrator has learned that his mother's insanity has been traced to Huntington's disease, and he is faced with a decision that faces more and more people today: Should he undergo testing to determine if he carries the dangerous gene? Young readers will find the path he chooses intriguing.

for various bodily structures. Genes not only perform certain duties within the cell but also join with other genes to reproduce both themselves and the whole chromosome.

Examine Figure 3.7 and note how the strands intertwine. The strands, similar to the sides of a ladder, are connected by chemical rings: adenine (A), guanine (G), cytosine (C), and thymine (T). The letters are not randomly connected: A joins with T, G with C. If a code were written as AGCTTGA, it must appear as:

A G C T T G A

T C G A A C T

Thus, one sequence determines the other.

A remarkable feature of DNA is its ability to reproduce itself and ensure that each daughter cell receives identical information. During mitosis the DNA splits as readily as a person unzips a jacket (Curtis & Barnes, 1998). Each single strand grows a new mate, A to T and G to C, until the double-helix model is reproduced in each daughter cell.

The four letter possibilities, AT, TA, GC, and CG, seem to limit genetic variation. But when we consider that each DNA molecule is quite lengthy, involving

FIGURE 3.7   (a) The chromosome structure of a male and (b) the chromosome structure of a female. The 23rd pair is shown in the bottom right box of each figure; note that the Y chromosome of the male is smaller. To obtain this chromosomal picture, a cell is removed from the individual's body, usually from the inside of the mouth. The chromosomes are magnified extensively and then photographed.

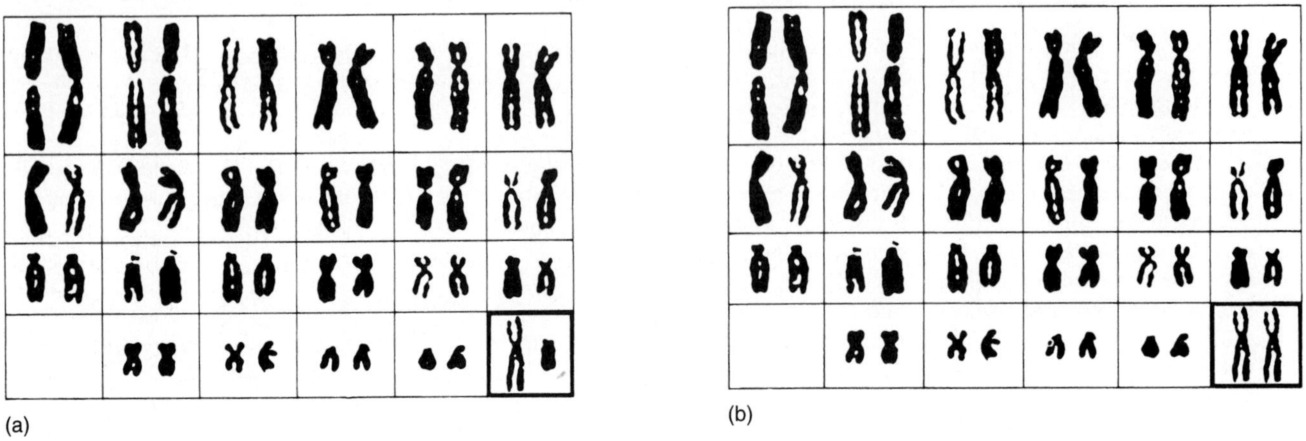

(a)

(b)

thousands, perhaps millions of chemical steps (TA, GC, AT, CG, AT, CG, TA), the possible combinations seem limitless. The differences in the DNA patterns account for the individual genetic differences among humans and for differences between species. (Figure 3.7 illustrates the chromosomal arrangement of a typical male and female.)

Estimates are that the entire human genome contains about 3 billion letters and is often referred to as the text of a book. Reading this book at the rate of one letter every second, plan to spend 11 years to finish it (Shreeve, 2005). The work of Watson and Crick, which led to a Nobel Prize in 1962, was first published in 1953 in the journal *Nature* and began with the words:

> *We wish to suggest a structure for the salt of deoxyribonucleic acid (DNA).*
> *This structure has novel features which are of considerable biological interest.*

And so began the DNA era!

Genetic Counseling

How much information is contained in this biological heritage? Each chromosome contains the equivalent of about 3 billion letters. Since the average word contains six letters, each chromosome incorporates information equal to about 500 million words. At about 300 words per typical printed page, this translates into the equivalent of about 2 million pages. The average book consists of about 500 pages. Thus the information in one human chromosome corresponds to that in 4,000 books. Francis Collins, the leader of the federally funded Human Genome Project, has stated that in 10 years we'll be able to predict what conditions most threaten us and that will lead to more specific preventative practices (In Smith, 2005). This enormous volume of information has led to changes in the practice of medicine with genetic testing and genetic counseling becoming more accessible.

There is little doubt that we're in the early stages of a genetic revolution (Patenaude, Guttmacher, & Collins, 2002). Yet genetic testing does not provide absolute answers. For example, should a woman decide on a hysterectomy to avoid a 40% chance of ovarian cancer, or a double mastectomy if the odds of getting breast cancer are 20%? These are serious, life-threatening issues that require informed answers. To help those who work with such clients, *The National Coalition*

James Watson. (1968). *The Double Helix*. Boston: Atheneum. This book has become a scientific classic. It is James Watson's personal, colorful look at the discovery of DNA and is guaranteed to hold your attention. If you are the least bit intimidated by the thought of reading about your genetic heritage, this book should eliminate your concerns. (Available in paperback.)

for Health Professional Education in Genetics (NCHPEG) has proposed a set of core competencies. They urge that health professionals working in this field recognize the limitations of their genetic expertise, thoroughly understand the implications of their work, and know when to make a referral to a genetics specialist, With these warnings, they identify three sets of competencies.

1. *Knowledge.* There are 17 guidelines for knowledge, ranging from understanding basic genetic terminology, recognition of a predisposition to genetic disease, and knowledge of referral services.
2. *Skills.* Gathering genetic family history and informing clients of the availability of genetic counseling are examples of needed skills.
3. *Attitudes.* Needed attitudes include an appreciation of the sensitivity of genetic information and an acceptance of one's limited expertise in the area of genetic information.

The task is challenging but exciting, with the promise of a rewarding future.

Guided Review

8. Cell division in which each daughter cell receives the same number of chromosomes as the parent cell is called _____.
9. A reduction division in which the number of chromosomes is halved is called _____.
10. The chemical key to life is _____.
11. The amount of _____ _____ is doubled in each mitotic division.
12. A remarkable feature of DNA is its ability to _____ itself.
13. In genetic coding, A is linked with ____ and G is linked with _____.
14. The genetic composition of a person is referred to as the _____, whereas the observed expression of a gene is called the _____.

The strong resemblance of these family members to one another is testimony to the role of heredity in our make-up. When you see the strength of heredity, as in this picture, how would you respond to the statement, "biology is destiny"?

How Traits Are Transmitted

In their analysis of genes and genomes, Hartl and Jones (2005, p. 3) state that the fundamental concept of genetics is that

inherited traits are determined by the elements of heredity that are transmitted from parents to offspring in reproduction; these elements of heredity are called genes.

The story behind the transmission of traits is fascinating.

Working in a quiet monastery garden, the Austrian monk Gregor Mendel provided the impetus for modern genetics. His great achievement was to demonstrate that inherited characteristics are passed on by discrete elements called *genes*. As a result of cross-breeding pea plants (for example, purple with white, yellow with green), Mendel discovered genetic principles that still guide us. By the last year of his experiments, it's estimated that Mendel had counted more than 300,000 peas (Henig, 2000)!

Answers

8. mitosis 9. meiosis 10. DNA 11. deoxyribonucleic acid 12. reproduce 13. T, C 14. genotype, phenotype

dominant (dominance)
Tendency of a gene to be expressed in a trait.

recessive
Gene whose trait is not expressed unless paired with another recessive gene; for example, both parents contribute genes for blue eyes.

mutations
Abrupt hereditary changes.

incomplete dominance
A genetic trait is not fully expressed.

codominance
Phenotypes of both alleles.

polygenic inheritance
Many genes contribute to the formation of a particular trait.

For example, cross-breeding purple with white produced all purple in the first generation. Consequently, Mendel called purple the **dominant** characteristic in this combination. When white appeared in later generations, he referred to white as the **recessive** characteristic. Studying his results, Mendel realized that the appearance and disappearance of various characteristics could be traced to separate factors. Some came from the maternal parent, others from the paternal parent, which led to his hypothesis that every individual carries pairs of factors for each trait. Members of each pair then separate from generation to generation. His discovery is called the *principle of segregation* and helps to explain why blue-eyed babies occasionally appear in typically brown-eyed families.

Mendel's work, first reported in 1865, was ignored until 1900 when other biologists discovered his work. Using his ideas, new strides were made. For example, abrupt changes in genes are possible, a phenomenon called **mutations.** Think of mutations as inherited accidents that may have adverse effects on any individual but that rarely affect evolutionary change (Jones, 1993). Other advances included the notion of **incomplete dominance,** that is, some characteristics seem to blend (red + white = pink). Occasionally **codominance** results in both pure characteristics appearing. Blood types are a good example: Type AB has red blood cells with the distinctive characteristics of both Type A and Type B. We now know, however, that most traits result from the interaction of many genes, and also that most genes influence more than a single trait (Curtis & Barnes, 1998). When many genes interact to produce a particular trait, the process is called **polygenic inheritance.** Such traits as height and weight are examples of polygenic inheritance.

Unfortunately, the line of transmission is occasionally broken and hereditary abnormalities occur.

Hereditary Disorders

Since hereditary abnormalities can reside either in the chromosomes or the genes, we'll analyze each case separately.

Examples of Chromosomal Disorders

The study of chromosomes is called **cytogenetics,** and thanks to new research techniques that enlarge prints of the chromosomes 2,000 to 3,000 times, our knowledge has increased tremendously. For example, we now know that chromosomal abnormalities usually occur when something goes wrong in normal chromosomal mechanisms and not through anything inherited (Rutter, 2006). These abnormalities typically appear by chance (given that there are so many cell divisions) or by damage to the DNA (radiation, and so on). Fertilization of older eggs may also be the cause, as in Down syndrome.

Down syndrome is caused by an extra chromosome; the person may have 47 chromosomes. This defect was identified in 1866 by a British doctor, Langdon Down; it produces distinctive facial features, small hands, a large tongue, and possible functional difficulties such as mental retardation, heart defects, and an increased risk of leukemia. The incidence of Down syndrome is closely related to the mother's age: Under age 30, the ratio is only 1 in 1,700 births; at age 35, the chances of a woman having a Down baby jumps to 1 in 400. Once a woman reaches the age of 45, the incidence increases to 1 in 30 (Watson, 2003).

Although the exact cause of Down syndrome remains a mystery, it may lie in the female egg production mechanism, which results in some eggs remaining in the ovary for 40 or 50 years. The longer they are in the ovary, the greater the possibility of damage. Research during the last 40 years has led to improvements in life expectancy, overall health, and quality of life of Down syndrome children (Hartl & Jones, 2005). Management of the mental retardation associated with Down syndrome has also advanced: better educational programs, early intervention

cytogenetics
The study of chromosomes.

Down syndrome
Genetic abnormality caused by a deviation on the twenty-first pair of chromosomes.

Down syndrome is caused by a deviation on the 21st pair of chromosomes. A child with the syndrome has distinctive facial features and is likely physically and mentally challenged. How has treatment of Down syndrome children changed dramatically?

techniques, and specific therapies (for example, speech programs), which in turn have produced better functioning and socialization.

Other disorders relate to the sex chromosomes. If you recall, the 23d pair of chromosomes are the sex chromosomes, XX for females, XY for males. Estimates are that 1 in every 1,200 females and 1 in every 400 males have some disorder in the sex chromosomes. Occasionally, a male possesses an XXY pattern rather than the normal XY. This is called **Klinefelter syndrome** (named after Dr. Harry Klinefelter in 1942), a disorder that may cause small testicles, reduced body hair, possible infertility, and language impairment. Klinefelter's occurs in about 1 in 1,000 male births; the condition may be helped by injections of testosterone. Another pattern that appears in males is XYY, which may cause larger size and increased aggression—about 1 in 1,000 male births (Bock, 1993).

Females occasionally possess an XO pattern (lack of a chromosome) rather than XX. This is called **Turner syndrome** and is characterized by short stature, poorly developed secondary sex features (such as breast size), and usually sterility (about 1 in 2,500 female births).

Examples of Genetic Disorders

This section discusses the incidence and characteristics of several specific genetic disorders. Even as this is being written, thanks to the Human Genome Project, new genetic discoveries are being announced daily. (For an excellent analysis of genetic disorders, see Hartl & Jones, 2005.)

Jews of Eastern European origin are struck hardest by **Tay-Sachs disease,** which causes death by the age of 4 or 5. At birth, the afflicted children appear normal, but development slows by the age of 6 months, and mental and motor deterioration begin. About 1 in every 25 to 30 Jews of Eastern European origin carries the defective gene, which is recessive; thus danger arises when two carriers marry. The disease results from a gene failing to produce an enzyme that breaks down fatty materials in the brain and nervous system. The result is that fat accumulates and destroys nerve cells, causing loss of coordination, blindness, and finally death. Today there are reliable genetic tests to identify carriers, and amniocentesis (see Chapter 4) can detect the genetic status of a fetus of carrier parents (Curtis & Barnes, 1998).

Sickle-cell anemia, which mainly afflicts those of African descent, appeared thousands of years ago in equatorial Africa and increased resistance to malaria. Estimates are that 10% of the African-American population in the United States carry the sickle-cell trait. Thus, two carriers of the defective gene who marry have a one in four chance of producing a child with sickle-cell anemia.

The problem is that the red blood cells of the afflicted person are distorted and pointed. Because of the cells' shape, they encounter difficulty in passing through the blood vessels. They tend to pile up and clump, producing oxygen starvation accompanied by considerable pain. The body then acts to eliminate these cells, and anemia results.

In the United States, **cystic fibrosis (CF)** is the most severe genetic disease of childhood, affecting about 1 in 2,000 children. About 1 in 30 individuals is a carrier. The disease causes a malfunction of the exocrine glands, the glands that secrete tears, sweat, mucus, and saliva. Breathing is difficult because of the thickness of the mucus. The secreted sweat is extremely salty, often producing heat exhaustion. About 30,000 children and adults have cystic fibrosis in the United States, and it kills more children than any other genetic disease (Ball & Bindler, 2006).

Cystic fibrosis has been deadly for several reasons: Its causes long remained unknown, and its carriers could not be detected. Thus until a child manifested the breathing and digestive problems characteristic of the disease, identification was impossible. The CF gene now has been identified, however, and new research offers hope. Discovery of the CF gene has made possible the detection of carriers, a tremendous legacy of the Human Genome Project.

Klinefelter syndrome
Males with the XXY chromosomal pattern.

Turner syndrome
Females with the XO chromosomal pattern.

Tay-Sachs disease
Failure to break down fatty materials in the CNS.

sickle-cell anemia
Chromosomal disorder resulting in abnormal hemoglobin.

cystic fibrosis
Chromosomal disorder producing a malfunction of the exocrine glands.

phenylketonuria (PKU)
Chromosomal disorder resulting in
a failure of the body to break down
the amino acid phenylalanine.

spina bifida
Genetic disorder resulting in the
failure of the neural tube to close.

sex-linked inheritance
Genes on the sex chromosome that
produce traits other than sex.

hemophilia
Genetic condition causing incorrect
blood clotting; called the "bleeder's
disease."

color blindness
Usually X-linked red/green color
blindness.

fragile X syndrome
Sex-linked inheritance disorder in
which the bottom half of the X
chromosome looks as if it is ready
to fall off; causes mental retardation
in 80% of the cases.

Hemophilia is an example of sex-linked
inheritance, which affected several of
the royal families of Europe (such as the
Romanovs of Russia, exemplified by the
family of Csar Nikolas, pictured here).

Phenylketonuria (PKU) results from the body's failure to break down the amino acid phenylalanine, which then accumulates, affects the nervous system, and causes mental retardation. Most states now require infants to be tested at birth. If PKU is present, the infants are placed on a special diet that has been remarkably successful.

But this success has produced future problems. Women treated successfully as infants may give birth to retarded children because of a toxic uterine environment. Thus at the first signs of pregnancy, these women must return to a special diet. The "cured" phenylketonuric still carries the faulty genes.

Spina bifida (failure of the spinal column to close completely) is an example of a genetic defect caused by the interaction of several genes with possible environmental involvement. During the formation of the nervous system (See Chapter 4), if the developing neural tube does not close, spina bifida results, which can cause mental retardation. Studies have shown that if women take extra folic acid when they're pregnant, the number of cases of spina bifida decreases (Blackman, 1997).

Disorders also occur because of what is known as **sex-linked inheritance.** If you recall, the X chromosome is substantially larger than the Y (about three times as large). Therefore, the female carries more genes on the 23rd chromosome than does the male. This difference helps to explain sex linkage. Think back now to the difference between dominant and recessive traits. If a dominant and a recessive gene appear together, the dominant trait is expressed. An individual must have two recessive genes for the recessive trait (say, blue eyes) to appear. But on the 23rd set of chromosomes, nothing on the Y chromosome offsets the effects of a gene on the X chromosome.

Perhaps the most widely known of these sex-linked characteristics is **hemophilia,** a condition in which the blood of hemophiliacs does not clot properly. Several of the royal families of Europe were particularly prone to this condition. Another sex-linked trait attributed to the X chromosome is **color blindness.** The X chromosome contains the gene for color vision, and, if it is faulty, nothing on the Y chromosome counterbalances the defect.

In 1970 a condition called **fragile X syndrome** was discovered. In this disorder, the end of the X chromosome looks ready to break off. In 1991 the gene for fragile X (FMR1) was discovered. Difficult to diagnose in the first year of life, fragile X seems to cause no physical problems. Fragile X appears in about 1 in 2,500 male births and 1 in about 5,000 female births. It affects males more severely than females, with developmental delays in speech and communication skills. As time passes, many of these children are learning disabled or mentally retarded (Hartl & Jones, 2005).

These are the more frequent chromosomal and genetic diseases, which are summarized in Table 3.2. (Other diseases also have, or are suspected of having, a strong genetic origin: diabetes, epilepsy, heart disorders, cancer, arthritis, and some mental illnesses.)

To end this part of our work on a more optimistic note, let's again turn our attention to the promising and exciting discoveries of the Human Genome Project.

THE HUMAN GENOME PROJECT

*The genome is the entire set of genetic instructions in the nucleus of every cell. (In fact, each cell contains **two** genomes, one derived from each parent: the two copies of each chromosome we inherit furnish us with two copies of each gene, and therefore two copies of the genome.) Genome size varies from species to species. From measurements of the amount of DNA in a single cell, we have been able to estimate that the human genome—half the DNA contents of a single nucleus—contains some 3.1 billion base pairs: 3,100,000,000 As, Ts, Gs, and Cs.* (Watson, 2003, p. 165)

TABLE 3.2   Chromosomal and Genetic Disorders

CHROMOSOMAL DISORDERS

Name	Effects	Incidence
Down syndrome	47 chromosomes; distinctive facial features, mental retardation, possible physical problems	Varies with age; older women more susceptible (under 30: 1 in 1,500 births; 35–39: 1 in 300 births)
Klinefelter syndrome	XXY chromosomal patterns in males; possible infertility, possible psychological problems	About 1 in 1,000 male births
Turner syndrome	One X chromosome missing in female, lack of secondary sex characteristics, infertile	About 1 in 2,500 female births
XYY syndrome	XYY chromosomal pattern in males; tend to be large, normal intelligence and behavior	About 1 in 1,000 male births

GENETIC DISORDERS

Name	Effects	Incidence
Tay-Sachs disease	Failure to break down fatty material in central nervous system; results in blindness, mental retardation, and death (usually by 4 or 5 years of age)	One in 25 Jews of Eastern European origin is a carrier
Sickle-cell anemia	Blood disorder produces anemia and considerable pain; caused by sickle shape of red blood cells	About 1 in 10 African-Americans is a carrier
Cystic fibrosis	Body produces excessive mucus, causing problems in the lungs and digestive tract; may be fatal; suspect gene recently identified	About 1 in 2,000 births
Phenylketonuria (PKU)	Body fails to break down amino acid (phenylalanine); results in mental retardation; treated by special diet	About 1 in 15,000 births
Spina bifida	Neural tube problem in which the developing spinal column does not close properly; may cause partial paralysis and mental retardation	About 1 in 1,000 births (depending on geographical area)

Human Genome Project
Attempt to identify and map the 50,000 to 100,000 genes that constitute the human genetic endowment.

As we mentioned at the opening of the chapter, the history of the **Human Genome Project** is one filled with animosity, anger, and lingering bitterness. The clash of personalities alone testifies to the intense feelings generated by the pursuit of biology's holy grail. Not to be lost in the telling of this story, however, is admiration for the sheer power of the human intellect. The steady and unrelenting search for knowledge—a network of hundreds of computers used in sequencing the genome, the irresistible accumulation of valuable data by such giants of biology as Watson, Collins, Venter, and Lander, among others, the genetic sequence of other species—all combined to make the search one of the most productive in a long and rich biological tradition. For example, among the more basic facts we now know are these:

- The busiest chromosome is chromosome 1, with 2,968 genes. The first letter (base) on chromosome 1 is G (Guanine).
- The most sparsely populated chromosome is the Y chromosome, which has only 231 genes.
- The DNA of any two humans is more than 99% identical.
- You have about 30,000 genes in the nucleus of about every cell in your body. (Red blood cells don't carry genes.)
- These 30,000 genes contain 3.2 billion base pairs (letters). (Smith, 2005)

The first complete draft of the human genome promises great potential, although much work remains to be done. Identify the various benefits to come from HGP, but also identify potential problems.

When you see the sheer numbers involved, it helps you to understand the difficulties entailed in identifying and sequencing the Human Genome.

How the Human Genome Project Began

Two gatherings of America's top biologists in the 1980s are credited as the forerunners of the project. In 1985, a group of scientists met at the University of California at Santa Cruz to discuss the possibility of mapping the human genome. Although many participants at this meeting were sure it *could* be done, they remained skeptical that it *should* be done, because of the enormous expense. Because of the widespread benefits that would come from the project, however, almost all the scientists present agreed that it deserved continued consideration. In March, 1986, a meeting of international scientists took place in Santa Fe, New Mexico. This meeting is considered to be the real beginning of the Human Genome Project. The National Institutes of Health (NIH), with the assistance of the Department of Energy (DOE), assumed leadership of the project (Shreeve, 2005). As a result of these meetings, the following goals were identified (McElheny, 2003).

- Continued mapping of the human genome—that is, mapping the many thousand genes present in each chromosome.
- Identification of all the genes in the genome.
- Advance DNA sequencing. (Sequencing is the process of determining the order of A, T, C, and Gs along a DNA strand.)
- Development of new and improved technologies.
- Continued investigation of the ethical, social, and legal aspects of the project.

On June 26, 2000, Dr. Francis Collins (director of the National Genome Research Institute) and Dr. J. Craig Venter (president of Celera Genomics) announced at a White House ceremony that they had completed a "rough draft of the human genome" (the total number of human genes. As we have seen, it requires over 3 billion chemical letters (A, T, C, G) to identify the DNA instructions by which an individual develops from an embryo to an adult.

Still, the rough draft of the human genome was only the beginning. It wasn't until three years later that the finished version appeared.

> *On April 14, 2003, the Human Genome Project announced the completion of its "finished version of the human code, two years ahead of the original projected finish in 2005. Timed to coincide with the fiftieth anniversary of the discovery of the DNA structure by Watson and Crick, the event was celebrated with a two-day orgy of symposia, speeches, and festivities in Washington with Francis Collins presiding and Watson himself the star of every gathering.* (Shreeve, 2005, p. 367)

Craig Venter was not invited to the celebration.

Much remains to be done, but the Human Genome Project is revolutionizing biology, medicine, and pharmacology, to say nothing of its ethical, legal, and social ramifications. For example, forms of hypertension, schizophrenia, and Alzheimer's have been targeted by an emerging drug therapy. The genes responsible for cystic fibrosis, Huntington's disease, and Duchenne muscular dystrophy (DMD) have been identified, as well as the breast cancer susceptibility gene (BRCA1). Some genetic defects have been identified only days after fertilization. Despite controversy and some disappointing results, gene therapy continues to offer promise for treating hemophilia, certain forms of cancer, and babies with defective immune systems. The future seems bright (Watson, 2003).

Although there are hundreds of diseases caused by a single gene, for thousands of other diseases, the genetic contribution is much more obscure. For example, some diseases need an environmental trigger (which may be the case for schizophrenia), whereas in other diseases, such as bipolar depression, several genes must interact (Watson, 2003).

Studies of genetic susceptibility will undoubtedly follow the same pattern. The genes that make people susceptible to certain diseases do not, by themselves, cause disease (Weissman, 2002). Rather, the combination of a particular environmental factor with a particular gene is needed (Smith, 2005). Once the mechanisms that cause a susceptibility gene to spring into action are more fully understood, such preventative measures as screening techniques and drug therapy will save many lives. Could it be possible that at birth people will be given a DNA test and then issued a small card or computer chip that indicates what type of health problems they are likely to encounter? An interesting footnote to the history of the Human Genome Project: On April 17, 2002, two years after the announcement of the successful mapping of the human genome, J. Craig Venter disclosed that his genes were among those used in the mapping effort (Shreeve, 2003). In 2007 Venter published his entire sequenced genome.

Ethical, Legal, and Social Implications

Unfortunately, this explosion of knowledge is also leading to uncertain, hotly disputed consequences. As genetic testing of embryos and prospective parents expands, the controversies these tests carry with them generate considerable concern (Smith, 2005; Watson, 2003). For example:

• The use of PGD (Preimplantation Genetic Diagnosis) has raised the issue of "designer babies." Assume a child is born with a major disorder of unknown origin and parents fear the consequences of a second child. Should the parents undergo several rounds of IVF entailing the immediate diagnosis of many embryos? When the problem is identified, the positive embryos are transferred.

With successful implantation and birth, blood cells from the second child can be transplanted to the first in hopes of curing the initial disease.

- Should companies be formed to recruit people to donate their DNA to help find genes that cause disease?
- If a family member is susceptible to a particular disease, do insurance companies have the legal right to deny this person, and perhaps the entire family, health insurance? Where are the lines drawn between public and private interests?
- How private/public is a person's medical history?

ELSI (Ethical, Legal, and Social Implications)
Program designed to study the ethical, social, and legal implications of the Human Genome Project.

Grappling with this and similar issues has led the *National Institutes of Health* and the *Department of Energy* to join forces and create a program for studying the ethical, legal, and social implications of the Human Genome Project—the **ELSI** program (Watson, 2003). Several of the issues that have been identified include the following.

- *Fairness in the use of genetic information* by insurers, employers, courts, schools, the military, and adoption agencies, among others. Who has access to this information, and how will it be used?
- *Privacy and confidentiality of genetic information.* Who owns and controls the information?
- *Psychological impact.* Is there any stigma attached because of a person's genetic make-up?
- *Genetic testing.* If there's a specific family history of a disorder, what is the role of genetic testing? How should people be informed about their predisposition to disease (Patenaude, Guttmacher, & Collins, 2002)?
- *Reproductive issues.* What role does genetic information play in decision making and reproductive rights?
- *Clinical issues.* What type of and how much education are necessary for health care providers? What are desirable standards and quality control measures?
- *Commercialization.* Who controls property rights and accessibility of data?

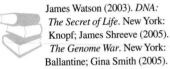

We strongly recommend three excellent accounts of the Human Genome Project: James Watson (2003). *DNA: The Secret of Life*. New York: Knopf; James Shreeve (2005). *The Genome War*. New York: Ballantine; Gina Smith (2005). *The Genomics Age*. New York: American Management Association.

Finally, a good way to summarize our work in this chapter is to remember that the outcome of genetic action depends on its interaction with environmental experiences.

Guided Review

15. _____ first made us aware of dominant and recessive characteristics.
16. When several genes contribute to a trait, this is called _____ inheritance.
17. Down syndrome is perhaps the best-known _____ disorder.
18. _____ _____ anemia and _____ _____ disease are examples of genetic disorders.
19. Mapping the human genes is the goal of the _____ _____ _____.
20. The results of the latest genetic research reinforce the belief that development is explained by the _____ of genes and the environment.

Answers   15. Mendel 16. polygenic 17. chromosomal 18. Sickle-cell, Tay-Sachs 19. Human Genome Project 20. interaction

CONCLUSION & SUMMARY

In this chapter we explored the biological basis of each person's uniqueness. We considered not only the power and beauty of nature in establishing our genetic endowment but also the growing influence of technology. The genes the mother and father provide unite to produce a new and different human being. Yet this new life still shows many of the characteristics of both parents. We saw how this newness and sameness has challenged researchers for decades.

Beginning with the discoveries of Mendel and still continuing, the secrets of hereditary transmission remain at the forefront of scientific endeavor, especially given the impetus of the Human Genome Project. Today's work, building on our knowledge of DNA, provides hope for the future while simultaneously raising legal and ethical questions that have yet to be resolved.

How does fertilization, both natural and assisted, occur?

- Knowledge of hormonal control of the menstrual cycle is crucial for understanding fertilization.

- The study of twins, especially monozygotic twins, has long fascinated psychologists.
- The increasing number of infertile couples has led to a growing demand for assisted fertilization.
- The most widely used assisted fertilization technique is AID (artificial insemination by donor).
- The success rate of assisted fertilization procedures has improved with increasing knowledge.
- Today's adoption procedures include both closed and open adoption.

What are the mechanisms of heredity, and what could go wrong?

- Mitosis and meiosis are the means of cell division.
- DNA is the chemical key to life.
- Understanding how traits are transmitted requires a knowledge of the workings of dominant and recessive genes.

- Chromosomal defects include Down syndrome, Klinefelter syndrome, and Turner syndrome.
- Genetic defects include Tay-Sachs disease, sickle-cell anemia, cystic fibrosis, phenylketonuria, and spina bifida.

What are the major features and anticipated uses of the Human Genome Project?

- The Human Genome Project is an endeavor to map all genes.
- HGP will have major implications for the identification, prevention, and medication of disease.
- Ethical, legal, and social issues require resolution in the light of new discoveries.

KEY TERMS

adoption
allele
artificial insemination by donor (AID)
assisted reproductive technologies (ART)
blastocyst
capacitation
chromosome
color blindness
closed adoption
codominance
cryopreservation
cystic fibrosis (CF)
cytogenetics
dizygotic
DNA (deoxyribonucleic acid)
dominant
Down syndrome
egg donation
ELSI

fallopian tubes
fragile X syndrome
gamete intrafallopian transfer (GIFT)
gene
genotype
hemophilia
Human Genome Project
identical
implantation
incomplete dominance
infertility
internal fertilization
intracytoplasmic sperm injection (ICSI)
intrauterine devices (IUDs)
in vitro fertilization (IVF)
Klinefelter syndrome
meiosis
mitosis
monozygotic

mutation
nonidentical
open adoption
ovulation
phenotype
phenylketonuria (PKU)
polygenic inheritance
recessive
RNA (ribonucleic acid)
sex-linked inheritance
sexually transmitted diseases (STDs)
sickle-cell anemia
sperm donation
spina bifida
surrogate motherhood
Tay-Sachs disease
Turner syndrome
zygote
zygote intrafallopian transfer (ZIFT)

chapter 3 Review

WHAT DO YOU THINK?

1. Several controversies have occurred lately about surrogate mothers and the children they bear. Do you have any strong feelings about surrogacy? Can you defend it? Regardless of your personal feelings, can you present what you see as the pros and cons of surrogacy?

2. In your reading, perhaps you noticed that the process of in vitro fertilization depended on research findings from studies of the menstrual cycle. Can you explain this, paying particular attention to the administering of hormones and the timing of their administration?

3. James Watson and Francis Crick received a Nobel Prize for their discovery of the double-helix structure of DNA. Why is the discovery of DNA so important in our lives? Can you think of anything you have read about in the newspapers or seen on television that derives from this discovery?

CHAPTER REVIEW TEST

1. **From ovulation to implantation takes about**
   a. seven days.
   b. two weeks.
   c. one month.
   d. nine months.

2. **The union of sperm and egg is known as**
   a. mitosis.
   b. fertilization.
   c. meiosis.
   d. mutation.

3. **In vitro fertilization takes place**
   a. in the fallopian tube.
   b. in the uterus.
   c. outside the woman's body.
   d. in the ovary.

4. **The process by which eggs are ripened and released is called**
   a. ovulation.
   b. mitosis.
   c. fertilization.
   d. implantation.

5. **Each sex cell carries a total of _____ chromosomes.**
   a. 23
   b. 24
   c. 47
   d. 46

6. **_____ twins are likely to occur when a woman's ovaries release two ripened eggs that are fertilized by separate sperm.**
   a. Nonidentical
   b. Identical

   c. Siamese
   d. Monozygotic

7. **Which factor is *not* thought to be a cause of infertility in men?**
   a. influenza
   b. low sperm count
   c. defective sperm
   d. genetic disease

8. **Which of these statements is true?**
   a. XX indicates male.
   b. XY indicates male.
   c. XO indicates male.
   d. X-indicates male.

9. **Which of these is an example of a genetic disorder?**
   a. sickle-cell anemia
   b. Turner syndrome
   c. Klinefelter syndrome
   d. Down syndrome

10. **When a natural mother relinquishes her child but retains input into the process of adoption, it's called _____ adoption.**
    a. closed
    b. foreign
    c. selected
    d. open

11. **Which of the following is an example of a chromosomal disorder?**
    a. spina bifida
    b. sickle-cell anemia
    c. phenylketonuria
    d. Turner syndrome

12. **_____ is the most widely used assisted fertilization technique.**
    a. IVF
    b. AID
    c. ATCG
    d. BRCA1

13. **Which combination is not possible?**
    a. AT
    b. TA
    c. GT
    d. GC

14. **DNA possesses the remarkable ability to _____ itself.**
    a. accommodate
    b. reproduce
    c. assimilate
    d. disengage

15. **Which of the following populations is more likely than others to be afflicted with sickle-cell anemia?**
    a. European-Americans
    b. African-Americans
    c. Asian-Americans
    d. Hispanic-Americans

16. **Down syndrome is caused by**
    a. the body's failure to break down amino acids.
    b. the fragile X syndrome.
    c. a deviation on the 21st pair of chromosomes.
    d. an XO pattern.

17. **An example of sex-linked inheritance includes**
    a. PKU.
    b. neural tube defects.
    c. Tay-Sachs disease.
    d. hemophilia.

18. **The Human Genome Project is an endeavor to identify and map**
    a. certain substances within cells.
    b. all human genes.
    c. cell divisions.
    d. sex-linked inheritance.

19. **Which of the following is not suspected of having a strong genetic origin?**
    a. polio
    b. epilepsy
    c. diabetes
    d. cancer

20. **The chromosome with the fewest genes is**
    a. chromosome 1
    b. x chromosome
    c. z chromosome
    d. y chromosome

Chapter 3 Review

Answers

1.a 2.b 3.c 4.a 5.a 6.a 7.a 8.b 9.a 10.d 11.d 12.b 13.c 14.b 15.b 16.c 17.d 18.b 19.a

PREGNANCY AND BIRTH

chapter

4

Chapter Objectives

After reading this chapter, you should be able to answer the following questions.

- What kinds of development occur during the prenatal period?

- What influences prenatal development, and what cautions should be taken?

- What are the circumstances and possible difficulties of the birth process?

Ellen and Kevin were delighted. The parents of a 3-year-old boy, they were now looking forward to their second child. Kevin, having shared in the birth of their first child, was calmer but even more excited as he looked forward to the events of this pregnancy and birth. Ellen, a healthy 31-year-old, was experiencing all the signs of a normal pregnancy. The morning sickness abated at 12 weeks. She felt movement at 17 weeks, and an ultrasound at 20 weeks showed normal development. Weight gain, blood glucose levels, blood pressure, and AFP (alpha-fetoprotein) test results were all within acceptable ranges.

Since this was Ellen's second pregnancy, she felt more comfortable with her changing body. Visits to the obstetrician were pleasant and uneventful. At 28 weeks, loosening ligaments caused her pelvis to irritate the sciatic nerve at the base of the spine. Her obstetrician recommended Tylenol, a heating pad, and rest. He also recommended a visit to an orthopedist to confirm the treatment. Ellen refused to take any medication and decided not to bother with a second opinion. Since she felt she could tolerate the pain for the 12 weeks until delivery, she would not be X-rayed or take even a mild painkiller. She rationalized that the back pain was acceptable because it accompanied a normal pregnancy.

At 31 weeks, Ellen noticed episodes of unusual movement and became concerned. A week later, fearing that the baby might be in distress, she called the obstetrician to describe the jabs, pokes, and excessive movements she was experiencing. The doctor immediately scheduled a biophysical profile: an eight-point check of the internal organs and another ultrasound.

Ellen nervously gulped the required 32 ounces of water an hour before the examination. Arriving at a glistening new medical center, she was quickly escorted to an examining room. The technician was both professional and serious as he looked for a problem (increasing Ellen's anxiety). The examination included a thorough check of the baby's heart chambers, a type of EKG (electrocardiogram) measurement, and an assessment of blood flow—all displayed in vibrant colors. The cord, internal organs, position of the baby, and body weight were all evaluated. Ellen was able to listen to the baby's heartbeat while watching the heart chambers function.

Later that day, Ellen's obstetrician called to tell her the results: no apparent medical problems, just an unusually active baby. Ellen and Kevin sagged with relief. They also received a bonus: a reassuring ultrasound image of their unborn child's face—in living color!

One of the authors (JFT) frequently (perhaps too often) tells an amusing story about the birth of his second child. Badly hurt in an automobile accident and temporarily using a wheelchair, he was determined to drive his wife to the hospital when the magic moment arrived. Sure enough, the time arrived (2 o'clock in the morning, of course), and he successfully maneuvered to the hospital. While he parked the car, his wife went in search of a wheelchair. As the two of them struggled down the corridor to the nurses' station, the puzzled nurse on duty looked from one to the other and tactfully asked, "Could you tell me which one of you I'm supposed to admit?"

Ultrasound is frequently used when questions arise about a pregnancy. Soundwaves directed onto the uterus bounce off the bones and tissues of the fetus and are formed into an image. Evaluate the significance of ultrasound in prenatal diagnosis.

The baby born after this less than auspicious beginning was Ellen, the subject of the chapter's opening. Her journey through the nine months of pregnancy was quite characteristic: normal prenatal development accompanied by occasional worrisome moments. Given current concern about the quality of life for a woman and her developing child, we can understand the importance placed on prenatal development. In fact, today's acceptance of the impact that these nine months have on an individual's future has led to greater emphasis on *prepregnancy* care. If you think about this for a moment, it makes considerable sense because some women don't realize they're pregnant for two or three months. By then, rapid growth has occurred (as we'll see, such growth is particularly true of the central nervous system), with the potential for serious damage if elements such as alcohol and drugs have been abused.

In this chapter, we first explore the prenatal world, that nine-month period that provides nourishment and protection and serves as a springboard for birth. Next we turn to those agents that can influence prenatal development. These are both physical and psychological and can be either positive or negative. We then look at birth itself, the completion of a journey that has involved remarkable development. For various reasons, some fetuses can't endure this nine-month journey, so our final focus in this chapter is the special case of these early, or premature, births. In the past few years, great advances—technological, medical, and psychological—have resulted in the survival of an increasing number of premature babies.

THE PRENATAL WORLD

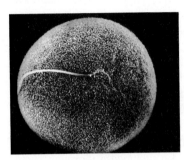

Fertilization through the embryonic period: the moment of fertilization. Can you describe the potential pitfalls facing successful fertilization?

implantation
Fertilized egg attaches and secures itself to uterine wall.

Giving birth is this particular combination of determination and compulsion.

—Alison Gopnik, Andrew Meltzoff, Patricia Kuhl

Although it may be difficult to imagine, you are the product of one cell, the zygote, or fertilized egg. Once the egg is released from the ovary, it passes into the fallopian tube. Fertilization occurs in the first part of the fallopian tube, about three days after the egg has entered the tube. After the union of sperm and egg takes place, in only a matter of hours (about 24–30), that one cell begins to divide rapidly. The initial phase of the event occurred in a very protected world—the prenatal environment.

The fertilized egg must now pass through the remainder of the fallopian tube to reach the uterus, a journey of about three to four days to travel five or six inches. During its passage through the fallopian tube, the zygote receives all its nourishment from the tube (Moore & Persaud, 2003). Figure 4.1 illustrates passage into the uterus and **implantation.**

FIGURE 4.1

Passage of the zygote onto the uterus

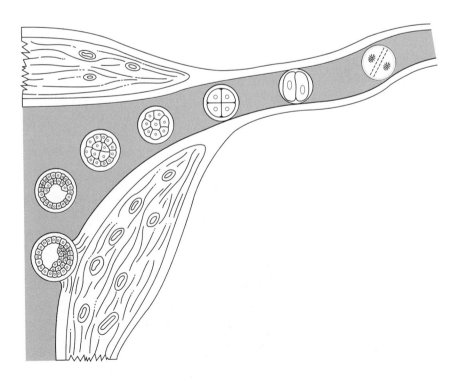

FIGURE 4.2

During the second week, the blastocyst becomes firmly implanted in the wall of the uterus, and the placenta, umbilical cord, and embryo begin to form from the blastocyst's outer layer of cells.

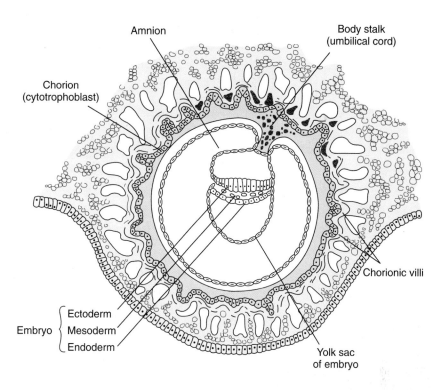

germinal period
First two weeks following fertilization.

blastocyst
The fertilized egg when it reaches the uterus (about 7 days after conception).

placenta
Supplies the embryo with all its needs, carries off all its wastes, and protects it from danger.

umbilical cord
Contains blood vessels that go to and from the mother through the arteries and veins supplying the placenta.

amniotic sac
Fluid-filled uterine sac that surrounds the embryo/fetus.

embryonic period
Third through the eighth week following fertilization.

cellular differentiation
Embryonic cells are destined for specific functions and thus differentiate themselves.

ectoderm
Outer layer of the embryo that gives rise to the nervous system, among other developmental features.

During the prenatal months, we can identify three fairly distinct stages of development: germinal, embryonic, and fetal.

Germinal Period

The **germinal period** extends through the first two weeks. The passage through the fallopian tube takes three to four days, and then the fertilized egg floats in the uterine cavity for about three more days before beginning implantation. During these days, it receives nourishment form the glands of the uterine wall (Leifer, 2003; Moore & Persaud, 2003). The zygote is now one week old and called a **blastocyst.** During the second week, the blastocyst becomes firmly implanted in the wall of the uterus. From its outer layer of cells, the **placenta,** the **umbilical cord,** and the **amniotic sac** begin to develop. The inner cell layer develops into the embryo itself. Figure 4.2 illustrates the developmental significance of the blastocyst.

The placenta and the umbilical cord serve critical functions during development. The placenta supplies the embryo with all its needs, carries off all its wastes, and protects it from danger. The placenta has two separate sets of blood vessels, one going to and from the baby through the umbilical cord, the other going to and from the mother through the arteries and veins supplying the placenta.

We can summarize the first two weeks following conception as follows:

Week 1: The zygote moves through the fallopian tube to the uterus, and rapid cell division begins within the first 30 hours.

Week 2: The blastocyst adheres to the uterine wall and begins to form the placenta, umbilical cord, and amniotic sac. (The amniotic sac will contain amniotic fluid, which is essentially fetal urine.)

Embryonic Period

In the **embryonic period,** from the third through the eighth week, a recognizable human being emerges. Perhaps the most remarkable change in the embryo is **cellular differentiation.** Three distinct layers are being formed: the **ectoderm,**

FIGURE 4.3

Development from the three layers of the blastocyst

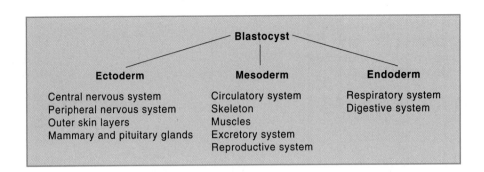

	Blastocyst	
Ectoderm	**Mesoderm**	**Endoderm**
Central nervous system	Circulatory system	Respiratory system
Peripheral nervous system	Skeleton	Digestive system
Outer skin layers	Muscles	
Mammary and pituitary glands	Excretory system	
	Reproductive system	

mesoderm
Middle layer of the embryo that gives rise to muscles, skeleton, excretory system.

endoderm
Inner layer of the embryo that gives rise to the lungs, liver, and pancreas, among other developmental features.

organogenesis
Formation of organs during the embryonic period.

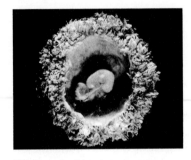

This 4-week-old embryo now has a beating heart, body buds are beginning to emerge, and the eye region is becoming discernible. Can you summarize the major accomplishments of the embryonic period?

which will give rise to skin, hair, nails, teeth, and the nervous system; the **mesoderm,** which will give rise to muscles, skeleton, and the circulatory and excretory systems; and the **endoderm,** which will give rise to lungs, liver, and pancreas. (See Figure 4.3 for details.)

Usually by the completion of the fourth week, the heart begins to beat—the embryo's first movement. The accompanying photograph show that, during the fifth week, eyes and ears begin to emerge; body buds give clear evidence of becoming arms and legs; and the head area is the largest part of the rapidly growing embryo.

During the sixth and seventh weeks, fingers begin to appear on the hands, the outline of toes is seen, and the beginnings of the spinal cord are visible. In the germinal period, the number and differentiation of cells rapidly increase; in the embryonic period, the organs are formed, a process called **organogenesis.** After eight weeks, 95% of the body parts are formed, and general body movements are detected.

Emergence of the Nervous System

At about the beginning of the third week, the first signs of the nervous system appear. For some reason we as yet don't understand, the mesoderm sends a chemical signal to the ectoderm. This process, *called neural induction,* causes a portion of the outer layer to become the *neural plate,* which leads to the formation of the nervous system. (And all of this has been going on before the woman realizes she's pregnant!) The neural plate now forms a groove and begins to fold in on itself, leading to the creation of the neural tube.

Speed of Nervous System Development

When you think of how complex a child's brain is, it's stunning to realize how quickly neural development occurs. The neuroscientist Marian Diamond (1999) summarizes the rapid growth in this way: If fertilization occurred on Monday, by Thursday the embryo would consist of 30 cells clustered together. By Saturday, this cluster of cells (the blastocyst) would have started digging into the woman's uterine wall. By Tuesday of the following week, the endoderm, mesoderm, and ectoderm would be emerging. Again, remember that all this happens before the woman misses her first period.

Summarizing then, the stages in this initial phase of nervous system development are as follows.

- The process begins with the induction of the neural plate (called *neural induction*), which can occur only during a limited time, usually about the beginning of the third prenatal week.
- The neural tube now forms, and its top expands into the brain, while the rest of the tube will become the spinal cord. Developmental biologists today are demonstrating that even in the early days of neural tube development our neurons know to what part of the brain they'll travel and what type of nerve cell they'll become (motor, vision, hearing, and so on) (Moffett, 2006).

- Nerve cells begin to form in the neural tube (a process called *cell proliferation*). For a baby to be born with the 100 billion cells we mentioned, nerve cells must be produced during pregnancy at an average rate of *250,000 per minute* for the entire period. During this same time, estimates are that 30,000 synapses are formed *every second* (Rose, 2005).

- The nerve cells at this stage are called *neurons,* and they begin to leave the neural tube and travel to their destination in the developing brain. This process is called *cell migration,* which typically commences during the seventh prenatal week. Some of the neurons travel distances in the brain that you may find hard to believe, for example, equal to the distance from Boston to San Francisco.

- The neurons now embark on their task of forming 1000 trillion connections in a child's brain.

- A pruning process quickly sets in, and million of neurons and connections perish, which is nature's way of insuring survival of the fittest neurons.

From these beginnings a picture of the brain appears with which you're familiar. The top of the neural tube leads to the formation of the two cerebral hemispheres and the four lobes of the cerebral cortex.

Think about the rapid development of the nervous system in these numbers:

- 200,000,000,000 brain cells in the fetus' brain by the fifth month
- 100,000,000,000 neurons (brain cells) in a newborn baby's brain
- One trillion glia (support) cells in a baby's brain
- 1,000 trillion connections in a baby's brain

We'd like to call your attention to one startling fact in these numbers: What happened to cause the fetus to lose 100,000,000,000 (one hundred billion) brain cells in the space of the four last months of pregnancy? The answer lies in the number of brain cells or neurons that nature produces in all our brains. Those neurons that *don't* make connections simply die. And—this may startle you—this exercise in survival (some connections die, some connections survive) continues throughout our lives, giving new and critical meaning to the expression "use it or lose it"—the fittest of our neurons are those that make connections and survive.

We can summarize development during the embryonic period as follows:

Weeks 3+: Rapid development of nervous system

Week 4: Heart beats

Week 5: Eyes and ears begin to emerge, body buds for arms and legs, embryo is about 3/8 inch long

Week 6 and 7: Embryo is about 1/2 to 3/4 inches long, fingers and toes visible, beginning of spinal cord, liver begins to form red blood cells

Week 8: Embryo is now about 1 inch long, about 95% of body parts differentiated—arms, legs, beating heart, nervous system

The embryonic period can be hazardous for the newly formed organism. During these weeks, embryonic tissue is particularly sensitive to any foreign agents during differentiation, especially beginning at the third or fourth week of the pregnancy. Estimates are that about 30% of all embryos are aborted at this time without the mother's knowledge; about 90% of all embryos with chromosomal abnormalities are spontaneously aborted.

At the end of this period, a discernible human being with arms, legs, a beating heart, and a nervous system exists. It is receiving nourishment and discharging waste through the umbilical cord, which leads to the placenta. The placenta itself never actually joins with the uterus but exchanges nourishment and waste products through the walls of the blood vessels (Moore & Persaud, 2003). The future mother begins to experience some of the noticeable effects of pregnancy: the need to urinate more frequently, morning sickness, and increasing fullness of breasts.

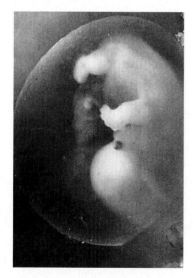

Coming to the end of the embryonic period, this 7-week-old embryo has begun to assume a more human appearance. It is now about 1 inch in length with discernible eyes, ears, nose, mouth, arms, and legs. Why is the time of organogenesis a particularly sensitive period?

AN INFORMED VIEW

Embryos for Sale

In the preceding chapter we mentioned the growing number of frozen embryos presently stored in fertility clinics throughout the United States, a number now believed to be at least 400,000 (Wade, 2007). In some cases the parents of these frozen embryos have donated their unused embryos to other infertile couples. To address the resulting legal, social, and moral questions, a new form of adoption has emerged in the United States.

In the summer of 2001, Senator Arlen Specter of Pennsylvania attached an amendment onto a family bill for U.S. Department of Health and Human Services. It provided one million dollars for *embryo adoption* (Spar, 2006). The first recipient of this money ($500,000) was an adoption program called *Snowflakes,* which derived not only money but also considerable publicity for its goal: matching frozen embryos with adoptive parents. (The name was chosen because each embryo is fragile and unique.)

As the program developed and techniques improved, 60% of the frozen embryos survived the thawing process. The use of these embryos resulted in a 22% successful implantation rate (*U.S. News and World Report,* 2007). By 2007, the program at Snowflake resulted in 45 women giving birth to 62 babies.

The history of this program is interesting. In 1990, the British government ruled that all embryos frozen for five years were to be destroyed. The law took effect in 1990, and the first destruction of the embryos was to occur in 1996. An American, Ron Stoddard, founder of Nightlight Christian Adoption, was appalled by the decision. He conceived the idea of public embryo adoption in the United States and formulated a process similar to that of open infant adoption (Spar, 2006). Prospective parents are charged about $10,000 for an agency fee and about $4,000–5,000 for medical bills.

The first Snowflake's baby was born on New Year's Eve, 1998. With the attendant publicity, by 2003 9,000 embryos were publicly available for adoption. Legislation has now been proposed to ensure a "presumption of parentage," which would transfer all parental rights to the new parents.

We strongly recommend Debora Spar's text *The Baby Business,* Cambridge, MA: Harvard Business School Press, which effectively describes how the baby business has become big business.

fetal period
Period extending from the beginning of the third gestational month to birth.

The fetus at 4½ months—a time of rapid growth and considerable activity. Can you justify the belief that prenatal learning is a real possibility?

Fetal Period

The **fetal period** extends from the beginning of the third month to birth. During this time, the fetus grows rapidly both in height and weight. The sex organs appear during the third month, and it is possible to determine the baby's sex. Visible sexual differentiation begins, and the nervous system continues to increase in size and complexity.

By the fourth month, the fetus is about 8 to 10 inches in length and weighs about 6 to 8 ounces. The fourth to the fifth month is usually the peak growth period. During this time, the mother begins to feel movement. The fetus now swallows, digests, and discharges urine. Growth is rapid during the fourth month to accommodate an increasing oxygen demand. The fetus produces specialized cells: red blood cells to transport oxygen and white blood cells to combat disease.

The fetus is now active—sucking, turning its head, and pushing with hands and feet—and the mother is acutely aware of the life within her. The marginal photo at left represents the fetus in the fourth month.

By the end of the fifth month, the baby is 10 to 12 inches long and weighs about a pound. The fetus sleeps and wakes as the newborn does, even manifesting a favorite sleep position. Rapid growth continues in the sixth month, with the fetus gaining another 2 inches and 1 pound, but slows during the seventh month. Viability, the ability to survive if born, is attained. After six months very few new nerve and muscle cells appear, since at birth the nervous system must be fully functioning to ensure automatic breathing.

Thus the foundation of the nervous system forms in the first few weeks following conception; by six weeks the reflexes are active and electrical brain-wave patterns appear. Touching the fetal forehead as early as nine weeks causes the fetus to turn away, and if the soles of its feet are stroked, the toes curl up. The entire body is sensitive to touch. By mid-pregnancy, the inner ear is fully developed, and the fetus reacts with movement to external sound.

During fetal testing, the fetal heart rate changes and movement increases, suggesting that the fetus has sensed tactile stimulation. Muscular development of the eyes enables the fetus to move its eyes during sleep. From about the 16th week the fetus is sensitive to any light that penetrates the uterine wall and the amniotic fluid.

Toward the end of pregnancy, a bright light pointed at the mother's abdomen causes the fetus to move. The fetus begins to swallow amniotic fluid early in the pregnancy and demonstrates taste by turning toward and swallowing more of a sweet substance injected into the amniotic fluid.

This description of fetal life leads to an inevitable conclusion: Given adequate conditions, the fetus at birth is equipped to deal effectively with the transition from its sheltered environment to the extrauterine world.

We can summarize these developments as follows:

Third month: Sex organs appear

Fourth month: Rapid growth, red blood cells, white blood cells; active sucking

Fifth month: Hears sound, sleeps, 10 to12 inches long, 1 pound

Sixth month: Rapid growth, 12 to 14 inches, 2 pounds

Seventh month: Growth slows, viability attained

Eighth and ninth months: Preparation for birth; senses ready to function, brain is 25% of adult weight

At the end of the ninth month, the fetus (just before birth) is about 20 inches long and weighs about 7 pounds, 6 ounces, and its brain at birth is 20–25% of its adult weight. Table 4.1 summarizes the course of prenatal development.

TABLE 4.1	Milestones in Prenatal Development
Age	*Accomplishment*
3 weeks	Nervous system begins to form
4 weeks	Heart begins to beat
5 weeks	Head continues rapid growth
8 weeks	Almost all body parts are differentiated
12 weeks	Possible to visually determine baby's sex Growth of head slows Formation of red blood cells by liver slows
14 weeks	Begins to coordinate limb movements Slow eye movements occur
16 weeks	Ultrasound shows clearly defined bone structure
20 weeks	Possible to hear heartbeat with fetoscope Baby covered by fine downy hair called *lanugo* Eyebrows and head hair visible Fetal movements called *quickening* are felt by mother
21 weeks	Rapid eye movements commence Substantial weight gain
24 weeks	Fingernails can be seen
28 weeks	Eyes open and close Lungs capable of breathing
32 weeks	Skin pink and smooth Chubby appearance
38 weeks	Nervous system can carry out some integrative functions Reacts to light Usually assumes upside-down position as birth approaches

Source: Leifer, 2003; Moore & Persaud, 2003; Olds, London, & Ladewig, 1996.

AN APPLIED VIEW

Stem Cells

A new scientifically promising but, to some, morally controversial body of research has appeared. *Stem cell research,* with all its potential for combating disease while simultaneously generating heated strife, has entered the arenas of legal, scientific, and moral dispute. How did it all begin?

On November 6, 1998, James Thomson, a professor at the University of Wisconsin's Primate Research Center, announced that he had developed the first line of human embryonic stem cells. As he reported:

> These cell lines should be useful in human developmental biology, drug discovery, and transplantation medicine. *(Thomson, 1998)*

Thomson fully realized the consequences of his discovery: what the implications were for the availability and use of a line of human stem cells. But he continued to "focus on the mechanics of an animal's development, how genes orchestrate the process, what chemical signals are involved, and how the combination leads to organized structures such as skin and bone" (Scott, 2006, pp. 5–6). The controversy would soon follow.

First, however, what exactly is this form of research that has generated such contention? To begin our discussion, we must carefully define what is meant by the various terms used in this research as defined by the National Institutes of Health.

- *Totipotent cells:* These are the cells that are formed from the immediate division of the fertilized egg and have the ability for about four or five days after fertilization to become any cell or tissue in the body.

- *Pluripotent cells:* These cells are capable of becoming almost any cell in the human body (with the exception of the placenta and supporting tissue) until they begin to

specialize, that is, give rise to a particular type of cell, such as blood or skin.

- *Multipotent cells:* These cells, formerly the pluripotent cells, begin to specialize, and their potential becomes limited to a particular type of cell (blood, skin, and so on).

If you recall our discussion of the days immediately following fertilization, the fertilized egg begins to divide about 24 hours following fertilization, travels through the fallopian tube, and at about the fourth day drops into the uterine cavity. At this point it becomes a *blastocyst,* consisting of an outer layer of cells called the *trophoblast* and an inner cell mass (ICM) that contains the pluripotent cells, which eventually becomes the embryo. When you hear the expression "embryonic stem cells," it is referring to the cells that have been removed from the inner cell mass.

You have undoubtedly also noticed that when the ICM is removed from the blastocyst, *the pluripotent cells must be prevented from specializing, while at the same time they must continue to divide.* Consequently, the culture into which they are placed holds the solution to this problem. (Note the similarity to the challenges facing the early pioneers of in vitro fertilization in determining the correct culture for the sperm and the egg.)

The application of this research abounds with moral, ethical, and legal issues. What are the obligations to the sick, who could benefit from this new knowledge? How much information should be provided to those who donate frozen embryos and those who may use them? On the other side of this ethical divide are those who argue for the sanctity of human life from the moment of conception. The four-day-old blastocyst certainly meets this criterion. Should there be more money, time, and research spent on adult stem cells as opposed to embryonic stem cells? Of one conclusion we can be sure: The controversy is far from over.

For a thoughtful discussion and overview of this issue, we recommend Christopher Scott, *Stem Cell Now* (2006). New York: Pi Press.

Guided Review

1. The fertilized egg passes through the _____ _____ on its way to the uterus.

2. When the zygote is 1 week old, it's called a _____.

3. The embryonic period extends from the _____ to the _____ week of development.

4. The three distinct layers during the embryonic period are the _____, the _____, and the _____.

5. The period beginning with the third month of pregnancy and extending to birth is known as the _____ period.

6. The growth of the nervous system commences with a process known as _____ _____.

7. A new form of adoption has appeared, called _____ _____.

Answers

1. fallopian tube 2. blastocyst 3. third, eighth 4. ectoderm, mesoderm, endoderm 5. fetal 6. neural induction 7. embryo adoption

INFLUENCES ON PRENATAL DEVELOPMENT

When we speak of "environmental influences" on children, we usually think of the time beginning at birth. But remember: At birth an infant has already had nine months of prenatal living, with all of this period's positive and negative features. Many women now experience the benefits of the latest and superior prenatal care. Diet, exercise, and rest are all carefully programmed to meet the needs of the individual woman. When women, especially pregnant teenagers, lack such treatment, the rates of prenatal loss, stillbirths, and neonatal (just after birth) mortality are substantially increased. What are some of the positive and negative influences that affect prenatal development?

Maternal Influences

Among the significant maternal influences on prenatal development are these: nutrition, weight, exercise, emotions and sense of self, and culture.

Nutrition

Examining pregnancy from a wellness perspective, we may identify several components that affect a woman's condition. As Leifer (2003, p. 58) notes:

> *Good nutrition is essential to establish and maintain a healthy pregnancy and to give birth to a healthy child. Good nutritional habits begun before conception and continued during pregnancy promote adaptation to the maternal and fetal needs.*

The physician usually recommends supplements to the pregnant woman's regular diet, such as additional protein, iron, calcium, sodium, fiber, folic acid, and vitamins. According to the 2005 Dietary Guidelines for Americans, a healthy diet emphasizes fruits, vegetables, whole grains, and low-fat or fat-free milk. It also includes lean meats, poultry, fish, beans, eggs, and nuts, as well as foods low in saturated fats, sodium, and cholesterol. Because a fetus depends on its mother for nourishment, most women today are keenly aware of the need to have a proper diet that will help them give birth to a healthy baby.

Weight

Women of childbearing age who wish to have children need to evaluate their weight and nutritional habits well before pregnancy. In this way, they can establish good eating habits and attempt to maintain normal weight for their size. How much weight to gain is always an important question for pregnant women. In a typical pregnancy, a woman will gain 25 to 35 pounds. If a woman is overweight beginning her pregnancy, a weight gain of 15 to 25 pounds is recommended (depending on health, nutritional status, and so forth). Underweight women are urged to reach their ideal weight plus 28 to 40 pounds during pregancy (Balcazar & Mattson, 2000; Grodner, Long, & DeYoung, 2004).

The weight that a pregnant woman gains is not distributed equally. Although a woman may gain 25 pounds, the newborn baby usually weighs only 7 to 8 pounds. The answer lies in the unequal distribution of weight gain a woman experiences: The uterus may gain 2.5 pounds, the breasts anywhere from 1.5 to 3 pounds, the placenta from 1.0 to 1.5 pounds, and so on.

Exercise

Moderate exercise during the prenatal period, as long as the woman is physically able, contributes to both mental health and general fitness. Among the guidelines suggested by the American College of Obstetricians and Gynecologists are these:

- Mild to moderate exercise during pregnancy is beneficial, but to avoid fatigue, do not engage in intense exercise.
- After the first trimester, avoid exercising in the supine position (lying on the back) to avoid decreasing cardiac output.
- Avoid any exercises that could affect balance.
- Be sure that diet matches energy demands.
- Be alert to any signs of overexertion: dizziness, fainting, pain, and so on (Olds, London, & Ladewig, 1996).

Emotions and Sense of Self

Noting that the primary process for pregnant women is coming to terms with their new role as a mother, that is, developing maternal identity and role competency, scientists (Arenson & Drake, 2007; Barnard & Solchany, 2002; Leifer, 2003) have frequently turned to the classic work of Ruth Rubin (1984) to explain the stressful emotional road many pregnant women travel. Rubin believed that women must master four tasks in the transition to motherhood.

1. *During the first trimester of pregnancy women focus on their personal well-being* and are alert to their health and avoiding the potential dangers of a faulty diet, drugs, and alcohol. During the second trimester, a woman's concern turns to her unborn child and the possible effects the environment can have on its development. Finally, in the third trimester, she has a sense of "oneness" with her child.

2. *Ensuring the acceptance of the child by others.* By this, Rubin meant the task of developing a physical and psychological haven for her child within the family. The mother, consciously or not, is aware that family relationships will require adjustment if her child is to receive unconditional acceptance.

3. *"Binding-in" is the process by which a woman and her unborn child establish a bond.* The process begins in the early days of the first trimester, when a woman alternates feelings of joy at the thought of giving birth with doubts and feelings of rejection. During the second trimester, when the expectant mother feels movement within her and when she sees the first ultrasound images, the sense of a relationship with the unborn child solidifies.

4. Learning to give of herself commences in the first trimester, when the woman becomes aware of the demands that her pregnancy will make on her: changes in body appearance, relationships, lifestyle, and many others. The realization of her role as a mother begins to take shape in the second trimester, whereas the third trimester brings feelings of anxiety: the pain and danger of delivery, worries about her competence, the sense of total commitment become more acute.

In spite of the worries and concerns associated with pregnancy, Rubin believed that mastering these tasks prepared a woman for the subsequent lengthy period of giving of one's self.

Today, we also ask, how do women *and* men negotiate the change in roles that is about to occur? How will they balance work and parenting, share domestic responsibilities, and just come to terms with the profound changes in their lives? Current advances in technology can be helpful, but they also can create anxiety when new parents are presented with a huge amount of information about how to parent.

Culture

In the United States, we live in a culturally diverse nation that is said to encourage newcomers to share our way of life, yet, even under the best of conditions, the path for many can be difficult. Even within specific racial or ethnic groups, tremendous cultural variation appears. When we examine cross-cultural data, we notice the dramatically different variations among different cultures. Being aware of and accepting of cultural differences is both important and beneficial to health care providers in their treatment of a woman and her family (Greenfield, Suzuki, & Rothstein-Fisch, 2006).

To ensure that a woman's journey through the prenatal months is as safe and satisfying as possible, we should consider certain basic ideas. For example, communication assumes paramount importance—not only language but also such behaviors as hand gestures, tone of voice, and so forth. How does the woman's family, as members of a particular culture, view the pregnancy? Is it seen as a natural, expected occurrence that doesn't require constant care? Does the woman's status change as a result of the pregnancy? Are there cultural dietary considerations that should be addressed? Are there spiritual beliefs that health care providers should be aware of?

Other Influences

developmental risk
Threat to children who may be susceptible to problems because of some physical or psychological difficulty ("at-risk" children).

In spite of good care, some children still experience problems, which introduces the concept of **developmental risk.** Developmental risk is a term used to identify those children whose well-being is in jeopardy. Such risks incorporate a continuum of biological and environmental conditions. These range from the very serious (genetic defects) to the less serious (mild oxygen deprivation at birth). What now seems clear is that *the earlier the damage (a toxic drug or maternal infection), the greater the chance of negative long-term effects.*

As we begin our discussion, remember that almost all drugs (including aspirin), unnecessary medication, and risky chemicals at work or at home—should be avoided. Most pregnant women today are also cautious about the amount of caffeine and sweeteners they use. For example, the FDA has cautioned pregnant women to moderate their consumption of caffeine-containing foods and beverages. These simple precautions eliminate danger for most women and their babies. Specifically, what causes a child to be *developmentally at risk?*

Teratogens

teratogens
Any agents that can cause abnormalities—for example, drugs, chemicals, infections, pollutants.

With regard to *developmental risk,* our major concern is with those substances that exercise their influence in the prenatal environment, a time of increased sensitivity. Teratogenic agents, which are any agents that cause abnormalities, especially demand our attention (Moore & Persaud, 2003). **Teratogens** that can cause birth defects are drugs, chemicals, infections, pollutants, or a mother's physical state, such as diabetic. Table 4.2 summarizes several of the more common teratogenic agents and the times of greatest potential risk. By examining Table 4.2, you can see that these teratogenic agents fall into two classes: infectious diseases and different types of chemicals.

Can you explain why the same teratogen can produce different effects at different prenatal ages?

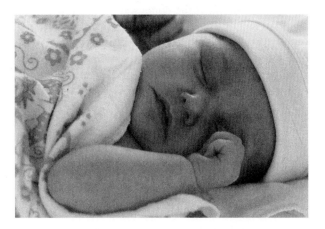

TABLE 4.2   Teratogens, Their Effects, and Time of Risk

Agent	Possible Effects	Time of Risk
Alcohol	Fetal Alcohol Syndrome (FAS), growth retardation, cognitive deficits	Throughout pregnancy
Aspirin	Bleeding problems	Last month, at birth
Cigarettes	Prematurity, lung problems	After 20 weeks
DES	Cancer of female reproductive system	From 3 to 20 weeks
LSD	Isolated abnormalities	Before conception
Lead	Death, anemia, mental retardation	Throughout pregnancy
Marijuana	Unknown long-term effects, early neurological problems	Throughout pregnancy
Thalidomide	Fetal death, physical and mental abnormalities	The first month
Cocaine	Spontaneous abortion, neurological problems	Throughout pregnancy
AIDS	Growth failure, low birth weight, developmental delay, death from infection	Before conception, throughout pregnancy, during delivery, during breast feeding
Rubella	Mental retardation, physical problems, possible death	First three months, may have effects during later months
Syphilis	Death congenital syphilis, prematurity	From five months on
CMV	Retardation, deafness, blindness	Uncertain, perhaps 4 to 24 weeks
Herpes simplex	CNS damage, prematurity	Potential risk throughout pregnany and at birth

Infectious Diseases

STORCH diseases
Syphilis, **t**oxoplasmosis, **o**ther infections, **r**ubella, **c**ytomegalovirus, **h**erpes.

Some diseases that are potentially harmful to the developing fetus and that are acquired either before or during birth are grouped together as the **STORCH** diseases (Blackman, 1997): **S**yphilis, **T**oxoplasmosis, **O**ther infections, **R**ubella, **C**ytomegalovirus, and **H**erpes. The potential risk of the disease lies in the timing of infection: the earlier the more serious. Estimates are that about 15% of all pregnant women experience some type of infectious disease. (Arenson & Drake, 2007).

Syphilis

syphilis
Sexually transmitted disease that, if untreated, may adversely affect the fetus.

Syphilis is sexually transmitted and, if untreated, may affect the fetus. It makes no difference whether the mother contracted the disease during pregnancy or many years before. If the condition remains untreated, about 25% of infected fetuses will die any time during or after the second trimester. (Another 25% die soon after birth.) Those who survive may be affected by serious problems such as blindness, mental retardation, and deafness (Blackman, 1997). Because of the advances in antibiotic treatments, the incidence of congenital syphilis has steadily decreased, although there has been a recent upsurge owing to an increase in numbers of cases among adolescents and heterosexuals (Leifer, 2003).

Toxoplasmosis

Toxoplasmosis
Infection caused by a protozoan; may cause damage to the nervous system; transmitted by animals, especially cats.

Toxoplasmosis is caused by a protozoan (a single-celled microorganism called *toxoplasma gondii*) that is transmitted by many animals, especially cats, or occasionally from raw meat. The infection is usually harmless in adults but can cause serious problems for the fetus. The results include both spontaneous abortion, premature delivery, and neurological problems such as mental retardation, blindness, and cerebral palsy. Low birth weight, a large liver and spleen, and anemia also characterize the disease. Although estimates are that as many as 20% to 30% of women have been exposed to the infection, the incidence of toxoplasmosis is about 1 per 1,000 live births (Moran, 2000).

Other Infections

This category includes such diseases as influenza, chicken pox, and several rare viruses, as well as measles, CMV, and herpes simplex.

- *Rubella (German measles):* When pregnant women hear the name German measles (the technical term is **rubella**), warning signals are raised, and with good reason. Women who contract this disease may give birth to a baby with serious defects: congenital heart disorder, cataracts, deafness, and/or mental retardation. The risk is especially high if the disease appears early in the pregnancy (when a spontaneous abortion may result). The infection appears in less than 1 per 1,000 live births. Also, any woman who had German measles as a child cannot assume that she is immune, so a woman who wishes to become pregnant should take the precaution of having a blood test, after which she should avoid becoming pregnant for at least three months.

- *Cytomegalovirus (CMV):* **Cytomegalovirus (CMV)** is a widespread STORCH infection that can cause damage ranging from fetal mental retardation to blindness, deafness, and even death. One of the major difficulties in combating this disease is that there is no specific treatment for it.

- *Herpes simplex.* In the adult, type I **herpes simplex** virus usually appears in the mouth, whereas type II herpes appears in the genital area. If the disease is passed on to the fetus (usually during the passage through the birth canal), the child develops symptoms during the first week following birth. The central nervous system seems to be particularly susceptible to this disease, with serious long-term consequences. The incidence is less than 1 per 1,000 live births.

The Special Case of AIDS

The final infection we wish to discuss is **AIDS (Acquired Immune Deficiency Syndrome).** To have an idea of the extent of the problem, consider the following figures (based on the most recent data from the National Centers for Disease Control and Avert, an international HIV/AIDS charity based in the United Kingdom).

- *People infected in 2003:* 5 million (800,000 children)
- *People living with HIV/AIDS:* 40 million (2.5 million children)
- *AIDS deaths in 2003:* 3 million (500,000 children)
- *Total number of AIDS deaths:* 22 million (4–5 million children)

In the United States, 7,000 to 8,000 women infected with HIV virus will give birth this year.

Statistics showing that only one in four babies born of mothers infected with HIV develops AIDS have long puzzled investigators. Studies have shown that these figures are directly related to the amount of the virus that the mother is carrying; that is, the more extensive the infection, the greater the chance that the baby will be born with the virus. Consequently, treatment with zidovudine ZDU—formerly called azidothymidine (AZT)—or other treatments early in the pregnancy may help to prevent the transmission of the virus.

An infected mother can pass the HIV virus to the fetus during pregnancy, during delivery, and after birth, occasionally through breast milk. We know today that AIDS is a disorder that cripples the body's disease-fighting mechanisms and that the virus causing it can lie dormant for years.

With regard to the fetus, estimates are that an infected mother transmits HIV from 30% to 50% of the time. Thus, 50% to 70% of fetuses remain unaffected.

---

rubella (German measles)
Typically mild childhood disease caused by a virus; pregnant women who contract this disease may give birth to a baby with a defect—congenital heart disorder, cataracts, deafness, mental retardation. The risk is especially high if the disease appears early in the pregnancy.

cytomegalovirus (CMV)
Virus that can cause fetal damage ranging from mental retardation, blindness, deafness, and even death. One of the major difficulties in combating this disease is that it remains unrecognized in pregnant women.

herpes simplex
Infection that can be contracted by a child during birth; the child can develop the symptoms during the first week following the birth. The eyes and the nervous system are most susceptible to this disease.

AIDS (Acquired Immune Deficiency Syndrome)
Condition caused by the HIV virus, which can invade a newborn baby's immune system, thus making it vulnerable to infections and life-threatening illnesses.

This cocaine-addicted baby was born prematurely and suffers from such behavior disturbances as tremulousness, irritability, and muscular rigidity. Evaluate and rank order the possible causes of infertility.

thalidomide
Popular drug prescribed during the early 1960s that was later found to cause a variety of birth defects when taken by women early in their pregnancy.

DES (diethylstilbestrol)
In the late 1940s and 1950s, DES (a synthetic hormone) was administered to pregnant women supposedly to prevent miscarriage. It was later found that the daughters of the women who had received this treatment were more susceptible to vaginal and cervical cancer.

diethylstilbesterol
Drug earlier administered to pregnant women to help them hold embryo or fetus; later found to increase the risk of genital cancer in the daughters of these women.

When the virus is transmitted, a condition called *AIDS embryopathy* may develop. This causes growth retardation, small head size (microcephaly), flat nose, and widespread, upward-slanted eyes, among other characteristics. AIDS is also associated with higher rates of preterm disease, low birth weight, and miscarriage. AIDS has a shorter incubation period in fetuses than in adults. Symptoms may appear as early as six months after birth and include weight loss, fever, diarrhea, and chronic infections. Once symptoms appear, babies rarely survive more than five to eight months.

Chemicals

In the United States, the following statistics remain a cause for alarm (Arenson & Drake, 2007).

- About 20% of pregnant women continue to smoke cigarettes.
- More than 13% of pregnant women report drinking alcohol.
- About 5.5% of pregnant women admit to using illicit drugs.

Also, a number of women continue to use drugs before they realize they are pregnant. Consequently, screening for substance abuse is typically done at the first prenatal visit.

Prescription drugs such as **thalidomide** have also produced tragic consequences. During the early 1960s, this drug was popular in West Germany as a sleeping pill and an antinausea measure that produced no adverse reactions in women. In 1962, physicians noticed a sizable increase in children born with either partial or no limbs. In some cases, feet and hands were directly attached to the body. Other outcomes were deafness, blindness, and occasionally, mental retardation. In tracing the cause of the outbreak, investigators discovered that the mothers of these children had taken thalidomide early in their pregnancies.

DES (diethylstilbestrol) is another example of a teratogenic drug. In the late 1940s and 1950s, DES (a synthetic hormone) was administered to pregnant women, supposedly to prevent miscarriage. Researchers found that the daughters of the women who had received this treatment were more susceptible to vaginal and cervical cancer. These daughters also experienced more miscarriages when pregnant than would be expected. Recent suspicions have arisen about the sons of DES women; they seem to have more abnormalities of their reproductive systems.

As knowledge of the damaging effect of these agents spreads, women have grown more cautious once they realize they are pregnant. We know now that these agents pass through the placenta and affect the growing embryo and fetus. We also know that certain prenatal periods are more susceptible to damage than others; for example, the embryonic period. Figure 4.4 illustrates times of greater and lesser vulnerability.

To keep a pregnancy as safe as possible, a woman should begin by avoiding the obvious hazards.

Smoking

Smoking negatively affects everything about the reproduction process: fertility, conception, possible spontaneous abortion, fetal development, labor and delivery, and a child's maturation. Smoking is probably the most common environmental hazard in pregnancy, and it results in a smaller than normal fetus. Babies of smoking mothers may have breathing difficulties and low resistance to infection, and they seem to suffer long-lasting effects after birth.

Maternal smoking produces a condition called *intrauterine growth retardation (IUGR)*. The birth weight of neonates whose mothers smoked during pregnancy is about 200 grams less than normal. Those infants whose mothers stopped smoking

FIGURE 4.4

Teratogens and the timing of their effects on prenatal development. The danger of structural defects caused by teratogens is greatest early in embryonic development. This is the period of organogenesis, which lasts for several months. Damage caused by teratogens during this period is represented by the dark-colored bars. Later assaults by teratogens typically occur during the fetal period and, instead of causing structural damage, are more likely to stunt growth or cause problems of organ function.

Modified from *The Developing Human: Clinically Oriented Embryology,* 5th ed. by K.L. Moore and T.V.N. Persaud, Copyright © 1993 W.B. Saunders Company, Philadelphia. Reprinted by permission.

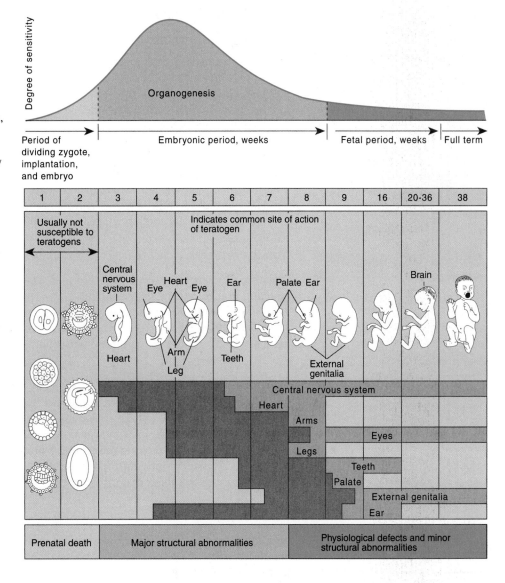

before the 16th week showed the greatest improvement in their birth weights (Moore & Persaud, 2003).

Alcohol

Women who consume alcohol daily during their pregnancy can produce damage in their babies, especially a condition called **fetal alcohol syndrome (FAS).** Identifying FAS depends on several characteristics (Moore & Persaud, 2003):

- A history of the mother's alcohol consumption
- Physical abnormalities of child (small head, widely spaced eyes, thin upper lip, and possible defects in limbs, joints, face, and heart)
- Growth deficiency (thin, short, gross reduction in brain weight)
- Central nervous system dysfunction (includes mild to moderate retardation, irritability, hyperactivity, and possible learning disabilities)

Recently, prenatal exposure to alcohol has been linked to so many different neurodevelopmental problems that the terms *alcohol-related neurodevelopmental disorder* and *alcohol-related birth defects* have been propsed to identify these children (American Academy of Pediatrics, 2000c). No safe amount of alcohol consumption has yet been identified (Arenson & Drake, 2007, p. 394).

fetal alcohol syndrome (FAS) Refers to the condition of babies whose mothers drank alcohol during pregnancy; babies manifest four clusters of symptoms: psychological functioning, growth factors, physical features, and structural effects.

Diagnosing Fetal Problems

Some women have a greater chance of developing difficulties during pregnancy or delivering a child with problems. To cope with these conditions, the rapidly expanding field of fetal diagnosis not only identifies problems but also offers means of treatment. About 1% of infants suffer from some genetic defect, whereas another 0.5% suffer from defective chromosomes. As a result, prenatal testing is steadily becoming more common, especially for older women.

For example, children born with cystic fibrosis or sickle-cell anemia acquire these diseases from parents who are both carriers. Tests are now available to determine whether a person is a carrier of a particular genetic disease. If both potential partners are carriers, the chances of children acquiring the disease can be calculated. Among the diagnostic tools now available are the following.

Amniocentesis

Probably the technique you have heard most about is **amniocentesis,** which entails inserting a needle through the mother's abdomen, piercing the amniotic sac, and withdrawing a sample of the amniotic fluid. (Amniocentesis may be done from the 15th week of pregnancy on.) The fluid sample provides information about the child's sex and almost 70 chromosomal abnormalities (Moore & Persaud, 2003).

Alpha-Fetoprotein (AFP) Test

Occasionally, AFP (a protein produced by a baby's liver) escapes from the spinal fluid in fetuses with neural tube problems (Jasper, 2000). It then passes into the mother's bloodstream. Spina bifida babies (see Chapter 3) show a raised level of AFP, which may be detected in the mother's blood by a test called MSAFP (Maternal Serum Alpha Fetoprotein). The test does produce false positives, however, which brings up the issue of further testing.

Fetoscopy

In a **fetoscopy,** a tiny viewing instrument called a *fetoscope* is inserted into the amniotic cavity, making it possible to see the fetus. If the view is clear, defects of hands and legs are visible. (Fetoscopy is usually performed after the 16th week.) Today, doctors avoid fetoscopy if possible because of potential injury to the fetus and use a relatively new method for obtaining fetal blood: *percutaneous umbilical blood sampling,* which draws pure fetal blood from the umbilical cord (Olds, London, & Ladeqwig, 1996). A needle is inserted through the abdomen and uterus into the blood vessels of the umbilical cord. Not only can this aid genetic diagnosis, it also permits blood transfusions to the fetus (Nightingale & Goodman, 1990).

Chorionic Villi Sampling (CVS)

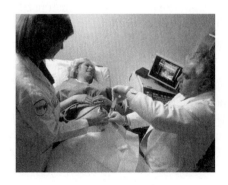

The outer layer of the embryo is almost covered with chorionic villi, fingerlike projections that reach into the uterine lining. A catheter (small tube) is inserted through the vagina to the villi, and a small section is suctioned into the tube. **Chorionic villi sampling (CVS)** is an excellent test to determine the fetus' genetic structure and may be given as early as 9 to 10 weeks. Results are available in 3 hours to 7 days, as compared with 2 to 4 weeks for amniocentesis.

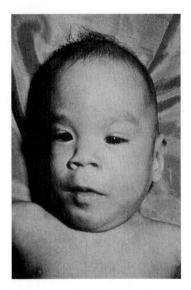

Babies born with fetal alcohol syndrome (FAS) manifest distinctive characteristics.

amniocentesis
Process of fetal testing that entails inserting a needle through the mother's abdomen, piercing the amniotic sac, and withdrawing a sample of the amniotic fluid.

fetoscopy
Procedure in which a tiny viewing instrument called a *fetoscope* is inserted into the amniotic cavity making it possible to see the fetus.

chorionic villi sampling (CVS)
Fetal testing procedure in which a catheter (small tube) is inserted through the vagina to the uterine villi, and a small section is suctioned into the tube.

Here a pregnant woman is having amniocentesis. Amniotic fluid is withdrawn and analyzed to determine any chromosomal abnormalities. Can you summarize the positive results of fetal diagnosis in spite of their invasive nature?

Ultrasound

ultrasound
Use of sound waves and special equipment to produce an image that enables a physician to detect internal structural abnormalities.

Ultrasound is a procedure that uses sound waves to produce an image that enables a physician to detect structural abnormalities, to guide other procedures (amniocentesis), to verify fetal viability, to determine the amount of amniotic fluid, and so on (Leifer, 2003). Useful pictures can be obtained as early as 7 weeks.

Guided Review

8. _____ _____ is the term used to describe children whose well-being is in jeopardy.

9. The acronym _____ indicates some of the potentially harmful diseases that can affect the developing fetus.

10. A harmful agent that can cause abnormalities in the developing fetus is called a _____.

11. _____ is the most common environmental hazard in pregnancy and can result in a smaller than normal fetus.

12. Amniocentesis can be used after the _____ week of pregnancy.

13. A comprehensive test to determine the fetus' genetic structure is _____ _____ _____.

THE BIRTH PROCESS

The odyssey that began nine months earlier for approximately four million American women each year reaches its climax at birth (Guyer et al., 1999) In spite of what you may have heard, no one knows exactly what causes labor to begin or why it begins about 280 days after the first day of the last menstrual period. What we do know is that birth practices over the years have changed remarkably. For example, ether was first used as an anesthetic on January 19, 1847, which caused considerable controversy, until Queen Victoria, the secular head of the Church of England, was administered chloroform in 1853 and 1857 when she was giving birth.

At the beginning of the 20th century, only 22% of babies were born in hospitals, a number that shot up rapidly until the middle of the century when almost 80% were hospital births. Women experienced increasingly heavy medication for the relief of pain until the gradual realization that the effects of drugs can be dangerous for the fetus. In the 1960s, the pill was growing in popularity, resulting in the more controlled timing of pregnancy and birth, a change that was accompanied by an expanding reliance on natural childbirth techniques. Louise Brown, the first "test-tube" baby, was born in 1978. And the changes continue to this day. (For an excellent discussion of these changes, see Ezzo and others, 2003).

When a person is born, one of the great shifts occurs among the interactions of the biopsychosocial framework (Cole, 1999). From the warm, cozy prenatal environment, the newborn enters a dry, cold world. The newborn must struggle for oxygen and nutrition. For the first time, the newborn encounters other human beings, and parents have their initial glimpse of their child. The interactions that lead to a particular parent-child relationship now commence.

Answers 8. Developmental risk 9. STORCH 10. teratogen 11. Smoking 12. 15th 13. chorionic villi sampling

Stages in the Birth Process

A woman usually becomes aware of the beginning of labor by one or more of these signs:

- The passage of blood from the vagina. Occasionally, with a softening of the cervix, the mucous plug is expelled with a small amount of blood called a *bloody show,* which usually signifies that labor will begin in about 24 to 48 hours (Arenson & Drake, 2007).
- The passage of amniotic fluid from the ruptured amniotic sac through the vagina.
- Uterine contractions and accompanying discomfort.

The first two clues are certain signs that labor has begun; other pains (false labor) are occasionally mistaken for signs of true labor. Three further stages of labor can also be distinguished:

1. *Stage One: Dilation.* The neck of the uterus (the cervix) dilates to about 4 inches in diameter. **Dilation** is the process responsible for labor pains and may last for 12 or 13 hours, or even longer. When labor begins, the duration of the contractions is about 30 seconds, which increases to about 60 seconds (range: 45–90 seconds) as labor continues (Arenson & Drake, 2007; Leifer, 2003).

   Think of the baby at this stage as enclosed in a plastic cylinder. It is upside down in the mother's abdomen, with the bottom of the cylinder under the mother's rib and the tip buried deep in her pelvis. The cervix is about 1/2 inch long and almost closed. Before the next stage, expulsion, occurs, the diameter of the cervix must be stretched to a diameter of 4 inches. (The comedienne Carol Burnett has said that the only way you can imagine this feeling is if you pulled your upper lip over your head!)

2. *Stage Two: Expulsion.* With the cervix fully dilated, the fetus no longer meets resistance, and the uterine contractions drive it through the birth canal. Uterine pressure at this stage is estimated to be 60 pounds. This **expulsion** phase should be completed about two hours after the cervix becomes fully dilated for those giving birth for the first time, about half that time for women who have previously given birth (Olds, London, & Ladewig, 1996). This is the phase when most fathers, if they are present, become exultant. They describe the appearance of the head of the baby (called *crowning*) as an unforgettable experience.

   Note that the times for expulsion (90 minutes and 30–45 minutes) are averages. If this second stage of labor is prolonged—with no evidence of a problem—surgical intervention remains unnecessary. Occasionally, women spend five or six hours (or more) in a normal first birth.

3. *Stage Three: Afterbirth.* In the **afterbirth** stage, the placenta and other membranes are discharged. This stage is measured from the birth of the baby to the delivery of the placenta and may last only a few minutes. If the spontaneous delivery of the placenta is delayed, the placenta may be removed manually. The woman's body now acts to shut down any excessive bleeding (Moore & Persaud, 2003, p. 132). Figure 4.5 illustrates the birth process.

When a pregnancy ends spontaneously before the 20th week, a spontaneous abortion, commonly called a **miscarriage,** has occurred. After the 20th week, the spontaneous end of a pregnancy is called a **stillbirth,** if the baby is born dead, or a premature birth, if the baby survives. Occasionally a pregnancy occurs outside the uterus. In an **ectopic pregnancy**, sometimes referred to as a *tubal pregnancy,* the fertilized egg attempts to develop outside the uterus, usually in one of the fallopian tubes. About 1 in every 200 pregnancies is ectopic.

---

dilation
Stage one of the birth process, during which the cervix dilates to about 4 inches in diameter.

expulsion
Stage two of the birth process, during which the baby passes through the birth canal.

afterbirth
Stage three of the birth process, during which the placenta and other membranes are discharged.

miscarriage
Term that describes the spontaneous lending of a pregnancy before the 20th week.

stillbirth
Term that describes the spontaneous end of a pregnancy after the 20th week; called a stillbirth if the baby is born dead.

ectopic pregnancy
Pregnancy in which the fertilized egg attempts to develop in one of the fallopian tubes (outside the uterus); this is sometimes referred to as a *tubal pregnancy.*

Stages in the birth process

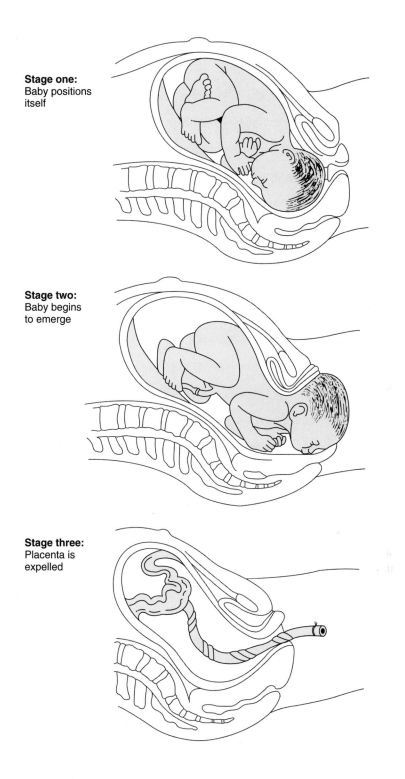

Stage one:
Baby positions
itself

Stage two:
Baby begins
to emerge

Stage three:
Placenta is
expelled

postpartum period
Typically refers to the 6-week
period following childbirth.

Immediately after birth and continuing for about six weeks, women enter
the **postpartum period,** a time of physical and psychological adjustment to
pregnancy and birth. Hormonal changes after birth, a sense of anticlimax after
completing something anticipated for so many months, sheer fatigue, and tension
about care of the baby (especially after a first birth) may cause temporary feelings of depression in the new mother (called *postpartum depression*). These
feelings usually leave quickly, but if they persist longer than two or three weeks
help should be sought.

While the biological processes involved in labor and birth are similar everywhere, the experience of giving birth varies in accordance with cultural traditions (Cole & Cole, 1996; Leifer, 2003). These expectations determine procedures and identify behaviors, emotions, and reactions to be expected.

For example, the Hmong women of Laos may attempt to avoid any internal examination and prefer to give birth in a squatting position, some Native American women remain upright, and Pueblo women may kneel during the birth process. Vietnamese women attempt to maintain self-control and even keep smiling during labor, but the Ibo of Nigeria consider childbirth as an illness. Japanese women usually will not ask for pain relief. Arabic women are extremely concerned with modesty and try to keep their bodies covered as much as possible. Knowing these cultural variations and preferences leads to more considerate treatment by those supporting the woman during child birth.

As Rogoff (2003, p. 66), noted, birth involves cultural practices surrounding labor and delivery (drugs for the mother, different positions, degree and kind of support). Consequently, cultural variations may well shape the biological characteristics of the species, as biological changes also shape cultural practices. Rogoff goes on to explain how a cultural innovation (cesarean section) saves a child whose head may be too large for the mother's birth canal. Thus the genes for large heads are preserved and passed on from generation to generation. You can see, then, how cultural technologies can contribute to nature and the resulting biological changes may produce cultural adaptations.

Birth Complications

For most women, the birth process, as painful as it may be, proceeds normally. Occasionally, however, problems arise. The following are a few of the more common complications.

Forceps Delivery

forceps delivery
Procedure in which the physician, for safety, withdraws the baby with forceps during the first phase of birth.

When certain conditions prevail—extreme fatigue, inadequate contraction strength, cardiac problems, and so on—the physician will withdraw the baby with forceps during the first phase of birth (Smith, 2000). A **forceps delivery** presents some danger of rupturing blood vessels or causing brain damage but, with new guidelines, forceps delivery is considered quite safe.

A decision about a forceps delivery depends on two conditions: those involving the fetus and those related to the mother. Is the fetus in distress? Is the baby in the correct position? Has the mother sufficient strength for the final push? Specifically, a forceps delivery may be called for when the woman has been in the second stage of labor for several hours or when an emergency arises for either the mother (shock, exhaustion) or the fetus (clear signs of fetal distress, such as a slowing heart rate).

Breech Birth

breech birth
Birth in which the baby is born feet first, buttocks first, or in a crosswise position (transverse presentation).

During the last month of pregnancy, most babies move into a head down (vertex) position. Most babies who don't turn during this time will be in **breech birth** presentation position. It's almost as if the baby were sitting in the uterus, head up and feet and buttocks down. Several conditions can contribute to a breech presentation: more than one fetus in the uterus, an abnormally shaped uterus, a placenta partially (or even fully) covering the uterine opening, and prematurity.

About four out of every hundred babies are born feet first, or buttocks first, whereas one out of a hundred is in a crosswise position (transverse presentation). Breech births can be worrisome because the baby must be carefully guided through the birth canal, but most breech babies are born well and healthy. The major concern is with premature babies who, given the size of their heads in proportion to the rest of their bodies, often require a cesarean birth. Today efforts are being made to reduce the increased number of breech births by cesarean section (Olds, London, & Ladewig, 1996).

Cesarean Section

cesarean section
Surgery performed to deliver the baby through the abdomen if for some reason the child cannot come through the birth canal.

If for some reason the child cannot come through the birth canal, surgery is performed to deliver the baby through the abdomen, in a procedure called **cesarean section.** For example, a cesarean may produce a healthier baby than does prolonged labor and difficult birth. Among the conditions suggesting a cesarean include: mother's health, fetal distress, the mother's pelvis too small for a safe vaginal delivery, the baby's abnormal presentation position, and previous cesareans that increase the possibility of uterine rupture (Smith, 2000).

A cesarean section is considered major surgery and is not recommended unless necessary. About one-fourth of all live births in the United States are cesarean, a figure many consider to be excessive. (In England, the cesarean birth rate is 12%, in Scotland 14%, and in Sweden 11%.) Leading obstetricians suggest that a 12% cesarean birth rate is a desirable goal. Today many women attempt a vaginal delivery following a cesarean if the conditions that caused the original cesarean are no longer a concern and if only one fetus is present. The success rate for a natural delivery after having had a cesarean is from 60% to 80%.

Anoxia (Lack of Oxygen)

anoxia
Condition involving lack of oxygen, which possibly can cause fetal brain damage or death.

If anything should happen during the birth process that interrupts the flow of oxygen to the fetus, brain damage or death can result. A substantial need for oxygen exists during birth because pressure on the fetal head can cause some rupturing of the blood vessels in the brain. After the umbilical cord is cut, delay in lung breathing can also produce **anoxia** (lack of oxygen). Failure here can cause death or brain damage. Controversy surrounds infants who have experienced anoxia and survived, but who show evidence of mental dullness. Whether the damage is permanent is difficult to predict (Carlson, 2004).

The Rh Factor

Rh factor
Involves possible incompatibility between the blood types of mother and child; if the mother is Rh-negative and the child Rh-positive, miscarriage or even infant death can result.

Rh factor refers to a possible incompatibility between the blood types of mother and child. If the mother is Rh-negative and the child Rh-positive, miscarriage or even infant death can result. During birth, some of the baby's blood inevitably enters the mother's bloodstream. The mother then develops antibodies to destroy fetal red blood cells. This usually happens after the baby is born, so the first baby may escape unharmed. During later pregnancies, however, these antibodies may pass into the fetus's blood and start to destroy the red blood cells of an Rh-positive baby.

Estimates are that about 10% of marriages are between Rh-negative women and Rh-positive men. For some time now, a protective vaccine called RhoGam (an RH immune globulin) has almost eliminated the possibility of Rh incompatibility when Rh-negative women are identified (Olds, London, & Ladewig, 1996). In a case where the first baby's blood causes the mother to produce antibodies, exchange blood transfusions may be given to the baby while still in the uterus.

The Special Case of Prematurity

prematurity
Early birth; condition that occurs less than 37 weeks after conception and is defined by low birth weight and immaturity.

The average duration of pregnancy is 280 days. Occasionally, however, some babies are born early; they are **premature,** or preterm, often called "preemies." Estimates are that 2% to 9% of newborns require care in a neonatal intensive care unit (NICU) (Goldberg & DiVitto, 2002). Formerly, these babies had high

AN INFORMED VIEW

Do Childbirth Strategies Matter?

A range of birth options is now available to couples. About 1% of women, for example, are choosing home births with the guidance of trained delivery specialists such as midwives. Midwives assist with about 50% of all nonhospital deliveries. One reason for the popularity of home delivery is that most babies experience few complications and little if any birth difficulty.

Hospital procedures are also changing. For example, birthing rooms may be available, which have a more relaxed and homelike atmosphere than does the typical delivery room. Some hospitals may provide birthing beds or birthing chairs for greater comfort. Still, between 95% and 99% of all births occur in hospitals.

Childbirth preparation typically involves the ideas of several theorists. For example, **prepared childbirth,** or the

Lamaze method, after French obstetrician *Fernand Lamaze,* is the most popular method used in the United States today. For several sessions, women are informed about the physiology of childbirth and instructed in breathing exercises and methods of muscle relaxation. These techniques are intended to relieve fear and pain.

Other strategies include the *Bradley* method, which focuses on breathing and the cooperation of a partner, and the *Kitzinger* method, which focuses on the use of sensory memory and relaxation techniques. Regardless of the technique used (or a combination of techniques), the basic principles of childbirth education include the following (Mullaly, 2000).

- Partner participation and support
- Learning about relaxation techniques to combat anxiety and pain
- Acquiring breathing patterns to help cope with pain and facilitate labor
- Knowledge about the birth process and any available options

Hospital, home, or birthing center? Each has its advantages and disadvantages. What is your reaction to these strategies and settings?

If you would like to have a more informed view on this issue, you may want to read one or more of the references in this chapter, such as Smith, 2000. You may also wish to learn more by going to our website at www.mhhe.com/dacey7.

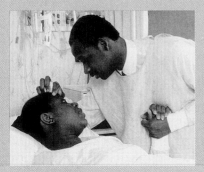

The presence of the father during birth can be a source of physical and psychological support for the mother. Many fathers present during the birth of their children have described it as "an unforgettable experience."

prepared childbirth
Combination of relaxation techniques and information about the birth process; sometimes called the *Lamaze method,* after its founder.

mortality rates, but with today's sophisticated technology their chances of survival are much greater (Feldman and others, 2002). Before we discuss the condition of these babies and the reasons for their early appearance, let's establish some pertinent facts.

Facts about Prematures

A preterm infant is one born before the completion of a 37-week gestation period and who "fits" one of three categories.

- *Borderline.* These infants are typically born between 37 and 38 weeks gestation and weigh about 5.8 to 7.3 pounds. In other words, they're similar to full-term babies, but just a little earlier and lighter.

- *Moderate.* These infants are born between 31 and 36 weeks gestation and weigh from 3.5 to 5.8 pounds. Thus these babies can be classified as low-birth-weight babies (LBW).

- *Extreme.* These infants are born between 24 and 30 weeks gestation and weigh from 1 to 3.5 pounds at birth. They are classified as very-low-birth-weight babies (VLBW) and account for 84% of neonatal deaths (babies of all gestational ages) (Putman, 2000).

This third classification—very low birth weight (VLBW)—is defined as below 1,500 grams (about 3 pounds). Babies in this class are particularly prone to infection of the amniotic fluid and death by pneumonia (Barton, Hodgman, & Pavlova, 1999). Their chance of survival improves during the first days after birth, but these babies are at significant risk for later death even after 84 days (Cooper and others, 1998).

Causes of Prematurity

About 300,000 to 400,000 of all infants born in the United States each year are classified as premature. Although it is still impossible to predict which women will begin labor prematurely, prematurity has been linked to certain conditions. For example, maternal risk for preterm labor is closely associated with infection. Also, once a woman has given birth prematurely, the risk of prematurity in the next pregnancy is about 25%. Multiple births (a growing phenomenon due to the increasing use of fertility drugs) also produce babies whose birth weights are lower than that of a single baby. Stress has likewise been identified as a cause of prematurity (Azar, 1999b), and *age* has shown a high correlation with prematurity. If the mother is under 17 or over 35, the risk is substantially increased.

Other causes include these:

- *Low socioeconomic status (SES).* In underdeveloped countries, as many as one infant in four is born prematurely. In the United States, more premature babies are born to poor than to affluent women.

- *Smoking* remains a significant factor in any discussion of prematurity. Growth delays and lung maturity are among the conditions attributed to smoking.

- *Alcohol* also increases the likelihood of prematurity. About 60% of American women drink. For those taking 10 drinks per week while pregnant, the chance of having a low-birth-weight baby doubles.

- Cervical problems, high blood pressure, unusual stress, diabetes, and heart disease may all be related causes. Even when all these causes are enumerated, explaining exactly what happened in any given pregnancy still is difficult, if not impossible.

Although these infants may differ from full-term babies in the early days of their development, the differences eventually may disappear. Most prematures reach developmental levels similar to those of full-term babies, although a little more slowly than usual.

However, too often a negative stereotype hinders their progress (Azar, 1999). The premature infant is seen as vulnerable, fragile, and less competent, *even after he or she has caught up with babies who experienced a normal birth.* For example,

M. C. Avery & G. Litwack (1983). *Born early.* New York: Little, Brown. Vital data, good writing, and a positive outlook make this an excellent introduction to the topic of prematurity. It has become a classic in the literature on premature birth.

With advances in the treatment of preemies (temperature control, nutrition), the outlook for these tiny, fragile babies has greatly improved.

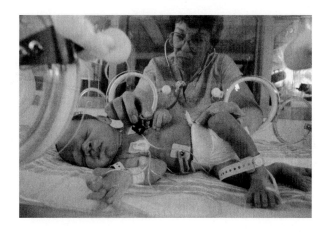

AN APPLIED VIEW | The Changing World of Prematures

Many of today's neonatal intensive care units reflect the research of Heidelise Als, a developmental psychologist at Boston Children's Hospital. Als's basic premise is that prematures lack the ability to keep the bodily systems in balance. Consequently, they can't prevent stimuli (noise, light, touch) from disrupting their inner sense of balance.

Formerly, pediatricians believed that prematures were too immature for stimuli to have any effect on them. Today, thanks to the work of Als (Als and others, 1986, Als, Duffy, & McAnulty, 1996), we realize that the premature baby's brain is too undeveloped to block stimuli from acting on the nervous, motor, and emotional systems, thus producing a disruption of needed and peaceful inner stability. For example, the baby gives clues to its upset by gagging, hiccoughs, changing color, increase in heart rate, and so on. Many NICUs (neonatal intensive care units) using Als's techniques carefully control and minimize such stimuli as lighting, sound, and even physical contact.

Als's research has shown that premature babies experiencing her techniques in NICU spend about one-half as

much time on respirators or oxygen tents as control babies. They were also able to breast feed or bottle feed up to a month earlier. These babies also showed more rapid weight gain and shorter hospital stays than did the control group.

With advances in the treatment of prematures (temperature control, nutrition), the outlook for these babies has greatly improved. Psychological insights into the their development have led to the conclusion that parental support and stimulation are needed during the baby's hospitalization to ensure that attachment proceeds as normally as possible.

When the premature infant can be taken from the incubator and given to the parent, a delicate moment has arrived. Some parents find it difficult to react positively to a premature; they feel guilty, occasionally harbor feelings of rejection, and must fight to accept the situation. They are simply overwhelmed. Usually this reaction passes quickly. On the occasion of this initial contact, parents should have been well prepared for holding a baby that is still entangled in wires and tubes.

observers were told that a healthy looking 9-month-old infant had been premature. They then described the baby as "weaker, less physically mature, less sociable, and less cognitively competent," a tendency called "prematurity stereotyping." Fortunately, studies indicate that by 12 to 18 months, most parents and their preterm babies have established a relationship quite similar to term infants and their parents (Goldberg & DiVitto, 2002).

Guided Review

14. Labor usually begins _____ days after the first day of the last menstrual period.

15. The spontaneous end of pregnancy is called a _____ if it occurs before the 20th week.

16. A fertilized egg that develops in a fallopian tube is called an _____ pregnancy.

17. _____ _____ can cause a woman to feel a little "down" for a few days following delivery.

18. Births occurring less than 37 weeks after conception are said to be _____.

19. After the 20th week of pregnancy, the spontaneous end of pregnancy resulting in death is known as a _____.

20. The baby's age and _____ help to categorize prematurity.

Answers   14. 280 15. miscarriage 16. ectopic 17. Postnatal depression 18. premature 19. stillbirth 20. weight

CONCLUSION & SUMMARY

In this chapter, you have seen how a human being begins his or her journey through the lifespan. Nature's detailed choreography of prenatal development provides a remarkably complex yet elegantly simple means of ensuring the survival of generations. Once conception occurs, uniting the genetic contribution of both mother and father, the developmental process is under way, sheltering the fetus for the first nine months in the protective cocoon of the womb.

Sometimes the process is interrupted and the uterine stay is shortened. Today, prematures, thanks to technological advances, have a heightened chance of survival and of normal physical and psychological development.

What kinds of development occur during the prenatal period?

- The germinal period is the time when the fertilized egg passes through the fallopian tube.

- The embryonic period is a time of rapid development and great sensitivity.
- The fetal period is a time of preparation for life outside the womb.
- The senses develop during the prenatal months and are ready to function at birth.

What influences prenatal development and what precautions should be taken?

- Developmental risk is a term that applies to those children whose welfare is in jeopardy.
- Teratogens are those agents that cause abnormalities.
- Infectious diseases and chemical agents are the two basic classes of teratogens.
- Today AIDS is recognized as a potential danger for newborns.

- Maternal nutrition and emotions are important influences during pregnancy.
- Advancing technology has provided diagnostic tools for the detection of many fetal problems.

What are the circumstances and possible difficulties of the birth process?

- Birth occurs as a series of three stages.
- Complications such as breech presentations, anoxia, and the Rh factor are among the difficulties that can develop during the birth process.
- Childbirth strategies are evolving that are designed to ease the transition from womb to world.
- Today, the outlook for prematures is much more optimistic than in previous times.

KEY TERMS

afterbirth (stage)
AIDS (Acquired Immune Deficiency Syndrome)
amniocentesis
amniotic sac
anoxia
blastocyst
breech birth
cellular differentiation
cesarean section
chorionic villi sampling (CVS)
cytomegalovirus (CMV)
DES (diethylstilbestrol)
developmental risk
dilation (stage)

ectoderm
ectopic pregnancy
embryonic period
endoderm
expulsion (stage)
fetal alcohol syndrome (FAS)
fetal period
fetoscopy
forceps delivery
germinal period
herpes simplex
implantation
mesoderm
miscarriage
organogenesis

placenta
postpartum period
premature
prepared childbirth
Rh factor
rubella
stillbirth
STORCH diseases
syphilis
teratogens
thalidomide
toxoplasmosis
trophoblast
ultrasound
umbilical cord

WHAT DO YOU THINK?

1. Considerable discussion has occurred recently about the possibility of prenatal learning. Where do you stand on this issue? Be sure to support your opinion with facts from this chapter.

2. You probably have heard how careful women must be when they are pregnant. They are worried

chapter 4 Review

about such things as smoking and drinking. Do you think we have become too nervous and timid about these dangers? Why?

3. Turn back to Table 4.2. From your own knowledge (relatives and friends, for example), indicate which of these teratogens you think are most common. Select one and explain why you think it is a common threat and what could be done to help prevent it. (Lead paint is a good example.)

4. Significant medical and ethical questions surround such techniques as fetal surgery. For instance, assume that a physician does not inform a woman that her fetus is a good candidate for fetal surgery. The baby is stillborn. Is the doctor guilty of malpractice or any crime? Can you think of other examples?

CHAPTER REVIEW TEST

1. It takes a fertilized egg about _____ to travel through the fallopian tube to the uterus.
   a. 3 days
   b. 14 days
   c. 30 days
   d. 9 months

2. It then takes another _____ days for the fertilized egg to implant.
   a. 3 days
   b. 7 days
   c. 14 days
   d. 30 days

3. The first two weeks following fertilization are called the _____ period.
   a. embryonic
   b. fetal
   c. germinal
   d. pregnancy

4. A (An) _____ is a one-week-old-zygote.
   a. fetus
   b. embryo
   c. blastocyst
   d. trophoblast

5. During the _____ period the nervous system develops rapidly.
   a. embryonic
   b. fetal
   c. gestational
   d. germinal

6. Which system does not develop from the mesoderm?
   a. muscular
   b. skeletal
   c. circulatory
   d. respiratory

7. Development is most vulnerable to outside agents during the _____ period.
   a. embryonic
   b. germinal
   c. fetal
   d. sensitive

8. The peak growth period for the fetus is during the _____ and _____ months.
   a. first, second
   b. fourth, fifth
   c. sixth, seventh
   d. eighth, ninth

9. Red blood cells transport _____ and white blood cells to combat disease.
   a. oxygen
   b. amniotic fluid
   c. teratogens
   d. villi

10. Which of the following statements is true?
    a. The earlier the damage, the greater the chance of negative long-term effects.
    b. The fetus is safe from all harm while in the womb.
    c. Babies are usually born on the day predicted.
    d. A fetus hears no sound until birth.

11. Toxoplasmosis is
    a. a sexually transmitted disease.
    b. a virus capable of causing deafness or cataracts.
    c. a disease capable of causing mental retardation or death.
    d. a problem caused by the genetic makeup of the father.

12. Which of the following does not result from exposure to rubella?
    a. congenital heart disorder
    b. hair follicle defects
    c. deafness
    d. mental retardation

13. _____ is not a STORCH infection.
    a. Rh disease
    b. CMV
    c. Herpes simplex
    d. Toxoplasmosis

14. It is almost impossible for a mother to pass the AIDS virus to her baby through
    a. delivery.
    b. handling.
    c. pregnancy.
    d. breast milk.

15. In a typical pregnancy, a woman will gain about _____ to _____ pounds.
    a. 25 to 30
    b. 30 to 35
    c. 35 to 40
    d. 40 to 45

16. A woman's emotions can affect her pregnancy indirectly by a release of her
    a. villi.
    b. teratogens.
    c. hormones.
    d. Rh factor.

17. _____ is a technique in which a needle is inserted through a pregnant woman's abdomen and into the amniotic sac in order to obtain a fluid sample.
    a. Ultrasound
    b. Chorionic villi sampling

c. Amniocentesis
d. Non-stress test

18. Prematurity is *not* associated with
   a. vitamin therapy.
   b. low SES.
   c. multiple births.
   d. cigarette use.

19. _____ was a pioneer in the technique of prepared childbirth.
   a. Leboyer
   b. Lamaze

c. DeCasper
d. Salk

20. Mental retardation, hyperactivity, and primary growth retardation can be symptoms of
   a. fetal alcohol syndrome (FAS).
   b. Rh factor.
   c. prematurity.
   d. anoxia.

21. Premature babies of very low birth weight are
   a. not normally at severe risk.
   b. not permitted visits by their parents.
   c. more likely to develop cerebral palsy.
   d. more likely to have problems later in life.

Chapter 4 Review

Answers

1. a 2. a 3. c 4. c 5. a 6. d 7. a 8. b 9. a 10. a 11. c 12. b 13. a 14. b
15. a 16. c 17. c 18. a 19. b 20. a 21. d

Part Three   Infancy

5
chapter

PHYSICAL AND COGNITIVE DEVELOPMENT IN INFANCY

Chapter Outline

Chapter Objectives

After reading this chapter, you should be able to answer the following questions.

- What are the major physical accomplishments of the infancy period?

- How do infants acquire information about their world?

- What are the differences between Piaget's view of cognitive development in infancy and that of information processing?

- How do infants acquire their language?

So you think you know what an infant is: small, helpless, appealing. Right? Let's see if the experts agree with you. John Watson an early and famous behaviorist thought he knew: Infants are a source of potential stimulus-response connections. He believed that if you turn your attention to an infant early enough, you can make that infant into anything you want—it's all a matter of conditioning! For example, One of Watson's most famous statements was this:

> *Give me a dozen healthy infants well-formed, and my own specified world to bring them up in and I'll guarantee to take any one at random and train him to become any type of specialist I might select—doctor, lawyer, artist, merchant-chief, and yes, even beggar-man and thief, regardless of his talents, penchants, tendencies, abilities, vocations, and race of his ancestors.* (Watson, 1930, p. 104)

Or consider Freud's interpretation of infancy. Freud believed that, from the first days of life, infants lead a stimulating sexual life:

> *Sexual life does not begin only at puberty, but starts with plain manifestations soon after birth.* (Freud, 1949, p. 26)

One of the most famous names in developmental psychology has been that of Jean Piaget. Discussing the origins of intelligence from a psychological perspective, he argues that we (humans) have a rich mental life from birth, if not sooner. He states:

> *In effect, if, as is probable, states of awareness accompany a reflex mechanism as complicated as that of the sucking mechanism these states of awareness have an internal history.* (Piaget, 1952b, p. 39)

Rather than seeing children as small sponges waiting for something to be poured into them (as Watson did), Piaget believed that children actively construct their own views of the world during these early years. Piaget was one of the first psychologists to question the apparently passive state of infants; he argued that infants are much more competent than originally thought, and during infancy they build the cognitive structures that are the foundation of their intelligence.

Why do the early interactions between parents and children have a powerful effect on all aspects of development?

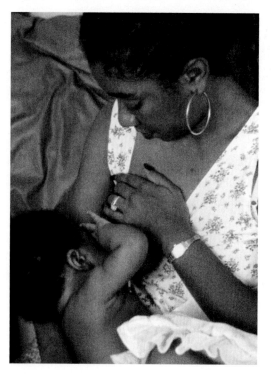

The well-known T. Berry Brazelton, one of America's most distinguished pediatricians, has formulated a concept of infancy that has led to a completely new vision of infant competence and behavior.

> *The Neonatal Behavioral Assessment Scale is based on the assumption that the newborn infant is both competent and complexly organized. In developing the scale, we were impressed by the newborn infant's ability to interact with the environment and by her capacity to deal selectively with environmental stimuli.* (Brazelton & Nugent, 1995, p. 7)

With his belief that infants are both competent and complex,

Brazelton, in his practice, his writings, and in television appearances, has been one of the leaders in changing our views of infancy. Thanks to his work and that of his colleagues (see Brazelton & Nugent, 1995), we now recognize how much infants contribute to their own development in these early years.

This chapter will help you to understand how infants are viewed in the 21st century. You'll first trace the infant's physical development and then examine the methods used to assess the well-being of infants following birth. Next you'll follow various paths of infant development: motor, perceptual, cognitive, and language. You'll also begin to discern the issues and themes discussed in Chapter 1. For example, the issue of stability is particularly important in any discussion of infancy; that is, do the events that occur in infancy leave an indelible mark that lasts a lifetime?

PHYSICAL DEVELOPMENT IN INFANCY

Newborn babies are beautifully programmed to fit their parents' fantasies and to reward the work of pregnancy.

—T. BERRY BRAZELTON

By their very coming into existence, infants forever alter the sleeping, eating, and working habits of their parents; they change who parents are and how parents define themselves . . . Parenting an infant is a "24/7" job. (Bornstein, 2002, p. 3)

Infancy is a time of rapid physical and nervous system development, accomplishments that ensure an infant's survival and ability to cope with its world. The typical newborn weighs about 7 1/2 pounds and is about 20 inches in length. In one year after its birth, an infant's length increases by one half, and its weight almost triples. Infancy sees exciting changes in psychomotor development as well as potential danger. For example, the National Center For Health Statistics reported that the infant mortality rate in 2005 was 6.8 deaths per 1,000 live births.

Developmental Milestones of Infancy

To visualize the rapid growth that occurs during infancy, see Table 5.1.

Growing children experience changes in shape and body composition, in the distribution of tissues, and in their developing motor skills, and these changes

TABLE 5.1	Physical Development in Infancy	
Age (mos.)	Height (in.)	Weight (lbs.)
3	24	13–14
6	26	17–18
9	28	20–22
12	30	22–24
18	32	25–26
24	34	27–29

then influence cognitive, psychosocial, and emotional development. For example, the infant's head at birth is about a quarter of the body's total length, but in the adult it is about one-seventh of body length. Different tissues (muscles, nerves) also grow at different rates, and total growth represents a complex series of changes. Underlying this rapidly unfolding and complex process is, of course, proper nutrition.

Nutrition

Considering the rapid growth and development that occurs during the first year of life, it's little wonder that appropriate nutrition is a key element for a healthy infant. In the first year, infants are expected to triple their birth weight and increase their length by about 50% (Grodner, Long, & DeYoung, 2004). To support this growth, infants require an ideal balance of all needed nutrients. But meeting these nutritional needs can be difficult because of an infant's small stomach and an immature digestive system (Ball & Bindler, 2006). To give you an idea of the delicate mix desired, think of the nutritional needs of the furiously developing nervous system and cells of the bodily organs.

These energy requirements demand an individualized combination of carbohydrates, proteins, minerals, and vitamins that should enable the infant to regain birth weight by 2 weeks after birth (Arenson & Drake, 2007; Farrell & Nicoteri, 2007). From birth to 6 months, infants display an amazing ability to assimilate and digest food, beginning with a few ounces of breast milk or formula to digesting pureed food at 6 months (Ball & Bindler, 2006). From 6 to 12 months infants continue to consume a wide variety of foods to satisfy increasing nutritional needs.

Breast Feeding

Doctors, nurses, and most mothers agree that human milk is the ideal food for infants under 6 months (Leifer, 2003). Breast milk contains a balance of nutrients that is typically digestible and the process itself (breast feeding) encourages mother-infant bonding.

> *Among the various forms of infant nourishment, breast milk is widely considered to be the most nutritionally beneficial during the postpartum period. Breast milk contains immunologic agents that protect infants against infectious diseases such as bacterial meningitis, diarrhea, respiratory ailments, and urinary tract infections.* (Jackowitz, Nobvillo, & Tiehen, 2007)

Breast feeding leads to two advantages that can't be duplicated by formula feeding. First is the protection against disease offered by a mother's milk. Breast-fed babies seem to have a lesser degree of illness than formula-fed babies, an important consideration in developing countries. Second, breast-fed babies are less at risk for allergic reactions than are formula-fed babies.

What conditions affect a woman's decision to breast feed? Farrell and Nicoteri (2007. p. 45) believe that a woman should be aware of the advantages and disadvantages of breast feeding. Among the influences she should consider are her sense of body image, sexuality concerns, cultural practices, family traditions, lifestyle (economics and the need to return to work), and drug and alcohol use.

One of the advantages of formula feeding is that others, including the father, can feed the baby. Commercial formulas are good, containing more proteins than breast milk. Assuming that the formula is appropriate, nutritional problems should not arise. In the United States, infants are usually well-nourished, either through breast or formula feeding

TABLE 5.2	Introducing Solid Foods
Age	*Foods*
0–4 months	Breast milk or formula
4–6 months	Iron-fortified cereals made with rice or barley
6–7 months	Strained fruits and vegetables Fruit juices, teething foods
8–9 months	Pureed meats, potatoes, rice, and pasta
10–12 months	Finger foods, toast strips, yogurt, and an increased variety of foods

Table 5.2 presents a recommended schedule for the introduction of solid food (Tamborlane, 1997).

In the course of one year, then, infants progress from either breast or bottle feeding to a variety of table foods.

Let's turn now to the remarkable role of the brain in development.

Brain Development

From the beginnings of the nervous system that we discussed in Chapter 4, a picture of the brain appears with which you're familiar. The top of the neural tube leads to the formation of the two cerebral hemispheres and the four lobes of the

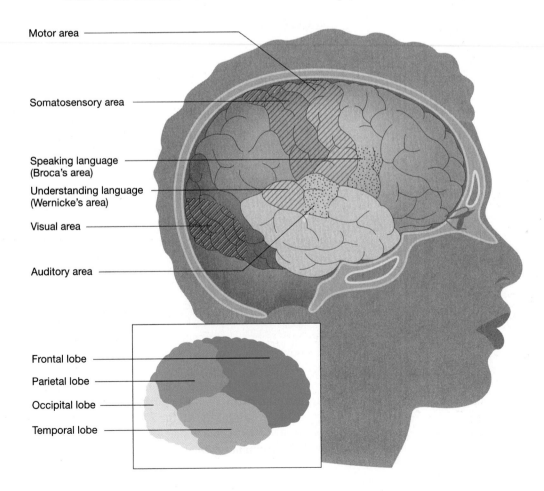

FIGURE 5.1a

Shown here are the brain's lobes and functional areas.

Motor area

Somatosensory area

Speaking language (Broca's area)

Understanding language (Wernicke's area)

Visual area

Auditory area

Frontal lobe

Parietal lobe

Occipital lobe

Temporal lobe

FIGURE 5.1b

FIGURE 5.1b

The human brain (*continued*)

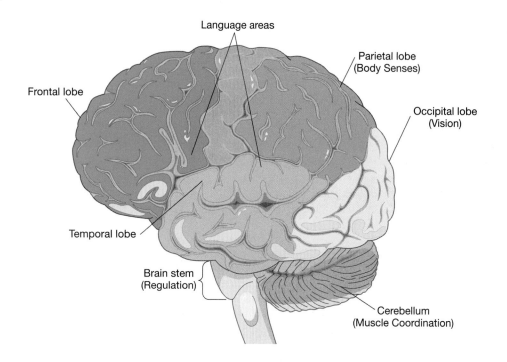

cerebral cortex. The rest of the tube turns into the spinal cord. Figure 5.1a and Figure 5.1b illustrate these features and suggest the functions of each.

What can we make of all this remarkable activity? Nature has taken breathtaking steps to insure that a baby will be able to adapt to its challenging environment at birth.

AN INFORMED VIEW

Building the Brain Structures

Tracing the evolutionary pathway of the brain leads to the conclusion that our brains developed in a bottom to top direction, starting with the brain stem and steadily moving to the more recent appearance of the cortical areas. The older areas of the brain (brain stem, hypothalamus) are closely linked to the urges and expression of rage, passion, and fear, whereas the cortical areas, devoted to thinking and problem solving, act as a brake on the limbic system. Figure 5.2 illustrates the appearance of several important brain structures that influence your child's life, from crying, regulating body temperature, eating habits, impulses, and thought processes.

- Starting in the lower regions of the brain (the cerebrum seems to sit on the spinal area), you can see the *brain stem,* which controls critical bodily functions such as breathing, states of sleep and wakefulness, and automatic muscular activities such as standing.
- In Figure 5.2, locate the *limbic system,* which includes the amygdala, hippocampus, and hypothalmus. The limbic system is deeply involved in emotional behavior and memory.
- The *amygdala,* which sits just above the brain stem, is a center for our emotional learning and remembering.

Studies of individuals with damaged amygdalas testify to the inability of these individuals to judge the emotional significance of events. In his popular book, *Emotional Intelligence,* Daniel Goleman notes that life without the amygdala is a life stripped of personal meanings.

- The *hypothalamus,* often called the "brain center" connects with many of the other brain areas and is particularly concerned with maintaining the body's internal conditions. For example, the hypothalamus seems to control thirst, hunger, body temperature, sex, and emotions, a full-time job by any standards!
- The *thalamus* acts as the main coordinator of input information. For example, as a child looks around, listens to sounds, and reacts emotionally, the thalamus acts to send this information to the proper brain areas.
- In Figure 5.2, you can see that attached to the brain stem is the *cerebellum,* whose major duty is to coordinate muscular movements. For example, if the cerebellum is damaged, control of fine movement is lost so that we cannot reach out and pick up an object.
- Finally, the *hippocampus* acts as a storage space for short-term memory until it can transmit its content to the frontal cortex.

FIGURE 5.2   The human brain—side and midline views

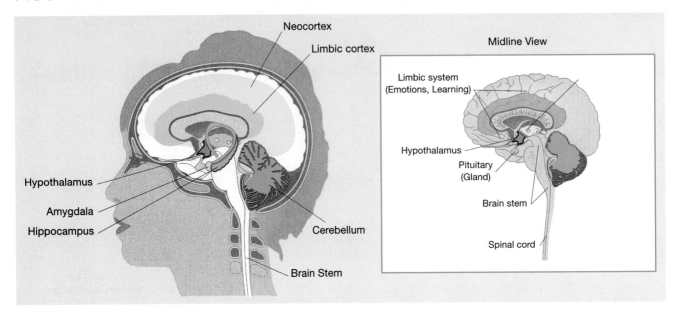

With these ideas in mind, we can now turn our attention to the unfolding story of how we're continuing to build our knowledge of brain development. As we have seen, nervous system development begins during the embryonic period, when neurons reproduce at the rate of about 250,000 per minute. During infancy, connections among the neurons begin to increase notably (as much as 100 to 1,000 connections for each of the billions of neurons). This growth rate translates into a brain size of about ½ pound at birth to about 1½ pounds at the end of the first year and then to about 3 pounds by five years (which is adult size) (Eliot, 2000).

Figure 5.3 shows the developmental pattern.

How We're Learning about the Brain

Today's brain researchers rely heavily on tools such as the following (Bear, Connors, & Paradiso, 2001; Gazzaniga, Ivry, & Mangun, 1998; Restak, 2001).

- *Electroencephalogram.* The nerve impulse is electrical, and when large numbers of neurons are active they produce enough electrical signals to be measured by electrodes placed on the scalp to identify different behavioral states—for example, deep sleep.

- *Computed Axial Tomography.* The Commonly used CAT scan is an advanced version of X-ray techniques, which presents three-dimensional pictures of the brain.

- *Positron Emission Tomography. PET* scans measure the amount of blood flow associated with brain activity. Tiny radioactive elements (about the same amount of radioactivity you would receive from a chest X ray) are injected into the blood stream and become tracers that the *PET* scan can detect.

- *Magnetic Resonance Imaging.* The increasingly popular *MRI* depends on the magnetic quality of blood to measure internal structures.

Another example of startling new breakthroughs in brain research is the ability to grow new brain cells to replace damaged brain cells (in mice). It was long thought that brain cells, once damaged, could never be replaced. However, recent research (Saltus, 2000) has discovered that neural brain cells migrate through the brain, attach to damaged nerves and transform themselves into the appropriate nerve cells. As a result, the future looks brighter for sufferers of such diseases as Parkinson's and Lou Gehrig's disease.

FIGURE 5.3

Brain development

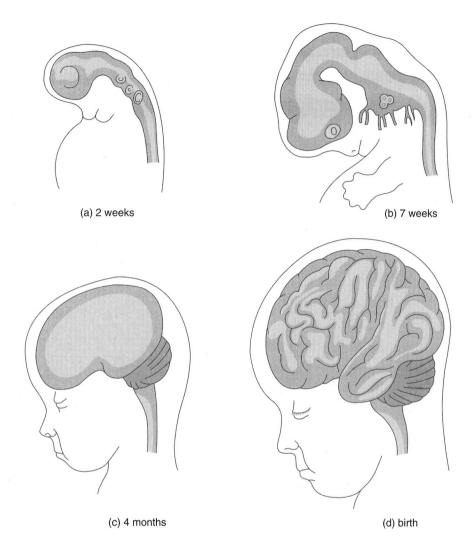

(a) 2 weeks

(b) 7 weeks

(c) 4 months

(d) birth

Unfortunately, some babies experience *Shaken Baby Syndrome (SBS)*. The National Center on Shaken Baby Syndrome puts the number of SBS babies at about 1,300 per year. Frustrated caregivers can shake babies so vigorously that enormous brain damage occurs, with the results that the baby's brain loses control over such vital functions as heart rate, respiration, blood pressure, and temperature.

An Infant's Brain, Neurons, and Communication

From your previous reading about neurons, you probably recall their importance in brain action. As a refresher, Figure 5.4 illustrates what they look like. In this figure, you can see that the communication process in the nervous system consists of the following steps.

- The messages (called *nerve impulses*) that travel along the neurons are electrical.
- For neurons to communicate with one another, the dendrites of one cell receive a message from the axon of another cell.
- To cross the space (called a *synapse*) between the axon and the dendrite, the nerve impulse needs the help of a chemical transmitter (called a *neurotransmitter*).
- Once the message has crossed the synapse, it resumes its journey as an electrical signal.

FIGURE 5.4   How neurons connect

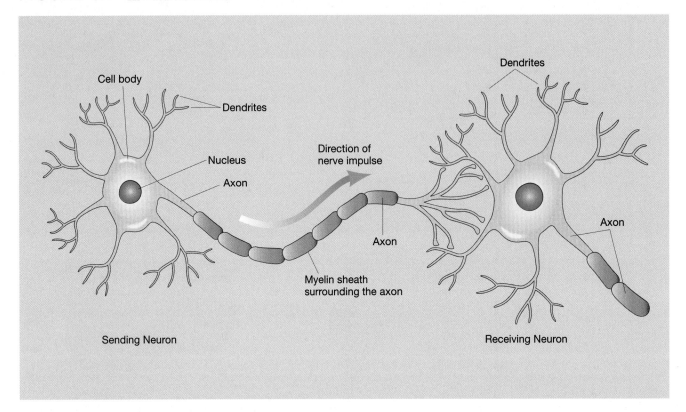

You'll recall that nature has manufactured billions of brain cells—more than will be needed to insure that the brain will be able to form enough connections for all the needed abilities and skills that demand new connections. The neurons that *don't* make connections simply die. And—and this may startle you—this exercise in survival (some connections die, some connections survive) continues throughout our lives, giving new and critical meaning to the expression "use it or lose it." The fittest of our neurons are those that make connections and survive. So the lesson here is not only for our children but also for all of us: Keep busy, seek challenges, stay alert.

Making Connections

Thanks to the prodigious research of the neuroscientists for the past two decades, we now know that infants absorb their experiences and use them to continually shape their brains. It happens this way: An infant "gobbles up" information from the outside world through its eyes, ears, nose, hands, and so on and translates it into nerve impulses that travel along neurons (axon of one cell to dendrites of another), making connection with the dendrites of other neurons along their pathways. The brain cells that receive this information survive; those that don't, die. It's as simple as that.

Environmental stimulation—teachers, parents, and other people and events—affect all parts of the brain. We'll stress throughout our work how important it is to talk *to* a baby. The language areas of the brain respond, resulting in superior language skills for the child. It's also important to surround an infant with a warm, emotionally supportive environment, which results in more connections in those parts of the brain responsible for developing emotions. The result? A child who is blessed with feelings of security and an emotional well-being that spreads throughout all aspects of her life.

AN INFORMED VIEW

Music and Your Brain

Are you a music lover? Aren't we all, to a greater or lesser extent, appreciative of music and pleased by its sounds? To help us understand why we derive such pleasure from music, recent brain research has begun to unravel the secrets of music appreciation.

Most modern neuroscientists believe that our love of music has deep roots. For example, Weinberger (2004) argues that we have been "making music" since the dawn of culture. More than 30,000 years ago, humans were already playing bone flutes, percussion instruments, and jaw harps. David Levitin (2006, p. 8), a product of today's rock world and currently a cognitive psychologist at McGill University, Laboratory for Music Perception, Cognition, and Expertise, argues that researchers are convinced that the secrets of human behavior will be unlocked by tracing the evolution of mind. Levitin's ideas are based on his belief that as our brains have evolved, so has the music we make with them.

Levitin's research points to findings suggesting music processing is distributed throughout the brain and is *not* confined to the right hemisphere. Agreeing with these research findings, Weinberger (2006) notes that music has a biological basis in a brain that is functionally organized for music. The inevitable conclusion is that many regions are involved in music processing. For example, (Levitin, 2006, pp. 84–85):

• Listening to music begins with subcortical activity that leads to activity in the auditory cortical areas on both sides of the brain.
• As you follow the music, the hippocampus (memory) and parts of the frontal lobe become engaged.
• If you react to the music with movement—tapping your feet—or even in your mind, the cerebellum contributes to the processing.
• If you perform music, the frontal lobe helps you in planning how to do it; the motor cortex guides any needed movements in your performance; and the sensory cortex gives you the needed feedback for a correct performance (for instance, pressing the right key).
• If you are reading music, the visual cortex becomes active, and if you are attempting to recall lyrics the language areas are stimulated.
• Any emotions you feel trigger activity in the amygdala.

Neuroscientific discoveries about the brain and music will continue to help us comprehend how both brain and mind evolved. Stay tuned!

Neonatal Reflexes

reflex
When a stimulus repeatedly elicits the same response.

Think of a **reflex** as an automatic response to certain stimuli and, as Rose (2005) notes, the previously unused reflexes now must be brought into play and under control. Popular examples include the eye blink and the knee jerk. All the activities needed to sustain life's functions are present at birth (breathing, sucking, swallowing, elimination). These reflexes serve a definite purpose: The gag reflex enables infants to spit up mucus; the eye blink protects the eyes from excessive light; an anti-smothering reflex facilitates breathing.

Infants must learn to breathe, adjust to feeding patterns, regulate their temperatures, and react to the stimuli of their new world (Rose, 2005). Breathing patterns are not fully established at birth, and sometimes infants briefly stop breathing. These periods are called **apnea,** and although there is some concern that apnea may be associated with sudden infant death, these periods are quite common in all infants. Usually they last for about 2 to 5 seconds; episodes that extend from about 10 to 20 seconds may suggest the possibility of a problem. Sneezing and coughing are both reflexes that help to clear air passages.

apnea
Brief periods when breathing is suspended.

Next in importance are reflexes associated with feeding. Infants suck and swallow during the prenatal period and continue at birth. They also demonstrate the rooting reflex, in which they'll turn toward a nipple or a finger placed on the cheek and attempt to get it into the mouth. Table 5.3 describes some of the more important neonatal reflexes.

neonate
Term for an infant in the first days and weeks after birth.

In the days immediately following birth until about two weeks to one month, the infant is called a **neonate.** During this period, babies immediately begin to use

TABLE 5.3	Neonatal Reflexes

Name of Reflex	How Elicited	Description of Response
Plantar grasp	Press thumbs against the balls of the infant's foot	Toes tend to curl
Babinski	Gently stroke lateral side of sole of foot	Toes spread in an outward and upward manner
Babkin	Press palm of hand while infant lies on back	Mouth opens; eyes close
Rooting	Gently touch cheek of infant with light finger pressure	Head turns toward finger in effort to suck
Sucking	Mouth contacts nipple of breast or bottle	Mouth and tongue used to manipulate (suck) nipple
Moro	Loud noise or sudden dropping of infant	Stretches arms and legs and then hugs self; cries
Grasping	Object or finger is placed in infant's palm	Fingers curl around object
Tonic neck	Place infant flat on back	Infant assumes fencer position: turns head and extends arm and leg in same direction as head
Stepping	Support infant in upright position; soles of feet brush surface	Infant attempts regular progression of steps

their abilities to adapt to their environment. Among the most significant of these are the following:

- *Infants display clear signs of imitative behavior at 7 to 10 days.* (Try this: Stick out your tongue at a baby who is about 10 days old. What happens? The baby will stick its tongue out at you!) Here neonates are telling us that they have the ability to imitate almost immediately after birth, an ability that should alert parents to immediately demonstrate desirable behavior for their children to learn and imitate. Infants' imitation of such tongue movements is well established in babies as young as a few hours to more than 6 weeks of age (Gopnik, Meltzoff, & Kuhl, 1999; Jones, 1996).

- *Infants can see at birth,* and, if you capture their attention with an appropriate object (such as a small, red rubber ball held at about 10 inches from the face), they will track it as you move the ball from side to side. Infants react to color at between 2 and 4 months; depth perception appears at about 4 to 5 months (Brazelton & Nugent, 1995).

- *Infants not only can hear at birth (and prenatally), but they also can perceive the direction of the sound.* In a famous yet simple experiment, Michael Wertheimer (1962) sounded a clicker (similar to those children play with) from different sides of a delivery room only 10 minutes after an infant's birth. The infant not only reacted to the noise but also attempted to turn in the direction of the sound, indicating that children immediately tune into their environment.

- Infants are *active seekers of stimulation.* Infants want—actually need—people, sounds, and physical contact to stimulate their cognitive development and to give them a feeling of security in their world. Remember that infants are engaged in a subtle, though powerful battle to establish control over their bodies. For example, they are struggling to regulate their bodily functions, such as eating, breathing, and heart rate. But for brief moments, perhaps for only

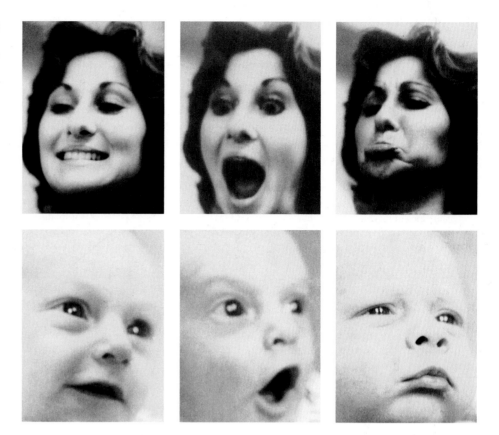

Sample photographs of a model's happy, surprised, and sad expressions, and an infant's corresponding expressions. How would you describe the effects on development that a mother's facial expressions have on a child?

Courtesy of Dr. Tiffany Field and Science. From Field et al., model and infant expressions from "Discrimination and Imitation of Facial Express by Neonates" in *Science*, Fig. 2, Vol. 218, pp. 179–181, October 8, 1982. Reprinted by permission of the American Association for the Advancement of Science.

15 or 20 seconds, they stop these efforts and pay close attention to the environment in a search for stimulation. This happens even when they are hungry.

One of the authors takes students to Children's Hospital of Boston for observation visits and finds a nurse bottle feeding an infant. Watching what happens when someone moves into the baby's field of vision, observers are surprised at the baby's reaction. *The baby stops sucking and stares intently at that person's face!* Not for long, but long enough to interrupt feeding. Now you may not be too impressed with this, but think about it. An infant's hunger drive is extremely powerful, yet, momentarily, the need for stimulation is even stronger, indicating that infants show a willingness, even a need, to interact with other human beings.

- *Infants, using these abilities, begin their efforts to master the developmental tasks of the first two years:* learning to take solid foods, learning to talk, learning to walk.

Neonatal Assessment Techniques

Although all infants are born with these reflexes and abilities, not all possess them to the same degree. For example, some neonates demonstrate much weaker reflex action than others, a condition that affects their chances of surviving. Consequently, efforts to develop reliable measures of early behavior, called *neonatal assessment*, have increased sharply.

Three basic classifications of neonatal tests are used to assess infant reflexes and behavior: the *Apgar scale, neurological assessment,* and *behavioral assessment.*

1. *Apgar Scale:* In 1953, Virginia Apgar proposed a scale to evaluate a newborn's basic life signs. The **Apgar** is administered 1 minute and again 5 minutes after

apgar
A scale to evaluate a newborn's basic life signs administered 1 minute after birth and repeated at 3-, 5-, and 10-minute intervals; it uses five life signs—heart rate, respiratory effort, muscle tone, reflex irritability, skin color.

Before continuing your reading, try to decide how competent you think a newborn baby is. In one view, infants are empty, unresponsive beings merely waiting for things to be done to and for them. They become active, healthy babies only because of maturation and the actions of those around them.

In another view, newborns are seen as amazingly competent and capable of much more than is now expected of them. Adherents of this belief view infants as "superbabies," capable of prodigious accomplishments from birth, if not before. Consequently, from the first months of an infant's life, infants need some form of education.

In a third view, infants are seen as neither passive objects nor as superbabies, designed for instant greatness. Newborn babies are seen as bringing abilities with them into the world, a cluster of competencies that enables them to survive but also permits them to engage in a wider range of activities than was previously suspected (Brazelton & Nugent, 1995).

The expectations that parents have for their babies determine how they treat them, and these expectations have important physical, cognitive, and psychosocial consequences. Babies "tune into" their environments—they react to the tone of an adult's voice, they sense how they're being handled (gently or roughly)—and are quite skillful in detecting the moods of those around them.

Ask your parents to think back on their childbearing days and to try to recall how competent they thought babies were. Ask them if it made any difference in how they treated you. If you have brothers or sisters or friends with children, ask them what they expected a newborn baby would be like? Combining their practical outlook on infancy with what you have read, decide which of these three views of infancy seems most realistic. Which will most help infants to fulfill their potential?

If you would like to have a more informed view on this issue, you may want to read one or more of the references in this chapter, such as Brazelton and Nugent's account of newborn behavior. You may also wish to learn more about it by going to our website at www.mhhe.com/dacey7.

---

birth. Using five life signs—heart rate, respiratory effort, muscle tone, reflex irritability, and skin color; an observer evaluates the infant by a 3-point scale. Each of the five dimensions receives a score of 0, 1, or 2. (0 indicates severe problems, whereas 2 suggests an absence of major difficulties.) A total of 8 or above indicates a successful transition to life outside the womb (Arenson & Drake, 2007).

neurological assessment
Identifies any neurological problem, suggests means of monitoring the problem, and offers a prognosis about the problem.

2. *Neurological Assessment.* **Neurological assessment** is used for three purposes:

- Identification of any neurological problem
- Constant monitoring of a neurological problem
- Prognosis about some neurological problem

Each of these purposes requires testing the infant's reflexes, which is critical for neurological evaluation and basic for all infant tests.

Brazelton Neonatal Behavioral Assessment Scale
Device to assess an infant's behavior; examines both neurological and psychological responses.

3. *Behavioral Assessment.* The **Brazelton Neonatal Behavioral Assessment Scale** (named after T. Berry Brazelton) has become a significant worldwide tool for infant assessment. Brazelton and Nugent (1995) believe that the baby's state of consciousness (sleepy, drowsy, alert, fussy) is the single most important element in the examination. The Brazelton test also permits us to examine the infant's behavior, which, as we have mentioned, is sensitive to cultural differences.

For example, during the administration of the Brazelton, one of the tests involves gently placing a piece of cheesecloth over the eyes and nose of the baby. This is intended to measure the baby's defensive reactions, so important for survival. Most African- and Anglo-American babies quickly turn their heads away or try to push the cloth away. Chinese-American babies, however, remain still and breath through their mouths (Brazelton & Nugent, 1995; Kagan, 1994). (For an excellent discussion of the role of culture in the origins of individual differences in neonatal behavior, see Nugent, Lester, & Brazelton, 1995).

All three of these assessment techniques provide clues about the infant's ability to function on its own and have proved to be invaluable tools in diagnosing problems in the early days of infancy. Tests such as these, plus careful observation, have given us much greater insight into infant development. These tests have also helped us to realize that infants are much more competent than we previously suspected.

Given the rapid development of the brain and the survival value of the reflexes, we should expect motor development to proceed rapidly, which is just what happens.

Motor Development

Parents are fascinated by their child's motor development: Is she sitting up on time? Shouldn't she be crawling by now? I wonder if she'll ever walk. Why can't she hold her head steady? Motor development occurs in both head-to-feet direction (called *cephalocaudal*), as well as a *proximodistal* direction (from the center of the body to the extremities).

For many years, research into infant locomotion has been at a standstill mainly because of the belief that neuromuscular maturation was the primary agent of motor development. Recently, however, modern investigators using high-speed film, computerized video recordings, and infrared emitting diodes have provided new insights into changes in coordination, balance, and strength in infants' locomotion.

Continuity of walking movements in the first year may be masked by underlying changes in the infant's muscle distribution, body fat, and the differential effect of gravity. For example, newborns with chubby legs stepped less than did slender-legged infants.

Here are several important characteristics of motor control.

Head Control

The most obvious initial head movements are from side to side, although the 1-month-old infant occasionally lifts its head when in a prone position. Four-month-old infants can hold their heads steady while sitting and will lift their head and shoulders to a 90-degree angle when on their abdomens. By the age of 6 months, most youngsters can balance their heads quite well.

Locomotion: Crawling and Creeping

Crawling and creeping are two distinct developmental phases. In **crawling,** the infant's abdomen touches the floor, and the weight of the head and shoulders rests on the elbows. Locomotion is mainly by arm action. The legs usually drag, although some youngsters push with their legs. Most youngsters can crawl after age 7 months.

Creeping is more advanced than crawling, since movement is on hands and knees and the trunk does not touch the ground. After age 9 months, most youngsters can creep.

Most descriptions of crawling and creeping are quite uniform. The progression is from propulsion on the abdomen to quick, accurate movements on hands and knees, but the sequence is endlessly varied. Youngsters adopt a bewildering diversity of positions and movements that can only loosely be grouped together.

Locomotion: Standing and Walking

After about age 7 months, infants when held support most of their weight on their legs. Coordination of arm and leg movements enables babies to pull themselves up

Note the steady development of body control in this picture, especially the head and upper body. Control of the lower body and legs follows by several months. Why is it important that control of the upper body appears early in development?

crawling
Locomotion whereby the infant's abdomen touches the floor and the weight of the head and shoulders rests on the elbows.

creeping
Movement on hands and knees; the trunk does not touch the ground; creeping appears from 9 months in most youngsters.

Most youngsters somewhere in the 7- to 9-month period begin to pull themselves up to a standing position. Their legs are now strong enough to support them while standing. Explain how locomotion contributes to other forms of development.

and grope toward control of leg movements. The first steps are a propulsive, lunging forward. Gradually a smooth, speedy, and versatile gait emerges. The world now belongs to the infant.

Once babies begin to walk, their attention darts from one thing to another, thus quickening their perceptual development (our next topic). Tremendous energy and mobility, coupled with a growing curiosity, push infants to search for the boundaries of their world. It is an exciting time for youngsters but a watchful time for parents, since they must draw the line between encouraging curiosity and initiative and protecting the child from injury. The task is not easy. It is, however, a problem for all aspects of development: What separates unreasonable restraint from reasonable freedom?

Finally, we want to call your attention to changes in theorizing about and research into motor development. Reflecting current thinking about development (see Chapters 1 and 2), recent studies have incorporated a multicausal explanation of motor development (Lockman & Thelen, 1993; Thelen, 1995; Thelen & Smith, 2006). For example, in analyzing the stepping reflex previously discussed (see p. 114), Thelen (1995) commented on the disappearance of this behavior by 2 or 3 months. Yet kicking, which has the same movement pattern as stepping, is *not* lost. How can these differences be explained? Thelen (1995) pointed to a change of posture, plus weight gain (the legs get heavier), plus the pull of gravity as the multicausal answer.

Table 5.4 summarizes milestones in motor development.

Neonatal Problems

Not all infants enter the world unscathed. Occasionally the developmental sequence that we have just discussed does not run smoothly. Among the most prominent of possible problems are the following.

TABLE 5.4	Milestones in Motor Development				
Age	Head Control	Grasping	Sitting	Creeping, Crawling	Standing, Walking
1–3 months	Can lift head and chest while prone	Grasps objects, briefly holds objects, carries objects to mouth	Sits awkwardly with support		
4–8 months	Holds head steady while sitting, balances head	Develops skillful use of thumb	Transition from sitting with slight support to brief periods without support	Crawling movements appear at about 7 months (trunk touches floor)	
8–12 months	Has established head control	Coordinates hand activities, handedness begins to appear	Good trunk control, sits alone steadily	Creeping (trunk raised from floor) begins at 9–10 months and continues until steady walking	Can stand and take steps holding on to something; by 12 months will pull self up
12–14 months		Handedness pronounced, holds crayon, marks lines	Can sit from standing position		Stands alone; begins to walk alone
18 months					Begins to run

AN APPLIED VIEW

Toilet Training—Easy or Difficult?

By the end of their child's infancy period, most parents begin to think about toilet training. One important fact to remember is that voluntary control of the sphincter muscles, which are the muscles that control elimination, does not occur until about the 18th month. For some children, however, control is not possible until about 30 months.

Evidence suggests that children are ready to participate in toilet training at about 18 months of age and may be be completely trained between 2 and 3 years of age. Attempting to train children before they are ready can only cause anxiety and

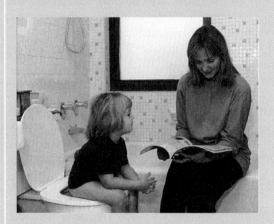

Toilet training should commence when bladder control and rectal muscles are sufficiently mature.

stress for the child and frustration for the parents (Brazelton & others, 1999).

Children really can't be trained; they learn when to use the toilet. Certain signs of readiness can alert parents when they can initiate the process. For example, necessary muscle control does not occur until well into the second year, and a child must be able to communicate, either by words or gesture, the need to use the bathroom.

At about 2 years, almost all children want to use the toilet, to become more "grown up," and to rid themselves of the discomfort of wet or soiled diapers. Parents should try to obtain equipment that the child feels most comfortable with—either a chair that sits on the floor or one that fits over the toilet seat.

Most parents expect their children to be toilet trained by the end of infancy, usually sometime between 2 and 3 years of age. Physiologically, most children are ready to learn control; socially it is desirable; psychologically it may be traumatic unless parents are careful. Here are several suggestions that can help parents (Gorski, 1999).

- Recognize the time of day and children's moods when they are most approachable.
- Work with children's attention span; plan distractions that will keep them comfortable on a potty chair.
- Accept a child's frustration level and work within those limits.
- Provide as much support and encouragement as a particular child needs.

Failure to Thrive

failure-to-thrive (FTT)
Condition in which the weight and height of infants consistently remain far below normal (the bottom 3% of height and weight measures).

There is general agreement today that **failure to thrive** should be defined on the basis of growth alone (Wolke, Skuse, & Reilly, 2007). The weight and height of failure-to-thrive (FTT) infants consistently remain far below normal. They are estimated to be in the bottom 3% of height and weight measures and account for about 3% of pediatric hospital admissions.

There are two types of FTT, organic and nonorganic. *Organic FTT* accounts for 30% of FTT cases, and the problem is usually some gastrointestinal disease, occasionally a problem with the nervous system. *Nonorganic FTT,* much more difficult to diagnose and treat, lacks a physical cause. Consequently, researchers have looked to the environment and identified problems such as poverty, neglect, abuse, and often ignorance of good parenting practices (Block et al., 2005).

The seriousness of this problem is evident from the outlook for FTT infants: Almost 50% of these infants will continue to experience physical, cognitive, and behavioral problems (Blackman, 1997). A recent follow-up study of FTT children at age 8 (Black et al., 2007) indicated that FTT increased vulnerability to short stature, poor arithmetic performance, and poor work habits. Home intervention helped by promoting maternal sensitivity and aiding children with their study habits.

Sudden Infant Death Syndrome

sudden infant death syndrome (SIDS)
Death of an apparently healthy infant, usually between 2 and 4 months of age; thought to be a brain-related respiratory problem.

Discussion of the survival value of reflexes introduces one of the most perplexing problems facing both parents and researchers, **sudden infant death syndrome (SIDS).** An estimated 2,500 infants 2 to 4 months old die each year from SIDS. There is little warning, although almost all cases are preceded by mild cold symptoms and usually occur in late winter or early spring (American Academy of Pediatrics, 2000a; American SIDS Institute, 2007). SIDS rarely occurs before age 1 month or after age 1 year; most victims are between 2 and 4 months old. Deaths peak between November and March. Boys are more vulnerable than girls, by a 3-to-2 margin (Stein & Barnes, 2002).

SIDS is particularly devastating for parents because of the lack of warning. These infants are apparently normal. Parents put them in a crib for a nap or for the night and return later to find them dead (hence the common name, "crib death"). You can imagine the effect this has on parents, particularly the feelings of guilt: What did I do wrong? Why didn't I look in earlier? Why didn't I see that something was wrong? Today, special centers have been established to counsel grieving parents. (One disturbing recent statistic has raised concern: There is a larger proportion of SIDS deaths in daycare centers than in parent care. For an analysis of this research, see Moon, Patel, & Shaefer, 2000.)

Although no definite answers to the SIDS dilemma have yet been found, current research points to a respiratory problem. Control of breathing resides in the brain stem, and autopsies have indicated that the SIDS infant may not have received sufficient oxygen while in the womb, a condition known as *fetal hypoxia*. Consequently, parents are being urged to be extremely cautious when their babies are sleeping: Keep them on their back as much as possible, be alert to overheating, and avoid soft, loose bedding (American Academy of Pediatrics, 2000; Klonof-Cohen, 1997; Stein & Barnes, 2002). These cautionary practices have resulted in a decrease in postneonatal SIDS mortality (Malloy & Freeman, 2000).

A startling twist in the analysis of SIDS deaths has recently led researchers to attribute *some* of these deaths to child abuse. One possible cause is called *Munchausen by proxy:* a parent deliberately injures or kills a child to attract attention. Munchausen by proxy is a variant of adult Munchausen, whereby victims inflict harm on themselves, again to seek attention and sympathy.

In a bizarre episode, researchers, baffled by unexplained illnesses in children who were being treated at an Atlanta hospital, hid video cameras in 41 rooms. In *more than half* of the cases mothers were inflicting injury on the child. One mother injected her child with her own urine; another gagged herself to vomit and then said the vomit was the child's; another injected chemicals into her child's feeding tube, causing chronic fatigue (Hall & others, 2000). Remember, however, in the vast majority of SIDS cases (estimates range from 95% to 98%), the parents are blameless. This bizarre finding will undoubtedly lead to more detailed studies.

Sleeping Disorders

Most sleeping disorders are less serious than FTT or SIDS. Nevertheless, infant sleeping problems negatively affect growth and trouble parents. As Ferber (2006, p. 3) stated:

> *The most frequent calls I receive at the Center for Pediatric Sleep Disorders at Children's Hospital in Boston are from a parent or parents whose children are sleeping poorly. When the parent on the phone begins by telling me "I am at the end of my rope" or "We are at our wits' end" I can almost predict what will be said next.*

Ferber went on to explain that typically the parent has a child between the ages of 5 months and 4 years who does not sleep readily at night and wakes repeatedly. Parents become tired, frustrated, and often angry. Frequently the relationship between the parents becomes tense.

Usually a sleeping disorder has nothing to do with parenting. Also, usually nothing is wrong with the child, either physically or mentally. Occasionally problems do exist; for example, a bladder infection or, with an older child, emotional factors causing night terrors. A sleep problem is not normal and should not be waited out.

Neonates sleep more than they do anything else (usually from 14 to 15 hours per day) and have three sleep patterns: light or restless, periodic, and deep. Little if any activity occurs during deep sleep (about 25% of sleep). Neonates are mostly light sleepers and have the brain wave patterns associated with dreaming (although infants probably do not dream).

Some internal clock seems to regulate sleep patterns, with most deep sleep spells lasting approximately 20 minutes. At the end of the second week, a consistent and predictable pattern emerges. Neonates sleep in short stretches, about 7 or 8 hours per day. The pattern soon reverses itself, and infants assume an adult's sleep schedule. Sleep patterns in infants range from about 16 to 17 hours in the first week to 13 hours at age 2. Adults also need to exercise caution when they take children into their own beds (called *cosleeping*). Agreement between the parents, safety considerations for the child, and a decision when cosleeping is to be discontinued all need to be considered (Ferber, 2006). (Almost all child specialist agree that cosleeping should cease by the age of 3 years.)

The American Academy of Pediatrics recommends the following procedures.

- Place infants on their backs on a firm mattress that meets current safety standards.
- Remove all pillows, quilts, and comforters, and any soft toys from the crib.
- If using a blanket, tuck it around the mattress and be sure it reaches only to the baby's chest.

Respiratory Distress Syndrome

respiratory distress syndrome (RDS)
Problem common with premature babies that is caused by the lack of a substance called *surfactant,* which keeps the air sacs in the lungs open.

T. Field (1990). *Infancy.* Cambridge, MA: Harvard University Press. A clear, simple, and carefully written account of infancy by a well-known commentator on these years.

The last of the disorders to be discussed is RDS—**respiratory distress syndrome** (also called *hyaline membrane disease*). Although this problem is most common with prematures, it may strike full-term infants whose lungs are particularly immature.

RDS is caused by the lack of a substance called *surfactant,* which keeps open the air sacs in the lungs. When surfactant is inadequate, the lung can collapse. Since most babies do not produce sufficient surfactant until the 35th prenatal week, you can see why it is a serious problem for premature infants. (Only 10% of a baby's lung tissue is developed at full-term birth.)

Full-term newborns whose mothers are diabetic seem especially vulnerable to RDS. Babies whose delivery has been particularly difficult also are more susceptible. The good news is that today 90% of these youngsters survive, and, given early detection and treatment, the outlook for them is excellent.

Guided Review

1. About _____% of the brain develops outside of the womb.
2. A _____ is a behavior in which a repeated stimulus elicits the same response.
3. The _____ is a neonatal assessment technique that measures how an infant interacts with the environment.
4. Motor development occurs in _____ and _____ directions.
5. The weight and height of _____ infants consistently remain below normal.

Answers   1. 75 2. reflex 3. Brazelton 4. cephalocaudal, proximodistal 5. FTT

PERCEPTUAL DEVELOPMENT

If you stop your reading for a moment and look around, you'll see some things that you recognize immediately: this text, a television set, shoes, paper, and so on. But you may also notice something that seems new or unfamiliar: for example, a new textbook or an unsolicited magazine. Our ability to recognize the familiar and to realize what we don't know depends on perception. Perceiving something means that:

- You can recall past experiences with a person, an object, or an event.
- You experience meaning.
- You have certain expectations about the person, object, or event.

Perception, then, implies more than a mere reaction to something; considerable processing is needed to obtain information from stimuli and to integrate multiple sources of information. Putting these ideas together defines **perception:** getting and interpreting information from stimuli.

We know now that babies not only receive stimuli, they interpret them. Perception begins our experience and interpretation of the world. It is also our basis for the growth of thought, the regulation of emotions, interactions in social relationships, and for progress in almost all aspects of development (Bornstein & Arterberry, 1999). Before attempting to trace perceptual development, let's explore the meaning of perception in more detail.

The Meaning of Perception

Infants are particularly ingenious at obtaining information from the stimuli around them. During infancy the capacity to take in information through the major sensory channels, to make sense of the environment, and to attribute meaning to information improve dramatically (Bornstein, 2002). Seeking information leads to meaning. Objects roll, bounce, or squeak—in this way infants learn what objects are and what they do. In the first year of life, infants discern patterns, depth, orientation, location, movement, and color (Bornstein & Arterberry, 1999). During infancy, babies also discover what they can do with objects, which furthers their perceptual development.

perception
Obtaining and interpreting information from stimuli.

habituation
Process in which stimuli that are presented frequently cause a decrease in an infant's attention.

Infants quickly begin to attend to the objects in their environments, thus constructing their views about how the world "works." Can you describe how motor development contributes to perceptual development?

Infants are born ready to attend to changes in physical stimulation. Stimuli presented frequently cause a decrease in an infant's attention (**habituation**). If the stimuli are altered, the infant again attends, indicating awareness of the difference. For example, if you show an infant a picture (flower, birds, anything attractive), the child is first fascinated, then becomes bored; the child has habituated. If you now change the picture, you again capture the child's attention.

In a classic study, Brooks and Lewis (1976) studied how infants responded to four different types of strangers: a male child and a female child, a female adult, and a female midget. In this way, facial configurations and height were varied. The infants reacted to the children by continuous looking and some smiling. They reacted to the midget with considerable puzzlement but no positive response such as smiling or movement toward her. They reacted to the adult by sporadic looking, averting their eyes, frowning, and even crying. Thus the infants used size and facial configuration cues.

We may conclude, then, that perception depends on both learning and maturation. An infant's perceptual system undergoes considerable development following birth, resulting from greater familiarity with objects and events in the world as well as from growth. Most of the research on infant perceptual development has concentrated on vision and hearing because of their importance and rapid development.

Visual Perception

Infants are born able to see and quickly exhibit a preference for patterns. Do infants prefer looking at some objects more than others? In a pioneering series of experiments, Robert Fantz provided dramatic documentation of an infant's perceptual ability. Fantz (1961) stated that the best indicator of an infant's visual ability is eye activity. Infants who consistently gaze at some forms more than others show perceptual discrimination; that is, something in one form holds their attention.

Using a "looking chamber," in which an infant lies in a crib at the bottom of the chamber and looks at objects placed on the ceiling, Fantz could determine

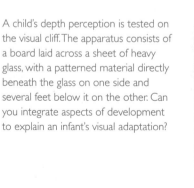

Fantz's "looking chamber" was an arrangement in which infants placed at the bottom of the chamber looked at objects placed at the ceiling above them. A researcher observed the infants' eyes by looking though a peephole at the top of the chamber.

the amount of time that infants fixated on different objects. In one of his experiments, Fantz tested pattern perception by using six objects, all flat discs 6 inches in diameter: face, bull's-eye, newsprint, red disc, yellow disc, and white disc. The face attracted the greatest attention (human faces are remarkably complex), followed by the newsprint, the bull's-eye, and then the three plain-colored discs (none of which received much attention). Infants, then, show definite preferences based on as much complexity as they can handle (Gibson & Pick, 2000, pp. 33–34).

Visual Adaptation

A child's depth perception is tested on the visual cliff. The apparatus consists of a board laid across a sheet of heavy glass, with a patterned material directly beneath the glass on one side and several feet below it on the other. Can you integrate aspects of development to explain an infant's visual adaptation?

Studying visual development spurs speculation about how growing visual skill helps infants to adjust to their environment. In their famous *visual cliff* experiment, Gibson and Walk (1960) reasoned that infants would use visual stimuli to discriminate both depth and distance.

The visual cliff is a board dividing a large sheet of heavy glass. A checkerboard pattern is attached flush to one half of the bottom of the glass, giving the impression of solidity. The investigators then placed a similar sheet on the floor under the other half, creating a sense of depth—the visual cliff.

Thirty-six infants from ages 6 to 14 months were tested. After each infant was placed on the center board, the mother called the child from the shallow side and then the cliff side. Twenty-seven of the youngsters moved onto the shallow side toward the mother. When called from the cliff side, only three infants ventured over the depth. The experiment suggests that infants discriminate depth when they begin crawling.

To conclude, we can state that by 2 to 4 months of age, infant perception is fairly sophisticated. Infants perceive figures as organized wholes; they react to the relationship among elements rather than single elements; they perceive color; and complex rather than simple patterns fascinate them. They scan the environment, pick up information, encode and process information (Gibson & Pick, 2000).

Auditory Perception

Infants display remarkable auditory abilities in the uterus and at birth (Siegler & Alibali, 2005). Hearing and auditory discrimination is well developed at birth since sounds are carried to the fetus through the amniotic fluid as a series of vibrations. Infants display a remarkable sensitivity to differences in the quality of sounds. For example, some babies may prefer music to other sounds and one type of music to another; they can discriminate their mothers' voices from those of other women. They also can locate where a sound comes from.

In his classic study (1961), Michael Wertheimer reported on his daughter's ability to localize sound at birth. On entering the delivery room, he first sounded a clicker on one side of the room and then the other. On first hearing the sound, his daughter turned her head in that direction, and then when Wertheimer moved to the other side, she turned in that direction.

Infants are more attentive to some sounds than others, especially speechlike sounds (Siegler & Alibali, 2005). Although significant in itself, this perceptual sensitivity underscores the importance of auditory perception in language development. For example, infants begin to differentiate the sounds of their language and tune into the speech they hear around them, suggesting a readiness to perceive the phonemes of their language (Bjorklund, 2005). It's as if nature has determined that infants must immediately attend efficiently to the important information in the speech surrounding them. Infants enter the world with substantial auditory capabilities, which develop rapidly. They attend to sounds, discriminate sounds, and they can localize these sounds.

Guided Review

6. The decrease in an infant's attention to stimuli presented frequently is called _____.

7. Newborn infants show a preference for _____.

8. A child's depth perception is tested on an apparatus called a _____ _____.

9. Neonates require about _____ hours of sleep per day.

10. Perception depends on _____ and _____ information.

Answers   6. habituation 7. patterns 8. visual cliff 9. 14 10. getting, interpreting

COGNITIVE DEVELOPMENT

As we witness the rapidly emerging scientific and theoretical breakthroughs of the 21st century, we also note that many of these recent discoveries apply to human cognitive development. To include these findings in our work, we have increased our discussion of the biological basis of cognition and its role in many human behaviors we were previously unaware of: genetic influences on behavior, the role of the brain in music processing, current biological insights into language development. These accomplishments have led to two major changes in studying cognitive development: an intensified examination of the brain's role in development and the sociocultural basis of cognitive development (Bjorklund, 2005).

Consequently, we'll present these views throughout our discussion of cognitive development. For example, we have enlarged our evaluation of brain development across all phases of development, and we formulated a larger role for the sociocultural view, one that begins with the seminal work of Lev Vygotsky. In this chapter, we begin with the compelling ideas of Jean Piaget. (Many of Piaget's conclusions about cognitive development were derived from observation of his own three children: Jacqueline, Lucianne, and Laurent.)

Piaget's Sensorimotor Period

Did you ever wonder what infants think about as they lie in their cribs, as they are carried to exciting new worlds, as they try to make sense of strange sounds directed at them? Probably not, but Piaget did, and his research made a lasting impression on studies of cognitive development. For the next few minutes consider the way that infants make sense of their world: how they react to all these wonderful sights, how they learn to understand the multitude of words that now surround them, how they interpret the manner in which they're handled—roughly or gently, lovingly or carelessly. What an incredible task! And yet, you did it, your parents did it, your friends did it, we all did.

Piaget (1967) believed that the period from birth to language acquisition is marked by extraordinary mental growth and influences the entire course of development. **Egocentrism** describes the initial world of children. Everything centers on them; they see the world only from their point of view. Very young children lack social orientation. They speak at and not to each other, and two children in conversation may be discussing utterly unrelated topics. (Likewise, egocentric adults know that other viewpoints exist, but they disregard them.) The egocentric child simply is unaware of any other viewpoint.

The remarkable changes of the **sensorimotor period** (about the first two years of life) occur within a sequence of six stages.

Stage 1

During the first stage, children do little more than exercise the reflexes with which they were born. For example, Piaget (1952b) stated that the sucking reflex is hereditary and functions from birth. At first infants suck anything that touches their lips; they suck when nothing touches their lips; then they actively search for the nipple. What we see here is the steady development of the coordination of arm, eye, hand, and mouth. Through these activities, the baby is building a foundation for forming cognitive structures (For a more extended discussion of the antecedents of these behaviors, see Smotherman & Robinson, 1996.)

Stage 2

Piaget referred to stage 2 (from about 1 to 4 months) as the stage of first habits. During stage 2, **primary circular reactions** appear, in which infants repeat some

egocentrism
Child focuses on self in early phases of cognitive development; term associated with Piaget.

sensorimotor period
Piaget's term for the first of his cognitive stages of development (0–2 years).

primary circular reactions
Infants repeat some act involving their bodies; term associated with Piaget's theory.

act involving their bodies. For example, they continue to suck when nothing is present. They continue to open and close their hands. Infants seem to have no external goal, no intent in these actions other than the pleasure of self-exploration. But they are learning something about that primary object in their world: their own bodies.

Stage 3

secondary circular reactions
Infants direct their activities toward objects and events outside themselves; term associated with Piaget's theory.

Secondary circular reactions emerge during the third stage, which extends from about 4 to 8 months. During this stage, infants direct their activities toward objects and events outside themselves. Secondary circular reactions thus produce results in the environment, and not, as with the primary circular reactions, on the child's own body.

For example, Piaget's son, Laurent, continued to shake and kick his crib to produce movement and sound. He also discovered that pulling a chain attached to some balls produced an interesting noise, and he kept doing it. In this way, babies learn about the world "out there" and feed this information into their developing cognitive structures.

coordination of secondary schemes
Infants combine secondary schemes to obtain a goal; term associated with Piaget's theory.

Stage 4

From about 8 to 12 months of age, infants **coordinate secondary schemes** to form new kinds of behavior. Now more complete acts of intelligence are evident (Piaget & Inhelder, 1969).

The baby first decides on a goal (finding an object that is hidden behind a cushion). The infant attempts to move objects to reach the goal. In stage 4, part of the goal object must be visible behind the obstacle. Here we see the first signs of intentional behavior.

tertiary circular reaction
Repetition with variation; the infant is exploring the world's possibilities; term associated with Piaget's theory.

Stage 5

Tertiary circular reactions appear from 12 to 18 months of age. In the tertiary circular reaction, repetition occurs again, but it is repetition with variation. The infant is exploring the world's possibilities. Piaget thought that the infant deliberately attempts to provoke new results instead of merely reproducing activities. Tertiary circular reactions indicate an interest in novelty for its own sake.

object permanence
Refers to children gradually realizing that there are permanent objects around them, even when these objects are out of sight.

How many times have you seen a baby standing in a crib and dropping everything on the floor? But listen to Piaget: Watch how the baby drops things, from different locations and different heights. Does it sound the same when it hits the floor as the rug? Is it as loud dropped from here or higher? Each repetition is actually a chance to learn. Thanks to Piaget, you will be a lot more patient when you see this behavior.

Stage 6

When infants begin to move things to get what they want, they are "coordinating secondary schemata." This is a clear signal of advancing cognitive development. Using data from Chapter 2 with this information, describe how Piaget's ideas explain a child's ability to coordinate secondary schemata.

During stage 6, the sensorimotor period ends, and children develop a basic kind of *internal representation*. A good example is the behavior of Piaget's daughter, Jacqueline. At age 20 months, she approached a door that she wished to close, but she was carrying some grass in each hand. She put down the grass by the threshold, preparing to close the door. But then she stopped and looked at the grass and the door, realizing that if she closed the door the grass would blow away. She then moved the grass away from the door's movement and then closed it. She had obviously planned and thought carefully about the event before acting. Table 5.5 summarizes the accomplishments of the sensorimotor period.

Progress through the sensorimotor period leads to four major accomplishments:

- *Object permanence:* Children realize that permanent objects exist around them; something out of sight is not gone forever.

- *Sense of space:* Children realize environmental objects have a spatial relationship.

TABLE 5.5	Outstanding Characteristics of the Sensorimotor Period

THE SIX SUBDIVISIONS OF THIS PERIOD

Stage 1 During the first month the child exercises the native reflexes, for example, the sucking reflex. Here is the origin of mental development, because states of awareness accompany the reflex mechanisms.

Stage 2 Piaget referred to stage 2 (from 1 to 4 months) as the stage of primary circular reactions. Infants repeat some act involving the body, for example, finger sucking. (Primary means first; circular reaction means repeating the act.)

Stage 3 From 4 to 8 months, secondary circular reactions appear; that is, the children repeat acts involving external objects. For example, infants continue to shake or kick the crib.

Stage 4 From 8 to 12 months, the child "coordinates secondary schemes." Recall the meaning of schema—behavior plus mental structure. During stage 4, infants combine several related schemata to achieve some objective. For example, they will remove an obstacle that blocks some desired object.

Stage 5 From 12 to 18 months, tertiary circular reactions appear. Now children repeat acts, but not only for repetition's sake; now they search for novelty. For example, children of this age continually drop things. Piaget interpreted such behavior as expressing their uncertainty about what will happen to the object when they release it.

Stage 6 At about 18 months or 2 years, a primitive type of representation appears. For example, one of Piaget's daughters wished to open a door but had grass in her hands. She put the grass on the floor and then moved it back from the door's movement so that it would not blow away.

As infants acquire the ability to form representations of objects, they begin to move through their environments more skillfully. Can you specify how the pertinent parts of Piaget's theory explain how children form representations of objects?

- *Causality:* Children realize a relationship exists between actions and their consequences.
- *Time sequences:* Children realize that one thing comes after another.

By the end of the sensorimotor period, children move from purely sensory and motor functioning (hence the name sensorimotor) to a more symbolic kind of activity.

Criticisms of Piaget

Although Piaget has left a monumental legacy, his ideas have not been unchallenged. Piaget was a believer in the stage theory of development; that is, development is seen as a sequence of distinct stages, each of which entails important changes in the way a child thinks, feels, and behaves. However, the acquisition of cognitive structures may be gradual rather than abrupt and is not a matter of all or nothing; for example, a child is not completely in the sensorimotor or preoperational stage. A child's level of cognitive development seems to depend more on the nature of the task than on a rigid classification system.

In one of the first important challenges to Piaget, Gelman & Baillargeon (1983), changed the nature of the task as follows:

- By reducing the number of objects children must manipulate.
- By allowing children to practice (for example, teaching children conservation tasks).
- By using materials familiar to children.

These researchers found that children can accomplish specific tasks at earlier ages than Piaget believed. Such criticisms have led to a more searching examination of the times during which children acquire certain cognitive abilities. For example, Piaget believed that infants will retrieve an object that is hidden from them in stage 4, from 8 to 12 months. Before this age, if a blanket is thrown over a toy that the infant is looking at, the child stops reaching for it as if it doesn't exist.

To trace the ages at which object permanence appears, Baillargeon (1987) devised an experiment in which infants between 3 1/2 and 4 1/2 months old were seated at a table where a cardboard screen could be moved back and forth, either forward (toward the baby) until it was flat on the table or backward (away from the baby) until the back of the cardboard touched the table.

Baillargeon then placed a painted wooden block behind the cardboard screen so that the infant could see the block when the screen was in a forward, flat position. But when the screen was moved backward, it came to rest on the block, removing it from the infant's sight. Occasionally Baillargeon secretly removed the block so that the screen continued backward until it rested flat on the table. The 4-1/2-month-old infants looked surprised at the change (they looked at the screen longer); even some of the 3-1/2-month-olds seemed to notice the "impossible" event. These findings suggest that infants may develop the object permanence concept earlier than Piaget originally thought.

Information Processing in Infancy

Piaget, as we have seen, argued forcefully that cognitive development proceeds by progression through discrete stages. Information-processing theorists, however, argue just as strongly that cognitive development occurs by the gradual improvement of such cognitive processes as attention and memory. Information processing theorists share several assumptions (Munakata, 2006).

- The first assumption relates to limited capacity—we can process only so much information at any one time (Borklund, 2005).
- The second assumption refers to the belief that all thinking is information processing. The major focus of these theories is on such functions as attention and memory, not on stages of development (Siegler & Alibali, 2005).
- Recent research (Chen & Siegler, 2000; Siegler, 1996, 1998; Siegler & Alibali, 2005) indicates that most children devise a wide variety of thinking strategies, and they select what they think is the most appropriate strategy. (This is the *adaptive strategy choice* model of Robert Siegler, 1996.) Those strategies that produce successful solutions increase in frequency, whereas those that do not decrease in frequency.

Figure 5.5 shows how these processes work in information-processing theory. Now let's examine how infants "use" these processes.

Infants and Attention

Attention enables children to decide what is important, what is needed, and what is dangerous. But it also helps them to gradually ignore everything else. Infants attend to different stimuli for a variety of reasons: intensity, complexity of the stimuli, visual ability, and novelty. Consequently, they find human faces, voices, and movements particularly fascinating.

FIGURE 5.5

An information-processing model

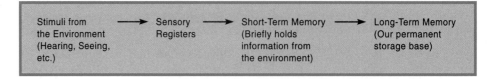

Infants quickly become skilled at discriminating facial expressions and responding accordingly (Flavell, 1999), which is why attention is often referred to as the "spotlight of the brain" (Andreasen, 2001). How do infants acquire this ability? What are the physiological and psychological mechanisms at work?

We should briefly mention the role of the brain since it is the biological basis of attention. When infants attend to something a series of interconnecting brain activities commences. For example, auditory receptors pick up the sound of the mother's voice, and the brain's reticular activating system brings the baby to a higher state of alertness. The limbic system now swings into action, which involves memory and emotion. Finally, cortical areas interpret what was said and how it was said. Was it directed at something? Was it soothing? Was it pleasant?

Psychologically, think about what attention means for the developing infant.

- *Their attention becomes selective;* that is, people (especially infants) can't attend to everything.

- *Their attention involves cognitive processing;* that is, infants don't just passively accept stimuli—they actively process incoming information.

- *Their attention is limited;* that is, infants especially can attend only to a limited number of things at the same time (Flavell, 1999).

When we consider these limitations during the infancy years, we realize that babies simply lack the cognitive maturity—call it an adequate gate-keeping mechanism—that permits them to control all the stimuli that assault them. A good rule of thumb to remember is that infants are drawn to stimuli of moderate intensity.

The adults around them must assume responsibility for monitoring the sights and sounds that their infants experience to shield them from too intense stimulation. Most mothers intuitively read their babies' signals and react appropriately, which reflects sensitive responsiveness to a child's needs. (See Brazelton & Nugent, 1995, for an analysis of an infant's ability to attend to and control stimuli.)

Infants and Memory

How important is memory in a person's life? Nobel Prize winner Eric Kandel has flatly stated that without memory we're really nothing—no sense of self, no sense of a personal history, no sense of certainty (Squire & Kandel, 2000). Here are four important discoveries that should guide your thinking about infant memory (Gazzaniga, Ivry, & Mangun, 1998; Squire & Kandel, 2000).

1. The brain as a whole is involved in memory; *memories don't reside in one particular location.*

2. Memories are reproduced (psychologists refer to this as *retrieval*) in the same manner as they were formed.

3. Memories are stored in the brain's *synapses,* which are the connections between neurons.

4. These synaptic connections can be strengthened through use, *and new synaptic processes can be formed by learning.*

Obviously, infants must have some ability to remember; otherwise, they could never learn about their world. They love to repeat actions that bring them pleasure. When does an infant begin to store information? To answer this question, we must first search our own memories and recall that the neurological basis must first be in place for permanent storage and conscious recall (Andreasen, 2001; Ratey, 2001; Squire & Kandel, 2001).

Psychologists have typically used habituation/dishabituation studies to analyze infant memory. For example, an infant sees a toy clown that is repeatedly placed before her—now she sees it, now she doesn't—until she's bored. Her attention shifts, and she looks away, which indicates habituation. Now a brightly colored toy monkey is presented to her. Immediately her attention centers on the novel toy.

R. Siegler and M. Alibali (2005). *Children's Thinking* (4th ed.). Upper Saddle River: Prentice Hall. An excellent, well-documented account of how children develop their thinking skills during infancy.

AN APPLIED VIEW

Infantile Amnesia

If memory seems to develop early in our lives, why do we have difficulty in remembering most of our experiences in infancy? You undoubtedly look with considerable skepticism at those individuals who claim to remember events from the first days of their lives. More common is a phenomenon called **infantile amnesia,** which refers to an inability to recall events from early in life. Infantile amnesia refers to our inability to remember much before the age of 4. Memories much before the age of 6 or 7 years are rare (Schneider & Bjorklund, 1998; Schneider & Pressley, 1997).

How do we explain this phenomenon? The passage of time is an inadequate explanation, as is a psychoanalytic interpretation that we tend to repress infant sexual experiences. Recent explanations point to the gradual maturation of the brain's frontal lobes, which seem to be involved in memory. A second explanation relates to language development. For example, you and I try to remember the names of people and events, but infants do not encode such information verbally. As infants listen to and begin to comprehend the stories they hear around them, they impose a logical construction on them that they tend to remember.

Another explanation may lie in the way that infants encode information compared to older children and adults. That is, do infants encode information in a way that they can later retrieve? Children often fail to encode important features of objects and events (Siegler & Alibali, 2005). The general knowledge we acquire as we mature helps us to encode information more precisely and clearly, thus making retrieval that much easier.

Finally, neuroscientists point out that neural circuits take several years to develop; thus infantile amnesia becomes a matter of storage not of retrieval. If the neural circuits, plus their synaptic junctions, aren't sufficiently mature, then memory, as we are coming to understand it, isn't yet functional (Eliot, 2000; Kandel, 2006; Squire & Kandel, 2000).

You can see that these recent explanations are not mutually exclusive, given that information storage is a fundamental property of neurons (Eliot, 2000, p. 334). For example, brain maturation is a must for healthy cognitive development; hearing others explain what's happening around them helps infants to encode information more meaningfully; improved coding helps children to retrieve information more rapidly and accurately.

infantile amnesia
Our inability to recall events from early in life.

This is one of those behavioral clues that tells us an infant can distinguish the new toy from the one that is now stored in memory.

After reviewing many studies of infant memory, the developmental psychologists Wolfgang Schneider and David Bjorklund conclude that infants demonstrate this type of memory (habituation) after the first few months following birth. By the end of the second year, an infant's memory more closely resembles that of older children. The habituation and novelty studies have also shown that a faster rate of habituation and a strong preference for novelty are related to higher IQs in childhood (For excellent discussions of current research into memory, see Kuhn, 2000; Samuelson & Smith, 2000).

Guided Review

11. Piaget's first stage of cognitive development is known as the _____ period.
12. _____ describes a phase of child development in which children perceive the world only from their point of view.
13. _____ _____ is achieved when a child realizes that an object out of sight is not gone forever.
14. A major assumption of information-processing theory is that children are not _____ recipients of stimuli.
15. Two important information-processes of infancy are _____ and _____.

LANGUAGE DEVELOPMENT

When people speak in a language that is totally unfamiliar to us, we have no way of understanding what they are trying to say. Prelinguistic infants are in an even worse situation. Not only do they not know what adults are trying to say, they do not even know that adults are trying to say something. They do not even know what "saying something" is. Without an understanding of linguistic symbols and how they work, it is all just noise. (Tomasello, 2003, p. 19)

A friend of one of us recently expressed amazement at the way his grandson was talking. "You know," he said, "it seems like only the other day that he was just making noises. But when I asked him today if we were still pals, he said, 'No, we're firefighters.' And he's not quite two." Here we see an excellent example of the tremendous growth of language during infancy.

AN INFORMED VIEW

The Brain's Language Areas

Understanding the brain's role in language seems to be a simple matter, probably because we're still learning about it! Beginning in 1864, we confidently identified certain parts of the brain as performing specific language functions. It was then that the French neurologist Paul Broca, working with stroke victims whose speech had been impaired and who suffered from paralysis of the right side of the body, determined that "we speak with the left hemisphere." *Broca's area* (in the left frontal lobe), as it came to be known, is thought to be responsible for the production of speech.

In 1876, the German psychiatrist Karl Wernicke described a section of the brain that receives incoming speech sounds. Called *Wernicke's area* (in the temporal lobe), it is responsible for interpreting and translating the speech sounds just heard and putting together the words for a reply. This composition is then passed on to Broca's area through a bundle of nerve fibers. The part of the brain identified as Wernicke's area (associated with interpretation and comprehension) seems to develop more rapidly than Broca's area does. The neural pathway connecting Wernicke's area to Broca's area develops even more slowly.

Children simply can't put their ideas into words because their brain won't let them. This makes practical sense if you think about that old saying: "He knows more than he's saying." Parents, psychologists, and linguists have long believed that children's speech doesn't accurately reflect what they know. Children know many more words and meanings than they can actually say. (So be careful what you say around them!)

But that isn't the end of it. The motor area of the brain now becomes involved and causes movements of the face, tongue, jaw, and throat. And, of course, our speech is often quite emotional. Putting it all together we have long thought that language production seemed to look like the diagram in Figure 5.6.

Think of it this way. Your child says something to you, which is immediately transferred to Wernicke's area. You understand what was said and think about a reply. When you decide to respond, your message is transferred to Broca's area

along a pathway of nerve fibers where a plan for vocalizing your ideas is formed. Parts of the motor cortex are now alerted, and the appropriate muscles of the mouth, lips, tongue, and the larynx swing into action, and you answer your child.

You can see from Figure 5.6 that language seems to be a function of the left cerebral hemisphere. John Ratey (2001), a clinical professor of psychiatry at Harvard Medical School, believes that language mainly resides in the left hemisphere for about 90% of the population. About 5% have their main language in the right hemishere, and another 5% split their language functions between both hemispheres. Remember, however, that both hemispheres are connected by the corpus callosum and both hemispheres are involved in language production. For example, the right hemisphere, mainly responsible for our emotional state, determines the emotional reactions of the speaker.

This so-called "classical" model of the brain-language relationship, however, has been challenged by recent research, so today no one is quite sure what Broca's area or Wernicke's area specifically does. Although we still accept the general idea that certain brain areas are responsible for certain behaviors, current studies have made us uncomfortable with the neat answer that "Broca's area does this" or "Wernicke's area does that." Thanks to data supplied by EEG studies, PET scans, CAT scans, and MRIs, a different picture is emerging. We now think that language functions are spread throughout the brain much more than we originally thought. Possible solutions to the problem of how these brain areas work together in our language world remain elusive. Questions of how the brain organizes movement and emotions as we listen, read, speak, and write still remain unanswered.

Finally, what can we make of all this? First, we are more certain than ever of the brain's critical role in language. Second, our belief in the "accepted" knowledge of the function of Broca's and Wernicke's areas persists, but in a more limited manner. Third, new data about the brain's role in language testify to an even greater complexity than we originally suspected.

FIGURE 5.6

The path of language production

Source: A. R. Damasio and H. Damasio,
Scientific American, September, 1992.

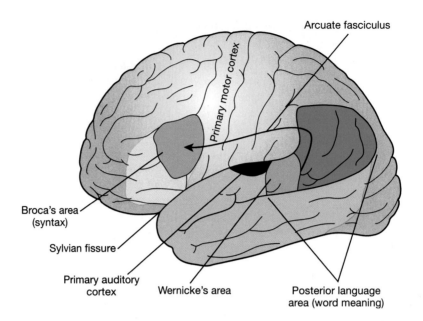

One of the most amazing accomplishments of an infant is the beginning of actual speech. The sounds, the words, the two- and three-word sentences, and the tremendous explosion of vocabulary are stunning achievements that we are still hard-pressed to explain. Think of it this way: With no formal training—in fact, often exposed to dramatically faulty language models—children learn words and meanings, and how to combine them in a logical, purposeful manner. Given this drive toward language and given that all children acquire their own language in a remarkably similar manner, we begin to suspect that nature plays a critical role, which leads us to consider the brain's function.

Acquiring Their Language

Children in all parts of the world go through a process in which they first emit sounds, then single words, two words, and finally fairly complex sentences. By the time they are about 5 years of age, they have acquired the basics of their language, an astonishing accomplishment. Here is an example, using English.

If I said to you, "Will you please *park* your car in the *driveway*?" I'm sure you would know exactly what I mean. When you leave I tell you that the quickest way home is to *drive* on the *parkway*. Again, you understand exactly what I'm getting at here. Think about it for a minute, and you'll realize that in spite of the switch in words, children easily master such intricacies.

Or consider this. After you finish reading this section, why don't you take a break and have dinner. I suggest that you eat some *ghotti,* it's always so tasty and it's good for you. If you follow my advice, what will you be having for dinner? (Put it all together—*gh* as in tough, *o* as in women, *ti* as in nation—and you'll have a delicious *fish* dinner.)

To guide you through the complexity of language development, here are several transitions that help to explain children's amazing accomplishments (Bloom, 1998).

- The first transition occurs at the end of the first year and continues in the second year with the appearance of words and the acquisition of a basic vocabulary.

- The second transition occurs when children change from saying only one word at a time to combining words into phrases and simple sentences about the end of the second year.

AN INFORMED VIEW | Infants and Their Language Development

The amazing competence of infants leads to some fascinating speculation, especially about language and reading. Reading? Yes, reading. Here's a question we'd like you to consider: Do children respond to certain books even *before* they're born? Although our concern in this chapter is with children from birth to two years of age, recent developmental research reaches from the womb into the world of children's literature. Beginning in the 1980s, Anthony De Casper at the University of North Carolina began experiments by having mothers read to fetuses in utero. Realizing that fetuses can hear sounds in the last months of pregnancy, De Casper and Spence (1986) determined to discover if listening to *The Cat in the Hat* (Dr. Seuss) in the womb would cause them to prefer this story after birth. He had 16 pregnant women read selections from *The Cat in the Hat* twice a day for the last six weeks of their pregnancies.

Approximately 52 hours after birth, the mothers read their babies the selections from *The Cat in the Hat* or different selections from *The King, the Mice, and the Cheese,* which had a different rhythm and pace. The infants reacted quite differently to the readings from *The Cat in the Hat.* (They sucked on a nipple at a significantly different rate to produce their mothers' voices reading *The Cat in the Hat.*) What does this tell us? Two clues to development emerge from this study.

1.   The human brain is programmed to learn before birth. If this is true, and research continually supports these findings, then the implications for those of us concerned with language and reading seem obvious. Far from being an exercise in futility, reading to the fetus during the last weeks of pregnancy becomes an exercise in learning. (For an excellent discussion of the consequences of prenatal taste, smell, and hearing see Eliot, 2000).

2.   The second conclusion we can reach concerns the effect that early exposure to literature has on memory. Obviously, the fetus and then the infant remembered the cadence of *The Cat in the Hat,* which then affected its behavior. As difficult as it may be to believe, by birth the fetus has 100 billion neurons in its brain. Does this imply that we bathe the fetus in a sea of literature? Of course not, but what it does imply is a recognition of how connections between and among neurons can be furthered by reading to the fetus and then the infant.

For example, an infant who is developing *object permanence* thinks an object is gone for good when it disappears and is surprised when it reappears. Janet and Allan Ahlberg's *Peek a Boo Book,* the board edition, is fascinating for children at this developmental stage. The baby peeks through die-cut holes to see members of the family: grandmother, daddy, mommy, and sister performing familiar chores. Jan Ormerod's *Peek a Boo!* also plays this ancient game by illustrating on each page a baby holding objects (such as mittens) up to its face. When the small child pulls open the flap, the baby appears in full.

- The final transition occurs when children move beyond using simple sentences to express one idea to complex sentences expressing multiple ideas and the relations between them.

Recall our previous comments about the number of brain connection formed in the early months and the powerful influence of the environment. Here we see the relationship between the environment and brain growth come to life in language development.

The Pace of Language Acquisition

How does this uniquely human achievement occur? Students of language, attempting to explain the richness and complexity of children's language, are convinced that this feat is possible because of two accomplishments. First, *children learn the rules of their language,* which they then apply in a wide variety of situations. Then, by the end of the second year, *children begin to fast map;* that is, they learn to apply a label to an object without anyone telling them. Even when children don't understand a word, they acquire information about it from the surrounding context (Bjorklund, 2005).

The process of acquiring language goes on at a furious pace until, at about the age of 5 for most children, they have acquired the fundamentals of their language. By the time children enter elementary school, they are sophisticated language users. After that it's a matter of expanding and refining language skills, a task that can often define success or failure.

A SOCIOCULTURAL VIEW

Context and Language

The Russian psychologist, Lev Vygotsky, whose ideas we discussed in Chapter 2 proposed a contextual view of language development that attracted considerable attention. Vygotsky (1978) believed that *speech* is one of the most powerful tools humans use to progress developmentally. Speech, especially inner speech, plays a critical role in Vygotsky's interpretation of cognitive development. In *Thought and Language* (1962), he clearly presented his views about the four stages of language development.

1. The first stage, which he called **preintellectual speech,** refers to such elementary processes as crying, cooing, babbling, and bodily movements that gradually develop into more sophisticated forms of speech and behavior. Although human beings have an inborn ability to develop language, they must then interact with the environment if language development is to fulfill its potential. Michael Cole (1996) employs a garden metaphor to help explain these issues: Think of a seed planted in damp earth in a jar and then placed in a shed for two weeks. The seed sprouts, a stem emerges, and then leaves appear. But for further development the plant must now interact with sunlight.

2. Vygotsky referred to the second stage of language development as "naive psychology," in which children explore the concrete objects in their world. At this stage, children begin to label the objects around them and acquire the grammar of their speech.

3. At about 3 years of age, **egocentric speech** emerges, that form of speech in which children carry on lively conversations, whether anyone is present or listening to them.

4. Finally, speech turns inward (**inner speech**) and serves an important function in guiding and planning behavior. For example, think of a 5-year-old girl asked to get a book from a library shelf. The book is just out of her reach, and as she tries to reach it, she mutters to herself, "Need a chair." After dragging a chair over, she climbs up and reaches for the book. "Is that the one?" "Just a little more." "OK." Note how speech accompanies her physical movements, guiding her behavior. In two or three years, the same girl, asked to do the same thing, will probably act the same way, with one major exception: she won't be talking aloud. Vygotsky believed she would be talking to herself, using inner speech to guide her behavior, and for difficult tasks she undoubtedly would use inner speech *to plan her behavior.*

In many cases, children who aren't permitted these vocalizations *can't accomplish the task!* In fact, the more complex the task, the greater the need for egocentric speech. Note how Vygotsky and Piaget disagreed about the function of egocentric speech: Piaget believed it simply vanishes; Vygosky believed it's an important transitional stage in the formation of inner speech.

preintellectual speech
Vygotsky's expression for crying, cooing, and babbling, which lead to more sophisticated forms of speech.

egocentric speech
Piaget's term to describe children's speech when they do not care to whom they speak or whether a listener is even present.

inner speech
Serves to guide and plan behavior; plays a critical role in Vygotsky's interpretation of cognitive development.

With this brief background, let's turn our attention to what we know about language development. All children learn their native language at about the same time and in a similar manner. During the infancy period, children at about 3 months use sounds in a similar manner to adults, and at about 1 year they begin to use recognizable words. The specific sequence of language development during infancy appears in Table 5.6.

TABLE 5.6   Language Development During Infancy

Language	Age
Crying	From birth
Cooing	2–5 months
Babbling	5–7 months
Single words	12 months
Two words	18 months
Phrases	2 years

Key Signs of Language Development

To begin our discussion, here's a question for you to think about: Since the fetus responds to sound, do you think it's possible that language acquisition begins *before* birth? When a newborn baby is presented with something new, its heart rate slows. Researchers asked several pregnant women to repeat the sentences *Hello, baby. How are you today?* while they rested. Each time the mother asked the question, the fetal heart rate slowed (Golinkoff & Hirsh-Pasek, 2000). It seems indeed that fetuses listen to their mothers' voices.

cooing
Early language sounds that resemble vowels.

During the first two months, babies seem to develop sounds that are associated with breathing, feeding, and crying. **Cooing** (sounds like vowels) appears during the second month. Between 5 and 7 months, babies play with the sounds they can make, and this output begins to take on the sounds of consonants and syllables, the beginning of **babbling.** Babbling probably appears initially because of biological maturation. At 7 and 8 months, sounds like syllables appear—da-da-da, ba-ba-ba (a phenomenon occurring in all languages), a pattern that continues for the remainder of the first year (Pinker, 1994).

babbling
Infant produces sounds approximating speech between 5 and 6 months.

Late in the babbling period, children use consistent sound patterns to refer to objects and events. These are called **vocables** and suggest children's discovery that meaning is associated with sound. For example, a lingering "L" sound may mean that someone is at the door. The use of vocables is a possible link between babbling and the first intelligible words.

vocables
Consistent sound patterns referring to objects and events.

phonology
Sounds of a language.

First Words

semantics
Meaning of words and sentences.

Around their first birthday, babies produce single words, about half of which are for objects (food, clothing, toys). Throughout the world children's first words express similar meanings. These words refer to people, animals, toys, vehicles, and other objects that fascinate children (Siegler, 1998). Children quickly learn the sounds of their language (**phonology**), the meanings of words (**semantics**), how to construct sentences (**syntax**), and how to communicate (**pragmatics**).

syntax
Grammatical ability to construct sentences.

pragmatics
Ability to communicate with others.

At 18 months, children acquire words at the rate of 40 per week (Woodward & Markman, 1998). This rapid increase in vocabulary lasts until about 3 years of age and is frequently referred to as the **word spurt.** Vocabulary constantly expands, but estimating the extent of a child's vocabulary is difficult because youngsters know more words than they articulate.

word spurt
Rapid increase of vocabulary from 18 months to 3 years.

Babbling—producing vowel and consonant sounds—encourages parents to interact verbally with their children. Why is a linguistic environment the richest environment a child can experience?

Estimates are that a 1-year-old child may use from two to six words, and a 2-year-old has a vocabulary ranging from 50 to 250 words. Children at this stage also begin to combine two words (Pinker, 1994). By first grade, children may understand 10,000 words, and by fifth grade they understand about 40,000 words (Woodward & Markman, 1998).

Holophrases

If you have the opportunity, listen to a child's speech when single words begin to appear. You will notice a subtle change before the two-word stage. *Children begin to use one word to convey multiple meanings.* For example, youngsters say "ball" meaning "give me the ball," "throw the ball," or "watch the ball roll." They have now gone far beyond merely labeling this round object as a ball. Often called **holophrastic speech** (one word to communicate many meanings and ideas), it is difficult to analyze. These first words, or **holophrases,** are usually nouns, adjectives, or self-inventive words and often contain multiple meanings. As mentioned previously, "ball" may mean not only the ball itself but "throw the ball to me."

When the two-word stage appears (anytime from 18 to 24 months), children initially struggle to convey tense (past and present) and number (singular and plural). They also experience difficulty with grammatical correctness. Children usually employ word order ("me go") for meaning, only gradually mastering inflections (plurals, tenses, possessives) as they begin to form three-word sentences. They use nouns and verbs initially and their sentences demonstrate grammatical structure. (Although the nouns, verbs, and adjectives of children's sentences differ from those of adults, the same organizational principles are present.)

Children begin to use multiple words to refer to the things that they previously named with single words. Rather than learning rules of word combination to express new ideas, children learn to use new word forms. Later, combining words in phrases and sentences suggests that children are learning the structure of their language.

Telegraphic Speech

At about 18 to 24 months of age, children's vocabularies begin to expand rapidly, and simple two-word sentences appear. Children primarily use nouns and verbs (not adverbs, conjunctions, or prepositions), and their sentences demonstrate grammatical structure. These initial multiple-word utterances (usually two or three words: "mommy milk"—give me the milk) are called **telegraphic speech.** Telegraphic speech contains considerably more meaning than superficially appears in the two or three words.

Word order and inflection (changing word form: for example, "word"/"words") now become increasingly important. During the first stages of language acquisition, word order is paramount. At first, children combine words without concern for inflections, and it is word order that provides clues as to their level of syntactic (grammatical) development. Once two-word sentences are used, inflection soon appears, usually with three-word sentences. The appearance of inflections seems to follow a pattern: first the plural of nouns, then tense and person of verbs, and then possessives.

A youngster's effort to inject grammatical order into language is a good sign of normal language development. Several things, however, signal delay or difficulty in language acquisition. When children begin to babble beyond 1 year, problems may be present. For example, deaf children continue to babble past the age when other children begin to use words (Cole & Cole, 1996).

As we complete this initial phase of examining infant development, remember that all phases of development come together in an integrated manner. Motor

---

holophrastic speech
Use of one word to communicate many meanings and ideas.

holophrase
Children's first words, which usually carry multiple meanings.

telegraphic speech
Initial multiple-word utterances, usually two or three words.

TABLE 5.7	Developmental Characteristics of Infancy

Age (months)	Height (in.)	Weight (lbs.)	Language Development	Motor Development	Cognitive (Piaget)
3	24	13–14	Cooing	Supports head in prone position	Primary circular reactions
6	26	17–18	Babbling: single syllable sounds	Sits erect when supported	Secondary circular reactions
9	26	20–22	Repetition of sounds signals emotions	Stands with support	Coordinate secondary schemata
12	29.5	22–24	Single words: mama, dada	Walks when held by hand	Same
18	32	25–26	3–50 words	Grasps objects accurately, walks steadily	Tertiary circular reaction
24	34	27–29	50–250 words, 2–3-word sentences	Walks and runs up and down stairs	Representation

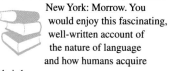

S. Pinker (1994). *The Language Instinct.* New York: Morrow. You would enjoy this fascinating, well-written account of the nature of language and how humans acquire their language.

development is involved when a child moves excitedly toward its mother on her return. Language development is involved when infants intensify their relationships with their mothers by words that are now directed toward her. Cognitive development is probably less obvious but just as significant: Children are excited by their mothers' return because they remember their mothers. Consequently, a sound principle of development remains—all development is integrated.

Finally, it's important to remember that about 5% of children under the age of 3 in the United States are diagnosed each year with a developmental delay. That is, they fall behind the normal child of the same age in one or more aspects of development: physical, cognitive, language, social, or emotional (Meltz, 2004).

Table 5.7 summarizes several of the developmental highlights we have discussed in this chapter.

Guided Review

16. _____ refers to sounds that approximate speech.
17. One word used to communicate many meanings is called _____ speech.
18. Vygotsky's work reflects a _____ view of language development.
19. A good sign of normal language development is a child's attempt to build _____ order into language.
20. For Vygotsky, _____ _____ plays a key role in cognitive development.

Answers

16. Babbling 17. holophrastic 18. cultural 19. grammatical 20. inner speech

CONCLUSION & SUMMARY

Our view of an infant today is of an individual of enormous potential, one whose activity and competence are much greater than originally suspected. It is as if a newborn enters the world with all its systems ready to function and eager for growth. What happens during the first two years has important implications for future development. Setbacks—both physical and psychological—will occur, but they need not cause permanent damage. From your reading in Chapter 1, you realize that human infants show remarkable resiliency.

What are the major physical accomplishments of the infancy period?

- Newborns display clear signs of their competence: movement, seeing, hearing, interacting.
- Infants' physical and motor abilities influence all aspects of development.
- Techniques to assess infant competence and well-being are widely used today.

- Motor development follows a well-documented schedule.
- Infants can develop problems such as SIDS and FTT for a variety of reasons.

How do infants acquire information about their world?

- Infants are born with the ability to detect changes in their environment.
- Infants are capable of acquiring and interpreting information from their immediate surroundings.
- Infants from birth show preferences for certain types of stimuli.

What are the differences between Piaget's view of cognitive development in infancy and that of information processing?

- Infants, even at this early age, attempt to answer questions about their world, questions that will continue to occupy them in more

complex and sophisticated forms throughout their lives.
- One of the first tasks that infants must master is an understanding of the objects around them.
- Piaget's theory of cognitive development has shed considerable light on the ways that children grow mentally.
- A key element in understanding an infant's cognitive development is the role of memory.

How do infants acquire their language?

- Infants show rapid growth in their language development.
- Language acquisition follows a definite sequence.
- Language behaviors in infancy range from crying to the use of words and phrases.

KEY TERMS

Apgar
apnea
babbling
binocular coordination
Brazelton Neonatal Behavioral Scale
cooing
coordination of secondary schemes
crawling
creeping
egocentric speech
egocentrism
failure to thrive

habituation
holophrases
holophrastic speech
infantile amnesia
inner speech
neonate
neurological assessment
object permanence
perception
phonology
pragmatics
preintellectual speech

primary circular reactions
reflex
respiratory distress syndrome
secondary circular reactions
semantics
sensorimotor period
sudden infant death syndrome (SIDS)
syntax
telegraphic speech
tertiary circular reactions
vocables
word spurt

WHAT DO YOU THINK?

1. The shift from considering an infant as nothing more than a passive sponge to seeing infants as amazingly competent carries with it certain responsibilities. We can't be overly optimistic about a baby's abilities. Why? What are some of

the more common dangers of this viewpoint?

2. Testing infants has grown in popularity these past years. You should consider some cautions, however. Remembering what you have read about infants in this chapter, men-

tion several facts you would be careful about.

3. You have been asked to babysit your sister's 14-month-old baby. When you arrive, the mother is upset because she has been repeatedly picking up things that the baby

has thrown out of the crib. With your new knowledge, you calm her down by explaining the baby's behavior. What do you tell her?

4. After reviewing the infancy work, what do you think about this period as "preparation for the future"? Select one phase of development (for

example, cognitive development) and show how a stimulating environment can help to lay the foundation for future cognitive growth.

CHAPTER REVIEW TEST

1. **Which of the following is not a reflex?**
   a. breathing
   b. sucking
   c. swallowing
   d. laughing

2. **A _____ reflex is elicited by gently touching the infant's cheek.**
   a. Moro
   b. rooting
   c. Babkin
   d. Babinski

3. **_____ is a brief period when an infant stops breathing.**
   a. Apnea
   b. Rooting
   c. Babbling
   d. Primary circular reactions

4. **Depth perception in infants appears at**
   a. birth.
   b. 7 to 10 days.
   c. 2 to 4 months.
   d. 4 to 5 months.

5. **The Brazelton test assesses an infant's**
   a. interaction with the environment.
   b. respiratory effort.
   c. reflex irritability.
   d. hearing.

6. **Neurological assessment is not used for which of the following purposes?**
   a. identification of a neurological problem
   b. treatment of a neurological problem
   c. monitoring a neurological problem
   d. prognosis about a neurological problem

7. **The final area of the brain to develop is the**
   a. sensory region.
   b. motor area.
   c. visual area.
   d. auditory area.

8. **_____ is a disorder caused by the lack of a substance called *surfactant.***
   a. SIDS
   b. RDS
   c. AIDS
   d. FTT

9. **When infants demonstrate a decrease in attention, this is called _____.**
   a. repression.
   b. habituation.
   c. egocentrism.
   d. permanence.

10. **The Brazelton test is a type of**
    a. survival assessment.
    b. motor assessment.
    c. play assessment.
    d. behavioral assessment.

11. **Infants from _____ show preferences for certain types of stimuli.**
    a. birth
    b. 10 days
    c. 2 months
    d. 6 months

12. **An infant's search for novelty during the sensorimotor period is seen in**
    a. object permanence.
    b. secondary circular reactions.
    c. coordination of secondary schemes.
    d. tertiary circular reactions.

13. **Infants initially show memory ability during**
    a. weeks 2 and 3.
    b. months 1 to 3.
    c. months 3 to 6.
    d. months 6 to 12.

14. **In the development of language, children about 1 year of age begin to use recognizable**
    a. vocables.
    b. holophrases.

c. phrases.
    d. sentences.

15. **According to Piaget, the acquisition of language in children depends on**
    a. cognitive structures.
    b. biology.
    c. reinforcement.
    d. language acquisition devices.

16. **By _____ months a child begins to run.**
    a. 9
    b. 12
    c. 24
    d. 18

17. **Which of the following is not a major accomplishment of the sensorimotor period?**
    a. reversibility
    b. sense of space
    c. causality
    d. time sequence

18. **_____ argue that cognitive development occurs by the gradual improvement of such cognitive processes as attention and memory.**
    a. Psychoanalysts
    b. Behaviorists
    c. humanists
    d. Information processing theorists

19. **A 2-year-old child may have a vocabulary of as many as _____ words.**
    a. 250
    b. 500
    c. 1,000
    d. 2,000

20. **_____ believed the roots of language and thought were separate and become linked only through development.**
    a. Chomsky
    b. Lenneberg
    c. Vygotsky
    d. Piaget

Answers
1.d 2.b 3.a 4.d 5.a 6.b 7.c 8.b 9.b 10.d 11.a 12.d 13.d 14.c 15.a 16.d 17.a 18.d 19.a 20.c

6 chapter

PSYCHOSOCIAL DEVELOPMENT IN INFANCY

Chapter Objectives

After reading this chapter, you should be able to answer the following questions.

- What is the role of relationships in psychosocial development?

- How do children develop and control their emotions?

- How would you assess the importance of attachment in psychosocial development?

- How does temperament affect the relationship between parents and their children?

John Bowlby knew. Bowlby, the founder of attachment theory, from his theorizing and research, came to realize how important an infant's relationships are to satisfactory and healthy psychosocial development. His work for the World Health Organization following World War II alerted him to the problems that arise when a child is separated from a mother figure.

Indeed, we held the view that the responses of protest, despair, and detachment that typically occur when a young child aged over 6 months is separated from the mother and in the care of a stranger are due mainly to loss of maternal care at this highly dependent, highly vulnerable stage of development. (Bowlby, 1969, p. XIII)

The reciprocal interactions between parents and their children are at the heart of the attachment process. What aspects of development is this mother encouraging?

Mary Salter Ainsworth knew. A former worker in Bowlby's lab in London, she was intrigued by his ideas and eventually devised a means of assessing the emotional bond between mother and child. As she looked back on her work, she summarized the importance of attachment in an infant's life as follows.

The implication is that the way in which the infant organizes his or her behavior toward the mother affects the way in which he or she organizes behavior toward other aspects of the environment, both animate and inanimate. The organization provides a core of continuity in development despite changes that come with developmental acquisitions, both cognitive and socioemotional. (Ainsworth, 1979, p. 936)

Indeed, the roots of attachment theory have burrowed deeply into the terrain of modern psychology:

But whatever the lingering controversies over attachment theory, it's now charting new directions for both mental-health practice and policy. New research in the neurobiology of bonding has put the theory on ever-stronger empirical footing. (Kendall, 2003, pp. 3, 5)

Beginning at about 6 months of age, infants show signs of distress when approached by a stranger. How do you explain this baby's fear of a stranger?

Children learn what to expect from others because, as we have seen, their rapid brain and cognitive development enables them to take in and interpret information, and some of this information is about how others, especially parents, treat them. Although they may not grasp everything that's going on around them, children understand the quality of their treatment: caring/cold, loving/hostile. *These initial relationships, then, are the foundation for a child's social development.*

These are the years that Erikson believed resulted in a sense of trust or mistrust. Infants develop the feeling that the world is a safe and secure haven or a place where a sense of confidence is never acquired, producing uncertainty about self and others.

To help us untangle this important network, we first discuss the meaning and the importance of relationships (such as the active role that infants play in their own development). Next, we'll explore the special relationship—attachment—that has attracted so much attention these past few years. We'll then examine how the temperaments of children and their parents structure the kind of relationships they form. Finally, we'll see how these forces interact to affect emotional development. Let's begin by looking at several basic ideas about relationships.

THE MEANING OF RELATIONSHIPS

Infancy implies beginnings, the early formation of characteristics, skills, and dispositions that may last a lifetime.

—Ross Thompson

Research into the role of relationships in development has increased substantially since the previous edition of this book, not only with regard to parent-child relationships but also with regard to other family members (Eisenberg, 2006). This explosion of interest has carried over from academic pursuits to a public fascination seen in popular magazines and numerous trade books (Rubin, Bukowski, & Parker, 2006).

To start us on our analysis, think of a relationship as *a pattern of intermittent interactions between two people involving interchanges over an extended period of time* (Hinde, 1993). A child's relationships incorporate many aspects of development: *physical aspects* such as walking, running, and playing with a peer; *language aspects,* which enable youngsters to share their lives; *cognitive aspects,* which allow them to understand one another; *emotional aspects,* which permit them to make a commitment to another person; and *social aspects,* which reflect both socialization and individuation. In other words, a relationship is a superb example of the influence of *biopsychosocial interactions.*

Infants are ready to respond to social stimulation, but it's not just a matter of responding passively. Infants in their own way initiate social contacts. Many of their actions (such as turning toward their mothers or gesturing in their direction) are forms of communication. Hinde (1993), too, noted that the interchange between infants and their environments is an active one. Those around infants try to attract their attention, but the babies actively select from these adult actions. In other words, infants begin to structure their own relationships according to their individual temperaments. They do this within the family context. The interactions occurring among the other family members—parent-parent, parent-other children, sibling-sibling—produce a ripple effect that colors the parent-child relationship. Marital conflict, for example, inevitably spills over into the relationship between parents and their children and may produce unexpected results such as physical illness or tension in the child (and may even affect his or her peer relations; Eisenberg, 2006). Consequently, the nature of the relationship between parents and their children emerges from the temperament and characteristics of each, and the interactions that occur (Rubin, Bukowski, & Parker, 2006).

For most people, relationships with other people are the most important part of their lives.

—Robert Hinde

Characteristics of the Developing Relationship

In their classic statement on the "earliest relationship" (parent-infant), Brazelton and Cramer (1990) list several characteristics that identify the emergence of a successful relationship:

synchrony
Ability of parents to adjust their behavior to that of an infant.

1. First is **synchrony,** which refers to the ability of parents to adjust their behavior to that of an infant. Immediately after birth, infants are mostly occupied by their efforts to regulate such systems as breathing and heart rate, which demand most of their energy and attention. Once parents recognize these efforts—the baby's "language" (Brazelton & Cramer, 1990)—they can use their own behavior—talking softly, stroking—to help their infants adapt to environmental stimuli. This mutual regulation of behavior defines synchrony.

symmetry
Infant's capacity for attention; style of responding influences interactions.

2. A second characteristic is **symmetry,** which means that an infant's capacity for attention and style of responding influence any interactions. In other words, how children interact with their parents reflects their temperaments. As Brazelton and Cramer (1990, p. 122) note, in a symmetric dialogue parents recognize an infant's thresholds, that is, what and how much stimuli an infant can tolerate.

entrainment
Term used to describe the rhythm that is established between a parent's and an infant's behavior.

3. A third characteristic is **entrainment,** which identifies the rhythm that is established between a parent's and an infant's behavior. For example, when the infant reaches toward the mother, the mother says something like "Oh, yes, Timmy." The sequence involved in entrainment leads to playing games, such as the mother making a face at the baby and the infant trying to respond similarly.

autonomy
Infants' realization that they have a share in controlling their interactions with others.

4. Finally, once infants realize that they have a share in controlling the interactions (about 6 months of age), they begin to develop a sense of **autonomy.** With these interactions, infants are beginning to form relationships and learn about themselves.

We turn now to the manner in which infants begin to develop their relationships.

How Do Children Develop Relationships?

Infants quickly focus on their mothers as they recognize them as sources of relief and satisfaction. Mothers, in turn, rapidly discriminate their infants' cries: for hunger, attention, or fright. Thus infants learn to direct their attention to their mothers, and a pattern of interactions is established. How do we explain this development? Three motives seem to be at work:

Infants immediately begin to take in information from their environment, and mothers are an important source of this information. From mothers, infants begin to develop a sense of how the world will treat them. Can you identify the multiple stimuli this mother is using?

- *Bodily needs*—food, for example—lead to a series of interactions that soon become a need for social interaction.

- *Psychological needs* can cause infants to interrupt one of their most important functions, such as feeding. Children, from birth, seem to seek novelty; they require increasingly challenging stimulation. For infants, adults become the source of information as much as the source of bodily need satisfaction.

- *Adult response needs.* Adults satisfy needs, provide stimulation, and initiate communication, thus establishing the basis for future social interactions.

How do these three influences—at work during the infant's early days—affect the development of relationships?

The Developmental Sequence

Bodily need satisfaction, a search for novelty, and adult responses to the infant's overtures form a basis for the appearance of social interactions similar to the following sequence.

- *During the first three weeks* of life, infants are not affected much by an adult's appearance. The only exception, as noted, is during feeding periods.

- *From about the beginning of the fourth week,* infants begin to direct actions toward adults. Emotional reactions also appear at this time, with obvious signs of pleasure at the sight and sound of adults, especially females.

- *During the second month,* more complex and sensitive reactions emerge, such as smiling and vocalizations directed at the mother, plus animated behavior during interactions.

- *By 3 months of age,* the infant has formed a need for social interactions. This need continues to grow and be nourished by adults until the end of the second or beginning of the third year, when a need for peer interactions develops (Hinde, 1987, 1992).

T. B. Brazelton and B. Cramer (1990). You should enjoy reading *The Earliest Relationship.* (Reading, MA: Addison-Wesley), an excellent, readable account of how relationships develop, presented from both a pediatric and a psychoanalytic perspective.

Guided Review

1. A relationship is a pattern of intermittent _____.
2. Infants quickly begin to _____ their relatonships.
3. _____ _____ is an important influence on developing relationships.
4. The nature of a relationship emerges from the _____ of the partners.
5. A relationship is an excellent example of _____ interactions.

We can usually label relationships, using adjectives such as warm, cold, rejecting, and hostile. But we must be cautious. Any relationship may be marked by apparently contradictory interactions. A mother may have a warm relationship with her child as evidenced by hugging and kissing, but she may also scold when scolding is needed for the child's protection. *To understand the relationship, we must understand the interactions.*

The Role of Reciprocal Interactions

We realize today that children are not born as passive sponges; they immediately seek stimulation from their environment and *instantly interpret, and react to, how they are being treated,* a process called **reciprocal interactions.** Think of it this way: You react to me in a particular manner and I change. As a result of the changes that occur in me, you change. Back-and-forth, on-and-on it goes, constantly changing

reciprocal interactions
Interactions that result in mutual changes

Answers

1. interactions 2. structure 3. Family context 4. characteristics 5. biopsychosocial

the relationship. Consequently, we can now examine an infant's psychosocial development from a totally new and exciting perspective. Not only do infants attempt to make sense of their world as they develop cognitively, they also "tune into" the social and emotional atmosphere surrounding them and immediately begin to shape their relationships with others.

Thinking about the type of interactions parents have with their children helps you to appreciate how the relationship has developed. For example, consider the kinds of things parents do with their children and the way they do them—all involving interactions. They play. They discipline. They explain. They provide correction and feedback. They answer questions. In other words, they're exercising their parental role in all these interactions with their children. Analyzing these interactions helps you to realize that parents change as a result of their child's behavior, and their children change in turn because of their parents' reactions. These *reciprocal interactions* demonstrate continuity over time and are a powerful force in the development of relationships (Freitag et al., 1996).

But infants also exercise some control over the interactions. We, as adults, respond to infants partly because of the way that they respond to us. An infant's staring, cooing, smiling, and kicking can all be employed to maintain the interactions. Thus these early interactions establish the nature of the relationship between parent and child, giving it a particular tone or style.

To understand the developing relationship between parents and infants, remember that infants "tune into" their environment from birth. Thus they react to far more than their parents' behavior; they react to the way their parents handle them, the tone of voice a parent uses, and the playful nature of interactions. Consequently, the quality of the interactions instantly begins to establish the nature of the relationship (Thompson, 2006).

Parental Roles: Expectations for a Relationship

Finally, parents bring basic preconceived ideas about the role they should play in their relationships with their children. Technically, *role* usually refers to behavior, or certain expectancies about behavior, associated with a particular position in society. Mothers and fathers have certain expectations about how parents should act. *How they exercise that power and how their children react to their suggestions and encouragements, their demands and commands, ultimately determine the success of the relationship.* In an ideal world, their ideas, their expectations, and their sense of their role as a parent should mesh perfectly with their child's personality and abilities (Chess & Thomas, 1999).

Ghosts in the Nursery

Let's pause for a moment and consider one source of their expectations about their parental role. Selma Fraiberg, a well-known child psychiatrist, has referred to the presence of *ghosts in the nursery,* which can have many consequences (1987). Do parents feel their own parents looking over their shoulder, telling them how to bring up their child, ideas that they may well have rejected or even rebelled against? Does their child remind them of someone from their past, and they begin to react as they did to that other person? Do they tend to imitate a friend whom they admire? Or have they been impressed by the ideas of some "expert" they have read about or have seen on television?

When parents are aware that ghosts from their past may influence them, they usually attempt to overcome these relics and move on to positive relations with their children. Many qualities, however, affect the nature of the relationship, such

Parents' own experiences and their expectations of their children's behavior help to shape the relationships they develop with their children. Can you summarize the experiences and the expectations that shape parental behavior?

FIGURE 6.1

The origin and development
of relationships.

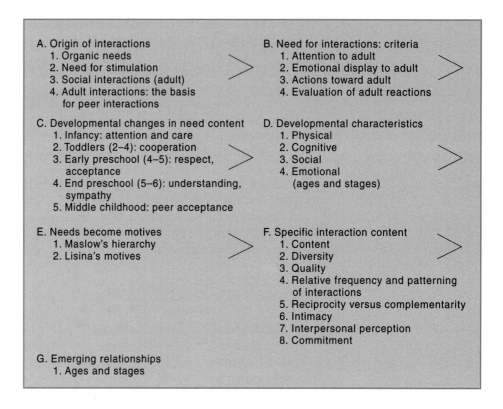

A. Origin of interactions
1. Organic needs
2. Need for stimulation
3. Social interactions (adult)
4. Adult interactions: the basis
for peer interactions

B. Need for interactions: criteria
1. Attention to adult
2. Emotional display to adult
3. Actions toward adult
4. Evaluation of adult reactions

C. Developmental changes in need content
1. Infancy: attention and care
2. Toddlers (2–4): cooperation
3. Early preschool (4–5): respect,
acceptance
4. End preschool (5–6): understanding,
sympathy
5. Middle childhood: peer acceptance

D. Developmental characteristics
1. Physical
2. Cognitive
3. Social
4. Emotional
(ages and stages)

E. Needs become motives
1. Maslow's hierarchy
2. Lisina's motives

F. Specific interaction content
1. Content
2. Diversity
3. Quality
4. Relative frequency and patterning
of interactions
5. Reciprocity versus complementarity
6. Intimacy
7. Interpersonal perception
8. Commitment

G. Emerging relationships
1. Ages and stages

as warmth, consistency, cultural traditions, and so on. Figure 6.1 illustrates the sequence by which the first interactions, combined with developmental changes, gradually lead to specific relationships.

As the interactions between mother and child increase and become more complex, let's now examine the attachment that develops between the two.

A SOCIOCULTURAL VIEW | *Different Cultures, Different Interactions*

As we have noted in our discussions of the effect of culture on development, from birth children are exposed to and shaped by the culture surrounding them. Their cultural context includes everything from sleeping arrangements and feeding practices to the child's value systems, school experiences, and interpersonal interactions. But the way in which children's needs are met within their culture varies tremendously (Saarni et al., 2006).

Parents from a particular culture share a common system of beliefs, values, practices, and behaviors that differ from those of parents in other cultures. These beliefs, in turn, lead to a determination of the kinds of events children should experience. For example, research has clearly demonstrated that infants in northern Germany are exposed to avoidant patterns of attachment. As one instance shows, these German infants are frequently left alone outside a shop while the mother briefly goes inside. In Japan, however, mothers remain in close proximity to their infants. Japanese infants are rarely separated from their mothers. Cultures also differ in

their reaction to eye contact. In most Western societies, looking into a baby's eyes is seen as "looking into a baby's soul." In some African societies, however, eye contact is discouraged. These different parental practices commence immediately following birth.

But merely identifying specific differences in raising children in different cultures limits our perspective on development. As Garcia Coll and others (1996) have noted:

In addition, studies of children of color need to move from conceptualizing developmental outcome as either negative or positive to a more balanced conceptualization that reflects both the strengths and weaknesses in developmental processes and competencies of these children (Garcia Coll et al., 1996, p. 1895).

(For a detailed and comprehensive examination of this subject, we recommend Special Issue on Race, Ethnicity, and Culture in Child Development, *Child Development*, 77(5), September/October, 2006.)

ATTACHMENT

attachment
Behavior intended to keep a child (or adult) in close proximity to a significant other.

ethology
Study of behavior in natural settings.

Because the roots of future relationships are formed during the first days of life, we may well ask: How significant is the mother-infant relationship in those first days and weeks after birth? Infants who develop a secure **attachment** to their mothers have the willingness and confidence to seek out future relationships. As Thompson (2006) notes, attachment figures are secure bases that encourage infants to explore their environments but remain reliable retreats when stress and uncertainty appear. Among the first researchers to recognize the significance of relationships in an infant's life were John Bowlby and Mary Salter Ainsworth. (For an excellent discussion of the history and background of the attachment movement, see Robert Karen [1994]. *Becoming Attached.* New York: Warner Books.)

Bowlby's Work

John Bowlby was a man not easily forgotten. With his shock of unruly white hair, confident manner, and brilliant mind, he was a commanding presence in the initial days of the attachment battles. Early in his professional career, Bowlby had been affected by the plight of children suffering from negative family experiences early in life (such as prolonged separation from their mothers).

Using concepts from psychology and **ethology** (the study of behavior in natural settings; Hinde, 1993), Bowlby formulated his basic premise: A warm, intimate relationship between mother and infant is essential to mental health, because a child's need for its mother's presence is as great as its need for food. A mother's continued absence can generate a sense of loss and feelings of anger. (In his 1969 classic, *Attachment,* Bowlby states quite clearly that an infant's principal attachment figure can be someone other than the natural mother.)

Background of Attachment Theory

Bowlby and his colleagues, especially James Robertson, initiated a series of studies in which children aged 15 to 30 were separated from their parents. (They had been placed either in hospitals or residential nurseries.) A predictable sequence of behaviors followed. *Protest,* the first phase, may begin immediately and persist for about one week. Loud crying, extreme restlessness, and rejection of all adult figures mark

Both parent and child bring their own characteristics to the relationship (facial expressions, movements, vocalizations), and as they do, the interactions between the two become more complex and an attachment slowly develops between the two. Can you discuss the many parental behaviors that help to produce attachment?

an infant's distress. *Despair,* the second phase, follows. The infant's behavior suggests a growing hopelessness: monotonous crying, inactivity, and steady withdrawal. *Detachment,* the final phase, appears when an infant displays renewed interest in its surroundings—but a remote, distant kind of interest. Bowlby describes the behavior of this final phase as apathetic, even if the mother reappears.

From observation of many similar cases, Bowlby defined attachment as follows:

Attachment behavior is any form of behavior that results in a person attaining or maintaining proximity to some other clearly identified individual who is conceived as better able to cope with the world. It is most obvious when the person is frightened, fatigued, or sick, and is assuaged by comforting and care-giving. At other times the behavior is less in evidence. (1982, p. 668)

Bowlby also believed that although attachment is most obvious in infancy and early childhood, it can be observed throughout the life cycle (Hamilton, 2000; Kerns et al., 2000; Waters et al., 2000). Table 6.1 presents a chronology of attachment behavior.

Attachment Research

A child's behaviors indicate attachment only when they are specifically directed at one or a few persons rather than to others. When infants first direct their attention to their mothers, they are attempting to initiate and maintain interactions with their mothers. Children also attempt to avoid separation from an attachment figure, particularly if faced with a frightening situation (Thompson, 2006; Waters & Cummings, 2000). Attachment theorists believe that a mother's (or some other adult's) sensitivity helps to determine the degree and quality of an infant's security. But, as we have seen in our discussion of reciprocal interactions, the child also contributes to the relationship.

J. Bowlby (1969). *Attachment.* New York: Basic Books. This is Bowlby's classic statement about attachment. It's very readable and is a reference with which you should be familiar.

TABLE 6.1	Chronology of Attachment Development	
Age	*Characteristics*	*Behavior*
4 months	Perceptual discrimination; visual tracking of mother	Smiles and vocalizes more with mother than anyone else; shows distress at separation
9 months	Separation anxiety; stranger anxiety	Cries when mother leaves; clings at appearance of strangers (mother is primary object)
2–3 years	Intensity and frequency of attachment behavior remains constant	Notices impending departure, indicating a better understanding of surrounding world
3–4 years	Growing confidence; tendency to feel secure in a strange place with subordinate attachment figures (relatives)	Begins to accept mother's temporary absence; plays *with* other children
4–10 years	Less intense attachment behavior, but still strong	May hold parent's hand while walking; anything unexpected causes child to turn to parent
Adolescence	Weakening attachment to parents; peers and other adults become important	Becomes attached to groups and group members
Adult	Attachment bond still discernible	In troubled times, adults turn to trusted friends; elderly direct attention to younger generation

Source: From John Bowlby, "Attachment and Loss: Retrospect and Prospect" in *American Journal of Orthopsychiatry,* 52: 664–678. Reprinted with permission from the *American Journal of Orthopsychiatry.* Copyright © 1982 by the American Orthopsychiatry Association, Inc.

The Strange Situation Technique

To assess the quality of attachment, a student of Bowlby's, Mary Salter Ainsworth, devised the **strange situation.** Ainsworth (1973, 1979; Ainsworth & Bowlby, 1991), who accepted Bowlby's theoretical interpretation of attachment, devised the strange situation technique to study attachment experimentally.

Ainsworth had a mother and infant taken to an observation room. The child was placed on the floor and allowed to play with toys. A stranger (female) then entered the room and began to talk to the mother. Observers watched to see how the infant reacted to the stranger and to what extent the child used the mother as a secure base. The mother then left the child alone in the room with the stranger; observers then noted how distressed the child became. The mother returned and the quality of the child's reaction to the mother's return was assessed. Next the infant was left completely alone, followed by the stranger's entrance, and then that of the mother. These behaviors have been used to classify children as follows:

- *Securely attached children,* who use their mothers as a base from which to explore. Separation intensifies their attachment behavior; they exhibit considerable distress, cease their explorations, and at reunion seek contact with their mothers.

- *Avoidantly attached children,* who rarely cry during separation and avoid their mothers at reunion. The mothers of these babies seem to dislike or are indifferent to physical contact.

- *Ambivalently attached children,* who manifest anxiety before separation and who are intensely distressed by the separation. Yet on reunion they display ambivalent behavior toward their mothers; they seek contact but simultaneously seem to resist it.

- *Disorganized/disoriented children,* who show a kind of confused behavior at reunion. For example, they may look at the mother and then look away, showing little emotion (Main, 1996).

Ainsworth also believed that attachment knows no geographic boundaries. Reporting on her studies of infant-mother attachment in Uganda, Ainsworth (1973) noted that of 28 infants she observed, 23 showed signs of attachment. She was impressed by the babies' initiative in attempting to establish attachment with their mothers and noted that the babies demonstrated this initiative even when no threat of separation or any condition that could cause anxiety existed. In tracing the developing pattern of attachment behavior, Ainsworth (1973) stated:

> *The baby did not first become attached and then show it by proximity-promoting behavior . . . rather . . . these are the patterns of behavior through which attachment grows.* (p. 35)

Ainsworth reported other studies, conducted in Baltimore, Washington, and Scotland, indicating that cultural influences may affect the ways in which different attachment behaviors develop. Nevertheless, although these studies used quite different subjects for their studies, all reported attachment behavior developing in a similar manner.

Continuing Attachment Research

An added tool in attachment research has been the development of the **Adult Attachment Interview (AAI),** which examines the responses of parents to determine if they maintain a coherent, relevant discussion of their early attachments (Main, 1996). Their answers are then linked to the quality of their children's attachment. Based on their responses, adults are classified as follows.

- *Autonomous.* These individuals value relationships, believe that their attachments help their development, and give consistent and coherent answers.

- *Dismissing.* These individuals denied the influence of attachments on their lives and showed memory lapses, and their positive expressions about their parents were inconsistent and contradictory.
- *Preoccupied.* These individuals speak of their parents in an angry, incoherent manner.
- *Unresolved/disorganized.* These individuals reflected a sense of unresolved loss in their answers.

Differences in responses to the questions of the AAI (that is, how truthful, clear, and orderly are the responses) predict the attachment categories of their infants (secure, insecure, and so on), both when the questions are asked *before and after birth* (Main, 1996).

Recent research (Adam, Gunnar, & Tanaka, 2004) into the relationship between adult attachment and parenting behavior offers several interesting conclusions. For example, a link was seen between adult attachment and maternal emotional well-being and parenting behavior.

Continued research into the application of the AAI has focused on asking respondents to look back on their own childhood attachment. During a one-hour interview, people are asked to support their memories by supplying evidence. For example, they are asked to furnish five adjectives describing their relationship to each parent. Later during the interview, they're questioned about specific incidents supporting their earlier answers. Parental responses have been coded into categories that relate to the quality of their infants' attachment (see Table 6.2).

Attachment researchers are also examining representational processes; that is, they're focusing on the relationship between early attachment and a child's drawings and stories in middle childhood. For example, when presented with instances of children who were separated from their mothers, secure 6-year-olds made up positive, constructive responses about the child in the story. But disorganized children gave frightened responses: "The mother is going to die," "The girl will kill herself." Continued studies (Lewis, Feiring, & Rosenthal, 2000; Weinfield, Sroufe, & Egeland, 2000) indicate that in high-risk samples (divorce, desertion, abuse, maternal depression) stability of attachment from the early years to adulthood was lacking.

Finally, researchers are placing greater emphasis on the cultural impact on attachment. Theorists have long held that culture influences specific behaviors and that there is a substantial core of attachment that is immune from cultural influence. Consequently, the more universal aspects of the theory are receiving closer scrutiny.

TABLE 6.2 The Adult Attachment Interview	
Adult Attachment Interview	*Strange Situation Response*
Secure/Autonomous: Coherent, values attachment, accepts any unpleasant, earlier experiences	*Secure*
Dismissing: Positive statements are unsupported or contradicted; they claim earlier unpleasant experiences have no effect	*Avoidant*
Preoccupied: Seems angry, confused, passive, or fearful; some responses irrelevant	*Resistant/Ambivalent*
Unfocused/Disorganized: Loses train of thought during discussion of loss or abuse; lapses in reasoning (speaks of dead people as alive)	*Disorganized/Disoriented*

AN INFORMED VIEW | Attachment and Children's Literature

As we have seen in our discussion of infancy in Chapters 5 and 6, certain developmental features lend themselves to desirable childcare practices. For example, we know that:

- The human brain is programmed to learn even before birth.
- Children of these years prefer certain kinds of objects, colors, forms, and so on.
- They continue to develop object permanence.
- They require definite signs of comfort and security from their parents.

When infants, in times of stress and uncertainty, feel that they lack a secure base to depend on, they develop feelings of doubt, lack of confidence, and so forth, reflecting Main's disorganized/disoriented category. To help these children, adults often turn to stories in children's literature. As one example, children in later infancy enjoy listening to the stories of Paul Galdone. Galdone

has retold and illustrated many familiar folktales through the years, such as *The Three Billy Goats Gruff, The Elves and the Shoemaker, The Three Little Pigs, The Little Red Hen, The Gingerbread Boy,* and *The Teeny-Tiny Woman.*

Fortunately, many of these enduring folktales have been reissued recently, so they continue to bring pleasure to a new generation of children. His characters are easily identifiable and nonthreatening. Most have pleasant, smiling faces—even his animals smile. When reading books like these to children in late infancy, caregivers provide them with a zone of comfortable security whether the wolf is destroying the pig's house or the gingerbread boy is running away from home.

If you would like to have a more informed view on this issue, you may want to read Barbara Travers and John F. Travers (2009), *Children's Literature: A Developmental Perspective.* New York: John Wiley. You may also wish to learn more about it by going to our website at www.mhhe.com/dacey7.

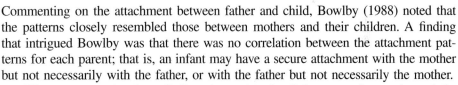

We have focused on the attachment between mothers and their children because most of the research has examined this relationship. What can we say about the attachment between fathers and their infants?

Fathers and Attachment

The interactions between a father and his child tend to be more physical than those between a mother and her child. The qualitatively different types of stimulation a child receives from each parent would seem to suggest implications for the staffing of day-care centers and preschool facilities. Can you expand on the notion of active, engaged fathering?

Commenting on the attachment between father and child, Bowlby (1988) noted that the patterns closely resembled those between mothers and their children. A finding that intrigued Bowlby was that there was no correlation between the attachment patterns for each parent; that is, an infant may have a secure attachment with the mother but not necessarily with the father, or with the father but not necessarily the mother.

We can summarize these findings by stating that fathers contribute substantially to the financial, social, and emotional healthy development of their children, but not by physical presence alone. The effect of a father's role in his child's life, especially a nurturing, caring father to whom the child is attached, cannot be overlooked. As Hetherington and Kelly noted (2002), a child doesn't become psychologically well-adjusted just because Dad is there. To instill stability and competence in a child requires active, engaged fathering over a period of time.

Differences in Mother/Father Behavior

Research has also focused on demonstrating the differences between mothers' and fathers' behavior (nurturant versus playful), the similarity between parental behaviors (both exhibit considerable sensitivity), and the amount of involvement in the infant's care. Mothers are more verbal, tend to offer toys, and play more conventional games. In a relaxed setting, both parents seem to have equal attractions as attachment figures. When infants are hungry or sick, however, they turn more to their mothers. Fathers, however, provide more unpredictable, less rhythmic, and more exciting stimulation than mothers do.

As you can tell from this brief summary, more research is needed to help us understand the dynamics of the interaction between fathers and their infants

(Parke, 2002). Although probably thousands of studies have been done about the mother-child relationship, to date only 17 known studies have compared the child's attachment to his father (Lewis, 1997). To conclude this section, we turn to Lewis' statement (1997) that the presence of an adult male, usually the father, is quite important for children's development. (For an excellent discussion of the father's role in development in our modern society, see Cabrera et al., 2000.)

Since we know that both adults and children contribute to the quality of attachment, let's turn now to the role that temperament plays in this process.

Guided Review

11. An early researcher into the significant relationships in an infant's life was _____.

12. Following separation from their mothers, Bowlby found a predictable sequence of behaviors: _____, _____, _____.

13. Attachment characterized by separation or stranger anxiety usually begins at the age of _____ months.

14. Adults' memories of their early attachments are assessed by the _____ _____ _____.

15. _____ is known for the strange situation technique.

TEMPERAMENT

One of the most important dynamics in parents' relationship with their children is temperament. **Temperament** technically refers to constitutionally based individual differences in emotional, motor, and attentional reactivity and self-regulation (Rothbart & Bates, 2006). Simply put, a child's temperament refers to a unique and stable style of behaving (Thompson, 1999). *Each child is different at birth and must be treated differently.*

Thus temperament is a critical personality trait, especially in the first days and weeks after birth, a trait that is both stable and fairly persistent. As a mother of 10-year-old identical twins said: "Even from birth, I could tell them apart by the differences in their reactions to things around them like faces, voices, and colors." In other words, their temperaments provided the clues to their identity.

The Origins of Temperament

Temperament appears to have a constitutional component that is observable, at least partially, during the first few days of life. Studies that used the same measure of temperament—Bayley's *Infant Behavior Record* (IBR)—all found significant genetic influences on temperament (Rothbart & Bates, 2006). For example, results of the *Colorado Adoption Project,* which compared matched adopted and non-adopted children, showed a clear genetic influence on temperament (Plomin et al., 1997). The ongoing *MacArthur Longitudinal Twin Study,* designed to study more than 330 same-sex twin pairs, has initially reported genetic influences on individual differences at 14 months of age; for example, behavioral inhibition and observed shyness showed a significant genetic influence (Emde et al., 1992). (For an excellent discussion of this topic, see Caspi, 1998).

temperament
A child's basic personality; technically refers to constitutionally based individual differences in emotional, motor, and attentional reactivity and self-regulation.

Answers

11. Bowlby 12. protest, despair, detachment 13. 9 14. Adult Attachment Interview 15. Ainsworth

Yet recent research (Rothbart & Bates, 2006) also testifies to changes in the expression of temperament over time. A child's family, the social environment, socioeconomic status, and cultural influences together weave a network of external forces that contribute to the shaping of temperament over the years. Examining this developmentally interactive process, Thompson (1999) reached the following conclusions.

- A child's temperament may mesh well or poorly with the demands of the social setting. As we'll see, this goodness-of-fit between temperament and environment has a major impact on personality and adjustment. But keep in mind also that a child's environment changes dramatically through the years, and these changes have powerful effects on development and adjustment (Putnam, Sanson, & Rothbart, 2002).
- Temperament influences how a child selects and responds to different aspects of the environment (individuals, settings, and so on). This in turn affects how people respond to the child. (Reciprocal interactions at work!)
- Temperament colors how a child perceives and thinks about the environment.
- Temperament may interact with environmental influences in a way we simply don't understand.

Thus temperament is a biologically based but developmentally evolving feature of behavior (Thompson, 1999).

The Dimensions of Temperament

To understand how researchers reached these conclusions, we turn to a description of the dimensions of temperament.

The Work of Mary Rothbart

As Kagan and Fox (2006) note, Mary Rothbart's ideas are currently dominating discussions of temperament. In a frequently quoted analysis of the structure of temperament, Rothbart (Rothbart & Bates, 2006) has identified several dimensions of temperament in infancy. These include:

- *Negative emotionality,* which refers to feelings of fear and sadness.
- *Surgency/extraversion,* which ranges from a positive approach to others to high-intensity pleasure.
- *Orienting/regulation,* which refers to such behaviors as low-intensity pleasure, cuddliness, and soothability

Examining these dimensions leads to clues for parenting children based on the children's temperamental characteristics: When do they need help to maintain self-control, require support, or need encouragement to approach novel activities?

Kagan's Biological Interpretation

In a different interpretation, Kagan (Kagan & Fox, 2006; Kagan & Snidman, 2004) describes temperament as *an inherited physiology that is preferentially linked to an envelope of emotions and behaviors (though the nature of that link is still poorly understood)* (Kagan & Snidman, p. 5). For example, Kagan has noted that 4-month-old infants who show a tendency to become upset at unfamiliar stimuli are more likely to become fearful and subdued during early childhood, a condition that Kagan has called *inhibition to the unfamiliar* (Kagan & Fox, p. 198). (An extension of Kagan's work by Putnam and Stifter [2005] examines not only a child's negative reactions but also positive expressions of behavior, called *approach tendencies.*)

Kagan has continued to develop his thesis that biology, especially the brain, is a major contributor to temperament. As he stated (Kagan, 2004, p. 40), most temperamental biases are due to heritable variations in neurochemistry or anatomy, although some may be due to unknown prenatal events. And yet, since our work is based on the critical role of reciprocal interactions, we can't overlook the interactions between biology and the environment.

Chess and Thomas's Goodness of Fit

Finally, we turn our attention to the work of two child psychiatrists, Stella Chess and Alexander Thomas (1987, 1999). These researchers were struck by the individuality of their own children in the days immediately following birth, differences that could not be attributed solely to the environment. Intrigued, they devised the **New York City Longitudinal Study** of 141 children. Chess and Thomas discovered that even with children as young as 2 or 3 months of age, they could identify and categorize three types of temperament:

- **Easy children,** characterized by regularity of bodily functions, low or moderate intensity of reactions, and acceptance of, rather than withdrawal from, new situations (40% of the children).
- **Difficult children,** characterized by irregularity in bodily functions, intense reactions, and withdrawal from new stimuli (10% of the children).
- **Slow-to-warm-up children,** characterized by a low intensity of reactions and a somewhat negative mood (15% of the children).

They were able to classify 65% of the infants, leaving the others with a mixture of traits that defied neat categorization. Table 6.3 summarizes their classification scheme.

If parents recognize similar characteristics in their children—the need for sleep at a certain time; a unique manner of reacting to strangers or the unknown; the intensity of concentration on a task—they can use their knowledge of such characteristics to build a **goodness-of-fit** relationship.

At different age periods, a child's psychological development—either goodness of fit or poorness of fit—may be consistent. But if circumstances change (either in the child or in the environment), goodness of fit could become poorness of fit. As Chess and Thomas state (1999, p. 4), "the consistency or change of

New York Longitudinal Study
Long-term study by Chess and Thomas of the personality characteristics of children.

easy children
Calm, relaxed children; term associated with Chess and Thomas.

difficult children
Restless, irritable children; term associated with Chess and Thomas.

slow-to-warmup children
Children with low intensity of reactions; may be rather negative when encountering anything new; term associated with Chess and Thomas.

goodness of fit
Compatibility between parental and child behavior; how well parents and their children get along.

TABLE 6.3 Categories of Temperament

Behaviors	Easy Children	Difficult Children	Slow-to-Warm-Up Children
Activity level	Varies	Low to moderate	Varies
Rhythmicity (Regularity)	Very regular	Irregular	Varies
Approach or withdrawal	Positive approach	Withdrawal	Initial withdrawal
Adaptability	Very adaptable	Slowly adaptable	Adaptable
Sensory threshold (level of stimulation necessary to produce a response)	High or low	Tends to be low	High or low
Quality of mood	Positive	Negative	Slightly negative
Intensity of reactions	Low or mild	Intense	Moderate
Distractibility	Varies	Varies	Varies
Persistence and attention span	High or low	High or low	High or low

goodness/poorness of fit over time is determined by the constancy versus the variability in the individual and his or her environment."

Poorness of fit exists when parental demands and expectations are excessive and not compatible with a child's temperament, abilities, and other characteristics. Poorness of fit produces stress and is often marked by developmental problems (Chess & Thomas, 1987, 1999). A simple way of phrasing this concept is to ask parents and their children how they get along together. (For additional discussion of this important topic, see Putnam, Sanson, & Rothbart, 2002).

Finally, the importance of parents' and children's temperaments in establishing a goodness-of-fit relationship (parents react differently to different children), has again demonstrated the significance of the concept of **sensitive responsiveness.** For example, as we have seen, babies are temperamentally different at birth. An example of sensitive responsiveness would be that although most infants like to be held, some dislike physical contact. How will a mother react to an infant who stiffens and pulls away, especially if previous children liked being held? Infants instantly tune in to their environment. They give clues to their personalities so that a mother's and father's responses to their child's signals must be appropriate for *that* child; that is, greater parental sensitivity produces more responsive infants.

sensitive responsiveness
Refers to the ability to recognize the meaning of a child's behavior.

Guided Review

16. An influential analysis of Temperament has been offered by _____ _____.

17. _____ and _____ are identified with the New York Longitudinal Study.

18. _____ refers to an individual's behavioral style in interacting with the environment.

19. Compatibility between parental and child behavior is known as _____ _____ _____.

20. Kagan's explanation of temperament depends on a _____ analysis.

EARLY EMOTIONAL DEVELOPMENT

While we were working on this section of the book, one of us (JFT) tried to relax by watching a hockey game on television. Bad choice. With a few seconds left in the game one of the players savagely swung his stick at the head of a member of the other team who immediately dropped to the ice, severely injured. Needless to say, there had been a history of bad blood between the two players, and the repercussions of this violent encounter are still being played out.

Still, it dramatically illustrated the powerful role that emotions play in our lives. What was there in the emotional development of this player that would cause him to act so brutally? Does the answer lie in brain functioning? Or do we turn to the environment for answers? Or, once again, do we search for the interactions between the two for an explanation of this fascinating aspect of human nature?

For example, current views of emotion consider not only the brain's role in emotional development but also the contributions of the body and the environment. Emotion is not the conveniently isolated brain function once thought. Rather, it's "messy, complicated, primitive, and undefined because it's all over the place, intertwined with cognition and physiology" (Ratey, 2001, p. 223).

Answers

16. Mary Rothbart 17. Chess, Thomas 18. *Temperament* 19. goodness of fit 20. biological

Lise Eliot (2000, p. 291) captured the enigmatic nature of emotion when she commented:

> *Each child is born with his or her own unique emotional makeup, what we often refer to as "temperament." But this innate bent is then acted upon by the unique environment in which children are reared—by parents, siblings, peers, and other caregivers . . . and by the forms of emotional display and social interactions they see modeled by those around them.*

From this mix of genes and experience comes a "one-of-a-kind" individual with a unique emotional disposition.

Defining Emotion

But what do we mean by *emotion?* Although philosophers and psychologists have trembled at the thought of defining emotion for almost as long as attempts have been made, the following definition hints at what underlies this emotional (!) term. For our purpose, we'll define emotion as follows:

> *Emotion is a feeling(s) and its distinctive thoughts, psychological and biological states, and range of propensities to act.* (Goleman, 1995, p. 289)

Goleman then goes on to ask the controversial question: Is it possible to classify the basic emotions? Answering his own question, he proposes several fundamental families of emotion, together with representative members of each family.

- *Anger:* fury, resentment, animosity.
- *Sadness:* grief, sorrow, gloom, melancholy.
- *Fear:* nervousness, apprehension, dread, fright.
- *Enjoyment:* happiness, joy, bliss, delight.
- *Love:* acceptance, trust, devotion, adoration.
- *Surprise:* shock, astonishment, amazement, wonder.
- *Shame:* guilt, embarassment, mortification, humiliation.

Although you may disagree with Goleman—what about blends such as jealousy?—efforts such as these undoubtedly will continue since Paul Ekman's discovery that specific facial expressions for fear, anger, sadness, and enjoyment are recognized by people of all cultures around the world, thus suggesting their universality (Ekman & Davidson, 1994). Once Ekman stated that emotions evolved for their adaptive value in dealing with fundamental life tasks and identified four of these emotions, the stage was set and the task was identified: Link these fundamental tasks with basic emotions.

Role of Emotions in Development

As you read about the impact of attachment and early relationships on psychosocial development, you can understand how a child's emotional life is also affected. For example, considering the path of early emotional development, Emde (1998) identifies several reasons that testify to the importance of emotions

- Healthy emotional development helps children to define their personal individuality. For example, in the goodness-of-fit work we examined, Chess and Thomas (1999) constantly returned to the theme of consistency. When consistency—either of environment or individual—is lacking, there exists a real possibility that goodness of fit may shift to poorness of fit. Emde states that positive emotions produce the consistency that helps to establish those boundaries for sensitivity and responsiveness that help children to feel right about their relations with the world.
- During the infancy years, emotions generate adaptive functions that help to define the meaning of a child's experiences. For example, infants' emotions

motivate them to either approach or withdraw from situations and to communicate their needs to those around them. When others respond, infants learn about social exchanges, which furthers their social development. These emotional interchanges help to explain why emotions are often referred to as the language of infancy (Emde, 1998).

Research has shown that from the first days after birth infants are sensitive to the quality and the discernible features of an emotional signal. To understand these early behaviors, we must carefully consider cultural differences in any attempt to interpret emotional communication. Appropriate emotions and behavior are heavily weighted with cultural values. For example, in a study of Asian and American children, Cole, Bruschi, and Tamang (2002) found appreciable differences in emotional expression. As one illustration, children from the United States expressed their anger more openly than did the children from the other cultures. The Asian children understood that one can feel differently than one reveals.

Let's now attempt to discover how emotions develop.

You would enjoy reading Daniel Goleman's remarkably clear analysis of emotions, *Emotional Intelligence* (1995). New York: Bantam.

In examining the manifestation of the various emotions, we must remember that *different* responses may be made to any *one* emotion. A smile, for example, may signal joy, scorn, a social greeting or some other emotion (Saarni, Mumme, & Campos, 1998). Also, different theorists may suggest slightly different schedules for the appearance of the various emotions, but the basic explanation of *how* they develop is identical. Emotional development occurs as the result of an infant's dispositional tendencies combined with a complex interaction between growing cognitive skills and social interactions. Table 6.4 illustrates the timing of several emotions.

Emotion Regulation

But we also know that as humans we are able to exercise considerable **emotion regulation** in our lives. In the first year of life, infants gradually develop the ability to inhibit or minimize the duration and intensity of emotional reactions. Two phenomena seem to be involved: a set of processes related to the appearance of emotions, and a second set of processes involving the management or mismanagement of the generated emotions (Campos, Frankel, & Camras, 2004, p. 377).

The topic of emotion regulation has recently attracted considerable attention—both theoretical and research—in the psychological literature (see Eisenberg, 2006;

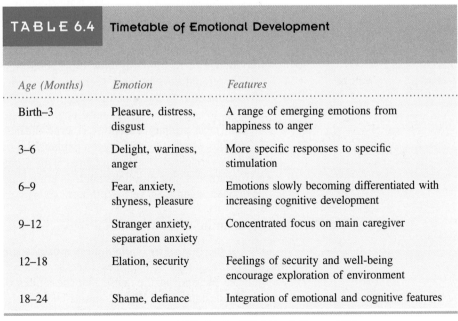

TABLE 6.4   Timetable of Emotional Development

Age (Months)	Emotion	Features
Birth–3	Pleasure, distress, disgust	A range of emerging emotions from happiness to anger
3–6	Delight, wariness, anger	More specific responses to specific stimulation
6–9	Fear, anxiety, shyness, pleasure	Emotions slowly becoming differentiated with increasing cognitive development
9–12	Stranger anxiety, separation anxiety	Concentrated focus on main caregiver
12–18	Elation, security	Feelings of security and well-being encourage exploration of environment
18–24	Shame, defiance	Integration of emotional and cognitive features

Source: Izard, 1994; Kopp, 1993; Luby, 2000; Sroufe, 1979; Thies & Travers, 2001.

Saarni et al., 2006). With renewed interest in the emotions themselves and their development, the concept of emotion regulation attempts to explain how and why emotions organize and facilitate other psychological processes (attention, problem solving, and so on) and also why they can exercise detrimental effects (Cole, Martin, & Dennis, 2004, p. 317).

As the authors cited above note, any psychological explanation of child development is suspect without recognizing the importance of emotions as motivators. One of the main problems in unraveling the complexity of emotion regulation is that of definition: What is an emotion? What is emotion regulation? Defined as biologically prepared capabilities that evolved and endured in humans because of their extraordinary value for survival (Cole, Martin, & Dennis, 2004, p. 317), emotions can help us analyze situations and prepare ourselves to act.

Emotion regulation, however, refers to changes associated with activated emotions—for example, children control their anger (Cole, Martin, & Dennis, 2004). Two types of emotion regulation are possible: first, emotion as regulating, such as a child reducing anger by distraction or a child's obvious anxiety, which lessens parental punishment. The second type of emotion regulation involves recognizing that emotion can be regulated, such as reducing stress through self-soothing. (We urge you to review *Child Development,* 75[2], pp. 315–394, for an excellent discussion of this topic.)

Analyzing Emotional Expressions

As children grow, the circumstances that elicit their emotions change radically; that is, the emotional experiences at different ages vary drastically. The amusement that a 6-month-old child shows when tickled by her mother is far different from a 16-year-old's amusement at a funny story told by a friend. We may label both "amusement," but is the emotion the same?

Remember also that complex new emotions appear as children grow. For example, as early as 2 or 3 years of age, children begin to display shame, guilt, and jealousy (Volling, McElwain, & Miller, 2002). These new emotions emerge from a child's increasing cognitive maturity, and, as they do, they have a strong influence on self-esteem (Dunn, 1994). For example, embarassment or shame at giving a wrong answer in school may weaken a child's sense of competence. Children's emotional competence is a good predictor of later social competence (Denham et al., 2003).

As emotions appear, children must grapple with the issue of regulating them. Impulse control (see Chapter 10) becomes an important learning experience early in life, strongly influenced by a child's temperament and how the environment (family, school, peers) reacts to emotional outbursts. We see here once again the importance of recognizing how biopsychosocial interactions affect behavior.

Emotional development seems to move from the general (positive versus negative emotions) to the specific—general positive states differentiate into such emotions as joy and interest; general negative states differentiate into fear, disgust, or anger. These primary emotions emerge during the first 6 months. Sometime after 18 months of age (recall Piaget's explanation of cognitive development), secondary emotions appear that are associated with a child's growing cognitive capacity for self-awareness. For emotions such as embarrassment to appear, children must have developed a sense of self (Rothbart, 1994).

The Smile

One of the first signs of emotion is a baby's smile, which most parents immediately interpret as a sign of happiness. Yet, as Sroufe (1995) notes, newborns' smiles don't indicate pleasure in the sense that the smiles of older infants do. These smiles are usually designated as "false" smiles because they lack the emotional warmth of the true smile. By the baby's third week, the human female voice elicits a brief, real

This 3-month-old infant is responding to its mother's face by smiling. In these interactions we see the roots of a child's psychosocial development. How does smiling contribute to psychosocial development?

smile, and by the sixth week the beginnings of the true social smile appear, especially in response to the human face.

Two-month-old infants are often described as "smilers," whereas frequent and socially significant smiles emerge around 3 months (Kagan & Fox, 2006). Babies smile instinctively at faces—real or drawn—and this probably reflects the human tendency to attend to patterns. Infants gradually learn that familiar faces usually mean pleasure, and smiling becomes a key element in securing positive reinforcement from those around the infant.

Summarizing, then: Infants smile at any high-contrast stimuli and at the human beings around them, and they discover a relationship between their behavior and events in the external world. When infants smile, they elicit attention from those around them and begin to associate the human face with pleasure.

As we conclude this chapter, we would like to emphasize that current research on emotional development reinforces the reciprocal interaction base of this book: Emotional expression appears immediately after birth, acquires definite meaning, and expands rapidly because of the socially interactive nature of emotional communication.

Guided Review

21. Emotions are particularly helpful in generating _____ functions.
22. Positive emotional developmental helps children to define their own _____.
23. _____ believes that each child is born with a unique emotional makeup.
24. A newborn's smiles are not identified as _____ smiles.
25. Inhibiting and minimizing emotional reactions is called _____ _____.

Answers

21. adaptive 22. individuality 23. Eliot 24. social 25. emotion regulation

CONCLUSION & SUMMARY

The role of relationships in development has achieved a prominent place in our attempts to understand children's growth. From the initial contacts with the mother to the ever-expanding network of siblings and peers at all ages, children's relationships exert a powerful and continuing influence on the direction of development.

We are slowly acquiring data about the function of relationships. For example, we have seen how important and persistent are the first interactions with parents and how significant are temperament and attachment. The interaction of these forces affects future relationships and the nature of emotional development. Recent research has led to significant findings about the quality of relationships.

What is the role of relationships in psychosocial development?

- Relationships involve almost all aspects of development.
- Infants, as active partners in their development, help to shape their relationships.
- To understand relationships, we must analyze and understand the reciprocal interactions involved.
- The development of social interactions seems to follow a definite schedule.
- Parents' role expectations affect their relationships with their children.

How would you assess the importance of attachment in psychosocial development?

- Bowlby and his colleagues, studying the separation of children from their parents, identified attachment as an important part of psychosocial development.
- Ainsworth's strange situation technique is designed to assess the security of an infant's attachment.
- Attachment is a cross-cultural phenomenon that knows no geographic boundary.
- Attachment develops early in life and offers clues to psychosocial development.

chapter 6 Review

- The *Adult Attachment Interview* helps to assess the quality of a child's attachment.
- The issue of attachment to fathers has attracted considerable interest.

How does temperament affect the relationship between parents and their children?

- Temperament refers to a child's unique way of interacting with the environment.
- An infant's temperament immediately affects interactions with adults.

- The work of Chess and Thomas helps us to understand the concept of goodness of fit.
- To maintain goodness of fit, parents must constantly adapt their parenting style to match the developmental changes in their children.

How do children develop and control their emotions?

- The brain plays a major role in the development and appearance of emotions.

- As emotional development occurs, children acquire a necessary degree of emotional regulation.
- Current research produced a schedule tracing the appearance of the various emotions.
- One of the first signs of emotional behavior is an infant's smile.

KEY TERMS

Adult Attachment Interview (AAI)
attachment
autonomy
difficult children
easy children
emotion regulation

entrainment
ethology
goodness of fit
New York Longitudinal Study
reciprocal interactions
sensitive responsiveness

slow-to-warm-up children
strange situation technique
symmetry
synchrony
temperament

WHAT DO YOU THINK?

1. Have you achieved a grasp of the extent of an infant's abilities: physical, social, and psychological? Do you think that infants are as we have described them in Chapters 5 and 6, or do you think that we have over— or underestimated their competencies?

2. Depending on your answer to question 1, explain how you interpret an infant's participation in developing relationships. That is, given an infant's ability to smile, coo, and make physical responses, how much control do you believe infants exercise in their interactions with adults?

3. As you read about the resurgence of interest in emotional development, how did you react to the developmental schedules that were presented? Do you think that theorists and researchers possess the skill and knowledge to be able to accurately identify the appearance of specific emotions at specific times?

4. Although Mary Ainsworth's research is the basis for our belief in the importance of attachment in social development, criticism has been directed at her studies because of the small number of subjects and the lack of consideration of the subjects' temperaments. Do you think these are valid criticisms? Do they raise questions in your mind about the universality of her conclusions?

CHAPTER REVIEW TEST

1. **An extended series of interactions doesn't necessarily imply a**

   _____.

   a. relationship
   b. goodness of fit
   c. friendship
   d. communication

2. **Which of the following statements is not in agreement with an understanding of psychosocial development?**

   a. All children are temperamentally similar at birth.

   b. Children instantly tune into their environment.
   c. Children give clues to their personalities.
   d. Children, from birth, engage in reciprocal interactions.

3. **A true relationship has**
   a. language aspects.
   b. cognitive aspects.
   c. physical aspects.
   d. all of these.

4. **More sensitive mothers have infants who are more**
   a. restless.
   b. nervous.
   c. detached.
   d. responsive.

5. **Parents and infants both exercise control over the**
   a. siblings.
   b. interactions.
   c. labeling.
   d. temperament.

6. **What parents see as their _____ affects parent-child relationships.**
   a. interactions
   b. function
   c. background
   d. role

7. **Children's _____ contribute significantly to their interactions with their environments.**
   a. ages
   b. gender
   c. temperaments
   d. culture

8. **Chess and Thomas described a child with a low intensity of reactions and a somewhat negative attitude as**
   a. slow to warm-up.
   b. difficult.
   c. easy.
   d. depressed.

9. **Constitutionally based individual differences are known as**
   a. interactions.
   b. attachments.
   c. temperament.
   d. parental signposts.

10. **The author of the strange situation test is**
    a. Ainsworth.
    b. Bowlby.
    c. Brazelton.
    d. Kagan.

11. **_____ is a characteristic that identifies the rhythm that is established between a parent's and an infant's behavior.**
    a. Synchrony
    b. Autonomy
    c. Entrainment
    d. Symmetry

12. **According to Bowlby, _____ behavior is any form of behavior that results in a person attaining or maintaining proximity to some other clearly identified individual who is conceived as better able to cope with the world.**
    a. detachment
    b. attachment
    c. protest
    d. emotional

13. **Which statement is true?**
    a. Only mothers have the potential to induce attachment.
    b. Fathers and mothers act quite differently with their infants.
    c. There is a sensitive period for parent-infant bonding.
    d. No sensitive period exists for parent-infant bonding.

14. **The study of behavior in natural settings is known as**
    a. ethology.
    b. physiology.
    c. anthropology.
    d. molecular biology.

15. **Bowlby's work on attachment began to notice the behavior of infants who experienced _____ from their mothers.**

    a. attention
    b. separation
    c. neglect
    d. habituation

16. **The true social smile appears at about _____ months.**
    a. 8
    b. 6
    c. 4
    d. 3

17. **Which is *not* a likely explanation of an infant's smile?**
    a. Infants smile at human beings around them.
    b. Infants smile at high-contrast stimuli.
    c. Infants smile at discovering a relationship between their behavior and external events.
    d. Infants smile at environmental noise.

18. **Inhibiting or minimizing the intensity of emotional reactions is known as emotion**
    a. guidance.
    b. latitude.
    c. regulation.
    d. short-circuiting.

19. **Chess and Thomas believe that positive emotions produce a _____ that leads to sensitive responsiveness.**
    a. happiness
    b. memory
    c. consistency
    d. phase

20. **One of the great adaptive values of emotions is that they _____ feelings and shared experiences.**
    a. communicate
    b. sublimate
    c. actualize
    d. repress

Answers

1.a. 2.a. 3.d. 4.d. 5.b. 6.d. 7.c. 8.a. 9.c. 10.a. 11.c. 12.b. 13.d. 14.a. 15.b. 16.d. 17.d. 18.c. 19.c. 20.a.

chapter

7

PHYSICAL AND COGNITIVE DEVELOPMENT IN EARLY CHILDHOOD

Chapter Outline

Chapter Objectives

After reading this chapter, you should be able to answer the following questions.

- What are the major physical and motor accomplishments of the early-childhood years?

- How do Piaget's views on cognitive development differ from information-processing theorists?

- What types of early childhood education seem most promising?

- How does children's language acquisition proceed during these years?

How would you describe the early childhood years? You would probably make comments like these: "Active little rascals aren't they?" "They are getting so smart!" "When did they learn to talk like that?" "Oh, they're so cute!" Do you think the experts would agree with you? Surprisingly, yes; perhaps their comments would be a bit more detailed, but, on the whole, they would say similar things.

With regard to physical development, T. Berry Brazelton, Professor of pediatrics at Harvard Medical School, summarizes the physical pace of these years as follows (Brazelton & Sparrow, 2001, p. 3).

> *Children were mostly under 4 . . . Freed from the pressure of their older sibling's domination, the 2- and 3-year olds raced from one activity to another. Watchful parents or caregivers needed to race back and forth with them to maintain conversation. Children were stimulated to keep up with each other's activities.*

Movement, constant activity, bursting exuberance—the early childhood years in action.

But what do the experts say about cognitive development? Let's turn to the grand master of cognitive development, Jean Piaget, for his views on the mental life of the early childhood child.

> *In the course of the second year (and continuing from Stage 6 of infancy), however, certain behavior patterns appear which imply the representative evocation of an object or event not present and which consequently presupposes the formation or use of differentiated signifiers, since they must be able to refer to elements not percepitbile at the time as well as to those which are present.* (Piaget & Inhelder, 1969, p. 53)

Did Piaget really write that way? Yes, because he wanted to be precise. If we translate his words, they simply tell us that children of these years have memory of objects or events not immediately present, and they also have the ability to label that memory in some way—an exciting developmental milestone.

Next we turn to the cognitive neuropsychologist Steven Pinker. From about 18 months to about 3 years, early childhood youngsters resemble language machines, accessing their languages at a phenomenal rate. Pinker characterizes language development during these years as the time when "all hell breaks loose." In Pinker's words (1994, p. 269):

> *Between the late 2s and the mid-3s, children's language blooms into fluent grammatical conversation so rapidly that it overwhelms the researchers who study it, and no one has worked out the exact sequence. Sentence length increases steadily, and, because grammar is a discrete combinatorial system, the number of synaptic types increases exponentially, doubling every month, reaching the thousands before the third birthday.*

In this photo of children playing together, how is development being stimulated?

Finally, we address the "cute" comment. In one of the great classics describing the early childhood years, Selma Fraiberg immortalized them as *The Magic Years*. Children believe that their thoughts and actions bring about the events they witness. Wonderful at times, such as when such "magic thought" enables children to see themselves as the heroic firefighter saving others, magical thought can also be upsetting, such as when children blame themselves for their parents' divorce. Our goal in this and the preceding chapter is to understand this magical world of the child.

These are "magic" years because children in their early years are magicians—in the psychological sense. Their earliest conceptions of the world are magical ones; they believe that their actions and thoughts can bring about events. Later, they extend this magic system and find human attribute in natural phenomena and see human or suprahuman causes for natural events or for ordinary occurrences in their lives. (Fraiberg, 1959, p. ix)

These, then, are the early childhood years—exciting, rewarding, and yet (as you'll see), challenging.

Have you ever seen a 2-year-old strutting around in one of those prophetic T-shirts that says:

Watch out—I just turned two!

Cries of frustration, frequently uttered by tired parents, don't mark parents as uncaring or heartless. Rather, they are a too-human reaction to the reality of dealing with a dynamo. Boundless energy, constant curiosity, and growing mental maturity all characterize children from 2 to 6 years of age. By age 2, typical children walk, talk, and eagerly explore their environment, gradually acquiring greater mastery over their bodies.

The rounded bodies of infancy give way to the slimmer torsos of early childhood, muscles begin to firm, bones begin to harden, and continued brain development provides a foundation for a world of symbolic promise. When these changes combine with feelings of confidence—"No, no, I can do it"—parents and other adults working with children of this age face challenges that can try their patience.

Cognitively, it's the time of Piaget's *preoperational period,* which traces a child's mental odyssey during these years. During these years, children also begin to form a theory of mind. Many of today's early-childhood youngsters also experience some form of preschool education. Finally, these are the years when children acquire their language so rapidly that we refer to the "language explosion."

In this chapter, we first trace the important physical changes of the period. We then analyze cognitive development and trace the growing symbolic ability of the early-childhood youngster. We conclude our discussion by analyzing how children of these years begin to control their environment by their use of rapidly developing language skills, which is often referred to as the language explosion.

PHYSICAL AND MOTOR DEVELOPMENT

One of the most obvious facts about grownups, to a child, is that they have forgotten what it's like to be a child.

—RANDALL JARRELL

Growth in childhood proceeds at a less frantic pace than in infancy. Children during this period grow about another 12 inches and continue to gain weight at the rate of about 5 pounds a year. Body proportions are also changing, with the legs growing faster than the rest of the body. By about age 6, the legs make up almost 45% of body length. At the beginning of this period, children usually have all their baby teeth; and at the end of the period, they begin to lose them. Boys and girls show about the same rate of growth during these years.

Features of Physical Development

Look at Figure 7.1, the human growth curve. (Note that 10 centimeters equal 4 inches.) This curve strikingly illustrates the regularity of physical growth. Most parts of the body (except the brain and the reproductive organs) follow this pattern.

Early childhood youngsters find the world a fascinating place. Giving these children the freedom to explore and learn, coupled with sensible restrictions, encourages the development of mastery. Suggest other constructive materials for children of this age to manipulate.

FIGURE 7.1

The human growth curve.

From John F. Travers, *The Growing Child,* Scott Foresman and Company, Glenview, IL 1982. Reprinted by permission of the author.

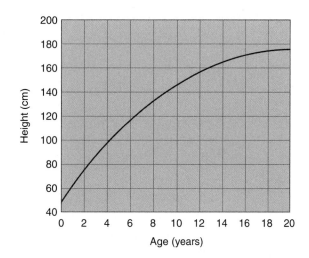

With the exception of the two spurts at infancy and adolescence, growth is highly predictable for almost all boys and girls, given satisfactory conditions.

Sequence of Early Childhood Growth

We know that different cells, tissues, and organs grow at different rates. (Some tissues never lose the ability to grow, such as hair, skin, and nails.) In humans, for example, body length at birth is about four times the length of the face at birth, so the head is relatively large. But the head grows more slowly than the trunk or limbs do, so that they gradually become proportional.

Parents and children alike are quite conscious of the appearance and loss of "baby" teeth and the arrival of the first permanent teeth. At about 2½ years, all the primary teeth have come through, which most children begin to lose between 5 and 6 years. At about this time, the first permanent teeth appear. Children continue to lose their primary teeth and gain new permanent teeth at about the same time. The timing can be different for some children, however, so that gaps between teeth may appear or new teeth arrive before the baby teeth have fallen out, causing a space problem that may require professional attention.

Continuing Brain Development

Thus the assembly of the general architecture of the brain occurs during the first two trimesters of fetal life, with the last trimester and the first few postnatal years reserved for changes in connectivity and function. The most prolonged changes occur in the wiring of the brain (synaptogenesis) and in making the brain work more efficiently (myelination) both of which show dramatic, nonlinear changes from the preschool period through the end of adolescence. (Nelson, Thomas, & DeHaan, 2006)

Arguing forcefully that brain development begins within weeks of conception and continues through adolescence, these authors believe that including the molecular biology of the brain in "development" adds a more holistic view of children.

Changes in brain development that occur during the early childhood period are interesting to trace. Microscopic examinations have repeatedly shown an increase in dendrites, accompanied by growth in the number of synapses. These changes, although not changes in structure, nevertheless help to explain the growing cognitive ability of 2- to 6-year-olds. The neural foundation is being laid for children to form more connections, providing a network that furthers cognition and learning.

The great task of the early childhood years is to form connections. Children of these years gobble up information from the outside word through their eyes, ears,

Children's rapidly developing motor skills are clearly seen in their drawings from uncontrolled scribbling to controlled "within the lines" attempts to their own creative expressions. Summarize the many developmental benefits of drawing.

FIGURE 7.2

Slowing growth of the brain.

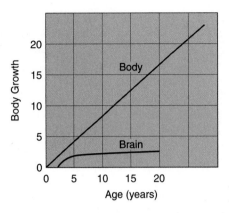

nose, hands and translate it into nerve impulses that travel along neurons (axon of one cell to dendrites of another), making connection with the dendrites of other neurons along its pathway. The brain cells that receive this information survive; those that don't, die. It's as simple as that. Two types of cells make up the brain: the neurons, which we have previously described in Chapter 5, and the glia cells, which are essentially support cells. The glia cells aid both the metabolism and the function of the neurons and also coat the axons with a substance called *myelin,* which controls the speed with which the axons transmit information (Ratey, 2001, p. 24).

For example, there probably is no more important stimulation than parents talking to their child. The language areas of the brain respond, resulting in superior language skills for a child. Children also need a warm, emotionally supportive environment, which results in more connections in those parts of the brain responsible for developing emotions. The result? Children who are blessed with feelings of security and an emotional well-being that spreads throughout all aspects of their lives. Consequently, we can say that continued brain growth during the early childhood years parallels cognitive and language accomplishments, another example of the continued effects of biopsychosocial forces (Andreasen, 2001; Eliot, 2000; Ratey, 2001; Rose, 2005).

For example, at 4 years of age, children understand much more about the world around them. They probably experience some type of preschool world, which they enjoy because they find pleasure in interacting with others. They're beginning to decide which of their playmates they like and which they don't; most importantly, they're learning *why* they like some and dislike others. They can run, jump, chase others, and PLAY! With their steadily growing cognitive abilities, they imagine all kinds of playmates and engage in fantastic activities.

During these years, children experience a slower brain growth pattern. In other words, whereas it took 2½ years to grow 75%, in the next 3½ years brain growth increases only 15%. Figure 7.2 illustrates this process.

Boys' and Girls' Brains

Boys and girls are different. Although this comes as no surprise to anyone, we are only now beginning to realize how subtle these dissimilarities are, particularly when we ask the question: Are there differences in brain structures between the sexes? As Rose (2005, p. 82) noted, any claims about differences in size and structure are so controversial that heated conclusions and interpretations are easily misappropriated. About the safest conclusion we can draw concerning structural differences is that any differences are few and tiny (Rose, 2005). Research must probe for answers in different domains, for example, neural connection, the neurochemistry of the brain, and the influence of sex-related hormones.

Still, questions remain, and in the final analysis variations between the sexes translate into different types of behavior, including interests, attitudes, even the kinds of books they like to read. What causes these differences? If in the biological structure, where do the answers lie? Or does it come down to a matter of nature versus nurture? Answering these questions has led scientists to focus on the manner in which girls' and boys' brains are wired and what this means for development and behavior.

As a result, several promising leads—both biological and environmental—have been investigated. For example, there is general agreement that the sex chromosomes— XX and XY—are the starting point to trace diversity between the sexes. What we now know (see Bear, Connors, & Paradiso, 2007) is that the smaller Y chromosome contains a gene identified as the *sex-determining region of the chromosome (SRY)*. A human child born with the Y chromosome and SRY develops as a male; otherwise, the individual develops as a female. (SRY, however, is not the only component in sex determination; other clusters of genes are also involved.) Thus, given the chromosomes of the parent, the stage is set for the development of the testes and the hormone that is responsible for producing a male fetus.

The next step in the process forces us to address a question posed by Bear, Connors, & Paradiso (2007): When and how during development does the fetus differentiate into one sex or the other? An important marker in our biological timetable is that at about the 7th or 8th month a surge of testosterone is produced and continues until about the 24th week of pregnancy. Remember, however, that both males and females manufacture testosterone; it is the surge we have described that 'masculinises' a brain otherwise destined to be female (Rose, 2005, p. 82). In other words, until that 7th week, the gonads remain undifferentiated.

Here we see for the first time the divergent paths that males and females begin to follow. With the ovaries producing the estrogens responsible for the female reproductive system and ultimately such secondary sexual characteristics as breast development, and with the testes directing the flow of testosterone leading to the male reproductive system and such secondary sexual characteristics as heavy beards, the differences between male and female have been established. Development now proceeds along recognizable pathways.

Role of the Environment

For better or worse, the brain is tightly bound to all aspects of children's lives. The neuroscientist Lise Eliot (2000) summarizes this reality when she notes that the genes may pass on the genetic program that forms the nervous system, the brain may direct your children's behavior, *but experience ultimately determines the extent of children's brain development.*

Brain enrichment is an idea whose time has come. Children are born with about 1,000 trillion connections in their brains, but by age 10 that number is down to 500 trillion, which under normal circumstances remains fairly constant for most of the remaining years. The original number was mainly due to nature's generous oversupply to insure that children would be able to make all the connections they needed. How did this come about? Eliot (2000) has summarized the process as follows.

Brain wiring involves an intricate dance between nature and nurture. Initially, genes direct the formation and the distribution of the neurons, but, thanks to the Human Genome Project (see Chapter 3), research has established that the number of functioning genes (about 25,000 to 30,000) is not up to the job of providing adequate wiring to insure survival.

It's at this point that nurture steps in and completes the wiring process. The heightened stimulation furnished by the environment now leads to the production of new neural connections, that is, continued vital brain wiring, additional synapses, and enriched brain activity. Unless these connections are repeatedly fired, nature has determined that they will perish, hence the truth of that old cliché, *use it or lose it*. Consequently, given the relative lack of knowledge concerning structural brain differences between the sexes, we are probably most comfortable in stating

FIGURE 7.3

Lateralization of handedness.

that any significant brain differences between the brains of males and females is undoubtedly due to the richness or paucity of environmental stimulation.

We know now that the brain is perfectly capable of rewiring itself, and, if not sufficiently stimulated, once-active neurons will fade and perish, or be commandeered by some other activity. We also realize that, although the hemispheres seem to be almost identical, there are important differences between the two. These differences are clues to a brain's organization. If you are right-handed, for example, your left cerebral hemisphere is lateralized for *handedness* and also for control of your speech—you are "left lateralized." Figure 7.3 illustrates *lateralization*.

Influences on Physical Development in Early Childhood

In an excellent overview of physical development, Tanner (1989) indicated how the interaction of heredity and environment produces the rate and kinds of physical growth. Among the chief contributing forces are the following:

- *Genetic elements.* Hereditary elements, as we have seen, are of immense importance to the regulation of growth. The genetic growth plan is given at conception and functions throughout the entire growth period.

- *Nutrition.* Active preschoolers need a well-balanced diet—bread, cereal, fruit, vegetables, meat, milk—and they also require wholesome snacks. Parents, for as long as possible, should restrict sweets and soda drinks. Almost as important, they should begin to develop good eating habits (Grodner, Long, & DeYoung, 2004).

- *Disease.* Short-term illnesses cause no permanent retardation of the growth rate, although they may cause some disturbance if the child's diet is consistently inadequate (an abundance of empty calories). Major disease usually causes a slowing of growth, followed by a catch-up period if circumstances become more favorable.

- *Psychological disturbance.* Stress can produce decided effects on physical development, beginning with the prenatal period. For example, stress and anxiety are associated with a predisposition to physical and mental disorders (Rutter & Taylor, 2002). During the early-childhood years, children experience the trauma of leaving home for preschool and kindergarten, adjusting to new adults and peers. If these events are coupled with any trouble at home (conflict, divorce), the impact on the children can be decidedly negative. There is always the danger that adverse experiences can—not always—cause a negative self-concept (Rutter & Rutter, 1993). (We'll explore this topic at greater length in Chapter 10.)

- *Socioeconomic status.* Children from different social classes differ in average body size at all ages. Tanner gives the example of differences in height between British children of the professional class and those of laborers. Children of the

The energy of the early-childhood years is seen in the physical activities of the period: constant motion followed by periods of rest and nutrition. Can you propose techniques by which the energy of these years can be safely and positively directed?

professional class are 1 inch or more taller at age 3 and 2 inches taller at adolescence. A consistent pattern appears in all such studies, indicating that children in more favorable circumstances are larger than those growing up under less favorable economic conditions. The difference seems to stem from nutrition, sleep, exercise, and recreation.

- *Secular trends.* During the past 100 years, the tendency has been for children to become progressively larger at all ages. This is especially true in Europe and America.

This brief overview of physical development again illustrates the importance of the biopsychosocial model. For example, you may be tempted to think that physical growth is essentially biological, mainly determined by heredity. Note, however, the roles played by nutrition and socioeconomic status. The interaction among biological, psychological, and social influences testifies to the power of the biopsychosocial model in explaining development.

Growing Motor Skills

When early-childhood children reach the age of 6, no one—neither parents nor teachers—is surprised by what they can do physically. Think back to the infancy period and recall how often we referred to what children couldn't do. Stand, walk, run. We tend to take the accomplishments of the 6-year-old for granted, but a great deal of neuromuscular development had to occur before these motor skills became so effortless.

We are concerned here with two types of **motor skills:** *gross* (using the large muscles) and *fine* (using the small muscles of the hands and fingers). Thanks to perceptual and motor development, 3- and 4-year-old children can hold crayons, copy triangles, button their clothes, and unlace their shoes. Table 7.1 summarizes the development of motor skills.

motor skills
Skills (both gross and fine) resulting from physical development enabling children to perform smooth and coordinated physical acts.

TABLE 7.1	The Emergence of Motor Skills	
Age	Gross Skills	Fine Skills
2	Runs, climbs stairs, jumps from object (both feet)	Throws ball, kicks ball, turns page, begins to scribble
3	Hops, climbs stairs with alternating feet, jumps from bottom step	Copies circle, opposes thumb to finger, scribbling continues to improve
4	Runs well, skillful jumping, begins to skip, pedals tricycle	Holds pencil, copies square, walks balance beam
5	Hops about 50 feet, balances on one foot, can catch large ball, good skipping	Colors within lines, forms letters, dresses and undresses self with help, eats more neatly
6	Carries bundles, begins to ride bicycle, jumps rope, chins self, can catch a tennis ball	Ties shoes, uses scissors, uses knife and fork, washes self with help

The physical picture of the early-childhood youngster is one of energy and growing motor skills. Adequate rest is critical, and parents should establish a routine to avoid problems. For example, to reconcile a rambunctious child with the necessity of sleep, parents should minimize stimulation through a consistent, easily recognized program: washing, brushing teeth, storytelling, and gentle but firm pressure to sleep. Careful and thoughtful adult care should prevent undue difficulties.

The Special Case of Drawing

Although we still lack considerable knowledge about children's aesthetic development, evidence suggests that sociocultural elements are influential (Szechter & Liben, 2007). Children love to draw, and their artwork has long attracted the attention of scholars as far back as John Ruskin in 1857 with his book, *The Elements of Drawing*. In a finely tuned sequence, which no one has to teach them, children move from the pincer movements of infancy to random scribbles to skillful creations. Learning to draw is like learning a language: Children acquire increasingly complex and effective drawing rules, which is one of the major achievements of the human mind (Willat, 2005, p. 1).

In analyzing children's art, one must remember that the drawings are the expression of *what children are capable of doing*. That is, the early-childhood youngster is limited in eye-hand coordination, motor ability, and manual dexterity. But a child's drawings, as crude as an adult may think they are, tells us much about the child's personality and emotional state.

For example, 2-year-olds grab markers and scribble enthusiastically (using dots and lines) and seem fascinated by their ability to produce lines as a result of their movements. Parents and preschool teachers should encourage this **random scribbling** as a necessary first step in children's creative growth. During this phase of random scribbling, which continues until about age 3, children are free from any evaluation of their drawings; they're simply having fun.

Three-year-olds hold a crayon with their whole hand and then begin to use their wrists, which permits them to draw curves and loops; this process is called **controlled scribbling.** Children become engrossed with geometric figures and

random scribbling
Drawing in which children use dots and lines with simple arm movements.

controlled scribbling
Drawing in which children carefully watch what they are doing, when before they looked away (random scribbling)

The early-childhood years are a time when children show a great love for drawing. Not only are their drawings a sign of motor development, but they also indicate levels of cognitive development and can be emotionally revealing.

AN INFORMED VIEW

Children and Their Drawings

Children love to draw and are fascinated by the illustrations in the books they read. One reason for the appeal of these illustrations is that many illustrators have adapted the style of children's drawings to their own work. Among them are Lois Ehlert (*Color Zoo, Chicka Chicka Boom Boom,* and so on), who constantly uses bright primary-colored geometric shapes to create letters and objects of nature. In Todd Parr's *The Feel Good Book,* the illustrations resemble the primitive drawings of small artists. Children's own art work has long attracted the attention of scholars for many reasons, ranging from artistic to psychological. (For an interesting discussion of this topic see Milbrath, 1998.)

We have previously mentioned the work of Rhoda Kellogg (1970), who taught preschool children for many years. During this time she collected over one million children's drawings and paintings that were done by thousands of children. You would enjoy reading Kellogg's description of children's art and derive insights from her work, such as her belief that the basic line formation and motifs that are appealing in children's art are *also to be found in the art of adults* (Kellogg, 1970, p. 44).

Kellogg believed that children's drawing passes through the following four stages, with the first stage of artistic development consisting of 20 basic scribbles.

1. *Placement,* which refers to where on the paper the child places the drawing (2 to 3 years).

2. *Shape,* which refers to diagrams with different shapes (about 3 years).

3. *Design,* which refers to a combination of forms (about 3 to 4 years).

4. *Pictorial,* which refers to representations of humans, animals, buildings, and so on (about 4 to 5 years).

By 2 years of age, children have achieved 17 placement patterns. At 3 years, they're using circles, crosses, squares and rectangles. By the time children are 4 years of age, they enter the pictorial stage.

As well-known artist, Mitsumasa Anno (in Marcus, 2002), points out, remarkable as it may seem, even children as young as 2 years *understand* when shown a simple drawing with circles for heads and rectangles for bodies and single lines for arms and legs that "this is Father, this is Mother." This is one of a child's first steps toward abstract understanding (You may also wish to learn more about children's art by going to our website at www.mhhe.com/dacey7.

begin to realize that their lines can represent objects. Now their art matches their cognitive development and reflects their growing symbolic power. For example, they'll point to their creation and say, "That's a man." This phase lasts until about age 4.

When children outgrow the scribbling stage, they then use dots, followed by curved lines to represent round areas and then move on to apply straight lines in their drawings (Willat, 2005). Four- and 5-year-olds show greater control and attention to what they are doing, deliberately attempting to create representations of objects. For example, they'll use a circle to represent a head or the sun. Artistic expression seems to peak by the end of the early-childhood period. During these years, children begin to paint and hold the brush with thumb and fingers. They hold the paper in place with the free hand. They give names to their drawings and begin to show representation (using one thing for another—see the cognitive section of the chapter).

After Kellogg's (1970) detailed analysis of children's drawings, she concluded that *child art contains the aesthetic forms most commonly used in all art.* Children's drawings not only are good clues to children's motor coordination but, as we'll see, also provide insights into their cognitive and emotional lives, another example of how a biopsychosocial perspective helps us to understand development.

Guided Review

1. The period of early childhood extends from the age of _____ to the age of _____.

2. During this period a child can grow as much as _____ inches and gain about _____ pounds per year.

3. By the end of this period, children begin to lose their _____ _____.

4. Hemispheric specialization is often referred to as _____.

5. By 2 to 2½ years of age, the brain has achieved about _____% of its adult weight.

6. SRY is a chromosomal region determining _____.

7. Much of our knowledge about the development of children's art is based on the millions of children's drawings collected by _____.

8. A child using his/her left hand to draw signals that the _____ cerebral hemisphere is lateralized for handedness.

9. Motor skills fall into two types: _____ and _____.

10. Kellogg believes that the themes found in children's drawings are also found in the art of _____.

COGNITIVE DEVELOPMENT

Physical developments, while observable and exciting, are not the only significant changes occurring during early childhood. Early-childhood youngsters expand their mental horizons by their increasing use of ideas and by their rapid growth in language. Although there is no denying this growing cognitive ability, explaining it is much more difficult. To help us understand what is happening in the cognitive world of these children and how it happens, we turn once more to Piaget.

Piaget's Preoperational Period

preoperational
Piaget's second stage of cognitive development, extending from about 2 to 7 years.

During Piaget's **preoperational** period, children of about 2 to 7 years begin to represent the objects and event of their environment. They remember and talk about their memories, which signals growing symbolic ability and language acquisition. They gradually acquire the basics of their language, a feat of such magnitude that its secret still eludes scholars. With no formal training, and often exposed to incorrect language models, children learn sounds; they combine the sounds into words; and, following a complex sequence of grammatical rules, they form sentences from the words. They put words in the correct order; they distinguish past from present, they identify plurals. They understand that we park in a driveway and drive on a parkway, that we play at a recital and recite at a play.

They become more comfortable with symbols, for example, reading and understanding what they read. They continue to explore and learn about their environment through their play. Yet their mental ability during these years remains limited. For Piaget, *preoperational* refers to children who cannot take two things into consideration at the same time (take something apart and put it together again), who cannot return to the beginning of a thought sequence (cannot comprehend how to reverse the action of 2 + 2), who cannot believe that water poured

Answers

from a short, fat glass into a taller, thinner one retains the same volume (can't mentally pour the water back)—these children are at a level of thinking that precedes operational thought.

An example of the limitations of preoperational thought is seen in the preschooler's notion of death. Studying 157 children ages 3 to 17 who had experienced a parent's illness and death, Christ (2000) discovered that children 3 to 5 years could not accept the finality of the parent's death. For months, they would ask when the parent was coming back. They needed repeated concrete explanations of what death meant.

Several examples of preoperational thinking are as follows.

- **Realism,** which means that children slowly distinguish and accept a real world. They now have identified both an external and internal world.

- **Animism,** which means that children consider a large number of objects as alive and conscious that adults consider inert. For example, a child who sees a necklace wound up and then released explains that it is moving because it "wants to unwind." Piaget believed that comparison with the thoughts of others slowly conquers animism as it does egocentrism.

- **Artificialism,** which consists of attributing human creation to everything. For example, when asked how the moon began, some of Piaget's subjects replied, "because we began to be alive." As egocentrism decreases, youngsters become more objective and they steadily assimilate objective reality to their cognitive structures. They proceed from a purely human or divine explanation to an explanation that is half natural, half artificial: The moon comes from the clouds, but the clouds come from people's houses. (The decline of artificialism parallels the growth of realism.)

Features of Preoperational Thought

For Piaget, the great accomplishment of the preoperational period is a growing ability to represent, which is how we record or express information. For example, the word "car" is a **representation** since it represents a certain idea. Pointing an index finger at a playmate and saying "Stick 'em up" is also an example of representation.

Other activities typical of preoperational children reflect their use of internal representation and include the following (Piaget & Inhelder, 1969).

Deferred Imitation. Preoperational children can imitate some object or activity that they have previously witnessed; for example, they walk like an animal that they saw at the zoo earlier in the day. Piaget gave the example of a child who visited his home one day and while there had a temper tantrum. His daughter Jacqueline, about 18 months old, watched, absolutely fascinated. Later, after the child had gone, Jacqueline had her own tantrum. Piaget interpreted this to mean that Jacqueline had a mental image of the event.

Symbolic Play. Children enjoy pretending that they are asleep, or that they are someone or something else. Piaget argued eloquently for recognizing the importance of play in a youngster's life. Obliged to adapt themselves to social and physical worlds that they only slightly understand and appreciate, children must make intellectual adaptations that leave personality needs unmet. For their mental health, they must have some outlet, some technique that permits them to assimilate reality to self, and not vice versa. Children find this mechanism in play, using the tools characteristic of symbolic play. (We'll discuss the role of play in greater detail in Chapter 8.)

Drawing. We have previously discussed drawing in a broad context, but here Piaget concentrated on its cognitive elements. Children of this age project their mental representations into their drawings. Highly symbolic, their artwork reflects the level of their thinking and what they are thinking. Encourage children to talk about their art.

---

realism
Refers to when children learn to distinguish and accept the real world; a form of Piagetian preoperational thinking.

animism
Children consider inert objects as alive and conscious; a form of Piagetian preoperational thinking.

artificialism
Children attribute human life to inanimate objects; a form of Piagetian preoperational thinking.

representation
Child's application of abstract thinking during Piaget's preoperational period.

deferred imitation
Imitative behavior that continues after the disappearance of the model to be imitated; a form of Piagetian preoperational thinking.

symbolic play
The game of pretending; one of five Piagetian preoperational behavior patterns.

drawing
According to Piaget, a skill that indicates a growing symbolic ability.

These children, playing doctor and patients, are furthering all aspects of their development. They are discovering what objects in their environment are supposed to do, they are learning about the give and take of human relationships, and they are channeling their emotional energies into acceptable outlets. What is the common thread that runs through all of these activities?

mental images
Internal representation of people, objects, or events.

reproductive images
Mental images that are faithful to the original object or event being represented; Piaget's term for images that are restricted to those sights previously perceived.

anticipatory images
Piaget's term for images (which include movements and transformation) that enable the child to anticipate change.

language
According to Piaget, a vehicle for thought for preoperational children.

egocentrism
Child focuses on self in early phases of cognitive development; term associated with Piaget.

Mental Images. Mental images appear late in this period because of their dependence on internalized imitation. Piaget's studies of the development of mental images of children between the ages of 4 and 5 showed that they fall into two categories. (1) **Reproductive images** are images restricted to those sights previously perceived. (2) **Anticipatory images** are images that include movements and transformations. At the preoperational level, children are limited to reproductive images.

A good illustration of the difference between the two types of images is Piaget's famous example of matching tokens. Piaget showed 5- and 6-year-old children a row of red tokens and asked them to put down the same number of blue tokens. At this age, children put one blue token opposite each red one. When Piaget changed the arrangement, however, and spread out the row of red tokens, the children were baffled because they thought there were more red tokens than blue. Thus, children of this age can reproduce but not anticipate, which reflects the nature of their cognitive structures and level of cognitive functioning.

Language. For preoperational children, language becomes a vehicle for thought. Children of this age need ample opportunities to talk with adults and with one another. (See the language section of this chapter.)

Limitations of Preoperational Thought

Although we see the steady development of thought during this period, preoperational thought still has limitations. To know an object is to act on it, to modify it, to transform it, and to join objects in a class. The action is also reversible. If two is added to two, the result is four; but if two is taken away from four, the original two returns. Preoperational children can't perform such operations on concepts and objects.

Several reasons account for the restricted nature of preoperational thought. In the period of preoperational thought, children cannot assume the role of another person or recognize that other viewpoints exist, a state called **egocentrism.** This differs from *sensorimotor egocentrism*, which is primarily the inability to distinguish oneself from the world. For example, children may believe that the moon follows *them* around; everything focuses on them.

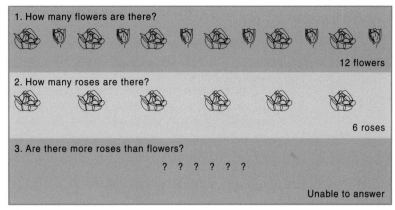

FIGURE 7.4

Lack of genuine classification.

From John F. Travers, *The Growing Child*, Scott Foresman and Company, Glenview, IL 1982. Reprinted by permission of the author.

centration
Feature of preoperational thought; the centering of attention on one aspect of an object and the neglecting of any other features.

classification
Ability to group objects with some similarities within a larger category.

conservation
Children conserve the essence of something even though surface features change.

FIGURE 7.5

Piaget used the beaker task to determine whether children had conservation of liquid. In 1, two identical beakers (A and B) are presented to the child; then the experimenter pours the liquid from B into beaker C, which is taller and thinner than A and B. The child is asked if beakers B and C have the same amount of liquid. The preoperational child says no, responding that the taller, thinner beaker (C) has more.

From John Santrock, *Child Development: An Introduction,* 9th ed., p. 245, Figure 8.8. Copyright © 2001 by The McGraw-Hill Companies. Reproduced with permission of The McGraw-Hill Companies, Inc.

In Piaget's classic experiment, a child is shown a display of three mountains varying in height and color. The child stands on one side of the table, looking at the mountains; a doll is then placed at various spots around the mountains. The child is next shown several pictures of the mountains and asked to pick the one that shows what part of the mountains the doll saw. Egocentric children pick the photo that shows the mountains as they saw them.

Another striking feature of preoperational thought is the centering of attention on one aspect of an object and the neglecting of any other features—called **centration.** Consequently, reasoning is often distorted. Preoperational youngsters are unable to decenter, to notice features that would give balance to their reasoning. A good example of this is the process of **classification.** At this stage, the classification seems rational, but Piaget and Inhelder (1969) provide a fascinating example of the limitations of classification at this age. If in a group of 12 flowers, there are 6 roses, preoperational youngsters can differentiate between the other flowers and the roses. But when asked if there are more flowers or more roses, they are unable to reply because they cannot distinguish the whole from the part (see Figure 7.4). This understanding does not appear until the third phase of classification, at about the age of 8.

Another limitation of the period is the lack of **conservation.** Conservation means understanding that an object retains certain properties, no matter how its form changes. The most popular illustration is to show a 5-year-old two glasses, each half filled with water. The child agrees that each glass contains an equal amount. But if you then pour the water from one of the glasses into a taller, thinner glass, the youngster now says that the new glass contains more liquid (see Figure 7.5). Youngsters consider only the appearance of the liquid and ignore what happened. They also do not perceive the reversibility of the transformation. In their minds they do not pour the water back into the first glass.

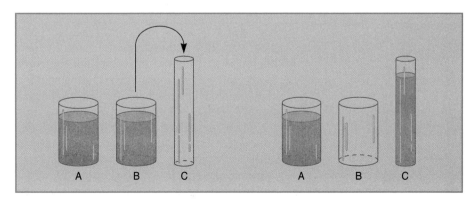

reversibility
A thought that can be retraced by an opposite action (2 + 2 = 4; 4 − 2 = 2).

Finally, preoperational thought lacks **reversibility.** A truly cognitive act is reversible if it can use stages of reasoning to solve a problem and then proceed in reverse, tracing its steps back to the original question or premise. The preoperational child's thought is irreversible and entangles the child in a series of contradictions in logic.

In the water-level problem, for example, the child believes that the taller, thinner glass contains more water. Youngsters cannot mentally reverse the task (imagine pouring the contents back into the original glass). At the conclusion of the preoperational period, children slowly decenter and learn reversibility as a way of mental life.

Challenges to Piaget

As you can well imagine, Piaget's theory, which has been with us for more than 70 years, has been tested, retested, challenged, and refuted in many respects. Training studies have repeatedly shown that early childhood youngsters possess more cognitive competence than Piaget believed. For example, 4-year-old nonconservers can be taught to conserve (Bjorklund, 2000).

Evidence continues to mount supporting the conclusion that Piaget underestimated the cognitive abilities of young children: They conserve, classify, and overcome egocentrism earlier than Piaget realized. For example, preschoolers show clear evidence that they understand basic concepts that Piaget believed were too advanced for them. As Siegler (1998) noted, although some preschoolers may not understand the number concept, they know a lot about numbers.

Information-Processing Theory

In Chapter 5, we noted that information-processing theorists argued that cognitive development occurred by improvement of such cognitive processes as attention and memory. Applying these concepts to children's development helps us to focus on what information children represent, how they process this information, how these cognitive changes affect their behavior, and what are the underlying psychological mechanisms responsible for these changes (Munakata, 2006).

During the early childhood years, the amount of information a child can attend to steadily increases. For example, studying what is called **span of apprehension** (how much information people can attend to at one time), Cowan and his colleagues (1999) compared first graders with fourth graders and discovered that the first graders could attend to 2.5 items, whereas fourth graders attended to 3 items. Such research raises the issue of the basic psychological mechanisms responsible. Can the difference between the two groups be attributed to capacity alone? More recent research has focused on the importance of a detailed knowledge base to explain the differences (Bjorklund, 2005, p. 125).

span of apprehension
The amount of information a person can attend to at one time.

Attention, as we have seen, involves a lengthy process in which children translate what they know into appropriate actions and then rely on these strategies to gather new information (Bjorklund, 2005). Selective attention becomes increasingly important as children move through the early-childhood years and they become more proficient in focusing on pertinent information. The selectivity with which children focus their attention on relevant items increases greatly between 3 and 8 years (NICHD, 2005b; Siegler & Alibali, 2005).

rehearsal
Mnemonic strategy that describes a person repeating target information.

Much the same holds true for memory. During the early childhood years, children begin to develop memory strategies, such as rehearsal, organization, and retrieval. For example, **rehearsal** (repeating target information) shows a clear developmental pattern. In a classic study, Flavell, Beach, and Chinsky (1966) studied list learning in 5-, 7-, and 10-year-olds. The results showed that as rehearsal increased with the older children, recall also improved. Eighty-five percent of the

organization
Memory strategy that entails discovering and imposing an easy-to-remember structure on items to be memorized.

10-year-olds displayed spontaneous rehearsal, whereas only 10% of the 5-year-olds did so.

Organization (discovering or imposing structure on a set of items to guide behavior) follows much the same developmental path as attention. When children are given a randomized list of items that can be sorted into categories (fruit, cars, tools, and so on), older children cluster the items and improve their recall. Preschool children, however, cluster items only by chance; but studies have shown that training exercises can improve their ability to organize (Bjorklund, 2005, p. 159).

Retrieval (obtaining information from memory) takes two forms: recognition and recall. Most children find recognition tasks fairly simple, but recall tests offer a more serious challenge. Helping younger children to recall demands that the circumstances under which they first acquired the material need to be repeated. Older children spontaneously use retrieval cues more often than preschoolers do.

retrieval
Obtaining information from memory.

Children's Theory of Mind

theory of mind
Children's understanding of others' thoughts, desires, and emotional states; emerges at about 2–3 years of age.

You can see, then, how rapidly improving cognitive processes such as attention and memory help children to acquire a theory of mind. Many developmental psychologists believe that today's cognitive psychology is actually the psychology of children's **theory of mind,** that is, the beliefs, desires, knowledge, and thoughts of children's mental states (Flavell, 1998). In other words, theory of mind describes children's understanding of other people's thoughts, desires, and emotional states, an ability that begins to emerge at about 2 to 3 years of age (Cole, 2006).

As children's cognitive processes show steady growth, their theory of mind also shows developmental changes (Bartsch & Wellman, 1995; Flavell, 1999):

- Around 2 years of age, children acquire a *desire psychology,* which is an expression of simple emotions and desires about what they're attending to. Cross-cultural studies consistently show a similar pattern of mental state language in children: desire, thinking, and knowing. Studying theory of mind development in Mandarin- and Cantonese-speaking children, Tardif and Wellman (2000) found that, although the pattern of development was similar, the Chinese-speaking children used desire terms much earlier than did English-speaking children.

- About 3 years of age, children begin to talk about beliefs and thoughts as well as desires. Nevertheless, they still explain people's behavior by desires rather than beliefs. This level of understanding is called *desire-belief* psychology.

- At approximately 4 years of age, children begin to understand that what people think and believe, as well as what they desire, affect how they behave. This level is referred to as *belief-desire* psychology.

For example, in a typical study (called a *false-belief* task) an experimenter showed a 5-year-old a candy box with pictures of candy on the cover. When asked what's in it, she replied, "Candy." She then looked inside and was surprised to find crayons, not candy. The experimenter then asked her what another child would expect to find in the box. "Candy," was the firm reply.

Next, the experiment was done with a 3-year-old, who said she expected to find candy inside. But when asked the second question, the three-year-old said, "Crayons!" She insisted that she thought the box always contained crayons. That is, children of this age don't realize that people think and act in accordance with the way they represent the world rather than the way the world actually is (Flavell, 1999).

How can we explain these differences? In their excellent meta-analysis, Wellman, Cross, and Watson (2001) analyze such competing explanations as early competence

AN APPLIED VIEW

Children and Their Humor

"Why did daddy tiptoe past the medicine cabinet?"
"Because he didn't want to wake the sleeping pills."

Jokes such as these have spurred Paul McGhee (1979, 1988; McGhee & Paniutsopoulous, 1995) to analyze children's humor and trace its developmental path. Noting that little is known about how children develop humor, McGhee turned to cognitive development as a possible explanation.

He begins by noting that the basis of most children's humor is incongruity, which is the realization that the relationship between different things just isn't "right." Using this as a basis, he traces four stages of incongruous humor. He treats stages as does Piaget: The sequence of stages remains the same, but the ages at which children pass through them vary.

- *Stage 1: Incongruous Actions toward Objects.* Stage 1 usually occurs sometime during the second year, when children play with objects. They are able to form internal images of the object and thus start to "make believe." For example, one of Piaget's children picked up a leaf, put it to her ear, and talked to it as if it were a telephone, laughing all the time. One of the main characteristics of stage 1 humor is the child's physical activity directed at the object.
- *Stage 2: Incongruous Labeling of Objects and Events.* Stage 2 humor is more verbal, which seems to be its most important difference from stage 1. McGhee (1979) notes that the absence of action toward objects is quite noticeable. Piaget's 22-month-old daughter put a shell on the table and said, "sitting." She then put another shell on top of the first, looked at them, and said, "sitting on pot." She then began to laugh. Children in this stage delight in calling a dog a cat, a foot a hand, and then start laughing.

- *Stage 3: Conceptual Incongruity.* Around age 3, most children begin to play with ideas, which reflects their growing cognitive ability. For example, stage 3 children laugh when they see a drawing of a cat with two heads.
- *Stage 4: Multiple Meanings.* Once children begin to play with the ambiguity of words, their humor approaches the adult level.

"Hey, did you take a bath?"

"No. Why, is one missing?"

Children at stage 4 (usually around age 7) understand the different meaning of *take* in both instances. Stage 3 children could not understand the following joke:

"Order! Order! Order in the court."

"Ham and cheese on rye, your honor."

Stage 4 youngsters appreciate its ambiguity.

You can see how cognitive development is linked to humor: The effective use of humor with children can help stimulate new learning and creative thinking, instill an interest in literature, facilitate social development, and enhance emotional development and adjustment (Franzini, 2002). Meltz (2005) has identified another interpretation of the emergence of the cognitive achievements we have mentioned.

- 6–12 months: Enjoys unexpected actions such as peekaboo.
- 12–15 months: Initiates humorous actions.
- 2 years: Makes deliberate mistakes.
- 3 years: Consciously misinterprets words and ideas
- 4–5 years: Begin to appreciate riddles but doesn't quite understand them.
- 6–7 years: Finds humor in knock-knock jokes and riddles.

or genuine conceptual change. We can't emphasize enough the importance of these competing claims, since they go to the heart of children's representations of the world. For example, conceptual change theorists argue that actual changes occur in children's conceptions of persons, whereas early-competence theorists believe that poor performance (such as that seen in the preceding example of the 3-year-old child) is due to developmental limitations of children's information-processing skills. As a result of their research, Wellman and his colleagues conclude that real and significant conceptual changes take place in children's thinking from 2½ to 5 years of age.

Finally, Flavell (1999) summarizes children's knowledge about mind as follows.

- Early childhood youngsters come to realize that only people are capable of thinking.

- Thinking is an internal, "in-the-head" process.

- People can think about objects not present to them.

- Other people are also capable of thinking.

Guided Review

11. According to Piaget, _____ is the means that permits children to assimilate reality to self.

12. Attributing life to inanimate objects is known as _____.

13. To understand that an object retains properties no matter how its form changes is called _____.

14. Researchers have used _____-_____ tasks to study a child's theory of mind.

15. When children understand that what people believe affects what they do, they are at the _____-_____ level.

EARLY-CHILDHOOD EDUCATION

Early-education programs, often referred to as preschool and kindergarten programs, usually take one of two directions. They are either physically, socially, and emotionally oriented or more cognitively centered, which is not to say that programs are exclusively social or cognitive; typically elements of both occur in all programs. As Gardner (2003) noted, two considerations are critical in any preschool program: assumptions about the minds of children and visions about the kind of society we desire. Early-childhood education today reflects a rich mixture of ideas from educational philosophy, educational psychology, and developmental psychology.

For example, the U.S. Department of Education, through the National Institute on Early Childhood Development and Education (ECI), has identified the "Three Rs" of early-childhood education as follows.

- *Relationships,* which implies loving relationships in early childhood, with parents and others, to encourage children's security and confidence in themselves.

- *Resilience,* which refers to a child's ability to meet challenges successfully, challenges that include violence, poverty, bias, and/or disability. The concern here is to discover why some children overcome these challenges better than others.

- *Readiness,* which combines good health, positive educational activities, and productive schools.

These goals have been identified to help young children physically, perceptually, cognitively, emotionally, and socially.

Although the writings of Rousseau, Froebel, Watson, Freud, Erikson, and others have helped shape current policy, given today's concern with educational achievement, many preschool programs rely particularly on the ideas of individuals such as Piaget and Montessori.

Piaget and Montessori

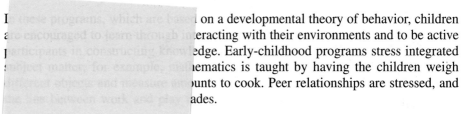 on a developmental theory of behavior, children are encouraged to learn through interacting with their environments and to be active participants in constructing knowledge. Early-childhood programs stress integrated subject matter; for example, mathematics is taught by having the children weigh different objects and measure amounts to cook. Peer relationships are stressed, and the line between work and play fades.

Answers

11. play 12. animism 13. conservation 14. false-belief 15. belief-desire.

Although Piaget never advocated using his developmental theory in this manner, you can see how his ideas could form the basis for early-childhood programs. His emphasis on a child's progression through intellectual stages of development has clearly defined program implications (use of concrete materials, and so on). Since Piaget's is an *interactive* theory, children's energy and activities can be directed at interesting cognitive outcomes rather than having children passively accept facts.

In contrast, Montessori (1912/2003; 1967) was a strong proponent of early-childhood programs. She believed that developing children pass through different physical and mental growth phases that alternate with periods of transition, suggesting that children possess different types of minds at different periods. These periods differ so sharply that Montessori referred to them as a series of new births.

She described three major periods of development. The first stage, which is called the **absorbent mind** phase to indicate a child's tremendous ability to absorb experiences from its environment, extends from birth to age 6. The second stage, which is referred to as the **uniform growth** phase to identify these years as a time of considerable stability, extends from age 6 to age 12. Finally, the third stage extends from 12 to 18 years.

A youngster reaches this level by what Montessori calls the **prepared environment.** For children under age 6, the prepared environment includes sensorial materials, such as rods to teach lengths, cubes to teach size, and bells to teach musical pitch, materials for the acquisition of cultural geography, history, art, and arithmetic, and materials and techniques necessary for the development of a child's religious life. Montessori also devised concrete materials to encourage learning in 6- to 12-year-old children.

The stages we have just described lead to what is perhaps the best known of Montessori's ideas, that of **sensitive periods.** Montessori believed that there are times when a child is especially *sensitive* or ready for certain types of learning. One of the earliest and most vital of these periods is concerned with the attainment of language, which, as we have seen, children acquire effortlessly, a good example of a sensitive period.

PROJECT HEAD START

Other preschool programs, such as Head Start, have also helped disadvantaged children. Originally conceived as part of President Lyndon Johnson's War on Poverty in the 1960s, **Project Head Start,** since its beginnings in 1965, has enrolled more than 24 million children in its programs. Head Start provides grants to local public and private non-profit and for-profit agencies to offer comprehensive child development services to economically disadvantaged children and families. In 2007, the Office of Head Start reported that with a budget of about seven billion dollars, one million children are registered in its almost 20,000 Head Start Centers (Office of Head Start, 2007).

From its beginnings, Head Start programs have attempted to improve the social and cognitive development of enrolled children by providing educational, health, nutritional, and other services. These Head Start centers supervise 50,000 classrooms and feature the characteristics of good preschools: low teacher-child ratio, specially trained teachers, availability of resources, and recognition of children's individual differences. The programs are all child centered and are designed to emphasize the well-being of individual children. They also provide children with age-appropriate, enriching, enjoyable experiences, which is especially desirable given the social needs of early childhood youngsters.

Their long-term benefits have been receiving recent scrutiny and the positive results of these early interventions have been clearly documented. For example, a 25-year evaluation of the BEEP Program—Brookline Early Education Program—demonstrated substantial gains in educational achievement, health, and general behavior. As the authors noted, participants in high-quality intervention programs are less likely to cost taxpayers money for health, educational, and public assistance

absorbent mind
Montessori's term for a child's ability to absorb experiences from the environment (0–6 years).

uniform growth
Montessori's term to describe the developmental period in which children show considerable stability.

prepared environment
Montessori's term for use of age-appropriate materials to further cognitive development.

sensitive periods
Montessori's term for ideal times of readiness for learning.

Project Head Start
Programs intended to provide educational and developmental services to preschool children from low-income families.

P. Hauser-Cram, D. Pierson, D. Klein Walker, and T. Tivnan (1991). *Early Education in the Public Schools*. San Francisco: Jossey-Bass. An excellent review of early childhood programs designed according to developmentally appropriate principles.

AN APPLIED VIEW

Good Preschools

An outstanding example of the principles we have been discussing can be found in the Reggio Emilia approach. Recognized in 1991 by *Newsweek* magazine as having exellent preschool programs, Reggio Emilia has been widely adopted in the United States, the United Kingdom, New Zealand, Australia, and many other countries (Edwards, Gandini, & Forman, 1998).

Following World War II in the community of Reggio Emilia, a young jounalist named Loris Malaguzzi, emotionally moved by the destruction he observed, determined to develop good schools for children aged about 1 to 3 years (the infant schools) and for preschoolers 3 to 6 years of age. With the support of the community of Reggio Emilia in northern Italy, an effort began to upgrade the community's schools using the ideas of Dewey, Piaget, Gardner, and Vygotsky.

Viewing children as curious and competent enabled teachers to devise a curriculum based on children's emerging interests and their desire to build relationships with others. This interpretation of the child as a competent learner leads to a strong child-directed curriculum in which skilled teachers guide children for several months in their pursuit of a theme that interests them.

The Reggio Emilia concept views the environment as another teacher, which transfers to the look and feel of the classroom. Classrooms become a place of happiness and motivation where children learn to cooperate in their search for solutions to problems and where they also learn to construct meaningful relationships with others. As Gardner noted (1999b, p. 87):

> If you walk into one of the preschools on a given morning, you will first be struck by the beauty and spaciousness of the building. Reggio buildings are ample, open, streaming with light; potted plants and inviting chairs and couches are strategically placed, adding color and comfort to the surroundings.

The educators at Reggio Emilia have developed and improved techniques for considering the ideas aspirations, and performances of children seriously. Can these ideas transfer to other parts of the world? As Gardner (1999b, p. 92) also recognized, *transplantation will not be easy* given its location, the dedication of its staff, and traditions from which these ideas emerged. It can be done but will reflect its own unique culture.

services. (For an excellent discussion of this program and comparison with other successful interventions such as the Perry Preschool Project and the Abecedarian Project see Palfrey and others, 2005.)

As you can tell from our discussion thus far, children of these years have marched firmly into a symbolic world, a major part of which is language.

Guided Review

16. Preschool programs are usually oriented to either _____ or _____/ _____/_____ development.

17. Two individuals who have had great influence on the nature of preschool programs are _____ and _____.

18. Since its beginning, Project Head Start has enrolled _____ children.

LANGUAGE DEVELOPMENT

Did you ever try to learn a second language, perhaps in high school or college? Do you remember the difficulties you experienced with everything, from pronunciation to vocabulary? Yet youngsters naturally and easily acquire language, a task of such scope and intricacy that its secrets have eluded investigators for centuries. During the early childhood period, language figuratively "explodes." At about the same age, children manifest similar patterns of speech development, whether they live in a ghetto or in a wealthy suburb.

Answers

16. cognitive, physical, social, emotional 17. Piaget, Montessori 18. 24 million

AN APPLIED VIEW

The Biological Basis of Language

Understanding the brain's role in language seems to be a simple matter, probably because we're still learning about it! Beginning in 1864, certain parts of the brain were identified as performing specific language functions. It was then that the French neurologist Paul Broca, working with stroke victims whose speech had been impaired and who suffered from paralysis of the right side of the body, determined that "we speak with the left hemisphere." *Broca's area* (in the left frontal lobe), as it came to be known, is thought to be responsible for the production of speech.

In 1876, the German psychiatrist Karl Wernicke described a section of the brain that receives incoming speech sounds. Called *Wernicke's area* (in the temporal lobe), it is responsible for interpreting and translating the speech sounds just heard and putting together the words for a reply. This composition is then passed on to Broca's area through a bundle of nerve fibers. But that isn't the end of it. The motor area of the brain now becomes involved and causes movements of the face, tongue, jaw, and throat. And, of course, our speech is often quite emotional.

Think of it this way. A child says something to you, which is immediately transferred to Wernicke's area. You understand what was said and think about a reply. When you decide to respond, your message is transferred to Broca's area along a pathway of nerve fibers, where a plan for vocalizing your ideas is formed. Parts of the motor cortex are now alerted, and the appropriate muscles of the mouth, lips, tongue, and the larynx swing into action and you answer your child.

Estimates are that language resides in the left hemisphere for about 90% of the population. About 5% have their main language activity in the right hemisphere, and another 5% split their language functions between both hemispheres. Remember, however, that both hemispheres are connected, and both hemispheres are involved in language production. For example, the right hemisphere, mainly responsible for our emotional state, determines the emotional reactions of the speaker.

Current studies have made us uncomfortable with the neat statement that "Broca's area does this" and "Wernicke's area does that." Thanks to data supplied by EEG studies, PET scans, CAT scans, and MRIs, a different picture is emerging. We now think that language functions are spread throughout the brain. (See Eliot, 2000, for an excellent discussion of this topic.)

How do these ideas translate into techniques for helping children with their language?

1. *Research and theory are clear that a child's environment influences the number of connections made in the brain.* Consequently, parents who speak *to,* not *at,* their children are providing an enriched language environment for their children.

2. *The type of stimulation parents and teachers use must be appropriate for a child's age and abilities.* Merely exposing children to language doesn't work. A 2-year-old listening to its mother on the telephone doesn't necessarily form connections in the language areas of the brain. Speech must communicate meaning and not merely be a source of noise.

3. *Remember that children's emotions are as involved in language development as are their ability to form words and move their lips and tongue.* As our knowledge of development during these crucial years has increased, we now realize that children, *from birth,* are remarkably sensitive to *how* they are spoken to and treated. They instinctively know when negative, harsh, and unpleasant talk is directed at them, which in turn affects all aspects of development.

4. *Parents and teachers must be good observers of a child's speech.* Children typically leave a trail of clues—at all ages—that point to definite behaviors as clearly as an arrow seeking its target. Respond to these cues with supportive speech. One of the biggest mistakes a parent can make is to ignore the channels of communication their children are trying to open with them. Such missed opportunities result in not only the loss of simple pleasures (such as a new word or idea) but also the loss of the chance to promote a warm relationship.

5. *Finally, remember the direction of brain growth mentioned earlier: Wernicke's area develops before Broca's, so children understand (receive) more than they speak (produce).* Consequently, parents in particular should talk constantly to their children to enrich their understanding of the meanings of words, and then encourage and support their efforts at speech.

Within a short span of time and with almost no direct instruction, children completely analyze language. Although refinements are made between ages 5 and 10, most children have completed the greater part of the process of language acquisition by the age of 4 or 5. Recent findings have also shown that when children acquire the various parts of their language, they do so in the same order. For example, in English, children learn *in* and *on* before other prepositions, and they learn to use *ing* as a verb ending before other endings such as *ed* (Hulit & Howard, 1997).

Language acquisition is a tremendous accomplishment; if you remember how you may have tried to learn a foreign language as an adult, you'll recall how difficult it was to acquire vocabulary and to master rules of grammar and the subtleties of usage. Yet preschool children do this with no formal training. By the time they are ready to

The attention that adults (especially parents) give children encourages positive interactions and leads to satisfactory and fulfilling relationships. Adult attention also furthers language development and enhances a child's self-concept. Do you agree with the statement that a linguistic environment is the most enriched environment?

fast mapping
Mental process whereby children use context to detect word meanings.

phonology
A language's sound system.

syntax
Rules of sentence structure.

semantics
Rules that describe how to interpret the meaning of words.

pragmatics
Rules that describe how people converse.

receptive language
Children's indication that they understand words without necessarily producing them.

expressive language
Language that children use to express their own ideas and needs.

enter first grade, most children have a vocabulary of about 8,000 words; use questions, negative statements, and dependent clauses; and have learned to use language in a variety of social situations. They are relatively sophisticated language users.

Language As Rule Learning

As children acquire the basics of their language, they are also learning the guidelines that make language such a powerful tool. For example, by the age of 4 or 5, children will have discovered that rules exist for combining sounds into words, that individual words have specific meanings, and that there are rules for combining words into meaningful sentences, and for participating in a dialogue. These rules help children to detect the meaning of a word with which they are unfamiliar. This mental process is called **fast mapping;** it enables children, upon only one exposure, to use context to figure out a word's meaning, thus causing continual rapid vocabulary development (see also Chapter 5).

We can summarize these accomplishments as follows.

- The rules of **phonology** describe a language's sound system—that is, how to put sounds together to form words.
- The rules of **syntax** determine sentence structure.
- The rules of **semantics** describe how to interpret the meaning of words.
- The rules of **pragmatics** describe how language is used in social contexts—that is, how people converse.

As we trace the path of language development in the early childhood years, remember a basic distinction that children quite clearly demonstrate. At about 1 year (the infancy period), children show an ability for **receptive language** ("show me your nose"—they receive and understand these words). Now, in early childhood, they produce language themselves, **expressive language** (McLaughlin, 1998). How do children acquire these language skills?

Simply by making noises with our mouths, we can reliably cause precise new combinations of ideas to arise in each other's minds.

—Steven Pinker

Pattern of Language Development

As mentioned earlier, all children learn language, and at similar ages they manifest similar patterns of language development. The basic sequence of language development during early childhood is that, at about 2½ years, most children produce complete sentences, begin to ask questions, and use negative statements. At about 4 years, they have acquired the complicated structure of their main language (and perhaps of another language), and in about two or three more years they speak and understand sentences that they have never previously used or heard.

As children grow, specifying the extent of their vocabularies is difficult. Do we mean spoken words only? Or do we include words that children may not use but clearly understand? Building a vocabulary is an amazing accomplishment. For example, the vocabulary of every language is categorized; that is, some words are nouns, some are verbs, still others are adjectives, prepositions, or conjunctions. If English had only 1,000 nouns and 1,000 verbs, we could form 1 million sentences ($1,000 \times 1,000$). But nouns can be used as objects as well as subjects. Therefore, the number of possible three-word sentences increases to one billion ($1,000 \times 1,000 \times 1,000$).

One billion sentences is the result of a starkly impoverished vocabulary. The number of sentences that could be generated from English, with its thousands of nouns and verbs, plus adjectives, adverbs, prepositions, and conjunctions, staggers the imagination. Estimates are that it would take trillions of years to say all possible

AN INFORMED VIEW

Reading Aloud to Children

Reading aloud to children is beneficial for them in many ways. It introduces them to vocabulary, grammar, and the literary elements so important for an appreciation of high-quality literature. Yet, reading aloud should be a time not only for instruction but also for child and adult to share a love of reading and language in a secure environment.

Reading is an accrued skill, which means that as long as children associate reading with pleasure and as long as they continue to read they will continue to improve their reading, increase their achievement level, and do well in school. Much of what a child learns is determined by the amount and richness of the language he hears from adults around him. As Trelease notes (2001), when you read to a child you introduce words that help the most when it's time for school and formal learning. You're also surrounding the child with books and print that bring enjoyment and satisfaction (Trelease, 2001).

To insure that reading aloud is a happy experience for both adult and child, the book should be a selection that both choose. Also, adults should be patient when the child wants to stop intermittently and talk about the book.

When we join our children in talks about the characters, in musing over what happens next, or in noticing the craft of the author, it is crucial to remember that these conversations are not detours around reading but are instead the essence of what it means to be thoughtful readers. To read well is to think well. *(Calkins, 1997, p. 48)*

As adults continue to read aloud to children, they should sense whether the child genuinely likes the book or would prefer another. Alternate choices should be available so that children can make another choice. (Young children readily listen to a favorite book over and over again.) Also, it may be wise for the reader to skim the book first to make sure the child is emotionally ready to hear, for example, that the dog is lost in the new large picture-book version written by Rosemary Wells of *Lassie Come Home,* or the cat is injured in Lynne Rae Perkins' *Broken Cat,* or the little boy is alone in a large Japanese department store in Toro Gomi's *I Lost My Father.*

Reading aloud to children: enjoyable, enriching, and (often) exciting.

English sentences of 20 words. In this context, the ability of children to acquire language is an astounding achievement. Although most youngsters experience problems with some tasks during this period—difficulty with reading or mathematics—they acquire language easily and in just a few years.

Language Irregularities

overextensions
Children's over-broad applications of words.

When speech emerges, certain irregularities appear in children's speech that are quite normal and to be expected. For example, **overextensions** mark children's beginning words. Assume that a child has learned the name of the house pet, *doggy.* Think what that label means: an animal with a head, tail, body, and four legs. Now consider what other animals "fit" this label: cats, horses, donkeys, and cows. Consequently, children may briefly apply *doggy* to all four-legged creatures; they quickly eliminate overextensions, however, as they learn about their world.

overregulation
Children's inappropriate use of language rules they have learned.

Overregularities are similarly fleeting phenomena. As youngsters begin to use two- and three-word sentences, they struggle to convey more precise meanings by mastering the grammatical rules of their language. For example, many English verbs add *ed* to indicate past tense.

> I want to play ball.
>
> I wanted to play ball.

Other verbs change their form much more radically.

> Did Daddy come home?
>
> Daddy came home.

Most children, even after they have mastered the correct forms of such verbs as come, see, and run, still add to the original form. That is, youngsters who know that the past tense of *come* is *came* still say:

> Daddy comed home.

Again, overregularities persist only briefly and are another example of the close link between language and thought. We know that from birth, children respond to patterns. They look longer at a human face than at diagrams because the human face is more complex. (Remember the Fantz study?) Once they have learned a pattern such as adding *ed* to signify past tense, they have considerable difficulty in changing the pattern.

An interesting development occurs as children's sentences grow longer: Children's use of word order becomes closely linked to grammar rather than merely reflecting meaning. That is, their language becomes more syntactic. Inflections such as *s* and *ed* are correctly added to words, and, thanks to Roger Brown's groundbreaking work (1973), we now know quite a bit more about these grammatical morphemes (*s, ed*). Brown studied 14 morphemes, including the three *s* inflections: plural (girl*s*), possessive (girl'*s*), and verb endings (run*s*).

Using these morphemes correctly requires considerable language sophistication. Children who correctly add *ed* to a word tell us in no uncertain terms that something happened in the past. Brown also discovered that *all* children acquire these 14 morphemes in the same sequence. For example, although the three *s* inflections look exactly alike, children learn the plural usage first, followed by the possessive, and finally the verb inflection.

During the early childhood years, children begin to display a growing mastery of meaning. As we mentioned, their vocabulary continues to increase quite dramatically, and they begin to combine words to refine their meaning. Yet they also display a sense of constraint in the way they use words; that is, they quickly learn to suggest the correct meaning for the correct word.

"That's right," suggesting correctness.

"That's right," suggesting direction.

Summarizing, then: As children come to the end of the early childhood period, several language milestones have been achieved.

- Children become skillful in building words; adding suffixes such as *er, man,* and *ist* to form nouns (the person who performs experiments is an *experimenter*).
- They begin to be comfortable with passive sentences (the glass *was broken* by the wind).
- By the end of the early-childhood period, children can pronounce almost all speech sounds accurately.
- As we have noted, this is the time of the "language explosion"; vocabulary has grown rapidly.
- Children of this age are aware of grammatical correctness.

Bilingualism

As migration patterns have increased rapidly, many societies are faced with problems that relate directly to language and cultural issues. As Snow and Kang (2006) note, migrants must learn to adapt to new and challenging situations, acquire a new language, and adjust to novel social, educational, and occupational settings as well. Migrant children, of course, are immediately faced with language issues in school, with friends, and with general social skills. The conclusion that such children have a risk of greater academic problems is solidly supported by research results. (For a summary of these results, see Snow & Kang, 2006). To sharpen our focus on these children, they are identified as L2/C2 learners.

- *L2 children.* Those children who need to acquire a second language.
- *C2 children.* Those children who need to adjust to a second culture.
- *L2/C2 children.* Those children who need to acquire both a second language and a second culture.

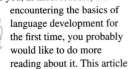

B. Moskowitz (1979). The Acquisition of Language, *Scientific American, 239,* 92–108. If you, as most readers, are encountering the basics of language development for the first time, you probably would like to do more reading about it. This article (still one of the best) is clear, thorough, and well written. You should find it easily in your library.

AN APPLIED VIEW

Meet Genie—A Child You'll Never Forget

The tranquility of Temple City, California, was shattered in November, 1970, by disquieting, almost unbelievable, news. Screeching headlines described the discovery of a young girl who had been "held prisoner" by her family for 13 years. Her mother, almost completely blind and feeling the ravages of an abusive marriage, sought assistance for the blind in the local welfare office. With Genie, she mistakenly stumbled into a social services office, where an alert eligibility worker became fascinated, not by the mother but by the girl.

No wonder. The 13-year-old girl weighed only 59 pounds and was 54 inches tall. She was even in worse condition than she looked. She wasn't toilet trained, she couldn't chew solid food, and she could barely swallow. She drooled continuously and had no compunction about spitting—no matter where she was. And these were Genie's less obnoxious characteristics. Perhaps most important of all, she couldn't talk.

After her discovery, investigators began to trace the road that led Genie to her present state. At about 20 months of age, she received a rare physical examination by a pediatrician who stated that she seemed a little "slow," which the father interpreted as meaning that she was profoundly retarded. With the physician's label ringing in his ears, Genie's father, Clark, developed a weird and abusive style of childrearing for his youngest child.

He kept her in a small bedroom tied to an infant's potty seat. Trapped in this harness, Genie couldn't move anything but her hands and feet. She sat there, day after day, month after month, year after year. At night, she was placed in a sleeping bag designed by her father that kept her arms motionless, much like a straitjacket. She was then placed in a crib with an overhead cover and wire mesh sides. She heard nothing—no human voices (only when her father swore at her), no radio, no language. When she made noise, her father beat her. She quickly learned to keep quiet rather than be beaten by a board her father kept in the room.

The room contained no other furniture, no pictures, one ceiling bulb. She was allowed to play with two dirty plastic raincoats, empty cottage cheese containers, and empty spools of thread. Her diet was baby foods, cereal, and an occasional soft-boiled egg. If she choked and spit out any food, Clark rubbed her face in it. Almost totally blind, Genie's mother was helpless; she was at the mercy of her husband. Finally, things became so bad that Clark relented and called Genie's maternal grandparents, who took Genie and her mother with them, which eventually led to Genie's discovery. Her parents were arrested. Despondent about the emotional valleys in his life, Clark killed himself. Genie was hospitalized and became the object of intensive and prolonged study.

The startling case of Genie illustrates the durability of language but also demonstrates its vulnerability. After treatment in the Children's Hospital of Los Angeles, Genie was placed in a foster home where she acquired language, more from exposure than any formal training. Estimates are that she has acquired as much language in eight years as the normal child acquires in three. She continues to have articulation problems and difficulty with word order.

Although Genie made remarkable language progress, difficulties persist. For example, she does not appear to have mastered the rules of language (her grammar is unpredictable), she continues to use the stereotypic speech of the language-disabled child, and she seems to understand more language than she can produce. Thus the case of Genie suggests that although language is difficult to retard, sufficiently severe conditions can affect progress in language. Here we see the meaning of *sensitive period* applied to language development.

If you'd like to learn more about this tragic case, read R. Rymer (1993). *Genie: A Scientific Tragedy*. New York: Harper. This is one of the best summaries of Genie's years of hell.

Many children in the United States who do not speak or write English as their native language face language problems on a daily basis. Our country has become more diverse ethnically and linguistically than ever before. Consequently, a major question facing language experts and educators is this: What is the most effective way to teach English to non-English speaking students while at the same time helping them to maintain the richness and cultural values of their own languages? The value of helping bilingual children maintain proficiency in both languages is also seen in brain research that testifies to the benefits bilingualism brings to brain development. For example, these children seem to be superior in ignoring misleading information.

Estimates of the number of English Language Learners (ELLs) in school range from 2 to 6 million (Marshall, 2002). But this figure is deceptive owing to differences within the ELL population that represent a wide range of economic and ethnic diversity. For many children, economic conditions dictate their access to resources that contribute to the acquisition of necessary English language skills. Ethnic diversity speaks for itself. Although the largest number of ELL students are of Hispanic/Latino origin (approximately 74%), the number of languages spoken within the ELL population literally know no boundary. Given the large number of these children, several different techniques of teaching needed language skills have been proposed.

A SOCIOCULTURAL VIEW

When English Is Not Spoken

Many schools in the country are today enrolling children of immigrant parents. Imagine the language problems facing these children, their parents, and grandparents. What can we do to help? Through TESOL (**T**eaching **E**nglish to **S**peakers of **O**ther **L**anguages) (Wong, 2006), teachers are encouraged to use their students' families and communities as resources (Kachru, 2005). Three questions guide their work.

1. What do we know about the nature of the language?
2. What do we know about the nature of the learner?
3. What are the aims of your instruction?

Probably the most effective step is to obtain as much information as possible about the cultures of the children so that we understand them at the significant or at least the intermediate level. In this way, adults who work with immigrant children can better appreciate the needs, attitudes, and values underlying their behaviors. Parents, grandparents, and other interested adults should also be encouraged to share books with the children even though they may not read or write English.

Wordless books, for example, that portray touching themes are excellent bridges for non-English speaking children to share with their families. Books such as those by Pat Hutchins, (*Changes, Changes*), Mitsumasa Anno (*Anno's, Journal*), Molly Bang (*The Grey Lady and The Strawberry Snatcher*), and Quentin Blake (*Clown*) are very helpful. By taking turns explaining to each other what is happening on each page both adult and child undertake a rewarding learning experience together.

Books by such well-known authors and illustrators as William Steig and Tomie dePaola are also available in other languages. Rebecca Emberley's *My Numbers/Mis Numeros* uses everyday objects and paints the objects in bright, vivid colors to encourage children to match English words with Spanish words. Step by step, teachers, librarians and interested adults are constantly exploring many innovative ways to encourage and motivate *all* children to be readers.

CDs, audiotapes, and *videotapes* of books for English language learners are available at public libraries. Examples of *videotapes* that are expertly produced and appeal to small children are *There Was an Old Lady Who Swallowed a Fly* (Simms Taback), *How Do Dinosaurs Say Good Night?* (Jane Yolen), and *Merry Christmas, Space Case* (James Marshall). The American Library Association annually selects videos, recordings, and software for all ages that are based on the recommendations of committees of librarians and educators from across the country who consider their originality, creativity, and suitability.

Recordings of books such as *The Frogs Wore Red Suspenders* (Jack Prelutsky), *Good Night Gorilla* (Peggy Rathmann), and *Martin's Big Words* (Doreen Rappaport) are also helpful as adults and young children follow the words of the book, together. In each recording, the narrator speaks slowly and distinctly so that the listener follows easily.

Bilingual Education Programs

In a landmark decision in 1974 (*Lau v. Nichols*), the U.S. Supreme Court ruled that Limited English Proficiency (LEP) students in San Francisco were being discriminated against because they were not receiving the same education as their English-speaking classmates. The school district was ordered to provide means for LEP students to participate in all instructional programs. The manner of implementing the decision was left to the school district under the guidance of the lower courts. This decision provided the impetus for the implementation of bilingual education programs in the United States.

With the bilingual technique, three major goals are identified (Brisk, 1998; Ovando & Collier, 1998):

- The continued development of the student's primary language.
- Acquisition of a second language, usually English.
- Instruction in content subjects using both languages.

Students are taught partly in English and partly in their native language. The objective here is to help pupils to learn English by subject matter instruction in their own language and in English. Thus they acquire subject matter knowledge simultaneously with English. Bilingual programs also allow students to retain their cultural identities while simultaneously progressing in their school subjects. In today's schools, bilingual education has become the program of choice.

Bilingual education programs can also be divided into two categories. First are those programs (sometimes called *transitional* programs) in which the rapid development of English is to occur so that students may switch as soon as possible to an all-English program. Second are those programs (sometimes referred to as *maintenance* programs) that permit LEP students to remain in them even after they have become proficient in English. The rationale for such programs is that students can use both languages to develop mature skills and to become fully bilingual. Transitional programs are the most widely used in the schools.

A third type of bilingual program, called **bilingual immersion,** has become increasingly popular in the United States (Brisk, 2005). Originally introduced in Canada in the 1960s, the program has children spend 90% of their day using the minority language in kindergarten and first grade. The majority language is introduced in grades two or three, and usage gradually increases until subjects are taught equally in both languages by grades four and five.

The controversy surrounding bilingual education programs recently came to a head in the state of California when voters decided to replace bilingual programs with structured English immersion (SEI). SEI programs have several variations, but each is characterized by extensive use of English and the use of English-as-a-second language (ESL) methodology (Baker, 1999).

Whatever program is chosen, a consensus seems to have gathered around techniques that in no way show disrespect to a student's language. For example, schools effective with culturally different populations are sufficiently flexible to accommodate a range of dialects that learners bring to school. Teachers are urged to allow dialects in social and recreational settings and encourage these students to use Standard English in school settings (Manning & Baruth, 2004).

Table 7.2. summarizes several of the outstanding characteristics of early-childhood youngsters.

bilingual immersion
Students are taught partly in English and partly in their own language.

Guided Review

19. Most children have completed the greater part of language acquisition by the age of _____.

20. _____ describes how to put sounds together to form words.

21. Calling all four-legged, furry animals *doggy* is an example of _____.

22. _____ was the first to determine that we "speak with the left hemisphere."

23. A popular method for teaching English to non-English speaking students is _____.

24. LEP refers to _____ _____ _____.

25. A program that has children initially spend 90% of their time using the minority language is called _____ _____.

Answers

19. 5 20. Phonology 21. overextension 22. Broca 23. TESOL. 24. Limited English Proficiency 25. bilingual immersion

TABLE 7.2			Some Developmental Characteristics of Early Childhood		
Age (yrs.)	Height (in.)	Weight (lbs.)	Cognitive Development	Language Development	Motor Development
2½	36	30	Continued symbolic development; thought still egocentric	Can identify object by use	Can walk on tiptoes; can jump with both feet off the floor
3	38	32	Discriminates 4 objects from 5; mental images are representations of objects	Answers questions; uses brief sentences	Can stand on one foot; jumps from bottom of stairs; rides tricycle
3½	39	34	Understands that thoughts differ from objects; some signs of conservation of number	Begins to build sentences	Continues to improve 3-year-old skills; begins to play with others
4	41	36	Continued growth of symbolic ability; proficient at counting	Names and counts several objects; uses conjunctions; understands prepositions	Walks downstairs, one foot to step; skips on one foot; throws ball overhand
4½	42	38	Begins to understand concept of time	Mean length of utterance 4.5 words	Hops on one foot; dramatic play
5	43	41	Some understanding of conservation of weight; begins to use rehearsal to help memory	Begins to show language mastery; uses words apart from specific situation	Skips alternating feet; walks straight line; stands for longer period on one foot
5½	45	45	Continuing signs of conservation; still tends to focus on perceptual aspects	Asks meaning of words; more complex sentences of 5 or 6 words	Draws recognizable person; continues to develop throwing skill

 # CONCLUSION & SUMMARY

Thus far in our discussion of the early childhood years, we have seen that although the rate of physical growth slows somewhat, it still continues at a steady pace. Physical and motor skills become more refined. Cognitive development during these years leads to a world of representation in which children are expected to acquire and manipulate symbols. Language gradually becomes a powerful tool in adapting to the environment.

What are the major physical and motor accomplishments of the early childhood years?

- Growth continues at a steady, less rapid rate during these years.
- Brain lateralization seems to be well established by the age of 5 or 6.

- Height is a good indicator of normal development when heredity and environment are considered in evaluating health.
- Increasing competence and mastery are seen in a child's acquisition of motor skills.

How do Piaget's views on cognitive development differ from those of information-processing theorists?

- These years are the time of Piaget's preoperational period and the continued appearance of symbolic abilities.
- During these years children develop a theory of mind.
- Children's growing cognitive proficiency is seen in their use of humor.

- Many current early childhood programs have a cognitive orientation.

What types of early-childhood education seem most promising?

- Many preschool programs are based on the ideas of Piaget and Montessori.
- Project Head Start was originally designed to offer educational and developmental services to disadvantaged children.
- Several positive social and emotional outcomes seem to be associated with Head Start programs.

chapter 7 Review

chapter 7 Review

How does children's language acquisition proceed during these years?

- Children acquire the basics of their language during these years with little, if any, instruction.

- All children seem to follow the same pattern in acquiring language.
- Migrant children in the USA whose native language is not English need a

carefully designed program to support their native language and to help them acquire English as efficiently as possible.

KEY TERMS

absorbent mind
animism
anticipatory images
artificialism
bilingual immersion
centration
classification
conservation
controlled scribbling
deferred imitation
drawing
egocentrism
expressive language
fast mapping

language
mental images
motor skills
organization
overextensions
overregulation
phonology
pragmatics
preoperational
prepared environment
Project Head Start
random scribbling
realism
receptive language

rehearsal
representation
reproductive images
retrieval
reversibility
semantics
sensitive periods
span of apprehension
symbolic play
syntax
theory of mind
uniform growth

WHAT DO YOU THINK?

1. As you can tell from the data presented in this chapter, early-childhood youngsters continue their rapid growth, although at a less frantic rate than during infancy. If you were a parent of a child of this age (boy or girl), how much would you encourage him or her to participate in organized, directed physical activities (swimming, dancing, soccer, and so on)? Be sure to give specific reasons for your answer.

2. As you read Paul McGhee's account of the development of children's humor, could you explain his stages by comparing them with Piaget's work? Do you think this is a logical way to proceed? Why?

3. When you consider the tragic case of Genie compared to the enormous language growth of most children, what comes to your mind? Does it change your opinion about how language develops? In what way? What do you think this case implies for the existence of a sensitive period for language development?

CHAPTER REVIEW TEST

1. **Glia cells are mainly _____ cells.**
   a. support.
   b. transmission
   c. synaptic
   d. embryonic

2. **By the age of 5 to 6 years, _____% of adult brain weight is present.**
   a. 70
   b. 80

   c. 90
   d. 100

3. **When children show a preference for one hand or the other, this illustrates brain**
   a. lateralization.
   b. synapses.
   c. dendrites.
   d. initiative.

4. **A frequent cause of psychological disturbance for children can be**

   a. brain adaptation.
   b. muscle growth.
   c. equilibration.
   d. stress.

5. **Using the large muscles is referred to as _____ motor skills.**
   a. fine
   b. peripheral
   c. gross
   d. anatomical

6. **Which of the following factors is not known to influence physical development?**
   a. genetic elements
   b. SES
   c. disease
   d. ethnicity

7. **Which of the following would not be considered a motor skill?**
   a. running
   b. skipping
   c. tying shoes
   d. concept formation

8. **Controlled scribbling appears at about age**
   a. 5.
   b. 3.
   c. 4.
   d. 2.

9. **Which of the following behaviors is not associated with the preoperational period?**
   a. symbolic play
   b. drawing
   c. language
   d. walks steadily

10. **A child's belief that inanimate objects are real and conscious is known as**
    a. artificialism.
    b. delusion.
    c. animism.
    d. centration.

11. **By the time children are ready to enter first grade they have a vocabulary of about _____ words.**

a. 8,000
b. 6,500
c. 3,000
d. 1,200

12. **McGhee notes that the basis of most children's humor is**
    a. irony.
    b. play on words.
    c. incongruity.
    d. sarcasm.

13. **Effective use of humor is not credited with stimulating**
    a. motor development.
    b. creative thinking.
    c. social development.
    d. emotional development.

14. **Montessori's ideas concerning _____ periods are important in planning preschool programs.**
    a. lengthy
    b. class
    c. sensitive
    d. time

15. **Project Head Start was initiated in the**
    a. 1960s.
    b. 1970s.
    c. 1980s.
    d. 1990s.

16. **When children produce language, the result is called**
    a. vocables.
    b. receptive language.
    c. phonetic output.
    d. expressive language.

17. **The rules of _____ describe how to put words together to form sentences.**
    a. phonology
    b. semantics
    c. syntax
    d. pragmatics

18. **The brain area thought to interpret speech is called**
    a. Broca's area.
    b. Wernicke's area.
    c. Lau's area.
    d. Bloom's area.

19. **A 3-year-old's statement that "Daddy comed home" is an example of**
    a. overextension.
    b. mispronunciation.
    c. overregulation.
    d. delayed development.

20. **Children who receive 90% of their instruction in a minority language are in _____ programs.**
    a. bilingual immersion
    b. sheltered language
    c. autonomous
    d. gramatically correct

Answers

1. a, 2. c, 3. a, 4. d, 5. c, 6. d, 7. d, 8. b, 9. d, 10. c, 11. a, 12. c, 13. a, 14. c, 15. a, 16. d, 17. c, 18. b, 19. c, 20. a

8 chapter

PSYCHOSOCIAL DEVELOPMENT IN EARLY CHILDHOOD

Chapter Objectives

After reading this chapter, you should be able to answer the following questions.

- What role does family play in development during these early-childhood years?

- How do children of this age acquire a sense of self?

- How do children come to understand the meaning of their gender?

- What is the value of play to children of these years?

New Orleans in 1911 was a teeming, exciting city. With the unending stream of ships plying the Mississippi River, with candy shops that enticed with their delicious sweets, and with music in the air everywhere, New Orleans was a delight for a child. On October 26, 1911, Mahalia Jackson was born into this stimulating atmosphere. She lived with 12 other people crammed into three rooms and a kitchen, and money was scarce. All the adults worked, freeing Mahalia to happily explore the city as a young child.

But when she turned 6 years of age, her mother died. Now living with a strict aunt, she was forbidden to sample the activity and adventures of this thriving community. Instead, she was given a long list of household chores to perform, which, if done carelessly, produced severe punishment. School was a part-time diversion, which she was soon forced to leave behind.

Displaying a fascination for music at an early age—singing in the church choir, listening to and being influenced by the great singer Bessie Smith—Mahalia soon established herself as a gospel singer. She quickly astonished churchgoers with her beautiful voice. Moving to Chicago with an aunt, she continued to enrich her voice and became a member of one of the first gospel groups that sang in different churches and social groups.

Soon invitations for solo performances began to pour in, and her career flourished until she became the famous woman the world came to know. How much of her success was due to love of family and love of music we can only speculate. But it seems safe to conclude that the early-childhood years contributed substantially to the formation of the revered singer.

During the early-childhood years, children blossom into quite distinctive personalities. Although personality differences are apparent at birth, they now flourish until even the most casual observer notices a child's "personality." Children of this age are entering a period in which they must learn to reconcile their individuality with the demands of the world around them. New abilities, new friends, new ideas come up against parental restrictions, and parents often find themselves searching for an ideal mix of firmness and love.

If you wish to know more about this charming and compelling person, see Laurainne Goreau, *Just Mahalia, Baby.*

Children's personalities take on definite shadings. Children's interactions with those around them begin to take shape, setting the stage for the kind of relationships that the children will form in the future. They now begin the process of widening their circle of relationships. Children from 2 to 6 will make new friends: in the family, in the neighborhood, in preschool. Some youngsters of this age are also faced with adjusting to a new sibling (or siblings), which can be a time of great frustration if not handled carefully.

How children accomplish all these things leads us to Erikson's stages of autonomy versus shame and doubt, and initiative versus guilt. If children are encouraged to *develop* as well as *control* their newfound abilities, they acquire feelings of competence and independence that can only further development. As Erikson noted, parental control during these years must be firmly reassuring so as to protect children from shame and doubt. They can then move on to using their growing sense of initiative in a manner that frees them from any sense of guilt.

To help you to understand these issues, in this chapter we examine the modern family, tracing the stages through which it proceeds (including the growing importance of day care and divorce), how children continue to develop their sense of self and gender identity, and the role of play in development. Our initial task, though, is to examine that great socializing agent—the family.

THE FAMILY IN DEVELOPMENT

When one is out of touch with oneself, one cannot touch others.

—ANNE MORROW LINDBERGH

Understanding and defining today's families became a difficult task once researchers began to analyze developmental data from a *systems* perspective. Careful evaluation has led to a realization that family life reflects a complex interaction over time among the effects of a family environment, the personality and temperamental characteristics of children, genetic influences, and resilience factors of children, all of which have different effects on individual children. When we consider the relationships that exist among these many variables, we realize that a family can't be viewed merely as a collection of individuals but as a system whose patterns of interactions become relatively stable (Eisler, 2002, p. 128–129).

For example, a modern family may have both parents working; it may be a single-parent family; it may comprise unrelated people living together; it may be a family with foster children; it may be a blended family (divorce and remarriage). It could also be a poor and homeless family. The older idea of homeless people being mostly alcoholic men has changed. The "new" homeless population is younger and much more mixed: more single women, more families, and more minorities. Distressed parents state they feel less effective and capable and are less affectionate in their interactions with their children. The developmental risks associated with poverty and economic difficulties are well known (NICHHD, 2005a).

Families with young children may be the fastest-growing segment of today's poor and homeless. They are also characterized by few social contacts, poor health, low school achievement, a high level of contact with the criminal justice system, and poverty. Today we recognize the powerful role poverty has in development owing to the multiple stresses that it causes. In a penetrating analysis of the environment of childhood poverty, Evans (2004) summarized the environmental inequities facing poor children: more family turmoil, violence, instability, separation, less social support, less access to books and computers, less parental involvement in school activities, and so on.

Despite the many changes that have occurred in any definition of *family*, the vast majority of individuals live in some type of "family," which testifies to the widely held belief in the strength of the family as the basic social structure.

Changing View of the Family

A good example of how culture and history change the structure of family life is seen in the following statement by Bornstein (2002, p. ix).

The family generally, and parenting specifically, are today in a greater state of flux, question, and redefinition than perhaps ever before. We are witnessing the emergence of striking permutations on the theme of parenting:

As social conditions change—working mothers, single-parent families—fathers have become more involved in child care. Children thus see their parents in roles different from the more stereotypical views of the past. As parental role expectations change, can you explain the possible effects on a child's development?

blended families, lesbian and gay parents, teen versus 50s first-time moms and dads. One cannot but be awed on the biological front by technology that now renders postmeno-pausal women capable of childbearing and with the possibility of designing babies.

Along with these changes identified by Bornstein have come several significant developmental discoveries—familial relationships, the importance of reciprocal interactions, the role of contextualism in interpreting development—that have produced changes in attempts to define family. Among these changes are the following (Parke & Buriel, 2006, p. 431).

- Focus currently is less on parent/child and more on the family as a social system.

- Recognition exists that family members influence one another both directly and indirectly. For example, a mother may influence a child indirectly by the nature of her relationship with the father.

- Different types of analysis are required to understand families. Not only individual relationships (for instance, mother/child) but also relationships among family members must be examined.

- The nature of parent/child relationships is bidirectional and not unidirectional; that is, influence runs both ways, from parent to child and from child to parent.

We turn now to the role of parents.

Parents and Their Children

Parents do many things—select clothes, limit television time, impose rules—but they alone can't determine the nature of the relationship with their children. Parents and children are in it together, for better or worse We'll wrestle with parent/child issues throughout the chapter, but if there's one thing we've learned about the relationships between parents and their children it's this: What's right means what works for parents and their children in their culture. Children of different ages, with different problems, and from different cultures require different types of parenting. We're quite sure now that parents and children actually *construct* their relationships; no one model fits all children and parents.

Certain forces exist, however, that seem to be particularly influential in the parent/child relationship (Bornstein, 2006). Among them are these:

- *Parents' characteristics affect parenting.* For example, personality, age, and stage of life are all important considerations.

- *Children's characteristics affect parenting.* For example, health, age, gender, and responsiveness all affect the bidirectional nature of parenting that we have mentioned.

- *Context affects parenting.* For example, social structure, socioeconomic status, culture, and family configuration are important determinants of the quality of parenting.

Let's turn now to Diane Baumrind's pioneering work on parenting style.

Parenting Behavior

Analyzing the relationship between parental behavior and children's competence, Baumrind (1967, 1971, 1986, 1991a/b) discovered three kinds of parental behavior: authoritarian, authoritative, and permissive:

authoritarian parents
Baumrind's term for parents who are demanding and want instant obedience as the most desirable child trait.

- **Authoritarian parents:** These parents are demanding, and for them instant obedience is the most desirable child trait. When there is any conflict between these parents and their children (Why can't I go to the party?), no consideration is given to the child's view, no attempt is made to explain why the youngster can't go to the party, and often the child is punished for even asking. It's a simple case of "Do it my way or else!"

authoritative parents
Baumrind's term for parents who respond to their children's needs and wishes; believing in parental control, they attempt to explain the reasons for it to their children.

- **Authoritative parents:** These parents respond to their children's needs and wishes. Believing in parental control, they attempt to explain the reasons for it to their children. Authoritative parents expect mature behavior and will enforce rules, but they encourage their children's independence and search for potential. In the resolution of socialization versus individuation, authoritative parents try to maintain a happy balance between the two. (For an excellent discussion of parental authority, see Garbarino & Bedard, 2001.)

AN INFORMED VIEW

The Puzzling Topic of Punishment

No child is perfect, which introduces the controversial subject of punishment. Most parents are puzzled about what to do when their children misbehave, and their reactions can range from using harsh physical punishment to a permissive, "hands-off" approach. Neither of these techniques is desirable, but what are some acceptable alternatives?

First, what is meant by punishment? Punishment may take one of two paths: Something unpleasant is done to a child (scolding, hitting), or something pleasant is withdrawn (removal from an exciting game). Either type of punishment can have certain effects:

- *Punishment confined to the immediate situation may have absolutely no effect in the future.* For example, most of you have been scolded for chewing gum in school; yet, if you look around your present classroom, you'll probably see some of your classmates chewing away.
- *Punishment may produce a future effect if it is sufficiently severe and causes intense, unpleasant emotional responses.* The danger here, of course, is that conditioned stimuli can cause negative, accompanying reactions: A child may fear a teacher, which then leads to a fear and dislike of all teachers and schools.

If parents punish their child, they should quickly have that child do something that they can praise. They should also be precise in what they punish so that their child knows exactly what behavior to avoid. For example, it makes little sense to say, "You're not going out with that crowd again." Who? Where? What was done? In addition, above all, no one parent should be singled out as "the punisher."

Most child experts, including pediatricians, oppose the use of corporal punishment for many reasons, chief of which is that it too often leads to child abuse. Nonphysical methods, such as positive reinforcement whenever possible, time-out, or removal of privileges are the desired methods (American Academy of Pediatrics, 1998). Still, spanking is used regularly by many parents who believe it is the most effective form of punishment. Would you spank your child? Were you spanked as a child?

If you would like to have a more informed view on this issue, you may want to read one or more of the articles referenced in this chapter, such as the analysis presented by the American Academy of Pediatrics (1998). You may also wish to learn more about it by going to our web site at www.mhhe.com/dacey7.

A particularly useful analysis of the role of punishment in child care can be found in American Academy of Pediatrics. (1998). Guidance for Effective Discipline, *Pediatrics,* 101(4), 723–728.

TABLE 8.1	Parental Behaviors and Children's Characteristics		

	PARENTAL BEHAVIORS		
	Authoritarian	*Authoritative*	*Permissive*
Children's characteristics	Withdrawn	Self-assertive	Impulsive
	Lack of enthusiasm	Independent	Low self-reliance
	Shy (girls)	Friendly	Low self-control
	Hostile (boys)	Cooperative	Low maturity
	Low need achievement	High need achievement	Aggressive
	Low competence	High competence	Lack of responsibility

permissive parents
Baumrind's term for parents who take a tolerant, accepting view of their children's behavior; they rarely make demands or use punishment.

- **Permissive parents:** These parents take a tolerant, accepting view of their children's behavior, including both aggressive and sexual urges. They rarely use punishment or make demands of their children. Children make almost all their own decisions.

Authoritative parents believe in control (they have definite standards for their children), maintain clarity of communication (the children clearly understand what is expected of them), encourage mature behavior (they want their children to behave in a way appropriate for their age), and are themselves nurturing (a warm, loving relationship exists between parents and children). In a longitudinal study from preschool to adolescence, Baumrind (1991c) found that authoritative parenting continued to be associated with positive developmental outcomes. Table 8.1 presents the relationship between Baumrind's classes of parenting behavior and children's characteristics.

Baumrind's findings have held firm over the years. As Holmbeck, Paikoff, and Brooks-Gunn (1995) stated, authoritative parents have adolescents who achieve better and demonstrate more positive social adjustment than do children whose parents adopted either authoritarian or permissive parenting styles.

Yet it's important to remember that Baumrind's findings don't necessarily indicate a cause-and-effect relationship between her categories and a child's characteristics. These findings apply to white, middle-class families with both parents present. Children reared in single-parent families may experience quite different parenting behaviors. We must also recognize that children's temperaments affect how they're treated. Baumrind has acknowledged the influence of temperament but has also argued that parenting behavior has a decided impact on a child's behavior.

No discussion of the family's influence on development would be complete without examining the role of siblings.

Siblings and Development

The two girls couldn't be more different. Twelve-year-old Christine was tall, blonde, smart, and athletically gifted. Nine-year-old Beth was tall, dark, smart, and couldn't walk across the room without falling over something. Christine, outgoing and nonchalant; Beth, quiet and intense. Christine, older and the center of attention, liked to tease Beth to the point of tears, a habit their parents tried to stop. As Christine grew older and her interests broadened (read "boys"), her relationship with Beth became much smoother, and both girls seemed to have worked out a comfortable way of living with each other.

siblings
Brothers and/or sisters.

Growing up with **siblings** (brothers and sisters) is quite different from growing up without them. Brothers and sisters, because of their behavior toward one another, create a different family environment. Siblings play a critical role in the socialization of children. For example, older siblings often act as caregivers for their younger brothers and sisters, which provides opportunities for them to learn about the needs of others (Eisenberg, Fabes, & Spinrad, 2006). Consequently, experience with siblings provides a setting in which the pattern of interactions that has been established transfers to relationships with others (Parke & Buriel, 2006).

Older siblings become models for younger children to imitate. They can become sounding boards for their younger brothers and sisters; that is, the younger siblings can try out something before approaching a parent. Older siblings often ease the way for younger ones by trying to explain to parents that what happened wasn't all that bad. In this way, bonds are formed that usually last a lifetime, longer in most cases than those between husband and wife or parent and child.

Sibling Relationships through the Years

About 80% of children have siblings, which means that they grow up in a special network of relationships that affects their development in unique ways.

—Judy Dunn

Several cultural factors contribute to the formation of a lifelong bond between siblings. For example, *longer lifespans* mean that brothers and sisters spend a longer period of their lives together than ever before, as long as 70 or 80 years! When parents have died, the siblings' own children have left and their spouses have died, siblings tend to tighten the bond and offer one another needed support. *Geographic mobility* means unavoidable separation. Friendships are lost; schools and teachers change; adjustments to new situations must be made, but the sibling relationship usually remains intact. *Divorce and remarriage* typically bring unhappiness and hurt, and the need for support. During these troubled days, siblings may well be a trusted source of support and stability. For many children, the one anchor to be found is a brother or sister.

Siblings play a major role in development. For those children with brothers and sisters, older siblings can act as models, help younger brothers and sisters in times of difficulty, and help smooth relations with adults. Describe how the interactions among siblings affect development.

Studying stability in sibling relationships, Dunn and her associates (1994) found considerable continuity from early childhood to the beginning of adolescence in the positive and negative feelings of siblings toward each other. Many reasons contributed to the stability of these behaviors, especially the ongoing family dynamics. The siblings seemed to grow closer with adversity; that is, when one sibling had troubles with someone at school or became ill, other siblings offered support and sympathy. Gender differences also appeared: Adolescent girls were closer to their younger sisters than were adolescent boys with their younger sisters. (For an excellent discussion of sibling relationships, especially with regard to parenting behavior, see Furman & Lanthier, 2002.)

How Siblings Help One Another

Siblings act as nonthreatening sounding boards for one another. New behaviors, new roles, and new ideas can be tested on siblings, and their reactions, whether positive or negative, lack the doomsday quality of many parental judgments. The emotional atmosphere is less charged. They exchange clothes as teenagers, borrow money before a paycheck, provide support in life's crises; in other words, they offer valuable services for one another.

sibling underworld
Familial subsystem, or coalition, of brothers and/or sisters.

Siblings also form subsystems that are the basis for the formation of powerful coalitions, often called the **sibling underworld.** Older siblings can warn their younger brothers and sisters about parental moods and prohibitions, thus averting problems. Older siblings frequently provide an educational service to parents by

A SOCIOCULTURAL VIEW

Families in Their Cultures

From birth, children are influenced by their culture in almost every way we can imagine: feeding practices, sleeping arrangements, accepted values, educational expectations, school experiences, and interpersonal relations. Yet, if we examine "culture" carefully, we see that two cultures affect children, the culture of the home and the culture of the society. Consequently, children are raised in a dual climate of culture within the home and the culture of the surrounding world (Greenfield, Suzuki, & Rothstein-Fisch, 2006).

Researchers also raise the interesting issue of cultural conflict in a country such as the United States, where the dominant culture values independence in its children and citizens, whereas the immigrant culture rewards interdependence as a goal of development. Consequently, children often face conflicting signals from home and the surrounding community with regard to values, attitudes, and behaviors (Greenfield, Suzuki, & Rothstein-Fisch, 2006, p. 659). These different paths of development require a sensitive understanding of diverse cultures to avoid conflict and also to help children preserve their cultural heritage while learning and adapting to a different culture.

Any analysis of the family's influence on development must consider parental goals. An example of this is seen in a culture's adoption of authoritarian parenting methods that aren't necessarily associated with negative child development. Chinese-American families use what appear to be authoritarian methods to foster harmonious relationships, and these methods are a sign of parental concern. Latino families may use authoritarian techniques to achieve the developmental goal of respect for others (Greenfield & Suzuki, 1998).

If we accept the basic concepts of developmental contextualism (see Chapter 2), we recognize that the interactions among the forces acting on children (genetic, environmental, behavioral, neural) change with age (Lerner & Ashman, 2006). For example, not only does our nervous system change as a result of our experiences, but our social relationships also change. The well-known cultural scholar, Barbara Rogoff, has taken this idea and used it as a basis for understanding cultural processes (2003, p. 11):

> Humans develop through their changing participation in the sociocultural activities of their communities, which also change.

Finally, it's important to remember that references to *culture* invariably refer to *cultural differences* and not *cultural deficits*.

Cultural differences are often seen in the relationships between parents and their children.

informing them of events outside the home that parents should be aware of. *Rivalry,* whatever the cause, may characterize any bond. An older sibling can contribute to that sense of inferiority that Erikson identified as the crisis of this period. Imagine the difficulty of a firstborn sibling forced to share parental attention, especially if the spacing between the children is close (less than two years). If the firstborns must also care for younger children, they can become increasingly frustrated.

The boyhood of President John F. Kennedy is a good example of the turbulence and support that siblings share. An older, stronger, and charming brother, Joe, at times made life miserable for the future president, resulting in quarreling and even fighting. John responded by frequently becoming the nasty little brother, irritating his older sibling when he could. Occasionally the two of them would join forces to torment the two younger brothers, Robert and Edward. Yet all four brothers shared a powerful bond that helped them survive the crises and tragedies that were to strike the Kennedy family.

Siblings of Children with Disabilities

Given the unique emotional bond that siblings share, the relationship between a child and a sibling with a disability takes on different meanings. If a disability limits peer interactions, the sibling relationship becomes the prime source of positive socialization with female children assuming more of the caregiving responsibility (Hauser-Cram, 2006, p. 293). Children with a disabled sibling spend about as much time together as in a typical sibling relationship, but the nature of the interactions changes significantly. More caregiving activities and more managerial behavior are evident, but generally the interactions reflected many of the functions that siblings provide for one another: help, support, and advice. As Hauser-Cram (2006, p. 297) noted:

The importance of the family context, however, carried additional implications for intervention. Given the existing empirical evidence, interventions focused on reducing parental stress, anxiety, and depression and increasing family communication and coping strategies may provide benefits for all members of the family.

Guided Review

1. Family members affect one another both _____ and _____.
2. Modern researchers see today's family as a _____ and not as a collection of individuals.
3. The sibling subsystem in a family is often called the _____ _____.
4. Parents who rely on verbal persuasion, positive reinforcement, and indirect methods of control are demonstrating _____ parenting behavior.
5. About _____ % of children have siblings.

Children of Divorce

Children develop within a complex network of family relationships. What they are exposed to during these years can have long-lasting consequences. Explain how family relationships have long-term developmental consequences.

The changes and stress associated with divorce typically cause multiple problems for all concerned—children, mothers, and fathers. Today's divorce rate is still about 50% of all first marriages and about 62% of remarriages. Sixty percent of the divorces in the United States involve children. Examining the current state of children of divorce, Wallerstein and her colleagues note that as a society we have not yet come to terms with a divorce culture (Wallerstein, Lewis, & Blakeslee, 2002). One reason for this is an ignorance of developmental change: Childhood is different, adolescence is different, and adulthood is different. As a result, there has slowly emerged an agreement that the effects of divorce are long term. Let's examine some of these ideas.

Families and Divorce

We think of divorce today as a sequence of experiences. The conflict and disagreements that lead to divorce undoubtedly begin long before the divorce itself, and children too often witness displays of hostility, anger, and arguments. Viewing angry adults is emotionally disturbing for children and may lead to childhood and adolescent problems such as aggression and poor psychological adjustment, problems that have proven to be long lasting (Friedman & Chase-Lansdale, 2002). Thus marital conflict is associated with a wide range of both internalizing problems such as depression and externalizing difficulties such as aggression (Jenkins et al., 2005).

After about two years, family arrangements usually stabilize, a remarriage may have occurred, and children and parents are on the road to adjustment

Answers   1. directly, indirectly 2. system 3. sibling underworld 4. authoritative 5. 80

FIGURE 8.1

Transitions in marriage.

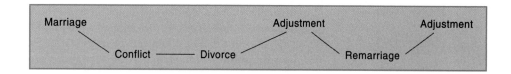

(although boys may still be more aggressive and disobedient). As we turn our attention to children's reaction to the divorce, remember that the divorce itself, that is, the actual separation, may *not* be the major cause of any problem behavior. Too many other factors have intervened (exposure to conflict, economic decline, erratic parenting, and so on). But how do early-childhood youngsters react to divorce?

Children's Adjustment to Divorce

Although studies of the age at which children experience the effects of divorce remain inconclusive, suspicion persists that early-childhood youngsters are particularly vulnerable. Unable to understand the reasons for the family upset, they are more adversely affected by the divorce than older children are (Hetherington & Stanley-Hagan, 2002). Their ability to engage in abstract thinking is still limited, and they lack that vital aspect of cognition—the ability to reverse their thinking. This colors their reaction to their parents' divorce; for example, they may think that *they* are responsible.

As we mentioned, in the two or three years following the divorce, most children adjust to living in a single-parent home. This adjustment, however, can once again be shaken by what a parent's remarriage means: losing one parent in the divorce, adapting to life with the remaining parent, the addition of at least one family member in a remarriage. Figure 8.1 illustrates these transitions in a child's life.

During the early-childhood years, children demonstrate intense separation anxiety and fear of abandonment by both parents, which leads to the tendency to blame themselves for the divorce (Hetherington & Stanley-Hagan, 1995; Lamb et al., 1999). Immediately following the divorce, mothers seem to show less affection toward their children and treat their sons more harshly (threatening them, for example). Fathers, conversely, seem to become more permissive and indulgent. As time passes, relationships stabilize, and life becomes more predictable.

There is growing concern that the effects of divorce may not be as temporary as we'd like to believe. In their follow-up of children of divorce, Wallerstein, Lewis, and Blakeslee (2000) stated that, as adults, these children are telling us "loud and clear" that the post-divorce years really count.

Divorced Fathers

As mentioned earlier, about 12% of all single parents are fathers, most of whom are divorced. The children in their families are usually older than those who remain with mothers and are more likely to be male. Fathers become the custodial parent when mothers are judged to be incompetent or simply don't want custody and the fathers accept the idea of single parenthood (Weinraub & Gringlas, 1995).

Fathers typically maintain their standard of living and have less difficulty with control. One of their chief challenges is with communication, in encouraging their children to talk about their feelings and problems. Their parenting is often less predictable than a mother's, probably because parenting is a less familiar role for them (Hetherington & Kelly, 2002).

Even when the mother has custody of the children, the father can—and should—remain an important figure in a child's life (Cabrera et al., 2000). Estimates are that only about a third of divorced fathers see their children once a week, a figure that decreases with time. This *retreat from parenthood* may be due to

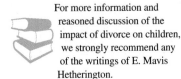

For more information and reasoned discussion of the impact of divorce on children, we strongly recommend any of the writings of E. Mavis Hetherington.

distance, finances, remarriage, and how the mother sees her role as *maternal gatekeeper*. Almost one-half of mothers with custody refuse to permit the father to see the child at all. They may be protecting the child from an incompetent father, or punishing the divorced father, or attempting to obtain increased monetary support (Parke & Brott, 1999).

Given that rapidly changing societal conditions affect parenting, let's now turn our attention to the search for quality day care.

Nonparental Child Care

In their thoughtful analysis of nonparental child care, Lamb and Ahnert (2006, p. 950) pose two questions intended to help researchers reshape their evaluation of modern child care:

- What type of and how much care do young children receive from adults other than their parents?
- What effects do such care arrangements have on their development?

These questions shape the direction of current research and evaluation, because we now realize that it is useless to ask simply whether day care is good or bad for children. Rather, researchers must examine the nature, extent, quality, and age at onset of care as well as the characteristics of the children from different backgrounds and needs (Lamb & Ahnert, 2006, p. 951).

There's nothing new about parents' search for superior nonparental day care. The need for good day care is one of the oldest problems faced by human society. Historically, it's possible to identify four characteristics of high-quality child care (Lamb & Ahnert, 2006, p. 955).

1. Child-care policies in many countries encourage female employment, thus increasing equal employment opportunities and economic self-sufficiency.

2. Child care, especially in preschools, provides a foundation for children of different cultures, an entry into the new culture.

3. Child care, if properly designed, can enrich children's lives.

4. Limited child care appears to have adversely affected fertility rates in several European countries, especially for well-educated women. As a result, countries such as Germany have made determined efforts to strengthen their child-care system.

Current economic conditions and the changing role of women in modern societies have resulted in more than two-thirds of women with children under 6 working (Clarke-Stewart & Allhusen, 2005). Consequently, one question remains to be answered: What happens to children while their mothers are at work? Obviously, someone must be caring for these youngsters, which raises questions about au pairs, nannies, and day care. How competent are the individuals who offer child-care services?

Au Pairs and Nannies

au pair
Young woman, from another country who provides child care services.

Au pairs are young women from other countries who want to spend time in the United States, typically for 12 months because of the length of their work permits (U.S. Bureau of the Census, 1996). (A recent decision by the United States Department of State permits extensions of 6, 9, or 12 months.) State department regulations stipulate that child-care services may be provided by a person for up to 45 hours working no more than 5½ days a week. Au pairs working with children under 2 years must have had at least 200 hours of prior experience with children of this age. They must also acquire 6 academic credits while in the USA, for which they

(a) Day care has become an important phenomenon in our society as more and more mothers join the workforce. Research indicates that developmental outcomes are closely linked to the quality of day care. (b) Among the variety of day-care settings, home day-care centers are quite numerous. Often run by a family member or a neighbor, they are smaller and more informal than large centers. Can you specify the influences on development in a day-care setting?

(a)

(b)

nanny
Professional child care provider, frequently a former nurse.

day care
Location providing services and care for children.

receive $500 from the host family. The United States Information Agency, which oversees the au pair process, recently stated that about 10,000 au pairs are working in the United States in any given year.

Au pairs must be at least 18 and not more than 25, and possess at least a secondary school certificate. They are screened, determined to be of good character, and have a driver's license (since the USA is such a car-oriented society). Compensation is based on the current minimum wage, and they receive about $140 per week plus room and board. The au pair-family relationship demands compatibility given the live-in arrangements and the daily contact. If problems arise, however, conditions can deteriorate quickly. (You may be interested in reading about the famous Louise Woodward case in Massachusetts; the au pair was accused of murder in the death of a child in her care due to "shaken baby syndrome.")

Nannies present a different picture. Older, usually better educated, and higher paid (about $300–$400 per week), they seem to provide a more stable environment for children. English nannies, for example, are often former nursery nurses with considerable experience. They typically receive careful developmental training, such as a course that discusses age characteristics, nutrition, work with exceptional children, how to handle problems, and so on. Many parents worry about the close relationship that develops between a child and a nanny, often feeling threatened by a growing attachment between the two. What's needed before care is begun is a frank discussion between the parents and the nanny about duties, responsibilities, and limitations, particularly regarding the need for privacy for both parties.

Facts about Day Care

Today, however, when we hear the term "caregiver," we tend to think of day care. What are the long-term developmental consequences of day-care placement? Is the day-care center healthy and stimulating? Is it safe?

Reliable facts about **day care** are hard to come by, chiefly because of the lack of any national policy that would provide hard data. Estimates are that there are over 116,000 licensed child-care centers in the United States and about 254,000 licensed child-care homes (Children's Foundation, 2003). (For a brief summary of the day-care movement in the United States, see Clarke-Stewart & Allhusen, 2005.)

The types of child-care arrangement vary enormously: One mother may charge another mother several dollars to take care of her child; a relative may care for several family children; churches, businesses, and charities may run large operations; some centers may be sponsored by local or state government as an aid to the less affluent; others are run on a pay-as-you-go basis. In 2003 the average annual cost of child care for one child in a child-care center was $4,000–$6,000. Almost everyone agrees that the best centers are staffed by teachers who specialize in day-care services (about 25% of day-care personnel).

AN APPLIED VIEW

Types of Day Care

Today the term *day care* has come to mean a variety of nonparental care arrangements: family day care, care by nonparental relatives, in-home babysitters, nursery schools, and day-care centers. But regardless of the type of day-care setting, the one key element that affects a child's development is the *quality* of care provided. Sorting out what is known about types of day-care centers, we can group them as follows (Clarke-Stewart & Allhusen, 2005).

Care in the Child's Home. In this type of care, a relative is usually the caregiver, and we probably know less about this care than any other. Although such an arrangement has several advantages (for example, the child is familiar with the setting and the caregiver, the schedule can be flexible), it also has several disadvantages (for instance, the caregiver is usually untrained, the child misses peer activities).

Family Day Care. Here caregivers provide service in their homes, which may or may not be licensed, and the number of children may range from 1 (family day-care home) to 12 (group day-care home). Family day-care homes are the most numerous and the least expensive. They are typically located near the child's home, so transportation is no problem. A family atmosphere exists that enables a child to interact with a limited number of children of various ages. A major disadvantage is that in this type of day care the provider is the least accountable of providers. These settings typically are informal, unprofessional, and short-lived, with little or no supervision (Clarke-Stewart et al., 1995; Clarke-Stewart & Allhusen, 2005).

Child-Care Centers. These centers are what people mean when they refer to "day care." They may be for profit (the number of these is increasing), or they may be nonprofit and they may provide for fewer than 15 or more than 300 children,

whom they group by age. Here is a summary of many of the day-care centers.

- *Private day-care centers* run for profit have no eligibility requirements and accept almost anyone who can pay the fee. Typically staffed by two or three people (usually not professionally trained), these centers may operate in a converted store or shop. They probably are minimally equipped with toys and educational activities and usually offer no social or health services.
- *Commercial centers* are also private and run for profit. These centers are a business. They may be part of a national or regional chain with uniform offerings and facilities. They usually are well equipped with good food and activities.
- *Community church centers* are often, but not always, run for children of the poor. The quality of personal care (attention, affection) is usually good, but church centers often have minimal facilities and activities.
- *Company centers* are often offered as fringe benefits for employees. They are usually run in good facilities with a well-trained staff and a wide range of services.
- *Public service centers* are government sponsored, well run, and have high quality throughout. Unfortunately, few of these are available, and they are designed to serve children of low-income families.
- *Research centers* are usually affiliated with a university and represent what the latest research says a day-care center should be. Most studies of day care have been conducted in these centers. But since the centers are of the highest quality, the results of such studies do not give a true picture of day care throughout the country.

Developmental Outcomes of Day Care

Two recent investigations have helped to shed light on how early child-care experiences influence development.

The National Institute of Child Health and Human Development (NICHD) studied over 1,000 families and their children beginning at 1 month of age and continuing through 36 months of age (NICHD, 1998, 1999, 2000, 2004). Data collected consisted of demographic information, child-care usage, children's behavioral functioning, mother-child interactions, and quality of the home environment.

Children were assigned to contrasting child-care groups. Those in the full-time child-care group experienced 30 or more hours of nonparental care per week beginning at 4 months of age. Children in the maternal-care group never averaged more than 10 hours per week of care by someone else (NICHD, 1998).

The researchers were intent on answering one question: Do different child-care experiences affect the cognitive and socioemotional development of children when they were 3-years old? Results indicated that nonparental care did *not* weaken the influence of family factors; developmental outcomes were similar for children with and without early-care experiences (NICHD, 1998). Although no significant differences were found between the two groups in attachment security (NICHD, 1999), some minor differences were found. For example, more hours in child care predicted less maternal sensitivity and less positive child engagement. Higher quality child care predicted greater maternal sensitivity.

In a later study of children 4.5 years and through kindergarten (NICHD, 2004), researchers focused exclusively on socioemotional adjustment. They found that the more time children spent in nonmaternal care over the first 4.5 years of life, the more likely they were to display behavior problems in preschool and kindergarten. The children also were more likely to show lower levels of social competence and greater chances of teacher conflict.

Another study by Watamura and colleagues (2003) discovered that stress-level hormones (cortisol) in infants and toddlers up to 3 years old and in day care showed an increase over the day. As Watamura and his colleagues asked: What do these findings imply for child development? Because of the increased stress level, it's possible that these children are more susceptible to physical and emotional illness. Although many 5-year-old children seemed to outgrow these effects, questions remain about the effect of increased neuroendocrine stress on brain development (Watamura et al., 2003, p. 1017).

Examining these results, Maccoby and Lewis (2003) offer four recommendations for nonparental care:

- Careful consideration should be given to practices that enhance the phenomenon of school attachment. School attachment has been linked to positive outcomes in sociomoral development and delinquency prevention.

- Day-care providers should give children more opportunities for them to plan activities and work with peers.

- Group care should emphasize intrinsic motivation.

- The experiences that children have in group care should support social development.

(For an extended discussion of these important results, see also Ahnert & Lamb, 2003; Brooks-Gunn, Han, & Waldfogel, 2002; Greenspan, 2003; Lamb & Ahnert, 2006; Langlois & Liben, 2003; Love et al., 2003.)

Another major study addressed the question: Does quality intervention at an early age aid the cognitive development of children born into poverty and hardship? The Carolina Abecedarian Project (Campbell & Ramey, 1994) studied 111 families and their infants. Based on such characteristics as parental education and income, the poor school achievement of older siblings, and other family problems, these 111 children had been identified as at risk for school failure. They were assigned to either a treatment or a control group. Both groups received identical nutritional supplements and health services.

Children in the treatment group were placed in a year-round day-care program until they entered school. During the first three years, instructors focused on improving the children's cognitive, language, and social skills. After three years, the program was expanded to include pre-reading and math concepts. A continuing thread through these years was the effort by parents and instructors to provide nurturing and supportive interactions with the children.

Follow-up studies have revealed continuing and significant differences between the two groups.

- At the end of the third year, the IQs of the children in the treatment group were significantly higher than those in the control group.

- By 15 years of age, those who were in the treatment group showed better academic progress, higher IQ scores, higher levels of grade retention, and less need for remedial services (Zigler & Hall, 2000).

- At age 15, twice as many members of the control group were in special education classes.
- At 21 years of age, 35% of the children who were originally in the treatment group, compared to 14% of the control group, attended college. Another 30% of the treatment group held good jobs (Clarke-Stewart & Allhusen, 2005; Wilgoren, 1999).

We can also conclude from this remarkable study that the earlier high-quality intervention is offered to children, the more satisfactory and long-lasting are the results. To test this belief, the researchers of the Carolina Project conducted a second study within the framework of the original. When the children of both groups entered kindergarten, half of the treatments and half of the controls were provided with a special teacher who offered additional educational activities to both groups. Little difference was found between these children and those who did not receive the supplementary treatment. In other words, waiting until 4 or 5 years of age may be too late.

The Effects of Day Care: Conclusions

What can we infer, then from the existing day-care research?

- In the United States, the majority of children under 5 years of age receive some kind of nonparental day care (Clarke-Stewart & Allhusen, 2005; Harvey, 1999; Zigler & Finn-Stevenson, 1999).
- Attendance in a child-care facility aided motor development and seemed to be associated with increases in height and weight. Children in child-care centers, however, contract more colds, flu, ear infections, and so on.
- Children who attend day-care programs are more independent of their mothers, but their attachment to their mothers is not damaged (Clarke-Stewart & Allhusen, 2005).
- Enrollment in day care during the early-childhood years does not aid or impede positive relationships with peers (Lamb & Ahnert, 2006).
- Children who attend day-care programs have advanced cognitive and language development (Clarke-Stewart & Allhusen, 2005).
- Nonparental child care seems to be associated with increased behavior problems, a result closely linked with the quality of care offered (Lamb & Ahnert, 2006).
- High-quality child care may have a positive effect on children's intellectual development, and care in a good child-care facility seems to have no negative effect on children's intellectual development (Clarke-Stewart & Allhusen, 2005, p. 86)

Table 8.2 illustrates those features associated with high-quality day care.

TABLE 8.2	Characteristics of High-Quality Day Care
Site Features	*Functional Features*
Good staff-child ratio	Concern with personal care
Superior staff education	Supervised motor activities
Good staff training	Attention to language
Higher staff wages	Opportunity for creativity
Attractive, safe environment	Social relationships encouraged

Finally, we repeat our earlier warning: Be cautious interpreting what you read and hear about the consequences of day care.

Guided Review

6. Nearly _____ of today's marriages will probably end in divorce.

7. A major factor in understanding children's reactions to divorce is their level of _____ _____.

8. High-quality day care has a positive effect on children's _____ achievement.

9. Research day care refers to centers usually associated with _____.

10. _____ day-care settings are the most numerous probably because they are the least _____.

THE SELF EMERGES

The development of self-awareness provides a window into the psychological growth of the child. Over the course of a few years, young children acquire capacities to engage with others intersubjectively, visually recognize their mirror images, attribute behavioral and psychological qualities to themselves, create autobiographical accounts, and situate themselves temporarily as individuals with continuity into the past and present.
(Thompson, 2006, p. 77)

With these words, Ross Thompson provides clues to the pathways that lead children to greater self-awareness with each phase of development.

Imagine for a moment you're looking in a mirror. What do you see? Don't laugh; *you* see *you.* But what exactly do you see? When you look in the mirror, you see yourself, of course. But there are two sides to this vision of yourself. The first is referred to as the "I" self, the part of you that is doing the actual looking. The second part of what you see is the "Me" self, the person who is being observed (Harter, 1993, 1998, 2006).

We have the great American psychologist, William James, to thank for this division of the self into two distinct parts. James believed that the "I" part of the self was the knower, that is, the "I" that thinks, makes judgments, recognizes it's separate from everything it sees, and controls the surrounding world. The "Me," in contrast, is the object of the "I's" thinking, judging, and so on. Think of the "Me" as your self-image, which helps you to understand how the "I" develops feelings of self-esteem: As a result of the "I" evaluating the "Me's" activities, the self is judged good or bad, competent or incompetent, masterful or fumbling.

The Development of Self

How do children construct a sense of *self,* this sense of who they are and what makes them different from everyone else? In a famous and ingenious study of self-development, the psychologists Michael Lewis and Jean Brooks-Gunn (1979)

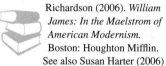

For an informative and enjoyable view of James's life and ideas, see Robert Richardson (2006). *William James: In the Maelstrom of American Modernism.* Boston: Houghton Mifflin. See also Susan Harter (2006) for an analysis of James's continuing legacy in modern studies of the self.

The infant shown here touching his nose and mouth against the mirror reveals the development of a sense of self, which most infants accomplish by about 18 months of age. What must occur for an infant to develop in this way?

Answers

AN APPLIED VIEW

When I and Me Are We

Born in Taiwan, adopted by American Caucasian parents with two children of their own, product of an American upbringing, Julia Ming Gale often looks in the mirror and asks herself, "Who am I?" In her mind she sees a young woman with curly red hair, green eyes, and freckles, an image that causes her considerable sadness. The Gales had lived in Taiwan for three years, studied the Chinese language, had many Chinese friends, and kept a number of Chinese items in their American home—books, scrolls, and furniture.

But Ming's world was Caucasian, and she couldn't recall a time when she didn't feel Caucasian, even though every time she looked in the mirror she faced an inescapable reality: the face looking back at her was Chinese. Periodic reminders of her Chinese heritage plagued her. Once when she was doing the dishes, her younger brother came in with a friend. He told his friend that she was the maid and didn't speak any English; her brother was joking, but Ming still remembers the hurt. Bewildered, she began to fantasize that her birth mother was some famous Asian woman.

Nevertheless, her inner self didn't want to be any more Chinese than she had to be, and she resisted any efforts her parents made to encourage the flourishing of her Chinese roots. She just wanted to be treated as another Caucasian. By the time she was 12, she learned she had been born in Taiwan, not in China, which only increased her sense of cultural rootlessness. She was bothered that she couldn't claim the culture she grew up in. She even tried to force herself to "go Chinese," but it didn't work. Wanting to be Caucasian, she couldn't bridge the gap between the two cultures.

When her parents realized what she was going through, they tried to help her reconcile her conflicts. Ming, at age 24, has slowly started to explore her Chinese background through language lessons, taking courses in Chinese history, and readings that show her interest in both China and adoption. The career she has chosen reflects her own background: helping Chinese adoptees discover their identities, to help them live with the duality that caused her so much pain.

In Ming's case two selves existed in conflict, and she spent 24 years trying to reconcile the differences between them. A novelist couldn't dramatize a better example to illustrate how knowing who they are shapes children's development, giving them the poise and assurance to undertake challenges they may otherwise shun. Too often children feel a conflict between the self they want to be and what they actually see themselves as, two different versions of the same self, *when "I" and "Me" are "We."*

devised different strategies for uncovering how children discover they are distinct from their surroundings.

- Working with infants between 5 and 8 months old, the investigators placed them before a mirror. The children looked at themselves intently, smiled at their images, and even waved at the mirror, but they gave no indication that they knew they were looking at themselves.

- Next, infants between 9 and 12 months reached out to the mirror to touch their bodies and turned toward other people or objects reflected in the mirror.

- The researchers then dabbed red rouge on the noses of infants between 15 and 18 months. When they saw themselves in the mirror, they pointed to their noses (on their own faces, not in the mirror) and tried to rub off the rouge.

- Finally, between 21 and 24 months, infants used their names and correctly applied personal pronouns. When placed with other same-sex infants in front of the mirror, they accurately identified themselves.

Changes in the Developing Self

After infants take this initial step on the path to self-development and understanding, the next phase centers on the early-childhood years. Children's increasing—even astonishing—ability to understand things provides them with ever-deepening insights into themselves. When asked to tell who she was, a 4-year-old replied as follows.

I go to preschool. I like it. I play with my brother a lot. I have dark brown hair. I like to talk. (Oh yes!)

These remarks are characteristic of preschoolers, particularly in the initial years of the period. Here are the comments of a 6-year-old girl when asked to describe herself.

I'm the youngest in my family. I'm happy most of the time. I like riding my bike. I eat a lot and I like different kinds of food. I have brown eyes. I have lots of freckles. I like almost everybody and I have lots of friends. Sometimes I get a little scared. When I'm a little older, I want to be a babysitter and I'll protect people. When I grow up I'm going to be a librarian.

These quotations are fairly sophisticated. Note the more abstract ideas of happiness, friendship, and protecting others, concepts that usually appear at later ages. Most children of her age focus on the physical—hair color, color of eyes, and so on—or on tangible objects such as food, toys, even freckles. As children grow, their sense of self isn't limited to their reflections in a mirror; they have acquired language and are able to tell us what they think of themselves. Their self-judgments reflect their changing cognitive and social maturity. As representational thinking continues to improve and they compare their performances with others, more realistic evaluations begin to appear (Harter, 2006).

Note how children change from identifying themselves by physical characteristics (hair or eye color) to more social and emotional characteristics (feeling good or bad about themselves). In these later years, they usually begin to compare themselves to others. Thompson (1999, 2006), attempting to explain these developmental changes, used a model of the self consisting of five features.

- As children begin to move through the early childhood years, they gradually learn that forms of self-awareness other than physical recognition exist. For example, verbal labeling becomes more important, conscience assumes a more compelling role, self-control steadily emerges, and so forth.

- At the core of self-development is a sense of *subjective self-awareness* that reflects William James "I-self." I'm the one doing the acting, thinking, and so on.

- But the self also includes *self-representation,* that is, who you think you are. As cognitive development continues, self-recognition deepens and becomes the basis for distinguishing yourself from others.

- An important element in self-development is *an autobiographical personal narrative* that integrates events in your life to the self.

- *Self-evaluations* steadily become more significant as children recognize the opinions of others. During the early-childhood years these various aspects of the self help children not only to better understand themselves but also to comprehend the thoughts and emotions of others.

I can't marry her. She's too much like myself. I hate myself.
—JERRY SEINFELD

- Finally, the *social self* is influenced by social interactions with others, and early-childhood youngsters gradually become interested in what others think of them.

THE ROLE OF GENDER IN DEVELOPMENT

Being born a boy or girl has implications that carry considerably beyond the chromosomal, hormonal, and genital differences. Virtually all of human functioning has a gendered cast—appearance, mannerisms, communication, temperament, activities at home and outside, aspirations, and values.
(Ruble, Martin, & Berenbaum, 2006)

In our modern society, a major concern is how children acquire their sense of gender in a way that they and their society find acceptable. "Acceptable" means many things to many people, and although gender roles for boys and girls, men and women, are slowly, even grudgingly, changing, sharp differences of opinion are still evident. For example, many parents want their children to follow traditional gender roles (sports for boys, dolls for girls), whereas other parents want to break down what they consider rigid gender-role stereotypes. In discussing these issues, let's first clarify the meaning of several terms used in any analysis of gender and development (Margolis, 2005; Zucker, 2002).

Definition of Terms

Developmental psychologists such as Unger and Crawford (1996) have urged that we use the terms *sex* and *gender* more carefully. In this new context, *sex* refers to biological maleness or femaleness (for example, the sex chromosomes), whereas *gender* suggests psychosocial aspects of maleness and femaleness (for example, changing gender roles).

Within this framework, we can now distinguish among gender identity, gender stereotypes, and gender role.

- **Gender identity** is a conviction that one belongs to the sex of birth.
- **Gender stereotypes** reflect narrow beliefs about the characteristics associated with being male or female.
- **Gender role** refers to culturally acceptable sexual behavior.

Theories of Gender Development

Let's now examine how the various theorists have explained gender development. Among the most popular of today's explanations and which have generated most of the research are the following (Bussey & Bandura, 1999).

- **Biological Explanations.** Biological explanations of gender development parallel physical and psychological sexual differentiation (Ruble, Martin, & Berenbaum, 2006, p. 888). Advocates of biological explanations of gender development have turned to the rapidly growing body of research relating to chromosomal and hormonal input. At about the sixth prenatal week, the fetal gonads develop and begin to secrete hormones that influence gender development. An important question then arises: Do hormones also cause gender differences in brain development? Perhaps the best way we can answer this question is to conclude that, although the evidence is limited, some structural differences are apparent (females seem to have a larger corpus callosum than males do), as well as some processing differences (females may process information with both hemispheres more than males do) (Eisenberg, Martin, & Fabes, 1996; Ruble & Martin, 1998). It's important, however, to remember that the brains of males and females are much more similar than they are different (Rose, 2005).

- **Social Learning Theory Explanations.** Social learning theorists believe that parents, as the distributors of reinforcement, reinforce appropriate gender-role behaviors. By their choice of toys, by urging "boy" or "girl" behavior, and by

gender identity
The conviction that one is either male or female.

gender stereotype
Narrow beliefs about the characteristics associated with being male or female.

gender role
Sexual behavior acceptable within one's culture.

Children quickly learn what objects, activities, and friends are gender appropriate. Can you design a model that integrates the various theories of gender development?

reinforcing this behavior, parents encourage their children to engage in gender-appropriate behavior. Today's social-learning theorists have incorporated cognition in their explanations (Bandura, 1997; Eisenberg, Martin, & Fabes, 1996; Ruble & Martin, 1998; Unger & Crawford, 2000). For example, if parents have a good relationship with their children, they become models for their children to imitate, encouraging them to acquire additional gender-related behavior. They also learn appropriate gender behavior from other social influences such as siblings, peers, media, and school (Ruble, Martin, & Berenbaum, 2006).

- **Cognitive Development Explanations.** Another explanation, quite popular today, is cognitive-developmental, which derives from Kohlberg's speculations about gender development (1966). Children first acquire their sense of gender identity and then seek appropriate behaviors (Lips, 2007). In other words, as a result of cognitive development—in a sense, constructing their own world—children begin to build the concepts of maleness and femaleness (Unger & Crawford, 2000).

- **Gender Schema Explanations.** A newer, and different, cognitive-developmental explanation is called *gender schema theory*. A *schema* is a mental blueprint for organizing information, and children develop a schema for gender. Children form a network of mental associations about gender, which they use as a guide to interpret and store information about male and female (Margolis, 2005; Ruble & Martin, 1998; Ruble, Martin, & Berenbaum, 2006). In other words, children use their cognitive abilities to form schema about gender and then shape any gender information coming from the environment to change and expand the existing schema. The gender schema then becomes a powerful tool in connecting many ideas that otherwise seem unrelated (Lips, 2007).

- **Psychoanalytic-Identification Explanations.** In traditional Freudian theory (see Chapter 2), children become sex typed usually from 4 to 6 years of age, because they identify with the same-sex parent. Fear of castration by the father because of the child's desire for the mother explains a boy's sex typing; explanations of identification for girls remains vague in this theory. More recent explanations rely on boys' and girls' different ways of knowing, which then translates into different ways of knowing boys as differentiated from girls, such as seen in Carol Gilligan's work (see Chapter 9).

Acquiring Gender Identity

One of the first categories children form is sex-related; there is a neat division in their minds between male and female. For example, children first indicate their ability to label their own sex and the sex of others between 2 and 3 years of age. By 4 years of age, children are aware that sex identity is stable over time. They then come to the realization that sex identity remains the same despite any changes in clothing, hair style, or activities (Lips, 2007; Ruble, Martin, & Berenbaum, 2006; Szkrybalo & Ruble, 1999).

Becoming Boys and Girls

Children move from the observable physical differences between the sexes and begin to acquire gender knowledge about the behavior expected of male and female. Depending on the source of this knowledge, gender role stereotyping has commenced and attitudes toward gender are being shaped. What do we know about the forces influencing this process?

Family

Evidence clearly suggests that parents treat boy and girl babies differently from birth by the toys they supply, by their room furnishings, and the type of gender behavior they encourage (Ruble, Martin, & Berenbaum, 2006). Adults tend to engage in rougher play with boys; give them stereotypical toys (cars and trucks),

Males and females grow up in quite different learning environments with important psychological implications for development.

—JEANNE BLOCK

and speak differently to them. By the end of the second year, parents respond favorably to what they consider appropriate sexual behavior (that is, stereotypical) and negatively to cross-sex play (boys engaging in typical girl's play and vice versa). Both mothers and fathers differentially reinforce their children's behavior: Parents reinforce girls for playing with dolls and boys for playing with blocks, girls for helping their mothers around the house and boys for running.

Parents usually are unaware of the extent to which they engage in this type of reinforcement (Lips, 2007). In a famous study (Will, Self, & Data, 1976), 11 mothers were observed interacting with a 6-month-old infant. Five of the mothers played with the infant when it was dressed in blue pants and called it "Adam." Six mothers later played with the same infant when it wore a pink dress and called it "Beth." The mothers offered a doll to "Beth" and a toy train to "Adam." They also smiled more at Beth and held her more closely. The baby was actually a boy. Interviewed later, all the mothers said that boys and girls were alike at this age and *should be treated identically.*

Since about 80% of children have siblings and spend considerable time with them, sibling relationships also exercise considerable influence. An older brother shows a younger brother how to hold a bat; a younger sister watches her older sister play with dolls; siblings quarrel among one another. Same-sex siblings seem to exercise a greater influence on gender-typed activities by modeling or reinforcing gender-appropriate behavior. The influence of other-sex siblings on gender typing is inconsistent, however (Maccoby, 1998; Ruble, Martin, & Berenbaum, 2006)

Peers

Boys and girls have different expectations about their friends; girls quickly learn that relationships are a crucial part of their lives, whereas boys are urged to be independent and self-reliant (Lips, 2007). When children start to make friends and play, activities foster and maintain sex-typed play. When children engage in "sex-inappropriate" play (boys with dolls, girls with a football), their peers immediately criticize them and tend to isolate them ("sissy; "tomboy"). Although we see increased diminishing of these stereotypes (girls in Little League and youth hockey, for example), the tendency to sexually compartmentalize behavior increases with age until most adolescents react to intense demands for conformity to stereotypical gender roles.

sex cleavage
Youngsters of the same sex tend to play and do things together.

Children learn about gender-appropriate behavior by observing their friends (Ruble & Martin, 1998; Ruble, Martin, & Berenbaum, 2006). During development, youngsters of the same sex tend to play together, a custom called **sex cleavage.** If you think back on your own experiences, you can remember your friends at this age—usually either all male or female. You can understand, then, how imitation, reinforcement, and cognitive development come together to intensify what a boy thinks is masculine and a girl thinks is feminine

The preference for same-sex peers has been neatly summarized by Ruble, Martin, and Berenbaum (2006, p. 877).

Preschool, kindergarten, and middle school children consistently like same-sex peers and prefer them as friends more than other-sex peers, and this tendency increases with age until adolescence, when other-sex interests become apparent and strong same-sex preferences decrease.

Even in adolescence, despite dating and opposite sex attraction, both males and females want to live up to the most rigid interpretations of what their group thinks is ideally male or female.

Media

Another influence on gender development, one that carries important messages about what is desirable for males and females and one that reaches into the home, is the media, especially television. Television has assumed such a powerful place in the socialization of children that it is safe to say that it is almost as significant as family and peers. What is particularly bothersome is the stereotypical behavior that it presents as both positive and desirable. The more television children watch, the more stereotypical is their behavior (Lips, 2007).

In spite of recent shows with female leads, the central characters of shows are much more likely to be male, the theme will be action-oriented for males, and the characters typically engage in stereotypical behavior (men are the executives and leaders, women are the housewives and secretaries). Much the same holds true for television commercials. There is little doubt that children notice the different ways that television portrays males and females. When asked to rate the behavior of males and females on TV, children aged 8 to 13 responded in a rigidly stereotypical manner: Males were brave, adventurous, intelligent, and make good decisions. Females, however, cried easily and needed to be protected (Lips, 2007).

With this brief examination of the biological and environmental forces that contribute to gender and the theories that attempt to explain the process, let's next look at what happens when gender stereotypes are formed.

Gender Stereotyping

Gender stereotyping is the belief that we have about the characteristics and behavior associated with male and a female. In other words, from an early age we form an idea of what a male and a female should be, begin to accumulate characteristics about male and female, and assign a label to that category: that rough, noisy person is a boy; that gentle, soft-spoken, obedient person is a girl (Liben, Bigler, & Krogh, 2002). Recent research (Ruble, Martin, & Berenbaum, 2006) confirms that gender stereotype knowledge of personal-social attributes appears between 3 and 5 years and peaks at about the time of entrance to first grade. (As a result of such stereotyping, the "feminine" boy or "masculine" girl often has difficulties with peers.)

Even the world of computer games mirrors society's stereotyping. In 1998, the top six selling computer games for girls were all Barbie games. One game, *Barbie's Fashion Designer,* sold an astonishing 500,000 copies in its first two months on the market (Brelis, 1998). Boys' games, however, take them into a virtual world where enemies are vanquished, space is explored, and aliens are battled. So the stereotype is further entrenched: Girls' games teach about social relationships and boy's games teach about power and mastery.

When the characteristics associated with a label create a negative image, problems arise. "Oh, girls can't do math; girls can't do science; girls are always crying, girls can't be leaders." At this point we start to treat the individual according to the stereotypes we associate with male or female. If you think about this for a moment, you can see some potential pitfalls, especially in the classroom.

Although sexual equality is widely accepted today—legally, professionally, and personally—gender stereotyping is still alive and well. As Yunger, Carver, and Perry (2004) note, acceptance by the same-sex peer group has a powerful effect on preadolescent children—how well children realize they are accepted by peers and how they reach different conclusions about themselves in relation to their sex with all that implies for happy, healthy development.

For an excellent summary of this topic, see Baron-Cohen's (2005) summary of the controversy surrounding former Harvard University President Lawrence Summers' remarks concerning the role of women in science.

Children may find toys aimed at the opposite-sex attractive. Many parents encourage the use of such toys to help their children avoid the development of stereotypical gender-role attitudes. Explain and illustrate several techniques to combat gender stereotyping.

AN INFORMED VIEW

The Emotional Life of Boys

"Nobody's going to make me do anything I don't want to do. If they try, they better be ready for trouble. I don't care what happens. I can take care of my self."

These macho words, spoken by a 13-year-old boy, illustrate the bravado that unfortunately too often leads to aggression. Boys exhibiting this kind of behavior have become a source of concern for those attempting to understand the causes for a dramatic increase in male violence. The horrifying murders at Columbine High School in Littleton, Colorado, brought to public attention a question that researchers and developmental psychologists have been wrestling with for several years: What happens in the development of some boys that leads to wild acts of violence, even murder?

The public's concern with causes of these brutal assaults is reflected in the popularity of such books as James Garbarino's *Lost Boys* (1999), Dan Kindlon's and Michael Thompson's *Raising Cain* (1999), and William Pollack's *Real Boys* (1998). There is a growing recognition that the emotional lives of some boys is so distorted that brutality and murder are inevitable results. Why? Among the reasons offered are these:

- Schools are "antiboy"; that is, they tend to ignore the physical restlessness and intense activity of boys.
- Many members of our society, especially fathers, encourage a tough-guy, macho image for their sons.
- Boys' environments are frequently a daily mix of aggression, fighting, bullying, and taunting.
- At the same time, other people, such as teachers, women, and psychologists, are urging boys to display greater sensitivity.

- The hero image—long neglected in our society—too often is seen in violent entertainment and sports figures.

Pollack (1998) stresses that parents, communities, and schools develop plans to help boys avoid feelings of alienation, prevent academic decline, and present image-enhancing role models. He identified two sources of a boy's reluctance to display his feelings.

1. The overuse of shame in the "toughening up" process of boys.
2. The emphasis society places on a boy separating emotionally from his mother at an unnecessarily early age (usually by 6 years).

The problem is not that we introduce our boys to the world—that's what parents should be doing—it's how we do it. We expect them to step outside the family too abruptly, with too little preparation for what lies in store, too little emotional support, not enough opportunity to express their feelings and often with no option of going back or changing course. That's because we believe disconnection is important, even essential, for a boy to "make the break" and become a man. (Pollack, 1998, p. xxiv)

If you would like to have a more informed view on this issue, you may want to read one or more of the articles referenced in this chapter. You may also wish to learn more about it by going to our website at www.mhhe.com/dacey7.

An important part of the early childhood years is the role of play in physical, cognitive, social, and self-development.

Guided Review

11. The "I" is the _____; the "Me" is the _____.
12. Children usually acquire a sense of self by _____ months of age.
13. When children develop a mental blueprint concerning gender, this is called _____ _____ _____.
14. Psychologists today are more alert to the proper use of the terms _____ and _____ to indicate the interaction of _____ and _____ to explain gender.
15. Gender stereotyping is reflected in the world of _____ games.

Answers

11. knower, known 12. 18 13. gender schema theory 14. sex, gender, biology, environment 15. computer

THE IMPORTANCE OF PLAY

A compelling argument for the importance of play in a child's life is seen in these words of Daniel Goleman (2006, p.178):

> *A simple sign that children feel they have a safe haven is going out to play. Playful fun has serious benefits; through years of hard play, children acquire a range of social expertise. For one, they learn social savvy, like how to negotiate power struggles, how to cooperate and form alliances, and how to concede with grace.*
>
> *All that practice can go on while playing with a relaxed sense of safety—even a mistake can trigger giggles, while in a schoolroom the same mistake might draw ridicule. Play offers children a secure space to try out something new in their repertoire with minimum anxiety.*

Why do children play? You'd probably answer that children play to have fun, to do things they've learned, or to relieve the anxieties of going to the dentist or doctor. In their play, children demonstrate each of these explanations: fun, learning, and emotions. When children play, they learn about themselves, others, and their world, and play becomes the medium through which these processes occur. We'll see later that play is linked to other developmental considerations such as physical, cognitive, emotional, and social development (Ginsburg, 2007). But for now, let's define play as *an activity that children engage in because they enjoy it for its own sake.*

Play may be one of the most profound expressions of human nature and one of the greatest innate resources for learning and invention.

—**MARTHA BRONSON**

The Meaning of Play

play
Activity that children engage in because they enjoy it for its own sake.

Play allows children to explore their environment on their own terms and to take in any meaningful experiences at their own rate and on their own level (for example, running through a field and stopping to look at rocks or insects). Children also play for the sheer exuberance of it, which enables them to exercise their bodies and improve motor skills. Such uninhibited behavior permits children to relieve tension and helps them to master anxiety (Watson, 1995).

You probably remember the story of the child playing dentist after a visit to a dentist's office. Keep in mind, however, in our discussion, the interactive nature of play: Children can't play certain kinds of games until they reach a specific cognitive level, but they can't reach that level without environmental encouragement, some of which comes through their play.

Play in childhood may also influence the learning skills and conscious learning interests of the future. What children learn as "fun" becomes the foundation for intrinsic motivation now and later. Think back yourself: What kind of play did you really enjoy? Do you think it contributed to your success today? (Discuss this in class; it should provide some entertaining moments.) Given the importance of play in the human lifespan, how have scholars interpreted this behavior?

Kinds of Play

In their efforts to understand the role of play in a child's life, theorists have presented several types of classification. For example, one of the earliest and most enduring schemes was proposed by in 1932 by Mildred Parten, who suggested six categories of play:

- *Unoccupied play,* in which children are seen as observers and not actually engaged in any activity.

- *Solitary play,* in which children play by themselves and are not involved with others.

TABLE 8.3		Types of Play	
Play Type	Age	Definition	Examples
Functional play	1–2 years	Simple, repetitive motor movements with or without objects	Running around, rolling a toy car back and forth
Constructive play	3–6 years	Creating or constructing something	Making a house out of toy blocks, drawing a picture, putting a puzzle together, using Legos
Make-believe play	3–7 years	Acting out roles	Playing house, school, or doctor; acting as a television character
Games with rules	6–11 years	Understanding and following rules in games	Playing board games, cards, baseball, etc.

Source: From Laura E. Berk (2007). *Child Development* (7th edition), p. 599. Copyright © Pearson Education/Allyn and Bacon. Reprinted by permission of the publisher and the author.

- *Onlooker play,* in which children watch others, do not become active themselves, but may call out suggestions or questions.
- *Parallel play,* in which children play beside but not with other children.
- *Associative play,* in which children play with others but seem more interested in the social interactions than the activity itself.
- *Cooperative play,* in which children play with others and are active participants in the goal of the activity.

Criticisms of Parten's work led to a growing realization of the complexity of play, and other typologies were suggested. For example, in 1983 Rubin, Fein, and Vandenberg proposed the classification shown in Table 8.3

Finally, in 2001 pediatrician Berry Brazelton and child psychiatrist Joshua Sparrow discussed play from the perspective of purpose and among many goals identified the following:

- To allow children to engage in wishful thinking.
- To learn about one's roles at different ages.
- To relieve pressure and stress.
- To build self-esteem
- To interact successfully with others.
- To have an outlet for painful or confusing feelings.

With these classification schemes in mind, we turn now to specific aspects of play.

Developmental Aspects of Play

With this interactive model in mind, we can see that children play for various reasons, such as the following.

Cognitive Development

Play aids cognitive development; cognitive development aids play. Through play, children learn about the objects in their world, what these objects do (balls roll and bounce), what they are made of (toy cars have wheels), and how they work. To use Piaget's terms, children "operate" on these objects through play and also learn behavioral skills that will help them in the future.

Once children leave infancy and enter the early childhood years, Piaget classified the games that children play as follows.

practice games
According to Piaget, games that are characteristic of the sensorimotor period.

symbolic games
According to Piaget, games that begin at 18–24 months.

games with rules
According to Piaget, games typical of the 7–11-year period.

For a more detailed presentation of Piaget's work on play see J. Piaget (1951). *Play, Dreams, and Imitation in Childhood.* New York: Norton.

- **Practice games,** which are mainly characteristic of the sensorimotor period, carry into the initial early-childhood years

- **Symbolic games,** which typically begin at about 18 to 24 months, are seen when children pretend to be asleep, or washing their hands. Piaget believed that during these years children use their growing symbolic ability to extend their real world.

- **Games with rules** begin during the early-childhood (symbolic) years but are more typical of the 7- to 11-year period.

Table 8.4 presents a schedule of appropriate games for various ages.

Vygotsky believed that play contributed significantly to cognitive development because children learn to use objects and actions appropriately and thus further their ability to think symbolically. Vygotsky (1978) also argued that children's imaginary situations provide zones of proximal development that function as mental support systems. Typically, adults provide these zones of proximal development by their suggestions, hints, and guidelines. But as Vygotsky noted, children tend to play at a level above their average age and above their daily behavior. (See Chapter 2 for an analysis of Vygotsky's work.)

Social Development

Play helps social development during this period, because the involvement of others demands a give-and-take that teaches early childhood youngsters the basics of forming relationships. Social skills demand the same building processes as cognitive

TABLE 8.4	Appropriate Games	
Age	*Appropriate Materials*	*Developmental Concerns*
Older toddlers (2 years)	Simple games with few pieces; game pieces that are not too small (2–4 inches); simple matching games with few pairs (lotto-type); giant dominoes; magnetic fishing games	Enjoy games that they can do alone or with one other child and/or adult
Prechool and kindergarten children (3 through 5 years)	More complex matching games (more pieces), including lotto; dominoes (picture, color number); simple card games (Concentration); first board games (4–5 years); picture bingo (matching letter/number bingo at about age 5); games involving construction or balancing	Development of turn taking, concentration, attention to detail, and understanding of rule-based interaction supported by early games; can play games in which outcome is determined by chance, not strategy; may play with one or two peers but may have difficulty losing
Primary school children (6 through 8 years)	Simple guessing or deductive games, strategy games, trading games, card games, bingo, dominoes, marbles, checkers, Chinese checkers; word games, arithmetic games (simple adding games)	Increasing interest in games but hate to lose; can play competitive games by age 8; increasing capacity for cooperative interaction and use of strategy nurtured by games, but games should have relatively few rules and not require complicated strategies

Source: Bronson, M. (1995). *The Right Stuff for Children Birth to 8.* Washington, D.C.: National Association for the Education of Young Children. Reprinted with permission.

AN INFORMED VIEW

Play, Fantasy, and Development

Children believe that their thoughts and actions bring about the events they witness around them, which is wonderful at times, such as when they see themselves as the heroic firefighter saving others. In Peter Sis's book, *The Firetruck,* Matt, the young narrator, is not the firefighter; he IS the fire truck.

As children grow, their interests turn away from real-life conditions; that is, the story needn't be about a real telephone but can describe a block of wood used as a telephone. By the age of 2½ to 3 years, make-believe is changing to include more complex, cognitive schemes. In other words, by about 4 years of age, children develop a relatively sophisticated understanding of the role that fantasy plays in their reading. Children of these ages easily relate to book characters and sometimes in pretend play, they assume these roles, and, as they do, they further such mental abilities as attention, memory, language, creativity, among other cognitive skills (Berk, 2002).

In *Max,* Bob Graham, the author and illustrator of this unusual story, revealed that in writing previous books, such as *Benny* and *Queenie One of the Family,* he tried to make the ordinary extraordinary; but in this book his problem is just the opposite: how to make this extraordinary family seem ordinary. And they are extraordinary. Max was born a superbaby—the son of superheroes Captain Lightening and Madam Thunderbolt, yet he had one problem: he couldn't get his feet off the ground. What finally prompted him to become a superhero makes *Max* a good story for children to read or to listen to.

Children especially relate to the escapades of animals at this age. Whether it's the lowly mouse in Kevin Henkes' stories, the ingenious pig in Ian Falconer's books, or the big lovable bear in Martin Waddell's stories, animals are considered human and children do not question their ability to talk or act like they do. As Brazelton and Sparrow (2001) note, children of these years express a mixture of fantasy and fears that frequently makes fantasy play safer than reality, thus providing a safe haven that reduces the stress and anxiety of everyday living.

skills; that is, children begin to share symbolic meanings through their use of pretend play (Rubin et al., 1999).

At 3 years of age, children prefer playmates of their own sex. Girls show a stronger preference than boys do at this age, but from 4 to 5 years it is boys who show a stronger sex preference, although mixed sex groups still occur. But gender differentiation from 3 to 5 years becomes ever more apparent. During free play sessions in preschool and day-care centers, children of the same sex are the close partners, a trend that advances the notion of "separate cultures." (For an excellent discussion of this topic see Maccoby, 1998.)

Why are some 5- and 6-year-olds more popular with their classmates than others are? Watching closely, you can discover the reasons: decreasing egocentrism, recognition of the rights of others, and a willingness to share. These social skills do not simply appear; they are learned, and much of the learning comes through play.

Emotional Development

The work of Freud and Erikson that we discussed in Chapter 2 suggests that play can provide an emotional release for children; that is, play helps children to master those intense, sometimes overpowering, experiences all children encounter. In their play, they avoid the right-or-wrong, life-and-death feelings that accompany interactions with adults. Children can be creative without worrying about failure and work out their emotional tensions through play.

Bronson (1995, p. 1) summarized these benefits of play nicely when she stated:

We are curious about the social and physical world and reach out to explore it. We manipulate and experiment to see what will happen and how things and people function. We try to master and control processes and produce desired effects by our own efforts. We also imitate what we perceive, and we play with these images in spontaneous variations on the captured themes.

AN APPLIED VIEW

Children and Their Toys

When parents shop for their children's toys, they should ask themselves a basic question: What kind of activities can this toy lead to? Too often, the answer is "nothing good." Today's toys frequently promote violence, involve candy, or depend on electronic technology, turning the child into a passive observer—push the button and watch.

From what we have said, you can see how important it is to provide appropriate play materials to match the needs and goals of children. As Bronson (1995) noted, the play materials we supply our children are loaded with multiple messages. They not only cause children to do certain things (because of the nature of the toy), they also convey clearly what parents think is acceptable. For example, some parents would never give a child a toy gun; others think guns are a normal part of growing up.

Play materials are typically grouped into four categories: social and fantasy; exploration and mastery; music, art, and movement; gross motor play. *Social and fantasy play materials* include items that encourage the use of imagination and the mental representation of objects and events, as well as a deeper understanding of people and the rules we live by. Play materials in this category are often used in dramatic play, solitary fantasy play, and role play.

Exploration and mastery play materials increase children's knowledge about the physical world, encouraging them to

devise ways to enrich their comprehension of "how things work." Puzzles, pattern making games, sand, water, and string encourage children's search for knowledge. *Music, art, and movement play materials* aid in the development of artistic expression and include arts, crafts, and instruments. Finally, *gross motor play materials* foster large-muscle development and skills and include playground and gym equipment, push-and-pull toys, and sports equipment.

Bronson (1995) suggests the following developmental guidelines for purchasing toys.

- *Birth to 12 months.* Simple toys such as rattles and mobiles are appropriate.
- *12 to 24 months.* In children's search for cause-and-effect relations and their need to learn self-control, blocks, stacking toys, and stuffed animals give them the opportunity to explore and experiment.
- *2 to 3 years.* Toys that make use of size, shape, color, and texture, balls that help motor skills to develop, and objects for pretend play are suited for these years.
- *3 to 5 years.* Simple board games, art materials, and building sets such as Lego are good for these years.

Guided Review

16. Any analysis of play must take into consideration that children play because they _____ it for its own sake.

17. Play is associated with four aspects of development: _____, _____, _____, and _____.

18. When parents buy toys, they should be concerned with the type of _____ the toy can lead to.

19. _____ theory reflects play's role in cognitive development.

20. The play material we furnish children are laden with _____ _____.

CONCLUSION & SUMMARY

At the beginning of the early-childhood years, most children meet other youngsters. By the end of the period, almost all children enter formal schooling. Their symbolic ability enriches all their activities, although limitations still exist. Given their boundless energy and enthusiasm, early-childhood youngsters require consistent and reasonable discipline. Yet they should be permitted to do as many things for themselves as possible to help them gain mastery over themselves and their surroundings.

By the end of the early-childhood period, children have learned much about their world and are prepared to enter the more complex, competitive, yet exciting world of middle childhood.

What role does family play in development during these years?

- The meaning of "family" in our society has changed radically.

- How parents treat their children has a decisive influence on developmental outcomes.
- Baumrind's types of parenting behavior help to clarify the role of parents in children's development.
- Research has demonstrated how divorce can affect children of different ages.
- Divorce plus remarriage produces a series of transitions to which children must adjust.
- Many children attend some form of day care, and the developmental outcomes of these experiences are still in question.

How do children of this age acquire a sense of self?

- The emergence of the self follows a clearly defined path.
- At the core of self-development is a sense of subjective self-awareness.

How do children come to understand the meaning of their gender?

- Various theories have been proposed to explain how children achieve their sense of gender.
- Youngsters acquire their gender identity during the early childhood years.
- Modeling is an important influence on children's gender development.
- Children initially seem to acquire an understanding of gender before they manifest sex-typed behavior.

What is the value of play to children of these years?

- Play affects all aspects of development: physical, cognitive, social, and emotional.
- The nature of a child's play changes over the years, gradually becoming more symbolic.

KEY TERMS

au pair
authoritarian parents
authoritative parents
day care
games with rules
gender identity

gender role
gender stereotypes
nanny
permissive parents
play
practice games

sex cleavage
sibling
sibling underworld
symbolic games

WHAT DO YOU THINK?

1. Given today's accepted changes in the gender roles of males and females, do you think that a boy or a girl growing up in these times could become confused about gender identity? Does your answer also apply to gender roles? Why?

2. Think back on your days as a child. Can you put your parents' behavior in any of Baumrind's categories? Do you think it affected your behavior? Explain your answer by linking your parents' behavior to some of your personal characteristics.

3. In this chapter you read about the "sleeper" effect of divorce (effects show up quite a bit later). Do you agree with these findings? Can you explain them by the child's age at the time of the divorce? (Consider all aspects of a child's development at that age.)

4. You probably have read about child abuse in some day-care centers. Do you think there should be stricter supervision? Why? By whom?

CHAPTER REVIEW TEST

1. During the early childhood years, a child's _____ becomes distinctive.
   a. walking
   b. personality
   c. socialization
   d. growth

2. A child who is aggressive and demonstrates a lack of responsibility is associated with _____ parenting behavior.
   a. authoritative
   b. permissive
   c. authoritarian
   d. doting

3. Today's homeless population is
   a. mostly alcoholic men.
   b. skid row inhabitants.
   c. younger and more mixed than previously.
   d. socially more limited.

4. About _____ of first marriages end in divorce.
   a. 75%
   b. 80%
   c. 50%
   d. 25%

5. Almost _____ of second marriages end in divorce.
   a. 48%
   b. 62%
   c. 74%
   d. 83%

6. Divorce is thought of today as a _____ of experiences.
   a. sequence
   b. repression
   c. assimilation
   d. amalgamation

7. After divorce, family conditions usually stabilize in about _____ years.
   a. two
   b. three
   c. four
   d. five

8. There are about _____ licensed child-care centers in the United States.
   a. 25,000
   b. 98,000
   c. 116,000
   d. 140,00

9. _____ are older, better educated, and higher paid care givers.
   a. Au pairs
   b. Babysitters
   c. Nannies
   d. Grandparents

10. In the United States, the majority of children under _____ years receive nonparental care.
    a. 2
    b. 3
    c. 4
    d. 5

11. The most important feature of day care is the _____ of care provided.
    a. time
    b. degree
    c. extent
    d. quality

12. Probably the best type of day care is found in the _____ center, which may not provide an accurate picture of all centers.
    a. research
    b. company
    c. commercial
    d. family-run

13. The American psychologist who discussed the "I" and "Me" elements of the self was
    a. Edward L. Thorndike.
    b. William James.
    c. B. F. Skinner.
    d. John Watson.

14. The beliefs that we have about the characteristics and behavior we associate with male and female is called
    a. accommodation.
    b. gender practices.
    c. gender stereotypes.
    d. gender equality.

15. In cognitive development theory, children first acquire their
    a. gender identity.
    b. appropriate gender behavior.
    c. psychic stability.
    d. conditioned behavior.

16. Social learning theory depends on the concept of _____ to explain the acquisition of appropriate gender behavior.
    a. schema
    b. assimilation
    c. reinforcement
    d. adaptation

17. When children of the same sex tend to play together, it is referred to as
    a. sex differentiation.
    b. sex cleavage.
    c. sex bias.
    d. sex dichotomy.

18. True play has no _____ goals.
    a. divergent
    b. coercive
    c. intrinsic
    d. extrinsic

19. Play materials are grouped into _____ categories.
    a. 4
    b. 6
    c. 8
    d. 10

20. Piaget classified games as practice, with rules, and
    a. complex.
    b. routine.
    c. simple.
    d. symbolic.

Answers

chapter

9

PHYSICAL AND COGNITIVE DEVELOPMENT IN MIDDLE CHILDHOOD

Chapter Outline

Chapter Objectives

After reading this chapter, you should be able to answer the following questions.

- How would you describe physical and motor development during these years?

- What are some of the competing views of cognitive development during the middle-childhood years?

- How do children develop thinking and problem-solving strategies?

- How would you trace children's progress in moral development?

- How does children's language change during these years?

*E*dison was as inquisitive as a young red squirrel—a nervous little question-box. As a boy, he ran down to the Milan shipyards (close to his Ohio home) and watched the men building boats for Great Lakes shipping. There he asked the shipbuilders hundreds of questions. "Why could you see a hammer hit a board before you could hear it, if you were at a distance?" "Why did you have to fit joints carefully?" "What was pitch made of?" Some of the questions the men could answer and some they couldn't. One of them jokingly said to Sam Edison, "It would save time to hire a man especial to answer your young one's questions." (Baldwin, 1995, p. 19)

Less than 40 years later, the person we think of as epitomizing the very idea of successful problem-solving behavior had tumbled to horrific financial depths. He experienced an estimated loss of 4.5 million dollars (when the dollar meant something). He suffered a humiliating plummet in status (forced to see his name dropped from the newly formed *General Electric Company*). He was subjected to ridicule because of "Edison's Folly" (a failed iron-ore milling adventure). And so Edison faced a questionable future (labeled a burnout—"His best days are behind him"). And yet, the waiting vultures could not take him down. Why? His determined drive, inner resilience, and immense intelligence carried him out of the grasp of his doubters and enabled him to rise like a phoenix from the ashes of his failures.

These two paragraphs, illustrating the intellectual spark that illuminated Edison's life, touch on the essential topics of this chapter: an inquiring mind from the earliest days, a supportive environment, a willingness to look at problems from a different perspective, determination that cannot be extinguished, and an acceptance of the risks accompanying novel ventures.

Why should we be so concerned about children's cognitive growth? In a highly technological world, the success and the survival of nations, let alone individuals, depend on a continued source of inquiring, creative minds. Science feeds on ideas, businesses need constant change, artistry (for example, painting, writing) thrives on innovative talent. But it isn't only these traditional fields that thirst for problem solvers; the way we relate to one another as individuals today needs reassessment. For example, the strains and demands of modern living (mothers

Cognitive theory has made us aware that children's language reveals much about their level of mental functioning. Can you incorporate your knowledge of heredity and environment to explain language development?

working, fathers more engaged in child care, children spending time with both parents following a divorce) frequently necessitate a new way of looking at relationships, which, in its way, is just as intellectually demanding as the work Edison was engaged in.

Cognitive complexities and subtle moral reasoning characterize the years between childhood and adolescence. These years see the emergence of talents that children have been previously nurturing and now, especially during the 9-to-11 year period, suspected skills become full-blown. Whether these talents be athletic, artistic, mathematical, musical, or whatever, parents, teachers, coaches, adults in general must be sensitive not only to children's abilities but also to their developmental needs and limitations—*they are still children.*

To help you discover clues to important developmental achievements, in this chapter we begin by tracing physical and motor development during the middle-childhood years. We then turn again to Piaget and analyze his concrete operational period, that time of cognitive development when youngsters begin to engage in truly abstract thinking. Here we pause and examine the world of intelligence, which has caused so much controversy. Today's children are expected to do much more with their intelligence than just sit and listen and memorize: They're expected to develop thinking skills and to solve problems. We'll explore both of these worlds (thinking and problem solving) and then trace the moral and language development of middle-childhood youngsters.

As observers of this phase of lifespan development, we can't allow ourselves to be deceived by an apparent lull in development. Too much is going on. Deep-seated developmental currents are changing the very process by which children reason and make their moral decisions. Think about what you read in this chapter; probe into what lies behind a child's behavior. It will help you to understand the developmental achievements that prepare a youngster to move from these last years of childhood to the different demands of adolescence.

PHYSICAL DEVELOPMENT

Always do right. This will gratify some people and astonish the rest.

—MARK TWAIN

In contrast to the rapid increase in height and weight during the first years of life, physical development proceeds at a slowed pace during middle childhood. Most children gain about 2 inches in height per year. The same pattern applies to weight gains. By 6 years of age, most children are at about seven times their birth weight. Changes in height and weight, however, are not the only noticeable physical differences.

Body proportion changes also. Head size comes more in line with body size. An adult's head size is estimated to be about one-seventh of total body size; the preschooler's is about one-fourth. This difference gradually decreases during the middle-childhood years. Also, the loss of baby teeth and the emergence of permanent teeth change the shape of the lower jaw. By the end of the period, the middle-childhood youngster's body is more in proportion and more like an adult's.

Changes in arms, legs, and trunk size also occur. The trunk becomes thinner and longer, and the chest becomes broader and flatter. Arms and legs begin to stretch but as yet show little sign of muscle development. Hands and feet grow more slowly than arms and legs do, which explains some of the awkwardness that we see during these years. Children are tremendously active physically and gradually display a steady improvement in motor coordination (Tanner, 1989). Among the most important changes are those in brain development.

The middle-childhood years are a time when children demonstrate considerable competence. Their continuing mastery of their bodies and their environment lead to emerging skills that are readily observable. As the skills and abilities of these years improve noticeably, can you identify potential problems with adult pressure?

Brain Development during the Middle Childhood Years

Neuroscience has provided fascinating glimpses into the brain's development and function; advances in our knowledge of the brain hold promise for improving the education of young children. When applied correctly, brain science may serve as a vehicle for advancing the application of our understanding of learning and development. (Katzir & Pare-Blagorv, 2006, p. 53)

As children begin their journey through the middle-childhood years, a perplexing—and frustrating—question troubles researchers: What has happened to any discernible links between structure and function? Does *this* region of the brain support *this* behavior? In earlier chapters you learned that memory involves the *whole* brain, and that we shouldn't concentrate solely on Broca's and Wernicke's areas to explain language development. Also, our recognition of the rapidly increasing complexity of the child's growing brain poses new challenges to be overcome. Consequently, as our knowledge of the developing brain expands almost on a daily basis, our certitude about many previous "facts" lessens. The middle-childhood years offer an excellent example of this dilemma.

In Figure 9.1, note the various brain lobes that we previously discussed in Chapter 5. Here we see the clearly defined brain regions whose development we traced earlier. Keeping these regions in mind, let's turn to several features of the brains of children 7 to 11 years of age. We know that memory is improving, attention is sharpening, decision making is becoming more mature, and problem solving is progressing. We also realize that these improvements are linked to brain development. For example, the frontal lobe continues its aggressive formation of neural circuits; the temporal lobe acts to help hearing become more acute thus focusing attention; [the parietal lobes function by coordinating more and more sensations] (Restak, 2001). These changes help to explain the middle-childhood youngster's rapidly advancing cognitive skills.

The Race toward Complexity

The child's brain is racing toward complexity as it increases the number of glial cells, and the myelination process keeps pace. (Myelin is the white, fatty sheath

FIGURE 9.1

The human brain.

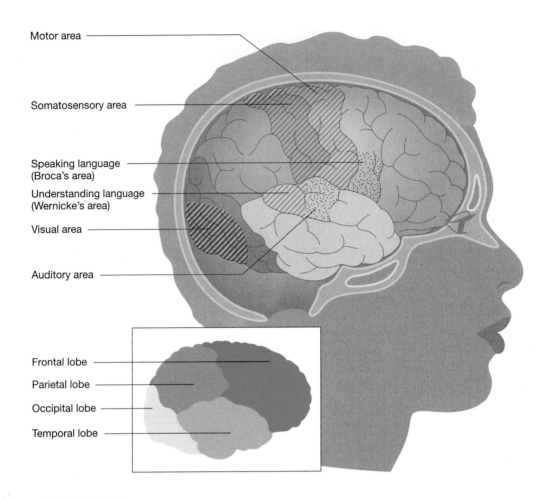

Motor area

Somatosensory area

Speaking language (Broca's area)

Understanding language (Wernicke's area)

Visual area

Auditory area

Frontal lobe

Parietal lobe

Occipital lobe

Temporal lobe

that provides a protective coating to the axon, much as a plastic wrapping protects electric wires) (Nelson, Thomas, & DeHaan, 2006; Rose, 2005). The cortical area is now about the thickness of six playing cards (about 2 millimeters) and, if stretched out, would be about the size of a dinner napkin (Hawkins, 2004).

Within this area, the neural process continues unabated: A vast network of pathways and interactions develops, with cells traveling great distances and always demanding more connections, and thus the number of synaptic connections grows at an amazing rate. Is it any wonder, then, that as Rose (2005, p. 122) notes, little is known about the details of the subtle changes that occur later in childhood. And then—the widening circle of middle-childhood experiences imposes itself on these neurophysiological changes to shape the unique and developmental paths of individual children.

Now, to return to those missing 100,000,000 neurons we mentioned in our earlier discussion of brain development: Nature has manufactured billions of brain cells more than will be needed to insure that the brain will be able to form enough connections for all the needed abilities and skills that demand new connections. Those neurons that *don't* make connections simply die. And—and this may startle some readers—this exercise in survival (some connections die, some connections survive) continues throughout our lives. So the lesson here is not only for our children, but also for all of us: Keep busy, seek challenges, stay alert.

The task of adults who are around children during these electrifying years is to provide the appropriate stimulation that will make them want to participate in this enticing world, thereby adding new connections and strengthening those already present. A good example of this principle is seen in John Fitzgerald's (2004) fascinating children's story, *The Great Brain*.

AN APPLIED VIEW

The Brain and Children's Literature

In John Fitzgerald's charming tale of Tom, *The Great Brain,* we see in fiction the playing out of many of the ideas we've been discussing. When Tom was 10 years old and living in a rural Indiana community, his father decided to install the first inside-the-house toilet in the town. When the only plumber in town came around to dig a cesspool, Tom charged all his friends a penny to watch. His little brother protested, but Tom told him that he had to keep thinking of new ideas so that his great brain would continue growing.

Next he decided to charge them to come into the house and flush the toilet. When his mother heard about it, she was furious and made Tom refund all the money. But after Tom gave back all the money he had collected, there were still 20 children demanding their money. He complained to his mother about all the "cheaters," but she made him use his own money to finish paying everyone. Tom's brother looked at him and decided that Tom would carry this financial catastrophe to the grave.

Undaunted, Tom's next adventure turned out much more satisfactorily. When two of his friends were lost in the twists and turns of a series of caves, the entire town came to help find them. For two days and a night they searched but couldn't find the boys. Everyone feared they were lost for good, but Tom's great brain went to work. His two friends had taken their dog Lucky with them. Lucky liked to play and romp through the fields with Tom's dog Brownie. Tom convinced the adults to let him go into the caves with Brownie and a pound of liver. He thought his dog would have a good chance of finding his pal Lucky. He smeared the liver over rocks on the way in, knowing that Brownie would use the smell to lead them out. The plan devised in Tom's great brain worked; he found his friends, Brownie led them out, and Tom became the town's hero.

With Tom's great brain continuing to dream up schemes, some crafty, some enormously helpful, people in his home town reluctantly resigned themselves to wondering what Tom's great brain would think of next. Of one thing they could be very sure: Tom's brain cells were forming and firing at the speed of light, brain connections were being made in numbers almost too many to register, allowing Tom to move on to bigger and better adventures. Is there a Tom in your family?

Nutrition

The physical picture of the middle-childhood youngster is one of energy and growing motor skills. Parents often worry that their child isn't eating enough, but given the slower growth rate of these years, less food is needed. Rather it's the quality of the food that's important; junk foods and excessive fats and sugars are to be avoided. Some parents in developed countries have children who are on vegetarian diets. In other cases, the children themselves dislike meat or avoid it because of their love of animals. The 2005 *Dietary Guidelines for Americans* urges that we think of a healthy diet as one consisting of:

- Fruits, vegetables, whole grains, and fat-free or low-fat milk and milk products.
- Lean meats, poultry, fish, beans, eggs, and nuts.
- A small amount of saturated fats, trans fats, cholesterol, sodium, and added sugars.

Children are now reaching a point in their lives where school schedules determine breakfast and lunch meals, snacking is becoming more frequent, and children make their own decisions on what they will eat (Farrell & Nicoteri, 2007). Peer influence is a growing and important element in children's decisions about what to eat: Should I bring a lunch, or shall I eat cafeteria food? Is soda OK, or should I have fruit juice?

Although growth slows during these years, several cautions are appropriate. For example, the body is preparing for the adolescent growth spurt, so the middle-childhood period is an ideal time to encourage good eating habits. Care is required regarding the type of snacks that are available for children. Soda and fat-laden chips and the like may lead not only to poor eating habits but also to obesity. Many schools find themselves involved in controversies concerning the use of vending machines. Although these machines are an easy and convenient way for school systems to raise money, their use has caused considerable concern across the country because of the increasing number of overweight children (Ball & Bindler, 2006).

Children's energy needs in these years is roughly 2,000 to 2,200 calories a day. To meet these needs and to satisfy children's longings for tasty snacks, here are a few suggestions (Grodner, Long, & DeYoung, 2004, p. 347).

- Ready-to-eat not overly sweet cereals.
- Apples, oranges, cheese, crackers, and some cookies.
- Fruit juice packs and low-fat chocolate milk packs.
- Peanut butter and jelly sandwiches.
- Smoothies and fruit shakes made with skim milk.

Careless use of available foods and snacks has led to a rising concern about obese children.

Obesity

To give you some idea of the seriousness of and concern about obesity in children, estimates are that 25 million children, 17 and under, are obese or overweight. To address this national problem, the Robert Wood Johnson Foundation plans to spend more than $500 million over the next five years to combat childhood obesity. Although children's needs for protein, vitamins, and minerals remains high, some children begin to accumulate empty calories from high-sugar and high-fat foods. Thus obesity, with its social, psychological, and medical consequences, looms on the horizon. (The best way to think of obesity is an excessive amount of fat on the body.) Recent research indicates that children who are overweight between the ages of 10 and 17 years probably will have a lifetime problem regardless of whether their parents were thin or fat (Whitaker & Dietz, 1997). Even with slim parents, children who are overweight during the preteen and teen years have a 64% chance of becoming obese adults. In the last 20 years, the number of overweight and obese children has increased almost 300% (Farrell & Nicoteri, 2007).

To help their children avoid obesity, parents should follow several safeguards (Ball & Bindler, 2006; Grodner, Long, & DeYoung, 2004).

- Carefully monitor television time; the sarcastic label "couch potato" is, unfortunately, all too true, given people's tendency to munch while watching.
- Encourage appropriate physical activity *on a year-round basis.*
- Serve as much fruit and vegetables as possible.
- Watch fat intake, because it is the most concentrated source of calories.
- Start early to make children aware of what they're eating.
- If a child is overweight, don't become obsessed with it; remember that obesity may well be a genetic problem.

Middle-childhood youngsters show steady growth, usually good health, and an increasing sense of competence. Physical growth is relatively slow until the end of the period, when girls' development may spurt. Actually, according to recent research, American girls are reaching puberty earlier than previously realized (Herman-Giddens et al., 1997). Nearly one-half of African-American girls and 15% of white girls begin to develop sexually by 8 years of age. In other words, girls in the second and third grades are facing issues of puberty (early breast development and growth of pubic hair), while, according to the American Academy of Pediatrics, the average age of a female's first period is 12.43 years.

Variables such as genetic influence, health, and nutrition may also cause wide fluctuations in the growth of these children. Two youngsters may show considerable physical variation and yet both are perfectly normal. Consequently, although most children achieve the major developmental milestones, development may well differ between cultures, subcultures, and ethnic groups.

A SOCIOCULTURAL VIEW

Exceptional Children

Working with children highlights the concept of individual differences, which reflects R. Bishop's (1997) belief that multiculturalism in its broadest sense includes those who have been marginalized by society. Here we would like to call your attention to the needs of exceptional children. Knowledge of developmental characteristics can guide us to choose appropriate materials that offer support for children who are exceptional and elicit understanding on the part of other children. Although you may have seen several methods for classifying exceptional conditions, the following are the most common categories of exceptionality

- *Sensory and physical disorders* (physical, orthopedic, and health impairments). These children have physical and/or health problems to the extent that it impairs their normal interactions with others. Sensory and physical disorders, of themselves, do not make children more susceptible to mental problems, but in the context of the nature of a child's world today, they can increase a child's vulnerability.

- *Mental retardation* (problems with intellectual functioning). Mental retardation is typically diagnosed by subaverage intellectual functioning, usually an IQ score below 70 on a traditional intelligence test and impairment in adaptive behavior, both of which begin in childhood (Hodapp & Dykens, 2006). For example, below-average performances are usually accompanied by limitations in two or more adaptive skills (academic, communications, inability to live on one's own, and so on) (Thies & Travers, 2001).

- *Communication disorders* (speech and language disorders). Assessing speech and language disorders in children is particularly challenging because of the expertise required in several disciplines: linguistics, audiology, child development, neuropsychology, pediatric neurology, and psychiatry (Bishop, 2006). The key element here is communication. For blind children the question is how to facilitate nonverbal communication; for the hearing impaired the question is how to access meaningful communication (Hindley & van Gent, 2005).

- *Learning disabilities* (difficulty with academic subjects with no specific mental or physical cause). Experts estimate that as many as one in five children has a learning disability, that is, those children who demonstrate a discrepancy between measured ability and actual achievement (Thies & Travers, 2001). Learning disabilities in reading and/or writing are among the most frequently occurring problems in school-age children (Berninger, 2006, p. 423).

- *Emotional and behavioral disorders.* This classification does not refer to the normal outbursts that all children experience. Rather they are much more intense and sufficiently disruptive to impair relationships, lead to aggressive acts that border on violence, and cause persistent problems in school. Attempting to address these issues, many school systems have turned to SEL programs (*Social, Emotional Learning*), which are intended to identify underlying causes of problem behavior while simultaneously supporting academic achievement (Kress & Elias, 2006).

- *Children who are gifted and talented.* With the growing sophistication of developmental research methods as we continue into the 21st century has come a realization that giftedness cannot be explained by high scores on traditional IQ tests. Today we recognize the extraordinary range of outstanding talent in varied and wide-ranging endeavors. (For a further discussion of this topic read Moran & Gardner, 2006.)

As you can see, these categories are far from exhaustive. Other disorders with which you are familiar, such as attention deficit hyperactivity disorder, defy neat classification. Does this disorder "fit" the emotional and behavioral category? Or the physical and sensory? Or the brain disorder class? Much the same is true of autism, with its developmental implications for communication, social interaction, intellectual functioning, and so on. Often classified with the *pervasive developmental disorders,* it is today referred to as *autism spectrum disorders,* with the term *autism* implying the need for more restricted diagnostic criteria (Lord & Bailey, 2006).

Children Who Are Exceptional

For teachers and parents, the concept of individual differences is part of their daily lives. Often, however, children are exceptional, and knowledge of developmental characteristics helps those working with them to better understand their needs. The notion of exceptionality has changed dramatically in recent years. At one time such children were either refused admission to public schools or educated in separate locations. Today, however, federal law mandates that children with special needs should be educated in the least restricted environment possible in which they can achieve success. *Least restrictive* means that students are to be removed from the regular classroom, home, and family as infrequently as possible. This procedure is also known as *inclusion* or *mainstreaming.*

These children's lives should be as normal as possible, and intervention should be consistent with individual needs and not interfere with individual freedom any more than is absolutely necessary. For example, children should not be placed in special classes if they can be served adequately by resource teachers, and they should not be placed in institutions if special classes will serve their needs just as well. Such treatment of children who are exceptional received powerful support from federal legislation, especially the passage of the *Education for All Handicapped Children* in 1975 (PL 94-142), which has been repeatedly amended and is now known as the *Individuals with Disabilities Education Improvement Act (IDEA)*. Along with *No Child Left Behind* legislation, these measure were designed to encourage and improve the educational improvement of all students.

Guided Review

1. During these years, the _____ process of the brain proceeds rapidly.
2 With regard to nutrition, the _____ of the food is extremely important.
3. The nutritional need of middle-childhood children must be carefully monitored to avoid _____.
4. Federal legislation to improve the educational need of exceptional children is known as _____.

COGNITIVE DEVELOPMENT

Middle-childhood youngsters now begin formal schooling, and their cognitive abilities help them to meet the more demanding tasks set by the school. One way of understanding how children's thinking enables them to master new challenges is to analyze Piaget's explanation of these years—the concrete operational period.

Piaget and Concrete Operations

Picture a 5-year-old child (in Piaget's preoperational stage), an 8-year-old child (in Piaget's concrete operational stage), six black tokens, and six orange tokens. Make a row of the black tokens. If you give the 5-year-old child the orange tokens with instructions to match them with the black tokens, the child can easily do it. When the tokens are in a one-to-one position, a 5-year-old can tell us that both rows have the same number.

• • • • • •

0 0 0 0 0 0

But if we spread the six black tokens to make a longer row, the 5-year-old will tell us that the longer row has more tokens!

• • • • • •

0 0 0 0 0 0

concrete operational period
Piaget's third stage of cognitive development, during which children begin to employ logical thought processes with concrete material.

Present the 8-year-old with the same problem. The child will think it is a trick—both rows obviously still have the same number. Why? This child is in Piaget's **concrete operational period,** and her thinking is much more flexible. Concrete operational children *operate mentally* on their environment. For example,

Answers   1. myelination 2. quality 3. obesity 4. IDEA

decentering
Process by which children in the concrete operational period can concentrate on more than one aspect of a situation.

conservation
The understanding that an object retains certain properties, no matter how its form changes.

seriation
Process by which children in the concrete operational period can arrange objects by increasing or decreasing size.

classification
Process by which children in the concrete operational period can group objects with some similarities within a larger category.

reversibility
Cognitive process by which children retrace their thoughts.

numeration
Process by which children in the concrete operational period grasp the meaning of number, the oneness of one.

they can reverse their thinking. During the period of concrete operations, children gradually employ logical thought processes with *concrete* materials, that is, with objects, people, and/or events that they can see and touch. They also concentrate on more than one aspect of a situation, which is called **decentering.**

Accomplishments of the Concrete Operational Period

Among children's cognitive achievements of these years are these:

- **Conservation** appears. If you think back to Piaget's famous water jar problem (see Chapter 7), children in the concrete operational stage now mentally pour the water back. By reversing their thinking in this manner, they *conserve* the basic idea: the amount of water remains the same.

- **Seriation** means that concrete operational children can arrange objects by increasing or decreasing size.

- **Classification** enables children to group objects with some similarities within a larger category. Brown wooden beads and white wooden beads are all beads.

- **Reversibility** enables children to retrace their thoughts.

- **Numeration** means that children understand the concept of numbers; for example, children understand oneness—that one boy, one girl, one apple, and one orange are all one of something.

Features of Concrete Operational Thinking

Children at the level of concrete operations can solve the water-level problem, but the problem or the situation must involve concrete objects; hence the name of the period. In the water-level problem, for example, children no longer concentrate solely on the height of the water in the glass; they also consider the width of the glass. But as Piaget noted, concrete operational children nevertheless demonstrate a true logic since they now can reverse operations. Concrete operational children gradually master conservation—that is, they understand that something may remain the same even if surface features change.

Figure 9.2 illustrates the different types of conservation that appear at different ages. For example, if preoperational children are given sticks of different lengths, they cannot arrange them from smallest to largest. Or if presented with three sticks, A, B, and C, they can tell you that A is longer than B and C, and that B is longer than C. But if we now remove A, they can tell you that B is longer than C, but not that A is longer than C. They must see A and C together. The child at the level of concrete operations has no difficulty with this problem.

Piaget's Legacy

As we end our analysis of Piaget's theory of cognitive development, what conclusions are possible?

- Piaget forced us to reconsider prevailing views on how children think.

- Thanks to Piaget we have a deeper understanding of children's cognitive development.

- He made us realize that children are active cognitively (not just passive recipients) as they construct their mental worlds.

- Piaget attempted to explain and not just describe children's thinking.

But, as we have seen, serious questions have emerged about Piaget's beliefs.

- By changing the nature of the task (for example, reducing the number of objects children must manipulate), researchers have found that children accomplish specific tasks at earlier ages than Piaget thought (Haith & Benson, 1998).

Middle-childhood youngsters are at Piaget's stage of concrete operations. Now they demonstrate increasing mental competence, such as classifying. Apply Piaget's ideas to a specific classroom subject such as social science.

FIGURE 9.2

Different kinds of conservation appear at different ages.

From John F. Travers, *The Growing Child,* Scott Foresman and Company, Glenview, IL 1982. Reprinted by permission of the author.

Conservation of	Example	Approximate age
1. Number	Which has more?	6–7 years
2. Liquids	Which has more?	7–8 years
3. Length	Are they the same length?	7–8 years
4. Substance	Are they the same?	7–8 years
5. Area	Which has more room?	7–8 years
6. Weight	Will they weigh the same?	9–10 years
7. Volume	Will they displace the same amount of water?	11–12 years

- By allowing children to practice (for example, teaching children conservation tasks) and by using familiar materials, young children can be trained to master concrete operational tasks.
- Research has rejected Piaget's belief that cognitive development proceeds through four discrete stages. For an excellent discussion of research on Piagetian concepts by French and Swiss psychologists, see Larivee, Normandeau, and Parent (2000). Their emphasis on individual differences reflects Robert Siegler's adaptive strategy choice model discussed on p. 242.

Although Piaget has left an enduring legacy, his ideas aren't the only explanation of cognitive development. Other psychologists, not entirely happy with Piaget's views, have devised new ways of explaining children's cognitive abilities.

New Ways of Looking at Intelligence

In our discussion of cognitive development from infancy through the middle-childhood years, we have identified limitations in Piaget's theory. Addressing these shortcomings, several recent theories have been proposed to explain intelligence and cognitive development. Two of these explanations, by Howard Gardner and Robert Sternberg, are particularly significant.

Gardner and Multiple Intelligences

multiple intelligences
Gardner's theory that attributes eight types of intelligence to humans.

Howard Gardner (1983, 1991, 1993, 1997, 2006) has forged a tight link between thinking and intelligence with his theory of **multiple intelligences,** which pluralizes the traditional concept of intelligence. Gardner (1993b, p. 15) defines *intelligence*

AN APPLIED VIEW

Footprints in the History of Intelligence

The story of Alfred Binet and his search for the meaning and measurement of intelligence is one of the most famous in the history of psychology. In 1904, Binet was asked by the Parisian Minister of Public Instruction to formulate some means of identifying the children most likely to fail in school. The problem was very difficult, because it meant finding some means of separating the normal from the truly retarded, of determining the lazy but bright who were simply poor achievers, and of eliminating the **halo effect** (assigning an unwarranted high rating to youngsters because they are neat and attractive).

Accepting this task meant that Binet had to begin with his own idea of intelligence, since it's impossible to fashion the means to measure something unless you know what that something is. Binet's view of intelligence contained three elements.

1. There is *direction* in our mental processes, which are directed toward the achievement of a particular goal and the discovery of adequate means of attaining the goal. In the preparation of a term paper, for example, you select a suitable topic and also the books and journals necessary to complete it.

2. We possess the ability to *adapt* by the use of tentative solutions, that is, we select and utilize some stimuli and test their relevance as we proceed toward our goal. Before writing the term paper, for example, you may make a field trip to the area you're researching, or to save time, you may decide to use relevant sources on the Internet or library resources.

3. We also possess the ability *to make judgments* and to criticize solutions. Frequently called *autocriticism,* this characteristic implies an objective evaluation of solutions. You may, for example, complete a paper, reread it, decide that one topic included is irrelevant, and eliminate it. This is autocriticism at work.

The items in Binet's early test reflected these beliefs. When an item seemed to differentiate between normal and subnormal, he retained it; if no discrimination appeared, he rejected it. Binet defined normality as the ability to do the things that others of the same age usually do. The fruit of his and his coworkers' endeavors was the publication in 1905 of the *Metrical Scale of Intelligence*.

Since their publication, Binet's mental-age scales have pointed the way for intelligence testing. The success of the Binet scale led a leading American psychologist, Lewis Terman, to adapt it for American usage. Terman's revision, called the Stanford-Binet, first appeared in 1916 and was revised in 1937, 1960, 1985, and 2003.

Another effort to measure intelligence appeared in the work of David Wechsler, who devised a series of tests intended to measure intelligence through the lifespan. Like Binet, Wechsler believed in a global theory of intelligence; that is, intelligent people, as measured on these tests, will be superior at anything they attempt. There are three forms of his test:

- *The Wechsler Adult Intelligence Scale–Revised (WAIS-111)* contains both verbal and performance items.
- *The Wechsler Intelligence Scale for Children-111 (WISC-111)* is designed for children 5 to 15 years old.
- *The Wechsler Preschool and Primary Scale of Intelligence–Revised (WPPSI-R)* is designed for children 4 to 6½ years old.

Considerable controversy has developed around these tests, mainly because those who have used them deviated from Binet's goal: to provide a means of identifying those students who needed help and *not* to classify people into rigid categories. Today we know that intelligence test scores change over the course of the lifespan for a variety of reasons. We also realize that these tests, which are highly verbal, are unfair to children from backgrounds different from those of middle-class white Americans. (For an extended discussion of these issues, see Travers and others, 1993.)

---

halo effect
Assigning a high grade to students because of their appearance (neat, attractive).

as the ability to solve problems or fashion products that are of consequence in a particular cultural setting or community. An especially intriguing aspect of his work is the insight it provides into those individuals who are capable of penetrating mathematical vision but who are baffled by the most obvious musical symbols. Gardner attempted to explain this apparent inconsistency by identifying eight equal intelligences and has argued forcefully that he has never identified additional intelligences, as is sometimes claimed (Gardner & Moran, 2006, p. 220).

1. *Linguistic intelligence.* The first of Gardner's intelligences is language—linguistic intelligence. For example, tracing the effects of damage to the language area of the brain, researchers have identified the core operations of any language: phonology, syntax, semantics, and pragmatics. Gardner considered language a preeminent example of human intelligence.

As we shall soon see, during these middle-childhood years children change their use of language to a more flexible, figurative form. Gardner

A child's intelligence may be expressed in many ways: physical, cognitive, psychosocial. Based on your knowledge and views of intelligence, evaluate the pros and cons of Gardner's theory.

commented on this by noting that middle-childhood youngsters love to expand on their accomplishments. They use appealing figures of speech: "I think I'll get lost," meaning that they're about ready to leave.

2. *Musical intelligence.* One has only to consider the talent and career of Yehudi Menuhin to realize that musical ability is special. At 3 years of age, Menuhin became fascinated by music, and by 10 he was performing on the international stage. The early appearance of musical ability suggests some kind of biological preparedness—a musical intelligence. The right hemisphere of the brain seems particularly important for music, and musical notation clearly indicates a basic symbol system. Although not considered intelligence in most theories, musical skill satisfies Gardner's criteria and so demands inclusion.

In regard to the middle-childhood years, Gardner noted that most children (except for those who are musically talented) cease musical development after school begins. For the talented, up to the age of 8 or 9, talent alone suffices for continued progress. Around 9 years of age, serious skill building commences, with sustained practice until adolescence, when these children must decide how much of their lives they want to commit to music. In general, society accepts musical illiteracy.

3. *Logical-mathematical intelligence.* Unlike linguistic and musical intelligences, logical-mathematical intelligence, Gardner believed, evolves from our contact with the world of objects. In using objects, taking them apart, and putting them together again, children gain their fundamental knowledge about "how the world works." By this process, logical-mathematical intelligence quickly divorces itself from the world of concrete objects. Children begin to think abstractly.

Gardner then used Piaget's ideas to trace the evolution of thinking. The development of logical-mathematical thinking, as explored by Piaget, is used as an example of scientific thinking. (You may want to review Piaget's ideas concerning the unfolding of intelligence to better understand Gardner's views.)

4. *Spatial intelligence.* Brain research has clearly linked spatial ability to the right side of the brain. Here Gardner relied heavily on Piaget, noting that an important change in children's thinking occurs during these years, especially with the appearance of conservation and reversibility. Middle-childhood youngsters can now visualize how objects seem to someone else. During these years, children can manipulate objects using their spatial intelligence, but this ability is still restricted to concrete situations and events.

5. *Bodily-kinesthetic intelligence.* Gardner stated that our control of bodily motions and the ability to handle objects skillfully are defining features of an "intelligence"—bodily-kinesthetic intelligence. You may be puzzled by this statement, given that we normally divide the mind and reasoning from our physical nature. This divorce between mind and body is often accompanied by the belief that our bodily activities are somehow less special. But Gardner urged us to think of mental ability as a means of carrying out bodily actions. Thus thinking becomes a way of refining motor behavior,

TABLE 9.1	Gardner's Multiple Intelligences
Type of Intelligence	*Meaning*
Linguistic	Communication, a preeminent example of human intelligence
Musical	Linked to brain location and a basic symbol system
Logical-mathematical	What we usually mean by "intelligence"
Spatial	Linked to brain location and symbol systems
Bodily-kinesthetic	Smooth development of bodily movements and adaptation
Interpersonal and intrapersonal	Linked to frontal lobe of brain; recognize what is distinctive in others
Naturalist	Ability to discriminate among categories

which raises the age-old question: Does increasing mental ability affect the performance of a bodily skill?

6 & 7. *Interpersonal and intrapersonal intelligence.* Gardner referred to interpersonal and intrapersonal intelligences as the personal intelligences. Interpersonal intelligence builds on an ability to recognize what is distinctive in others, whereas intrapersonal intelligence enables us to understand our own feelings. Autism is a good example of a deficit in this intelligence. Often competent in a certain skill, autistic children may be utterly incapable of ever referring to themselves.

8. Gardner recently identified the eighth of his intelligences as *naturalist intelligence,* by which he meant the human ability to discriminate among living things as well as a sensitivity to our natural world. (Table 9.1 summarizes Gardner's theory.)

Sternberg's Triarchic Model of Intelligence

Robert Sternberg (1988, 1990, 1995, 2006; Sternberg-Davidson, 1995) has designed a **triarchic model** of intelligence, which focuses on the following three aspects of intelligence.

1. *The components of intelligence.* These are the information-processing skills or components that contribute to intelligent behavior: **metacomponents,** which help us to plan, monitor, and evaluate our problem-solving strategies; **performance components,** which help us to execute the instructions of the metacomponents; and **knowledge-acquisition components,** which help us to learn how to solve problems in the first place (Sternberg, 2003). For example, consider writing a term paper. The metacomponents help you to decide on the topic, plan the paper, monitor the actual writing, and evaluate the final product. The performance components help you in the actual writing of the paper. You use the knowledge-acquisition components to do your research.

2. *Experience and intelligence.* The second contribution to intelligent behavior is experience, which improves our ability to deal with novel tasks and to use pertinent information to solve problems. Think of the first time you used a word processing program—nervous, hesitant, afraid of making mistakes—and compare those days to the rapid and expert techniques you now use. As tasks become more familiar, many parts of the task become automatic, requiring little conscious effort (Sternberg, 2003, p. 509).

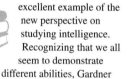

H. Gardner (1983). *Frames of Mind.* New York: Basic Books. Gardner's book, which is available in paperback, is an excellent example of the new perspective on studying intelligence. Recognizing that we all seem to demonstrate different abilities, Gardner makes an appealing case for the existence of several intelligences.

triarchic model of intelligence
Three-tier explanation of intelligence proposed by Robert Sternberg.

metacomponents
Sternberg's term for intelligence components that help us to plan, monitor, and evaluate our problem-solving strategies.

performance components
Sternberg's term for intelligence components that help us to execute the instructions of the metacomponents.

knowledge-acquisition components
Sternberg's term for intelligence components that help us to learn how to solve problems in the first place.

FIGURE 9.3

The triarchic model of intelligence

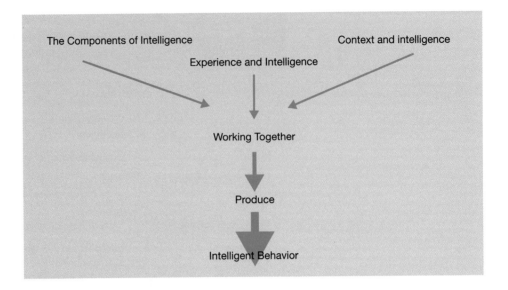

3. *The context of intelligence*. The third contribution to intelligent behavior in Sternberg's model refers to the ability to adapt to our culture. We learn how to do those practical things that help us to survive in our society, such as changing the washer in the kitchen sink, driving a car, getting along with others. In other words, intelligence must be viewed in the context in which it occurs (Bjorklund, 2005, p. 449). Thus the context of intelligence enables us:

    *   to *adap*t to our environment.
    *   to *create* and/or *shape* our environment.
    *   to *select* new environments (Sternberg, 2003).

    Figure 9.3 summarizes the triarchic theory of intelligence.

A SOCIOCULTURAL VIEW | Immigrant Children and Tests

Children's ability to take tests often powerfully influences the results of the test, especially intelligence tests. Tests can scare students or cause them anxiety. Test anxiety may come from parental pressure, their own concerns, or the testing atmosphere. At any rate, merely taking a test may affect a child's performance, which often is especially true for pupils with different cultural experiences. Language, reading, expectations, and behavior all may be different and influence their test performance.

These children want to succeed, as reflected in interviews with many of them: Almost 50% were doing one to two hours of homework every night. (Twenty-five percent of the Southeastern Asian students reported more than three hours each night.) We have spoken throughout our work of the need for sensitive responsiveness. Here is an instance in which being sensitive to the needs of multicultural children will only aid their adjustment and achievement in school.

The goals are clear; the task itself is difficult. Since social and cultural groups differ in the extent to which they share the values that underlie testing and the values that testing promotes,

any national testing system raises questions of equity (Madaus, 1994). The values of the test makers and the test takers aren't necessarily identical. For example, different cultural groups may have different intellectual traditions that tests, of whatever design, may not measure. As Madaus (1994) pointed out, who gains and who loses once again raises the issue of equity.

When children feel comfortable, they do better; this is particularly true for test taking. Multicultural children need information about why the test is being given, when it is being given, what material will be tested, and what kinds of items will be used. These are just a few topics to consider. In addition, language should not be a barrier to performance. For example, children need to understand the terms in the directions of the test—what "analyze" means; what "compare" means; what "discuss" means.

Helping multicultural students in this way means extra time and effort for teachers. But it is teaching, just as teaching English or history is teaching. As more and more multicultural students become users of classroom tests, they shouldn't do poorly because they don't understand the mechanics of the test.

Sternberg (Sternberg & Davidson, 1996) has also turned his attention to what he calls *successful intelligence,* which refers to the kind of intelligence needed to achieve important goals. Successful intelligence demands more active involvement by individuals as opposed to the inert intelligence measured by tests and consists of analytical, creative, and practical aspects. As Sternberg stated (1996, p. 32), successfully intelligent people capitalize on their intellectual strengths and compensate for and correct their weaknesses; this functionality should become the goal of teachers, parents, and the workplace.

Guided Review

5. The concrete operational period is characterized by the following cognitive accomplishments: conservation, classification, seriation, numeration, and _____.

6. Sternberg's triarchic model of intelligence includes _____, _____, and _____ _____ components.

7. _____ is associated with the theory of multiple intelligences.

8. Gardner describes an ability to recognize what is distinctive in others as an example of an _____ intelligence.

THINKING AND PROBLEM SOLVING

As our society moves from an industrial base to one committed to information technology, the skills that children need to adapt to these new directions likewise change. Unless parents and teachers equip themselves with the ability to teach innovative skills, children will be woefully unprepared to meet new demands (Ceci, 1996). Since a swift proliferation of knowledge characterizes information technology, mastery of available content will not suffice once children leave home and school and attempt to become productive citizens. Rather, they need thinking skills and problem-solving strategies that enable them to adapt to constant change; that is, critical thinkers are self-correcting—they discover their own weaknesses and act to remove obstacles and faults.

Children and Thinking Skills

Once children have accumulated knowledge, they must plan what to do with the material, just as a carpenter who has secured a desirable piece of wood and now has to decide how to shape it. Children need to shape their facts so that they squeeze as much value from them as possible. It's not enough just to obtain knowledge. Children need to apply what they have learned, to integrate it with other facts, and then to stand back and ask themselves if they could do any better. Parents and teachers attempting to help children improve their thinking skills shouldn't focus merely on questions or on facts. They should try to stretch children's thinking abilities by asking questions that require application, analysis, synthesis, and evaluation such as those based on thinking skills programs.

Answers   5. reversibility 6. metacomponents, performance, knowledge acquisition 7. Gardner 8. interpersonal

1. Imagine that you were lucky enough to obtain two tickets to a great Broadway musical for $100. As you walk down the street to the theater, you discover that you have lost the tickets. You can't remember the seat numbers. Would you go to the ticket window and buy another pair of tickets for $100?

2. Imagine that you are on the way to the theater to buy tickets for a great Broadway play. They will cost you $100. As you approach the ticket window, you discover that you have lost $100. Would you still pay $100 for the tickets?

These questions, originally posed by Tversky and Kahneman (1981) elicit some interesting answers. How did you answer them? Among their subjects, 46% answered yes to question 1, while 88% answered yes to question 2. Note that many more people said they would buy new tickets if they had lost the money rather than the tickets. Yet the two situations are almost identical—in each instance you would have lost $100.

How can we explain the difference in the responses? Tversky and Kahneman believed that the way a problem is framed helps to explain our response. As they stated:

> The frame that a decision-maker adopts is controlled partly by the formulation of the problem and partly by the norms, habits, and personal characteristics of the decision-maker. *(1981, p. 453)*

The point here is that our personal characteristics (such as motivation, persistence, and the like) and how questions and problems are structured influence our decisions. We can help children reach better decisions by teaching them the skills and strategies discussed in this chapter.

A Thinking Skills Taxonomy

In 1956, Benjamin Bloom and his colleagues published a classic work entitled *Taxonomy of Educational Objectives, Handbook 1: Cognitive Domain.* (Think of a taxonomy as a classification scheme.) Bloom's taxonomy has enjoyed widespread acceptance and today forms the core of many thinking skills programs. The main purpose of the taxonomy is to provide a classification of the goals of our educational system (Bloom, 1956, p. 1). The taxonomy consists of three major sections: the cognitive, the affective, and the psychomotor domains. Our concern here is with the cognitive taxonomy, which is divided into the six major classes listed below:

1.00 *Knowledge*—recall of specific facts

2.00 *Comprehension*—understanding what is communicated

3.00 *Application*—generalization and use of abstract information in concrete situations

4.00 *Analysis*—breakdown of a problem into subparts and detection of relationships among the parts

5.00 *Synthesis*—putting together parts to form a whole

6.00 *Evaluation*—using criteria to make judgments

The use of a taxonomy of thinking skills provides a useful organization of knowledge about thinking and facilitates answering questions such as:

*   What do we know about children—their developmental paths, needs, and interests?

*   What is in the nature of the subject matter that can help to shape objectives?

*   What does the psychology of learning tell us about the appropriate placement of objectives in the learning sequence? Do the ways that students learn suggest a series of steps that must be mastered?

With today's interest in thinking skills, many concerned parents and teachers have turned to Bloom's categories of analysis, synthesis, and evaluation as the best means available for their children to master higher order thinking skills. Table 9.2 provides some examples of Bloom's ideas and samples of the kinds of questions you can ask your students to sharpen their thinking skills. (We used the American Civil War as an example.)

TABLE 9.2	Using Bloom's Taxonomy

Level of Thinking	Sample Questions
Knowledge—recalling specific facts	When did the Civil War begin? When was the Civil War completed? Who was President of the Confederacy during the Civil War?
Comprehension—understanding what is communicated	Why would Americans want to fight against each other? Can you give me a brief summary of the Civil War in your own words?
Application—generalizing and using abstract information	Why did the North want to keep a large army around Washington? Where would you put the Southern cities on this map?
Analysis—dividing a problem into subparts	Can you think of several causes of the Civil War? What were the main features of the Battle of Gettysburg?
Synthesis—putting together parts to form a whole	Why do you think Lee surrendered at Appomattox? Could you write a few sentences describing Lee's personality?
Evaluation—using criteria to make judgments	Many people criticize Grant for losing so many men. Do you think Lincoln made the right decision in putting him in charge of the Union armies? Do you think Lincoln made a mistake in leaving McClellan as head of the Army of the Potomac for so long?

From S. Elliott, T. Kratochwill, J. Littlefield, and J. Travers, *Educational Psychology: Effective Teaching, Effective Learning,* 3rd ed., pp. 299, 301. Copyright © 2000 by Stephen N. Elliott. Reproduced by permission.

Helping children improve their thinking skills introduces the important role played by questions. *Parents and teachers should not focus merely on questions about facts; rather they should stretch their children's thinking abilities by asking questions that require application, analysis, synthesis, and evaluation.*

Using Questions to Improve Thinking Skills

Even before Socrates, questioning was one of teaching's most common and effective techniques. Teachers and parents ask hundreds of questions, especially about science, geography, history, and literature. Using questions is a specific example of how to help children improve their thinking skills. Good questions cause children to pay *attention*, to *process* information, to *organize* their ideas, and to *compose* an answer, a neat summary of thinking and problem solving.

Three issues are critical in framing thoughtful questions (Cruickshank, Bainer, & Metcalf, 1995).

1. *How to ask questions.* Questions should be clearly and concisely phrased. You could well follow Michael Gelb's advice (1996) to use a reporter's classic questions: *What? Where? When? Who? How? Why?* The language of the question must be appropriate for the children's cognitive level and focus their attention on clear objectives. In other words, don't muddy the waters by introducing unnecessary words or expressions (Cooper, 2006). Also, avoid questions that merely require a "yes" or "no" answer. Effective questions cause children to *think about* what's asked and to compose an answer. Finally, ask only one question at a time. Too often adults think about another aspect of the material they're using and piggyback one or more questions on to the original.

2. *Obtaining good answers.* One of the best ways to encourage children to give their best responses is *to give them enough time to answer*. Research has shown that a wait time of about 3 to 5 seconds results in the best answers (Cooper, 2006; Cruickshank, Bainer, & Metcalf, 1995).

| TABLE 9.3 | Using Bloom's Taxonomy to Frame Questions |

Level of Thinking	Examples of Questions
Knowledge	Who did _____? When was _____ completed? Identify the _____ in the list. What does 2 + 6 equal?
Comprehension	Provide a good title for the story you read. In your own words, what was the main theme of the story?
Application	Use the word correctly in a sentence. Design a model that illustrates your understanding of the concept.
Analysis	Categorize all of the elements of the problem. What is the function of _____? How is A related to B?
Synthesis	Identify the common pattern resulting from all the pictures. Summarize the various points that were made by stating a rule. Integrate the various pieces of information to create a profile of the person.
Evaluation	Judge the best method for testing the hypothesis. Rank order the projects, using stated criteria, from best to worst. Decide which problems were solved correctly.

From S. Elliott, T. Kratochwill, J. Littlefield, and J. Travers, *Educational Psychology: Effective Teaching, Effective Learning,* 3rd ed., pp. 299, 301. Copyright © 2000 by Stephen N. Elliott. Reproduced by permission.

3. *Following-up the responses.* Once children have responded, you (parents, teachers, adults) must react. Try to avoid saying "OK" and then moving on. You should clarify, expand, and synthesize when you can. Never let an incorrect answer stand.

Parents and teachers are the primary motivators of a middle-childhood youngster's cognitive potential to think critically. By appealing to a child's enthusiasms and abilities, adults encourage these youngsters to begin using "a thinking disposition" and to use their thinking abilities to attack the problems they face, both in and out of school.

Give careful attention to the level of thought your question is demanding. Table 9.3 illustrates the use of Bloom's taxonomy in organizing questions.

Problem-Solving Strategies

One of the authors of this text (JFT) recently was asked to give a talk to a group of parents on thinking skills and problem-solving strategies for children. To begin, I presented the following problem.

Two motorcyclists are 100 miles apart. At exactly the same moment they begin to drive toward each other for a meeting. Just as they leave, a bird flies from the front of the first cyclist to the front of the second cyclist. When it reaches the second cyclist, it turns around and flies back to the first. The bird continues flying in this manner until the cyclists meet. The cyclists both travel at the rate of 50 miles per hour, while the bird maintains a constant speed of 75 miles per hour. How many miles will the bird have flown when the cyclists meet?

Examining this problem, you may immediately begin to calculate distance, miles per hour, and constancy of speed. Actually, this is not a mathematical problem; it's a word problem. Carefully look at it again. Both riders will travel for one hour before they meet; the bird flies at 75 miles per hour; therefore, the bird will have flown 75 miles. No formula or calculations are needed, just a close examination of what is given.

The talk to the parents was in the evening. They were tired, and not too attentive. Then they became downright mad at themselves for not getting the correct answer. Now I had their attention, and the parents were determined not to be tricked again. I next asked them to think of something that had frustrated them recently—in other words, a problem—and how they had felt if they couldn't reach a solution. Finally, I reminded the parents that their children have similar feelings when they are baffled by an arithmetic word problem, or bewildered about how to start a term paper.

Characteristics of Good Problem Solvers

Solving a problem occurs when a person has a particular goal in mind that can't be attained immediately because obstacles are present. Thus there are four criteria needed for problem solving to occur: goals, obstacles, strategies for overcoming the obstacles, and an evaluation of the results (Bjorklund, 2005). We know a great deal about problem-solving strategies today, and this knowledge can be of great value to children. To give you one example, simply reassuring them that there's nothing to be afraid of when they face a problem and urging them to look for the facts that are given in a problem greatly improves their problem-solving abilities.

As children move into the middle-childhood years (7 to about 12 years), memory shows marked improvement. Many developmental features come into play during these years to enhance memory skills. Attention dramatically improves as children learn to shut out distractions and concentrate on the immediate task. Their short-term memory span increases as they acquire and use various memory strategies. They are becoming more capable of transferring ever increasing amounts of information to long-term memory by strengthening synaptic connections (Squire & Kandel, 2000).

Siegler (2000) notes that children's speed in processing information increases as their cognitive skills grow, they continue to improve their ability to develop and apply many memory strategies, and they constantly expand their knowledge base. Finally, they show marked improvement in developing memory strategies for specific topics (science, math, and so on).

Improving Children's Problem-Solving Strategies

Obviously some people are better at problem solving than others are, owing to intelligence, experience, and/or education. But it's possible to improve anyone's ability to solve problems, even children's. Some children and adults don't do well with problems because they're afraid of them. "I'm just not smart enough"; "I never could do these." Here is a good example. Group the following numbers in such a way that when you add them, the total is 1,000.

$$8\ 8\ 8\ 8\ 8\ 8\ 8\ 8$$

Some children won't even bother trying; others will make a halfhearted effort; still others will attack it enthusiastically. What is important is how you think about a problem. In the eights problem, think of the only number of groups that would give you 0 in the units column when you add them—five. Try working with five groups and you will eventually discover that:

$$888 + 88 + 8 + 8 + 8 \text{ gives you } 1,000$$

Many of the daily problems children face are vague and ill defined, and if children lack problem-solving strategies, solving those problems is next to impossible. Research (Siegler & Alibali, 2005) indicates that most children devise a variety of strategies to solve their problems, and, depending on the nature of the task, they'll select what they think is the most appropriate strategy. This is the *adaptive strategy choice model* (Siegler, 1996; Siegler & Alibali, 2005). Those strategies that produce successful solutions increase in frequency, while those that do not decrease in frequency.

Children have multiple strategies available at all ages, but poor problem solvers often jump at the first clue. Among the most common sources of error are the following:

- *Failure to observe and use all the relevant facts of a problem.* Did you account for each word in the language problem?

- *Failure to adopt systematic, step-by-step procedures.* The problem solver may skip steps, ignore vital information, and leap to a faulty conclusion. Did you make a check, or some other mark, against each word?

- *Failure to perceive vital relationships* in the problem. Did you discover any pattern that could lead to the correct answer?

- *Frequent use of sloppy techniques in acquiring and applying vital information.* Did you guess at the meanings of any of the words? Did you try to eliminate the irrelevant words?

Following is a strategy to help children overcome these mistakes, by developing effective problem-solving techniques.

The DUPE Model

DUPE
Problem-solving model (**D**etermine a problem exists, **U**nderstand its nature, **P**lan for its solution, and **E**valuate the solution).

Teaching children the basics of problem solving will improve their abilities to recognize and solve problems, both in and out of the classroom. Can you specify the positive outcomes of teaching children to use a strategy such as the DUPE model?

Many models have been proposed to help people solve a wide variety of problems. Often these models employ acronyms to assist people in problem solving (for example, SAC—Strategic Air Command; NATO—North Atlantic Treaty Organization; HOMES—the names of the Great Lakes: Huron, Ontario, Michigan, Erie, Superior). For our purposes we'll use an acronym that you'll remember easily and transfer to any problems (or teach to a child). The acronym is **DUPE** and its intent is to convey the message: *Don't let yourself be deceived.* The meaning of each letter is as follows.

D—Determine that a problem exists. Too often children fail to realize that a problem lies hidden in the words of a story, or in the description of a science project or in the simple presentation of a math example. How would you go about solving this problem?

> *There is a super psychic who can predict the score of any game before it is played. Explain how this is possible.*

This problem, taken from Bransford and Stein (1993), poses a challenge to most of us because, as the authors noted, a reasonable explanation is difficult to generate. If you are having difficulty, it is probably because you have made a faulty assumption about the nature of the problem. You were not asked about the final score; the score of any game before it is played is 0 to 0. We deliberately presented a tricky problem to stress that you must attend to details.

U—Understand the nature of the problem. Realizing that a particular problem exists is not enough; you must also comprehend the essence of the problem if your plan for solution is to be accurate. For example, we frequently hear that a pupil's classroom difficulties are due to hyperactivity. Thus the problem is determined; but understanding the cause of the hyperactivity—physical, social, psychological—requires additional information. Here is an example of the need to understand the nature of a problem.

AN APPLIED VIEW

The Role of Memory

Most children have good memories that can be improved with adult help, which, in turn, helps them in solving problems. All memory strategies, however, are not equally effective. The appropriateness of the strategy depends on what you are asked to do. Try this memory problem. *The following list contains 25 words. Take 90 seconds to study these words. When time runs out, write as many of the words as you can without looking at the list.*

paper	fruit	street	wheel
white	step	juice	time
spoke	shoe	car	note
ball	word	judge	run
banana	touch	hammer	table
dark	page	bush	official
walk			

How did you do? Or more importantly from our perspective, how did you do it? Were these among the strategies you used?

1. Rehearse each word until you have memorized it: car, car, car.

2. Rehearse several words: paper, white, spoke; paper, white, spoke.

3. Organize the words by category. Note that several words are related to cars; others could be grouped as fruit; still others could be categorized as relating to books.

4. Construct a story to relate as many of the words as possible.

5. Form images of words or groups of words.

You may have tried one or a combination of these strategies, but note that you were not told to memorize them in any particular manner. If you had received specific instructions, each of these strategies would not have been equally effective. For example, when we are asked to remember a particular telephone number, the tendency is to rehearse it for as long as we need to recall it. If you had been directed to memorize the words in the list in a certain order (for instance, the way that they were presented), grouping them by categories would not have been efficient. Thinking of a story to link them in the correct order would have been much more efficient.

B. Bransford & B. Stein (1993). *The IDEAL problem solver.* New York: Freeman. An excellent little book that explores the mysteries of problem solving in an engaging and practical way.

Tom either walks to work and rides his bicycle home or rides his bicycle to work and walks home. The round trip takes one hour. If he were to ride both ways, it would take 30 minutes. If Tom walked both ways, how long would a round trip take?

This problem illustrates a basic problem-solving strategy of dividing a problem's information into subgoals to help understand what's required. Think for a moment: What are the givens? How long would it take to ride one way? (15 minutes.) How long is a round trip? (1 hour.) How long does it take to walk one way? (45 minutes.) How long is the round trip if Tom walked both ways? (45 + 45 = 90 minutes.)

P—Plan your solution. Now that you know that a problem exists and you understand its nature, you must select strategies that are appropriate for the problem. It is here that memory plays such an important role (Siegler, 1998). The accompanying box illustrates various memory strategies that aid memory.

E—Evaluate your plan, which usually entails two phases. First examine the plan itself in an attempt to determine its suitability. Then decide how successful your solution was.

The Big6 Skills Method

Another popular technique of problem solving currently in use across the country is the Big6 skills program. Used to teach students to make decisions and solve problems, the technique consists of the following six stages (Eisenberg & Berkowitz, 2003).

1. Task Definition

2. Information Seeking Strategies

3. Location and Access

4. Use of Information
5. Synthesis
6. Evaluation

The authors state that their technique incorporates many of the features of information and technology and has particular relevance for curricular activities. The six stages need not be followed in a rigid manner but can be used as needed to help students to select appropriate resources, to discriminate between needed and superfluous information, and to evaluate their progress and success.

Guided Review

9. A program designed to aid the development of thinking skills was devised by _____.

10. A memory strategy in which you go over material repeatedly is called _____.

11. The adaptive strategy choice model was proposed by _____.

12. Many of a child's daily problems are _____.

13. The letters in DUPE mean _____, _____, _____, and _____.

MORAL DEVELOPMENT

The capacity to evaluate the actions of self and others as good or bad is one of the psychological qualities that most distinguishes Homo sapiens from the higher apes. (Kagan, 1984, p. 113)

The developmental psychologist Jerome Kagan, long a stalwart proponent of developmental ideas, argues that some ideas are classified as good or bad and that these evaluations are related to feeling states. Morality will always be of primary concern to humans; however, its definition and developmental pathways are numerous, complex, and interactive, so formulating a neat and relatively straightforward explanation remains a tortuous task.

For example, we want children to be good, truthful, kind, wise, just, courageous, and virtuous. We also want them to behave, *in all circumstances,* according to an internalized code of conduct that reflects these desirable characteristics. Internalization of moral standards, which entails a shift from reliance on external controls to internal mechanisms, is a significant milestone in the socialization process (Koenig, Cicchetti, & Rogosch, 2000). How do children reach this ideal state? As we attempt to answer this question, we would like you to keep three issues in mind as we study children's moral development.

1. *How do children think about moral development?* Here we'll present the theories and relevant research that shed light on this question. We'll then trace the powerful influence of gender and social class on children's thinking about moral issues.

2. *How do children feel about moral matters?* The role of emotions in morality deserves our attention because of the manner in which emotions interact with how children think and behave in moral situations. To make this more meaningful,

Answers

think of yourself for a moment. For example, how do you "feel" when you know you hurt someone else by something you said, even if you didn't mean to? The answer is that you feel awful. So do children when they do the same thing.

3. *How do children behave in moral situations?* Do children's thoughts and emotions dictate how they act morally? This is an intriguing question, one that both fascinates and frustrates us, and one that will challenge our ingenuity to answer.

As we begin our analysis of children's moral progress, remember that moral behavior is a complex mixture of *cognition* (thinking about what to do), *emotion* (feelings about what to do or what was done), and *behavior* (what is actually done). To untie this tightly formed knot, psychologists today have appealed to a variety of theoretical explanations, ranging from psychoanalytic to cognitive to behavioristic views. Within these theoretical perspectives consideration is given to issues such as emotion, culture, gender, individual judgment, social influences, and personal reflection (Turiel, 2006).

The Path of Moral Development

A summary of children's moral development should help to put the theories and research in a more meaningful perspective.

- Initially, young children (birth to about 2 or 3 years) begin to learn about right and wrong from their parents; these teachings immediately begin to interact with children's natural inclination to do good. So from an early age—as soon as possible—most parents try to combine direction with understanding. Continually forcing children to obey, as we know, loses its effectiveness as they grow older. During these early years, modeling is especially effective. Lacking cognitive sophistication, young children who have a good relationship with their parents usually are enormously impressed by what they see their parents doing.

- The next phase (about 2 to 6 years) reflects children's growing cognitive maturity and their developing ability to decide what's right or wrong. They now begin to interact with a variety of authority figures—teachers, counselors, religious advisors, coaches, directors—who make reasonable demands on them. These individuals assume great importance in children's lives and usually reinforce parental concerns about moral behavior. By their directions, explanations, expectations, and by pointing out the consequences of children's behavior for others (a process called *induction*), they provide welcome support to parents' efforts.

  Yet telling the truth remains a difficult developmental task for children. Studying 72 children from 3 years 1 month to 6 years 3 months, Polak and Harris (1999) found a decided increase in children's use and understanding of deceptive strategies. Growing deception occurred in a three-step process. First, the younger children showed a clear tendency to deliberately deny obvious misdemeanors. Next, as understanding of deceptive strategies grows, denial of misdeeds becomes more widespread. In these first two phases, however, the children find it difficult to sustain their deception by pretending ignorance. It isn't until the third phase that children become more clever at feigning ignorance.

- As children move into the next phase (about 7 to 11+ years), they interact more frequently and intensely with their siblings in their family lives, with their schoolmates in classroom experiences, and with their friends in games and other social activities. Here they again encounter the reality of rules not established by parental edict. (For an excellent discussion of the differential impact of peers and parents in moral development, see Walker, Hennig, & Krettenauer, 2000). As a result they learn about making and following regulations as well as deriving insights into those children who break the rules. In this way, children are both participants (in games and activities where they must obey the rules) and authority figures (occasionally they will be among those who make the rules). In a sense, they are reflecting the relationship between truth and rightness (Chandler, Sokol, & Wainryb, 2000).

Parents and Moral Development

Are parents influential in their children's moral development? A team of psychologists at Pennsylvania State University probed the question of why children show marked differences in their sensitivity to moral issues, differences that have been widely documented (Dunn, Brown, & Maguire, 1995). The researchers concentrated on uncovering the possible reasons for these differences. Studying 6-year-old children, they made two important findings.

1. Children whose mothers treated them reasonably but firmly after transgressions seemed more sensitive to matters of right and wrong. These mothers also insisted that their children consider the harm or discomfort done to the *other* child.
2. Those children with older siblings who were friendly and supportive seemed more morally mature.

These findings testify to the significant input parents have into their children's moral development, which begins with the type of family relations they encourage.

In the current controversy swirling around explanations of moral development—psychoanalytic, social learning, cognitive developmental—the issue of parental versus peer influence has arisen as a major rallying point. Which of these forces is more decisive in stimulating the moral maturity of children? In a careful study of 60 children, 60 parents, and 60 friends, Walker, Hennig, and Krettenauer (2000) concluded that parent/child and peer/child relationships have a role to play and both are highly significant.

Let's now turn our attention to how children think about matters of right and wrong.

A cadet does not lie, cheat, or steal, or tolerate those who do.

—The West Point Honor Code

Piaget's Explanation

Youngsters realize that the opinions and feelings of others matter: What they do might hurt someone else. By the end of the middle-childhood period, children clearly include intention in their thinking. For 6-year-olds, stealing is wrong because they might get punished; for the 11- or 12-year-old, stealing may be wrong because it takes away from someone else. During these years, children move from judging acts solely by the amount of punishment to judging acts based on intention and motivation.

Marbles and Morality

As might be expected, Piaget examined the moral development of children and attempted to explain it from his cognitive perspective (Piaget, 1932). Piaget formulated his ideas on moral development by observing children playing a game of marbles. Watching the children, talking to them, and applying his cognitive theory to their actions, he identified how children actually conform to rules.

While observing the children playing marbles Piaget also asked them their ideas about fairness and justice, what is a serious breach of rules, and how punishment should be administered. From this information, he devised a theory of moral development:

*   Up to about 4 years, children are not concerned with morality. Rules are meaningless, so they are unaware of any rule violations.
*   At about 4 years, they begin to believe that rules are fixed and unchangeable. Rules come from authority (for example, parents, God) and are to be obeyed

without question. This phase of moral development is often called *heteronymous morality* (or *moral realism*). Children of this age make judgments about right or wrong based on the consequences of behavior; for example, it is more serious to break five dishes than one. They also believe in *immanent justice;* that is, anyone who breaks a rule will be punished immediately—by someone, somewhere, somehow!

- From 7 to about 11 years of age, children begin to realize that individuals formulate social rules, which can be changed. This phase is referred to as *autonomous morality* (or *the morality of reciprocity*). At this age, children think punishment for any violation of rules should be linked to the intent of the violator. The person who broke five cups didn't mean to, so should not be punished any more than the person who broke one.

Piaget's ideas about moral development led to the advancement of a more complex theory devised by Lawrence Kohlberg.

Kohlberg's Theory

Among the more notable efforts to explain a child's moral development has been that of Lawrence Kohlberg (1975, 1981). Using Piaget's ideas about cognitive development as a basis, Kohlberg's moral stages emerge from a child's active thinking about moral issues and decisions. Kohlberg formulated a sophisticated scheme of moral development extending from about 4 years of age through adulthood.

moral dilemma
Modified clinical technique used by Kohlberg whereby a conflict is posed for which subjects justify the morality of their choices.

To discover the structures of moral reasoning and the stages of moral development, Kohlberg (1975) employed a modified clinical technique called the **moral dilemma,** in which a conflict leads subjects to justify the morality of their choices.

In one of the best known, a husband needs a miracle drug to save his dying wife. The druggist is selling the remedy at an outrageous price, which the woman's husband cannot afford. He collects about half the money and asks the druggist to sell the drug to him more cheaply or allow him to pay the rest later. The druggist refuses. What should the man do: Steal the drug or permit his wife to die rather than break the law?

By posing these conflicts, Kohlberg forces us to project our own views.

Kohlberg's theory traces moral development through six stages by successive transformations of cognitive structures. Middle-childhood youngsters are typically at Kohlberg's *preconventional level of morality.* Only as they approach ages 10 to 12 do they begin to edge into the *conventional level of morality,* where acts are right because that's the way it's supposed to be (determined by adult authority). The *postconventional level of morality* comes at age 13 and over. Only a small number of adults reason at the postconventional level.

According to Kohlberg, moral judgment requires us to weigh the claims of others against self-interest. Thus youngsters must overcome their egocentrism before they can legitimately make moral judgments. Consequently, we again see how the blend of cognitive development and cultural beliefs shape the nature of moral thinking (Narvaez et al., 1999).

Finally, anyone's level of moral development may not be the same as their moral behavior. To put it simply, people may know what is right but do things they know are wrong. Research suggests that when children are in a stage of developmental transition, Kohlberg's moral concepts are less influential in moral decision making; that is, children are unsure how to interpret actual events (Thoma & Rest, 1999). Table 9.4 summarizes Kohlberg's theory.

Not all students of moral development agree with Kohlberg. Strenuous objections have been made to Kohlberg's male interpretation of moral development, especially by Carol Gilligan.

TABLE 9.4   Kohlberg's Stages of Moral Development

Level I. Preconventional (about 4 to 10 years)

During these years children respond mainly to cultural control to avoid punishment and attain satisfaction. There are two stages:

Stage 1. Punishment and obedience. Children obey rules and orders to avoid punishment; there is no concern about moral rectitude.

Stage 2. Naive instrumental behaviorism. Children obey rules but only for pure self-interest; they are vaguely aware of fairness to others but obey rules only for their own satisfaction. Kohlberg introduces the notion of reciprocity here: "You scratch my back, I'll scratch yours."

Level II. Conventional (about 10 to 13 years)

During these years children desire approval, both from individuals and society. They not only conform, but also actively support society's standards. There are two stages:

Stage 3. Children seek the approval of others, the "good boy-good girl" mentality. They begin to judge behavior by intention: "She meant to do well."

Stage 4. Law-and-order mentality. Children are concerned with authority and maintaining the social order. Correct behavior is "doing one's duty."

Level III. Postconventional (13 years and over)

If true morality (an internal moral code) is to develop, it appears during these years. The individual does not appeal to other people for moral decisions; these decisions are made by an "enlightened conscience." There are two stages:

Stage 5. An individual makes moral decisions legalistically or contractually; that is, the best values are those supported by law because they have been accepted by the whole society. If there is conflict between human need and the law, individuals should work to change the law.

Stage 6. An informed conscience defines what is right. People act, not from fear, approval, or law, but from their own internalized standards of right or wrong.

Source: Based on L. Kohlberg, "A Cognitive-Developmental Analysis of Children's Sex-Role Concepts and Attitudes" in *The Development of Sex Differences*, edited by E. Maccoby, Stanford University Press, Stanford, Calif., 1966.

Gilligan's *In a Different Voice*

The importance Kohlberg placed on justice triggered serious doubts by those who believe that he ignored gender differences. Carol Gilligan (1982), in particular, questioned the validity of Kohlberg's theory for women. She argued that the qualities Kohlberg associated with the mature adult (autonomous thinking, clear decision making, and responsible action) are qualities that have been traditionally associated with "masculinity" rather than "femininity."

Characteristics that supposedly define the "good woman" (gentleness, tact, concern for the feelings of others, display of feelings, caring) all contribute to a different concept of morality. As a result, the different images of self that boys and girls/men and women acquire lead to different interpretations of moral behavior: women, concerned with caring and a strong interpersonal focus; men, raised with the belief that rights and justice are paramount.

According to Gilligan, two sequences of moral development were of primary importance: learning to treat others fairly (justice) and to help those in need (care) (Turiel, 2006). Thus women's moral decisions are based on an *ethics of caring* rather than a *morality of justice,* which led Gilligan to argue forcefully for a different sequence for the moral development of girls and women similar to the following.

- Initially, any moral decisions a girl has to make centers on the self and her concerns are pragmatic: Will it work for me?

- Gradually, as her attachment to her parents continues, self-interest is redefined in light of "what one should do." A sense of responsibility for others appears (the traditional view of women as caretakers), and goodness is equated with self-sacrifice and concern for others. Gilligan believes that women, with growing maturity, begin to include concern for self with their concern for others. In other words, is it possible to be responsible to one's self as well as to others? Women

AN APPLIED VIEW | Moral Development at Home and in the Classroom

Many schools are now using moral dilemmas as a teaching tool in their classrooms. These are thought-provoking dialogues that probe the moral bases for people's thinking. They're real or imaginary conflicts involving competing claims, for which there is no clear, morally correct solution. As you can imagine, both teachers and parents are interested in using them to further children's moral development. Here are several suggestions.

• *With younger children,* they might try something like this: Set the scenario with a newly arrived foreign student. Yasmin has just arrived from Lebanon, and some classmates, because of differences in language and customs, are mocking her. Ask children what they would do if their friends would no longer play with them if they were friendly with Yasmin. Would they risk their friendships by being nice to the new girl?

Because most younger children have had little experience in resolving moral dilemmas, at first adults should act as a guide during the discussion and only later introduce more complex issues that require resolution at the stage above their present moral level.

• *Asking why* helps children to identify the dilemma and discover their level of moral reasoning. For example, after discussing Hong Kong's reunion with China with your older students, why not ask them what people should do if, while working on a Hong Kong newspaper, they were forbidden to write a story critical of the Chinese government. Their family's lifestyle and security could be at stake. Yet the writer feels strongly about freedom of the press. (Ask your students why theirs is a good solution.)

• *Complicating the situation* adds a new dimension to the problem. Pose this problem to older children: Imagine an official in the Cuban government with family in the United States. He is torn between trying to retain power in Cuba and moving to the United States and rejoining his family. Begin by discussing loyalty, then gradually introduce complications, such as civil conflict, family ties, regional or national commitment, and then ask, "What would you have done?"

Effective discussions of moral dilemmas also require an atmosphere, both at school and in the home, conducive to moral instruction, which can be encouraged by attention to the following four points.

1. *You must create an atmosphere of trust and fairness in which children are willing to reveal their feelings and ideas about the moral dilemma with which the group is wrestling.* Adults must work to bring children to the point where they will share their beliefs with others.

2. *Such an atmosphere results from respecting children and valuing their opinions.* Adults who are decent and fair in their relations with children and treat them with respect can do much to create a positive atmosphere for moral instruction.

3. *Adults must be sensitive to what children are experiencing.* They must be alert especially to those who find a discussion painful, for whatever reason. Make every effort to provide a forum—within the group or in private conversation—for them to express their feelings on their terms.

---

now realize that recognizing one's needs is not being selfish but rather being honest and fair, that is, the idea of doing good includes others but also one's self.

• Finally, women resolve the conflict between concern for self and concern for others because of their maturing ability to view their relationships from a broader perspective, which results in a guiding principle of nonviolence. Harmony and compassion govern all moral action involving self and others, which ultimately defines both femininity and adulthood.

To both their credit, neither Gilligan nor Kohlberg argued for the superiority of either a male or a female sequence of moral development. Nevertheless, does the difference in emphasis on what constitutes the basis of moral development—caring or justice—carry the seeds of inevitable clashes of opinion when boys and girls/men and women look at moral issues? It shouldn't, because the replies of boys and girls to moral dilemmas show both justice and caring themes.

Continuing to refine Gilligan's ideas about the sequence of moral development for women, Gilligan, Lyons, and Hanmer (1990) noted that adolescent girls face problems of connections: What is the relationship among self, relationships, and morality? Must women exclude themselves and be thought of as a "good woman," or exclude others and be considered selfish? The answer seems to reside in the nature of the connections that women make with others.

Finally, we must return to the notions of habit and reflection in the expression of moral beliefs. Although habit, in the sense of doing the right thing that a child did in the past, usually suffices, circumstances change. As they do, children (especially as they grow older) must decide if the habits of the past still are sufficient in a time of new temptation. For example, Prencipe and Helwig (2002) found that, as children age, they tend to see the family context as distinct from governmental legislation in the teaching of values.

Whether boy or girl, middle-childhood youngsters, through their rapid cognitive development, are aware of right and wrong. How do we know this? They write answers to questions; they talk to us. Thus, language development is another clue to their growing maturity.

Guided Review

14. According to Piaget, when children believe that anyone who breaks a rule will somehow be punished, this is called _____ _____.
15. The phase of moral development when children realize that individuals formulate social rules is known as _____ _____.
16. A _____ _____ was Kohlberg's clinical technique whereby a conflict leads subjects to justify the morality of their choices.
17. Middle-childhood youngsters are, for the most part, at Kohlberg's _____ level of morality.
18. _____ has challenged Kohlberg's theory as it applies to women.

LANGUAGE DEVELOPMENT

You must be familiar with the picture: The 2- or 3-year-old sitting there solemnly examining an open book—probably upside-down! But this picture conveys the importance of reading in our society—in school for knowledge, on computers for practical usage, at home for pleasure. You can tell from our discussion of language development from infancy through the middle-childhood years that language and reading are not simultaneous accomplishments. Rather, reading is built on solid language skills and facilitated by advancing cognitive abilities (Bjorklund, 2005; Siegler & Alibali, 2005).

For example, children (and adults) are rather limited information processors. Consequently, we're faced with the dilemma of understanding how good readers distribute their attention across the many processes needed for efficient reading. It's a formidable task. Children must learn to identify letters, connect them to sounds, decipher spelling patterns, and, finally, comprehend what all of this means. The key to this complex process seems to be that good readers process printed words automatically and use their cognitive processes for comprehension. *Automaticity* refers to the ability to automatically process lower level perceptual information needed to decode words so that the reader can concentrate on using more complex cognitive processes for comprehension (Bjorklund, 2005; Siegler & Alibali, 2005).

Answers

Changes in Usage

By the time children enter kindergarten they have a vocabulary of about 8,000 words and have acquired most of the basic grammar of their language. They use questions, negative statements, clauses, and compound sentences (Gleason, 2005). During the middle-childhood years, they communicate constantly with their peers, and their language is rich with jokes, riddles, aggressive statements, and forms they learn from television and movies. They appear to be quite sophisticated in their knowledge, but `considerable development is still to come. By the end of the period, middle-childhood youngsters understand about 50,000 words and are similar to adults in their language usage (McLaughlin, 1998).

One of the most obvious examples of developmental change in language during these years is an increase in pragmatic sophistication, which illustrates the interaction between language and socialization. Children are not only continuing to add new words to their vocabulary, but they are devising new ways to use these words. These changes help to explain the transition from the *learning to read* stage to the *reading to learn stage,* which occurs during grades 4 through 8 (Bjorklund, 2005*).

Stage Models of Reading Acquisition

In attempting to explain the acquisition of reading skills, theorists are divided between those who adhere to a stage model of reading acquisition and those who believe in a nonstage explanation. **Stage theorists** state that children's abilities and tasks change qualitatively over time. **Nonstage theorists,** in contrast, argue that reading should unfold naturally, much as a child's language develops.

An example of stage theory is seen in the work of one of today's leading reading specialists, Jeanne Chall, who has proposed a stage model leading to reading proficiency (Chall, 1983; Chall, Jacobs, & Baldwin, 1990). The features of the middle-childhood stages are seen as follows.

- *Stage One: ages 6 to 7 years.* Children learn the relationship between letters and sounds and begin to read simple text. They usually experience direct instruction in letter-sound relations (phonics) and use high-frequency words in their reading.

- *Stage Two: ages 7 to 8 years.* Children demonstrate greater fluency in reading simple stories. They combine improved decoding skills with fast-mapping in their reading selections.

- *Stage Three: ages 9 to 13 years.* Reading is now used as a tool to obtain knowledge (science and social science textbooks, novels, magazines).

The two major goals of reading acquisition are seen in Chall's stages: efficient word identification and the comprehension of increasingly difficult material.

Reading As Component Processes

Nonstage theorists describe reading acquisition as a seamless process in which there is considerable overlapping of skill development—that is, continuous development within various reading categories. Most current theories of reading development view efficient reading as the assembly, coordination, and automatic use of several component processes (Paris & Paris, 2006, p. 50). For example, in the *No Child Left Behind* federal legislation, five components were identified as essential: the alphabetic principle, phonemic awareness, oral reading fluency, vocabulary, and comprehension.

In another, but similar scheme, Whitehurst and Lonigan (1998) have proposed nine components of successful reading: familiarity with the child's language, knowledge of the conventions of print (left to right, top to bottom), knowledge of letters, linguistic awareness (awareness of phonemes, syllables, and so on), the relationship of sounds to letters, emergent reading (pretending to read), emergent writing, (pretend writing), print motivation (interest in and attention to "breaking the code"), and a

---

stage theorists
Those who believe that children's abilities and reading tasks change qualitatively over time.

nonstage theorists
Those who believe that children's reading should unfold naturally, similar to language development.

mixture of other cognitive skills. Regardless of the classification formula used, most reading specialist agree that the acquisition and integration of these components are basic requirements for successful reading (Paris & Paris, 2006).

Children and Their Books

Children love to read. Walk into any bookstore or library in the country and you will find children devouring books. This wonderful sight provides opportunities for teachers, librarians, and parents. What should they be reading? Why? Who selects the books for them, for their school libraries, and for the children's section in the public library? What criteria do they use? Providing the type of help for teachers, librarians, and parents that matches the developmental levels of children, their needs, desires, and interests is a serious business, one that affects the lives and futures of millions of children each year.

Children, in this technologically oriented society, benefit from stories in print—books—to help them understand themselves, others, and the relationships that will color their lives. The world of books offers them an exciting, challenging kaleidoscope of fiction and nonfiction that can only enrich their lives. The stories that children will read portray characters, themes, and conflicts that reflect their personal experiences.

Examining the essential features of a story isn't enough, however. Is the child ready for this story? Is a child's developmental level adequate for understanding and enjoying a particular story? What are the developmental characteristics that prepare a child to successfully enter the world of books. The goal of those who work with children—teachers, parents, librarians—is to match these developmental characteristics with the appropriate literature, thus engaging children and ultimately improving children's reading skills and inspiring their love of books. *The underlying structure for children's book selection is based on a developmental framework.* The secret of selecting the appropriate book for a child is not only the knowledge teachers, parents, and librarians have about children's literature, but also what they know about the developmental level of the children they are serving.

What is the child like? Is she in the middle years, active, curious and competitive? Or is he just learning to walk and talk, and is fascinated by sounds and colors? Perhaps the child is a dreamer and likes to create her own stories or spend hours building with a Lego set. The secret to leading a child to the right book is not only to know the books but also to know the child. Only then is the concept of goodness of fit complete. (Goodness of fit here refers to the match between a child's developmental level and appropriate literature and is based on the concept originally developed by the child psychiatrists Stella Chess and Alexander Thomas, 1987, 1999; see Chapter 6.) Consequently, the traditional genres (categories) of children's literature become more meaningful when viewed through a developmental lens.

We believe that understanding development provides teachers, parents, and librarians a desirable depth of knowledge in selecting appropriate books for children. But we also believe that grasping the range and application of developmental data provides insights into the problems and triumphs of the children depicted in the stories they're reading. In this way, young readers sense they're not alone in understanding and coping with the happenings of their own journey through the lifespan. Consequently, to help children read, speak, and write well, and listen intelligently, adults should know as much as possible about the relationship between development and reading. (For a more detailed discussion of these ideas, see Travers and Travers, 2008.)

The Issue of Literacy

Young readers may be classified as emergent, developing, or independent. Don't think of these categories as neat, separate compartments but merely as descriptive tools. Let's look briefly at each of these categories.

AN APPLIED VIEW

Spinoff: Dialogic Reading

Reading aloud to children, often and enthusiastically, is a wonderful way to introduce small children to books long before they can actually read. Even in infancy, children benefit enormously from listening to stories. For preschoolers, listening to adults read aloud introduces them to vocabulary, grammar, and meaning so important for an appreciation of quality literature. How we as adults read aloud to children is "every bit as important as how often we read to them" (Whitehurst in Arnold, 2005, p. 30). He urges that adults practice *Dialogic Reading,* which is a strategy that stresses the value of shared reading. Adults ask children open-ended questions and then ask them to expand on their answers (Arnold, 2005, p. 31).

Bandura's work (see Chapter 2), especially his belief that imitation is a natural skill for children, makes clear that when an adult reads aloud to a child or a class, she becomes a role model. Much of what children learn is determined by the amount and richness of the language they hear from adults. Early readers are usually those children whose parents frequently read to them when they were young. Yet, reading aloud should not only be a time for instruction but a time for child and adult to share a love of reading in a comfortable, warm environment.

Goodness of Fit in Reading

As adults who read aloud to children, we should sense whether the book that we select to read to them is a genuine goodness of fit. If necessary, alternate choices should be available so that the child can help us make another choice. (Small children readily listen to a favorite book read to them over and over again because

of repetition, familiar themes, and security). Also, It may be wise for the adult to skim the book first to determine that the child is emotionally ready to appreciate the story's theme. For example, will the child become upset to discover that the dog in Rosemary Wells's new large picture book edition of *Lassie Come Home* is lost or that the cat is injured in Lynne Rae Perkins' *Broken Cat?* Perhaps learning that the little boy is alone in a large Japanese department store in Toro Gomi's *I Lost My Father* will cause the listener to be overly concerned.

To insure that reading aloud is a happy experience for both the adult and small child, the book should be a selection that both choose. Adults should also be patient when the child wants to stop intermittently and talk about the book.

> When we join our children in talks about the characters, in musing over what happens next, or in noticing the craft of the author, it is crucial to remember that these conversations are not detours around reading, but are instead, the essence of what it means to be thoughtful readers. To read well is to think well. *(Calkins, 1997, p 48)*

Young children when they are emotionally comfortable with the books that have been read to them will glow with familiarity when they enter preschool. To discover that they recognize many of the books on the classroom or library shelves and have already made the acquaintance of *Curious George,* or *Madeline, Babar,* or *Clifford the Big Red Dog,* they no longer feel like strangers in their new environment; they see familiar faces in the crowd.

---

emergent readers
Children who can identify letters and recognize some common words; they know what books "do," and they attempt to read by using semantic and syntactic cues.

developing readers
Children who are beginning to understand the relationship between sound and symbol and pay close attention to the print in their efforts at decoding.

independent readers
Children who can read ably and without assistance using all the cueing systems.

- **Emergent readers** are at the beginning of the reading adventure. From stories read to them, they learn that books tell interesting stories and that words and pictures lead to understanding. There seems to be a developmental continuum from preschoolers to proficient readers, which is referred to *as emergent literacy* (Spira, Bracken, & Fischel, 2005). These are the years when the skills, knowledge, and attitudes that are the developmental precursors to formal reading are formed (Whitehurst & Lonigan, 1998). As Bjorklund (2005, p. 393) noted, emergent literacy refers to the developmental continuum of reading skills, from those of the preschooler to those of the proficient reader.

- **Developing readers** are becoming true readers. They have established the habit of reading for meaning, and are encouraged to use their own experiences to enrich the meaning of stories. They have learned to use words, illustrations and their own knowledge, supplemented by analyzing letter-sound associations within the story's context, to predict word meanings.

- **Independent readers** are those children who read on their own and when they are alone. These children are competent, confident readers who use all their skills to derive as much meaning from their reading as possible.

The Scope of Literacy

Literacy—the ability to read and write—is becoming an increasingly heated topic as worried parents and concerned teachers focus on the language skills of their children.

Reading in middle childhood encourages academic success and lays the groundwork for a lifelong pleasure. Given what you know about the competition from television, devise and evaluate several methods to encourage children's reading.

Teachers have always been aware that children must learn specific skills so they will be outstanding problem solvers, write fluently, and read with comprehension as well as be technically knowledgeable when they enter today's information-oriented marketplace. Among the literacies identified as particularly significant and that describe the scope of emergent literacy are these:

1. Basic literacy (reading, writing, listening, and speaking).

2. Scientific literacy (knowledge of science, scientific thinking, and mathematics).

3. Technological literacy (the ability to understand and work with computers, networks, and software).

4. Visual literacy (the ability to decipher, interpret, and express ideas using images, charts, graphs, and video).

5. Information literacy (the ability to find, evaluate, and use information effectively).

6. Cultural literacy (knowledge and appreciation of the diversity of peoples and cultures).

7. Global awareness (understanding and recognition of the interrelations of nations, corporations, and politics around the world).

Discussion of the use of technology, censorship, and literacy reinforces the mission of teachers and parents to be strong collaborators in the biopsychsocial education of the whole child in the 21st century. You can understand why reading is so important to children of these years. In this fast-paced technological society a youngster with a reading problem is a youngster in trouble. Table 9.5 summarizes several of the language accomplishments of the middle-childhood years.

TABLE 9.5	Typical Language Accomplishments of Middle Childhood
Age (years)	Language Accomplishment
6	Has vocabulary of several thousand words; understands use and meaning of complex sentences; uses language as a tool; possesses some reading ability.
7	Improving motor control helps writing skills; can usually print several sentences; begins to tell time; losing tendency to reverse letters (b, d).
8	Motor control continues to improve, aiding both printing and writing; understands that words may have more than one meaning (*ball*); uses total sentence to determine meaning.
9	Describes objects in detail; little difficulty in telling time; writes well; uses sentence content to determine word meaning.
10	Describes situations by cause and effect; can write fairly lengthy essays; likes mystery and science stories; acquires dictionary skills; possesses good sense of grammar.

Guided Review

19. Middle-childhood youngsters begin to use language for their own _____.
20. The most obvious language accomplishment of these years is in the development of _____.
21. A noted stage theorist of reading acquisition is _____.
22 When children learn that books tell interesting stories, they are called _____ readers.
23. When children read on their own or when they're alone, they're called _____ readers.

Answers

19. purposes 20. pragmatics 21. Chall 22. emergent 23. independent

CONCLUSION & SUMMARY

From our discussion so far, we know several things about middle-childhood youngsters. But are they capable of meeting the problems they face? Yes and no. They can assimilate and accommodate the material they encounter but only at their level. For example, elementary school youngsters up to the age of 10 or 11 are still limited by the quality of their thinking. They are capable of representational thought but only with the concrete, the tangible. They find it difficult to comprehend fully any abstract subtleties in reading, social studies, or any subject.

With all of the developmental accomplishments of the previous six or seven years, youngsters want to use their abilities, which means that they sometimes experience failure as well as success, especially in their school work. Physically active, cognitively capable, and socially receptive, much is expected of these children, especially in school, as we shall see.

How would you describe physical and motor development during these years?

• These are good years physically as middle-childhood youngsters consolidate their height and weight gains.

• Middle-childhood youngsters develop considerable coordination in their motor skills.

What are some of the competing views of cognitive development during the middle-childhood years?

• Among the major cognitive achievements of this period are conservation, seriation, classification, numeration, and reversibility.

• Children of this age show clear signs of increasing symbolic ability.

• Sternberg and Gardner have proposed new ways of explaining intelligence.

How do children develop thinking and problem-solving strategies?

• Children today need critical thinking skills to adapt to sophisticated, technological societies.

• Good problem solvers have several observable characteristics.

• The DUPE model offers suggestions for improving problem-solving skills.

How would you trace children's progress in moral development?

• Piaget formulated a four-stage theory of moral development that is tightly linked to his explanation of cognitive development.

• Kohlberg proposed six levels of moral development that follow a child's progress from about 4 years of age to adulthood.

• Gilligan has challenged the male-oriented basis of Kohlberg's work.

How does children's language change during these years?

• Children's language growth during these years shows increasing representation and facility in conversing with others.

• During these years children develop several strategies to help them with their reading.

chapter 9 Review

chapter 9 Review

KEY TERMS

classification
concrete operational period
conservation
decentering
developing reader
DUPE
emergent reader

halo effect
independent reader
knowledge-acquisition components
metacomponents
moral dilemma
multiple intelligences
nonstage theorists

numeration
performance components
reversibility
seriation
stage theorists
triarchic model of intelligence

WHAT DO YOU THINK?

1. Imagine an 11-year-old boy—let's call him Tim—who lives in the suburbs of a large northeastern city. He shows signs of becoming a great baseball player (a pitcher). His father realizes that his son could eventually win a college scholarship and go on to become a professional if he continues to develop. He decides that Tim should not play pickup games with his friends, because he might hurt himself. He also decides that the family should move to the South so Tom can play ball all year. Neither his wife nor Tim's sister wants to move. As a family friend, you have been asked for advice. What would you suggest?

2. You are a fourth-grade teacher and you turn to Janice and say, "Janice, Barbara is taller than Janie, who is taller than Liz. Who's the tallest of all?" Janice just looks at you. You sigh and think, "Where's Piaget when I need him?" How would you explain Janice's behavior?

3. Billy (9 years old) cuts through the parking lot of a supermarket on the way home from school. In the bike rack by the wall he sees a beautiful racing bike that he really wants. It seems to be unlocked, and no one is around. Using Kohlberg's work as a guide, what do you think is going through Billy's mind?

CHAPTER REVIEW TEST

1. **Psychological characteristics of middle childhood include all but**
   a. seriation.
   b. numeration.
   c. moral reasoning.
   d. random scribbling.

2. **The protective coating around the axon is**
   a. dendrite.
   b. myelin.
   c. synapse.
   d. neural induction.

3. **The energy needs for children of these years is**
   a. 1,000—1,200 calories.
   b 2,000—2,200 calories.
   c. 3,000—3,200 calories.
   d. 4,000—4,200 calories.

4. **Which of these is out of order? Conservation of**
   a. number.
   b. volume.
   c. liquids.
   d. length.

5. **The acquisition of the number concept is known as**
   a. classification.
   b. seriation.
   c. numeration.
   d. conservation.

6. **Sternberg's theory is based on components, experience, and**
   a. context.
   b. gender.
   c. age.
   d. chromosomes.

7. **A popular Taxonomy of Educational Objectives was devised by**
   a. Sternberg.
   b. Gardner.
   c. Piaget.
   d. Bloom.

8. **Howard Gardner's theory of multiple intelligences includes _____ equal intelligences.**
   a. 4
   b. 5
   c. 8
   d. 10

9. **In Sternberg's theory, learning how to solve problems is a function of**
   a. metacomponents.
   b. genetic endowment.

c. environment.

d. knowledge-acquisition components.

10. **When we plan, monitor, and evaluate our problem-solving strategies, we are using**

   a. knowledge-acquisition components.

   b. performance components.

   c. metacomponents.

   d. general intelligence.

11. **Mental age scales were used by _____ in creating his intelligence test.**

   a. Binet

   b. Bloom

   c. Gardner

   d. Piaget

12. **Recognizing what is distinctive in others is an example of which of Gardner's intelligences?**

   a. linguistic

   b. interpersonal

   c. logical-mathematical

   d. bodily-kinesthetic

13. **Which of Gardner's intelligences results from contact with the objects of the world?**

   a. musical

   b. interpersonal, intrapersonal

   c. linguistic

   d. logical-mathematical

14. **One problem with tests is that test takers and test makers may differ in their**

   a. relationships.

   b. circumstances.

   c. conditions.

   d. values.

15. **The adaptive strategy choice model was devised by**

   a. Bjorklund.

   b. Bransford.

   c. Skinner.

   d. Siegler.

16. **Gilligan's developmental sequence is based on**

   a. social justice.

   b. female superiority.

   c. an ethic of care.

   d. moral reasoning.

17. **Piaget's ideas on moral development came from**

   a. structured interviews with children.

   b. moral dilemmas.

   c. an ethic of care.

   d. observations of children playing marbles.

18. **The major change in language development during the middle childhood years is in _____ sophistication.**

   a. pragmatic

   b. phonetic

   c. syntactic

   d. semantic

19. **A belief that reading should develop naturally much as language does is characteristic of _____ theorists.**

   a. nonstage

   b. stage

   c. quantitative

   d. trait

20. **Processing lower level information quickly and with a minimum of cognitive input is called**

   a. emergent.

   b. independent.

   c. automaticity.

   d. inputting.

Answers

10

chapter

PSYCHOSOCIAL DEVELOPMENT IN MIDDLE CHILDHOOD

Chapter Outline

Chapter Objectives

After reading this chapter, you should be able to answer the following questions.

- What are the key elements in children acquiring a personally satisfying and competent sense of self?

- How influential are peers during these years?

- What are some effects that different schools and teachers have in the middle-childhood years?

- Does television affect, either positively or negatively, children's development?

- What are some of the major stressors of the middle-childhood years?

The two boys were sitting on the top row of the spectator seats, talking quietly until the game began. (Let's call them Jack and Bill.) It was a beautiful spring afternoon, and baseball was in the air as the two high school teams prepared to get the game underway. The two boys stopped talking for a moment and waved at one of the players, obviously a friend of theirs. As the umpire motioned the first batter of the visiting team into the batter's box to start the game, a tall, striking-looking man paused at the foot of the stands and scanned the seats. Seeing the two boys in the top row, he quickly climbed the steps to join them.

"Hi guys. What are you doing here? No classes today for you private school softies?"

Both boys laughed; they obviously were at ease with the older man and his brand of humor. Jack then replied, "No, we started exams today and got out at noon. We're about a week ahead of Phil (the adult man's son). But don't forget, we started earlier in September."

"Sure, Sure, Sure. All I get from you two are excuses, excuses, excuses."

Bill turned to him and said, " Well, at least Phil has a longer season; I'd love to still be playing." (Both boys played varsity baseball on their school team.)

The man shrugged and said, "I dunno. If the season ended sooner, I wouldn't feel I had to come here and watch that kid of mine make a fool of himself. Game after game; sometimes I wonder what's wrong with him. But, you know, fathers are supposed to be here."

Both boys stared at the field and didn't say anything. They liked Phil's father. He was nice to them and always was glad to see them, but they couldn't understand his reaction to Phil. Nothing that Phil did seemed to please his father. And to make matters worse, his father had no hesitation in criticizing—sometime belittling—Phil in front of others, including Phil's friends.

Just as his father finished speaking, Phil entered the batter's box. Both Jack and Bill noticed how Phil glanced up at his father as he moved to the plate. "Here we go again," said his father, "I suppose it'll be another strikeout."

Jack and Bill were too respectful to say what they thought, but both of them, when they were talking later, mentioned how glad they were that their fathers either voiced their support or kept quiet when things went bad. Jack summed up their feelings nicely. "I don't know how Phil takes that, day after day. If that were my father, I wouldn't even go out for team. No one needs that kind of stuff."

The preceding story, unfortunately true, involved a friend of one of the authors. Too often we tend to overlook the long-term consequences of the way parents, teachers, and adults in general sometimes treat children. Phil, the son in the story, today is a timid, anxious man with little drive and no confidence in himself. Will he ever achieve anything to the extent he might have if his self-concept hadn't been so severely shaken during those early years? As Erikson noted, middle-childhood years are the years when children are ready for "entrance into life"; their sense of industry leads them to form productive relationships with others, thus helping them avoid any feelings of inferiority.

We have encountered too many similar cases over the years not to recognize the importance of a child's self-esteem. Consequently, in this chapter, we study its role in healthy development, while simultaneously avoiding many of the pitfalls and exaggerated claims surrounding any discussion of this important topic. For example, if parents do this or don't do that, will their children be geniuses, presidents, Mars-walking astronauts, or Hollywood movie stars? Well, maybe, but unfortunately it just doesn't work that way, as we'll see.

Among the prime influences on a child's developing sense of self is peer

Support and encouragement are needed during the middle-childhood years if a realistic sense of self-esteem is to develop. Can you identify those parental behaviors that encourage the development of positive self-esteem?

opinion, which at this age is becoming a powerful motivator of behavior. School, with its important network of social contacts and the emphasis placed on achievement, provides constant feedback that powerfully affects a child's feeling about self. The media, especially television with its stereotypical models, furnish children with artificial, often self-destructive, goals of what the self should be. Finally, all children face occasional stress, and some children find themselves under unrelenting pressure. How these children cope with stress leaves an indelible mark on their feelings about themselves.

THE CHANGING SENSE OF SELF

If we have our own "why" of life, we can bear almost any "how."

—FRIEDRICH NIETZSCHE

The development of self-awareness provides a window into the psychological growth of the child. Over the course of a few years, young children acquire capacities to engage with others intersubjectively, visually recognize their mirror images, attribute behavioral and psychological qualities to themselves, create autobiographical accounts, and situate themselves temporally as individuals with continuity into the past and future. (Thompson, 2006)

Thompson's elegant description of the developmental pathway of the self offers a succinct account of a child's growing complexity, the gradual transformation of concrete chronicles of self (I have blonde hair, brown eyes) into more subtle psychological characterizations (I'm a true friend, I get along well with others). These different shadings of the self continue to develop as cognitive maturity and social awareness sharpen and both self-concept and self-esteem contribute to a child's keener understanding of *who* and *what* "I" am.

The Developing Self-Concept

self-concept
Person's evaluation of his/her self.

William James is alive and well in modern psychology! Although James was at the height of his intellectual powers as far back as the 1890s, his ideas remain with us today. His discussion of the I-Self and the Me-Self in his *Principles of Psychology* (1890/1981) has produced a burst of renewed interest in any discussion of the development of **self-concept** (Harter, 2006). James believed that children are not born with a sense of an unchanging self. Rather the self develops through the years as the result of contact with a myriad of sources and experiences.

For example, Thompson (2006), in his analysis of self-development in a temporal manner, reflects the constancy of James's I-Self and Me-Self. As children pass through the middle-childhood years and with growing cognitive maturity, they identify the present self with the past self and the self that will exist in the future. That is, the same "I" functions in each of these temporal contexts (Thompson, 2006, p. 79).

How does this happen? To answer this question, we return to Harter's conviction that the self is both a *cognitive* and a *social* construction (Harter, 2006, p. 506). Erikson has described the middle-childhood years as a time when children use their tools and skills and acquire a feeling of satisfaction at the completion of satisfactory work (1963, 1968). This developing sense of competency leads them to understand the perspective of others, which then, either positively or negatively, influences self-development (see Selman, this chapter, p. 266). As these two forces, cognitive and social, begin to coalesce toward the end of the middle-childhood period, a more realistic form of self-evaluation contributes to continued self-development.

self-esteem
How children rank themselves compared to others (self-worth).

In this chapter, we continue our narrative by demonstrating the tight link between realistic self-esteem and the attainment of competence. What do we mean by children's **self-esteem?** A good way to describe this concept is as the sense of worth and value that children place on themselves. During the middle-childhood years, children's developing sense of self helps to shape their personal goals. For example, any discrepancy between the perceived ideal self and the real self can be a strong motivating force. As we have seen, thanks to their growing cognitive ability, children become more objective during these years, and, as they do, they begin to compare their achievements with those of others. In a sense, children are discovering how they "measure up" against others. They come to realize that, for example, although they may excel at math, someone else is a much better writer and someone else is an outstanding athlete.

Children during these years begin to employ a complex and sophisticated self-evaluation that results in a more balanced assessment of personal strengths and weaknesses. They recognize that they have both desirable and undesirable qualities. Consequently, their perceptions of self and self-esteem are tightly interwoven with their satisfaction with their appearance, their need for support from those they love and trust, and a belief in their own competence.

Self-Esteem and Competence

Susan Harter, a developmental psychologist at the University of Denver, has been a long-time student of the self, self-development, self-concept, and self-esteem, and her research has been a beacon in an otherwise murky field. Studying 8- to 13-year-old children, Harter and her colleagues identified five types of **competence** that seem to be central to a child's level of self-esteem: scholastic competence, athletic competence, likability by peers, physical appearance, and behavioral conduct (Harter, 1999). Trying to determine what produces a child's sense of self-esteem, Harter posed a basic question.

> *How do children's evaluations of their competency affect the level of their self-esteem?*

Devising a questionnaire that tapped children's perceptions of their competence, the researchers used items such as the following.

> *Some kids have trouble figuring out the answers in school.*

but

> *Other kids can almost always figure out the answers.*

Children would then indicate which of the answers best described them, thus creating a profile of their feelings of competence. The results were fascinating.

Children don't feel they do equally as well in all the five types of competence that Harter identified. Most children show a "sawtooth" profile, indicating that they feel good about themselves in some activities but not so good in others. Not only that, but some children who have noticably different profiles have quite similar levels of self-esteem. Other children, with similar profiles, have vastly different levels of self-esteem. Here's an example of the children's profiles.

competence
Measure of children's level of self-esteem; related to scholastic competence, athletic competence, peer popularity, physical appearance, and behavior.

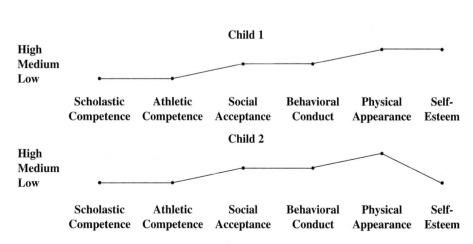

You can see in this example that each child has a similar profile but a much different level of self-esteem. Each child's self-esteem was affected only by the things he or she viewed as important (social acceptance, looks, and so on). The first child does not see school or athletics as important and so not doing well academically or athletically doesn't matter. The other child, however, probably does value sports and studies and feels inadequate, with an accompanying loss of self-esteem.

In the second phase of her study, Harter probed to discover how what others think about children affects their self-esteem. She used questions similar to the following:

Some kids have classmates that like the kind of person they are.

but

Other kids have classmates who do not like the kind of person they are.

The results were as you probably anticipated. Children who receive considerable support from the important people in their environment had a high regard for themselves. Those who obtain little, if any, support from their significant others showed the lowest self-esteem. Taken together, these findings provide penetrating insights into how children acquire their sense of self-esteem.

Ever the honest researcher, Harter proposed several troublesome questions about the information she and her colleagues uncovered. For example, in all her studies there was a strong link between what children thought of their physical appearance and their level of self-esteem. In fact, what children think of their looks is the leading predictor of their self-esteem. As Harter asks, is self-esteem only skin deep?

Harter asked her subjects whether they felt that their appearance determined their self-esteem or that their sense of worth lead them to favorably evaluate their looks. She discovered that those who believed their looks determined their self-esteem felt worse about their appearance, had lower self-esteem and were more subject to bouts of depression (Harter, 1993, 1998, 2006).

In summary, then, children and young adolescents for whom personal appearance and the opinion of others determined their sense of self had lower levels of self-esteem. Those who believed that their sense of self caused others to think highly of them and who felt that their sense of self-esteem led to feelings of competency had higher levels of self-esteem. The lesson is clear for those working with children: To help children enhance their self-esteem, encourage them to examine their sense of worth carefully but not to look through the glass darkly.

Parents and educators must walk a thin line between providing the necessary support and encouragement for children to face "the great battle of life," on the one hand, and recognizing the equally necessary task of keeping children's feet securely planted in reality, on the other. We again want to emphasize the need to praise and recognize children's honest achievements. (For some serious questions regarding the specific effects of self-esteem, see Baumeister and others, 2007.)

But if an adult's reactions are an island of praise in a sea of neutral, even negative evaluations, eventually children will ignore them. Children shouldn't be subjected to a salvo of criticisms, but reactions to their efforts can't be transparently false. You can't fool children; they cut right through any sham, especially if something is meaningful to them. It's better to be honest. "You didn't do that well this time, but I know if you study (practice, rehearse, whatever the activity) hard, you'll do better next time." Honest evaluation, coupled with support and encouragement, go a long way toward deserved self-esteem.

There is, however, a flip side to this positive look we've taken at the self. For their own good, and the good of those around them, children must develop self-control.

Children and Self-Regulation

The capacity for conscious and voluntary self-regulation is central to our understanding of what it is to be human. It underlies our assumptions about choice, decision making, and planning. Our conceptions of freedom and responsibility depend on it. Among all living things, we hold only ourselves legally and morally responsible accountable for our actions. (Bronson, 2000, p. 1)

Just exactly what is this significant aspect of our psychosocial development known as *self-regulation?* As you may imagine, self-regulation refers to many different types of behaviors: mastering fear, controlling eating, restricting drinking, keeping your temper in check, and refusing drugs.

self-control
Self-restraint exercised over impulses, emotions, and desires.

A dictionary definition of **self-control** is a good starting point: restraint exercised over one's own impulses, emotions, and desires. A more psychologically based definition would be this: an individual's capacity to initiate, terminate, delay, modify the form or content, or modulate the amount or intensity of a thought, emotion, behavior, or physiological reaction, or redirect thought or behavior toward a new target (Compas et al., 2002, p. 939). In other words, children should possess the ability to control their actions in appropriate ways; they must develop a sense of inner control (Dacey & Fiore, 2000). How to develop these vital coping skills is a key element in psychosocial development.

The Development of Self-Regulation

If you think of coping as involving conscious efforts to regulate *emotion, cognition, behavior, physiology,* and the *environment* in response to events or circumstances (Compas et al., 2002), you realize that these categories match our *biopsychosocial* model almost perfectly. Consequently, the skills that constitute emotional, cognitive, and social control are developmental in nature. As Bronson (2000, p. 3) noted, the characteristics of self-regulation vary with age and development. Children at ages 3, 6, and 10 years demonstrate different controls at each age level because of the psychosocial development that has occurred. Not only are there generalized age differences, but parents and teachers must be aware of the individual differences that appear because of temperament and experience.

In their analysis of the development of self-regulating behavior, Siegler, Deloache, and Eisenberg (2006, p. 388) suggest three age-related patterns of change.

- The change from caregiver regulation to greater self-regulation, a shift that occurs because of neurological changes, learning, and social awareness.
- Cognitive maturity that enables children to devise strategies to control their negative emotions.
- As the preceding two changes appear, children are better able to choose appropriate strategies.

Thus with age and maturing developmental systems, most children gradually acquire the ability to adjust to themselves and their environments.

Children and Impulse Control

For children to be successful in any of their endeavors and enjoy pleasant relationships with others, they must exercise restraint in deciding what to do, how to do it, what to say, and how to say it. In other words, controlling their impulses becomes an increasingly important feature in their lives. A considerable body of research exists today that shows that children with behavior problems often demonstrate maladaptive social information processing (Runions & Keating, 2007). For example, if children interpret others' behavior to be hostile, how do they react? These children also manifest more aggressive response planning to perceived hostility.

impulsivity
Child's lack of ability to delay gratification.

bully
Cruel, bossy person who has aggressive reaction patterns and considerable physical strength.

Psychologists have found the study of impulsivity alluring, similar to standing at a window and peering into the depths of a child's personality. And what they see not only is revealing but also has serious long-term developmental implications. (You may also have seen **impulsivity** referred to as a child's lack of ability to delay gratification or, of course, self-control.) Children who are reflective as opposed to impulsive seem destined to achieve at higher levels, attain greater emotional maturity, and gain appreciable personal popularity (Mischel & Mischel, 1983).

Impulsivity and Development

What do we know about impulsivity and the developmental path it follows? Like the tributaries of a river joining to form the major body, the streams of research into impulsivity converge on delay-of-gratification studies. Picture this setting: Children are placed in a position in which they are presented with something they enjoy—candies, toys—and told if they don't eat the candy or play with the toy until the researcher returns, they can have two pieces of candy or an even bigger toy. The researcher then leaves the room, and observers watch the children through one-way mirrors. The results were as you would expect: Some children ate the candy immediately or played with the toy; others resisted by trying to distract themselves.

AN APPLIED VIEW

The Bully

Is there any reader who did not have nightmares sometime during school about that "monster" who loved to tease, humiliate, threaten, and fight? Tough boys see themselves as very popular, very aggressive, and very competent (Rodkin & Farmer, 2000). Many of their peers see them in that same way, which raises the disturbing topic of bullies. Even today most middle-school principals list bullying among their major worries.

Who is the **bully?** Olweus (1993, 1995) identified bullies as those who are overly aggressive and possess considerable physical strength. Four causes are apparent in the development of a bully:

- *Indifference* (usually by a parent), in itself a form of silent violence.
- Parents who are *permissive* with an aggressive child.
- Parents who typically resort to *physical punishment.*
- A *temperamentally aggressive* child.

One survey of about 16,000 students (grades 6 through 10), estimated that more than one in three children was either a bully or a victim (Nansel et al., 2001). In this study, bullying was defined as verbal or physical behavior intended to harm another. Boys and younger students were usually the participants, and the most frequent type of bullying was belittling others about looks or speech. Children who are bullied also demonstrate a low level of self-esteem (Arsenault et al., 2006).

The range of bullying behavior seems to be growing. For example, the most common forms of bullying have been physical, verbal, and emotional. Today, however, new types of bullying have appeared. *Racial* bullying targets children because of their race or color. An even more recent kind of intimidation has emerged from the technological world: the *cyberbully.*

Similar to traditional forms of bullying, its goal is the abuse of another by using the Internet. Email, chat rooms, cell phones, and so on all become tools for cyberbullies to harass their victims night and day, seven days a week. As Willard (2006, p. 55) states, "these devastating effects include low self-esteem, poor academic performance, depression, and, in some cases, violence, even suicide."

Be alert for this type of behavior; often teachers and parents are the last to know, since the victim is reluctant to talk about it. Among Olweus's suggestions for dealing with bullies are the following:

- Supervise recreation periods more closely.
- Intervene immediately to stop bullying.
- Talk to both bully and victim privately, and insist that if such behavior does not stop, both school and parents will become involved.

Children of these years particularly enjoy reading stories about others of their age who face similar problems. For example, Author Jerry Spinelli, the popular author of the award-winning *Maniac Magee,* introduces his readers to Crash Coogan in his novel, *Crash.* Crash Coogan is intimidating because he is a seventh-grade football star, big, powerful, and a bully who can't resist tantalizing the weak and defenseless. Penn Webb, a peaceful Quaker, a cheerleader and the new kid in school, is easy for him to torment. Even more annoying to Crash is the fact that the prettiest girl in the class prefers Penn to him. How Crash finally reveals his hidden generosity of spirit in a heroic gesture has all the ingredients of a good story: action, conflict, and a plot that is realistic for middle-school students.

The truly amazing part of this work, however, was the follow-up research. The same children who displayed impulsivity at 4 years of age were the more troubled adolescents; they had fewer friends; they experienced more psychological difficulties such as lower self-esteem; they were more irritable and aggressive, and less able to cope with frustration. The 4-year-olds who delayed their gratification could better handle frustration; were more focused and calm when challenged by any obstacle; and were more self-reliant and popular later on as adolescents. The behavior of the 4-year-olds on delay-of-gratification tests predicted success in both elementary and secondary schools, and even turned out to be a powerful predictor of how they would do on their SATs (Mischel & Mischel, 1983). (For an update on this concept, see Peake, Hebl, and Mischel, 2002.)

Middle-childhood youngsters bring to their interactions with those outside the family the characteristics that they formed within the family circle. With this fact in mind, let's turn now to the impact of peers on development.

Guided Review

1. A feeling of confidence and satisfaction with one's self is defined as _____.
2. Harter's work attempted to link level of self-esteem with various types of _____.
3. Level of self-esteem is affected powerfully by what children think of their _____ _____.
4. The best predictor of future antisocial behavior is _____ _____.
5. Conscious effort to control behavior is known as _____.

THE INFLUENCE OF PEERS

peers
Youngsters who are similar in age, usually within 12 months of one another.

We typically use the word **peers** to refer to youngsters who are similar in age, usually within 12 months of one another. But equal in age does not mean equal in everything—for example, intelligence, physical ability, or social skills. Nevertheless, interactions with peers constitute an important developmental context for children, providing a range of experiences that affect their adaptation across the lifespan (Rubin, Bukowski, & Parker, 2006).

During middle childhood, peer relationships become increasingly important for social development. Children are attracted to those who share their interests, who play well with them, and who help them to learn about themselves. Can you specify and integrate the many influences that come together to affect a child's choice of friends?

Understanding children's relationships with their peers requires an analysis of several levels of social complexity (Cillessen & Bukowski, 2000).

- *Individual.* Each child brings a unique blend of skills and temperament to any relationship, which structures the type and quality of interactions between partners. (Here you may want to review the relationship discussion in Chapter 6.)
- *Interactions.* These vary with the particular social situation and the characteristics of the partners.
- *Relationships.* Any relationship is influenced by, once again, the characteristics of the children involved, as well as past and anticipated interactions (Stepp, 2000).
- *Groups.* Groups, through shared beliefs, help define the type and the range of relationships and interactions (Rubin et al.,1999).

During these years, the interactions involving peers increases dramatically to about 30% of all social interactions. The size of the peer group increases with a lessening of adult supervision in a variety of settings: malls, schools, telephones, email. **Aggression** becomes more verbal and personally hostile. Children of these years become much more concerned with acceptance by their peer group, and gossip is more prevalent (who's in, who's out). Friendship assumes a greater role in determining acceptance or rejection (Rubin, Bukowski, & Parker, 2006; Rubin et al., 1999).

Children's Friendships

Middle-childhood youngsters, with the abilities that we have traced, can reach logical conclusions about their friends. (For an excellent discussion of this topic, see Dunn, Cutting, and Fisher, 2002.) Children of this age search for **friends** who are psychologically compatible with them. As Rubin (2002) noted, peers are a powerful influence on almost all aspects of development. Children begin to realize, especially toward the end of the middle-childhood period, that friends must adapt to one another's needs. One explanation of these developmental changes in peer relations is seen in Selman's theory of social perspective taking.

Social Perspective Taking

In his efforts to clarify children's interpersonal relationships, Selman proposed a theory of **social perspective-taking** levels that springs from a social cognitive developmental framework. Selman (1980) stated that you can't separate children's views on how to relate to others from their personal theories about the traits of others. Thus, children construct their own version of what it means to be a self or other.

As a result of careful investigations of children's interactions with others, and guided by such theorists as Piaget, Flavell, Mead, and Kohlberg, Selman identified several levels of social perspective taking and noted that in the middle-childhood years a youngster gradually realizes that other people are different and have ideas of their own, thanks to a diminishing egocentrism. By the end of middle childhood, a youngster's views of a relationship include self, someone else, and the kind of relationship between them, and also the desire to conform becomes important, especially at the end of the period. Table 10.1 summarizes a child's thinking at each level.

Peers in Middle Childhood

Once upon a time, a child's world of peers tended to be misunderstood, undervalued, or even largely ignored. A generation or two ago, mothers and fathers didn't worry about all that much about their children's social lives. While parents genuinely hoped for the best, as long as a child wasn't getting into fistfights and his school grades stayed decent, the

aggression
Hostile or destructive behavior directed at another person.

friend
Nonfamilial relationship that offers feelings of warmth and support.

social perspective taking
The idea that children's views on how to relate to others emerge from their personal theories about the traits of others.

TABLE 10.1 Social Perspective Taking

Level 0: 3–6 years. Undifferentiated and egocentric; children have no accurate idea of relations.	**Friendship** depends on physical closeness.
Level 1: 5–9 years. Differentiated and subjective; focus remains on self.	**Friendship** depends on someone doing what a child wants, or a child does what someone else wants.
Level 2: 7–12 years. Relationships become more reciprocal.	**Friendship** depends on desirable interactions, a "meeting of the minds."
Level 3: 10–15 years. Recognizes that interpersonal interactions include self, others, and the relationship.	**Friendship** includes mutual interest and sharing.
Level 4: 12+ years. Accepts complexity of individuals, interactions, and relationships.	**Friendship** depends on open and flexible relationships to satisfy complex needs.

friendships (s)he formed or didn't form were not a matter of great interest. Teachers and other adults who worked with children likewise remained largely silent on the subject of peer relationships. (Rubin, 2002, p. 3)

Today, that picture has changed. Think of the world these children are now encountering. Their physical and cognitive abilities enable them to move steadily, although slowly, toward others, such as neighborhood friends. Upon entering school, they increase their contacts and begin to realize that other children have ideas that differ from their own.

School entrance changes children's lives dramatically. Their interactions with others contain revealing clues about the path of their future social development. During these years some children still find it difficult to tear themselves away from their mothers and have considerable difficulty in relating to their peers. Where is the problem here, with the mother or the child?

In one of the schools we visited, we noticed the mother of a fifth-grade boy walking him to school every day while holding his hand. We discovered that the boy, while not a problem in school, was having difficulty with the other boys in his class and tended to drift off by himself or play with younger children. How to reach the mother, of course, was the issue, because the boy was doing fairly well in school and was causing no difficulties. The matter was resolved by having the teacher gently point out the growing independence of boys of this age and by having the mother become a "room mother," where she could see the typical behavior of fifth-grade boys.

Getting along with peers is a major step in social development and research findings are consistent with the conclusion that peer rejection directly impairs children's adjustment. Peers more often direct negative behaviors and verbal harassment toward rejected children (Buhs & Ladd, 2001), which also makes it more likely that that rejected children will be excluded from social activities (Dodge et al., 2003).

Given the increase in friends during the school years, we should examine the role of schooling itself. How does it influence the development of middle-childhood youngsters?

One's friends are that part of the human race with which one can be human.

—George Santayana

Guided Review

6. Children who are within 12 months of age of one another are called _____.

7. Equal in age does not mean equal in _____.

8. Understanding children's relationships requires an analysis of different levels of _____ _____.

9. Selman's theory is referred to as _____ _____ _____.

10. Because of diminishing _____, children in middle childhood gradually come to see that other points of view exist.

SCHOOLS AND MIDDLE CHILDHOOD

We start the 21st century with ideas that had not gained widespread attention until after the middle, or near the end, of the 20th century. In the study of learning, new ideas include situated cognition, constructivism, social constructivism cultural-historical perspectives, and various other cognitive and Vygotsky-inspired approaches to learning to name but a few. We weave into our studies of learning concerns about metacognition and self-efficacy, topics that were not found to be of great interest until closer to the end of the past century, though such topics were easily found in James' Principles of Psychology *and Dewey's* How We Think. *In our new century the perspectives of other social and behavioral sciences are now more common.* (Berliner, 2006, p. 3)

These words of the noted educational psychologist David Berliner aptly identify the challenges facing our schools today. Common sense dictates that any environment in which children sharpen their intellectual skills, learn how to get along with others, work with a diverse cultural group of peers, and assess their self-concepts in competition with others must have a powerful effect on development.

Are Schools Really That Important?

It's only recently that researchers have looked beyond the academic and the intellectual to examine how school influences a child's identity, self-esteem, beliefs, and behavior

Same-sex preferences persist in unsupervised activities during the middle-childhood years, although schools strive for mixed activities. Suggest reasons why same-sex preferences remain so persistent during these years.

(Eccles & Roeser, 1999). Given the physical, cognitive, and social changes that occur in children of these years, it's only reasonable to expect schools to play an influential role. As an example of the cognitive changes that occur, consider this:

> *A 7-year-old came home tearfully one day from school to question her parents about something they had protected her from since birth: Her classmates had told her that there was no Santa Claus. When her mother and father admitted that what she heard was true, she stared at them dolefully while reaching an even more disheartening conclusion—"This probably means that there's no Easter Bunny or Tooth Fairy either!"* (Sameroff & Haith, 1996, p. 3)

This conversation is as revealing as it is emotional. Think for a moment about what's happening here: A child's loss of an imaginary but treasured figure is logically extended to other similar creatures. In Mary Olson's book for early elementary children, *Nice Try, Tooth Fairy,* Emma writes a series of letters to the tooth fairy asking for her tooth back. She would like to show it to her grandfather. The tooth fairy responds by leaving her a tooth from an elephant, a skunk, and so forth, all of which Emma rejects. Then we see the humor develop when the tooth fairy turns the house upside down looking for the tooth! This book is a big hit with children from 5 to 7, when losing a tooth is a major topic of their conversation.

Developmental psychologists refer to this change in thinking as the *5-to-7 shift,* in which a child's thinking after age 7 differs from thinking before age 5 (Sameroff & Haith, 1996). After all, a first-grader's thinking is *quite* different from a preschooler's and is reflected in the types of stories they enjoy. Children's attitudes, interests, attention span, and cognitive abilities all combine to produce multiple benefits from the carefully selected stories they're now capable of reading.

One of the few attempts to examine a school's effect on intellectual development has been the work of Michael Rutter, an internationally respected researcher of children's issues. In a massive and meticulously conducted study of school effectiveness, Rutter found startling differences between schools in their impact on children (1983). His data led to several conclusions.

- Children are more likely to show good behavior and good scholastic achievement if they attend some schools rather than others.
- Differences between the schools are not due to the size or age of the buildings or the space available.
- Differences between the schools are due to a school's emphasis on academic success, teacher expectations of student success, time-on-task, skillful use of rewards and punishment, teachers who provide a comfortable and warm classroom environment, and teachers who insist on student responsibility for their behavior.

These criteria graphically demonstrate that *good instructional leadership* is critical, which means that principals, teachers, students, and parents agree on goals, methods, and content. Home-school cooperation supports good leadership, which in turn produces *an orderly environment* that fosters desirable discipline, academic success, and personal fulfillment. When *teachers sense the support of parents and administrators,* they intuitively respond in a manner that promotes student achievement and adjustment, encourages collegiality among teachers, and produces a warm, yet exciting atmosphere (Elliott et al.; 2000; Travers Elliott, & Kratochwill, 1993).

Do Teachers Make a Difference?

Do teachers really make a difference? Unfortunately, some people are still under the illusion that teaching is a relatively simple task. Teachers talk; students listen, which completely ignores the complicated interactions between teachers and students, interactions that involve personalities, intelligence, abilities, and motivation. In his charming little classic, *The Teacher in America* (1954), Jacques Barzun, a renowned historian, painted a much different picture. As a young man, he had been assigned to teach a class in naval history by an admiral who patted him on the shoulder, saying "Don't worry about it, any damn fool can teach naval history."

Barzun admitted to a certain nervous encouragement by these friendly words, but deep within his subconscious he sensed something wasn't quite right; the admiral was wrong. "I had visited a midshipmen's school and heard a petty officer who was not a damn fool, but not a teacher either, conduct a class in naval history. He had his nose in a book and was reading aloud: 'On the eleventh of February, Commodore Perry made for an anchorage 12 miles farther up Yedo Bay. This is important; take it down: On - the - eleventh - of - February - Commodore - Perry - made - for - an – anchorage . . .'."

This surely was not the most exciting of classes; the petty officer was simply out of his element. Barzun then wryly commented, if someone such as Charles Dickens, famous for his public readings, had held that textbook of naval history in his hands, the class would have *seen* Commodore Perry steaming up the bay; they wouldn't have to have been told what was important.

In a sense, Barzun's delightful example summarizes many of the difficulties in understanding the importance, the complexity, and the far-reaching consequences of teaching. Parents entrust their children to individuals who, for the most part, are strangers. Parents may have some word-of-mouth information about a certain teacher, but usually they make a "leap of faith" that this stranger will instruct without coercion, motivate without demanding, regulate without terror, and communicate without deceit.

AN APPLIED VIEW

A Personal Recollection

Let me introduce a personal note about a school whose leadership did not aspire to such goals. One of my first teaching assignments, an elementary school in a very old building, depressed me the moment I walked in. I had been teaching biology in a stimulating secondary school with an enthusiastic principal and dedicated teachers when I received an enticing offer to move to the elementary level in another city. When I checked into the school (no faculty meeting before school opened, by the way), I was welcomed by one of the secretaries. As I recall, I didn't see the principal for about a week, and then the meeting consisted of a few questions concerning the whereabouts of my records for the personnel department, all delivered as she walked down the corridor.

Teachers in the individual classrooms were doing as well as they could, using their own money to buy decorations for their rooms and even purchasing curriculum materials, a practice much more common than I had realized. Straining to make their classrooms as pleasant as possible for their students, the teachers realized the school would be the most cheerful setting that most of the children would see all day. I admired my colleagues, but owing to a lack of leadership, we all seemed to be on individual missions; no sense of collegiality existed among faculty members. By the end of the year, quite frankly, I was discouraged and wondered if I should return for another year.

I finally decided to stay, because the children were wonderful, willing, and eager students. I'm sure the other teachers, some of whom had been there for several years, felt the same way. When I returned the following September, a new principal had been appointed, and it was as if someone had waved a magic wand over the school. A preschool meeting was called, and you could almost feel the excitement coming from this new leader as she communicated her delight at educating a new generation of learners. Interactions between home and school immediately improved; team projects were encouraged; achievement was emphasized; objectives were discussed and committees formed. Perhaps equally as important, this principal fought long and hard with the central administration for more money and resources.

It's hard to describe the changed atmosphere. With the influx of new materials, a clean building freshly painted, a sense of direction, motivation running high, and discernible leadership, the year began and ended with the feeling that great things could be accomplished. Children finding themselves in a similar setting can only benefit enormously from such an *under-the-roof* school culture. And what should be particularly exciting is that many readers of this text can be an integral part in creating and maintaining schools that make a difference.

President John Kennedy once said that life is unfair, and, unfortunately, weak schools do indeed exist. When visiting less effective schools (such as the one where I taught), an observer is immediately struck by the lack of communication among all the leading players. The atmosphere, whether by intent or not, seems designed to isolate all participants. Everyone and everything seems compartmentalized. Students lack commitment to the school itself or its teachers, teachers lack any degree of collegiality, issues are not discussed, decisions are delivered from above. Parental involvement is actively discouraged. Luckily, dedicated teachers and inspired CAN make a difference.

Teaching As a Complex Process

Before entering a classroom for the first time, teachers should possess a wide range of skills (Borko & Putnam, 1996). They must have acquired the management skills and routines that enable them to provide students with a healthy learning environment and the motivation to become productive learners. Teachers must have earned an expertise in the subjects they teach and developed insights into the nature of the students for whom they have responsibility. These skills are in addition to the multiple and varied other competencies that are expected: knowledge of the individual differences in development that are played out in the classroom each day; the social skills that are vital to smooth student-teacher relationships and productive parent-child-teacher relationships; the ability to maintain positive relationships with colleagues and superiors. No small task, indeed!

In addition to these multiple tasks, researchers have recently proposed a hidden network of concepts that give added depth to any analysis of the art and science of teaching. Thanks to this research, those responsible for preparing our teachers have come to realize that the *knowledge* and *beliefs* of teachers act as a filter through which all the skills we have mentioned must pass (Hoy, Davis, & Pape, 2006). Teachers find themselves, as we all do, functioning in and affected by several "nested ecosystems," similar to those proposed by Brofenbrenner, which we discussed in Chapter 1. In Figure 10.1, you'll see an ecological model of the knowledge and beliefs of teachers based on these ideas.

It is evident that schools differ on a variety of quite different features, and there are strong suggestions that these differences may have an important influence on children's behavior and scholastic progress.

—MICHAEL RUTTER

FIGURE 10.1

Ecological model of teachers' knowledge and beliefs.

Handbook of Educational Psychology by Woolfolk Hoy, A., Davis, H., & Pape, S. J. Copyright © 2006 by Taylor & Francis Group LLC-Books. Reproduced with permission of Taylor & Francis Group LLC-Books in the format Textbook via Copyright Clearance Center.

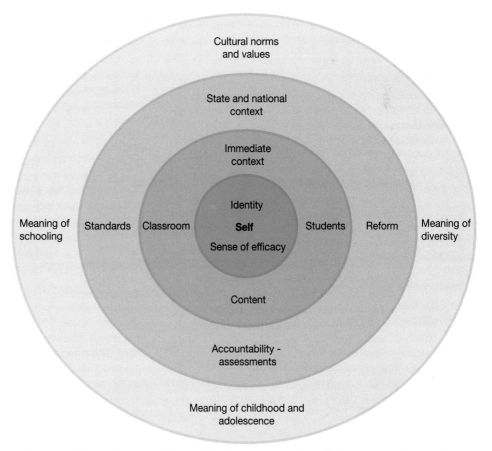

Source: Bronfenbrenner, U. (1986). Ecology of the family as a context for human development: Research perspectives. **Developmental Psychology,** 22, 723–742.

But today's parents face many challenges as they attempt to insure as effective an education as possible for their children. More than 60% of families in the United States with children from 5 to 14 years have mothers who are working (NICHD, 2004). Since parental work hours don't match the shorter school day, what arrangements can be made? Studying 933 children (approximately 7 years of age), the NICHD study examined five types of out-of-school care: before-and after-school programs, extracurricular activities (sports, music and dance lessons, clubs), sitters, fathers, and nonadult care. The results were unexpectedly clear: Children who consistently participated in extracurricular activities during kindergergarten and first grade obtained higher scores on cognitive tests than did those who were involved in the other four possibilities, a significant finding for both parents and educators.

Our schools should develop the reasoning faculties of our youth, enlarge their minds, cultivate their morals, and instill in them percepts of virtue and order.

—THOMAS JEFFERSON

Let's now examine several issues that affect children's development in our schools.

A SOCIOCULTURAL VIEW | Poverty, Culture, and Education

Research has demonstrated a powerful relationship between poverty and a child's health, behavior, and achievement. For example, poor children repeat grades and drop out of high school more than twice as much as their nonpoor peers do (Duncan & Brooks-Gunn, 2000).

In his biting commentary on current conditions in America's schools, Jonathan Kozol (1991) drew some vivid comparisons. In schools populated with children of the poor, students are crowded into small, squalid spaces, and in some cities overcrowding is so bad that some schools function in abandoned factories. Students eat their lunches in what was previously the building's boiler room. Reading classes are taught in what used to be a bathroom; science classes have no microscopes; one counselor serves 3,600 students in the elementary grades. In the high school of this district, a single physics section exists for 2,200 students; two classes are being taught simultaneously in one classroom.

According to Kozol:

The city was so poor there had been no garbage pickup for four years . . . On the edge of the city is a large chemical plant. There is also a very large toxic waste incinerator, as well as a huge sewage treatment plant . . . The city has one of the highest rates of infant mortality in Illinois, the highest rate of fetal death, and also a very high rate of childhood asthma.

The schools, not surprisingly, are impoverished. The entire school system had been shut down after being flooded with sewage from the city's antique sewage system. I did meet several wonderful teachers

in the school, and I thought the principal of the school was excellent. The superintendent is also a very impressive person. *(Kozol, 1991, p. 5)*

A more affluent district in the same state presents a different picture. A greenhouse is available for students interested in horticulture; the physical sciences department offers 14 courses; there are 18 biology electives. The school's orchestra has traveled to the former Soviet Union. Beautifully carpeted hallways enourage students to sit and study; computers are everywhere. The ratio of counselors to students is 1 to 150. Parents of these students recently raised money to send the school choral group to Vienna. Given these different conditions, is it any wonder that different educational outcomes are inevitable?

These conditions can either be improved or made worse by the family's belief in education. As Garbarino and Benn noted (1992), parents may not be present in the classroom, but they have a profound influence on the way their children view school and learning. The extent to which the family supports the school's objectives directly affects their child's academic performance. Too often low parental expectations for their children reflect the parents' own educational experiences. If parents had encountered difficulties in school, they may exercise a negative impact on their children's attitudes, expectations, and performance. The reverse also holds true.

Our discussion points to an inescapable conclusion: Schools must be as good as possible because they frequently are the only escape routes from poverty, crime, and violence.

Schools and Development

As children pass through the elementary grades, they no longer satisfy society's needs by playing happily and behaving nicely. Now they face challenges to achieve, and, like it or not, they face daily competition. They not only experience steady developmental changes, but they also encounter constant subject matter change. It's almost as if knowledge that had been forced below a level of consciousness has burst through restraining barriers and, as if to make up for lost time, has exploded before their eyes. Children, in the midst of all these discoveries, have a unique opportunity to acquire learning that will shape their future as never before.

Consequently, recognizing the psychosocial developmental pathways that children must follow, schools today, perhaps as always, must grapple with 10 timeless themes.

1. How to Help Children Learn to Develop Good Relationships

2. How to Help Children Learn to Acquire Effective Thinking Skills

3. How to Help Children Learn to Be Part of the Solution, Not the Problem

4. How to Help Children Learn to Look at Things Differently

5. How to Help Children Learn to Be Goal-Oriented

6. How to Help Children Learn to Achieve Academic Success

7. How to Help Children Learn the Difference between Right and Wrong

8. How to Help Children Learn to Know and Accept Differences in Others

9. How to Help Children Learn to See the Real Self

10. How to Help Children Learn to Bounce Back and Keep Trying—Issues of Stress and Resiliency

Schools, Development, and Learning

learning
Process that results in the modification of behavior.

With all the demands made on modern schools, we occasionally forget that children go to school to learn, which raises the interesting question: What does **learning** have to do with development? Children learn. They learn in school, often with difficulty, and out of school, usually with ease. One of my students, Liz (a first-year college student) does fairly well on her classwork but rebels against reading assignments. Yet this same student has a part-time sales position in the jewelry department of a well-known large store, which requires her to spend hours reading about emeralds, jade, and diamonds. She does this cheerfully and successfully.

Or consider Ellen, an 11-year-old sixth-grader who complains constantly that "I can't do math; I just don't like it." This same student—for reasons hard to understand—was selected to head the school bank (a cooperative banking project in conjunction with a local bank in an effort to introduce students to the idea of money management). She performed flawlessly.

Summarizing 40 years of research on schooling, Eccles and Roeser (1999) reach several conclusions.

- Although school resources are important, the organizational, social, and instructional processes have the greatest impact on children's development.

- Schools produce their effects at different levels: the school as a whole, the classroom, and interpersonal interactions.

- Children's perceptions of the school are powerful predictors of their adjustment, adaptation, and achievement.

- A school's effects on behavior are determined by individual, psychological processes.

AN APPLIED VIEW

Translating Knowledge into Practice

One of the best illustrations of how scientists think and how the great scientists shift their thinking from the highly technical to the practical applies to the Nobel Prize winner Richard Feynman (Gleick, 1992). Admittedly a genius, Feynman showed his abilities early in life. Fascinated by mathematics and an inveterate tinkerer, as a boy of 10 or 11 years he designed his own radios, invented a burglar alarm for his house, and invented a gadget for rocking his sister's cradle. He taught himself the tricks of mental arithmetic and speculated about the possibility of using atomic power for rockets. Even while deeply immersed in the atomic bomb project, Feynman, always intrigued by puzzles, taught himself how to pick locks, open safes, and infuriate his colleagues.

But it was the *Challenger* disaster and Feynman's ability to convert the highly technical to the readily understandable that demonstrated the utility of scientific thinking. (In 1986 the space shuttle *Challenger* disintegrated 73 seconds after lift-off and crashed into the Atlantic Ocean.) Considerable speculation about the disaster had centered on the O-rings that were designed to keep gases from escaping from the rocket. Feynman believed that at low temperatures (32°F), the O-rings would become brittle and permit gases to escape with disastrous consequences.

Appointed a member of the committee to uncover what had caused the tragedy, Feynman became disgusted by the bureaucratic thinking that was gripping the committee. To dramatize his ideas, on the morning of one of the hearings, he rose early, found a taxi, and cruised Washington, searching for a hardware store that would be open. He bought a C-clamp and a pair of pliers. When the hearing began, he asked for a glass of ice water and dropped a piece of O-ring into the glass. Onlookers immediately detected changes in the O-ring, changes that made failure of the critical seals inevitable. Feynman's simple experiment demonstrated scientific thinking at its best, the translation of theory into action.

You're probably saying to yourself: That's fine thinking for a Nobel prize winner, but students in grade school? The answer is yes. Good science instructors teach children to think in a similar manner: Don't be satisfied with the obvious. Do other, better solutions exist? What steps do I take for answers? Remember, it's not the subject matter that's important; it's the way of thinking. Disturbed by estimates that fewer than 10% of high school graduates have the skills necessary to perform satisfactorily in college-level science courses, science teachers today are using a more "hands-on" approach to their teaching. Instead of having students memorize lengthy formulas, they have them doing experiments starting in the early grades.

Guided Review

11. The middle-childhood years are the time of the _____ - _____ shift.

12. A massive study showing that schools do indeed make a difference in children's development was conducted by _____ _____.

13. Teaching is often described as a _____ process.

14. Teachers' skills and abilities are filtered through a screen of _____ and _____.

15. Children's _____ of school affects their adjustment and achievement.

Are there other influences that affect achievement, learning, and development in school? Study after study suggest, clearly and precisely, the negative effects that television viewing exercises on school achievement. (For an excellent summary of these studies see Comstock and Scharrer, 2006.)

Answers

11. 5, 7 12. Michael Rutter 13. complex 14. knowledge, beliefs 15. perception

TELEVISION AND DEVELOPMENT

Do you have a television set in your home? Did you laugh at what appears to be a ridiculous question? In 2005, Nielsen Media Research estimated that (for 2006):

- 95 million American homes subscribed to cable television, which is 86% of all households with a television set.
- Of the 110.2 million American households that owned at least one television set, 81% had 2 or more sets and 50% had 3 or more sets.
- Children 2–11 years of age watched on the average 23.4 hours per week.

Although today's children are immersed in a media world (movies, television, video games, CDs, audiotapes, videotapes), television is the most widely used medium and undoubtedly has a greater effect on development than do other media. Is television viewing as extensive as claimed? With 1,600 television stations, with more than 224 million television sets, and with most homes having a choice of at least 10 channels (many of them offering programs 24 hours per day), America is a land of television viewers (Comstock & Scharrer, 1999, 2006). Are there developmental effects from all of this viewing?

Television and Cognitive Development

The moment we concede that children learn from watching television, certain questions arise:

- How active are children in the process?
- To what do they attend?
- How much do they understand?
- How much do they remember?

Answering these questions gives us insight into how TV watching and cognitive development are associated. For example, when you studied Piaget's work, especially his views on operations, you saw how he insisted that children were active participants in their cognitive development. They actively construct their cognitive world.

AN APPLIED VIEW

The Extent of Television Watching

For an idea of the role that television plays in our society, try to answer these questions, which have been drawn from several national surveys.

1. What percentage of American homes have a TV set?
2. How long (on the average) is the set on per day?
3. By age 85, how many years of television has the average viewer seen?
4. How many hours of TV does the average viewer watch per week?
5. By age 18, a student has watched how many hours of TV?

6. By age 15, how many killings has a child seen on television?
7. Television viewing reaches a peak at _____ years of age.

If you had any doubts about the huge extent of television viewing, these figures should dispel them.

Answers 1. 99 2. 7 hours 3. 9 years 4. 28 hours 5. 15,000 hours 6. 13,000 killings 7. 12

Television has become one of the great means of socialization in a child's life. Thus, recognizing the relationship between program content and a child's age, adults should be particularly careful in what children watch. Can you describe how the various theories of development explain television's effect on development?

Cognitive theorists, reflecting Piaget's views, believe that children understand what they see according to their level of cognitive development. The cognitive structures that children form can be altered by what they see on television. Children attend to what they see; they learn from what they see; and they remember what they see. They can also apply these new ideas in new settings.

Among the many specific findings, we know that:

- *Television viewing seems to have little effect on vocabulary during the middle-childhood years,* has little impact on creativity, and seems to be inversely associated with mental ability particularly during the middle-childhood years (Comstock & Scvharrer, 2006).

- *Children remember what is said,* even when they are not looking at the screen. Auditory attention is also at work—voices, sound changes, laughing, and applause (Huston & Wright, 1998).

- *The amount of time spent looking at the set is directly related to age.* By age 4, children attend to TV about 55% of the time, even when there are many other distractions in the room (Comstock, 1993). During the early years of the middle-childhood period, viewing time remains steady and begins to decline from years 10 to 13, the "adolescent downward slope" (Comstock & Scharrer, 2006; Huston & Wright, 1998).

- *Television viewing and school achievement* are positively and negatively related. The amount of time spent viewing television seems to be a key factor: Anything over 30 hours per week seems to interfere with academic achievement. (For an excellent discussion of the relationship between viewing time and reading, see Huston and Wright, 1998).

prosocial behavior
Socially supportive behaviors such as friendliness, self-control, and being helpful.

In their excellent analysis of the most significant features of human learning, Bransford and colleagues (2006) introduce the concept of *implicit learning*, which has meaningful implications for children's television viewing. They define implicit learning as information that is acquired effortlessly and occasionally

AN INFORMED VIEW

Television and Positive Outcomes

There is another side to television's role in development, however: its potential for the development of **prosocial behavior,** which furthers all aspects of development. Nancy Eisenberg (1992, 2006; Eisenberg & Fabes 1996), who has done so much to further our thinking about this important topic, has defined prosocial behavior as voluntary behavior intended to benefit others (such as helping, sharing, and comforting).

Prosocial behavior, although it may have an ulterior motive (such as rewards or approval), may also include elements of altruistic behavior, that is, behavior motivated by concern and sympathy for others (Eisenberg & Fabes, 2006; Hastings et al., 2000; Hoffman, 2000). Viewing programs specifically designed to promote prosocial behavior leads to changes in children's behavior. However, research shows that it's easier to measure cognitive viewing than social/emotional outcomes of television viewing. Given the uncertainty of the research, do you think that it's possible to increase prosocial behavior by television viewing, or are most shows too violent and sexual?

If you would like to have a more informed view on this issue, you may want to read one or more of the references (such as Eisenberg & Fabes, 2006) in this chapter. You may also wish to learn more about it by going to our website at www.mhhe.com/dacey7.

without conscious recollection of the learned information or having acquired it. Indeed, a substantial amount of media learning is implicit. The effects are indirect, involve automatic attentional processes, and, as we have mentioned, are beyond the conscious awareness of those processing the information (Bransford et al., 2006)—conclusions strongly supported by Bandura's theory of social cognitive learning (see Chapter 2).

Television and Violence

Aspects of the media have been consistently linked to violence and aggression. More than 3,500 studies have examined the association between media violence and violent behavior. *All but 18 have shown a positive relationship* (American Academy of Pediatrics, 2001). Consequently, we cannot ignore the possible long-term negative effects of violence on TV, particularly when we realize the power of observational learning (Bransford et al., 2006). Most children watch television with few, if any, parental restrictions. (Our concern here is with middle-childhood youngsters who tend to watch adult shows.) Once the negative effects of television viewing are introduced, the issue of aggression and violence inevitably assume major importance.

- *Aggression* is behavior intended to harm or injure a person who is motivated to avoid such harm. (For an excellent overview of the developmental origins of aggression see Tremblay, Hartup, and Archer, 2005.)
- *Violence* is thought to be an aggressive act that has extreme harm as its goal (Walsh & Barrett, 2006, p. 357).

With the growing sophistication of technology, the effects of media on children, particularly with respect to aggression and violence, have drawn considerable attention. James Garbarino (1999) summarizes the potential danger of television viewing:

> But the fact of the matter is, psychological, physical, and sexual violence exists in homes and neighborhoods throughout the country, regardless, of geography. Such violence occurs in small towns and suburbs, in cities and rural areas. And images of it are accessible to almost every child in America simply by turning on the television. (p. 107)

Geographical boundaries matter little in our time of instant communication. Barbara Rogoff (2003, p. 328) notes that television's spread to other parts of the world demonstrates that events almost anywhere can be seen almost anywhere, and our electronic programs are seen worldwide. In light of our discussion of television's impact, TV's violent content has enormous implications.

The effects of viewing televised violence are more intense for children than for adults, particularly if the children believe that the televised violence is real. Another major concern, of course, is the possibility of children becoming desensitized because of their exposure to a steady diet of televised violence. Over time, children can begin to lose their sense of reality and fantasize about their own aggressive behavior.

Michael Rich (1999) provides the following five questions to guide children's television viewing.

1. What is the purpose of this show?
2. What techniques are used to attract the children's attention?
3. What values are being presented?
4. Will children interpret the show's message differently from adults?
5. What is lacking in the presentation?

STRESS IN CHILDHOOD

stress
Anything that upsets a person's equilibrium—psychologically and physiologically.

Children today are growing and developing in a climate of **stress** that impinges on every part of their lives: physical, cognitive, psychosocial. They are more likely to successfully survive tension and anxiety if, as children, their needs are met. Building on the concept that children (and all of us for that matter) function more effectively and happily when our needs are satisfied, Abraham Maslow (1987), a humanistic psychologist at Brandeis University, proposed a meaningful, helpful, and practical model for providing appropriate experiences for healthy development. His ideas were built around a hierarchy of five needs, which are illustrated in the accompanying diagram. (See Figure 10.2.)

Let's look at each of these in turn, beginning with physiological needs.

1. Physiological Needs. Physiological needs, such as hunger and sleep, when they are unsatisfied, dominate our lives. Unless they are satisfied, everything else recedes. Children who frequently don't eat breakfast or suffer from poor nutrition, or adolescents who are extremely sensitive about their weight and diet endlessly, experience sharp drops in their energy levels and are less likely to be motivated. For several years JFT taught the upper elementary grades in a large city school system, where many of the children had no breakfast before coming to school.

FIGURE 10.2

Maslow's hierarchy of needs.

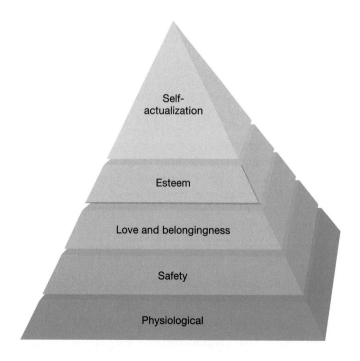

Self-actualization

Esteem

Love and belongingness

Safety

Physiological

Until he discovered the cause, he was amazed that at about 11:00 o'clock many of the children would simply put their heads down on their desks, too tired and sleepy to even think about school work. How can children remain motivated under these conditions?

2. Safety Needs. Children who are free from fear and anxiety, both physical and psychological, usually are highly motivated. Imagine the feelings of those children who are subject to daily abuse of whatever kind, whether it's neglect, a home atmosphere marked by the uncertainties of excessive drug or alcohol use, physical trauma, or psychological sarcasm and ridicule. Too often adults fail to recognize the terror that children experience. For example, if children are threatened by a bully at school, their safety needs are not being met.

3. Love and Belongingness Needs. Feelings of being alone, not being part of the group, or not having any sense of belongingness raise real threats to a child's self-esteem. *Children need to feel they are wanted and accepted.* If these needs remain unsatisfied, children may go to great lengths in their efforts to be accepted. A newly arrived neighbor, when he discovered JFT's work with children, stopped him in the driveway one fall morning after the local school had been in session for about six weeks. His son, about 10 years old, seemed to be in constant trouble in school.

After JFT talked to everyone involved, it seemed clear to him that the boy wanted to be accepted so badly that he was acting up in school to attract the attention that he thought would win him acceptance. Being accepted was the most important and intense goal of his life. Once the parents understood the cause of his behavior (frequent family moves for business), they helped by inviting his classmates to their home, making a serious attempt to participate in school activities and make friends with the other parents, and encouraging their son to join the many teams and clubs available to the community. They worked to stabilize their son's life and help him gain the acceptance he so ardently wanted.

4. Esteem Needs. The opinions of others and a child's own self-judgment act to produce a sense of self-esteem, which, if positive, leads to a continuous desire to excel. Deserved reinforcement (praise, rewards, and so on) goes a long way to stimulating and maintaining motivation. Try to provide opportunities for children to satisfy their esteem needs by following this guideline: Help children to achieve and receive *deserved* reinforcement and recognition.

5. Need for Self-Actualization. By self-actualization, Maslow means the tendency, regardless of the satisfaction of other needs, to feel restless unless we are doing what we think we are capable of doing. We're all familiar with stories of the starving artist or the inventor who goes without sleep and food. Since self-actualization is the peak of the needs hierarchy and usually characterizes the adult years, encourage children to recognize their potential, and guide them into activities that will enable them to feel both competent and fulfilled.

Here is an example of how Maslow's hierarchy of needs translates into practical suggestions for helping children. If you think of the horrific events involving New York's Twin Towers and the attack on the Pentagon on 9/11/2001, you can well imagine the stress that children of all ages experienced. We know from children's drawings made many weeks after the attack that children were battling all types of fear. Children of the middle-childhood years (7 to 11), with their growing cognitive ability, understand in much greater detail the reality of what they're seeing and hearing. Yet it's still a limited cognitive ability; that is, they can't grasp the complexities of the anxiety they sense around them, which can cause confusion and uncertainty in their minds. Some suggestions for helping children of these years cope with stress include these:

- *Talk to them; listen to them.* Explain in as much detail as you think they can grasp about what is bothering them, what they can do, what to watch out for. Don't let them withdraw into themselves; encourage them to express their feelings; give them your undivided attention. Children are constantly giving you clues about how they feel. Observe them and learn to read the signs that indicate stress, anxiety, pleasure, and the like.

- *Stress that their home, their school, their friends' homes are good places to be*—safe, comfortable, and friendly. John Dacey and Lisa Fiore, in their thoughtful book, *Your Anxious Child* (2000), note that when children are anxious they encounter four problems:

  a. They find it harder than other children do to calm themselves in stressful situations.

  b. Although many of them may be more intelligent or creative than other children, they can't use their abilities when faced with stress.

  c. They become discouraged easily and tend to generate feelings of helplessness.

  d. Even when succeeding—academically, emotionally, athletically—they don't recognize and accept their progress.

You can help children overcome feelings of anxiety by being alert to the clues that they give and by following the suggestions we have discussed.

Teachers and parents can help to provide the critical emotional security children need in stressful times. These steps should help you reinforce and build into children's lives feelings of security that contribute to their sense of need satisfaction on the path to eventual self-actualization. Your support at all times, particularly in times of stress, will aid children in developing the coping skills that will serve them well in times of need.

But first, let's link what is known about childhood development to stress. We begin by admitting that no definition of stress exists that satisfies everyone. Let's use this definition: *Stress is anything that upsets our equilibrium—both psychologically and physiologically.*

Types of Stress

When we face stress, we all react differently. To begin with, not all of us would agree on what stress is. For example, some people are probably terrified of flying, whereas others see it as a pleasant, relaxing adventure. Although many reasons help to explain different responses, we can isolate several important individual differences. Table 10.2, based on Brenner's practical work (1984), remains an excellent example of specific childhood stressors.

Why Children React Differently to Stress

Stress, regardless of the source, produces a variety of reactions. Think of your own childhood when your parents were really angry with you. How did you react? Some children react in the same ways to anything stressful: with high anxiety, fear, avoidance, weakness, or even vomiting. Others rationalize that they'll do better next time and get on with their lives. Still others aren't bothered at all; they mentally shrug and say to themselves, "They'll get over it." Although we could list many reasons for these varied responses, several important individual differences are at work.

- *Sex.* Whether it's temporary separation, divorce, or hospitalization, boys are more vulnerable to stressful events in their lives. Boys are more likely to be exposed to the conversations and tensions surrounding separation, divorce, or illness, or any other stressor, whereas parents frequently try to shelter girls from as much unpleasantness as possible. Also, parents may not be as sympathetic to the signs of a boy's distress as they are to a girl's (Rutter, 1996).

- *Age.* Children of different ages respond differently to distress. Below the age of 6 months, they simply don't have the cognitive capacity to recognize the

TABLE 10.2	Specific Childhood Stressors

Type	Example
Two-parent families	Changes associated with normal growth: new siblings, sibling disputes, moving, school, working parents
One-parent families	Multiple adults, lack of sex-role model, mother vs. father
Multiparent families	New relationships, living in two households
Death, adoption	Parental death, sibling death, possible institutional placement, relationships with different adults
Temporary separation	Hospitalization, health care, military service
Divorce	Troubled days before the divorce; separation, the divorce itself
Abuse	Parental, sibling, institutional; sexual, physical, emotional
Neglect	Physical (food, clothes), emotional (no response to children's needs for attention and affection)
Alcoholism	Secrecy, responsibility for alcoholic parent, suppress own feelings

temperament
The manner of interacting with the environment.

Children need emotional support from those in their environment. Even under the most difficult circumstances (divorce, death of a parent, hospitalization), the presence of a "significant other" can help a child to cope, to deal with stress in an appropriate manner for the child's developmental level. What aspects of development do adults have to consider in helping children through a stressful period?

various types of stress. During the early childhood years (2–6), children don't really understand what's happening and tend to blame themselves for any problems. But in middle childhood—particularly toward the end of this period—children are exposed to wider range of stressors: tobacco, alcohol, other drugs, exposure to violence, accidents. Their greater cognitive ability makes them more vulnerable to the stress caused by a parent's death. However, they have much better coping resources than younger children.

- *Temperament.* Recall that children are all born with unique **temperaments,** differences that affect the way they interact with the environment. Consequently, their temperament influences the intensity of their reactions after a stressful event, such as parental separation (Kagan, 1994, 2006). In other words, there seem to be inborn temperamental differences that influence children through the later years, and probably for life.

Courage is the price life exacts for granting peace.

—AMELIA EARHART

Let's focus now on one of the stressors we've mentioned—abuse—which unfortunately has become a major problem in modern society.

Abused Children

child abuse
Infliction of injury to a child; commonly includes physical abuse, sexual abuse, emotional maltreatment, and neglect.

physical abuse
Nonaccidental physical injury to a child.

sexual abuse
Any sexual activity between a child and adult, whether by force or consent.

emotional maltreatment
Emotional ill-treatment; a form of child abuse.

neglect
Lack of care; a form of child abuse.

battered child syndrome
Kempe and associates' term for classic physical abuse of children.

Most people consider the United States to be a nation of child lovers, thus the recognition of **child abuse** always comes as a shock. Before we begin to discuss this topic, we should agree on what is meant by the term. Four major types of abuse are commonly identified: **physical abuse, sexual abuse, emotional maltreatment,** and **neglect** (Cicchetti & Toth, 1998). Among these types, estimates are that in 2004, 152,250 children and adolescents were confirmed victims. (Some estimates are much higher.)

Child abuse has always been with us, but it has been a matter of public awareness only for the past 40 years. Although child abuse is an age-old problem, not until recently did it become widely publicized. In the 1920s, Dr. John Caffey, studying bone fractures and other physical injuries, suggested that parents might have caused the injuries. The skepticism that greeted his conclusions prevented him from officially reporting his findings until the late 1940s. In 1961, C. Henry Kempe and his associates startled the annual meeting of the American Academy of Pediatrics by their dramatic description of the **battered child syndrome.**

Unfortunately, there are no universal legal or scientific definitions of child abuse (Emery & Laumann-Billings, 2002). Physical and sexual abuses that leave evidence are easy to detect and describe (if they are reported), but other forms of abuse that emotionally wound youngsters are perhaps never detected. In a diverse population, some parents may not consider certain practices as abusive. For example, in Cambodia, fever may be treated with *cao gao*, whereby hot coins are rubbed over a child's back or chest (Wyckoff, 1999).

Parental Characteristics

You may well ask: What kind of person could ever hurt a child? Although the parental characteristics leading to child abuse are not rigidly defined, several appear with surprising frequency. Here are some of the most frequently found characteristics (Cicchetti & Roth, 1998; Rogosh et al., 1996):

- The parents themselves were abused as children.
- They are often loners.
- They refuse to recognize the seriousness of the child's condition.
- They resist diagnostic studies.
- They believe in harsh punishment.
- They have unreasonable expectations for the child. (Children should never cry or drop things.)
- They lack control and are often immature and dependent.
- They feel personally incompetent.

The most consistent feature of the histories of abusive families is the repetition, from one generation to the next, of a pattern of abuse, neglect, and parental loss or deprivation. In each generation, we find, in one form or another, a distortion of the relationship between parents and children that deprives children of the consistent love and care that would enable them to develop fully. Parents perceive the child as disappointing or unlovable, especially in times of stress and crisis. Finally, for most children, no lifeline exists; that is, no helpful sources can be accessed in times of crisis.

Dissatisfaction with attempts to identify the characteristics of individual abusers has led today's researchers to explore the importance of *multiple pathways* and *multiple factors* in the development of family abuse. As a result, three kinds of typologies have been suggested (Emery & Laumann-Billings, 2002, p. 331).

- *Type 1: Generally violent and antisocial.* These abusers tend to be violent across situations and victims.

- *Type 2: Family only.* These abusers are violent almost exclusively with family members and are usually less violent and aggressive than Type 1 abusers.

- *Type 3: Dysphoric, borderline batterers.* Typically violent only within the family; they are often depressed and socially isolated.

The Special Case of Sexual Abuse

The hallmarks of child sexual abuse are its secret nature and the very frequent denial of the abuse by the abuser, once it is alleged to have happened. These two factors play a central role in the process of the abuse and its aftermath. Sexual abuse includes a far wider spectrum than incest, occurs both within the family and outside it, but, in either circumstance, the abuser is frequently already known to the child. (Glaser, 2002)

What is sexual abuse? Probably the most lasting of the many definitions was originally proposed by Schecter and Roberge in 1976: Sexual abuse is defined as the involvement of dependent, developmentally immature children and adolescents in sexual activities they do not truly comprehend, to which they are unable to give informed consent or that violate the social taboos of family roles. Many abused children have been abused more than once by the same abuser, the majority of whom are male.

Obtaining reliable data about the sexual abuse of children is extremely difficult. One example of a lack of good data relates to child abuse in day-care settings. Estimates are that the incidence rate of the sexual abuse of children under the age of 6 years in day care is 5.5 per 10,000 children, compared to 8.9 per 10,000 children abused at home. The accuracy of these figures is indeed questionable, and the topic cries out for extensive, objective research (Jackson & Nuttall, 1997).

Effects of Sexual Abuse

Abused children feel that they have lost control and are helpless when an adult sexually abuses them. All their lives, children have been taught to obey adults, so they feel forced to comply. This is particularly sensitive, because most abusers are known to the family: a relative, a friend, or some authority known to the children. For example, in a survey of one county in the state of Massachusetts, one-third of the rape victims under 17 were attacked by fathers, stepfathers, male relatives, or mothers' boyfriends. (About 80% of the victims were girls.) From 50% to 60% of the other children were assaulted by someone familiar to them (Hart, 2000).

What are the developmental effects of an adult's violation and betrayal of a child? Different ages seem to suffer different types of effects (Kendall-Tackett et al., 1993). For example, the highest rate of problems was found in the 7- to 13-year-old group. Forty percent of the abused children of this age showed serious disturbances; 17% of the 4- to 6-year-old group manifested some disturbance. About 50% of the 7- to 13-year-old group showed greatly elevated levels of anger and hostility, compared with 15% of the 4- to 6-year-olds. Increased anxiety, fear, and distress were common to all age groups. A sad consequence of abuse is that many of these children blame themselves for it or for not stopping it or not disclosing it earlier.

Sexual abuse is a problem that every reader will find repugnant. Yet we can offer some positive conclusions. We are now better able to identify these children and provide help. Treatment techniques offer hope for the future. As the problem becomes more widely publicized, parents, teachers, and concerned adults are becoming more sensitive to the possibility of the occurrence of sexual abuse (Lynskey & Fergusson, 1997).

As we examine these children who have experienced severe stress, what can we learn from them that would benefit others? There are no guarantees of successful coping, for obvious reasons: the intensity of the stress, the immaturity of the children, and the amount of support they receive (Liem et al., 1997). Indeed, abused and neglected children are more than four times as likely to develop personality disorders in early adulthood (Huff, 2004). Yet we also know that a small number of children seem oblivious to stress, at least for a time, which leads us to the topic of resilient children.

Resilient Children

Thanks to continuing research we have come to realize that many children can adapt to stress and develop adequate or competent social, emotional, and cognitive functioning despite the challenge of powerful stressors (Friedman & Chase-Lansdale, 2002). As an illustration of this finding, consider this:

> *The mother of three children was beset by mental problems. She refused to eat at home because she was sure someone was poisoning her. Her 12-year-old daughter developed the same fear. Her 10-year-old daughter would eat at home only if the father ate with her. Her 7-year-old son thought they were all crazy and always ate at home. The son went on to perform brilliantly in school and later in college and has now taken the first steps in what looks like a successful career. The older daughter is now diagnosed schizophrenic, whereas the younger girl seems to have adjusted after a troubled youth. How do we explain these different reactions?*

resilient children
Children who sustain some type of physiological or psychological trauma yet remain on a normal developmental path.

First, understand what **resilient** means. Although many definitions have been proposed over the years, the following definition presents the key elements of resiliency in a relatively simple manner.

> *Resilience is characterized by good outcomes in spite of serious threats to adaptation or development.* (Masten, 2001, p. 228)

Resilient children have endured terrible circumstances and come through, not unscathed but skilled at fending off feelings of inferiority, helplessness, and isolation (Heller et al., 1999). What we know about these children points to their ability to recover from either physiological or psychological trauma and return to a normal developmental path (Cicchetti & Toth, 1998).

Identifying Resilient Children

Who are these resilient children who grow up in the most chaotic and adverse conditions, yet manage to thrive? Clues may be found in a remarkable long-term study conducted by Emmy Werner and Ruth Smith (1992, 2001). They studied all the children (837) born on the Hawaiian island of Kauai in the year 1955. What's unusual about this study is that the authors studied 505 of these children from their prenatal days until they were 31–32 years of age. (The drop in numbers from the original 837 was due to some of the subjects dying, some moving to other islands or to mainland United States.)

Of the 505 individuals followed over the 30+ year span, one in three was born with the odds stacked dramatically against them. They either experienced birth problems, grew up in poverty, or were members of dysfunctional families (desertion, divorce, alcoholism, mental illness). Two children out of three in this particularly

For an excellent discussion of resiliency and development, see Kathleen Thies (2006). Resiliency. In K. Theis and J. Travers (eds.), *Handbook of Human Development for Health Care Professionals*. Sudbury, MA: Jones & Bartlett.

vulnerable group encountered four or more risk factors before they were 2 years old and developed serious learning and/or behavior problems. *Nevertheless, one of three of these high-risk children developed into a competent, confident young adult by the age of 18.* What protective factors were at work in these children that let them overcome daunting adversity?

Characteristics of Resilient Children

Remember that the children we're focusing on here were battered by stressful events including desertion, divorce, discord, drugs, alcoholism, mental illness, neglect, and abuse. These conditions delivered a series of sledgehammer blows to their development, yet one of three of these children turned out to be a success in their personal and professional lives. They made good marriages, had happy families, and were good workers. What personal characteristics were at work here?

One way to answer this question is to search for the characteristics that mark the lives of resilient children. The following features are the results of many years of research. (See Garmezy & Rutter, 1983, 1985; Werner & Smith, 1992, 2001).

- *They possess temperaments that elicit positive responses from those around them.* They are the easy children described in Chapter 4: Eating and sleeping habits are quite regular; they show positive responses when people approached them; they adapt to changes in their environment. They exhibit a considerable degree of self-regulation (Bronson, 2000). In spite of their suffering, they are friendly, likable children who possess an inner quality that protects them from their hostile surroundings and enables them to reach out to an adult who could offer critical support.

- *Many of these children have a special interest or talent.* For example, some are excellent swimmers, dancers, and artists. Others have a special knack for working with animals. Still others show talent with numbers quite early. Whatever their interest, it served to absorb them and helped to shelter them from their environment. They use their talent to take advantage of the support systems available to them, whether in school, church programs, or community. These activities seem to provide the encouragement and stability often lacking in their home lives.

- *They are sufficiently intelligent to acquire good problem-solving skills,* which they then use to make the best of things around them; they attract the attention of helpful adults; they do well in school, where they are usually popular. Interestingly enough, their obvious competence elicits support from others, which produces a good sense of self. In turn, higher levels of self-esteem at age 18 produce individuals less inclined to have later bouts of emotional disturbance. In other words, they use their abilities to adapt successfully to their circumstances.

- When children from troubled families (now the successful adults) recaptured the times when they were struggling and now linked them to their present happy circumstances, *they usually mention some person—grandparent, aunt, neighbor, teacher, religious figure, coach—who appeared on the scene in the nick of time.* The support, warmth, advice, and comfort offered by this friend in need usually was crucial (Dacey & Fiore, 2000).

- Children who are buffeted by events outside of the family, such as economic hardships, often find that one parent—frequently the mother—forms a tight bond with them. Her behavior in accepting the hard times and doing everything she can to overcome crippling adversity sets a lasting example for her children. Here, as in everything else we've discussed, you can see the benefits and power of modeling.

TABLE 10.3	Characteristics of Resilient Children

Age	Characteristics
At birth	Alert, attentive
1 year	Securely attached infant
2 years	Independent, slow to anger, tolerates frustration well
3–4 years	Cheerful, enthusiastic, works well with others
Childhood	Seems to be able to remove self from trouble, recovers rapidly from disturbance, confident, seems to have a good relationship with at least one adult
Adolescence	Assumes responsibilities, does well in school, may have part-time job, socially popular, is not impulsive

Such characteristics—a genuinely warm, fairly easy-going personality, an absorbing interest, and the ability to seek out a sympathetic adult—help to distance them emotionally from a drugged, alcoholic, or abusive parent (sometimes a parent with all of these problems). You can understand, then, how our efforts to learn more about resilient children also help us to provide paths of intervention and prevention of undesired outcomes of adverse conditions (von Eye & Schuster, 2000).

You will be informed and encouraged by reading E. Werner and R. Smith (1992). *Overcoming the Odds: High-risk Children from Birth to Adulthood*. Ithaca, NY: Cornell University Press.

> *There is no single set of qualities or circumstances that characterizes all such resilient children. But psychologists are finding that they stand apart from their more vulnerable siblings almost from birth. They seem to be endowed with innate characteristics that insulate them from the turmoil and pain of their families and allow them to reach out to some adult— a grandparent, teacher, or family friend—who can lend crucial emotional support.* (Werner & Smith, 1992)

Table 10.3 summarizes the characteristics of resilient children.

Guided Review

20. Anything that upsets our equilibrium, both psychological and physiological is known as _____.
21. The highest rate of problems resulting from sexual abuse was found in children aged _____ to _____.
22. _____, _____, and _____ are examples of external sources of stress.
23. Gender must be considered in responding to stress. _____ are more vulnerable to stress than _____ are.
24. Children who succeed under adverse conditions are called _____ children.

Answers   20. stress 21. 7, 13 22. Family, school, peers 23. Males, females 24. resilient

CONCLUSION & SUMMARY

In this chapter, we followed middle-childhood youngsters as they moved away from a sheltered home environment and into a world of new friends, new challenges, and new problems. Whether the task is adjusting to a new sibling, relating to peers and teachers, or coping with difficulties, youngsters of this age enter a different world.

But the timing of their entrance into this novel environment is intended to match their ability to adapt successfully, to master those skills that will prepare them for the next great developmental epoch, adolescence. With their entrance into a widening world, middle-childhood youngsters require those skills that will enable them to deal with their widening social world.

Inevitably, though, they face times of turmoil, which, as we have seen, can come from internal or external sources. For some youngsters, these periods of stress are brief interludes; for others, there is no relief for years. Children cope uniquely using temperamental qualities and coping skills as best they can.

What are the key elements in children acquiring a personally satisfying and competent sense of self?

- The link between self-esteem and competence grows stronger

during the middle-childhood years.
- The development of self-control becomes a key element in a child's success, both cognitively and psychosocially.

How influential are peers during these years?

- During the middle-childhood years, children begin to form close friendships.
- Children who have difficulty with their peers are often bothered by personal problems.
- Middle-childhood youngsters learn to recognize the views of others.
- Children form and test social relations during these years.

What are some effects that different schools and teachers have in the middle-childhood years?

- Children must learn to adjust to a wide variety of classmates, many of whom may be children of different cultures.
- School-age children are encountering considerable change in both curriculum and instructional methods.

Does television affect, either positively or negatively, children's development?

- Television is the school's great competitor for children's time and attention.
- Some children spend more time watching television than they do in school-related activities.
- Controversy surrounds the issue of the effects of television violence.
- Television is also credited with the potential for encouraging prosocial behavior.

What are some of the major stressors of the middle childhood years?

- Children react differently to stress according to age, gender, and temperament.
- Some children, called resilient children, overcome the adverse effects of early stressors.
- Several theories have been proposed to explain how children become violent.
- Children acquire coping skills that enable them to adjust to stress in their lives.

KEY TERMS

aggressive behavior
battered child syndrome
bullies
child abuse
competence
friend
impulsivity

observational learning
peer
peer victimization
prosocial behavior
resilient children
self-control

self-esteem
sexual abuse
social perspective-taking
stress
temperament
transformation

WHAT DO YOU THINK?

1. Recall Harter's studies investigating the association between self-esteem and physical appearance. Would you agree that the association is as strong as she found in her subjects? Could you make

additional suggestions for helping children find other means of evaluating themselves?

2. It is generally accepted that friendships and groups become more important during the middle-childhood

years. With your knowledge of the developmental features of these years, do you think children of this age are ready for group membership?

3. For individuals to experience stress, they must understand the

forces that are pressing on them. Do you think middle-childhood youngsters are capable of such an interpretation of the events surrounding them?

4. Great concern exists today about the increasing rate of violence among children. Do you think the problem is as serious as the media indicate?

From your knowledge of this topic, do you think the predictors of early criminal behavior are useful?

CHAPTER REVIEW TEST

1. **Children who have similar levels of competence may have quite different levels of**
   a. cognitive development.
   b. friendship.
   c. television viewing.
   d. self-esteem.

2. **A peer is defined as one who is**
   a. equal in intelligence.
   b. in the same grade.
   c. within 12 months of age.
   d. in a nearby house.

3. **Which of these differences between schools has little effect on children's development?**
   a. emphasis on academic success
   b. teacher expectations
   c. time-on-task
   d. size of school

4. **Impulse control at 4 years of age predicted**
   a. the nature of interactions with siblings.
   b. future academic success.
   c. the health of child.
   d. physical competence.

5. **Friends provide certain resources for children that adults lack. Which of these is not a resource provided by friends?**
   a. membership in the sibling underworld
   b. opportunity for learning skills
   c. chance to compare self with others
   d. chance to belong to a group

6. **Selman's theory of interpersonal relationships is known as**
   a. observational learning.
   b. social perspective taking.
   c. linguistic interpretation.
   d. accommodation.

7. **A critical factor in effective schools is**
   a. condition of the school.
   b. recreational facilities.

   c. number of tenured teachers.
   d. good instructional leadership.

8. **Teachers find themselves functioning in**
   a. nested ecosystems.
   b. experiential consciousness.
   c. assimilated environments.
   d. interactive restrictiveness.

9. **The author of a scathing criticism of schools in low SES environments is**
   a. Bruner.
   b. Skinner.
   c. Kozol.
   d. Deming.

10. **Toward the end of the middle-childhood period, television viewing time begins to**
    a. increase.
    b. stabilize
    c. decline.
    d. compete.

11. **Television can also further _____ behavior.**
    a. regressive
    b. accommodating
    c. subliminal
    d. prosocial

12. **Which of these is not considered a severe stressor of childhood?**
    a. parental alcoholism
    b. school life
    c. abuse
    d. separation from parent

13. **Child abusers often share parental characteristics. Which of these is not such a characteristic?**
    a. perpetrator abused as a child
    b. have unreasonable expectations for the child
    c. often immature and dependent
    d. low SES

14. **Abused children feel they have lost**
    a. memory.
    b. appetite.

   c. control.
   d. time.

15. **Which is not a long-term effect of sexual abuse?**
    a. permissive parenting
    b. depression
    c. negative self-concept
    d. sexual problems

16. **Although middle-childhood youngsters are more exposed to stressful situations, they possess a better ability to**
    a. cope.
    b. ignore.
    c. retreat.
    d. achieve.

17. **Stress has the tendency to upset our**
    a. denial patterns.
    b. equilibrium.
    c. sublimations.
    d. trust.

18. **Which of the following does not account for individual differences in the reaction to stress?**
    a. age
    b. sex
    c. temperament
    d. athletic ability

19. **Children react differently to stress according to all but**
    a. age.
    b. gender.
    c. temperament.
    d. race.

20. **Among the protective factors for resilient children is**
    a. temperament.
    b. interactive error.
    c. geographic mobility.
    d. assimilation.

Answers

1. d 2. c 3. d 4. b 5. a 6. b 7. d 8. a 9. c 10. c 11. d 12. b 13. d 14. a 15. a 16. a 17. b 18. d 19. d 20. a

PHYSICAL AND COGNITIVE DEVELOPMENT IN ADOLESCENCE

11
chapter

Chapter Outline

Chapter Objectives

After reading this chapter you should be able to answer the following questions.

- How should we define adolescence?

- What are the leading theories that attempt to explain adolescence?

- What are the key factors of physical development in adolescence?

- How does cognition develop during the adolescent years?

Peter and Lynn are wide awake at 2 in the morning, but they are not having a good time. They are having a teenager. Matty, their son, was due home two hours ago. He is 16, his curfew is midnight, and they have heard nothing from him. They are wide awake and angry, and most of all, they are worried.

But this is not going to be one of those nights that changes anyone's life. Nobody is going to die. Nothing of this night will be on the news. This is the ordinary night nobody writes about. Matty is going to come home in another half hour, hoping his parents have long since gone to sleep, so he can assure them tomorrow that he was in "only a little past 12." When his hopes are dashed by the sight of his wide-awake parents, he will have an excuse about somebody's car and somebody else's mother and a third person who borrowed the first person's jacket with his car keys and left the party early, and maybe it's just because it's now nearly three in the morning, but the story will sound to Peter and Lynn so freshly made up that all its pieces barely know how to fit together.

Lynn won't be thinking about it now, but only six years ago—not a long time to her—she had been struck by how independent Matty had become. This clingy kid who seemed to need her so much had become a little 10-year-old fellow full of purpose and plans, in business for himself, with a sign on his bedroom door—"Adults Keep Out." A part of her missed the little boy who didn't want to be left alone, but a bigger part of her was pleased for both of them by this development. But six years later, at 2:30 in the morning, it will not occur to her to say, "Matty, my son, I'm so impressed by the way you are able to take care of yourself, by how much you can do for yourself, by the way you just go wherever you want to and come home whenever you want to, by how little you seem to need your dad and me. You're really growing up, son. Your dad and I just wanted to stay up until 2:30 in the morning to tell you how proud we are!" No, what will occur to Lynn to say is something more like "This isn't a hotel here, buddy!" Peter and Lynn want something more of Matty now than they wanted when he was 10. (Kegan, 1994, pp. 15–16)

Are adolescents today forced to deal with too many pressures?

Harvard psychologist Robert Kegan believes we all want a lot from teens like Matty. We want him "to be employable, a good citizen, a critical thinker, emotionally self-reflective, personally trustworthy, and possessed of common sense and meaningful ideals. This is a lot to want. It grows out of our concern for ourselves, our concern for others who live with Matty, and our concern for Matty himself. Will he be up to all these expectations?" (1994, p. 19).

Kegan suggests that, in general, our expectations of our teenagers are too high. There is considerable evidence today that the great majority of adolescents pass safely through this stage of life and become reasonably happy adults who make contributions to their families, friends, and communities. Nevertheless, some researchers are finding that our youths are under greater stress than in previous decades (for example, Reisberg, 2000) and that this situation is reflected in an increase in a variety of high-risk behaviors (see the Applied View box on page 293). In this and the next chapter, we look closely at the most revealing studies and try to come to some conclusions about the nature of adolescence today. We begin by looking at some ways to better define our subject.

WHAT IS ADOLESCENCE AND WHEN DOES IT START?

> *"Who are you?" said the caterpillar. Alice replied, rather shyly, "I—I hardly know, Sir, just at present—at least I know who I was when I got up this morning, but I must have changed several times since then."* (Lewis Carroll, Alice in Wonderland, 1865)

puberty
Relatively abrupt and qualitatively different set of physical changes that normally occur at the beginning of the teen years.

In writing his brilliant story, Carroll presaged in many ways current views of adolescence. For example, Graber and Brooks-Gunn (1996) stated that current approaches to studying adolescence frequently consider the precursors and outcomes of a variety of transitions, a constellation of events that define the transition period, or the timing and sequence of events that occur within a transitional period. For example, **puberty** and school events are frequently studied as key transitions signaling the entry into adolescence; finishing school or beginning one's full-time job are examined as transitional events that define the exit from adolescence or entry into adulthood. . . . The term **transition-linked turning points** is used to characterize this framework. (pp. 768–769)

transition-linked turning points
Constellation of events that define the transition period or the timing and sequence of events that occur within a transitional period.

Lerner (2002; see Chapter 1) characterized the adolescent transition as being distinguished by four traits:

- *Relative plasticity.* There is always the potential for change, although past and contemporary contextual conditions may oppose severe limitations.
- *Relationism.* The basis for change lies in the multiple levels of the individual's relationships with others.
- *Historical embeddedness.* No level of organization functions as a result of its own isolated activity. All change is meaningful only in the context of the historical time in which it occurs.
- *Diversity and individual difference.* In the past, developmental psychology has emphasized the ways that all humans are alike (that is why we have behaviorist and stage theories). More and more, the emphasis is on the variety of ways individuals learn to cope with themselves and their environments.

In this chapter, some of the theories and research that we review conform to these newer views and some do not. Nowhere can the science of developmental psychology be seen to be more in transition than in its study of adolescence. Therefore, although we attempt to report the best of the newer work, we also retain an interest in the older, still classic contributions.

At what point did your adolescence begin? Many answers have been offered:

- When you began to menstruate, or when you had your first ejaculation.
- When the level of adult hormones rose sharply in your bloodstream.
- When you first thought about dating.
- When your pubic hair began to grow.
- When you became 11 years old (if a girl); when you became 12 years old (if a boy).
- When you developed an interest in the opposite sex.
- When you (if a girl) developed breasts.

- When you passed the initiation rites set up by society: for example, confirmation in the Catholic Church; bar mitzvah and bas mitzvah in the Jewish faith.
- When you became unexpectedly moody.
- When you became 13.
- When you formed exclusive social cliques.
- When you thought about being independent of your parents.
- When you worried about the way your body looked.
- When you entered seventh grade.
- When you could determine the rightness of an action, independent of your own selfish needs.
- When your friends' opinions influenced you more than your parents' opinions.
- When you began to wonder who you really are.

Although at least a grain of truth exists in each of these statements, they don't help us much in defining adolescence (Coleman & Roker, 1998). For example, although most would agree that menstruation is an important event in the lives of women, it really isn't a good criterion for determining the start of adolescence. The first menstruation, called **menarche,** can occur at any time from 8 to 16 years of age. We would not say that the menstruating 8-year-old is an adolescent, but we would certainly say the nonmenstruating 16-year-old is one.

Probably the most reliable indication of the onset of adolescence is a sharp increase in the production of the four hormones that most affect sexuality: progesterone and estrogen in females, testosterone and androgen in males. But determining this change would require taking blood samples on a regular basis, starting when youths are 9 years old. Not a very practical approach, is it?

Clearly, identifying the age or event at which adolescence begins is not a simple matter. We will need to look at it much more closely, from the standpoints of biology, psychology, and sociology (biopsychosocial interactions). An American psychologist was the first to offer a specific theory to explain development in the teen years, one based almost entirely on biology.

G. Stanley Hall (1844–1924) is known as the father of adolescent psychology. Building on Charles Darwin's theory of evolution, Hall constructed a psychological theory of teenage development, published in two volumes and entitled *Adolescence* (1904). A major aspect of his theory was his speculation that this stage of life is characterized by "storm and stress," that most teens are by nature moody and untrustworthy. This stereotype has had many advocates ever since (Kegan, 1994).

Some researchers agree that adolescents tend to be more emotional and antagonistic than children are, since increased brain activity is bound to contribute to a sense of confusion. Adolescents participate in society at a time when their brains are experiencing increased nerve activity in the prefrontal cortex (Arnstein & Shansky, 2004). This may influence adolescents' perception that the world is "so unfair!" Although Hall is to be admired for his efforts to bring objectivity to adolescent psychology through the use of empiricism, it has been suggested that he had several personal agendas. He was a strong preacher against what he viewed to be teenage immorality and was especially concerned that educators try to stamp out the "plague of masturbation," which he considered to be running rampant among male youths. Here is a little speech that he recommended high school teachers and clergy give to their youthful charges:

If a boy in an unguarded moment tries to entice you to masturbatic experiments, he insults you. Strike him at once and beat him as long as you can stand, etc. Forgive him in your mind, but never speak to him again. If he is the best fighter and beats you, take it as in a good cause. If a man scoundrel suggests indecent things, slug him with a stick or a stone or anything else at hand. Give him a scar that all may see; and if you are arrested, tell the judge all, and he will approve your act, even if it is not lawful. If a villain shows

menarche
Onset of menstruation.

Is interest in the opposite sex the best sign that a young person has reached puberty? What other indicators could you name?

AN APPLIED VIEW

An Average Day in the Life of Some North American Teens

Today (and every other day this year), some teens get into trouble:

- 8,441 teens become sexually active.
- 2,756 teens become pregnant.
- 1,340 babies are born to teen mothers.
- 2,754 babies are born out of wedlock.
- 638 babies are born to mothers receiving late or no prenatal care.
- 2,699 babies are born into poverty.
- 95 babies die before their first birthday.
- 2 children younger than 5 are murdered.
- 248 children are arrested for violent crimes.
- 176 children are arrested for drug abuse.
- 12,720 children are arrested for alcohol abuse or drunk driving.
- 135,000 children take guns to school.
- 2,350 children are in adult jails.
- 167,500 students ages 16 to 24 drop out each school day.

However, today (and every other day this year), teenagers have engaged in many kinds of activities that enrich their own lives and those of the people around them. The great majority of them never engage in the kinds of misbehaviors noted in this list.

It is impossible to know exactly how many are involved in altruistic activities. (It is interesting that we know much more about teenagers' negative actions, isn't it?) Here are some examples of what we mean:

- Have joined a service-oriented club (for example, Scouts, 4-H, Future Farmers of America).
- Became members of Junior Achievement.
- Competed in an athletic event.
- Became a candy-striper (volunteer nurse's aide).
- Joined Students Against Drunk Driving.
- Taught another teen in a peer tutor program.
- Served food in a shelter for the homeless.
- Volunteered at a day-care center or a nursing home for the elderly.
- Answered phones on a drug abuse or suicide hot line.
- Delivered newspapers, stocked supermarket shelves, or in some other way earned money at a part-time job.

Obviously, we would wish that all adolescents were more interested in the ideals represented by these activities. Can you think of ways that you could help make this happen?

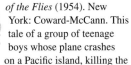

A book that also deals with the stereotype of lack of civility among adolescents is William Goldman's *Lord of the Flies* (1954). New York: Coward-McCann. This tale of a group of teenage boys whose plane crashes on a Pacific island, killing the adults, is excellent reading. You watch the subgroups develop and proceed to the shocking ending.

you a filthy book or picture, snatch it; and give it to the first policeman you meet, and help him to find the wretch. If a vile woman invites you, and perhaps tells a plausible story of her downfall, you cannot strike her; but think of a glittering, poisonous snake. She is a degenerate and probably diseased, and even a touch may poison you and your children. (1904, p. 136)

Is adolescence typically a stage during which hormones run rampant, causing irrational and antisocial behavior? It is true that some misbehavior occurs (see the accompanying Applied View box), but there is also evidence that it is a time when many good deeds are done.

Guided Review

1. Graber and Brooks-Gunn hold that the precursors and outcomes of a variety of transitions are one kind of _____ _____ _____.

2. Lerner characterized the adolescent transition as being distinguished by four traits: relative plasticity, historical embeddedness, diversity and individual difference, and _____.

3. G. S. Hall, the father of adolescent psychology, saw child development paralleling the development of the human race, with adolescence being a time both of civilization and of storm and _____.

Answers

THEORIES OF ADOLESCENCE

If men and women are to understand each other, to enter into each other's nature with mutual sympathy, and to become capable of genuine comradeship, the foundation must be laid in youth.

—HAVELOCK ELLIS

In this section, we review the theories of three famous adolescent theorists. These theories were not chosen because they fully explain adolescence but because they have done such a good job of spurring our thinking about the nature of this period. Thus it is with theories in general: They are respected not because they are true but because they are generative.

True, my theory is no longer accepted, but it was good enough to get us to the next one!

—DONALD HEBB

Anna Freud's Psychological Theory

The daughter of Sigmund, Anna Freud (1895–1983) believed that his definition of adolescence was too sketchy. She suggested (1968) that her father had been too involved with his discovery that sexuality begins not at puberty but in early infancy. As a result, he overemphasized the importance of that earlier stage in the total developmental picture. Anna Freud spent the major part of her professional life trying to extend and modify psychoanalytic theory as applied to adolescence. Anna Freud saw the major problem of adolescence as being the restoration of the delicate balance between the ego and the id, which is established during latency and disrupted by puberty. Latency, she felt, is the time when children adopt the moral values and principles of the people with whom they identify. Childhood fears are replaced with internalized feelings of guilt that are learned during this period. The id is controlled during latency by the strength of the superego. At puberty, however, the force of the id becomes much greater, and

AN INFORMED VIEW | Is Bias Built into Adolescent Research?

Hall is hardly the only adolescent psychologist who can be accused of bias in his thinking. In a fascinating study, Enright and colleagues (1987) looked at 89 articles published during two economic depressions and two world wars to see if these events had an influence on research. The results were striking:

> In times of economic depression theories of adolescence emerge that portray teenagers as immature, psychologically unstable, and in need of prolonged participation in the educational system. During wartime, the psychological competence of youth is emphasized and the duration of education is recommended to be more retracted than in depression. *(p. 541)*

Is it likely that youths were viewed as immature during financial depressions in order to keep them from competing with adults for scarce jobs? Is their maturity seen as greater during wartime because they are needed to perform such adult tasks as soldiering and factory work? If so, is this societal bias conscious or unconscious? What do you think? Perhaps a search of the popular press for articles about teens, some written in war times and some when the economy was stagnant, would enlighten your thinking.

As you read the other theories in this chapter, see if you can spot what you believe to be biases in them. Do they emphasize some aspects of adolescent life at the expense of others? Is one more moralistic than the others?

A SOCIOCULTURAL VIEW

In Western cultures, extended schooling keeps children out of full-time productive work, so they do not start observing and participating in the adult economic world as they do in, for example, Guatemala. Schooling has become a substitute for adult roles. For instance, a college student spends years studying nursing (or chemistry or psychology), but he or she is not a nurse (chemist, psychologist). Extended schooling, then, artificially stretches the period from childhood to adulthood. This delay or waiting period is unique in human history. Combined with the decreasing age of reaching menarche in middle-class Western girls, adolescence can be prolonged more than 10 years! Compare this with the Efe, hunters and gatherers in Zaire, who marry and assume adult roles soon after puberty.

Is adolescence just a theoretical construct (see Chapter 2)? Is it peculiar to cultures with extended schooling? Has an extended adolescence altered our definition of maturity? What if our increasing need for high-level education were to extend adolescence into the middle or even late 20s? Would this change the meaning of adolescence? What do you think?

---

the delicate balance is destroyed. The problems brought about by this internal conflict cause the adolescent to regress to earlier stages of development. A renewed Oedipal conflict (see Chapter 2) brings about fears that are entirely unconscious and often produce intense anxiety. Therefore, the unconscious defenses of the ego tend to multiply rapidly, especially the typical ones of repression, denial, and compensation. The problem, of course, is that the use of these defense mechanisms causes new stresses within the individual and tends to further increase the level of anxiety.

Anna Freud described two additional adolescent defense mechanisms:

- *Asceticism,* in which, as a defense against the sexual, "sinful" drives of youth, the teenager frequently becomes extremely religious and devoted to God.
- *Intellectualization,* in which the adolescent defends against emotionality of all kinds by becoming extremely intellectual and logical about life.

Anna Freud may be seen as emphasizing the psychological aspect of the biopsychosocial model.

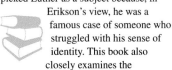

Erik Erikson's Psychosocial Theory

According to Erik Erikson (1902–1994), the main task of the adolescent is to achieve a **state of identity.** Erikson (1963, 1975), who originated the term **identity crisis,** used it in a special way. In addition to thinking of identity as the general picture one has of oneself, Erikson referred to it as a state toward which one strives. If you were in a state of identity, the various aspects of your self-image would be in agreement with one another; they would be identical.

Repudiation of choices is another essential aspect of a person's identity. Striving for identity means that we have to repudiate (give up) all the other possibilities, at least for the present. All of us know people who seem unable to do this. They cannot keep a job, they have no loyalty to their friends, or they are unable to be faithful to a spouse. For them, "the grass is always greener on the other side of the fence." Thus, they must keep all their options open and must not repudiate any choices, lest one of them should turn out to have been "the right one."

Erikson suggested that identity confusion is far more likely in a democratic society because so many choices are available. In a totalitarian society, youths are

Sidebar:

Erikson wrote a fascinating book on Martin Luther: *Young Man Luther* (1958). New York: Norton. Erikson picked Luther as a subject because, in Erikson's view, he was a famous case of someone who struggled with his sense of identity. This book also closely examines the Protestant Reformation and so may appeal to you if you are interested in the beginnings of the Protestant religions.

state of identity
If individuals were in a state of identity (an ideal circumstance), the various aspects of their self-image would be in agreement with each other; they would be identical.

identity crisis
Erikson's term for those situations, usually in adolescence, that cause us to make major decisions about our identity.

repudiation
Striving toward a state of identity means committing to one lifestyle and repudiating (giving up) all the other possibilities, at least for the present.

Do you think that members of the Hitler Youth Corps were victims of "premature foreclosure"? Do you believe that they had a real choice in deciding who they were?

identity status
Marcia's four aspects of identity formation.

usually given an identity, which they are forced to accept. The Hitler Youth Corps of Nazi Germany in the 1930s is an example of a national effort backed by intense propaganda to get all the adolescents in the country to identify with the same set of values and attitudes. In democratic societies, where more emphasis is placed on individual decision making, choices abound; some children may feel threatened by this overabundance of options. Nevertheless, a variety of choices is essential to the formation of a well-integrated identity.

Erikson saw adolescence as a period of moratorium—a "time out" period during which the adolescent experiments with a variety of identities, without having to assume the responsibility for the consequences of any particular one. The moratorium period does not exist in preindustrial societies. Erikson stated that indecision is an essential part of the moratorium. Tolerance of it leads to a positive identity. Some youths, however, cannot stand the ambiguity of indecision. This leads to "premature foreclosure." The adolescent who makes choices too early usually comes to regret them. He or she is especially vulnerable to identity confusion in later life.

Although some youths tend to be overly idealistic, Erikson believed that idealism is essential for a strong identity. In young people's search for a person or an idea to be true to, they are building a commitment to an ideology that will help them unify their personal values. They need ideals to avoid the disintegration of personality that is the basis of most forms of mental illness.

Identity Status

Erikson's ideas on adolescence have generated considerable research on identity formation. The leader in this field is James Marcia, who has made a major contribution to our understanding through his research on **identity status.** He and his colleagues have published numerous studies on this topic (Berzonsky & Kuk, 2000; Marcia 2002; van Hoof, 1999; Waterman, 1999).

Marcia believes that two factors are essential in the attainment of a mature identity. First, the person must undergo several crises in choosing among life's alternatives, such as the crisis of deciding whether to hold or to give up one's religious beliefs. Second, the person must come to a commitment, an investment of self, in his or her choices. Since a person may or may not have gone through the crisis of choice and may or may not have made a commitment to choices, four combinations, or statuses, are possible for that person to be in.

Status 1. Identity confusion: No crisis has been experienced and no commitments have been made.

Status 2. Identity foreclosure: No crisis has been experienced, but commitments have been made, usually forced on the person by the parent.

Status 3. Identity moratorium: A number of crises have been experienced, but no commitments are yet made.

Status 4. Identity achievement: Numerous crises have been experienced and resolved, and relatively permanent commitments have been made.

Table 11.1 summarizes these definitions.

Erikson's eight stages (in addition to the six described in this book thus far, there are the stages of generativity and integrity) follow one another in a more or less unchangeable sequence. Research indicates that Marcia's identity statuses have a tendency toward an orderly progression, but not so clearly as Erikson's stages. Carol Gilligan and others have focused on possible gender differences in identity formation. They have concluded that women are less concerned than men with achieving an independent identity status. Women are more likely to define themselves by their relationships and responsibilities to others. Society gives women the predominant role in transmitting social values from one generation to the next. This

TABLE 11.1	Summary of Marcia's Four Identity Statuses			
	IDENTITY STATUS			
	Confusion	*Foreclosure*	*Moratorium*	*Achievement*
Crisis	Absent	Absent	Present	Present
Commitment	Absent	Present	Absent	Present
Period of adolescence in which status often occurs	Early	Middle	Middle	Late

role requires a stable identity, and therefore a stable identity appears to be more important to women than it is to men.

John Hill's Biopsychosocial Theory

The early work of psychologist John Hill (1987) in developing a biopsychosocial theory of adolescence has led to research on a wide range of adolescent issues (Collins et al., 2001; Grant et al., 1998; Keel et al., 2001; Meschke et al., 2000). Figure 11.1 illustrates his theory. The concentric rings are meant to portray the interrelatedness of the three factors. Biological factors are in the center because they are present at birth, as are some of the psychological factors. However, all the psychological and social factors begin playing a part immediately after birth. The major point is that each is embedded in the other two. The meaning of each is inextricably connected to that of the other two. A fourth factor running through the others is time—not only the aging process from early to late adolescence but also the events going on during this historical period.

FIGURE 11.1

John Hill's theory of adolescence.

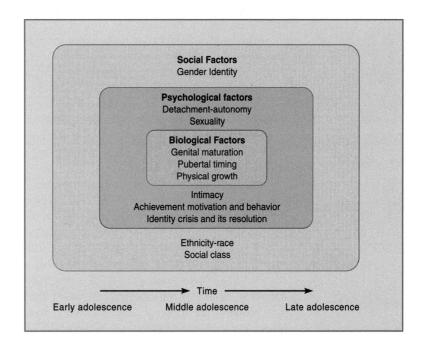

The biological factors Hill considered important are covered later in this chapter, and the social factors are reviewed in Chapter 12. However, some additional comment on Hill's conception of the psychological factors is required here. By detachment, Hill did not mean emotional independence from parents, as did many other theorists of his time. According to their view (which was primarily psychoanalytic), because teens are shifting their sexual attachments from their parents to their peers, there is bound to be a lot of "storm and stress." It was seen as natural for parents and their adolescent children to fight with each other on a regular basis. Hill rejected this view on the basis of actual research of his own and others. He saw the shift as more a matter of moving from dependence to interdependence (see Chapter 12).

The nature of the shift, he felt, was more a matter of growing autonomy, which means "independence in decision making and feelings of confidence in personal goals and standards of behavior" (1973, p. 37). There is a lessening of dependence, but the emphasis should be placed on increases in autonomy. As to sexuality, once again Hill disagreed with the psychoanalytic view, which was that change in one's sense of a sexual self follows a gradual, continuous pattern. He argued that puberty is brought on not only by physiological changes of a rather abrupt nature (menarche, nocturnal emissions, the growth spurt). Rather, the social changes involved in acquiring the new self-concept of adolescence force teens to view themselves in a whole new light sexually. Thus, the change is discontinuous, not gradual.

The new adolescent ability to become intimate with another, Hill believed, is basically tied to sexuality. It begins with feelings of affection for a close friend (which are not overtly sexual but are more intimate than the feelings that characterized earlier relationships). For most people, intimacy and sexual attraction then move to focus on opposite-sex friends. The integration of intimacy and sex, Hill believed, is one of the basic tasks of adolescence.

Achievement motivation and behavior are related to the standard of excellence individuals set for themselves and the relative proficiency they see themselves as having. Achievement behavior is different from achievement motivation, because the former may be affected by other motives, too (having a good time, for instance). This difference is a particularly good example of the role that social context may play. For example, a girl may be highly motivated to play the violin, but if her friends treat that activity with contempt, and if she cares more and more about their opinions as she passes into adolescence, then the violin is likely to be relegated to its case.

Finally, Hill paid Erikson the compliment of saying that his concept of identity integrates much of what is known about adolescence. Hill felt that the six psychological factors he highlighted (see Figure 11.1) fit well with and added to the concept of psychological identity. He did caution, however, that more research would be needed to determine if the adolescent years are always the time in which identity issues are most likely to be addressed (Adams et al., 1996). His concern has been borne out: It is now clear that many young people, especially college students, do not come to a clear identity crisis until they are in their early 20s, if then.

Although much progress in understanding the building blocks of adolescence has been made since Anna Freud, Erik Erikson, and John Hill theorized about it, it is abundantly clear that our progress would have been far less without their splendid insights.

In summary, it may be said that the adolescent's personality is undergoing many changes, but these changes are probably no more traumatic than at any other stage of life. There is the danger of overreliance on defense mechanisms. Another danger is staying in the moratorium period too long. The major concern is to begin to form an adult identity, which means choosing certain values and repudiating others. It is considered necessary to work one's way from identity confusion through the moratorium to an achieved identity, while avoiding foreclosure. In the next two sections of this chapter, we deal with the two foundations of adolescence: physical and cognitive development.

Guided Review

4. Anna Freud sees adolescence as a time to restore the delicate balance between the ego and the id and sees _____ and intellectualization as two defense mechanisms unique to the period.

5. The phrase "identity crisis" is associated with the theorist _____ _____ and is his fifth stage of development.

6. Identity status is achieved through crises and commitment in four stages: identity confusion, identity foreclosure, identity _____, and identity achievement.

7. Marcia believes that to attain a mature identity, a person must undergo several crises in choosing from life alternatives and come to a _____ in his or her choices.

8. James Hill was the first to see that the causations of adolescent changes are always embedded in the intricate interactions among _____, _____, and _____ forces.

PHYSICAL DEVELOPMENT

Theories tend to present models of development that are useful in specific areas, such as physical development (Sturdevant & Spear, 2002). To better understand physical development in adolescence, we answer the following questions in this section: What parts of our body are involved? When does puberty start? What are the effects of timing?

The girls are clearly beginning to look like young ladies, while the boys with whom they have thus far played on scarcely equal terms now seem hopelessly stranded in childhood. This year or more of manifest physical superiority of the girl, with its attendant development of womanly attitudes and interests, accounts in part for the tendency of many boys in the early teens to be averse to the society of girls. (King, 1914, p. 13)

Gretchen, my friend, got her period. I'm so jealous, God. I hate myself for being so jealous, but I am. I wish you'd help me just a little. (Judy Blume, Are You There, God? It's Me, Margaret, 1991)

Your Reproductive System

Today more is known about many aspects of puberty, such as how the organs of our reproductive system function together. Just as important, we are learning how to present this knowledge to adolescents effectively.

Answers

4. asceticism 5. Erik Erikson 6. moratorium 7. commitment
8. biological, psychological, social

Prior to the 20th century, it appears that children moved directly from childhood into adulthood with no period of adolescence in between.

The Female Sexual System

The parts of the female sexual system are defined here and are illustrated in Figure 11.2.

- *Bartholin's glands.* A pair of glands located on either side of the vagina. These glands provide some of the fluid that acts as a lubricant during intercourse.
- *Cervix.* The opening to the uterus located at the inner end of the vagina.
- *Clitoris.* Comparable to the male penis. Both organs are similar in the first few months after conception, becoming differentiated only as sexual determination takes place. The clitoris is the source of maximum sexual stimulation and becomes erect through sexual excitement. It is above the vaginal opening, between the labia minora.
- *Fallopian tubes.* Conduct the ova (egg) from the ovary to the uterus. A fertilized egg that becomes lodged in the fallopian tubes, called a fallopian or ectopic pregnancy, cannot develop normally and if not surgically removed will cause the tube to rupture.
- *Fimbriae.* Hairlike structures located at the opening of the oviduct that help move the ovum down the fallopian tube to the uterus.
- *Hymen.* A flap of tissue that usually covers most of the vaginal canal in virgins.
- *Labia majora.* The two larger outer lips of the vaginal opening.
- *Labia minora.* The two smaller inner lips of the vaginal opening.
- *Mons pubis* or *mons veneris.* The outer area just above the vagina, which becomes larger during adolescence and on which the first pubic hair appears.
- *Ova.* The female reproductive cells stored in the ovaries. These eggs are fertilized by the male sperm. Girls are born with more than a million follicles, each of which holds an ovum. At puberty, only 10,000 remain, but they are more than sufficient for a woman's reproductive life. Because usually only 1 egg ripens each month from the midteens to the late forties, a woman releases fewer than 500 ova during her lifetime.
- *Ovaries.* Glands that release one ovum each month. They also produce the hormones estrogen and progesterone, which play an important part in the menstrual cycle and pregnancy.
- *Pituitary gland.* The "master" gland located in the lower part of the brain. Not strictly part of the sexual system, nevertheless it controls sexual maturation and excitement and monthly menstruation.
- *Ureter.* A canal connecting the kidneys with the bladder.

FIGURE 11.2

Female reproductive system.

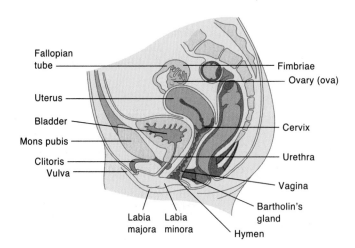

- *Urethra.* A canal leading from the bladder to the external opening through which urine is excreted.
- *Uterus.* The hollow organ (also called the *womb*) in which the fertilized egg must implant itself for a viable pregnancy to occur. The egg attaches itself to the lining of the uterus, from which the fetus draws nourishment as it matures during the nine months before birth.
- *Vulva.* The external genital organs of the female.

The Male Sexual System

The parts of the male sexual system are defined here and are illustrated in Figure 11.3.

- *Cowper's glands.* Located next to the prostate glands. Their job is to secrete a fluid that changes the chemical balance in the urethra from an acidic to an alkaline base. This fluid proceeds up through the urethra in the penis, where it is ejaculated during sexual excitement just before the sperm-laden semen. About a quarter of the time, sperm also may be found in this solution, sometimes called *preseminal fluid.* Therefore, even if the male withdraws his penis before he ejaculates, it is possible for him to deposit some sperm in the vagina, which may cause pregnancy.
- *Epididymis.* A small organ attached to each testis. It is a storage place for newly produced sperm.
- *Foreskin.* A flap of loose skin that surrounds the glans penis at birth, often removed by a surgery called circumcision.
- *Glans penis.* The tip, or head, of the penis.
- *Pituitary gland.* The "master" gland controlling sexual characteristics. In the male it controls the production of sperm, the release of testosterone (and thus the appearance of secondary sexual characteristics such as the growth of hair and voice change), and sexual excitement and maturation.
- *Prostate gland.* Produces a milky alkaline substance known as semen. In the prostate the sperm are mixed with the semen to give them greater mobility.
- *Scrotum.* The sac of skin located just below the penis, in which the testes and epididymis are located.
- *Testes.* The two oval sex glands, suspended in the scrotum, that produce sperm. Sperm are the gene cells that fertilize the ova. They are equipped with a taillike structure that enables them to move about by a swimming motion. After being ejaculated from the penis into the vagina, sperm attempt to swim through the

FIGURE 11.3

Male reproductive system.

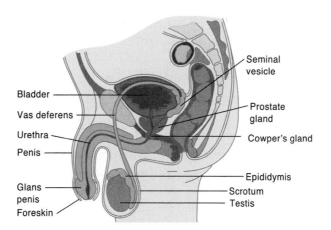

cervix into the uterus and into the fallopian tubes, where fertilization takes place. If one penetrates an egg, conception occurs. Although the testes regularly produce millions of sperm, the odds against any particular sperm penetrating an egg are enormous. The testes also produce testosterone, the male hormone that affects other aspects of sexual development.

- *Ureter.* A canal connecting each of the kidneys with the bladder.
- *Urethra.* A canal that connects the bladder with the opening of the penis. It is also the path taken by the preseminal fluid and sperm during ejaculation.
- *Vas deferens.* A pair of tubes that lead from the epididymis up to the prostate. They carry the sperm when the male is sexually aroused and about to ejaculate.

When Does Puberty Start?

Is the beginning of adolescence marked by any one physiological event? The sequence of bodily changes in puberty is surprisingly constant. This holds true whether puberty starts early or late and regardless of the culture in which the child is reared. Table 11.2 lists the sequences of physiological change.

Which of these physical events in the life of the adolescent might we choose as the actual beginning of puberty? Change in **hormonal balance** is first, but its

hormonal balance
One of the triggering mechanisms of puberty that may be used to indicate the onset of adolescence.

TABLE 11.2	Sequence of Physiological Change in Females and Males

FEMALES

- Change in hormonal balance
- Beginning of rapid skeletal growth
- Beginning of breast development
- Appearance of straight, pigmented pubic hair
- Appearance of curly, pigmented pubic hair
- Menarche (first menstruation)
- Maximum growth spurt (when growth is at its fastest rate)
- Appearance of hair on the forearms and underarms

MALES

- Change in hormonal balance
- Beginning of skeletal growth
- Enlargement of the genitals
- Appearance of straight, pigmented pubic hair
- Early voice changes (voice "cracks")
- First ejaculations (wet dreams, nocturnal emissions)
- Appearance of kinky, pigmented pubic hair
- Maximum growth spurt
- Appearance of downy facial hair
- Appearance of hair on the chest and underarms
- Late voice change (the voice deepens)
- Coarse, pigmented facial hair

Note: For more on these physiological changes, see Muuss (1996).

beginning is difficult to pinpoint. Measuring skeletal growth, genital growth, pubic hair, breast development, voice change, or a growth spurt is complex. Menarche has been suggested as the major turning point for girls, but many women do not recall menarche as a particularly significant event. Hormonal changes actually precede menarche by about two years, or as early as 8 or 9 years of age. Sometimes the first ejaculation is suggested as the beginning of adolescent puberty for males, but this, too, is often a little-remembered (and possibly repressed) event.

Despite the fact that puberty is primarily thought of as a physical change in an adolescent, the psychological impact can be significant (Dorn et al., 1999; Kosan, 2000). This is especially true with menstruation. Even in these "enlightened" times, too many girls experience menarche without being properly prepared. As a result, an event in a young girl's life that should be remembered as the exciting, positive beginning of the transition to adulthood is instead viewed as a negative, sometimes frightening, experience. When menarche comes early (before 11 years of age), it is more likely to be associated with depression and substance abuse than when it comes later (Beousang & Razor, 2000; Stice, Presenell, & Bearman, 2001). The same is very likely also the case for a male's first ejaculation. Accurate and accessible information about the changes our bodies undergo benefits adolescents, for whom physical changes often lead to sexual activity (Bingham & Crockett, 1996).

Given our understanding of the physiology of adolescents and differences in individual psychology and culture, we would have to conclude that no single event but, rather, a complex set of events marks the onset of puberty, a process whose effects may be sudden or gradual. Thus, biology alone cannot give us a definition of adolescence; we will need to include psychological and social factors to achieve that.

The Secular Trend

secular trend
Phenomenon (in recent centuries) of adolescents entering puberty sooner and growing taller and heavier.

The average teenagers 100 years ago were physically similar in most ways to the more late maturers of today. This fact is part of the phenomenon called the **secular trend.** The secular trend refers to the decreasing age of the onset of puberty. In Western countries, the average age of menarche has declined about three months per decade over the past 100 years. In the United States, 17 was the average age of puberty in the late 18th and early 19th centuries. By the beginning of the 20th century, it was 14.5.

Today the average age of menarche is 12.5, about the same as it was 50 years ago (Posner, 2006). However, researchers do not agree about racial and ethnic differences and early puberty (Chumlea et al., 2003; Obeidallah et al., 2000). Obesity

AN APPLIED VIEW | Dealing with Early or Late Development

Turner, Runtz, and Galambos (1999) found an increased risk of sexual abuse for the early-maturing female. Significantly early to late development has been linked to eating disorders in both boys and girls (Kaltiala-Heino et al., 2001) and to psychological distress and delinquency in boys (Ge, Conger, & Elder, 2001; Williams & Dunlop, 1999), so it is important for practitioners working with adolescents to be aware of the negative reactions to their physical change (or lack of it). If you know a teen who is significantly early or late in body development, be on the lookout for psychological problems. If you find evidence of such problems, make arrangements for the youth to have access to appropriate professional attention.

However, you should understand that "normal" covers a wide band of developmental time. We should help teens who "hate" their bodies because they are not perfectly average to be more accepting. Finally, if you do believe there is a problem, say nothing to the teen until you have an experienced person's advice on the best course of action.

This is a picture of typical male and female growth at the turn of last century (King, 1914). What conclusions can you draw from it?

in childhood is linked with early puberty (Lee et al., 2007; Anderson, Dallal, & Must, 2003), yet most researchers feel that improved nutrition, sanitation, and health care are responsible for optimal, healthy development. There is some evidence that breast development is continuing to occur earlier, however, and that this places even more stress on early maturers. For example, premature development of breasts may make young teens subject to cultural "sexualization." Suspected causes for earlier occurrence of these aspects of puberty are

• Lack of exercise—obesity can promote hormone production.

• More fat in diet—same result.

• Presence of hormonelike chemicals in milk and meat (although the evidence for this is scanty (Kaplowitz, 2000).

The findings of the Dorn and associates (1999) study found that girls misreport the onset of menarche by as much as several months. This suggests that girls experience menarche as a series of developmental experiences rather than a single event. Dekovic (1999) found no evidence that childhood conflict influences the timing of puberty. However, Ellis and associates (1999) found that factors of family relationships are associated with starting puberty later. These include fathers' presence in the home, fathers providing more childcare, greater supportiveness with the parenting dyad, and more father and mother affection with the daughter. It is clear that the processes of development and the role of puberty are complicated and occur concurrently (Dorn & others, 2003).

Figure 11.4 details the age ranges considered normal for development. Adolescents who experience these changes earlier or later may have no medical problem, but consulting a doctor is probably a good idea. If a glandular imbalance exists, the doctor can usually remedy the problem with little difficulty.

In summary, we may say that the vast majority of human bodies proceed toward maturity in the same way, but that in the last few centuries the timing of the process in females has changed radically. Although timing is affected mainly by biology, psychological and social forces clearly influence it, too. An example of the biological consequences of psychological and social factors is the eating disorder.

What are some ways that "late maturers" often suffer?

Three books that provide additional information are (1) Judy Blume's *Are You There, God? It's Me, Margaret* (1991). New York: Bradbury. Although written for teens, this book has a wealth of insights into pubertal change, at least for females. (2) R. H. Curtis's *Mind and Mood: Understanding and Controlling your Emotions* (1986). New York: Scribner's. According to Curtis, knowing more about emotions and how they affect the body can help in understanding and controlling them. (3) McCoy and Wibbelsman's *The Teenage Body Book* (1992). Los Angeles, CA: The Body Press. This is an excellent reference book for teenagers and those who work with them.

Body Image and Eating Disorders

Although still rather rare, eating disorders are so serious (about one-third of those who develop an eating disorder die) that it is necessary to review what we know about them here. Eating disorders are the third most common chronic condition among adolescents. The two main types, anorexia and bulimia nervosa, have in common the profound concern about shape and weight (Jimerson et al., 2002). While some symptoms are unique to one disorder, there are numerous parallels between anorexia and bulimia.

FIGURE 11.4

Normal age ranges for puberty.

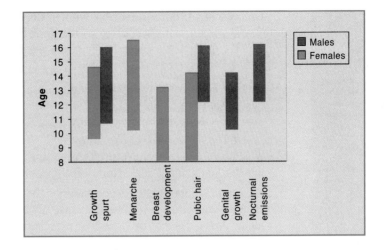

anorexia nervosa
Syndrome of self-starvation that mainly affects adolescent and young adult females.

Gender, puberty, weight, and age all affect body image and eating behaviors in adolescents. Young boys believe that their sexual appeal is based on their ability to develop their bodies. Postpubertal males tend to have high self-esteem and are confident in their ability to control their own lives. In contrast, postmenarcheal females often experience dissatisfaction with their new size and shape. This dissatisfaction can lead to feelings of inadequacy, loss of control, and decreased self-esteem, which are all risk factors for eating disorders (O'Dea & Abraham, 2000).

Anorexia nervosa is a syndrome of self-starvation that mainly affects adolescent and young adult females, who account for 95% of the known cases. Professionals suspect that many males may also be victims (for example, those who must maintain a low weight for sports), but their illness is covered up (O'Dea & Abraham, 1999). "The essential features of anorexia nervosa are that the individual refuses to maintain a minimally normal body weight, is intensely afraid of gaining weight, and exhibits significant disturbance in the perception of the shape or size of his or her body. In addition, post menarcheal females with this disorder are amenorrheic. (The term *anorexia* is a misnomer, because loss of appetite is rare.)" (American Psychiatric Association, 2000, p. 238.)

Health professionals have seen an alarming rise in the incidence of this disorder among young women in the last 15 to 20 years. Whether anorexia nervosa has actually increased or whether it is now being more readily recognized has yet to be determined. According to the *DSM-IV-TR* (American Psychiatric Association, 2000), the specific criteria for anorexia nervosa are these:

- Refusal to maintain body weight at or above a minimally normal weight for age and height (for instance, weight loss leading to maintenance of body weight less than 85% of that expected; or failure to make expected weight gain during period of growth, leading to body weight less than 85% of that expected).

- Intense fear of gaining weight or becoming fat, even though underweight.

- Disturbance in the way in which one's body weight or shape is experienced, undue influence of body weight or shape on self-evaluation, or denial of the seriousness of the current low body weight.

bulimia nervosa
Disorder is characterized by "episodic binge eating accompanied by an awareness that the eating pattern is abnormal, fear of not being able to stop eating voluntarily, and depressed mood and self-deprecating thoughts following the eating binges."

- In postmenarcheal females, amenorrhea—that is, the absence of at least three consecutive menstrual cycles. (A woman is considered to have amenorrhea if her periods occur only following hormone, such as estrogen, administration.)

Bulimia nervosa is a disorder related to anorexia nervosa and sometimes combined with it. It is characterized by "binge eating and inappropriate compensatory methods to prevent weight gain. In addition, the self-evaluation of individuals with bulimia nervosa is excessively influenced by body shape and weight" (American Psychiatric Association, 2000).

Christy Henrich, a gymnast, died of anorexia. What do you imagine were some of the causes of her death?

Bulimia has been observed in women above or below weight, as well as in those who are normal. According to the *DSM-IV* (American Psychiatric Association, 2000), the specific criteria of bulimia are these:

- Recurrent episodes of binge eating. An episode of binge eating is characterized by both of the following: eating, in a discrete period of time (for example, within any 2-hour period), an amount of food that is definitely larger than most people would eat during a similar period of time and under similar circumstances.

- A sense of lack of control over eating during the episode (for instance, a feeling that one cannot stop eating or control what or how much one is eating).

- Recurrent inappropriate compensatory behavior in order to prevent weight gain, such as self-induced vomiting; misuse of laxatives, diuretics, enemas, or other medications; fasting; or excessive exercise.

- The binge eating and inappropriate compensatory behaviors both occur, on average, at least twice a week for three months.

- Self-evaluation is unduly influenced by body shape and weight.

- The disturbance does not occur exclusively during episodes of anorexia nervosa.

Despite their clinical differences, anorectics and bulimics share emotional and behavioral traits. The most characteristic symptoms specific to these disorders are the preoccupation with food and the persistent determination to be slim, rather than the behaviors that result from that choice (Jimerson et al., 2002).

The Athletic Body and Eating Disorders

The gymnastic training system encourages young female athletes to keep their weight down, and many gymnasts live on diets of fruits, laxatives, and painkillers. In 1976, the average age of a U.S. gymnast was 18, with an average weight of 106 pounds. In 1992, the average age of a U.S. gymnast was 16, with an average weight of 83 pounds—a drop of 23 pounds! Cathy Rigby, a former gymnast who won a gold medal at the 1968 Olympics, fought a 12-year battle with anorexia and bulimia. Now recovering from her illness, Cathy states that gymnasts are trained to be slim through fear, guilt, and intimidation (Ryan, 1995). This trend appears to continue. In a study of college athletes, Picard (1999) found that females involved in sports that stress a lean figure, place restrictions on weight, and compete at higher levels demonstrated more symptoms of disordered eating and were at higher risk for developing an eating disorder.

The Role of Stress

The relationship between stress and emotional illness is well established. Therefore, it is important to know to what extent adolescents feel that their lives are stressful. The most reliable source for this information is the Higher Education Research Institute, which has been studying this question for the last 35 years (Reisberg, 2000). Of the over 260,000 students interviewed at 462 colleges by the institute, 30% say they feel "overwhelmed by all I have to do." This is up from 16% in 1985. The concern is almost twice as great among women (39%) than among men (20%). A significant part of this pressure comes from the need to work. In 1982, 16% of entering freshmen felt they would have to get a full-time job while attending college; in 1999, that figure had risen to 25%.

Many adolescents who find that sports teams at schools are not available to them are looking for alternatives to sitting on the couch and watching television. As a result, fitness programs for teens are becoming popular in places such as the

YMCA. Another strong argument in favor of noncompetitive sports is that they tend to promote higher levels of self-esteem among adolescent girls (Bowker, Gadbois, & Cornock, 2003).

Other teens are turning to long hours at work as a means of spending their high level of energy, not always with good results. Teenagers are working more and more, and as a result, they are getting injured more frequently on the job. Over two-fifths of their occupational fatalities occur when they are engaged in work prohibited by child labor laws (Wright, 2000). For children under 18, national laws prohibit:

- driving a motor vehicle.
- operating power-driven equipment.
- working in hazardous jobs such as wrecking, roofing, mining, excavating, demolition, logging, and saw milling.
- working in meat packing or slaughtering.

In addition, children under 16 may not:

- bake or cook.
- work on a ladder or scaffold.
- load or unload trucks, railroad cars, or conveyors.
- work in a warehouse.
- work in construction, building, or manufacturing.

Guided Review

9. Puberty is a relatively abrupt and qualitatively different set of physical changes in boys and girls that usually occurs at the beginning of the _____ years.

10. Although there is a rather wide normal range of development as relates to the onset of puberty, early- or late-maturing children can be affected socially and _____.

11. _____-maturing boys are often peer group leaders.

12. One hundred years ago the average-maturing girl was physically much like the late-maturing girl today. This phenomenon is called the _____ _____.

13. _____ _____ is a syndrome of self-starvation characterized, in part, by an intense fear of becoming obese, disturbance of body image, and significant weight loss.

COGNITIVE DEVELOPMENT

I was about 12 when I discovered that you could create a whole new world just in your head! I don't know why I hadn't thought about it before, but the idea excited me terrifically. I started lying in bed on Saturday mornings till 11 or 12 o'clock, making up "my secret world." I went to fabulous places. I met friends who really liked me and treated me great. And of course I fell in love with this guy like you wouldn't believe! (Susan Klein, an eighth-grade student)

Answers

Adolescence is a complex process of growth and change (see, for example, Rushton & Ankney, 1997). Because biological and social changes are the focus of attention, changes in the young adolescent's ability to think often go unnoticed, yet growth spurts in the parietal and frontal lobes of the brain, as well as subcortical regions, make possible tremendous changes in the quality of a teenager's thinking. It has recently been discovered (Seltz, 2000) that there are actually two growth spurts, one at around 12 and 13 and a second in the later teen years. It is during early and middle adolescence that thinking ability reaches Piaget's fourth and last level—the level of abstract thought (see Chapter 2). To understand how abstract thought develops, we have to know more about cognition itself.

Variables in Cognitive Development: Piaget

Let us pause to review Jean Piaget's theory (described in Chapter 2). He argued that the ability to think develops in four stages:

1. The *sensorimotor* stage (birth to 2 years), in which the child learns from its interactions with the world.

2. The *preoperational* stage (2 to 7 years), in which behaviors such as picking up a can are gradually internalized so that they can be manipulated in the mind.

3. The *concrete operational* stage (7 to 11 years), in which actions can be manipulated mentally, but only with things. For example, a child of 8 is able to anticipate what is going to happen if a can is thrown across the room without actually having to do so.

4. The *formal operational* stage (11+ years), in which groups of concrete operations are combined to become formal operations. For example, the adolescent comes to understand democracy by combining concepts such as putting a ballot in a box and hearing that the Senate voted to give money for the homeless. This is the stage of abstract thought development.

It was Piaget who first noted the strong tendency of early adolescents toward democratic values because of this new thinking capacity. This is the age at which youths first become committed to the idea that participants in a group may change the rules of a game, but once agreed on, all must follow the new rules. This tendency, he believed, is universal; all teenagers throughout the world develop this value.

Having considered Piaget's ideas about adolescent cognition in some detail earlier in this book, let us turn now to a review of the findings of those researchers who have been diligently following him.

Culture and gender can also influence cognitive development. Piaget's theory seems to assume that the ideal person at the end point of cognitive development

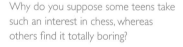

Why do you suppose some teens take such an interest in chess, whereas others find it totally boring?

resembles a Swiss scientist. Most theorists focus on an ideal end point for development that, not too surprisingly, ascribes their own valued qualities to maturity.

To better understand how cultural identity affects the academic achievement of African Americans, Chavous and associates (2003) compared black adolescents based on their educational beliefs, performance, and level of completion. They found that not only do African-American youths have different interpretations of their racial identities, but these beliefs may lead them down different paths of educational achievement. For instance, some adolescents who had positive group pride but felt as though society viewed their race negatively had the highest rates of post–high school achievement. Perhaps, in this case, they were motivated by their determination to overcome discrimination.

Piaget (1973) acknowledged that his description of the end point might not apply to all cultures, since evidence had showed cultural variation. If one stresses the influence of context (sociocultural and individual) on development, as Vygotsky (1978) and Barbara Rogoff (1990) do, then one sees multiple directions for development rather than only one ideal end point. For example, it may well be that for some agricultural societies, sophisticated development of the concrete operational stage would be far more useful than minimal formal operational thinking. That is, an understanding of the complicated workings of a machine may be concrete, but that does not make that type of thinking inferior to another person's ability to do formal operations. Thus, believing that the formal operations stage is always superior would be intellectual snobbism.

Gender also plays a role in the definition of formal operations. Gilligan (1982) said that most theories of development define the end point of development as being male only and that they overlook alternatives that more closely fit the mature female. She believed that, if the definition of maturity changes, so does the entire account of development. Using men as the model of development, researchers see independence and separation as the goals of development. If women are used as the models, the goals of development are relationship with others and interdependence. Gilligan contends that this gender difference also leads to distinctions in the development of thinking about morality.

Emotions and Brain Development

spindle cell
Neurons that play a large role in emotion.

reticular activation system (RAS)
Complex sub-cortical system that protects the brain from being overwhelmed.

Researchers continue to study how complex emotions such as self-awareness, morality, feelings of free will, and social emotions are initiated by the brain. Some believe that cigar-shaped neurons known as **spindle cells** play a large part in how the brain creates emotion (Blakeslee, 2003). These cells are responsible for sending socially relevant signals across the brain. This function whereby the subcortex filters out all but new and/or really important information is known as the **reticular activation system (RAS).** The RAS protects the brain from being overwhelmed by extraneous data. Despite the great similarities among various mammals' brains, it turns out that only humans and great apes have spindle cells. These cells are not even present at the time of birth. Instead, they gradually appear as children develop a concept of moral and social judgments, and then develop more rapidly during adolescence.

All morality consists in a system of rules, and the essence of all morality is . . . in the respect which the individual acquires for these rules.

—JEAN PIAGET

Connections between neurons are responsible for communication between the body and the brain. Information is transformed into feeling and self-awareness. Some information or stimuli are turned into social emotion along the path. It is through this pathway that the most basic aspects of human nature such as love, sadness, fear, excitement, and anger are processed (Blakeslee, 2003).

Adolescent Egocentrism

adolescent egocentrism
Reversion to the self-centered thinking patterns of childhood that sometimes occurs in the teen years.

Parents often feel frustrated at the seemingly irrational attitudes and behaviors of their adolescent children. One explanation is the reemergence of a pattern of thought that marked early childhood, egocentrism. **Adolescent egocentrism,** a term coined by Elkind (1978), refers to adolescents' tendency to exaggerate the importance, uniqueness, and severity of social and emotional experiences. Their love is greater than anything their parents have experienced. Their suffering is more painful and unjust than anyone else's. Their friendships are most sacred. Their clothes are the worst or the best. Developmentally speaking, adolescent egocentrism seems to peak around the age of 13 (Elkind & Bowen, 1979), followed by a gradual and sometimes painful decline.

imaginary audience
Adolescents' perception that the world is constantly scrutinizing their behavior and physical appearance.

Elkind sees two components to this egocentrism. First, teenagers tend to create an **imaginary audience** (Vartanian & Powlishta, 2001). They feel they are on center stage, and the rest of the world is constantly scrutinizing their behavior and physical appearance. This accounts for some of the apparently irrational mood swings in adolescents. The mirror may produce an elated, confident teenager ready to make an appearance. Then one pimple on the nose can be cause for staying inside the house for days. In fact, school phobia can become acute during early adolescence because of concerns over appearance.

> **Young teenagers today are being forced to make decisions that earlier generations didn't have to make until they were older and more mature, and today's teenagers are not getting much support and guidance.**
>
> —DAVID ELKIND

personal fable
Adolescents' tendency to think of themselves in heroic or mythical terms.

The second component of egocentrism is the **personal fable.** This refers to adolescents' tendency to think of themselves in heroic or mythical terms (Frankenberger, 2000; Vartanian & Powlishta, 2001). The result is that they exaggerate their own abilities and their invincibility. This type of mythic creation on the part of an adolescent can sometimes lead to increased risk-taking, such as drug use, dangerous driving, and disregard for the possible consequences of sexual behavior. Many teenagers simply can't imagine an unhappy ending to their own special story.

Another explanation for these seemingly irrational behaviors and attitudes may be found in the adolescent brain. In a study conducted by Yurgelun-Todd (1998), adults and adolescents were shown photos depicting fear. The adults accurately identified the emotion; however, most adolescents incorrectly identified the pictured emotion. Their inaccurate responses included emotions such as anger and worry. After studying brain scans of the teens and adults, Yurgelun-Todd found that the amygdala (the part of the brain that is responsible for emotional responses) played a large role in the teens' reactions. In contrast, the prefrontal cortex (the part of

Some students prefer divergent thinking to convergent thinking, and for others, the reverse is true. Can you think of any explanations for that?

AN INFORMED VIEW

What's Your View: Should Critical Thinking about Interpersonal Problems Be Taught in Our Schools?

Critical thinking is of tremendous importance to teens, as they learn to cope with the changes that life brings. One arena in which this skill is of great usefulness is in working out interpersonal problems. Here, too, we may easily see how an understanding of the concept of bidirectionality (see the section on contextualism in Chapter 1) also plays a role. The roots of interpersonal problems almost always involve bidirectional causes. Most teens are well aware of how the actions of others affect them but sometimes fail to see how their own actions may bring about negative reactions. Here is where following the five phases of critical thinking comes in. Practicing this procedure can greatly alleviate some of the hurt feelings and misunderstandings that inevitably occur.

Many educators agree that teaching critical thinking as it applies to school subjects is appropriate but cannot agree that they should also apply these lessons to real-life teen problems. If you were a secondary teacher (or counselor or administrator), would you include adolescent interpersonal relations in your teaching of critical thinking? What's your view?

If you would like to have a more informed opinion on this issue, you might want to read one of the articles on the subject referenced in Chapter 9.

the brain that is responsible for reason and thought) played a large role in the adults' responses. These differences between the adolescent and adult brain may explain why teens are often seen to be so emotional (Baird et al., 1999; Killgore & Oki, 2001).

Critical Thinking

Although we discussed critical thinking at some length in Chapter 9, we should make a number of points about its role in adolescence. The distinction between convergent and divergent thinking is helpful here, because critical thinking is made up of these two abilities.

convergent thinking
Thinking used to find one correct answer.

Convergent thinking is used when we solve a problem by following a series of steps that close in on the correct answer. For example, if we were to ask you to answer the question "How much is 286 times 469?" you probably could not produce it immediately. However, if you used a pencil and paper or a calculator, you would almost certainly converge on the same answer as most others trying to solve the problem. Only one answer is correct. Critical thinking uses convergent thinking. **Divergent thinking** is just the opposite. This is the type of thinking used when the problem to be solved has many possible answers. For example, what are all the things that would be different if it were to rain up instead of down?

divergent thinking
Thinking used when a problem to be solved has many possible answers.

Other divergent questions are "What would happen if we had no thumbs?" and "What should we do to prevent ice buildup from snapping telephone lines?" Divergent thinking can be right or wrong, too, but considerably greater leeway exists for personal opinion than with convergent thinking. Not all divergent thinking is creative, but it is more likely to produce a creative concept. To be a good critical thinker, analyzing statements accurately is not enough. Often you will need to think divergently to understand possibilities and implications of those statements, too. In the next section, we make a distinction between critical and creative thinking, but it is important that we not make too great a distinction. Paul (1987) describes this concern well:

Just as it is misleading to talk of developing a student's capacity to think critically without facing the problem of cultivating the student's rational passions—the necessary driving force behind the rational use of all critical thinking skills—so too it is misleading to talk of developing a student's ability to think critically as something separate from the student's ability to think creatively.... The imagination and its creative powers are continually called forth. (p. 143)

AN APPLIED VIEW | Video Games and Cognitive Development

The emergence of video games as a popular pastime among children and adolescents in the late 1970s created a firestorm of controversy. Parents and educators were warned that there may be detrimental consequences to prolonged exposure.

Research from the early 1990s offers a different perception of this form of play. Strong evidence indicates that just as various forms of play in all societies prepare children for the demands of adulthood, video games are an important cultural artifact to teach skills that relate to the mastery of computer technology. Video games may also enhance hand-eye coordination, decision making, numerical concepts, and the ability to follow directions. Additionally, video games have been shown to improve divided attention in both expert and novice video game players. In 1998, the video game industry topped $6.3 billion.

Despite rating systems and parental disapproval, adolescents find violent video games to be highly accessible. Most of the games are used on home computer systems. Research has found that parents prefer not to engage in dialogue with their teens regarding the violent and aggressive nature of these games (Leland, 1998). Recent research by Wiegman and van Schie (1998) found that children, especially boys, who favored aggressive video games showed more aggression and less pro-social behavior. Also, children with lower intelligence were more likely to play aggressive video games. However, it cannot be overlooked that even violent and aggressive video games provide opportunities for visualization and learning through analysis of clues (Leland, 1998).

Creative Thinking

This is the story about a very curious cat named Kat. One day Kat was wandering in the woods where he came upon a big house made of fish. Without thinking, he ate much of that house. The next morning when he woke up he had grown considerably larger. Even as he walked down the street he was getting bigger. Finally he got bigger than any building ever made. He walked up to the Empire State Building in New York City and accidentally crushed it. The people had to think of a way to stop him, so they made this great iron box, which made the cat curious. He finally got inside it, but it was too heavy to get him out of again. There he lived for the rest of his life. But he was still curious until his death, which was 6,820,000 years later. They buried him in the state of Rhode Island, and I mean the whole state. (Ralph Titus, a seventh-grade student)

The restless imagination, the daring exaggeration, the disdain for triteness that this story demonstrates—all are signs that its young author has great creative potential. With the right kind of encouragement, with the considerable knowledge we now have about how to foster creativity, this boy could develop his talents to his own and society's great benefit (Dacey, 1989a, 1989c, 1998; Dacey & Lennon, 1998; Esquivel, 1995). Creative thinking appears to have many elements—divergent thinking, fluency, flexibility, originality, remote associations. We will look more closely at these elements when we get to adult creativity later in this book, but one element that seems to be of special importance in adolescence is the ability to demonstrate both abstract and logical thinking. The combination of thought processes contributes to creative endeavors.

Creativity, Giftedness, and the IQ

As Feldman (1979, 1994) has pointed out, many studies of "giftedness" have been conducted, but only a few of exceptionally creative, highly productive youths have been undertaken. This is a serious omission because, as you will see later in this book, adolescence is a sensitive period in the growth of creative ability. Feldman believes that this unfortunate situation is mainly the fault of "the foremost figure in the study of the gifted," Lewis M. Terman. Terman (1925) was well known for

Many gifted teens use art to express their feelings. What is there about art that makes it preferable to other forms of expression.

Child prodigies are distinguished by the passion with which they pursue their interests. Here we see young Wolfgang Amadeus Mozart performing for a group of admiring adults. He was not merely precocious—able to perform at levels typical of older children; he was prodigious—able, at a young age, to write music that professional musicians still perform.

precociousness
Ability to do what others are able to do, but at a younger age.

prodigiousness
Ability to do qualitatively better than the rest of us are able to do; such a person is referred to as a prodigy.

his research on 1,000 California children whose IQs in the early 1920s were 135 or higher. Terman believed these children to be the "geniuses" of the future, a label he kept for them as he studied their development over the decades. His was a powerful investigation and has been followed by scholars and popular writers alike. Precisely because of the notoriety of this research, Feldman argues, we have come to accept a numerical definition of genius (an IQ above 135), and a somewhat low one at that. Feldman notes that the *Encyclopaedia Britannica* now differentiates two basic definitions of genius: the numerical one fostered by Terman and the concept first described by Sir Francis Galton (1870, 1879): "creative ability of an exceptionally high order as demonstrated by actual achievement."

Feldman says that genius, as defined by IQ, really refers only to **precociousness**—doing what others are able to do, but at a younger age. **Prodigiousness** (as in child prodigy), however, refers to someone who is qualitatively higher in ability than the rest of us. This is different from simply being able to do things sooner. Further, prodigiousness calls for a rare matching of high talent and an environment that is ready and open to creativity. If such youthful prodigies as Mozart in music or Bobby Fischer in chess had been born 2,000 years earlier, they may well have grown up to be much more ordinary. In fact, if Einstein had been born 50 years earlier, he might have done nothing special—particularly because he did not even speak well until he was 5!

So if prodigies are more than just quicker at learning, what is it that truly distinguishes them? On the basis of his intensive study of three prodigies, Feldman states that:

Perhaps the most striking quality in the children in our study as well as other cases is the passion with which excellence is pursued. Commitment and tenacity and joy in achievement are perhaps the best signs that a coincidence has occurred among child, field, and moment in evolutionary time. No event is more likely to predict that a truly remarkable, creative contribution will eventually occur. (1979, p. 351)

In summary, critical and creative thinking are similar in that they both employ convergent and divergent production. The main difference between them is that critical thinking aims at the correct assessment of existing ideas, whereas creativity is more aimed at the invention and discovery of new ideas. Although each requires a certain amount of intelligence, creativity also depends on such traits as metaphorical thinking and an independent personality.

Robert Sternberg (2000a, 2000b) said the intelligent person can recall, analyze, and use knowledge, whereas the creative person goes beyond existing knowledge and the wise person probes inside knowledge and understands the meaning of what is known (see Chapter 18). It should be noted that these conclusions appear to hold true not only for adolescence but also for all periods of the lifespan.

Mental Health Issues

A number of psychologists and psychoanalysts (most notably Freud) have suggested that the distressing, turbulent, unpredictable thoughts deemed normal in adolescence would be considered pathological in an adult. This disruptive state is partly characteristic of the identity stages of confusion and moratorium. Identity confusion is sometimes typified by withdrawal from reality. Occasional distortions in time perspective can occur. Mental disturbance also often makes intimacy with another person impossible. These characteristics are also seen in the moratorium stage, but they tend to be of much shorter duration. Mental health issues are pertinent for numerous reasons. Many adult disorders originate in childhood events, childhood mental illness is common, and many of these illnesses have a poor prognosis (Gerhardt et al., 1999; Wells et al., 2001).

How common and how serious are these problems? The picture is not clear. Researchers have concluded that true psychopathology (mental illness) is relatively rare during adolescence. It is impossible to determine the frequency of mental illness, however, because of current disagreements over its definition. The summary of numerous studies gives us considerable reason to believe that "adolescent turmoil," though common, does not really constitute psychopathology. Studies do indicate that, when adolescents become seriously disturbed and do not receive appropriate treatment quickly, the chances of their "growing out" of their problems are dim (Dacey, Kenny, & Margolis, 2006; Findling et al., 2001; Woodward, 2001).

Students suffering from serious physical ailments, such as deformities and immobility, often experience academic and emotional problems. A study by Lumley and Provenzano (2003) found that academic performance of these students can be improved through written descriptions of their emotional states. Such written disclosures led to significantly better grade point averages in subsequent semesters and a general decrease in the negative feelings associated with stress.

Because stress is difficult to detect, but for obvious symptoms (for example, stomachaches, headaches, diarrhea), it is especially important for adults to recognize the warning signs of stress in adolescents so they may receive the support they need. Some adolescents may resist help at first for reasons of pride, embarrassment, or sheer will, but they will appreciate the persistence of caring friends and family later.

Adolescent suicide represents the third leading cause of death among teenagers (Shaffer & Pfeffer, 2001). "It is estimated that each year, approximately 2 million U.S. adolescents attempt suicide, and almost 700,000 receive medical attention for their attempt" (Shaffer & Pfeffer, 2001, p. 25). Adolescent males are five times as likely to commit suicide as adolescent females. In addition, Native-American, Native-Alaskan, and Hispanic teens have higher rates of suicides than do white and African-American teens. Although African-Americans have lower rates of suicide than whites do, their rate of attempts has shown a sharp rise over the past decade.

A number of factors increase the likelihood of a suicide attempt (Shaffer & Pfeffer, 2001). The overwhelming number of adolescents who commit suicide suffer from some associated psychiatric disorder, such as a pathological level of anxiety. These teens may have poor parent-child communication, have experienced a recent stressful life event, and/or have a history of suicide attempts, substance abuse, and pathology and suicidal behavior. Gay, lesbian, and bisexual teens and teen survivors of childhood sexual and physical abuse are at higher risk because of such factors as family conflict and ostracism at school. In addition, suicide completers and attempters are more likely to be friends with peers who have attempted suicide, use drugs, or have psychiatric symptoms (Ho et al., 2000). Antisocial behavior in adolescence has also been linked to ADHD (Pisecco & others, 2001).

Research has shown that adolescents diagnosed with ADHD may have lower self-esteem, which contributes to antisocial behavior, yet ADHD does not explain why some adolescents direct violent behaviors at others and at themselves. King (2000) suggests the following warning signs for adolescent suicide. Nine out of 10 adolescents who commit suicide give warning signs.

- Depressed mood
- Substance abuse
- Loss of interest in once-pleasurable activities
- Decreased activity and attention levels
- Distractability
- Withdrawal from others
- Sleep or appetite changes
- Morbid ideation (for example, thinking about death)
- Verbal cues ("I wish I were dead") or written cues (notes, poems)
- Giving possessions away
- A previous suicide attempt
- Low self-esteem or a recent relationship breakup
- Being homosexual
- Coming from an abusive home
- Easy access to a firearm
- Low grades
- Exposure to suicide or suicidal behavior by another person

The transition from junior high school to high school can be a stressful time for adolescents (Eccles, 2003). The stress may come from many different sources, such as peers, parents, siblings, and teachers. It is a time when more emphasis is placed on grades and academic achievement. It is also a time of increased pressure to date and experiment with cigarettes, drugs, and alcohol. Researchers have found that, the more teens feel a sense of belonging in their schools, the easier the transition. Support from family, particularly parents, is critical.

Types of Mental Disorders

The National Institute of Mental Health has reported that the incidence of mental health problems among adolescents is about 1 in 10 youth and rising (Child and Adolescent Mental Health Government Guide, 2002; Haliburn, 2000). Adolescents suffer from a wide range of mental health disorders that affect their normal development and functioning. The most common of these mental health disorders are anxiety disorders (13% of children 9 to 17), depression (8% of adolescents), and attention deficit hyperactivity disorders (3–5% of school-aged children) (Child and Adolescent Mental Health Government Guide, 2002). Other disorders adolescents can experience can include eating disorders, autism and other pervasive developmental disorders, conduct disorders, and substance abuse disorders. Many teens are not treated for mental disorders, because their parents and even their doctors often hope they will "grow out of it." Figure 11.5 details the reasons for treatment for all those who actually received it.

Research has looked at a number of factors that may affect adolescent mental health issues, such as age, gender, culture, poverty, and genetics, to name a few (Kovas et al., 1997).

In addition, the diagnosis and treatment of adolescents' mental health disorders are very important for the long-term development of the youth. The failure to treat these mental health issues can lead to a range of academic, social, emotional, and behavioral problems as well as suicide and delinquency (Child and Adolescent Mental Health Government Guide, 2002; Haliburn, 2000).

A source on this subject is Gibson's *The Butterfly Ward* (1980). New Orleans: Louisiana State University Press. This set of short stories tells what it is like to be between sanity and insanity. It is a sensitive look at the world of the mentally ill, both in and out of institutions.

FIGURE 11.5

Reasons for mental health treatment in the past year among youths ages 12 to 17 in 2002.

Source: Department of Health and Human Services, 2003, p. 34.

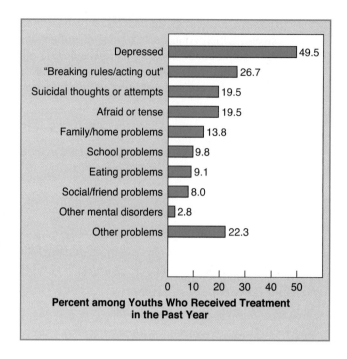

Percent among Youths Who Received Treatment
in the Past Year

Depressed — 49.5
"Breaking rules/acting out" — 26.7
Suicidal thoughts or attempts — 19.5
Afraid or tense — 19.5
Family/home problems — 13.8
School problems — 9.8
Eating problems — 9.1
Social/friend problems — 8.0
Other mental disorders — 2.8
Other problems — 22.3

Many of these mental health illnesses can be treated effectively with a range of medications and therapies. For example, studies have reported that ADHD can be successfully treated with stimulant medications and different forms of psychotherapy (Barkley, Conner, & Kwasnik, 2000; Child & Adolescent Mental Health Government Guide, 2002).

In conclusion, adolescence is not a time of turmoil and distress for most teens. Rates of mental disturbance among teens are very similar to rates of disturbance among adults. The high levels of stress adolescents experience impact daily functioning and have implications for healthy social and emotional development.

AN INFORMED VIEW | *Is the New Emphasis on Testing Helping or Hurting Students?*

Currently there is an angry debate among those concerned about the role of "high stakes testing" in our schools. On the one side are those who believe that more testing is needed to improve standards. As the CEO of IBM, Louis Gerstner, put it, "Too little is expected of American students, and as a consequence too little is delivered. . . . in the future, students must become workers, not shirkers" (1994, p. 173). Those in this position argue that tests should be used to promote the hard work that leads to cognitive growth.

Many developmental psychologists oppose this point of view (Crain, 2004). They believe that testing pressures force teachers to teach for the test, reducing opportunities to deal with developmental differences in their pupils. Crain, the author of a text on theories of development, presents this case:

As testing gains power, child-centered teachers in particular are finding their autonomy and flexibility severely

curtailed. They have little opportunity to tailor education to the child's deepest interests when so much of what they must teach is determined by the tests. . . . From a developmental perspective, we must reduce this tyranny and put testing in a broader perspective. Tests provide useful information, but there are more basic considerations. Is education in accord with the child's basic growth tendencies—does she have opportunities to pursue interests and develop capacities that seem most important to her at her own phase of development? *(2004, pp. 390–391)*

What do you think? If you would like to have a more informed opinion on this subject, you may want to read one or more sources on this subject (for example, Crain, 2004; Quality Counts, 2004; Rosenbaum, 2004).

Guided Review

14. In exploring cognitive development, we examine Piaget's four stages of cognitive development: sensorimotor, preoperational, _____ operational, and formal operational.

15. Formal operational means that a person can form _____ mental operations.

16. Elkind presented the concept of adolescent egocentrism, which includes an _____ _____ and the personal fable.

17. Thinking skills can be separated into convergent (coming together with a single correct answer) and _____ (exploring the many possible answers to a question).

18. David Feldman claims that some children are precocious (doing what others do, but at a younger age), while other children are _____ (having a qualitatively greater ability than the rest of us).

19. _____ _____ is sometimes typified by withdrawal from reality.

Answers

14. concrete 15. abstract 16. imaginary audience 17. divergent 18. prodigious 19. Identity confusion

CONCLUSION & SUMMARY

Defining adolescence is a complex task. Deciding when it begins and ends is even more complicated. We know that any definition must be biopsychosocial in order to be comprehensive. We know that, biologically, there is a marked increase in the flow of sex-related hormones, as well as a maximum growth spurt and the appearance of secondary sex characteristics. Psychologically, a new sense of self and the formation of the identity take shape, and cognitive changes such as formal operations, the personal fable, and the imaginary audience occur. The social world of the teen undergoes many changes, including the inauguration of new privileges and new responsibilities. These changes constitute the bare bones of a definition, but even all the information in this and the following chapter only begin to tell the whole story.

We wish that all children could complete puberty with a normal, healthy body and body image. We wish they could negotiate adolescence so successfully that they become energetic, self-confident adults.

Unfortunately, we know that this is not always the case. Some youths suffer from a negative self-concept because, although they differ from the norm only slightly in their body development, they perceive this as "catastrophic." Others deviate significantly from the norm because of some physiological problem. Of particular concern for females is our society's obsession with thinness. Taken together, the various aspects of puberty can cause the adolescent quite a bit of chagrin.

The only solution is to get some perspective on these problems. The good news is that, just when they need it, most adolescents develop improved mental abilities that enable them to get a more realistic view of themselves. Cognitive development is a complex matter, one about which we understood very little before the middle of the last century. Our best evidence is that the intellect develops in stages. Contrary to earlier beliefs, thinking in childhood, adolescence, and adulthood are qualitatively different from each other. Furthermore, cognitive development has a number of other aspects: social cognition, information processing, egocentric thinking, critical thinking, creative thinking, and mental health.

How should we define adolescence?

- Most experts state that the majority of adolescents are happy and productive members of their families and communities.

- Hall's interpretation of adolescent development was greatly influenced by his observation that it is a period of storm and stress.

- It is likely that youths are viewed as immature during financial depressions in order to keep them from competing with adults for scarce jobs; their maturity is seen as greater during wartime because they are needed to perform such adult tasks as soldiering and factory work.

What are the leading theories that attempt to explain adolescence?

- Anna Freud believed that the delicate balance between the superego and the id, being disrupted by puberty, causes the adolescent to

- regress to earlier stages of development.
- According to Erik Erikson, human life progresses through eight "psychosocial" stages, each of which is marked by a crisis and its resolution. The fifth stage applies mainly to adolescence.
- Although the ages at which one goes through each Eriksonian stage vary, the sequence of stages is fixed. Stages may overlap, however.
- John Hill's biopsychosocial theory, with its emphasis on the six factors of dependence, autonomy, sexuality, intimacy, achievement, and identity, offers the most inclusive theory of adolescence.

What are the key factors of physical development in adolescence?

- Theories of adolescence in the early 20th century were largely based on personal bias, because little empirical data existed.
- Those who work with adolescents need complete knowledge of the reproductive systems of both sexes.
- The order of physical changes in puberty is largely predictable, but the timing and duration of these changes are not.
- The normal range in pubertal development is very broad and includes early, average, and late maturers.
- The adolescent's own perception of being normal has more influence on self-esteem than objective normality.
- Maturity of appearance affects whether adolescents are treated appropriately for their age.
- Early maturing is usually a positive experience for boys but may be negative for girls.
- Late maturing is often difficult for both boys and girls.
- Two of the most disruptive problems for adolescents are the eating disorders known as anorexia and bulimia nervosa.
- Adolescent girls develop eating disorders more than any other group.
- Developmental, cultural, individual, and familial factors are associated with the development of eating disorders.
- Teens are working longer and longer hours, and this has resulted in a serious increase in injuries on the job.

How does cognition develop during the adolescent years?

- Piaget focused on the development of the cognitive structures of the intellect during childhood and adolescence.
- The infant and child pass through Piaget's first three stages: sensorimotor, preoperational, and concrete operational.
- Piaget's highest stage of cognitive development, that of formal operations, begins to develop in early adolescence.
- Adolescents focus much attention on themselves and tend to believe that everybody is looking at them. This phenomenon is called the imaginary audience.
- Many adolescents also hold beliefs about their own uniqueness and invulnerability. This is known as the personal fable.
- Critical thinking combines both convergent thinking, in which there is only one correct answer, and divergent thinking, in which there are many possible answers to a problem.
- Effective decision making, a formal operational process, is a part of critical thinking.
- Creative thinking includes divergent thinking, fluency, flexibility, originality, and remote associations.
- Conventional schooling often has a dampening effect on students' willingness to risk doing creative, metaphorical thinking.
- Criticism of genius, as defined by IQ, holds that IQ indicates only precociousness but cannot account for prodigiousness.
- The idea that those who develop mental illness during adolescence will "grow out of it" is not supported by research. Depression can be an especially dangerous illness at this age.
- Adolescence is not a time of turmoil and distress for most teens. Rates of mental disturbance among teens are very similar to rates of disturbance among adults.

KEY TERMS

adolescent egocentrism
anorexia nervosa
bulimia nervosa
convergent thinking
divergent thinking
hormonal balance
identity crisis

identity status
imaginary audience
menarche
personal fable
precociousness
prodigiousness
puberty

repudiation
reticular activation system (RAS)
secular trend
spindle cell
state of identity
transition-linked turning points

WHAT DO YOU THINK?

1. Should children be taught about their bodily functions in school? Should this teaching include sexuality? If so, at what grade should it start?

2. How do sociocultural influences impact adolescent cognitive

development? How do these influences differ for girls and boys?

3. Why do you suppose people develop eating disorders?

4. Why should adolescents be more prone than other age groups to having "imaginary audiences" and "personal fables"?

5. Do you believe you can "disinhibit" (free up) your creative abilities? How should you start? Why don't you?

6. What are some of the ways we can help adolescents to have better mental health?

CHAPTER REVIEW TEST

1. **Which of these is part of the male reproductive system?**
   a. fimbriae
   b. vas deferens
   c. cervix
   d. ova

2. **What controls sexual characteristics in both males and females?**
   a. pituitary gland
   b. Bartholin's glands
   c. Cowper's glands
   d. epididymis

3. **What marks the onset of puberty?**
   a. menarche for females; first ejaculation for males
   b. the growth spurt for females and males
   c. the beginning of breast development for females; the enlargement of the genitals for males
   d. No single event marks the onset of puberty.

4. **Adolescents who are dependent and childlike, who feel a growing dislike for their bodies, and who become more introverted and self-rejecting because of it are most likely to be**
   a. early-maturing males.
   b. early-maturing females.
   c. average-maturing males.
   d. late-maturing females.

5. **The identity status in which numerous crises have been experienced and resolved and relatively permanent commitments have been made is called**
   a. identity moratorium.
   b. identity achievement.
   c. foreclosed identity.
   d. confused identity.

6. **The decreasing age of the onset of puberty is referred to as**
   a. early physical maturation.
   b. early psychological maturity.
   c. the evolutionary trend.
   d. the secular trend.

7. **Specific criteria for anorexia nervosa include**
   a. weight loss of at least 25% of original body weight.
   b. onset before age 25.
   c. distorted attitudes toward eating and weight.
   d. All these answers are correct.

8. **One of the traits by which Lerner characterized the adolescent transition is**
   a. independence.
   b. eating disorders.
   c. relative plasticity.
   d. negative body image.

9. **From the standpoint of adolescence, the most important of Erikson's eight stages is the stage of**
   a. identity.
   b. autonomy.
   c. intimacy.
   d. industry.

10. **What occurs during Piaget's formal operational stage?**
    a. Concrete operations combine to become formal operations.
    b. Preoperations turn into formal operations.
    c. Parts of the sensorimotor stage turn into formal operations.
    d. The preoperational stage and the sensorimotor stage combine to become formal operations.

11. **One of the criticisms of Piaget's theory of cognitive development is that it**
    a. is too broad.
    b. does not address abstract thought.
    c. is too complex.
    d. does not account for culture and gender influences.

12. **To think of oneself in heroic or mythical terms is known as**
    a. egocentrism.
    b. imaginary audience.
    c. the personal fable.
    d. invincibility.

13. **When teenagers believe they are being scrutinized for their behavior and physical appearance, they are**
    a. egocentric.
    b. creating a personal fable.
    c. creating an imaginary audience.
    d. exaggerating their abilities and skills.

14. **According to John Hill's biopsychosocial theory, which three factors are most involved?**
    a. biological, achievement, and social
    b. biological, psychological, and sexual
    c. intimacy, dependency, and autonomy
    d. biological, psychological, and social

15. **To solve problems that have only one correct answer, we are using**
    a. divergent thinking.
    b. convergent thinking.
    c. creative thinking.
    d. critical thinking.

16. **New ideas are to creative thinking as existing ideas are to**
    a. convergent thinking.
    b. critical thinking.
    c. divergent thinking.
    d. preoperational thinking.

Answers

12

chapter

PSYCHOSOCIAL DEVELOPMENT IN ADOLESCENCE

Chapter Objectives

After reading this chapter you should be able to answer the following questions.

- **What changes have occurred to American families and their roles in adolescent life in recent years?**

- **What is the nature of peer relations during the teen years?**

- **How do teens deal with sexual relations?**

- **What new information do we have about sexually transmitted infections?**

- **How is the modern teenage parent dealing with the stresses that parenthood entails?**

- **What recent information do we have on adolescent illegal behavior?**

n the last chapter and in this one, evidence is presented of a serious increase in several types of high-risk behaviors (such as eating disorders, binge drinking, use of illegal substances, and unprotected sex) among a significant group of today's adolescents. In a comparison of these youths with their parents, who became adults in the 1970s, William Pfaff (1997) offers a possible explanation for this phenomenon:

> *The post-1960s generation felt itself liberated to set its own principles of life. . . . People now were to be free, independent, 'self-actualizing' individuals.*
>
> *What counted was each person's freedom to do whatever he or she wanted to do, within the professed limitation that it did not restrict anyone else's freedom to do whatever they wanted to do. All this, as we now know, did not work out in an entirely positive way. . . .*
>
> *. . . A great many of the children of [today's] generation feel that they have been deserted by their parents. They have been given no standards. . . . This new generation is saying: You failed to transmit to us positive values in which you believed. We now must look for them elsewhere.* (p. 15)

Is Pfaff's description of the situation today the explanation for the increase in high-risk activities? He is describing a relatively momentary trend in family life, one that seems likely to change as today's teens become parents. As you read the various sections of this chapter, ask yourself whether you believe Pfaff's explanation is sufficient, or whether you think there could be other forces, perhaps more biological or psychological, that also play a role in why adolescents are behaving as they are.

The topics in this chapter examine the evidence, pro and con, on Pfaff's position. Following a discussion of the changing life of the family, we look closely at peer relations and sexuality. We also cover four topics of psychosocial development that no one is happy about: sexually transmitted infections, teenage pregnancy, substance abuse, and criminal behavior.

CHANGING AMERICAN FAMILIES AND THEIR ROLES IN ADOLESCENT LIFE

> *It is, after all the simplest things we remember: a neighborhood softball game, walking in the woods at twilight with Dad, rocking on the porch swing with Grandma.*
>
> *Now, no one has time to organize a ballgame. Our woods have turned to malls. Grandma lives three states away. How will our children have the same kind of warm memories we do?* (Barbara Meltz)

Of all the changes in American society in recent years, those affecting families have probably been the most extensive (also see Chapter 8). Let's begin with a look at the changing roles of families in modern society.

Loss of Functions

In 1840, the American family fulfilled six major functions (Sebald, 1977). Table 12.1 lists those functions and suggests which elements of society now perform them.

Today professionals have taken over the first five functions—economic-productive, educational, religious, recreational, medical. It appears that the family has been left to provide but one single function—affection—for its members. In the 19th century, parents and children needed each other more than now, for the following three major reasons:

- *Vocational instruction.* For both males and females, the parent of the same sex taught them their adult jobs. Most men were farmers and most women, housewives. Parents knew all the secrets of work, secrets passed on from generation

TABLE 12.1	The Changing Roles of Families
Former Family Roles	*Societal Elements That Perform Them Now*
Economic-productive	Factory, office, and other business
Educational	Schools
Religious	Church or synagogue
Recreational	Commercial institutions
Medical	Doctor's office and hospital
Affectional	Still the family's role

to generation. Today nearly 100% of men work at jobs different from their fathers, and an increasing percentage of women are not primarily housewives, as their mothers were.

- *Economic value.* Adolescents were a vital economic asset on the farm; without children, the farm couple had to hire others to help them. Work was a source of pride to the children. It was immediately and abundantly clear that they were important to the family. Today, instead of being an economic asset, most children pose an economic challenge to the family's resources.

- *Social stability.* When families almost never moved from their hometowns, parents were a crucial source of information about how to live in the town, knowing all the intricacies of small-town social relationships. One depended on one's parents to know what to do. Today, when the average American moves every five years, the adults are as much strangers in a new place as the children. In fact, with Dad, and now frequently Mom, driving out of the neighborhood to work, the children may well know the neighborhood better than their parents do.

In a recent study, Youngblade and associates (2007) argue it is important to consider factors closest to adolescents, including family, school, and the larger community

A humorous look at adolescence and the family in earlier times may be found in Carson McCullers's *The Member of the Wedding* (1946). New York: Bantam Books. Twelve-year-old Frankie yearns desperately to join her brother and his bride on their honeymoon. She learns a great deal about the transition from childhood to maturity from the devoted housekeeper.

AN APPLIED VIEW

How Well Do Parents Know What Their Teens Are Doing?

The *Who's Who* organization recently (1997) surveyed 3,370 teenagers 16- to 18-year-olds, all of whom have an A or a B average and are planning to attend college. Because these students are among the highest achievers in the United States, one might assume that their parents would be reasonably well aware of their activities. As the following chart reveals, there are some serious discrepancies.

At least three important questions are posed by these data: Why is there such a great distance between what the teens say they do and what their parents believe? Might these "good students" be underreporting their actual activities? As you will see in other chapters of this book, in some cases these students' rates of behavior are lower than for more ordinary students, and in some cases higher—Why do you suppose this is so?

Do You Think That Your Child . . .	Parental Myth	Teen Reality
Has contemplated suicide?	9%	26%
Has cheated on a test?	37	76
Has had sex?	9	19
Has friends with drug problems?	12	36
Has driven a car while drunk?	3	10
Has worries about pregnancy?	22	46

Source: *Who's Who Special Report,* 1997.

in terms of healthy or optimal adolescent development. Drawn from the 2003 National Survey of Children's Health, data from 42,305 adolescents were examined. The researchers found that one of the most important ways to influence positive social, emotional, and academic outcomes in adolescents was including parents in the effort.

Effects of Divorce

A smoothly functioning family can provide support and nurturance to an adolescent during times of stress (Youngblade et al., 2007). But when the family is itself in a state of disarray, such as during a divorce, not only is the support weakened, but the family often becomes a source of stress (Pelton & Forehand, 2001; Sun, 2001).

Divorce has become commonplace in American society. Even with slight decreases in the divorce rate in recent years, more than 1 million divorces still occur every year, which is roughly half the number of marriages performed during the same time (Munson & Sutton, 2006). Divorce tends to occur most in families with a newborn, second most in families with an adolescent present. Estimates suggest that divorce affects as much as one-third to one-half of the adolescent population.

What, then, are the effects of divorce on the development of the adolescent? Unfortunately, conclusions are often based as much on speculation as on research findings, owing to problems in the research. Divorcing parents often refuse to let themselves or their children participate in such studies, which makes random samples difficult to obtain.

Nevertheless, the divorcing family clearly contributes additional stress to a developing adolescent. One obvious effect is economic. The increased living expenses that result from the need to pay for two domiciles most often leads to a significant decrease in the standard of living for the children. Most adolescents, particularly young adolescents, are extremely status conscious, and status is often obtained with the things money can buy (clothes, stereos, cars, and so on). Young adolescents may well resent being unable to keep up with their peers in this regard. Older adolescents

Divorce has many negative effects on children. Can you think of any positive effects?

are better equipped to cope with this type of additional stress, both psychologically and financially, because they can enter the workforce themselves.

Simons and associates (1999) found that adolescent adjustment problems may often be attributed to divorce-related issues. For example, both girls and boys from divorced families tend to be more depressed than their same-aged peers from intact families. Divorce increases the mother's chances of being depressed, which often reduces the quality of her parenting. Another obvious effect of a divorce is the absence of one parent. Often custodial rights are given to one parent (usually the mother), and so the children are likely to lose an important source of support (usually that of the father). What support the noncustodial parent provides is sometimes jeopardized by the degree of acrimony between the divorced parents. One or both of the parents may attempt to "turn" the adolescent against the other parent. This sometimes results in disturbing, negative tales about a mother or father, forcing adolescents to cope with adult realities while they are still young.

Such distractions also can disrupt the disciplinary process during adolescence. Under any circumstances, administering consistent and effective discipline during this time often requires the wisdom of King Solomon. A difficult job for two parents becomes the primary responsibility of one. Preoccupied parents, perhaps feeling guilty over subjecting the child to a divorce, find it difficult to provide the consistent discipline that the child was used to previously. It should be noted however, that for adolescents in general, decreased contact with parents also produces these problems. Despite the popular belief that parental remarriage increases a child's ability to tackle academic challenges, Jeynes (1999) found that those from reconstituted families often scored lower academically than their peers from single-parent divorced families.

Not surprisingly, adolescents from divorced families tend to be vulnerable as a result of the stressors both during and after divorce (Hetherington, 2005). For instance, the absence of a father may lead to aggressive behavior and poor adjustment. Imitating feuding parents may be another cause of aggressive behavior. In addition to father absence and parental conflict, economic distress is a common result of divorce. Adolescents who experience poverty as a result of increased financial stress on the family are more prone to depression and feelings of abandonment owing to the new pressures of one of their single parents, usually their mother, having to get a job. Children in nontraditional families, such as children with same-sex parents and adopted children, often experience unique stresses owing to societal assumptions about families and what is best for children (Willemsen, 2005).

Some adolescents are able to adapt to the stress of a divorce. Researchers attribute their resilience to personality characteristics such as self-esteem, access to support systems, family unity, and a good relationship with peers and at least one parent (Thompson, 1998).

Because the father typically leaves a family during divorce, there are often more negative effects for males than for females (Hetherington & Kelly, 2000, 2002; Hetherington & Stanley-Hagan, 1989). Wolfinger (1998) found an increased likelihood of problem drinking in men owing to parental divorce. The chances of being a smoker were also greatly increased as a result of divorce. During the teenage years, the father often assumes primary responsibility for disciplining the male adolescents in the family. An abrupt change in disciplinary patterns can lead some adolescents to exhibit more antisocial and delinquent behavior. For example, divorce may force adolescents into growing up faster and disengaging from their families. Early disengagement from a family can actually be a good solution for teens, if they can devote themselves to school activities and rewarding relationships with friends or teachers (Hetherington et al., 1989). The single-parent family is likely to influence the timing of when a girl leaves home. A study conducted by Cooney and Mortimer (1999) indicated that girls from a single-parent home are more likely to leave home after high school. The likelihood of this departure is increased if the adolescent has a child of her own or if she is responsible for a great deal of the housework.

The absence of a biological father can also influence adolescent girls in terms of sexual activity and pregnancy rate. Ellis and associates were able to isolate and measure the impact of a father's absence (Ellis et al., 2003). They interviewed parents and adolescents from the United States and New Zealand and measured family dynamics (including race, socioeconomic status, and methods of discipline), psychosocial adjustment, educational achievement, and sexual behavior of the adolescents. The researchers concluded that a father's absence does increase the likelihood of earlier sexual behavior and pregnancy among adolescent girls. Further, in both countries, the earlier in the daughter's life that her father left, the higher the rate of early sexual behavior and teen pregnancy.

Despite the negative aspects we've outlined, you should keep in mind that not all aspects of a divorce have a negative impact on adolescents. Divorce is often a better alternative than keeping a stressful, unhappy family intact. In fact, a few studies that have compared adolescents from the two groups have shown that teenagers from divorced families do better in general than adolescents from intact but feuding families (Hetherington et al., 1989). This inference has recently been challenged by Wallerstein and associates (1999), who studied 131 children of divorce in California. They concluded that most of the children were unhappy as a result of the divorce. They stated that "children don't care if parents sleep in separate beds if the household runs well and if the parenting holds up" (p. 2).

Hines (1997) summarizes the research findings:

> *For the adolescent undergoing multiple developmental changes, divorce and its related transitions present additional challenges, promoting growth for some and constituting developmental vulnerabilities for others. A review of the literature on adolescent development, family relations and the impact of divorce on adolescents reveals that adolescents experience divorce differently from younger children and that a positive parent-adolescent relationship can ameliorate the negative effects of divorce.* (p. 375)

Nurturing Parent

authoritarian parenting
Parents strive for complete control over their children's behavior by establishing complex sets of rules.

permissive parenting
Parents have little or no control over their children and refrain from disciplinary measures.

authoritative parenting
Parents are sometimes authoritarian and sometimes permissive, depending to some extent on the parents' mood.

nurturing parenting style
Parents use indirect methods and modeling to influence their child's behavior.

As we discussed in Chapter 8, most family researchers have agreed that three styles of parenting exist (Mupinga, 2002): the **authoritarian, permissive,** and **authoritative parenting** styles. In an extensive study of 56 families in which at least one of the adolescents was highly creative (Dacey, 1998; Dacey, Kenny, & Margolis 2006; Dacey & Lennon, 1998), a picture of a fourth style clearly emerged. The parents in these families were found to be devotedly interested in their children's behavior, but they seldom make rules to govern it. Instead, by modeling and family discussions, they espouse a well-defined set of values and expect their children to make personal decisions based on these values.

After the children make decisions and take actions, the parents let the children know how they feel about what was done. Even when they disapprove, they rarely punish. Most of the teens in the study said that their parents' disappointment in them was motivation enough to change their behavior. All of the parents agreed that, if their child were about to do something really wrong, they would stop him or her, but that this virtually never happens. This has been termed the **nurturing parenting style** (Dacey & Packer, 1992). Only some of the parents in the study were found to be highly creative, but all appeared committed to this approach.

The success of nurturing parents is based on a well-established principle: People get better at what they practice. These parents provide their children with ample opportunities to practice decision-making skills, self-control, and, most vital of all, creative thinking. They serve as caring coaches as their children learn how to live. This research demonstrates the profoundly positive effects a healthy family can have on a person.

Guided Review

1. Five functions that were provided by the family but are now provided elsewhere are educational, religious, recreational, medical, and _____.

2. Within families that experience divorce, there are some interesting gender differences. Divorce generally has more adverse effects on _____ than on _____.

3. In a study on parenting styles in which at least one of the adolescents in a family was highly creative, parents were found to employ a style of parenting called _____.

4. Divorce tends to occur most often in families with a newborn and second most in families with an _____.

5. The three styles of parenting most often identified by researchers are authoritarian, permissive, and _____.

PEER RELATIONS

Important debates have existed in the field of adolescent psychology concerning the value and influence of peer and parental relationships during adolescence. Recent research has helped to resolve some of these debates. The importance of parent and peer relationships and the ways in which peer relationships change during the adolescent years are the focus of this section.

Developmental Patterns of Peer Groups

Peer groups are important in adolescent development. Although it is clear that friendships are vital throughout life, there seems to be something special about the role of the peer group during adolescence.

The role of peers as a source of activities, support, and influence increases greatly (Dumont & Provost, 1999). Perhaps it is for these reasons that adults and the media have been interested in and anxious about the role of the peer group.

Galambos and associates (2003) studied how parental techniques and peer relations affect adolescent behavior. The study included three parenting styles of control (support, behavioral control, and psychological control) and two behavioral patterns (externalization and internalization). Externalizing behaviors include physical actions such as smoking, shoplifting, drinking, and such, whereas internalizing behaviors include emotional troubles such as depression and anxiety.

It was found that deviant peers increase the risk of adolescents experiencing externalizing and internalizing problems. However, parenting can reduce this risk. Behavioral control such as discipline and limit setting were the most effective parental techniques for reducing adolescents' externalizing behavior. No significant technique was found for parents to reduce the risk for their children's internalizing problems, however. Brown (1990) described four specific ways in which the peer group changes from childhood to adolescence.

- As previously mentioned, adolescents spend much more time with peers than do younger children. As early as sixth grade, the early adolescent begins withdrawing from adults and increases time spent with peers. During high school,

Answers   1. economic 2. boys, girls 3. nurturing 4. adolescent 5. authoritative

Although rigidly segregated into gender groups during middle childhood, boys and girls become much more willing to interact with each other as adolescence proceeds.

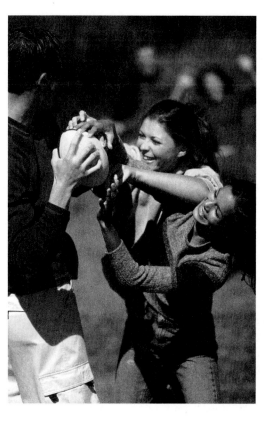

middle adolescents spend twice as much time with their peers as they spend with parents and other adults.

- Adolescent peer groups receive less adult supervision and control. Teenagers try to avoid close supervision by parents and teachers, are more independent, and find places to meet where they are less closely watched. Even at home, teenagers seek privacy and places where they can talk to friends without being overheard by parents and siblings.

- Adolescents begin interacting more with peers of the opposite sex. Although boys and girls participate in different activities and friendship groups during middle childhood, the sexes mix increasingly during the adolescent years. Interaction with members of the opposite sex seems to increase at the same time as adolescents distance themselves from their parents.

- During adolescence, peer groups become more aware of the values and behaviors of the larger adolescent **subculture.** They also identify with certain **crowds,** which are groups with a reputation for certain values, attitudes, or activities. Common crowd labels among high school students include "jocks," "brains," "druggies," "populars," "nerds," "burnouts," and "delinquents." Interestingly, although the adolescent subculture changes over time, these crowds seem to exist in some form across all periods in which the adolescent subculture has been studied.

subculture
A subgroup within a culture, in this case a social culture.

crowds
Groups known for certain values, attitudes, or activities.

Brown and associates (1997) made an important distinction between crowds and cliques, which are subgroups within crowds:

Some might suppose that crowd labels are little more than vague, stereotypical categories, and because the constraints on selecting a crowd for

AN APPLIED VIEW

Internet Bullies

"You're a zit-face! "Everyone at school hates you!" "Better not show up tomorrow, or you'll be sorry!" These are actual messages sent anonymously over electronic media.

Sometimes peers provide just the opposite of support. Of growing concern is the use of cell phones and instant messaging on computers for the purpose of bullying. Bullying has long been a problem in schools. But now, with the ability to communicate easily and anonymously via electronics, there has been a sharp rise in hurtful statements among teens, with no obvious way to reduce the problem (Harmon, 2004). As electronic devices become even more pervasive, culture will have to develop a means of dealing with this pernicious form of bullying.

oneself are substantial, the crowd niche would matter less to adolescents than their clique niche. Remember, however, that the clique affiliation indicates merely who an adolescent's close friends are; crowd affiliation indicates who an adolescent is—at least in the eyes of peers. It is a very personal evaluation of the adolescent by those whose opinions matter. Thus, it is not surprising that adolescents resist being labeled or pigeonholed as part of one crowd. (p. 184)

It is well known that teenagers, especially girls, spend a lot of time talking to their peers, much of it over the telephone. A recent study by Boehm and associates (1999) reviewed the issues discussed by adolescent girls around the country while calling a peer hotline. Peer relationships was the most frequently discussed topic (46%–60%), followed by family problems (10%–20%). The concerns of the girls were quite similar.

Functions of Peer Groups

In contrast with the popular view that peers are a negative influence during adolescence, peer influence serves important social and psychological functions. When adolescents do not have the chance to be part of a peer group, they miss out on important learning experiences. Kelly and Hansen (1990) described six important positive functions of the peer group. The group can help teens to:

- *Control aggressive impulses.* Through interaction with peers, children and adolescents learn how to resolve differences in ways other than direct aggression. Observing how peers deal with conflict can be helpful in learning assertive, rather than aggressive or "bullying," behavior.

- *Obtain emotional and social support and become more independent.* Friends and peer groups provide support for adolescents as they take on new responsibilities. The support adolescents get from their peers helps them to become less dependent on their family for support.

- *Improve social skills, develop reasoning abilities, and learn to express feelings in more mature ways.* Through conversation and debate with peers, adolescents learn to express ideas and feelings and expand their problem-solving abilities. Social interactions with peers give adolescents practice expressing feelings of caring and love, as well as anger and negative feelings.

- *Develop attitudes toward sexuality and gender-role behavior.* Sexual attitudes and gender-role behaviors are shaped primarily through peer interactions. Adolescents learn behaviors and attitudes that they associate with being young men and women.

- *Strengthen moral judgment and values.* Adults generally tell their children what is right and what is wrong. Within the peer group, adolescents are left to make decisions on their own. The adolescent has to evaluate the values of peers and decide what is right for him or her. This process of evaluation can help the adolescent develop moral-reasoning abilities.

- *Improve self-esteem.* Being liked by a large number of peers helps adolescents feel good about themselves. Being called up on the telephone or being asked out on a date tells adolescents that they are liked by their peers, thereby enhancing feelings of positive self-esteem.

It is clear that the formation of intimate friendships is an important adolescent goal. One of the most important aspects of these friendships during adolescence is the growing trend for them to become sexual.

Guided Review

6. Brown describes four ways in which the peer group changes from childhood to adolescence. These are (1) adolescents spend more time with peers; (2) adolescent peer groups receive less adult supervision; (3) adolescents begin interacting more with peers of the _____ _____; and (4) peer groups become aware of values of the larger adolescent subculture.

7. Girls from _____ _____ are more likely to leave home after high school than peers.

8. The influences of the peer group serve important social and _____ functions.

9. Whereas peers teach adolescents about social relationships outside the family, adults provide a source of guidance in forming _____ and setting goals.

SEXUAL BEHAVIOR

Certainly, the need to manage juvenile sexuality has confronted every civilization, and our own civilization's track record is . . . suspect. Demographers tell us that, within a very few years, over 50 percent of the births in the U.S. will be illegitimate, [most] to adolescents.

—THE WASHINGTON POST WRITERS GROUP

Few aspects of human behavior changed more in the last century than sexual behavior. Until the 1980s, the popular belief about sex was "They're talking more about it now, but they're not doing anything more about it!" This may have been true years ago, but no longer.

Evidence shows that the forces that traditionally kept the majority of adolescents from engaging in sex are no longer powerful. In her study of female teen magazines, Durham (1998) indicates that not only do magazines contain many articles pertaining to teen sex, but they also support social stereotypes that girls should be sexually subordinate to boys. An argument against such stereotypes can be found in the research of Feiring and associates (2002), who concluded that girls are more likely to report initiating physical sexual aggression than boys. Available data show that U.S. adolescents are becoming sexually active at increasingly earlier ages. Early sexual activity appears to have declined recently, however, probably the result of a growing concern about AIDS and other sexually transmitted diseases. A study conducted by the National Survey of Family Growth (HHS News, 1997a) indicates that, in the current group of 15- to 19-year-olds, the percentage who have had sex is about 50%, down from a peak of 55% several years earlier. Results of studies vary, but the most likely percentage of college sophomores who are no longer virgins is about 75% for both males and females. In their comparison of the sexual risk-taking behaviors of athletes and their nonathletic counterparts, Savage and Holcomb (1999) found that athletes were less likely to have engaged in risk-taking behaviors. They were also less likely to be sexually active. Gender and racial differences also affect odds of sexual risk (Miller & others, 2002).

Answers 6. opposite sex 7. single-parent families 8. psychological 9. values

Stages of Sexuality

Many psychologists believe that human sexuality usually moves from self-involvement (masturbation) to sexual involvement with others. They believe that sexual awareness develops in three steps. Research by scholars from various areas of psychology agree that human sexual development occurs in stages (DeLamater & Friedrich, 2002):

1. Love of one's self (**autosexuality**).
2. Love of members of one's own sex (**homosexuality**).
3. Love of members of the opposite sex (**heterosexuality**).

These stages appear to be natural, although some argue that it is as natural to stay in the second stage as to go on to the third.

In the autosexual stage, the child becomes aware of himself or herself as a source of sexual pleasure and consciously experiments with masturbation. The autosexual stage begins as early as 3 years of age and continues until the child is about 6 or 7, although in some children it lasts for a considerably longer period of time.

When the child enters kindergarten, the homosexual phase comes to the fore (please note that this does not necessarily refer to sexual touching but, rather, to the direction of feelings of love). For most children from the age of 7 to about 13, best friends are usually people of the same sex. Feelings become especially intense between ages 10 and 12, when young people enter puberty and feel a growing need to confide in others. They tend to be more trusting with members of their own sex, who share their experiences. Occasionally these close feelings result in overt sexual behavior (one study found this to be true more than one-third of the time). In most cases, however, it appears that such behavior results from curiosity rather than latent homosexuality of the adult variety.

The great majority of teenagers move into the third stage, heterosexuality, at about 13 or 14 years, with girls preceding boys by about a year. We discuss these three phases in the following sections.

autosexuality
Stage at which the child becomes aware of sexual pleasure and consciously experiments with masturbation.

homosexuality
Love of members of one's own sex.

heterosexuality
Love of members of the opposite sex.

Autosexual Behavior

Masturbation is probably universal to human sexual experience (Halpern et al., 2000; Schwartz, 2002; Wiederman et al., 1996). Although most people still consider it an embarrassing topic, it has always been a recognized aspect of sexuality. Most 4- to 5-year-olds masturbate, are chastised for it, and stop, then start again at an average age of 14. If masturbation is so popular, why has it been considered such a problem?

Although most psychiatrists feel that no intrinsic harm exists in masturbation and believe it to be a normal, healthy way for people to discharge their sexual drive, some teens (mainly boys) feel such a sense of shame, guilt, and fear that they develop the "excessive masturbation" syndrome. In this case, masturbation is practiced even though the child feels very bad about it. These feelings are reinforced by solitude and fantasy, which leads to depression and a debilitating sense of self-condemnation. A recent result of these feelings is a sharp increase in 900 phone sex calls. Some teens are now being treated for an addiction to making 900 calls.

In summary, most psychiatrists argue that masturbation in childhood is not only normal but helpful in forming a positive sexual attitude. It cannot be obsessive at 4, so it should be ignored at that age. However, it can be obsessive at 14, and if the parents suspect this to be the case, they should consult a psychologist.

Homosexual Behavior

The Psychoanalytic Theory of Homosexuality

Freud's **psychoanalytic theory of homosexuality** suggested that, if the child's first sexual feelings about the parent of the opposite sex are strongly punished, the child may identify with the same-sex parent and develop a permanent homosexual orientation. Because researchers have noted many cases in which the father's suppression of the homosexual's Oedipal feelings was not particularly strong, this theory is not held in much regard today.

The Learning Theory of Homosexuality

The **learning theory of homosexuality** offers another explanation: Animals that are low on the mammalian scale follow innate sexual practices. Among the higher animals, humans included, learning is more important than inherited factors. According to this theory, most people learn to be heterosexual, but, for a variety of little-understood reasons, some people learn to be homosexual.

The Biopsychosocial Theory of Homosexuality

No direct proof exists that people become homosexual because of genetic reasons. However, a number of studies (Greenberg & Bailey, 2001; McKnight & Malcolm, 2000) have offered some evidence of genetic predisposition (an inborn tendency). Some theories argue that the fetus's brain reacts to sex hormones during the second through sixth months of gestation in a way that may create such a predisposition. In other words, those who favor a **biopsychosocial theory of homosexuality** suggest that, if the biological predisposition is present and certain psychological and social factors (as yet unknown) are in place, then the contention of many homosexuals that their sexual orientation was not a matter of choice is confirmed. According to Sandra Bem's "exotic becomes erotic theory," genetic inheritance influences temperament. This interacts with a long chain of psychological factors that influence whether the person will be homosexual or heterosexual. Because our current culture strongly favors heterosexuality, most people turn out that way. In another cultural setting, things might be different, he believes. Further support for the idea of genetic predisposition can be found in Bem and associates (2001) and in Dawood and associates (2000).

In general, the mental health of gay, lesbian, and bisexual adolescents is frequently dependent on how they perceive their parents' acceptance of their sexual orientation. Floyd and associates (1999) found that perceived parental acceptance was the best predictor of the youth's overall sense of well-being.

Clearly, some of the stereotypes about homosexuals are untrue and unfair. What generalizations, if any, do you believe can fairly be made about all homosexuals?

AN INFORMED VIEW

Is Homosexuality a Matter of Choice?

In the past, efforts to determine whether there are physical differences between straight and gay men may have been unsuccessful because the strength of the subjects' sexual feelings were not taken into account. Recently, however, researchers at the University of Chicago (ascribe Newswire, 2003) have detected a connection between *strong sexual feelings* in men and the metabolism levels in their brain. Previous testing on rats showed that both the hypothalamus and the neurotransmitter serotonin are strongly connected with sexual activity. Based on this knowledge, the researchers predicted that differences in the hypothalamus may reflect biological differences between homosexual and heterosexual males.

To study these differences, the researchers carefully selected eight exclusively homosexual males and eight exclusively heterosexual males in their 20s and 30s. All men were given Prozac in order to block the entry of serotonin in their brains. A brain scan was then given to each man 90 minutes after he received the drug or placebo to determine how his brain reacted to the lack of serotonin.

It turned out that the brains of heterosexual men have a significantly higher reaction to Prozac. This finding suggests that serotonin does work differently in the brains of men with strong sexual preferences. The research confirms the notion that sexual orientation is related to the physiology of the hypothalamus.

An as yet unpublished study related to the biopsychosocial theory has been carried out by Northwestern University psychologists J. Michael Bailey and Meredith Chivers. Although heterosexual men and gay men can be distinguished on the basis of their erectile responses to pictures of nude men and women, similar research on women has not been conducted until very recently. The researchers showed erotic films to heterosexual, bisexual, and lesbian women. Then the researchers measured genital and subjective arousal and found that women, unlike men, showed the same genital responses to different kinds of erotic stimuli, regardless of their sexual orientation. The films depicted two males, two females, or a male and a female engaging in sexual activity. Nevertheless, the different groups of women in the study responded in similar ways (reported in Benson, 2004b).

Does this fundamental sex difference between sexual arousal patterns in men and women reflect biological differences in the two sexes, or are the differences more likely to be caused by contradictory socialization trends for males and females? This fascinating question has yet to be answered.

There are, however, those who believe that despite this research, homosexuality is a matter of free choice and that those who choose it are behaving in an immoral way: Homosexuals don't have to be that way; they want to. What's your view? Do you think interviewing some gays and lesbians on this question would deepen your understanding?

If you would like to have a more informed opinion on this issue, you might want to read one of the articles on the subject referenced in this chapter (for example, Bem, 1996, 2001; D'Augelli & Patterson, 1995; Freud, 1996).

Heterosexual Behavior

At the beginning of this section, we presented some statistics on teen sexuality that may have surprised you. To get a clearer picture of this situation, you will need to look at the data that a number of other studies have provided on heterosexual teen behavior.

First Coitus

Although sexuality develops throughout life, most people view first intercourse as the key moment in sexual development. When this moment occurs is influenced by numerous factors (Lerner & Simi, 1997). For example, risk behaviors such as drug and alcohol abuse, attending rave parties, and delinquency are often associated with coitus (Ngai et al., 2006). Additionally, Schwartz (2002) found that males and females have considerable levels of sexual exploration before their first coitus.

Early first coitus is highly associated with a number of adverse outcomes. The National Center for Health Statistics found that 22% of girls who had had sex before they turned 15 described their first encounter as "not voluntary," and over one-third stated that their partner had been a male over 18, which constitutes statutory rape in most states (HHS News, 1997b). Brady and Halpern-Fisher (2007)

AN APPLIED VIEW

How to Talk to Teens about Sex (or Anything Else, for That Matter)

Adolescents are more likely to talk to adults who know how to listen—about sex, alcohol, and other important issues. But certain kinds of responses, such as giving too much advice or pretending to have all the answers, have been shown to block the lines of communication.

Effective listening is more than just "not talking." It takes concentration and practice. Following are six communication skills that are useful to anyone who wants to reach adolescents. By the way, these skills can also enhance communication with other adults.

Rephrase the person's comments to show you understand. This is sometimes called reflective listening. *Reflective listening* serves four purposes:

- It assures the person you hear what he or she is saying.
- It persuades the person that you correctly understand what is being said (it is sometimes a good idea to ask if your rephrasing is correct).
- It allows you a chance to reword the person's statements in ways that are less self-destructive. For example, if a person says, "My mother is a stinking drunk!" you can say, "You feel your mother drinks too much." This is better, because the daughter of someone who drinks too much usually can have a better self-image than the daughter of a "stinking drunk."
- It allows the person to "rehear" and reconsider what was said.

Watch the person's face and body language. Often a person will assure you that he or she does not feel sad, but a quivering chin or too-bright eyes will tell you otherwise. A person may deny feeling frightened, but if you put your fingers on his or her wrist, as a caring gesture, you may find that the person has a pounding heart. When words and body language say two different things, always believe the body language.

Give nonverbal support. This may include a smile, a hug, a wink, a pat on the shoulder, nodding your head, making eye contact, or holding the person's hand (or wrist).

Use the right tone of voice for what you are saying. Remember that your voice tone communicates as clearly as your words. Make sure your tone does not come across as sarcastic or all-knowing.

Use encouraging phrases to show your interest and to keep the conversation going. Helpful little phrases, spoken appropriately during pauses in the conversation, can communicate how much you care:

"Oh, really?"
"Tell me more about that."
"Then what happened?"
"That must have made you feel bad."

Remember, if you are judgmental or critical, the person may decide that you just don't understand. You cannot be a good influence on someone who won't talk to you.

---

analyzed survey reports from 275 adolescents and found that both oral and vaginal sex have adverse effects, especially for females.

When do most Americans first experience intercourse? The statistics vary, but all research confirms that this experience occurs at a younger age than it did for previous generations (Gebhardt et al., 2006; Kinsman et al., 1998; Stevens-Simon & Kaplan, 1998). A more recent study of nearly 1,400 sixth graders found that, at the beginning of the school year, 30% had had sexual intercourse, and an additional 5% had done so by the end of the year (Kinsman et al., 1998). From these data, it seems clear that the downward extension of sexual experience is continuing. Table 12.2 offers a national picture for high school students and young adults.

Sexual Abuse

When adolescents are abused, typically it is by someone they know and trust. It is often just a continuation of abuse that started during childhood. The most common type of serious sexual abuse is incest between father and daughter. This type of relationship may last for several years. The daughter is often manipulated into believing it is all her fault and that, if she says anything to anyone, she will be seen as a bad person, one who may even be arrested and jailed. The outcome is an adolescent at greater risk for running away, having eating problems, being a sexual victim, and engaging in substance abuse (Conners, 2001; Whitbeck et al., 2001; Yoder et al., 2002).

A SOCIOCULTURAL VIEW | Adolescent Sexual Activity: A Look at Risk Factors in Three Ehtnic Groups

Perkins and associates (1998) studied the sexual activity of adolescents in three ethnic groups. They were interested in whether there were differences among African Americans, Latinos, and European Americans concerning the effects of risk factors on sexual activity. Examples of risk factors included alcohol use, religiosity, grade point average, and sexual and physical abuse. Perkins and his colleagues found a "relationship between the level of risk and the rate of sexual activity for adolescents, regardless of ethnicity." Heavy alcohol use was the strongest risk factor associated with increased sexual activity for males and females from all ethnic groups. Sexual and physical abuse were also strong predictors of increased sexual activity in females from all ethnic groups. These results suggest that ethnic group is much less important than has been thought. Further, it emphasizes the role of other nonsexual causes for teenage sexual behavior. The results emphasize the need to help eliminate or decrease risk factors in adolescents' lives if we are to ensure their safety.

TABLE 12.2　Avoiding Pregnancy

Most sexually experienced women and their partners use a contraceptive, primarily the pill or condoms.

BY AGE

More than 7 out of 10 sexually active girls age 15 to 17 use contraceptives, a figure that rises to nearly 9 out of 10 young women 20 to 24.

Age	Pill	Condom	Other*	Total (%)
15–17	38	29	5	72
18–19	52	24	8	84
20–24	60	13	15	88

BY RACE AND ETHNICITY

Young Hispanic women age 15 to 19 trail blacks and whites in use of contraceptives.

Race	Pill	Condom	Other*	Total (%)
Hispanic	37	26	2	65
Black	58	17	2	77
White	45	28	8	81

BY INCOME

Seven out of 10 low-income young women age 15 to 19 use contraceptives, as do 8 of 10 higher-income women.

Income Level	Pill	Condom	Other*	Total (%)
Low**	41	27	3	71
High	47	27	9	83

*Other methods include the diaphragm, sponge, spermicide, and IUD.
**Low-income means from 100–199% of the poverty level. For example, a family of four that earned $14,000 to $28,000 in 1992 would be considered low income.
Source: Leeming and associates (1996), *Issues in Adolescent Sexuality.* Needham Heights, MA: Allyn & Bacon.

Most sexual offenses are discussed with a friend or with no one. Very few are reported to parents, police, social workers, or other authorities. It has also been found that the effects of abuse may influence a youth's future relationships. Directly following the experience, children may engage in "acting out" behaviors (for example, truancy, running away, sexual promiscuity), but symptoms may persist for years, and into adulthood (Deblinger et al., 2006; Hussey et al., 2006).

Adolescents not only are the victims of sexual abuse; they also are perpetrators of it (Murphy et al., 2001). Male adolescents and adults are most often behind reported abuses (Salter et al., 2003). Abusive acts also include sexual coercion, in which both males and females bear responsibility (Oswald & Russell, 2006).

Research has led to increased awareness of how to support victims of sexual abuse, including family pressures, reporting systems, legal definitions, and treatment of victims (Malloy et al., 2007). These may help us better understand and intervene, so that victims can receive professional attention earlier, which may reduce the long-term effects of abuse.

Sexuality in the lives of late adolescents and young adults in the beginning of this century is very different from in earlier decades (although perhaps not so different from several centuries ago). What is the relationship between this fact and the problem covered in the next section about sexually transmitted infections? That is a complex question.

Guided Review

10. Some psychologists describe three stages of human sexuality. These include auto-sexuality, _____, and heterosexuality.

11. Currently the three theories that attempt to explain homosexuality include psychoanalytic theory, _____ theory, and the biopsychosocial theory of homosexuality.

12. It is estimated that, by the end of adolescence, more than 80% of the boys and _____% of the girls will have been sexually active.

13. Rather than talking to _____ about sexual abuse, teens choose to talk with friends or tell no one at all.

14. Considering some of the reasons for adolescent sexual activity, it is not surprising that nearly 70% of twelfth-graders report having had _____ _____.

SEXUALLY TRANSMITTED INFECTIONS

sexually transmitted infections (STIs)
Class of infections that are transmitted through sexual behavior.

AIDS (acquired immune deficiency syndrome)
Condition caused by a virus that invades the body's immune system, making it vulnerable to infections and life-threatening illnesses.

In this section, we cover research on AIDS and other infections that are sexually contagious.

AIDS

Not long ago, when people thought about **sexually transmitted infections (STIs)**, gonorrhea came to mind. In the 1970s, it was herpes. Today, **AIDS (acquired immune deficiency syndrome)** causes the most concern (CDC, 2000b).

Answers   10. homosexuality 11. learning 12. 70 13. parents 14. sexual intercourse

First diagnosed in 1979, AIDS quickly approached epidemic proportions. Can you find any data in your local media about the current status of the AIDS epidemic?

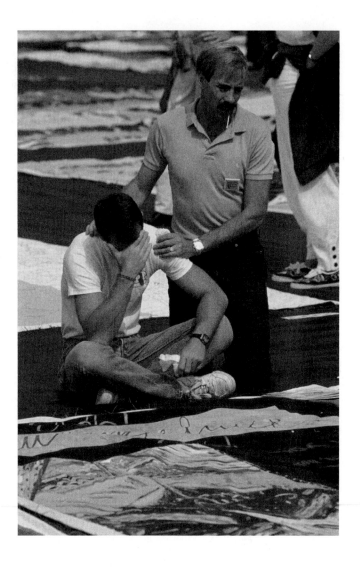

human immunodeficiency virus (HIV)
Virus that leads to AIDS.

AIDS was first diagnosed at Bellevue–New York University Medical Center in 1979 and has quickly approached epidemic proportions. What is known about AIDS is that a virus attacks certain cells of the body's immune system, leaving the person vulnerable to any number of fatal afflictions such as cancer and pneumonia. In addition, the disease can directly infect the brain and spinal cord, causing acute meningitis.

The virus that leads to AIDS—**human immunodeficiency virus (HIV)**—is transmitted through the transfer of substantial amounts of intimate bodily fluids such as blood and semen. The virus is most likely to be transferred through sexual contact, the sharing of hypodermic needles, and, much less likely, blood transfusions (a test for AIDS is now available at blood banks and hospitals). In addition, the virus can be transmitted from an infected mother to an infant during pregnancy, during birth, or through breast feeding. In fact, there were more than 80,000 orphans in the year 2000 in the United States as the result of the effects of AIDS (Children's Defense Fund, 1999). Table 12.3 shows the concentrations of AIDS in each of several age groups, as well as the percentages of cases by race/ethnicity.

In the initial stages of the spread of the disease in this country, HIV has most often been found in certain segments of the population such as male homosexuals and intravenous drug users and, to a much lesser degree, among hemophiliacs. But that is changing. In some Central African countries, where AIDS is thought to have originated, HIV is found equally among men and women throughout the population. After a slow start, large-scale education efforts by grassroots organizations, as

TABLE 12.3	AIDS Cases by Age and Race/Ethnicity				
Age	White	Black	Hispanic	Asian/Pacific Islander	American Indian/ Alaska Native
Under 5	1,011	4,212	1,524	31	25
5–19	1,632	2,865	1,267	51	32
20–29	51,716	46,951	25,878	910	497
30–39	148,406	122,459	62,760	2,376	1,058
40–49	85,040	76,415	32,809	1,509	471
50–59	26,796	21,791	9,823	481	113
60+	10,219	8,027	3,514	188	37

Source: *Center for Disease Control, Surveillance Report,* Vol. 12, No. 1, 2000.

well as by state and federal government agencies, have begun to get these messages out, but the problems remain extremely serious (Shuey et al., 1999).

First, as mentioned, the virus has been identified with a few select groups. If you're not gay or a drug user, you might think you don't have to consider preventive measures. However, a person exposed to HIV may not show any symptoms for as many as 15 years. Further, this same person can expose other people to the virus during this incubation phase. Some people have reacted to this by becoming more particular about their sexual partners. Monogamous relationships were on the rise again during the 1980s, after the "liberated" days of the sexual revolution of the 1960s and 1970s. And as condom use increases, the educational message seems to be getting through. But many still ignore the dangers, and the consequences may be years away.

This may be particularly true among adolescents. Adolescents currently constitute only about 1% of all diagnosed cases of AIDS in the United States (CDC, 2000a). But given the long incubation period and the research findings that suggest that adolescents are not very well informed about AIDS, many researchers think this may be an underestimation. Adolescents are also more prone than the general public to misconceptions and prejudices generated by the frightening new disease.

For example, some adolescents have the misconception that AIDS can be transmitted through casual contact such as kissing or hugging someone with AIDS, or sharing their utensils or bathroom facilities. Such misconceptions unnecessarily increase fear and anxiety in everyone. AIDS prevention efforts aimed at adolescents often have as their main goal the dispelling of such myths (Cohall et al., 2001).

Other Sexually Transmitted Infections

Often pushed from the public eye by the attention focused on HIV and AIDs, other sexually transmitted infections (STIs) have quietly become a "hidden" epidemic in America (Centers for Disease Control and Prevention, 2002). The CDC (Centers for Disease Control and Prevention, 2002) reports that there are more than 65 million people living in America with STIs. Cates (1999) found that there are approximately 15 million new cases of STIs each year, with adolescents accounting for approximately 4 million of these new cases. Many of these people, young and old, are not aware of the symptoms of the diseases or that there are successful treatments for some forms of STIs. The risks and consequences to one's health when untreated can range from mild discomfort to infertility and death.

Some of the more common STIs (other than AIDS) include the following:

chlamydia
Bacterial infection that may cause infertility; now the most common STI, there often are no symptoms.

- *Chlamydial infection.* **Chlamydia** is the most common reported form of STIs and is found among all racial and ethnic groups in the United States. There are 2 million people currently infected, an estimated 3 million new cases are reported each year, and approximately 40% of all cases are young people (Cates, 1999; Centers for Disease Control and Prevention, 2002). Chlamydia is a bacterial infection that often has no symptoms but if untreated can have serious health consequences. Chlamydia rates are the same for men and women. This STI may be one of the most dangerous STIs for women because it is a major cause of infertility in women, it can lead to pelvic inflammatory disease, and women with chlamydia are at higher risk of becoming infected by the HIV virus than are women without chlamydia.

gonorrhea
Well-known venereal infection accounting for between 1.5 and 2 million cases per year.

- *Gonorrhea.* The well-known venereal disease **gonorrhea** infects 650,000 persons per year in the United States (Cates, 1999). Approximately the same number of cases go unreported each year because of lack of information about the disease or a lack of symptoms of the disease in the infected person. Although men and women are infected at equal levels, the highest rates of infection are among adolescents, young adults, and African-Americans (Centers for Disease Control and Prevention, 2002). Gonorrhea showed a 13% increase among adolescents between 1997 and 1999, with the highest rate of infection being among females 15 to 19 and males 20 to 24 years old (Centers for Disease Control and Prevention, 2002). Gonorrhea is caused by bacteria, and the most common symptoms are painful urination and a discharge from the penis or the vagina. Untreated, gonorrhea can lead to pelvic inflammatory disease, infertility, and tubal pregnancies in women (Centers for Disease Control and Prevention, 2002). However, gonorrhea can be successfully treated with antibiotics.

pelvic inflammatory disease (PID)
Infection that often results from chlamydia or gonorrhea and frequently causes prolonged problems, including infertility.

- *Pelvis inflammatory disease.* **Pelvic inflammatory disease (PID)** frequently causes prolonged problems, including infertility. It is usually caused by untreated chlamydia or gonorrhea. These infections spread to the fallopian tubes, resulting in PID. The scarring the infection causes often prevents successful impregnation. More than 1 million new cases per year occur in the United States (*Sexually Transmitted Diseases Handbook,* 1997), with the infection rate highest among teens. Women who are most likely to get it are those who use an intrauterine device for birth control, have multiple sex partners, are teenagers, or have had PID before. PID is so widespread that it causes $2.6 billion in medical costs per year!

genital herpes
Incurable sexually transmitted infection, with about 500,000 new cases every year.

- *Genital herpes.* The **genital herpes** simplex type-2 virus is one of the most common STIs in the United States, and it is incurable. Fleming (1997) reported that one in five Americans is infected with genital herpes, and McQuillan (2000) estimates that the prevalence rates of herpes among 14- to 19-year-olds is 19% the U.S. population. In addition, adolescents and young adults are at high risk for infection, and white teens 12 to 19 years old showed the greatest increase in infection during the 1990s (Fleming and others, 1997). Women are four times as likely than men to be infected with the virus (Centers for Disease Control and Prevention, 2002). The virus is spread during skin-to-skin contact, and the major symptom of genital herpes is an outbreak of genital sores, which can occur as often as once a month. Unlike chlamydia, problems associated with herpes are mainly emotional and social, rather than medical, except for newborns and people with HIV. People with herpes often experience embarrassment and low self-esteem about their bodies.

syphilis
Sexually transmitted infection that presents a great danger in that in its early stage there are no symptoms; if untreated, it can be fatal.

- *Syphilis.* Like gonorrhea, **syphilis** is no longer the killer it was before penicillin. However, this sexually transmitted infection still accounts for 70,000 new

FIGURE 12.1

The relative percentage of new cases of each type of STI in the United States each year.

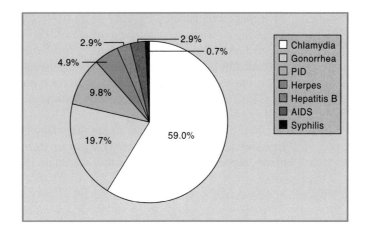

hepatitis B
Viral infection transmitted through sex or shared needles.

cases per year, with men accounting for 50% more of the new cases than women (Cates, 1999; Centers for Disease Control and Prevention, 2002). In addition, African Americans have infection rates for syphilis that are 30 times higher than infection rates for white Americans. Syphilis is caused by bacteria, and the first sign is a chancre ("shan-ker"), a painless open sore that usually shows up on the tip of the penis or around or in the vagina. The disease must be treated with antibiotics or it can be fatal.

• *Hepatitis B.* About [300,000] 120,000 new cases of **hepatitis B** occur each year in the United States (Cates, 1999). This serious viral disease is transmitted through sexual contact and through the sharing of infected needles. Hepatitis B is an incurable disease that attacks the liver and can lead to chronic liver disease, increased risk of HIV infection, and even death (Centers for Disease Control and Prevention, 2002).

A number of other less well-known STDs such as human papillomavirus (HPV), trichomoniasis, bacterial vaginosis, and chancroid are also present within the U.S. population. These STIs are not as widespread as the ones previously listed and have less serious health-related consequences (Centers for Disease Control and Prevention, 2002).

Figure 12.1 depicts the relative percentage of new cases of each type of STI in the United States each year.

Studies have shown that adolescents and young adults are the age group at greatest risk for STI infection because of their multiple sex partners and risky behaviors (CDC, 2002). In addition, certain racial and ethnic segments of the U.S. population are at greater risk for STI infection. The discrepancy in the rate of infection among African-Americans, Native-Americans, Latino-Americans, and European-Americans may be attributed to the lack of prevention and education programs and medical resources available for some of these groups (CDC, 2002).

The AIDS crisis and the STI epidemic have several features in common. On the negative side, misconceptions contribute to both problems. Many young people believe that only promiscuous people get STIs and that only homosexuals get AIDS. Having multiple sex partners does increase the risk of contracting STIs, but most people do not view their sexual behavior, no matter how active, as being promiscuous. Recent research also suggests machismo gets in the way of proper condom use, an effective prevention technique for all STIs. A "real man" doesn't use condoms. And, finally, when people do contract a disease, strong social stigmas make accurate reporting difficult.

On the positive side, the preventive and educational measures are basically the same for AIDS and other STIs: Dispel the myths, increase general awareness and acknowledgment of the problem, and encourage more discriminating sexual practices. Sexual education programs have actually succeeded in reducing the number

Three books that should be of interest to you are (1) Jean Auel's *Clan of the Cave Bear* (1986). New York: Bantam Books. Auel's wonderful imagination and excellent knowledge of anthropology make this book on the beginnings of the human family a winner. (2) Mary Calderone and John Ramsey's *Talking with Your Child about Sex* (1982). New York: Ballantine. This offers a creative interpretation of human sexuality in a family setting. (3) Erich Fromm's *The Art of Loving* (1956). New York: Harper & Row. Perhaps the best book on love ever written!

of teenage pregnancies by 20% since 1991 (National Campaign to Prevent Teen Pregnancy, 2001). Perhaps some of the educational efforts made on behalf of AIDS prevention and treatment will have a helpful effect on the current STI epidemic. Historically the health focus on STIs has been on treatment, typically with antibiotics, but recently the Public Health Service has shifted its focus to prevention for all STIs. So perhaps comprehensive efforts of this kind that emphasize all STIs will prove fruitful.

In summary, it seems safe to say that major changes in adolescent sexual practices have occurred in recent decades. Many of them must be viewed with considerable alarm, especially when we consider the tragic increases in STIs and pregnancy.

Guided Review

15. The nature of our concern about sexually transmitted infections has changed since the spread of AIDS, or _____ _____ _____ syndrome.

16. HIV attacks the body's _____ _____, thus leaving the person vulnerable to a number of fatal afflictions.

17. Other sexually transmitted infections include chlamydia, _____, pelvic inflammatory disease, syphilis, genital herpes, and hepatitis B.

18. Studies show that the age group at greatest risk for sexually transmitted infections is _____.

THE TEENAGE PARENT

"You're pregnant," the doctor said, "and you have some decisions to make. I suggest you don't wait too long to decide what you'll do. You appear to be at about 8 weeks already."

"It can't be true!" I replied. I was trying to convince myself that the clinic doctor was wrong. It wasn't supposed to be like this! I didn't want to be lectured by the doctor. I totally resented him. How could I let myself be seen like this?

I had feared this answer. I suppose I had known the truth all along, but I really didn't want to face it. I didn't want an abortion; that much I was sure of. Besides, where would I get the money?

For ages now, I had been hoping my period would come any day. Now the truth was in the open! I walked out of the office and headed aimlessly down the street. I looked around and saw only ugliness. I thought about my mother and how disappointed she would be. It all hurt so much.

"How could this have happened to me?" I thought. "Good girls don't get pregnant—only the ones who stayed out late and hung around with reckless boys. I wasn't part of that category!

I looked down at my belly and thought about my family. Would they understand? After all, they had plans for my future. They would be destroyed by the news.

Except for the youngest adolescents, birthrates for adolescents have been dropping in recent years. Nevertheless, there is still considerable reason for concern. What are some of the risks faced by teenagers giving birth?

"I'm not a tramp," I said to myself. "Then again, I'm only 16 and who would believe that Ben and I really are in love?"

The feelings of this unmarried girl are all too typical. Each year, about 1 million teenage girls in the United States become pregnant. About half of those pregnancies result in live births; one-third result in abortions; and one-sixth result in miscarriages (Annie Casey Foundation, 1998) (see Table 12.4). Miller and associates (2001) report a series of factors that place some teens at greater risk for pregnancy: poverty, unsafe communities, a single-parent house-hold, a history of sexual abuse, and teenage siblings who are sexually active or are parents.

TABLE 12.4	Teenage Pregnancy Rates Affected by Use of Contraceptives, Women Ages 15–19
Decline in Pregnancies (1995–2002)	24%
Reason	
86%	Improved contraception use (e.g., use of contraceptives, methods of contraception, multiple methods)
14%	Delay in first intercourse
Age-specific influences	
15–17 year-olds	Delays in sexual activity
18–19 year-olds	Improved contraception use

Source: Alan Guttmacher Institute: *U.S. Teen Pregnancy Rates are Down Primarily Because Teens are Using Contraceptives Better,* December 2006.

Guided Review

19. Of the 1 million teenage births in the United States each year, about _____ of these pregnancies result in live birth.

20. Teenagers are at a _____ (greater/less) risk for pregnancy if they live in a single-parent household.

21. Contrary to the stereotype, most teenagers who become pregnant had been in a relationship for at least _____ _____.

Answers

ILLEGAL BEHAVIOR

Although substance abuse and criminal behavior are not necessarily developmental in nature, we include brief sections on them in this chapter because they often play a role in other aspects of development during adolescence. For the most part, that role clearly is negative.

Substance Abuse

It is difficult to say precisely how widespread substance abuse is. Studies differ from year to year, from region to region, and, disappointingly, from one another (even when year and region are the same). Nevertheless, there have been some sound studies.

In its recent study of 68,000 teenagers, the Department of Health and Human Services (2004) looked at drug and cigarette use and mental health. Figures 12.2 and 12.3 summarize the department's findings on drug use.

Recent research points to some alarming evidence that excessive alcohol use during one's teen years can impair later brain functioning (Cleveland & Wiebe, 2003). Because teenagers' brains continue to develop throughout adolescence, the

FIGURE 12.2

Past month illicit drug use among youths aged 12 to 17, by race/ethnicity, 2002.

Source: Substance Abuse & Mental Health Administration (2003). *Data on Drug Use,* 13.

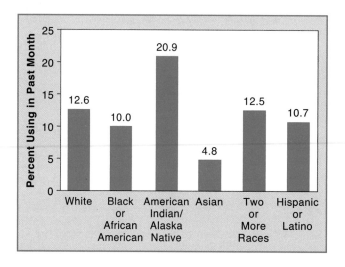

FIGURE 12.3

Annual numbers of new users of ecstasy, LSD, and PCP, 1965–2001.

Source: Substance Abuse and Mental Health Administration (2003). p. 13.

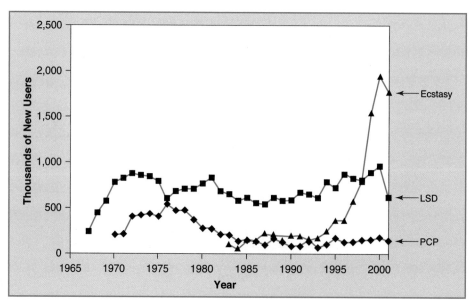

FIGURE 12.4

Lifetime cigarette use among youths aged 12 to 17, by gender, 1965–2002.

Source: Substance Abuse and Mental Health Administration (2003), p. 26.

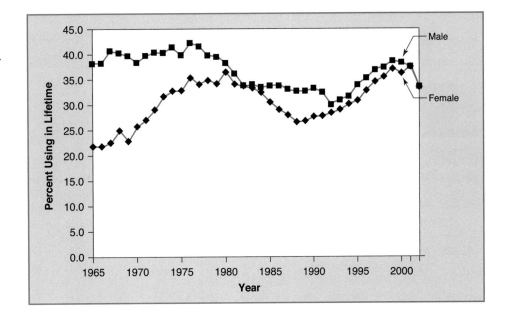

Two excellent books on this topic are: (1) Cohen and Cohen's *A Six-Pack and a Fake I.D.: Teens Look at the Drinking Question* (1986). New York: M. Evans. According to the authors of this book, the decision to drink or not to drink is personal rather than moral. (2) Harris's *Drugged Athletes: The Crisis in American Sports* (1987). New York: Four Winds Press. Harris provides an overview and discusses specific problems of drugs in sports at all levels.

toxic effects of alcohol abuse can damage their memories, learning abilities, and language skills. In another study, teenagers who begin drinking before 14 are three times more likely to injure themselves while drinking than those who begin drinking after 21. These injuries include falls, burns, unintentional wounds, and automobile accidents (Hingson et al., 2000) Figure 12.4 indicates that use of cigarettes has not changed much in general since 1965, although girls now smoke as much as boys.

Not surprisingly, school context influences the prevalence of smoking and drinking among adolescents (Cleveland & Wiebe, 2003). If a school has many substance-using students, then other students are more likely to imitate the negative actions of their peers. Use of new tobacco products such as kreteks (5.8%) and bidis (5.0%) has become popular among high school students. The overall prevalence of tobacco use was 34.8% among high schoolers, with males using all forms of tobacco more than females (CDC, 2000b; McCool et al., 2001).

The CDC (2000b, 2001) predicts that, if this pattern of tobacco use continues, an estimated 5 million Americans who were 18 years old or younger in 1995 could suffer from a smoking-related illness that could cause premature death.

Criminal Behavior

Although the national crime rate for individuals has remained level for the last three years, the amount of gang violence has increased by more than 50% (FBI, 2003). Some believe that the recent rise in gang homicide is a result of cities' cutting back on gang prevention and enforcement programs (Fox, 2003). Without these programs in place, today's youth may view the elements of gang life as attractive, without knowing about the bloodshed that occurred when gang participation peaked 10 years ago. Furthermore, the level of gang violence may increase as more influential gang leaders return from their prison sentences and reestablish their power. To stop the resurgence of gang violence, many criminologists propose that cities must reinvest in prevention programs such as boys and girls clubs and youth athletic leagues, as well as to restore the strength of police antigang units.

Gangs often offer youths the fulfillment of basic needs (Flannery, 1998; Hasan, 1998; Short, 2001). Some of their functions clearly coincide with those of the larger society. Gangs typically provide protection, recognition of the desire to feel wanted, and rites of passage that mark achievement, status, and acceptance, such as the initiation rite of a potential gang member.

AN INFORMED VIEW

Youth Violence

The problem of youth violence has been receiving increasing attention over the past several years. Since 1994, homicide arrests of young people have decreased, mostly because of an overall decline in the use of firearms. Researchers from the U.S. Department of the Surgeon General (2001), however, in a major study of adolescent violence, have found that arrest rates for aggravated assault are almost 70% higher today than they were in 1983. Recent tragedies involving young people who commit violent crimes, such as the Columbine high school shootings in Colorado, have caused parents, teachers, and researchers to ask why these incidents are occurring and what can be done to prevent them.

Researchers have identified two major paths of youth violence that they call early-onset and late-onset trajectories. The **early-onset trajectory** refers to children who commit their first violent crime before puberty (about age 13); the **late-onset trajectory** begins after puberty. Early-onset youngsters generally commit more serious crimes for a longer time than do late-onset youths, sometimes continuing this pattern into adulthood. However, the majority of youth violence is late onset and stops before the adult stage.

Many factors affect how likely a young person is to engage in violent acts. These risk factors are found in family interactions as well as in peer and school influences. During childhood, risk factors include family and individual characteristics, such as poverty, antisocial parents, or aggressive behavior. During adolescence, however, these risk factors become more peer-oriented, including associations with delinquent friends or gang membership.

As you might expect, researchers are also concerned with finding out which factors might protect young people from becoming perpetrators of violent crime. Again, these factors exist across a number of different areas, such as individual characteristics, family, and peer groups. Examples of these protective factors include outgoing behaviors, high IQ, and commitment to school.

Many are quick to blame the occurrence of youth violence on the changing American family, including working mothers and nontraditional households. Others might say that youth aggression results from increased portrayals of violence in the media, such as on television, in movies, and in song lyrics. Do you think that this is the case? Is youth violence the result of these social changes?

---

early-onset trajectory
Refers to criminal behavior that begins before puberty.

late-onset trajectory
Refers to criminal behavior that begins after puberty.

The gang provides many adolescents with a structured life they never had at home. What makes the gang particularly cohesive is its function as a family substitute for adolescents whose strong dependency needs are displaced onto the peer group. The gang becomes a family to its members.

The formation of juvenile gangs typically follows a sudden increase in this country of new ethnic groups due to immigration. The children of new immigrants have a difficult time breaking through cultural barriers such as a new language and racism. Perceiving their prospects of succeeding in the new society as bleak, some of these children form gangs, which provide the structure and security discussed but also serve as an outlet to attack the society that seemingly will not accept them. In times past, these gangs were composed of Jewish-, Irish-, and Italian-Americans. Today's gangs are frequently formed by Latinos, Asian-Americans, and African-Americans. The gang becomes a vehicle for tearing its members away from the main social structures and authorities, in particular the family and school.

As early as the early 1960s, Leonard Bernstein's *West Side Story* signaled society's concern that glib sociological excuses would only worsen the handling of behavior disorders. Public opinion and public institutions are turning back to a punishment model.

—JOHN MEEKS

America's youth used to own the most guns. However, it has recently been determined that those 65 years of age and older are more likely to own guns in America (AARP, 2004). The rate of gun of ownership in this age bracket has been increasing since the late 1990s, but it wasn't until 2002 that the margin for older citizens owning guns passed their younger counterparts. One possible explanation of this reversal is that younger Americans are buying fewer guns.

To what can we attribute the appeal of gang membership? Numerous studies have pointed to factors such as financial trouble, family involvement in a gang, drug and alcohol use, and social pressures (Lauber et al., 2005). Violence has also been attributed to neglect and lack of physical affection (Field, 2002). Fortunately, research shows parenting practices can reduce children's involvement with gangs (Walker-Barnes & Mason, 2004). In addition, programs and interventions help reduce violence and raise awareness in schools and communities (Wright & Fitzpatrick, 2006).

Guided Review

22. Recent research indicates that excessive alcohol use during one's teen years can impair later _____ functioning.

23. Some of the functions of a gang include protection, recognition of desire to feel wanted, rites of passage that mark _____, status, and acceptance.

24. Gangs can be cohesive because of their function as a _____ _____ for adolescents with strong dependency needs.

25. Gangs can become a vehicle for tearing their members away from the main _____ _____ of society.

Answers

22. brain 23. achievement 24. family substitute 25. social structures

CONCLUSION & SUMMARY

For each of the aspects of social interaction reviewed in this chapter—family interactions, peer relations, sexual behavior, sexually transmitted infections, teenage parenthood, criminal behavior—all adolescents must deal with one consistent trend: fast-paced change. Some of this change derives from ground swells in today's society, and some results from the nature of adolescence itself. Here again we see the biopsychosocial model demonstrated.

There are many changes going on in the American family. Many functions formerly fulfilled by the family are now the province of other agencies. The stress of divorce has a variety of outcomes, many of which we are learning to understand and deal with. The nurturing parenting style appears to promote many desirable traits.

Interactions among teenage peers change with each generation. Gang behavior is a growing threat to healthy development, yet perhaps nothing has had a more resounding impact on adolescent life than the recent changes in our attitudes toward sexuality. The four areas of greatest change have been in homosexuality, sexually transmitted infections (including AIDS), the earlier and more widespread participation in sex by teenage females, and the increase in pregnancy and childbearing among younger teenagers.

Some observers have suggested that the biggest problem facing adolescents today, and one intertwined with those just listed, is the difficulty in knowing when childhood and youth have ended and adulthood has begun. When the societal lines between these stages of development are blurred, youths cannot be blamed for not knowing how to behave. We will look into this phenomenon more fully in Chapter 13.

As to a comprehensive definition of adolescence (the goal of this section of the book), we have seen that only by including biological, psychological (both cognitive and affective), and social factors can we begin to define this complex stage of life. We have reviewed numerous such factors: the sequence of physiological changes that occur in virtually every teen's body as well as the timing of those changes; the remarkable advances made in cognitive abilities; the social and emotional alterations that occur in relations with family, peers, and the larger society. Together these provide markers for the onset of the adolescent period. You should be aware, however, that a really adequate biopsychosocial definition cannot be presented in two chapters of a book, or even in one whole book. We learn more about this complex subject every day, and so our definition must be considered still in process.

What changes have occurred to American families and their roles in adolescent life in recent years?

- American families have lost five of their six main functions; the only remaining one is providing affection for family members.

- A number of effects of divorce pertain only to adolescents.
- There are four recognized parenting styles: authoritarian, permissive, authoritative, and nurturing.

What is the nature of peer relations during the teen years?

- Peer groups provide adolescents with a source of social activities and support, as well as an easy entry into opposite-sex friendships.
- The biological, psychological, cognitive, and social changes of adolescence affect the development of a teenager's peer relationships.
- Peer groups serve to control aggressive impulses, encourage independence, improve social skills, develop reasoning abilities, and form attitudes toward sexuality and sexual behavior. They may also strengthen moral judgment and values and improve self-esteem.
- Peer groups also aid in the development of self-concept and allow an adolescent to try out a new identity.

How do teens deal with sexual relations?

- Many teenagers are becoming sexually active at increasingly younger ages.
- Sexuality develops in three stages, from love of self to love of members of the same gender to love of members of the opposite gender.
- Masturbation is believed to be a harmless and universal form of human sexual expression.

- Homosexual behavior has been surrounded by many myths throughout history.
- Several theories suggest different origins of homosexual orientation: psychoanalytic, learning, and biopsychosocial.
- Many researchers now believe that homosexual orientation may already be set by adolescence.
- Many teens still obtain a great deal of information and misinformation about sex from their peers.
- Youths from stable family environments are less likely to engage in premarital sexual relations.
- Effective listening skills are essential for parents who wish to maintain good communication with their adolescents.
- Teenagers misuse sex for many non-sexual reasons, including a search for affection, rebellion against parents, venting anger, and alleviating boredom.
- Many adolescent runaways and prostitutes are the products of sexual abuse, often by someone they know, a family member, or a parent.

What new information do we have about sexually transmitted infections?

- Today a high prevalence of sexually transmitted infections (STIs) is found in sexually active adolescents.
- AIDS (acquired immune deficiency syndrome) causes the most concern, because it is currently incurable and fatal. As yet, it is not very common in adolescents, but because it usually lies dormant for 10 to 15 years, it is a cause for great concern.

- Other STIs that affect adolescents are increasing in epidemic proportions, including chlamydia, gonorrhea, genital herpes, syphilis, and hepatitis B.
- In spite of increased availability and information about contraceptive methods, many teenagers continue to engage in unprotected sex.

How is the modern teenage parent dealing with the stresses that parenthood entails?

- Except for the youngest adolescents, birthrates for adolescents have been dropping in recent years. With rare exceptions, this situation causes a lot of heartache for the youngest teenage parents, their parents, and their child.
- It has been found that teens are at a greater risk if they live in poverty, unsafe communities, a single-parent household, or have a history of sexual abuse.

What recent information do we have on adolescent illegal behavior?

- Drug and alcohol abuse is still prevalent among teens. Tobacco use is on the rise again as is use of marijuana, cocaine, and LSD.
- Gangs typically have a high degree of cohesion and organization, a consistent set of norms, clearly defined leaders, and coherent organization for warfare.
- Gangs have become much more violent in the past decade, probably in part as a response to increased drug trafficking.

KEY TERMS

AIDS (acquired immune deficiency syndrome)
authoritarian parenting
authoritative parenting
autosexuality
biopsychosocial theory of homosexuality
chlamydia
crowds

early-onset trajectory
genital herpes
gonorrhea
hepatitis B
heterosexuality
homosexuality
human immunodeficiency virus (HIV)
late-onset trajectory

learning theory of homosexuality
nurturing parenting style
pelvic inflammatory disease (PID)
permissive parenting
psychoanalytic theory of homosexuality
sexually transmitted infections (STIs)
subculture
syphilis

WHAT DO YOU THINK?

1. Do you think that your adolescent peer group followed the developmental patterns described in this chapter?

2. What are some of the most important effects that your teenage peer group had on your life?

3. Do you agree with the theorists who claim that there are three stages in the development of love and sexuality and that this development is natural?

4. In what ways do you believe family life in the United States will be different in 50 years from the ways it exists today?

5. If you were the mayor of a medium-size city, what actions would you take to try to reduce the incidence of sexually transmitted infections?

6. A number of large, urban high schools are creating day-care facilities for the babies and children of

high school students. Do you think public schools should be providing these services? What services, if any, should junior and senior high schools provide to teenage parents?

7. In what cases should juvenile offenders be tried as adults? Should they always be treated as adults? Should they be treated differently because of their age? What things need to be considered?

CHAPTER REVIEW TEST

1. **Brown (1990) states that the peer group can change in four ways during adolescence: adolescents spend more time with peers; they receive less adult supervision; they interact more with peers of the opposite sex; and they**
   a. interact with peers in a work setting.
   b. become sexually active.
   c. begin to identify with certain crowds.
   d. interact more with peers in school and service activities.

2. **Most family researchers have agreed that the three styles of parenting are**
   a. authoritarian, permissive, and devoted.
   b. permissive, aggressive, and impassive.
   c. authoritarian, authoritative, and permissive.
   d. aggressive, impassive, and devoted.

3. **What reason is cited in the text for why there may be a decline in early sexual activity?**
   a. concern about AIDS and other STIs
   b. prevailing conservative attitudes
   c. more people devoting time to making money
   d. increasing influence of religion

4. **The first stage of sexuality**
   a. is heterosexuality.
   b. is homosexuality.
   c. is autosexuality.
   d. depends on the individual.

5. **Parents who practice a nurturing parenting style are**
   a. interested in their child's behavior but seldom prescribe rules, relying instead on modeling and family discussions to instill a well-defined set of values.
   b. controlling but loving in guiding their children through development.
   c. nurturing but providing little structure in the family.
   d. nurturing yet strictly controlling of the way in which the family functions.

6. **The genetic theory on homosexuality claims that**
   a. people learn to be homosexual.
   b. as children homosexuals identified with the same-sex parent.
   c. persons born with a predisposition toward homosexuality can be influenced by the environment to either select or avoid homosexuality.
   d. many homosexuals are in denial about their genetically predisposed orientation.

7. **Although he has a girlfriend, Steve wants to prove to his friends that he can "score" with a number of different girls in school. Steve's nonsexual motive for sex is to**
   a. get affection.
   b. confirm his masculinity.
   c. ensure the fidelity of his girlfriend.
   d. obtain greater self-esteem.

8. **A female adolescent who "acts out" by running away, engaging in sexual promiscuity, or damaging her school performance may be a victim of**
   a. drug abuse.
   b. peer pressure.
   c. extreme loneliness.
   d. sexual abuse.

9. **A recent 6% decline in AIDS has been attributed to**
   a. safe sex.
   b. powerful new drugs.
   c. better practices.
   d. none of these.

10. **Intravenous drug users, homosexual men, and inner-city heterosexuals are groups most at risk for contracting**
    a. syphilis.
    b. genital herpes.
    c. hepatitis B.
    d. gonorrhea.

11. **Each year in the United States approximately _____ teenage girls become pregnant.**
    a. 25,000
    b. 250,000
    c. 500,000
    d. 1,000,000

12. **Sara is an African-American teenager who grew up in a poor, single-parent home and has low occupational aspirations. Sara fits the profile of a**
    a. drug abuser.
    b. gang member.
    c. pregnant teenager.
    d. domestic abuse victim.

13. **Risk factors that predict teenage pregnancy are**
    a. early school failure.
    b. early behavior problems.

    c. both a and b
    d. neither a nor b

14. **Factors that affect teenage pregnancy include**
    a. poverty.
    b. a history of sexual abuse.
    c. teenage siblings who are sexually active.
    d. all of these.

15. **John joins a gang because it serves as a pseudo-family for him. Most likely, John has strong _____ needs that are being displaced onto the peer group.**
    a. dependency
    b. friendship
    c. financial
    d. All of the answers are correct.

16. **Recent research indicates that gangs have which of these characteristics?**
    a. They possess a consistent set of norms and expectations that are understood by all gang members.
    b. Members have lower expectations of success than do nonmembers.
    c. Members are as likely to have divorced parents as are nonmembers.
    d. Members are more likely to score high on IQ tests than are nonmembers.

Answers

1. c 2. c 3. a 4. c 5. a 6. c 7. b 8. d 9. b 10. c 11. d 12. d 13. c 14. d 15. d 16. a

PHYSICAL AND COGNITIVE DEVELOPMENT IN EARLY ADULTHOOD

13
chapter

Chapter Outline

Chapter Objectives

After reading this chapter you should be able to answer the following questions.

- How are American youths being initiated into adulthood today?

- What are the significant factors affecting physical development in early adulthood?

- How does cognition change during the early adult years?

- What patterns of work typify young adults today?

Yudia cannot believe how rapidly her feelings keep changing. One moment she is curious and excited; the next, nervous and afraid. Tonight begins her *igubi,* the rite that celebrates her induction into adulthood. Yudia has longed for this day most of her 11 years, but now she wonders if she really wants the responsibilities of a grown-up.

Though it seems much longer, only a week has passed since the excruciating beginning of her initiation. The memory of it is already dimming: the bright fire, her women relatives pinning her down on the table, her grandmother placing a thin sharp stone against her vulva, the searing pain.

The women had held and consoled her, empathizing fully with her feelings. Each had been through the same agony. For them, too, it occurred shortly after their first menstruation. They had explained to her that this was just the beginning of the suffering she must learn to endure as an adult woman. All during the past week, they had been teaching her—about the pain her husband would sometimes cause her, about the difficulties of pregnancy and childbirth, about the many hardships she must bear stoically, for she is Kaguru, and all Kaguru women accept their lot in life without complaint.

It has been a hard week, but tonight the pleasure of the *igubi* will help her forget her wound. There will be singing, dancing, and strong beer to drink. The ceremony, with its movingly symbolic songs, will go on for two days and nights. Only the women of this Tanzanian village will participate, intoning the time-honored phrases that will remind Yudia all her life of her adult duties.

In a large hut less than a mile from the village, Yudia's male cousin Mateya and seven other 13-year-old Kaguru boys huddle close, even though the temperature in the closely thatched enclosure is a stifling 110°. Rivulets of sweat flow from their bodies and flies dot their arms, backs, and legs. They no longer pay attention to the flies or the vivid slashes of white, brown, and black clay adorning all their faces. Their thoughts are dominated by a single fear: Will they cry out when the elder's sharpened stone begins to separate the tender foreskin from their penises? Each dreams of impressing his father, who will be watching, by smiling throughout the horrible ordeal.

Three months of instruction and testing have brought the young men to this point. They have learned many things together: how to spear their own food, how to tend their tiny gardens, how to inseminate their future wives, and most important, how to rely on themselves when in danger.

The last three months have been exhausting. The boys have been through many trials. In some, they had to prove they could work together; in others, their skill in self-preservation was tested. For most of them, being out of contact with their mothers was the hardest part. They have not seen any of the female members of their families since they started their training. Unlike Yudia's initiation, which is

What are some of the reasons that initiation into adulthood differs so greatly in various parts of the world?

designed to draw her closer to the adult women of the tribe, Mateya's initiation is designed to remove him from the influence of the females and to align him with the adult men.

Now it is evening. Mateya is the third to be led out to the circle of firelight. Wide-eyed, he witnesses an eerie scene. His male relatives are dancing in a circle around him, chanting the unchanging songs. The grim-faced elder holds the carved ceremonial knife. Asked if he wishes to go on, the boy nods yes. Abruptly the ritual begins: The hands of the men hold him tight; the cold knife tip touches his penis; a shockingly sharp pain sears his loins; he is surprised to hear a piercing scream; then, filled with shame, he realizes it comes from him.

Thus far, Yudia's and Mateya's initiations have been different. Mateya's has been longer than Yudia's. She is being brought even closer to the women who have raised them both, but Mateya must now align himself with the men.

The initiations are similar, though, in that both youths have experienced severe physical pain. In both cases, the operations were meant to sensitize them to the vastly greater role sex will now play in their lives. Furthermore, their mutilations made them recognizable to all as adults of the Kaguru tribe.

At this "coming out" ceremony, males and females also receive new names, usually those of close ancestors. This illustrates the continuity of the society. The beliefs of the tribe are preserved in the continuous flow from infant to child to adult to elder to deceased and to newborn baby again. When all is done, Yudia and Mateya can have no doubt that they have passed from childhood to adulthood.

INITIATION INTO ADULTHOOD

You grow up the day you have your first real laugh—at yourself.

—ETHEL BARRYMORE

The horrors of the college fraternity initiation have been softened by legal restrictions and by more humane attitudes. Nevertheless, most of us have heard of cases of maimings and even deaths of young men who have been put through **hazing,** the initiation rite that precedes full acceptance into fraternity membership. Hazing continues to exist not only in fraternities but among athletes and school leaders as well (Campos, Poulos, & Sipple, 2005).

hazing
The practice of initiating individuals into group membership through arduous and demeaning tasks.

Why do some people, and the groups they wish to be associated with, seem to enjoy holding initiation rites so much? And why are so many adolescents, many of them otherwise highly intelligent and reasonable, willing and eager to endure such pain? Is it simply because they want to join the group, to feel that they belong? There seems to be more to it than that. Throughout the world, adolescents readily engage in such activities because they seem to want to be tested, to prove to themselves that they have achieved the adult virtues of courage, independence, and self-control. And the adults seem to agree that adolescents should prove they have attained these traits before being admitted to the "club of maturity."

The Transition to Adulthood in the United States

How are youths inducted into adulthood in the United States? Whereas a physical experience, as described in the opening vignette, makes the transition painfully clear, Western initiation rites have generally become social or secular in nature. Are such initiation rites adequate? Changing times bring changes in priorities, and while young adults may have more opportunities than in the past, they often have less structure to guide them in their pursuits.

This is not to say that Americans have no activities that signal the passage to maturity. We have a number of types of activities, which usually happen at various stages and ages of adolescence. Here is a list of the types and some examples of each:

Religious

Bar mitzvah or bat mitzvah

Confirmation

Participating in a ceremony, such as reading from the Bible

Physical

Menarche (first menstruation)

Nocturnal emissions (male "wet dreams")

First sexual encounter

Beginning to shave

Social

"Sweet Sixteen" or debutante parties

Going to the senior prom

Joining a gang, fraternity, or sorority

Being chosen as a member of a sports team

Moving away from one's family and relatives

Joining the armed forces

Getting married

Becoming a parent

Voting for the first time

Educational

Getting a driver's license

Graduating from high school

Going away to college

Economic

Getting a checking or credit card account

Buying a first car

Getting a first job

This list offers a good example of the biopsychosocial approach. Some of the items are mainly biological (menarche), some psychological (going away to college), and some social (getting married). Which activities help in the passage from adolescence to adulthood? How might we improve this passage? In this and Chapter 14, we look at the developmental trends and needs of young adults, which will help us to better answer these important questions.

Implications of the Lack of an Initiation Ceremony

There is increasing evidence for the existence of a maturity status called "adultoid" (Dacey & Kenny, 1997; Galambos and Tilton-Weaver, 2000) or "emerging adulthood" (Arnett, 2000). Each of these terms refers to a time period before long-term adult identities are formed. Emerging adulthood is typically noted between ages

AN APPLIED VIEW

The Components of Maturity

Think of the woman and the man who are the most mature persons you know—people with whom you are personally familiar or people who are famous. Then ask yourself, "Why do I think these people are so much more mature than others?" In the spaces to the right, for both the male and the female, create a list of the characteristics that seem to distinguish them in their maturity.

How much do the lists differ? Is male maturity significantly different from female maturity? Which of the two people is older? Which of the two do you admire more? Which of the two are you more likely to want to imitate? Were you able to think of many candidates for this title of "most mature adult," or was it difficult to think of anyone? Are either or both of the people you picked professionals? Are either or both of these persons popular with their own peer group? What is the significance of your answers to you?

Female	Male
1.	1.
2.	2.
3.	3.
4.	4.
5.	5.
6.	6.
7.	7.
8.	8.
9.	9.
10.	10.

18 and 25 (Arnett, 2000). A level of (or lack of) maturity, sometimes marked by rebellious, problem behavior, is evident as young adults try on different identities. However, researchers Hagan and Foster (2005) argue that delinquency is a developmental phase and that attention to the emotions specific to that period can lead to fewer related problems in adulthood.

In the 1960s and early 1970s, American youths sought to establish their identities by imitating the very rituals of the preindustrial tribes described earlier in this chapter. Known as "hippies" and "flower children," they attempted to return to a simpler life. Many of them returned to the wilderness, living on farms and communes away from the large cities in which they were brought up. Many totally rejected the cultural values of their parents. The most famous symbol of their counterculture was the Woodstock musical marathon in 1969. With its loud, throbbing music, nudity, and widespread use of drugs, the event was similar to many primitive tribal rites, yet these self-designed initiation rites also seem to be unsuccessful as passages to maturity. Most of the communes and other organizations of the youth movement of the 1960s have since failed.

Organized sport is another attempt to initiate young adults into American life. The emphasis on athletic ability has much in common with the arduous tasks given to tribal youths. In particular, we can see a parallel in the efforts by parents to get their children to excel in athletics. Fathers (and often mothers) are seen exhorting the players to try harder, to fight bravely, and when hurt to "tough it out" and not cry (Malcolm, 2006).

Thus, in delinquency, the counterculture, and sports, we see evidence that members of several age groups today yearn for the establishment of some sort of initiation rite. Adolescents and adults alike seem to realize that something more is needed to provide assistance in this difficult transitional period. But what?

Traditional initiation rites are inappropriate for American youths. In preindustrial societies, individual status was decided by tribe. Social scientists call this an *ascribed identity*. The successes or failures of each tribe determined the prestige of its members. Family background and individual effort usually made little difference. In earlier times in the United States, the family was the prime source of

Sports teach coordination, cooperation, fair competition, and other skills needed by adults. Can you think of ways that sports might serve as initiation rites?

status. Few children of the poor became merchants, doctors, or lawyers. Today, personal effort and early commitment to a career path play a far greater role in an individual's economic and social success. This is called an *achieved identity* (see Chapter 11). For this reason (and others), preindustrial customs are not compatible with Western lives today.

Guided Review

1. Rites of passage use _____ to capture elements of adult life that have been denied youths and are now accessible to them as they are initiated into adulthood.

2. In the United States today, initiation activities occur in religious, _____, social, educational, and _____ settings.

3. A level of (or lack of) maturity, sometimes marked by rebellious, problem behavior, is evident as young adults try on different identities in _____ _____.

4. In _____, counterculture, and sports we see evidence that adolescents yearn for the establishment of some form of initiation rite.

PHYSICAL DEVELOPMENT

Psychologist Malcolm Knowles (1989) has stated:

> As I see it, there are four definitions of "adult." First, the biological definition: We become adult biologically when we reach the age at which we can reproduce. . . . Second, the legal definition: We become adult legally when

Answers   1. rituals 2. sexual, economic 3. emerging adulthood 4. delinquency

You might enjoy a book by Maya Angelou on this subject: *I Know Why the Caged Bird Sings* (1969). New York: Random House. Ms. Angelou recounts her childhood in rural Arkansas. Her strength and resilience model the building of a strong personal and cultural identity.

we reach the age at which the law says we can vote, get a driver's license, marry without consent. . . . Third, the social definition: We become adult socially when we start performing adult roles. . . . Finally, the psychological definition: We become adult psychologically when we arrive at a self-concept of being responsible for our own lives, of being self-directing. From the viewpoint of learning, it is the psychological definition that is most crucial.

Let us begin our exploration of young adulthood with a consideration of Knowles's first criterion, physical development. We address three main questions about physical development in this section: When is peak development reached? What is organ reserve? What are the effects of lifestyle?

The Peak Is Reached

Early adulthood is the life period during which physical changes slow down. Table 13.1 provides some basic examples of physical development in early adulthood.

In sports, young adults are in their prime condition in terms of speed and strength. A healthy individual can continue to partake in less strenuous sports for years. As the aging process continues, however, the individual will realize a loss

TABLE 13.1	Summary of Physical Development in Early Adulthood

HEIGHT
Female: maximum height reached at age 18.
Male: maximum height reached at age 20.

WEIGHT (AGE 20–30)
Female: 14-pound weight gain and increase in body fat.
Male: 15-pound weight gain.

MUSCLE STRUCTURE AND INTERNAL ORGANS
From 19–26: Internal organs attain greatest physical potential. The young adult is in prime condition as far as speed and strength are concerned.
After 26: Body slowing process begins. Spinal disks settle, causing decrease in height. Fatty tissue increases, causing increase in weight. Muscle strength decreases. Reaction times level off and stabilize. Cardiac output declines.

SENSORY FUNCTION CHANGES
The process of losing eye lens flexibility begins as early as age 10 and continues until age 30. This loss results in difficulty focusing on close objects.
During early adulthood, women can detect higher-pitched sounds than men.

NERVOUS SYSTEM
The brain continues to increase in weight and reaches its maximum potential by the adult years.

Source: U.S. Census Bureau, 1996.

of the energy and strength felt in adolescence. Early adulthood is also the time when the efficiency of most bodily functions begins to decline. For example, cardiac output and vital capacity start to decrease.

Organ Reserve

organ reserve
That part of the total capacity of our body's organs that we do not normally need to use.

Organ reserve refers to that part of the total capacity of our body's organs that we do not normally need to use. Our body is designed to do much more than it is usually called upon to do. Much of our capacity is held on reserve. As we get older, these reserves grow smaller. The peak performance capacity of each of our organs (and muscles, bone, and so on) declines. A 50-year-old man can fish all day with his 25-year-old son and can usually take a long walk with him without becoming exhausted, but he has no chance at all of winning a footrace against him.

This is why people are aware of little decline during the early adult years and often do not experience a sharp decline in most of their everyday activities even into middle age. Our organ reserves are diminishing, but we are unaware of it because we call on them so seldom.

Of course, some individuals regularly try to use the total capacity of their organ reserves. Professional athletes are an example. Here again we see the biopsychosocial model in action. Biology sets the limits, but psychological factors (for example, personal pride) and social factors (for instance, the cheering crowd) determine whether the person "gives it her all."

The Effect of Lifestyle on Health

Young adults are healthier than older adults in just about every way. All the body's systems reach peak functioning at this age. Less illness occurs, too. For example, young adults have fewer hospitalizations and visits to the doctor's office than older adults, and those that do occur are caused mainly by injuries. According to the Centers for Disease Control (CDC) (2004), there are approximately one and a half times fewer reported AIDS cases during young adulthood than in middle adulthood. Non-Hispanic whites and non-Hispanic blacks make up more than half these reported cases. (It is important to note that, although most AIDS diagnoses are made 8–12 years after infection, the majority of diagnoses are made in individuals over age 35.)

Good health is clearly related to factors such as genetics, age, and the medical treatment locally available. But these factors are generally beyond the control of the individual. Increasingly, people are beginning to realize that their style of life plays an enormous role in their own health.

The impact of lifestyle on health is dramatically illustrated by the observations in the book *The Healing Brain* (Ornstein & Sobel, 1987). These researchers determined that the miraculous technological gains in medicine over the last 100 years have not had as great an impact on health as one might think. It is true that at birth we can expect many more years of life than people could a century ago. However, a person who has reached the age of 45 today has a life expectancy of only a couple years more than the person who had reached 45 years of age 100 years ago, in spite of all the money and effort now spent on medicine after that age.

As a counterexample, Ornstein and Sobel offer the people of Nevada and Utah, two states and populations that are similar in geography, education, income, and availability of medical treatment, yet Nevada's death rate is 40% higher than Utah's. Utah is largely composed of Mormons who live a relatively quiet and stable lifestyle, including very low incidences of smoking and drinking. In Nevada, people drink and smoke much more heavily, and it shows. The rates of cirrhosis of the liver and lung cancer are 100% to 600% higher in Nevada than in Utah. A man who reaches the age of 45 in Utah can expect to live 11 years more than the man who reaches age 45 in Nevada. The point is that simple, cost-free choices under the control of the individual are much more effective at improving health than all the expensive, time-consuming medical advances of the past century. Perhaps our priorities are misplaced.

Based on this information, we could conclude that a simple difference in style of life can have more of an effect on health than medical advances. Let's look at the influence on health of some specific lifestyle choices.

Choices of Foods

cholesterol
Substance in the blood (including HDLs and LDLs) that may adhere to the walls of the blood vessels, restricting the flow of blood and causing strokes and heart attacks.

Nutrition plays an important role throughout human development. In middle adulthood, however, increasing evidence demonstrates the influence of nutrition on two major health concerns, heart disease and cancer. Medical science has established a link between heart disease and a substance in the blood, **cholesterol.** Cholesterol, specifically low-density lipoprotein (LDL), has been found to leave deposits along the walls of blood vessels, blocking the flow of blood to the heart and brain. The main culprit in high levels of "bad" cholesterol has been found to be diets high in fat. High-density lipoprotein (HDL) is known as "good" cholesterol, because it may actually protect against build-up of dangerous plaque. Changes to the typical American diet that contains 40% fat, such as eating fish and poultry instead of red meat, choosing lowfat yogurt and cheese, drinking skim milk instead of whole milk, and avoiding transfats (for example, hydrogenated oils) will lower cholesterol in the body. Exercise is also very helpful and cannot be emphasized enough for its impact on health in later life.

A similar link has been found between diet and certain types of cancer, such as cancer of the breast, stomach, intestines, and esophagus. The American Cancer Society has a set of recommendations for an improved, healthy diet. It also recommends lowering fat intake to no more than 30% of the daily caloric total and following a diet that is high in fiber, a substance that helps the digestive process. High-fiber foods include leafy vegetables such as cauliflower, broccoli, and brussels sprouts, as well as whole-grain cereals and breads. The proliferation of new products that feature lower levels of fat and higher levels of fiber indicates that the American public is taking this new knowledge to heart (no pun intended).

Obesity has become an epidemic in this country. The CDC (2006) reports that "although one of the national health objectives for the year 2010 is to reduce the prevalence of obesity among adults to less than 15%, current data indicate that the situation is worsening rather than improving." Anyone who is 10% over the normal weight for his or her height and build is considered overweight. Anyone who is 30% over the normal weight is considered obese. Between 1976 and 1980 and 2003 and 2004, the prevalence of obesity among adults aged 20–74 years increased from 15.0% to 32.9% (CDC, 2006). However, slight changes in home, school, and work environments make it possible to live a healthier life in a Super Size Me society and reverse the obesity trend (Segelken, 2005). Placing healthy food choices in vending machines is one simple step that is rapidly catching on around the country.

Use of Alcohol

Most people consume alcohol to attain the relaxed, uninhibited feeling that alcohol tends to produce. The fact is, alcohol dulls the senses. Specifically, it decreases reaction times in the brain and nervous system. Continued drinking may affect the sex life of males, by making it difficult for them to attain and keep an erection.

AN INFORMED VIEW

Can Drinking Alcohol Have Positive Effects?

In most articles you may have read about alcohol consumption, it has been associated with a variety of negative biological and psychological effects. Earlier research seemed to indicate that alcohol had no redeeming qualities. More recently, studies have indicated that moderate use of alcohol may have some beneficial effect. For example, anticlotting properties of alcohol may account for decreased risk of coronary disease and heart attack (Klatsky, 1999, 2001).

Do you think the consumption of alcohol can have positive physiological and social effects? What advice would you get if you called your local board of health? The Alcoholics Anonymous Central Service Office? The Ask-a-Nurse Hotline?

If you would like to have a more informed opinion on this issue, you might want to read one of the articles by Klatsky on the subject referenced in this box.

Even though problems associated with alcoholism (for example, with family, the law, and one's health) have been highlighted in the popular press, binge drinking in college remains stable and at a high level (Johnston et al., 2005). Binge drinking has been defined as five or more drinks in a row for men and four or more drinks in a row for women, one or more times during a two-week period (Wechsler, 1994). However, researchers have identified a need for new definitions that more accurately reflect actual college drinking practices (LaBrie, Pedersen, & Tawalbeh, 2007). The practice is harmful not only for those who drink but also for those in their immediate environment. For example, bingeing is associated with injuries from fights and automobile accidents. Depression may also contribute to problem drinking in early adulthood (Aalto-Setala, Marttunen, & Tuulio-Henriksson, 2003).

Ironically, some research has indicated that a daily, moderate intake of alcohol may be beneficial (although not for those over the age of 50—see Chapter 15). Such small amounts of alcohol seem to produce a protein in the blood that helps lower cholesterol. Unfortunately, the addictive qualities of alcohol make it impossible for many people to drink only in moderate amounts. This is why researchers are interested in factors outside of formal treatment that may influence recovery. Culturally distinct populations have specific needs that can inform efforts to prevent addiction (Bezdek, Croy, & Spicer, 2004).

Use of Tobacco

Although the use of tobacco has been falling rapidly, at about 1% per year since 1987, it continues to be the leading preventable cause of death in the United States. Currently more than 400,000 deaths per year have been attributed to cigarette smoking in this country (CDC, 2000b), adding up to over $50 billion in medical costs. Every year, more people die from smoking than from alcohol, AIDS, drug abuse, murders, car accidents, suicides, and fires—combined (CDC, 2000b). Cigarette smoking has been proven to cause lung and esophageal cancer, heart disease, and chronic lung disease. It also contributes to various other types of cancers (kidney, bladder, and pancreatic). Smokers are 14 times more likely to die from cancer of the lungs and twice as likely to die of a heart attack than nonsmokers. Cigarette smoke is a combination of tar, nicotine, carbon monoxide, and various other chemicals. Smoking increases heart rate and blood pressure, it constricts blood vessels, and it reduces oxygen supply to tissue, thereby straining the heart.

Cigar smoking has been somewhat fashionable with young adults, but more exotic forms of smoking tobacco have risen in popularity. Hookahs, for example, are waterpipes used to smoke flavored tobacco and are found in trendy bars and restaurants. Many people think this type of tobacco contains little or no nicotine, but it actually contains more toxins and is equally addictive.

Peer pressure from friends is the major reason that young adults smoke. Some young adults see smoking as a way of appearing older and more mature. Others, especially girls, believe that smoking will either help them lose weight or keep them from gaining weight. As is the case with nonsmokers, increased physical activity can offset weight gain (Colditz & Stein, 2005). Among young women, smoking is associated with being less athletic and more social, studying less, getting lower grades, and generally disliking school more than nonsmoking females.

You may also involuntarily be exposed to the dangers of tobacco use. A growing body of research is documenting the deleterious effects of passive smoking. Passive smoking is the breathing in of the smoke around you that others produce. More than 4,000 chemical compounds have been identified in tobacco smoke. Each year, an estimated 3,000 nonsmoking Americans die of lung cancer owing to breathing in secondhand smoke (CDC, 2000a). (The role of smoke in the health of children is covered in Chapter 4.) Evidence also indicates that children can be affected when their mothers smoke. The CDC reports that approximately 300,000 young children are plagued with lower respiratory tract infections owing to the effects of secondhand smoke. This evidence has led to legislation prohibiting smoking in certain public areas such as elevators, airplanes, and restaurants and the designation of smoking areas in workplaces and sports arenas.

The message does seem to be reaching the public. Overall, fewer people smoke now than at any time in the past 25 years (with the exception of teenage females). Numerous stop-smoking programs spring up all the time. These programs run the gamut from classic behavioral techniques to hypnosis. But perhaps the most telling evidence that smoking is on the decline in the United States is the reaction of the giant tobacco companies. In recent years these companies have increasingly targeted foreign markets (a growing ethical controversy, because these markets are typically Third World countries) while diversifying their domestic market with different and healthier products.

Physical Fitness

One of the most popular trends of recent years has been the so-called fitness craze. Health benefits are the obvious reason for this enthusiasm for exercise. Studies have shown that women who increase their physical activity by 2.5 hours a week can add months to their lives (Fitzpatrick, 2003). Moderately intense exercise, such as brisk walking, also reduces the risk of stroke, osteoporosis, some types of cancer, and diabetes.

Many corporations are now providing the time and facilities for employees to build regular exercise into their workday. The idea is that work time lost in this way is more than made up for by more productive employees, who end up losing less time because of illness. Health insurance programs often offer free access to exercise facilities or rebate for membership, looking at the long-term gain of having healthier members.

The pressure felt by young people, especially women, to stay physically fit and attractive is enormous. While eating disorders among young adults are fairly common, recent research has found that perceptions differ about women and men with anorexia nervosa and relate to powerful ideas about culture and gender (McVittie, Cavers, & Hepworth, 2005). These findings underscore the relationship between physical and intellectual well-being and have strong implications for healthy development.

Guided Review

5. Early adulthood is the time when the efficiency of most bodily functions begins to _____.

6. Although physical ability has peaked, bodily responses in adulthood are supplemented by _____ _____—that is, the part of the total capacity of our body's organs that we do not normally need to use.

7. Our lifestyle affects our health, mainly through our choices of foods, use of alcohol, use of tobacco, and _____ _____.

8. Cholesterol, a substance in the blood related to heart attack, can be controlled by _____.

9. Even though problems associated with alcoholism have been highlighted in the media, _____ _____ in college remains stable and at a high level.

10. Use of _____ has been falling rapidly, yet continues to be the leading preventable cause of death in the United States.

11. Eating disorders among young adults are becoming _____ common.

COGNITIVE DEVELOPMENT

Young adult learners are presented with opportunities that differ from those of years ago. For instance, technology provides younger students with online learning methods and curriculum designed to address a variety of learning styles. Increased pressures for high performance have led to innovative problem-solving strategies being taught in higher education and the workplace (Schmidt, Vermeulen, & Van der Molen, 2006; White, 2006). An example of an individual encouraging innovative problem-solving is vacuum inventor James Dyson, in England. He is helping to create the Dyson School of Design Innovation—where young adults will explore engineering through projects and relationships with mentors in the field. Students and mentors will be encouraged to succeed and fail, if necessary, in their endeavors. In addition to learning factors, an emphasis in research has been on the relationship between intellectual and ethical growth.

Intellectual/Ethical Development

Perry (1968a, 1968b, 1981) studied the intellectual/ethical development of several hundred Harvard University students, a group of males ages 17 to 22. These students responded to several checklists on their educational views and were interviewed extensively on the basis of their responses. The results of these studies led Perry to suggest a sequence of intellectual and ethical development that typically occurs during the transition from late adolescence to early adulthood. This sequence consists of nine positions, which indicate progress from belief in the absolute authority of experts to the recognition that one must make commitments and be responsible for one's own beliefs.

Perry's nine stages are divided among three broader categories, as follows:

I. **Dualism** ("Things are either absolutely right or absolutely wrong.")

- *Position 1:* The world is viewed in such polar terms as right versus wrong, we versus they, and good versus bad. If an answer is right, it is absolutely right. We get right answers by going to authorities who have absolute knowledge.

dualism
Perry's initial phase of ethical development, in which "things are either absolutely right or absolutely wrong."

Answers 5. decline 6. organ reserve 7. physical fitness 8. diet 9. binge drinking 10. tobacco 11. more

- *Position 2:* The person recognizes that uncertainty exists but ascribes it to poorly qualified authorities. Sometimes individuals can learn the truth for themselves.
- *Position 3:* Diversity and uncertainty are now acceptable but considered temporary because the authorities do not know what the answers are yet. The person becomes puzzled as to what the standards should be in these cases.

II. **Relativism** ("Anything can be right or wrong depending on the situation; all views are equally right.")

- *Position 4a:* The person realizes that uncertainty and diversity of opinion are often extensive and recognizes that this is a legitimate status. Now he or she believes that "anyone has a right to an opinion." It is now possible for two authorities to disagree with each other without either of them being wrong.
- *Position 4b:* Sometimes the authorities (such as college professors) are not talking about right answers. Rather, they want students to think for themselves, supporting their opinions with data.
- *Position 5:* The person recognizes that all knowledge and values (including even those of an authority) exist in some specific context. It is therefore relative to the context. The person also recognizes that simple right and wrong are relatively rare, and even they exist in a specific context.
- *Position 6:* The person apprehends that because we live in a relativistic world, we must make some sort of personal commitment to an idea or a concept, as opposed to looking for an authority to follow.

III. **Commitment** ("Because of available evidence and my understanding of my own values, I have come to new beliefs.")

- *Position 7:* The person begins to choose the commitments that he or she will make in specific areas.
- *Position 8:* Having begun to make commitments, the person experiences the implications of those commitments and explores the various issues of responsibility involved.
- *Position 9:* The person's identity is affirmed through the various commitments made. There is a recognition of the necessity for balancing commitments and the understanding that one can have responsibilities that are expressed through a daily lifestyle. Perry (1981) described this position:

This is how life will be. I will be whole-hearted while tentative, fight for my values yet respect others, believe my deepest values right yet be ready to learn. I see that I shall be retracing this whole journey over and over—but, I hope, more wisely. (p. 276)

Some students move through these stages in a smooth and regular fashion; others, however, are delayed or deflected in one of three ways:

- **Temporizing.** Some people remain in one position for a year or more, exploring its implications but hesitating to make any further progress.
- **Escape.** Some people use opportunities for detachment, especially those offered in positions 4 and 5, to refuse responsibility for making any commitments. Because everyone's opinion is "equally right," the person believes that no commitments need be made and, thus, escapes from the dilemma.
- **Retreat.** Sometimes, confused by the confrontation and uncertainties of the middle positions, people retreat to earlier positions.

Perry's theory has been criticized because all the subjects of his research were male. However, his work spurred considerable research on females, which we now overview.

---

relativism
Second phase in Perry's theory; attitude or a philosophy that says anything can be right or wrong depending on the situation; all views are equally right.

commitment
Third phase in Perry's theory, in which the individual realizes that certainty is impossible but that commitment to a certain position is necessary, even without certainty.

temporizing
Some people remain in one position for a year or more, exploring its implications but hesitating to make any further progress.

escape
Others refuse responsibility for making any commitments because everyone's opinion is "equally right."

retreat
According to Perry's theory of ethical development, when someone retreats to an earlier ethical position.

"Women's Ways of Knowing"

In a continuing collaborative study, Belenky, Bond, and Weinstock (1997) set out to answer the questions "Do female ways of knowing develop differently than those of males? If so, how do they come to learn and value what they know?" The study was rooted in Perry's work and the work of Carol Gilligan, whose groundbreaking research on the morality of care and responsibility versus the morality of rights and justice was covered in Chapter 9.

Belenky and her associates conducted a series of lengthy and intense interviews with 135 women of diverse socioeconomic backgrounds. The researchers found five general categories of ways in which women know and view the world. Though some of the women interviewed clearly demonstrated a progression from one perspective to the next, the researchers contend that they are unable to discern a progression of clear-cut stages, as did Perry and Gilligan. The five perspectives are silence, received knowledge, subjective knowledge, procedural knowledge, and constructed knowledge.

silence
Belenky's first phase of women's thinking, characterized by concepts of right and wrong.

1. **Silence.** Females in the silence category describe themselves as "deaf and dumb." These women feel passive and dependent. Like players in an authority's game, they feel expected to know rules that don't exist. These women's thinking is characterized by concepts of right and wrong, similar to the men in Perry's first category of dualism. Questions about their growing up revealed family lives filled with violence, abuse, and chaos. The researchers noted that "gaining a voice and developing an awareness of their own minds are the tasks that these women must accomplish if they are to cease being either a perpetrator or victim of family violence" (Belenky et al., 1986, p. 38).

received knowledge
Belenky's second phase of women's thinking; characterized by being awed by the authorities but far less affiliated with them than in the first phase.

2. **Received knowledge.** Women in the received knowledge category see words as central to the knowing process. They learn by listening and assume truths come from authorities. These women are intolerant of ambiguities and paradoxes, always going back to the notion that there are absolute truths. Received knowers seem similar to the men that Perry described as being in the first stage of dualism, but with a difference. The men Perry interviewed felt a great affiliation with the knowing authority. The women of this perspective were awed by the authorities but far less affiliated with them. In contrast to the men of Perry's study, women of received knowledge channel their energies and increased sense of self into the care of others.

subjective knowledge
Belenky's third phase of women's thinking; characterized by some crisis of male authority that sparked a distrust of outside sources of knowledge and some experience that confirmed a trust in women thinkers themselves.

3. **Subjective knowledge.** The researchers noted that women in the subjective knowledge category often had experienced two phenomena that pushed them toward this perspective: some crisis of male authority that sparked a distrust of outside sources of knowledge and some experience that confirmed a trust in themselves. Subjectivists value their "gut," or firsthand, experience as their best source of knowledge and see themselves as "conduits through which truth emerges" (p. 69). The researchers note that subjectivists are similar to males in Perry's second category of relativism in that they embrace the notion of multiple truths.

procedural knowledge
Belenky's fourth phase of women's thinking; characterized by a distrust of both knowledge from authority and the female thinker's own inner authority, or "gut."

4. **Procedural knowledge.** The women in the procedural knowledge category have a distrust of both knowledge from authority and their own inner authority, or "gut." The perspective of procedural knowledge is characterized by an interest in form over content (how you say something rather than what you say). Women in this category also have a heightened sense of control. This category is similar to Perry's position 4b, where students learn analytic methods that authorities sanction. But analytic thinking emerges differently in women because they are less likely to affiliate with authorities.

The researchers describe women as having two kinds of procedural knowledge: separate knowing and connected knowing. These terms are reminiscent of Gilligan's work. Separate knowers are analytical and try to separate the self, to reveal the truth. Connected knowers learn through empathy with others.

constructed knowledge
Belenky's fifth phase of women's thinking; characterized by an integration of the subjective and procedural ways of knowing (Perry's types 3 and 4).

5. **Constructed knowledge.** Those in the constructed knowledge category have integrated the subjective and procedural ways of knowing (Perry's types 3 and 4). Women of this perspective note that "all knowledge is constructed and the knower is an intimate part of the known" (p. 137). They feel responsible for examining and questioning systems of constructing knowledge. Their thinking is characterized by a high tolerance of ambiguity and internal contradiction. Indeed, the women whose ways of knowing are of this perspective often balance many commitments and relationships, as well as ideas.

I think the one lesson I have learned is that there is no substitute for paying attention.

—DIANE SAWYER

The work of Perry and Belenky and her associates (as well as that of Piaget, Kohlberg, and Gilligan, discussed earlier in this book) has greatly advanced our knowledge of intellectual and ethical development in the late adolescent and early adult years. It has also produced much controversy. Many questions remain to be answered. For example, does socioeconomic level make any difference? What about cultural background? We hope that the research in this area will provide further insights into how we can help youths progress through this period successfully. We could say the same for the next aspect of development we will review, work in young adulthood.

Guided Review

12. Perry examined the intellectual and ethical changes in Harvard males and found them to move through three broad categories of change. These categories include _____ (things are absolutely right or wrong), relativism (all views are equal), and _____ (holding to beliefs based on the best available evidence and values).

13. Perry describes nine stages within these three categories. Some students move through the stages smoothly; others are delayed by _____, escape, and _____.

14. Belenky and her colleagues, building on Perry's work and the work of Carol Gilligan, examined the _____ and _____ development of women.

15. Belenky and others found five general categories of ways in which women view the world. The five perspectives include silence, _____ _____, subjective knowledge, procedural knowledge, and _____ _____.

PATTERNS OF WORK

Waste of time is thus the deadliest of sins. Loss of time through sociability, idle talk, luxury, or more sleep than is necessary for health (six hours) is worthy of absolute moral condemnation. Thus inactive contemplation is also valueless, or even reprehensible if it is at the expense of one's daily work. (Max Weber, *The Protestant Ethic and the Spirit of Capitalism*, 1904–1905)

Answers

12. dualism, commitment 13. temporizing, retreat 14. ethical, intellectual 15. received knowledge, constructed knowledge

AN APPLIED VIEW

Choosing a Career

One of the most stressful and rewarding aspects of one's college experience is career planning. Though a daunting task if left until the spring semester of senior year, it can be a time of exploration, reflection, and excitement if the pursuit is spread out over four years of school. In Kim Hays's "Coping with College" series (2004), she gives a general time line for career planning during the college years. Though she warns that this timetable may not suit all needs, it provides an excellent overview of what to expect as one navigates his or her options.

Freshman and sophomore years are most conducive to exploration of major and career choices. Hays says that "even students who begin college knowing what they want to major in may question their choice at one point." Questioning at this early stage is normal and even advisable; committing to a major without proper exploration of other options often leads to regret later on. Hays suggests speaking with other students or

perusing career-related periodicals to assist in career investigation. By the end of sophomore year, exploration should be coming to a close as the student begins to feel more committed to a major and career path. Failure to choose foci at this time makes it difficult for the student to pursue in-depth his or her chosen path.

Junior year should be used to solidify choices and begin taking advantage of opportunities in the student's chosen field. Hays suggests that juniors develop some career-related experience to help bridge the gap between college and that first job. The best way to do this is through summer jobs, internships, and co-op placements in a specific field related to one's major. Often colleges offer course credit for completed internships and co-ops that meet university standards. If these preliminary exploratory steps have been completed, beginning the job search in one's senior year is no longer formidable.

Weber, a philosopher and economist, was a leading spokesperson on the role of labor at the turn of the 20th century. How differently we view that role today! Changes in the world of work have been coming more rapidly in recent years than ever before. Working in the United States today is complicated. The rest of this section is devoted to explicating the major trends, their causes, and their likely results.

The Phenomenon of the Dual-Career Family

dual-career family
Family in which both the mother and the father are working, usually full time.

The traditional family pattern of the husband who goes off to work to provide for his family and the wife who stays home and manages that family is almost extinct. Now, work has become a means for attaining power (Blustein, 2000). Economic realities and the women's movement have led to the development of a growing family dynamic—the **dual-career family.** The goals of the American Dream, achievement and self-sufficiency, have not changed. What has changed, however, is recognition of challenges related to career opportunities for women (Rosser, 2004; Schmader, Johns, & Barquissau, 2004).

Despite their increased presence in the workforce, women are still considered responsible for the maintenance of the family. Women often choose jobs that meet family needs and demands. Women tend to work shorter hours and change the nature of their work more often than men do.

However, another changing aspect of the American family is the increasingly active role of fathers in the raising of their own children. Paternal child care, where the father cares for children while their mother works outside the home, is receiving more attention in the field because of its implications for child development, marital relations, and the family's economic situation. According to Averett, Gennetian, and Peters (2000), paternal child care occurs most often in families where (1) a mother's expected market wage on her return to the workplace is high or (2) when the cost of nonmaternal care is comparatively low. The occurrence of paternal child care also strongly depends on factors such

On the average, a working wife does about 80% of the caretaking chores in a family, as opposed to the 20% done by a working husband. Can you predict the likely consequences of this ratio?

as the father's work schedule in a dual-career family, the amount of opportunities for employment outside of the home that exist for the father, and the extent to which both fathers and mothers identify with more traditional gender roles, which dictate that the mother should provide the majority of care to their children, rather than their fathers.

Today it is more difficult for some people to define themselves according to their jobs. As the number of two-income households continues to grow, women are taking many of the new high-growth jobs, although this is almost exclusively an upper- and middle-class white phenomenon (Fouad & Brown, 2000). It affects men's traditional image as chief provider in the family (Mirchandani, 2000), and men are taking on more responsibility for the family (Barnett, 2001).

Home-Based Work

As a result of recent technological advances, the possibility of working out of one's home is increasing in popularity. In dual-career households with young children, home-based work can be an effective way to balance a full-time career with caring for or supporting a family. According to a recent study, Mirchandani (2000) found that two contradictory views of the home-based work situation exist. It seems that by working at home, individuals can sometimes successfully integrate their work responsibilities and child care and/or domestic duties, thereby having to rely less upon child care providers and saving money on commuting expenses. Conversely, in other families, in order to work at home, an individual must continue to keep the areas of paid work and child care distinct. For example, some home-based workers find that they still need to find child care outside of the home so that they can still devote uninterrupted time to their jobs. In the same study, Mirchandani reported that another potential drawback of home-based work is that since there is no clear end to the workday, as in a traditional 9-to-5 job, there is increased possibility for around-the-clock workaholism. The realities of work and home demands are a constant challenge to many young adults, and directly impact other aspects of development.

AN INFORMED VIEW

Working Mothers and Work–Family Conflict

As we have previously discussed, mothers who work outside the home often experience some degree of work–family conflict. For some women, this conflict is manageable; they are able to balance their roles as mothers and workers in a way that causes a low amount of stress. However, for other women, work and family demands come into conflict in such major ways that they grow unhappy or unfulfilled. Since every family is different, it is important to look at the number of factors that might influence a mother's feelings about her various roles.

- *Interpersonal relationships.* Women's work status can affect interpersonal relationships in positive and negative ways. In a study of women managers, most felt that their demanding careers reduced the amount of time that they were able to spend with their friends (Grant, 2000). In terms of support from their spouses, however, women reported a broad range of responses. A large percentage of women said that they enjoyed enhanced self-esteem and personal development as a result of working and that these qualities improved their marital relationships. However, a number of the other women said that their husbands felt threatened by their successful careers and increased earning power, which caused more conflict in their marriages.
- *Work environment.* The type of environment in which a woman works can have an impact on her ability to balance domestic and professional duties. When women work in jobs where they have a lot of control, such as decision-making authority, they are better able to handle the psychological stresses of a large workload than women who do not have this kind of control (Bliese & Castro, 2000).

- In another study, employees who were especially trusted by their managers felt that their jobs were more meaningful and empowering than did other employees (Gomez & Rosen, 2001). Individuals who feel that their work is an important, valuable part of their identity are more likely to have warmer, more caring interactions at work and at home (Thompson & Bunderson, 2001). However, when either work or home responsibilities are not important to the identity of the employee, she will likely experience more frustration and conflict.
- *Societal influences.* According to Jacobs and Gerson (2001), conflict between work and family is often the result of rigid employee policies. For example, most jobs are still organized around a traditional, 9-to-5 work schedule. Some other examples of rigid policies are nonpaid family leave time and the expectation of weekend and overtime work. Jacobs and Gerson argue that businesses ought to adopt more flexible policies in order to accommodate the domestic responsibilities of their employees.

On balance, would you say that the dramatic increase in dual-earner families in recent decades has been for the better or not—from the standpoint of women, their partners, and their families? What kinds of things do you think need to be done so that all may benefit more fully from a mother's full-time job? Should some mothers simply not work, or else work only part time? If you would like to have a more informed opinion on this issue, you might want to read one of the articles on the subject referenced in this box.

A SOCIOCULTURAL VIEW

Should Psychologists Pay More Attention to Culture?

Developmental psychologists, urged on by the contextualists, are starting to pay more attention to cultural and ethnic influences. However, most of this work has compared whites and African-Americans. Mio has challenged this view: "As such, American Indians, Latinos, and Asians have been left out of this discussion. Such exclusion does not make scientific sense, as it makes conclusions about race relations less generalizable. It also comes with a cost, as the excluded groups are

often asked to give up their respective ethnicities to join the discussion" (Mio, 2004).

The U.S. Census reports (U.S. Census Bureau, 2006) offer ample evidence of how restricted this view has been. As the population figure (Figure 13.1) indicates, Americans of Hispanic origin are now the largest ethnic minority group in the United States.

FIGURE 13.1   Population in Selected Race and Hispanic Origin Groups, by Age: United States, 1980–2005

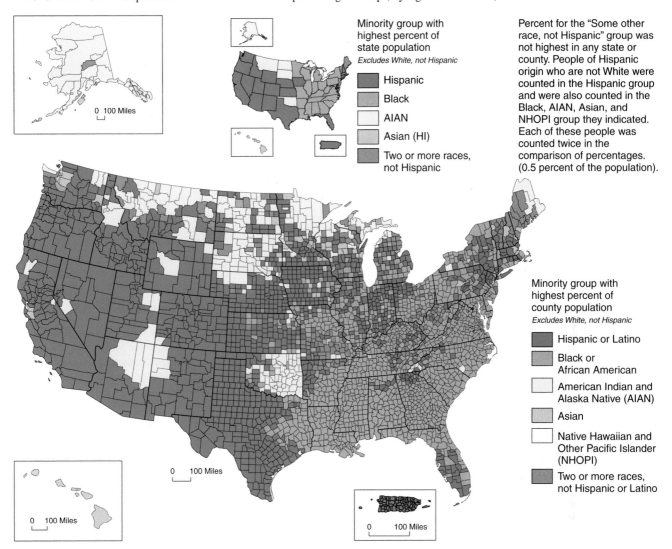

Minority group with highest percent of state population
Excludes White, not Hispanic

- Hispanic
- Black
- AIAN
- Asian (HI)
- Two or more races, not Hispanic

Percent for the "Some other race, not Hispanic" group was not highest in any state or county. People of Hispanic origin who are not White were counted in the Hispanic group and were also counted in the Black, AIAN, Asian, and NHOPI group they indicated. Each of these people was counted twice in the comparison of percentages. (0.5 percent of the population).

Minority group with highest percent of county population
Excludes White, not Hispanic

- Hispanic or Latino
- Black or African American
- American Indian and Alaska Native (AIAN)
- Asian
- Native Hawaiian and Other Pacific Islander (NHOPI)
- Two or more races, not Hispanic or Latino

0 100 Miles

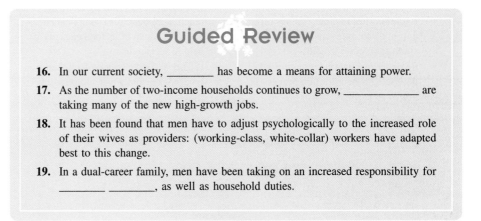

Guided Review

16. In our current society, _____ has become a means for attaining power.

17. As the number of two-income households continues to grow, _____ are taking many of the new high-growth jobs.

18. It has been found that men have to adjust psychologically to the increased role of their wives as providers: (working-class, white-collar) workers have adapted best to this change.

19. In a dual-career family, men have been taking on an increased responsibility for _____ _____, as well as household duties.

Answers

CONCLUSION & SUMMARY

We began this chapter by comparing how youths are inducted into adulthood in pre-industrial tribes in other parts of the world and in the modern United States. We concluded that our situation is much more complex than that of the tribes and that the absence of clear initiation rites still causes problems for us.

Young adulthood is a period during which many changes are taking place. The peak of physical development is reached, and the decline of certain abilities begins. These declines are almost never apparent, however, because of organ reserve. Our style of life has a powerful effect on this development, including our diet, our use of alcohol, drugs and nicotine, and physical fitness.

The major change occurring in the area of cognitive development involves progress from dualistic thinking through relativism to the ethical/intellectual stage of commitment. Research also suggests that there are five "women's ways of knowing."

The nation's workers experience a very different environment than their predecessors of 50 years ago, as we leave the industrial age and enter the age of "information processing." Many problems still must be solved—especially the treatment of persons of color and women.

How are American youths being initiated into adulthood today?

- Initiation rites in other cultures offer a formal ceremony marking the transition from child to adult.
- Some researchers have suggested parallels to the initiation process in the crimes juveniles are often required to commit in order to become a member of a gang, and in the sequence of experiences that so often lead to drug addiction.
- The purpose of initiation rites in pre-industrial societies is to cushion the emotional disruption arising from the transition from one life status to another.
- Entry into adulthood is far more complex for adolescents today, largely due to the increase of sophisticated technologies and the need for many more years of formal education.
- Organized sports, the adolescent counterculture, and delinquency all provide some sort of trials that must be passed for acceptance into adulthood.
- Five types of activities signal the passage to maturity in America today: religious, physical, social, educational, and economic.

What are the significant factors affecting physical development in early adulthood?

- Early adulthood is the period during which physical changes slow down or stop.
- The human body is designed to do much more than it is usually called on to do. Much of its total capacity is held in "organ reserve."
- Lifestyle, food choices, alcohol and tobacco use, and physical fitness are enormous factors in the health of a young adult.

How does cognition change during the early adult years?

- Perry suggested three categories of intellectual and ethical development that typify transition from late adolescence to early adulthood: dualism, relativism, and commitment. By avoiding the three obstacles that might impede their progress (temporizing, escape, and retreat), young adults should be able to achieve commitments that are the hallmark of the mature person.
- Belenky and associates suggest women know and view the world through five perspectives: silence, received knowledge, subjective knowledge, procedural knowledge, and constructed knowledge.

What patterns of work typify young adults today?

- The traditional family pattern of the husband who goes off to work to provide for his family and the wife who stays home and manages that family is almost extinct now.
- Women often choose jobs that fit in well with the needs of their family. Women tend to work shorter hours and change the nature of their work more often than men do.
- Economic realities and the feminist movement have given rise to dual-career families, in which both husband and wife work outside the home.

KEY TERMS

cholesterol
commitment
constructed knowledge
dual-career family
dualism

escape
hazing
organ reserve
procedural knowledge
received knowledge

relativism
retreat
silence
subjective knowledge
temporizing

WHAT DO YOU THINK?

1. Do you remember any experiences from your own youth that were particularly helpful in your transition to adulthood?

2. Societal changes have led to a change in the nature of initiation rites into adulthood. Are young adults better off today as a result, or should we try to return to the societal structures of the past?

3. The media offer countless advertisements to help a person look younger, feel better, be better. Why are these ads so effective? What do they say about Western society?

4. Most college students are making the transition from Perry's category of dualism to relativism and, finally, to commitment. What types of behaviors might you observe from a college student at each of these levels of intellectual development?

5. Many of the problems in the American family today have been attributed to the phenomenon of the dual-career family. Is there any truth to this perception? In what ways do two working parents alter (positively and negatively) the family's operation as a unit?

 CHAPTER REVIEW TEST

1. **A bar mitzvah or bat mitzvah is an example of a(n) _____ rite of passage.**
   a. religious
   b. physical
   c. social
   d. educational

2. **Many adolescents are willing to endure pain to be initiated into groups because**
   a. they want to be tested.
   b. they want to prove to themselves that they are courageous.
   c. they want to prove to themselves that they have self-control.
   d. all of these.

3. **Because we seldom call on its total capacity, people often are not aware of the decline of their _____ during early adulthood.**
   a. aerobic capacity
   b. blood pressure
   c. heart rate
   d. organ reserve

4. **Research indicates that heart disease and cancer are linked to**
   a. nutrition.
   b. other related diseases.
   c. childhood habits.
   d. none of these.

5. **Lack of exercise, snacking, and use of labor-saving devices are the main causes of**
   a. leukemia.
   b. cancer.
   c. obesity.
   d. diabetes.

6. **A survey among college students on alcohol use showed that alcohol consumption was directly related to**
   a. low grade-point average.
   b. poor relations with peers.
   c. memory loss.
   d. length of time needed to earn a college degree.

7. **What is the major reason that young adults smoke?**
   a. stress
   b. economic reasons
   c. peer pressure
   d. get a fix

8. **According to the Centers for Disease Control and Prevention (CDC, 2004), there are approximately _____ times fewer reported AIDS cases during young adulthood than in middle adulthood.**
   a. one and a half
   b. two
   c. two and a half
   d. three

9. **Among young adult females, maximum height is usually reached at age _____; for males, it is age _____**
   a. 18, 25.
   b. 19, 16.
   c. 18, 20.
   d. 18, 18.

10. **Research indicates that obesity has become an epidemic in the United States. Anyone who is over _____% above normal weight is considered obese.**
    a. 10
    b. 20
    c. 25
    d. 30

11. **Cigarettes, cigars, and trendy pipes called _____ are equally addictive and contain nicotine that is toxic to the human body.**
    a. hookahs
    b. tubas
    c. poppers
    d. none of these

12. **Perry's stages of dualism, relativism, and commitment refer to a person's**
    a. relationship development.
    b. intellectual and ethical development.
    c. ability to make moral decisions.
    d. interpersonal relationships.

13. **In a study of women's perspectives on knowledge (Belenky & others), received knowledge is**
    a. the view that words are central to the knowing process.
    b. an experience that resulted in a distrust of outside sources of knowledge.

c. a distrust of knowledge from authority.

d. learned passivity and dependency in relationships.

14. **Belenky's category of procedural knowledge is most similar to which of Perry's stages?**
    a. dualism
    b. commitment

c. affirmation

d. relativism

15. **The ability to recognize that certainty is impossible but that _____ to a certain position is necessary, even without certainty, describes Perry's third stage.**
    a. aspiring
    b. commitment

c. ambivalence

d. disgust

16. **Today, women are taking on many of the**
    a. middle-level jobs.
    b. new, high-growth jobs.
    c. old, less-skilled jobs.
    d. none of these

Answers

1.a 2.d 3.d 4.a 5.c 6.a 7.c 8.a 9.c 10.d 11.a 12.b 13.a 14.d 15.b 16.b

PSYCHOSOCIAL DEVELOPMENT IN EARLY ADULTHOOD

14 chapter

Chapter Objectives

After reading this chapter you should be able to answer the following questions.

- **What factors affect American marriages and families?**

- **What challenges do young adults face in developing a healthy personality?**

- **What are the relationships between sexual identity and gender roles?**

- **How do young adults deal with the interpersonal relationships of sexuality and love?**

When things go wrong in society, we immediately inquire into the condition of family life. When we see society torn apart by crime, we cry, "If only we could return to the good old days when family was sacred." But were the good old days so good? Was the family ever free of violence? Many people who go to therapy these days were raised in the so-called golden age of the family, and they tell stories of abuse, neglect, and terrifying moralistic demands and pressure. Looked at coldly, the family of any era is both good and bad, offering both support and threat. This is why adults are so ambivalent about visiting their families and spending time with them: They want the emotional rewards of the sense of connection, but they also want the distance from painful memories and difficult relationships.

You may disagree with this assessment of the American family, but most researchers agree that the rapid changes this institution has been experiencing may well be cause for concern, if only because the family is the foundation from which so many other social and emotional elements of our lives spring. No aspects of young adult lives are more vital than those dealt with in this chapter: marriage and the family, work and leisure, and personal development.

MARRIAGE AND THE FAMILY

When two people are under the influence of the most violent, most divisive, and most transient of passions, they are required to swear that they will remain in that excited, abnormal, and exhausting condition continuously until death do them part.

—GEORGE BERNARD SHAW

Changing American Marriages and Families

Finding critics of marriage is not difficult (for example, www.nomarriage.com). Not many Americans are concerned, though. Almost 95% of Americans get married at some point in their lives. To better understand the present situation, let us take a look at the trends in marriage and family relations.

The U.S. Census Bureau defines a family as "a group of two or more people (one of whom is the householder, the person in whose name the housing unit is owned or rented) who reside together and who are related by birth, marriage, or adoption" (American Community Survey, 2005). The average U.S. family consists of 3.18 people, down from 3.58 in 1970. Latino families are larger, with an average of 3.92 members, than either African-American or non-Latino white families, which average 3.42 and 3.02 members, respectively.

About 54% of all American adults (under 11 million people) are married and living with their spouses, according to the U.S. Department of Commerce (2005). About 31% of men and 25% of women had never been married. Nearly 30% of all children under 18 years of age live with just one parent, and, of them, 84% live with their mother. One of the major changes in the families of young adults is that the number of single parents has increased. For example, the percentage of single mothers rose from 12% in 1970 to 26% in 2003 (U.S. Census Bureau, 2004). Trends in the rates of first marriage, divorce, and remarriage since the early 20th century reflect patterns of change in economic and social conditions in the United States. These changes can be clearly seen in Table 14.1. One of the most interesting trends has been the change in the average age at first marriage. At the turn of the 20th century, the average age for females was almost 22 years; for males, almost 26 years. With the exception of the late Depression and war years, the trend *had* been toward earlier marriages.

This trend led demographers to make erroneous predictions. For example, they predicted that marriages in 1990 would come even earlier, at about age 20 for both males and females. Several other investigators said the same thing in the late 1960s. But these miscalculations demonstrate only the difficulty of predicting the behavior of human beings.

The modern American family is quite different from those of 100 years ago. Those families were larger, and family members were much more likely to live near one another in the same city or town. What are the advantages and disadvantages of this tendency?

TABLE 14.1	Median Age at First Marriage, by Sex, 1890–2003	
Year	Men	Women
2003	27.1	25.3
2002	26.9	25.3
2001	26.9	25.1
2000	26.8	25.1
1999	26.9	25.1
1998	26.7	25.0
1996	27.1	24.8
1994	26.7	24.5
1990	26.1	23.9
1985	25.5	23.3
1980	24.7	22.0
1970	23.2	20.8
1960	22.8	20.3
1950	22.8	20.3
1940	24.3	21.5
1930	24.3	21.3
1920	24.6	21.2
1910	25.1	21.6
1900	25.9	21.9
1890	26.1	22.0

Source: From "America's Families and Living Arrangements: 2003" in *Current Population Reports,* P-20 (No. 553), U.S. Census Bureau, Washington, D.C., 2004.

The average age at first marriage in the United States has gradually increased since the record lows during the mid-1950s (Table 14.1). Small increases in the age at first marriage occurred from 1955 to 1975. However, sharper increases have occurred in the last two decades. This U-shaped curve (from a higher age in the 1890s to a relatively low age in the 1950s back to a higher age today) is an excellent example of contextualism (see Chapter 1). One example of the effect of the current context for marriage is the rising number of women who have entered the workforce during this period.

An interesting change has been the nearly triple rise in the proportion of young adults who have not married during the past four decades. Eighty-six percent of men aged 20 to 24 years had never married in 2004, up from 36% in 1970. In this same time period, the rate went from 11% to 57% for men 25 to 29 years old and from 6% to 32% for men aged 30 to 34. As expected, because men marry later, men have higher proportions of the never-married in all age groups (U.S. Census Bureau, 2006).

Another aspect of young adult relationships is cohabitation, which involves sharing a residence and personal assets, and sometimes having a child, without being married. In the years between 1990 and 2000, there was a 71% increase in the number of unmarried partners who were living together (U.S. Census Bureau, 2001). This figure includes both heterosexual and homosexual domestic partners. In comparison, there was only a 7% increase in the number of married couples during the same period of time. However, the recent jump in the number of unmarried, cohabiting couples will undoubtedly affect all these findings.

More Americans are marrying outside of their racial groups, according to the major 1990 U.S. Census data (Reyes, 1997). White men who had served in the military were three times as likely to marry outside their racial group as men who had never served. White women in the military were seven times as likely to marry outside their racial group as men who had never served.

The recent trend in increased divorce rates is probably caused, at least in part, by four factors:

1. Liberalization of divorce laws.

2. Growing societal acceptance of divorce and of remaining single.

3. Reduction in the cost of divorces, largely through no-fault divorce laws.

4. Broadening educational and work experience of women, which has contributed to increased economic and social independence, a possible factor in marital dissolution.

Other factors that affect divorce rates are ethnicity, the wife's workforce participation, the husband's employment status, and residence status. Changes in gender equity, for example, will have a great impact on marriage and families. Personal goals and support from nonfamily members affect a person's desire to get, or remain, married. Related to the role that networks of nonrelatives and friends play in providing support to a family, one study of school-age children in a U.S. city presented evidence of a social support system available to parents and their children. Such a network exists across ethnic groups, although the exact nature of the network is not always the same. For example, middle-class European Americans are more likely than other ethnic groups to involve friends or neighbors in their social or community activities. However, Latinos and African Americans are more likely to spend time with extended family members who live in the household or nearby. Children who are part of such an extended social network are more likely to perform better in school, and to be more socially competent and happier than children in families who lack this support system (Marshall et al., 2001).

Who contributes the most to offsetting the negative effects of isolation and stress many face in their lives? Looking at the ability of family and friend support to the psychological well-being of Latino college students, Rodriguez and associates (2003) found that "friend support made a slightly greater contribution to well-being than family support" (p. 236). In addition, friend support but not family support protected against the negative effects of psychological distress.

Researchers have also asked the question "When a marriage produces a sense of well-being, is that due to the state of marriage itself or because mentally healthy people are more likely to marry than those with problems?" Horvitz and associates (1996) completed a study of 450 males and females age 12, 15, and 18 years old in a longitudinal study that took place from 1982 to 1994. They concluded that

> with controls for premarital rates of mental health, young adults who get married and stay married experience higher levels of well-being than those who remain single... When both male-prevalent and female-prevalent outcome measures are used, both men and women benefit from marriage. (p. 895)

However, decreased marital satisfaction has long been linked to the addition of children to the marriage. The transition to parenthood has been implicated as a risk factor for married couples. Some researchers view this transition as a crisis period that slowly improves as the child grows older.

Cox and associates (1999) observed couples before and after the birth of their first child to determine the impact of the child on the marriage. Several interesting findings emerged:

- Couples reported higher marital satisfaction if the pregnancy was planned.

- Lower marital satisfaction was reported by couples who had depressive symptoms before the birth of the child.

Three marvelously well-written books that deal with this subject area are (1) John Fowles's *The Magus* (1985, revised edition). Boston: Little, Brown. This is surely one of the best psychological mystery stories ever written. (2) Mary Gordon's *Final Payments* (2006). New York: Random House. (3) John Updike's *Rabbit, Run* (1960). New York: Knopf. This is the first of four books that chronicle the development of an ordinary man whose nickname is "Rabbit."

- Marital satisfaction decreased over time for parents of girls.
- Marital satisfaction was higher if at least one partner demonstrated positive problem-solving communication skills.

It is clear that marriage presents challenges as well as rewards—emotional, physical, and material. The concept of marriage is something that bears consideration and definition. Some would argue that there is a great need for redefinition as well.

Types of Marriage

monogamy
Standard marriage form in the United States and most other nations, in which there is one husband and one wife.

polygamy
Marriage in which there is one husband but two or more wives.

polyandry
Marriage in which there is one wife but two or more husbands.

group marriage
Marriage that includes two or more of both husbands and wives, who all exercise common privileges and responsibilities.

homosexual marriages
Though not accepted legally, the weddings of homosexuals are now accepted by some religions.

Attitudes toward marriage, and therefore types of marriage, vary greatly throughout the world. Despite many variations in the ways humans begin their married lives, there are basically four kinds of marriage throughout the world: monogamy, polygamy, polyandry, and group marriage.

Monogamy is the standard marriage form in the United States and most other nations, in which there is one husband and one wife. In **polygamy,** there is one husband but two or more wives. In earlier times in this country, this form of marriage was practiced by the Mormons of Utah. There are still some places in the world where it exists, but the number is dwindling. **Polyandry** is a type of marriage in which there is one wife but two or more husbands. The rarest type of marriage, it is practiced only in situations where there are very few females. **Group marriage** includes two or more of both husbands and wives, who all exercise common privileges and responsibilities. In the late 1960s this form of marriage received considerable attention, but it accounts for a minuscule percentage of the world's population and has lost considerable popularity in recent years.

Homosexual marriages, although not officially sanctioned in many parts of the world, are beginning to be accepted in some U.S. states, either as civil unions/domestic partnerships (CA, CT, NH, NJ, VT) or as fully sanctioned marriages (MA). Other states have less-than-comprehensive statewide recognition of same-sex relationships (HI, ME, WA).

Same-sex marriages, according to Rutter and Schwartz (2000), can provide individuals with an intimate, mature relationship. Kurdek (1998) conducted a longitudinal study that compared heterosexual married couples with gay and lesbian cohabiting couples. The study examined whether there were differences between the groups with regard to relationship quality. The quality of the relationship comprised five dimensions: constructive problem solving, intimacy, equality, autonomy, and barriers to leaving. Although there were some differences between the groups, the findings suggest that, overall, married heterosexual couples "are more similar to than different from cohabiting gay or lesbian partners." At the same time, though, this type of relationship presents a number of unique challenges to the couple.

Two lesbian women hold their Vermont License and Certificate of Civil Union at the town hall in Williston, VT. They were among the first to take advantage of the new state legislation providing same-sex couples with legal benefits similar to marriage in July of 2000.

Aside from prejudice and lack of understanding from society at large, in the United States many social service networks and agencies are unprepared to offer services to gay and lesbian men and women (p. 148).

Guided Review

1. The sharpest increases in the average age at first marriage have occurred in the last two decades. One reason for this trend may be that higher numbers of women have entered the _____ during this time.

2. Of Latinos, African-Americans, and whites, _____ have the largest families.

3. Societal acceptance of divorce and of remaining single has been (increasing, decreasing, staying about the same) lately.

4. Four factors are attributed to a recent trend in increased divorce rates. These factors include _____ of divorce laws, growing social acceptance of divorce, reduction in cost of divorces, and the broadening educational and work experience of women.

5. Basically, four types of marriage exist in the world: monogamy, polygamy, _____, and group marriage.

PERSONAL DEVELOPMENT

In this section, we discuss the theories of Daniel Levinson and Erik Erikson. Each of these theories is classic and offers insights into the development of the adult personality that are still of great value. We also consider gender differences in individuation.

The Adult Life Cycle: Levinson

Yale psychologist Daniel Levinson, who died in 1994, was one of the most respected researchers in adult developmental psychology. Working with his colleagues at Yale, he derived a theory of adult development based on intensive interviews with 40 men and 40 women. Levinson found that intensive interviewing and psychological testing with a small number of representative cases provided him with information to formulate a theory of adult development.

Key to Levinson's (1978, 1986, 1990a) theory of adult development is the notion of **life course.** *Life* refers to all aspects of living—everything that has significance in a life. *Course* refers to the flow or unfolding of an individual's life. Life course, therefore, looks at the complexity of life as it evolves over time.

Equally important to Levinson's theory is the notion of **life cycle.** Building on the findings of his research, Levinson proposed that there is "an underlying order in the human life course; although each individual life is unique, everyone goes through the same basic sequence" (1986, p. 4). The life cycle is a general pattern of adult development, whereas the life course is the unique embodiment of the life cycle by an individual.

Through his studies, Levinson further defined the life cycle as a sequence of eras. Each era is biopsychosocial in character: It is composed of the interaction of the individual, complete with his or her own biological and psychological makeup, with the social environment. Each era is important in itself and in its contribution

life course
Levinson's term. Life refers to all aspects of living—everything that has significance in a life; course refers to the flow or unfolding of an individual's life.

life cycle
Levinson's term; the life cycle is a general pattern of adult development, whereas the life course is the unique embodiment of the life cycle by an individual.

Answers   1. workforce (or job market) 2. Latinos 3. increasing 4. liberalization 5. polyandry

Responsibility for Self

One of the clearest indexes of maturity is the ability to be responsible for your own life and behavior. This exercise asks a number of questions involving responsibility for your own behavior.

1. Name two major purchases you have made in the past year by yourself without a strong influence by anyone else.
2. Wherever it is that you live, do your parents support you, or do you pay for your own housing?
3. Are you completely in charge of what time you come home at night, or do you have to answer to someone else?
4. Are you the sole person who decides what clothing you wear?

5. To what extent have your parents influenced your career—that is, whether you have chosen to go to college or work, the acceptability of your grades or pay, and so on?
6. Are you able to make independent decisions about your sex life? Do you let your parents know what you have decided?

You might compare your answers with those of some of your friends to get a relative idea of how responsible you are for your life.

---

transition
Levinson's concept that each new era begins as an old era is approaching its end; that "in-between" time is a transition.

life structure
The underlying pattern or design of a person's life at a given time.

structure-building
During structure-building periods, individuals face the task of building a stable structure around choices they have made.

structure-changing
Process of reappraising the existing life structure and exploring the possibilities for new life structures characterizes the structure-changing period.

to the whole of the life cycle. A new era begins as the previous era approaches its end. That in-between time is characterized as a **transition.**

The intricacies of Levinson's theory of adult life course and life cycle are further elaborated by his concept of the adult **life structure**—the underlying pattern or design of a person's life at a given time. Levinson noted that "a theory of life structure is a way of conceptualizing answers to a different question: 'What is my life like now?'" (1986, p. 6). The primary components of a life structure are the relationships that an individual has with significant others. Levinson regarded relationships as actively and mutually shaped. Life structure may have many components, but generally only one or two components are central in the structure at a given time. The central component is the one that most strongly influences the life structure of the individual.

The evolutionary sequence of the life structure includes an alternating series of **structure-building** and **structure-changing** transitions. During the structure-building periods, individuals face the task of building a stable structure around choices they have made. They seek to enhance the life within that structure. During this period of 5–7 years, the stability of the life structure affords individuals the freedom to question their choices and to consider modifying their life.

The process of reappraising the existing life structure and exploring new life structures characterizes the structure-changing period, whichusually lasts around five years. Its end is marked by the making of critical life choices around which the individual will build a new life structure. Levinson noted that the individual decides at this point, "This I will settle for" (1986, p. 7).

In considering the periods of stability and change in the adult life cycle, Levinson noted, "We remain novices in every era until we have had a chance to try out an entry life structure and then to question and modify it in the mid-era transition" (1986, p. 7). Individuals enter into new stages of adult development as they become focused on certain developmental tasks. Levinson captured the evolution of the focus of an individual and the flowing quality of adult development. Unlike most theories of child development,, Levinson's study of adult development recognized a coexistence of growth and decline.

Seasons of a Man's Life: Levinson

Levinson made two separate studies, one of men (1978) and one of women (1990b) (both to be further described in Chapter 16). In his first study (of men) 40 male subjects ranging in age from 35 to 45 were selected, representing four categories (10 each): blue-collar workers paid on an hourly basis, middle-level executives, academic biologists, and novelists. Of course, this sample cannot be considered to represent the average male in the United States, but the diversity of the people selected in social class origins; racial, ethnic, and religious backgrounds; education; and marital status does make it typical of a great deal of American society today.

The study concentrated on the choices made by each man during his life and how he dealt with the consequences of his choices, especially as they affected occupation, marriage, and family. After studying these components, Levinson suggested that there are four main seasons of male life: (1) childhood and adolescence—birth to 22 years; (2) early adulthood—17 to 45 years; (3) middle adulthood—40 to 65 years; and (4) older adulthood—60 years and older.

Obviously, considerable overlap occurs between each of the stages Levinson theorized, and substages help with the transitions necessary for development. Figure 14.1 gives a description of various stages and substages. Levinson concentrated on the early and middle adult periods, leaving further consideration of the childhood and late adult periods to others.

He believed that "even the most disparate lives are governed by the same underlying order—a sequence of eras and developmental periods" (1978, p. 64). The purpose of these developmental transitions is to cause greater individuation. **Individuation** refers to how we develop a separate and special personality, derived less and less from our parents and teachers and more from our own behavior. This idea is reinforced by recent research, which suggests that problems in earlier stages of development affect ego and status attainment in adulthood (Chen & Kaplan, 2003; Krettenauer et al., 2003).

Although Levinson hypothesized more than 10 substages in the course of a man's life, he chose to concentrate on three specific phases in male development. These are the novice phase, the settling-down phase, and the mid-life transition (the last two are discussed in Chapter 16).

individuation
Refers to our becoming more individual; we develop a separate and special personality, derived less and less from our parents and teachers and more from our own behavior.

FIGURE 14.1

Model of Levinson's theory. Levinson's initial phase of human development extends from ages 17 to 33 and includes the early adult transition, entering the adult world, and the age-30 transition.

From *The Seasons of a Man's Life* by Daniel Levinson. Copyright © 1975, 1978 by Daniel J. Levinson. Used by permission of Alfred A. Knopf, a division of Random House, Inc. and reprinted by permission of SLL/Sterling Lord Literistic, Inc.

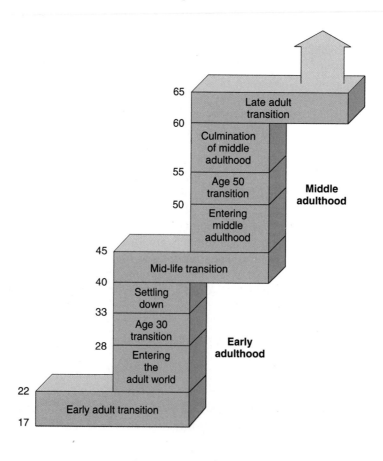

A solid relationship with an older mentor is crucial to the career success of a young adult, according to Levinson. Why is it, do you think, that older males are more likely to take a mentoring attitude toward their younger colleagues than are older females toward their younger colleagues?

The Novice Phase

The **novice phase** of human development extends from age 17 to 33 and includes the early adult transition, entering the adult world, and the age-30 transition (see Figure 14.1). In this phase of life, four major tasks are to be accomplished. The man in the novice phase should form:

1. *The dream.* "Most men construct a vision, an imagined possibility that generates vitality" (p. 91).
2. *Mentor relationships.* Each man should find someone who is older, more experienced, and willing to make suggestions at each of the choice points in his early adult life.
3. *An occupational decision.* A man should begin to build on his strengths and to choose a vocation that values those strengths.
4. *Love relationships.* Each man should make decisions on a marriage partner, number of children desired, and the type of relationship that he wants to have with his wife and children.

novice phase
Period of ages 17–33 that includes early adult transition, according to Levinson.

The Mentor

mentoring
The act of assisting another, usually younger, person with his or her work or life tasks.

The concept of **mentoring** has received considerable attention in recent years (Cannister, 1999; Johnson, 2002; Thompson & Kelly-Vance, 2001). Cannister (1999) found that young men involved in mentor relationships reported improved spiritual well-being over time, compared with peers without mentors.

Levinson found that after each man selects a dream, mentor relationship, occupation, and love relationship, at around age 30 (plus or minus two years), he comes to reexamine his feelings about these four major tasks. Important decisions are made at this time, such as an alteration of the dream, a change in mentor, a change in occupation, and sometimes a change in marital status. For some, this transitional period proves to be very smooth. In most cases, however, it challenges the very foundations of life itself. Although he often keeps it to himself, the typical male at this stage undergoes a serious period of self-doubt. Fortunately, most emerge from these doubts with a clearer understanding of their strengths and weaknesses and a clearer view of what they wish to make of themselves.

The racial group to which one belongs plays an important role in one's concept of self. For college students, the campus climate is usually a significant influence on their views of themselves. In a study examining racial differences in perception of general campus climate, Reid and Radhakrishnan (2003) found that "racial minority students, particularly African-Americans, perceived more negative general campus, racial, and academic climates than [did] White students." The study concluded that one's academic and racial experiences were "the best predictors of their perception of the general campus climate" (p. 263).

An insightful book on this topic is Robert Bly's *Iron John* (2004). Reading, MA: Addison-Wesley. A teacher of both poetry and philosophy, Bly combines the two in this fascinating tale of a journey into the self. Among other insights, he explores the modern young man's grief over his inability to become close to his father.

Yearn to understand first and to be understood second.

—Confucius

Thus, for Levinson, the transition from late adolescence to early adulthood (and for the years to come) tends to proceed in stages as orderly as those we have seen in the earlier stages of life. More variation occurs as we grow older, because we are affected by our own individual decisions. Even if we have had a hard childhood, with alcoholic parents and traumatic accidents, we should be developing the ability to be in charge of our lives. As we grow older, we have the opportunity, and indeed the responsibility, to reinvent ourselves. Of course, how we reinvent ourselves is influenced by culture. Some have suggested that Levinson's theory is culturally limited to the United States. What do you think? The next theorist we will cover, Erikson, offered his own views.

Intimacy versus Isolation: Erikson

We last talked about Erikson's theory in Chapter 11, where we discussed his fifth stage (adolescence), identity and repudiation versus identity confusion. Now we consider his sixth stage, intimacy and solidarity versus isolation. This stage applies to what he defined as young adulthood, ages 18 to 25.

In his definition of intimacy, Erikson stated that it should include:

1. Mutuality of orgasm
2. with a loved partner
3. of the other sex
4. with whom one is able and willing to share a mutual trust
5. and with whom one is able and willing to regulate the cycles of
   a. work
   b. procreation
   c. recreation

   so as to secure to the offspring, too, all the stages of a satisfactory development (1963, p. 266).

Erikson pointed out, however, that sexual intercourse should not be assumed to be the most important aspect of intimacy between individuals. He was talking about the ability to relate one's deepest hopes and fears to another person and to accept another's need for intimacy in turn.

Those who have achieved the stage of **intimacy** are able to commit themselves to concrete affiliations and partnerships with others and have developed the "ethical strength to abide by such commitments, even though they may call for

intimacy
Erikson's stage that represents the ability to relate one's deepest hopes and fears to another person and to accept another's need for intimacy in turn.

The 1960s were a time when many grass-roots action groups, such as Students for a Democratic Society, came into being. An example of a grass-roots action group that is currently in operation would be the Green Party that runs candidates for elective office. Can you name others?

solidarity
Erikson's term for the personality style of persons who are able to commit themselves in concrete affiliations and partnerships.

distantiation
The readiness of all of us to distance ourselves from others when we feel threatened by their behavior.

isolation
The readiness all of us have to isolate ourselves from others when we feel threatened by their behavior.

significant sacrifices and compromises" (1963, p. 262). This leads to **solidarity** between partners.

The counterpart of intimacy is **distantiation**—the readiness we have to distance ourselves from others when we feel threatened by their behavior. Distantiation is the cause of most prejudices and discrimination. Propaganda efforts mounted by countries at war are examples of attempts to increase distantiation. It is what leads to **isolation.**

Most young adults vacillate between their desires for intimacy and their need for distantiation. They need social distance because they are not sure of their identities. They are always vulnerable to criticism, and because they can't be sure whether the criticisms are true or not, they protect themselves by a "lone wolf" stance.

Although intimacy may be difficult for some males today, Erikson believed that it used to be even more difficult for females. "All this is a little more complicated with women, because women, at least in yesterday's cultures, had to keep their identities incomplete until they knew their man" (1978, p. 49). Today less emphasis in the female gender role is placed on getting married and pleasing one's husband, and more emphasis is on being true to one's own identity. A growing number of theorists, however, many of them feminist psychologists, argue that females still have a harder time "reinventing" themselves, because of the way our society educates them. In the next section, we present their position.

Guided Review

6. Daniel Levinson's theory looks at adult development by examining life _____ (the unique development of the individual) and the life _____ (the general pattern of adult development).

7. Life structure is the underlying pattern or design of a person's life at a given time. It is _____ in character, with a primary component being the _____ that an individual has with significant others.

8. Erik Erikson's sixth stage of psychosocial development, intimacy versus isolation, focuses on building a _____, as opposed to Levinson's more career-oriented approach.

SEXUAL IDENTITY AND GENDER ROLES

The problem lay buried, unspoken, for many years in the minds of American women. It was a strange stirring, a sense of dissatisfaction, a yearning that women suffered in the middle of the 20th century in the United States. Each suburban wife struggled with it alone, as she made the beds, shopped for groceries, matched slipcover material, ate peanut butter sandwiches with her children, chauffeured Cub Scouts and Brownies, lay beside her husband at night—she was afraid to ask even of herself the silent question—"Is this all?" (Friedan, 1963, p. 1)

This paragraph, which opened Betty Friedan's famous book *The Feminine Mystique,* marked the beginning of a major reexamination of the female gender role. Today we are still undergoing societal inquiry into the appropriate gender roles of both sexes. But are we any nearer to the answers we seek?

Consider this statement that the famed Greek philosopher Aristotle made more than 2,000 years ago: "Woman may be said to be an inferior man." Most of us would

Answers 6. course, cycle 7. biopsychosocial, relationships 8. partnership

The beginning of the "feminist revolution" in the 1960s opened an era of changing views toward gender roles. Do you believe that society's views of gender roles are significantly different today from what they were 10 years ago?

disagree with his viewpoint publicly, but the underlying attitude is still widespread. People today are far less willing to admit to a belief in female inferiority, but many still act as though it were so. However, the influence of the women's movement, as well as of science and other forms of social change, is profoundly affecting the way we view sexual identity and gender role (Harding, 1998).

First, we should make a distinction between the two. Sexual identity results from those physical characteristics that are part of our biological inheritance. They are the genetic traits that make us males or females. Genitals and facial hair are examples of sex-linked physical characteristics. Gender role, in contrast, results largely from societal and cultural traits in fashion at any one time. For example, women appear to be able to express their emotions through crying more easily than men do, although no known physical cause accounts for this difference.

People may accept or reject their sexual identity, their gender role, or both. For example, Jan Morris, a British author, spent most of her life as the successful author James Morris. Although born a male, she deeply resented the fact that she had a male sexual identity and hated having to perform the male gender role. She always felt that inside she was really a woman. The cause of these feelings may have been psychological—the result of a childhood event. Or the cause may have been genetic—something to do with hormone balance. Such rejection is rare, and there is no one distinct cause. Morris decided to have a transsexual operation that changed her from male to female. The change caused many problems in her life, but she says she is infinitely happier to have her body match her feelings about her gender role.

Some people are so unhappy with their sexual identity that they have it changed surgically. Renee Richards—(a) before the surgery and (b) the female tennis star—used to be a man by the name of Richard Raskind. What kinds of changes in self-concept would such a person have to make, do you think?

(a)

(b)

Aspects of Gender Role

Some people are perfectly happy with their sexual identity but don't like their gender role. Gender role itself has three aspects:

- *Gender-role orientation.* Individuals differ in how confident they feel about their sexual identity. Males often have a weaker gender-role orientation than females. (This will be discussed later in the chapter.)
- *Gender-role preference.* Some individuals feel unhappy about their gender role, as did Jan Morris, and wish either society or their sex could be changed. The feminist movement of the last few decades has had a major impact on many of the world's societies in this regard.
- *Gender-role adaptation.* Adaptation is defined by whether other people judge individual behavior as masculine or feminine. If a person is seen as acting "appropriately" according to his or her gender, then adaptation has occurred. People who dislike their gender role or doubt that they fit it well (for example, the teenage boy who fights a lot because he secretly doubts he is masculine enough) may be viewed as poorly adapted.

The Traditionalist View

The traditional view holds that sexual identity is the result of interaction between sex chromosome differences at conception and early treatment by the people in a child's environment. Once culture has had the opportunity to influence a child's sexual identity, it is unlikely to change, even when biological changes occur. Even in such extreme cases of **chromosome failure** as gynecomastia (breast growth in the male) and hirsutism (abnormal female body hair), sexual identity is not affected. In almost all cases, those with one of these problems desperately want medical treatment so they can keep their sexual identity.

Some research indicates that people's gender roles evolve, in part, because of relationships with important individuals. For example, according to Bohannon and Blanton (1999), mothers and daughters share similar attitudes toward gender, marriage, and family issues. Furthermore, although these attitudes often change over time, owing to social and other environmental factors, these attitudes change for both groups in similar ways. As a result of this study, the authors hypothesized that mothers influence the development of their daughters' gender role attitudes in early life, whereas daughters may influence the development of their mothers' gender role attitudes as they both mature.

Evolutionary Psychology

A more recent theory that also reflects the biological viewpoint is known as *evolutionary psychology.* Proponents of this view hold that behaviors, including those typically seen in the two genders, are programmed into our genes (Bjorklund & Pellegrini, 2002; Buss, 2001; Grossman & Kaufman, 2002). Gender-bound behaviors are thought to have evolved over the millennia because they serve some useful purpose. Hence, males and females are genetically predisposed to react to the environment in specific ways. In this regard, we are no different from other mammals. In most species, for example, the male is responsible for guarding the family group (herd, pride), and the female is responsible for watching over the young. Likewise, over the many centuries of human development, males have been rewarded for being competitive and females for being cooperative. As you would expect, many researchers and feminists disagree with this biological explanation, arguing that gender-related behaviors are more likely the result of learning that occurred in childhood (Harding, 1998).

chromosome failure
Biological changes such as enlarged breasts in males and abnormal body hair in females.

An excellent reference book on this topic is Judy Blume's *Letters to Judy: What Your Kids Wish They Could Tell You* (1987). New York: G. P. Putnam's Sons. Blume offers letters from young adults who confide their concerns over the stresses of friendships, families, abuse, illness, suicide, drugs, sexuality, and other problems.

For more on this subject, read *Adulthood* (1978). New York: Norton. Edited by Erikson, this collection of essays explains what it means to become an adult and is written by experts from a wide variety of fields.

Androgyny

One gender-role researcher, Sandra Bem (1999), argued that typical American roles are actually unhealthy. She said that highly masculine males tend to have better psychological adjustment than other males during adolescence, but as adults they tend to become highly anxious and neurotic and often experience low self-acceptance. Highly feminine females suffer in similar ways.

Bem believed we would all be much better off if we were more androgynous. The word is made up of the Greek words for male, *andro,* and for female, *gyne.* It refers to the ability to behave in a way appropriate to a situation, regardless of one's sex. For example, when someone forces his way into a line at the movies, the traditional female role calls for a woman to look disapproving but to say nothing. The androgynous female would tell the offender in no uncertain terms to go to the end of the line. When a baby left unattended starts to cry, the traditional male response is to try to find a woman to take care of its needs. The androgynous male would pick up the infant and attempt to comfort it.

Androgyny is not merely the midpoint between two poles of masculinity and femininity. Rather, it is a more functional level of gender-role identification than either of the more traditional roles. Figure 14.2 illustrates this relationship. Not surprising, Joensson and Carlsson (2000) found that people who were more androgynous were rated as more creative than people who were either strongly masculine or feminine.

Before we look at the relationship between gender roles and sexuality, we need to examine one other factor. This is the difference between female and male identity.

Male versus Female Identity

> *Identity precedes intimacy for men. . . . For women, intimacy goes with identity, as the female comes to know herself as she is known, through her relationships with others.* (Gilligan, 1982, p. 12)

According to this view, because females are trained to believe in the necessity of their maintaining relationships within the family, and because this role often involves self-sacrifice, women find it harder to individuate—that is, to develop a healthy adult personality of their own. For the young adult male, identity formation involves establishing himself as an independent, self-sufficient adult who can compete and succeed in the world.

For the young adult female, career and self-assurance are not emphasized to the same degree. Gaining the attention and commitment of a man is often viewed as a more important aspect of a woman's identity, and intimacy is the major goal. This is seen as unhealthy. Recent research has noted gender differences in identity development, in the United States and other countries (Bergh & Erling, 2005), though this idea is not new.

This point of view arose in the 1960s, primarily with Betty Friedan's book. The **feminist movement** fostered a new commitment to women's issues and to studies of women themselves. For example, as a result of her research on the female perspective (see Chapter 9), Harvard psychologist Carol Gilligan and others (1982, 1990) have come to believe that

> *for girls and women, issues of femininity or feminine identity do not depend on the achievement of separation from the mother or on the progress of*

androgyny
Functional level of gender-role identifications that incorporates male and female qualities.

feminist movement
The efforts of some women to secure more equitable standards in workplace, society, and home.

FIGURE 14.2

Relationships among the three gender roles.

From R.J. Sternberg, "The Triangular Theory of Love" in *Psychological Review,* 93: 119–135. Copyright 1986 by the American Psychological Association. Adapted with permission of the American Psychological Association and the author.

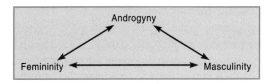

For most young adults, society's gender roles determine the kind of careers they can have. What, if anything, should be done about this?

individuation. Since masculinity is defined through separation while feminin-ity is defined through attachment, male gender identity is threatened by intimacy while female gender is threatened by separation. (1982, p. 9)

Research has also pointed to two other concerns about women's identity forma-tion. One has been the tendency of society to "objectify" women, which means seeing them as a particular type of creature or object rather than as individuals. This may relate to a difference in the way men and women view sexuality. As Everaerd and associates describe the difference, "The contrast between men and women would then be that in [sexual] experience, women process more situational cues and men more physiological cues" (2000, p. 88). In other words, the better part of a man's sexual drive comes from the inside, whereas for women, it tends to come from stimuli in the outside world. Thus, men are more likely to view their partners as the object of their physiological drive. Psychoanalyst Erich Fromm (1955) suggested that "to be considered an object can lead to a deep inner sense that there must be something wrong and bad about oneself" (p. 323). There can be little doubt that women have suffered as a result of this difference: Take, for exam-ple, the fact that males perpetrate an extremely high percentage of sexual abuse (Calhoun & Wilson, 2000). These authors report that on average, over half the women on the nation's college campuses record having experienced some sort of sexual victimization. Hamby and Sugarman (1999) found that males are more likely to cause psychological, as well as physical, abuse.

Another concern involves the ability to admit vulnerability. Men are taught to avoid showing any signs of vulnerability, whereas women are taught being vulner-able can be a virtue. In fact, some (Jacobs & Speckhardt, 2004) have argued that the so-called sexual revolution has brought gains as well as setbacks. Greater artic-ulation of sexual "rights" might shed light on societal opinions relating to gender. Obviously more work is needed to resolve this question of the role of gender in the development of the adult personality. Erikson (1963) himself appears to have endorsed this point of view, by stating that

there will be many difficulties in a new joint adjustment of the sexes to changing conditions, but they do not justify prejudices which keep half of mankind from participating in planning and decision making, especially at a time when the other half [men], by its competitive escalation and acceleration of technological progress, has brought us and our children to the gigantic brink on which we live, with all our affluence. (p. 293)

For example, recent studies have repudiated the old idea that both sexes respond to stress with a "fight-or-flight" response (see Chapter 16). That is, when we are threatened, ancient structures that have evolved in our brains cause us to want to attack or run away. This appears to be truer of males than of females. Because women have higher concentrations of oxytocin in their brains, they are more likely to respond when threatened with a **bend-and-bond response.** In other words, they are more likely to seek a compromise solution to a conflict, which is followed by a sense of improved relationship with the potential enemy (Douglas, Johnstone, & Russell, 2000; Neumann et al., 2000).

This gender difference is reflected in a number of ways. Let's take, for example, the question: "Are there gender differences in empathy and forgiveness in conflict resolution?" This is the question that propelled researchers Toussaint and Webb (2005) to survey 127 community residents. The researchers found that while men showed lower levels of empathy than women did, it was more important for them in terms of forgiveness and resolving conflicts.

Are such gender differences cast in concrete? Apparently not. Despite our new understanding of the differences in male and female biology, society and its new child-rearing practices are clearly guiding males toward less aggressive gender roles and away from placing such a high value on competition. As a result, developmental theorists are coming to agreement on a view of identity that holds that men and women are really more like each other, especially in our need to interrelate, than we have realized. It may be that males and females have seemed so different only because we have been taught to think so—the self-fulfilling prophecy.

In each of the theories described in the following section on personality, the roles of biological, psychological, and social forces are evident. No one force completely dominates. Once again, we see the power of the biopsychosocial theory, which points to the complex interaction of all three forces in the explanation of human behavior.

bend-and-bond response
The more typically female response to threats is to seek a compromise, rather than the male response of "fight-or-flight."

Guided Review

9. With regard to gender roles, many people are not willing to admit a belief in female _____ but act as if it were so.

10. *Sexual identity* refers to our physical characteristics, whereas *gender roles* refers largely to the specific social _____ in fashion at a given time in a culture.

11. The three parts of gender identity are gender-role _____, gender-role preference, and gender-role adaptation.

12. Erik Erikson believed that gender differences are _____ determined, based on his experiments with girls and boys as they played with building blocks.

13. According to Bem, _____ is characterized by more functional levels of role identification than by either male or female roles.

INTERPERSONAL RELATIONS

As young adults relate to one another, two of the most important human conditions with which they must deal are sexual behavior and love.

Answers 9. inferiority 10. characteristics 11. orientation 12. biologically 13. androgyny

Sexuality

Another example of the effect of social forces on sexual behavior is in the declining rates of sexual activity among young adults. According to a study by the Centers for Disease Control and Prevention (2000a), young people are having sex less frequently and with fewer partners than they did a decade ago. They also report using contraception, such as condoms, more often than ever. Researchers think that this may be due to increases in sex education across the country, particularly with regard to contraceptive use and abstinence. Social forces are also reflected in the experimental qualities of dating, such as examining gender roles, identity, and sexuality (DeGenova & Rice, 2005). Although dating practices may bolster one's confidence and sense of identity, it may keep people from forming deeper, more committed relationships.

Some experts suggest that pack dating (Gabriel, 1997) may be an attempt, in part, to deal with the risk of disease. Although HIV infection rates appear to be relatively low on campuses, rates of other STIs, such as venereal warts and chlamydia, are soaring. Because HIV can remain dormant for up to 15 years before becoming AIDS, we really don't know its incidence. Choosing a sex partner from a small circle of friends allows a person to know the histories and habits of the potential partners, which could possibly reduce the risk of contracting an STI.

Another explanation for pack dating is that students simply don't have time for relationships. Many students hold at least one job while carrying a full course load, and others are focused on earning grades that will help get them into graduate school.

However, not all college students engage in pack dating. Some choose to become emotionally and physically involved with only one partner and enjoy spending time alone with that person. Knox, Zusman, and Nieves (1998) were interested in learning why people choose a particular person to date or to marry. They found that both men and women felt it was important to choose a partner similar to themselves in terms of age, values, and education. They also found that men and women valued different characteristics in a partner. Women also stressed the importance of occupation and religious values as well as the desire to have children. Men, however, were more influenced by the physical attractiveness of a partner. Other research has investigated same-sex attraction and the biological and social factors that influence relationships in adulthood (Dickson, Paul, & Herbison, 2003). Most researchers agree that sexual development is a lifelong process (DeLamater & Friedrich, 2002).

Marital Practices

Intercourse between a husband and wife is the only type of sexual activity totally approved of by American society. Sexual closeness also tends to lessen significantly with the birth of each child, except in cases where the couple has taken specific steps to maintain the quality of their sexual relationship.

A number of findings of the Janus Report (Janus & Janus, 1993) are relevant to the marital behavior and attitudes of young adults. Among the most important findings are

- Women who lived with their spouses before marriage are more likely to be divorced than women who didn't; men, less likely. Couples still married lived together, on the average, for a shorter period of time before marriage than those who are now divorced.

- Among the divorced, men cite sexual problems as the primary reason for the divorce three times more frequently than women. Women cite extramarital affairs twice as frequently as men. But both cite emotional problems as the most frequent cause of divorce.

● Among the divorced respondents, 39% of the men and 27% of the women report using no contraception.

Another important question that we might ask has to do with frequency of sexual relations among young adults. There is an old joke, which suggests the following guidelines: under 25, twice daily; between 25 and 35, try weekly; between 35 and 45, try weekly; between 45 and 55, try weekly; after 55, try, try, try. This joke is a good example of an inaccurate stereotype. In fact, as we will detail later, young adults engage in sex with each other at about the same rate as adults over the age of 55 and less than middle-aged adults. Most adults are more sexually active when they have a regular partner, but because of the much higher average age of marriage mentioned earlier in this chapter, a fairly high percentage do not have sex at all or only rarely.

As Everaerd and associates (2000) have stated, "But frequency follows desire, and not the other way around. Desire will vary with sexual sensitivity and availability of attractive partners, and will generally decrease in the long-lasting relationships and with age" (p. 82). Thus, statistics about the frequency of the sexual activity among young adults do not necessarily describe very well what most of them are doing.

In the next section we turn to an examination of the deepest aspect of human relationship, love. The words written about love over the course of human history are uncountable. In this book, we will limit ourselves to describing the developmental aspects of this emotion: the seven forms of love that psychologist Robert Sternberg has suggested and psychoanalyst Erich Fromm's definition of the essence of love.

Forms and Factors of Love: Sternberg

passion
Sternberg's term for a strong desire for another person and the expectation that sex with them will prove physiologically rewarding.

intimacy
Sternberg's term for the ability to share one's deepest and most secret feelings and thoughts with another.

commitment
Sternberg's term for the strongly held conviction that one will stay with another, regardless of the cost.

Sternberg (1997) argued that love is made up of three different components:

● **Passion.** A strong desire for another person, and the expectation that sex with them will prove physiologically rewarding.
● **Intimacy.** The ability to share one's deepest and most secret feelings and thoughts with another.
● **Commitment.** The strongly held conviction that one will stay with another, regardless of the cost.

Each of these components may or may not be involved in a relationship. The extent to which each is involved defines the type of love that is present in the relationship. Sternberg believed that the various combinations actually found in human relations produce seven forms of love (see Table 14.2).

TABLE 14.2	Sternberg's Seven Forms of Love
Liking	Intimacy, but no passion or commitment
Infatuation	Passion, but no intimacy or commitment
Empty love	Commitment, but no passion or intimacy
Romantic love	Intimacy and passion, but no commitment
Fatuous love	Commitment and passion, but no intimacy
Companionate love	Commitment and intimacy, but no passion
Consummate love	Commitment, intimacy, and passion

From R.J. Sternberg, "The Triangular Theory of Love" in *Psychological Review,* 93: 119–135. Copyright 1986 by the American Psychological Association. Adapted with permission of the American Psychological Association and the author.

If you were about to marry, would you want to have premarital counseling? Why or why not?

This is not to say that the more of each, the better. A healthy marriage usually includes all three, but the balance among them is likely to change over the life of the marriage. For example, early in the marriage, passion is likely to be high relative to intimacy. The physical aspects of the partnership are new, and therefore exciting, although probably not enough time has passed for intimacy to develop fully. This is a dangerous time in the marriage, because when intimacy is moderate, the couple may misunderstand each other in many situations or may make unpleasant discoveries about each other. Such problems are often much more painful than they are later, when deeper intimacy and commitment have developed.

Passion, Sternberg states, is like an addiction. In the beginning, the smallest gesture can produce intense excitement. As the relationship grows older, however, larger and larger "doses" are needed to evoke the same feelings. Inevitably, passion loses some of its power. Of course, wide differences exist among couples. Some never feel much passion, whereas others maintain at least moderately passionate feelings into old age. Some appear to have strong commitments from the earliest stage of their association (love at first sight?), whereas others waver for many years.

Research indicates that love has biological and neurochemical roots (Anderson & Middleton, 2006). People who experience feelings of love, commitment, and satisfaction in their relationship are actually reaping the rewards of brain chemistry.

For an expanded view of this subject, read Robert Sternberg's "The triangular theory of love," *Psychological Review, 93,* 129–135, and "Love as a story," *Journal of Social and Personal Relationships, 12* (4), 5, 541–546. These articles, too, offer a penetrating view of this most elusive topic.

Sternberg's theory has numerous implications for couples, as well as for marriage therapists. For example, more and more couples are engaging in premarital counseling. In this, they analyze with their counselor the three factors of love and how each person feels about them. This often helps them to avoid later problems and to get their relationship off to a good start. For some, it provides information that makes them realize that, although their passion is high, their intimacy and commitment may not be, and they wait until these develop or decide not to get married at all. It is hoped that findings such as those made by Sternberg will improve counseling efforts, which will in turn help to bring about a decrease in our nation's high divorce rate. One caution: At least one review of Sternberg's model (Szuchman & Muscarella, 2000) states that, although "conceptually interesting," the model has yet to be empirically validated.

Another way of looking at conceptions of love is offered by Robert Sternberg's expansion of his triangular theory of love. He suggests (2000) that, through young adulthood, everyone develops a personal "love story." He has identified a number of these love stories.

- The travel story ("I believe that beginning a relationship is like starting a journey that promises to be both exciting and challenging.")

- The gardening story ("I believe any relationship that is left unattended will not survive.")

- The horror story ("I find it exciting when I feel my partner to be somewhat frightened of me.")

AN APPLIED VIEW

Are You a Good Lover?

I want to step out of my role as an author for a moment to write as a psychotherapist (John Dacey). Since 1973, I have had a small practice—no more than four clients a week—mostly consisting of marriage counseling. In the course of trying to help individuals to improve or save their marriages, one question almost inevitably occurs to the client: "Am I a good lover?" At first, most men will say that they think they are. As they become more trusting and self-analytical in the counseling setting, the majority realize they have serious doubts about the question. Women are much more likely to be aware of a lack of confidence in this area right from the beginning. I have met very few people, within my practice or in my social life, who are without doubts about themselves as a lover.

The problem is, it's a bad question. In fact, there's no such thing as a good lover.

I believe we can get a lot of help in understanding this issue from the contextualist approach (see Chapter 1). As you will recall, this model recommends that we consider several criteria when examining human relationships:

- *Bidirectional causation.* Most human behavior is the result of *interactions* with others. That is, I do what I do because you did what you did because I did what I did, and so on. There is seldom one clear initial cause of why we behave as we do. I have found that, in helping my clients, the question should not be "Am I a good lover?" but, rather, "Are we good lovers to each other?"

- *Historical imbeddedness.* All actions are meaningful only in the context of the historical time in which they occur. There are times during a relationship when the partners take good care of each other, sexually and otherwise. There are other times, when one or both are sick, tired, or distracted, and then, for a time at least, they are not good lovers to each other. Remember the biopsychosocial model: Over time, all three factors (biological, psychological, social) will play a role in how good a partner we are able to be.

- *Goodness of fit.* No matter how much a person might want to be a good lover, the relationship is limited by the extent to which it fits the needs of the two partners. All lovers differ in their preferences, tastes, interests, and values. Some difference in these areas is likely to add spice to the interaction. But if the differences are too great, then the level of intimacy is necessarily limited, and the individuals will be unable to be good lovers to each other no matter how much they might try. They are likely to continuously invalidate each other's personality, which inevitably causes great pain.

- *Probability.* Human interactions are complex and ever-changing. As a result, no one is a good lover all of the time. All we can hope for is that the components that make up our partnership allow us to be good lovers to each other *most of the time.* It seems to me that the greatest joy in life is to participate in a loving relationship that has a high probability of success. Only then are we likely to have much chance of being a "good lover."

- The business story ("I believe close relationships are like good partnerships.")
- The pornography story ("It is very important to be able to satisfy all my partner's sexual desires and whims.") (2000, p. 54)

Sternberg argues that, even when couples have similar values and interests, they may still have love problems because they are operating from significantly different love stories.

Validation: Fromm

In his highly enlightening book on this subject, *The Art of Loving* (1956), Erich Fromm gave us a highly respected understanding of the meaning of love. First, he argued, we must recognize that we are prisoners in our own bodies. Although we assume that we perceive the world around us in much the same way as others, we cannot really be sure. We are the only ones who truly know what our own perceptions are, and we cannot be certain they are the same as those of others. In fact, most of us are aware of times when we have misperceived something, such as hearing a phrase differently than everyone else.

Thus, we must constantly check on the reality our senses give us. We do this thousands, maybe millions, of times every day. Let us give you an example. We assume you are sitting or lying down while you are reading this book. Did you make a conscious check of the surface you are sitting or lying on when you got on it? Probably not. Nevertheless, your brain did. You know that if it had been cold, sharp, or wet, you would have noticed. That it is none of these things is something your unconscious mind ascertained without you having to give it a thought.

With some mentally ill people, this is a major problem. Their "reality checker" isn't working right. They cannot tell fact from imagination. They dwell in "castles in the air," out of contact with the real world. We need the feedback from all our senses, doing repeated checks at lightning speeds, to keep in contact with reality.

Fromm's point is this: As important as these "reality checks" on our physical environment are, how much more important are the checks on our innermost state—our deepest and most important feelings and thoughts! To check on the reality of these, we must get the honest reactions of someone we can trust. Such a person tells us, "No, you're not crazy. At least I feel the same way, too!" Even more important, these individuals prove their insight and honesty by sharing with us their own secret thoughts and feelings. In Fromm's words, others give us **validation.**

validation
Fromm's term for the reciprocal sharing of deep secrets and feelings that allows people to feel loved and accepted.

Validation is essential to our sanity. We are social animals, and we need to know that others approve of us (or, for that matter, when they don't). When someone regularly makes you feel validated, you come to love him or her. This is the essence of what Erikson has called intimacy. Intimacy fulfills what Maslow calls the need for self-esteem (see Chapter 2).

There is, however, great risk in receiving validation. The person who gives it to you is able to do so only because you have let him or her in on your deepest secrets. This gives the person great power, for good or for ill. Because that individual knows you and your insecurities so well, he or she has the capability to hurt you horrendously. This is why many divorces are so acrimonious. No one knows how to get you better than a spouse with whom you have shared so many intimacies. This is why it is said, "there is no such thing as an amicable divorce."

Nevertheless, we truly need love and the validation that leads to it. As studies of mental illness make clear, those who try to live without love risk their mental health.

Guided Review

14. Unlike previous generations of young adults, who tended to pair off for social events, today _____ _____ is more common.

15. Research on marital intercourse indicates that sexual closeness between many couples tends to (lessen, increase) significantly with the birth of each child.

16. According to the Janus Report, _____ are more likely to cite sexual problems as the primary reason for divorce than _____.

17. Research indicates that, as couples spend more time in a relationship, their feelings of love, commitment, and safety (decrease, stay about the same, increase).

18. Robert Sternberg examined the nature of love, claiming that love is made up of three different components: passion, _____, and commitment.

19. A healthy marriage, according to Sternberg, involves _____ among all three of his components.

20. Erich Fromm's concept of _____ is closely related to what Erikson calls intimacy.

Answers

14. pack dating 15. lessen 16. men, women 17. increase 18. intimacy 19. balance 20. validation

chapter 14   Review

CONCLUSION & SUMMARY

By now you can see that the study of human development is mainly the study of change. Few chapters in this book, however, have described a more changing scene than this one.

Americans are getting married later for a variety of reasons. They are staying married for shorter periods, are having fewer children, and are more reluctant to remarry if they become divorced or widowed. As we discussed previously, the functions of the family itself have changed tremendously, and some have even predicted the family's demise.

Perhaps the liveliest area in developmental study in recent years has been the field of personality research. More and more we are realizing that, just as in childhood and adolescence, adulthood has predictable stages. Distinct life cycles apparently exist, the goals of which are individuation and maturity. As we do more research, differences between male and female development are becoming apparent.

Next we looked at definitions of sexual identities and gender roles and at specific aspects of each. We examined Erikson's studies and looked into the concept of androgyny.

Pack dating is an important change in the interpersonal relationship patterns among young adults. It is difficult to categorize the current sexual practices of young adults because their partnerships tend to change more than previously. Love, too, may be variously explained—for example, with the theories of Sternberg and Fromm.

What factors are affecting American marriages and families?

- Almost 95% of Americans get married at some point in their lives.
- Basically four kinds of marriage exist throughout the world: monogamy (one husband, one wife), polygamy (two or more wives), polyandry (two or more husbands), and group marriage (two or more of both husbands and wives). Homosexual marriages are also continuing to gain acceptance.

What problems do young adults face in developing a healthy personality?

- Levinson suggested that adults develop according to a general pattern known as the life cycle. Each individual's personal embodiment of the life cycle is known as his or her life course.
- Levinson also described stages of development unique to men.
- According to Erikson's theory, early adulthood is defined in terms of intimacy and solidarity versus isolation.

What are the relationships between sexual identity and gender roles?

- Sexual identity results from those physical characteristics and behaviors that are part of our biological inheritance.

- Gender role, on the other hand, results partly from genetic makeup and partly from the specific traits in fashion at any one time and in any one culture.
- Views of acceptable gender-role behaviors have changed considerably during the past 20 years. Androgyny is now considered an acceptable alternative to masculine and feminine gender roles.
- Men are more likely to react to stress with a "fight-or-flight" response, whereas women are more likely to react with a "bend-and-bond" response.

How do young adults deal with the interpersonal relationships of sexuality and love?

- Dating trends include group dating as well as the tendency to pair off for social events.
- Stimuli for male sexual behavior are rooted primarily in internal motives, whereas for females, external stimuli tend to be more powerful.
- Sternberg argues that love is made up of three different components: passion, intimacy, and commitment.
- Fromm states that people need to have their deepest and most important thoughts and feelings "validated" by others who are significant to them.

KEY TERMS

androgyny
bend-and-bond response
chromosome failure
commitment
distantiation
feminist movement
group marriage
homosexual marriages
individuation

intimacy
isolation
life course
life cycle
life structure
mentoring
monogamy
novice phase
passion

polyandry
polygamy
solidarity
structure-building
structure-changing
transition
validation

WHAT DO YOU THINK?

1. Which of the four types of marriage described in this chapter do your parents have? Your grandparents?

2. Which of the types of marriages described in this chapter are likely to exist 100 years from now?

3. Levinson believed that forming a mentor relationship is an essential part of the novice phase. Have you formed such a relationship? What are its characteristics?

4. To be intimate, you must know your own identity. But to achieve an identity, you need the feedback you get from being intimate with at least one other person. How can this catch-22 be resolved?

5. How would you explain the change from pair to pack dating? How can you tell if you are truly in love?

 ## CHAPTER REVIEW TEST

1. **Since 1890, the average age at first marriage in the United States has**
   a. increased for males and decreased for females.
   b. increased for females and decreased for males.
   c. increased for both males and females.
   d. decreased for both males and females.

2. **A group marriage can be defined as**
   a. when there is one husband and two or more wives.
   b. when there is one wife and two or more husbands.
   c. when one husband marries two or more sisters.
   d. when there are two or more of both husbands and wives, who all exercise common privileges and responsibilities.

3. **The recent trend in increased divorce rates may be caused by which of the following?**
   a. liberalization of divorce laws
   b. growing societal acceptance of divorce and remaining single
   c. increases in the educational and work experience of women
   d. all of these

4. **The role of a _____, according to some theorists, is to provide an individual with guidance during life transitions, assistance with decision making, and a clearer view of what the individual wishes to make of himself or herself.**
   a. teacher
   b. mentor

   c. partner
   d. sibling

5. **Compared with the baby-boom generation, the dating practices of young adults are quite**
   a. different.
   b. superior.
   c. inferior.
   d. similar.

6. **In Sternberg's conceptualization of love, when a person is able to share his or her deepest feelings and thoughts with another, that person is experiencing**
   a. passion.
   b. commitment.
   c. intimacy.
   d. true love.

7. *Androgyny* **refers to**
   a. persons who are more likely to behave in a way appropriate to a situation, regardless of their sex.
   b. women who have higher than average male elements in their personalities.
   c. men who have higher than average female elements in their personalities.
   d. the midpoint between the two poles of masculinity and femininity.

8. **If someone forced his way into a line at a football game, an androgynous female**
   a. would accept the fact that he probably had good reason to cut in line.
   b. would be angry but not let her feelings show.
   c. would look disapproving.

   d. would tell the offender to go to the end of the line.

9. **According to Levinson, the purpose of the developmental periods in our lives is to cause greater individuation, which is**
   a. our developing separate and special personalities, derived less and less from our parents and teachers and more from our own behavior.
   b. the realization that one does not need to be in a relationship to attain happiness.
   c. the recognition of our distinct interests.
   d. the inability for peers to have great influence on major life decisions.

10. **Erikson used the term** *distantiation* **to describe**
    a. the distance we keep between ourselves and others during personal conversation.
    b. our ability to distance ourselves from our families of origin.
    c. the time we need to progress from one developmental stage to the next.
    d. the readiness all of us have to distance ourselves from others when we feel threatened by their behavior.

11. **Whose theories find fault with Erikson because of his belief that women are judged through their relationships with others?**
    a. Erikson and evolutionary psychologists
    b. Gilligan and Erikson
    c. Friedan
    d. Bem and Erikson

chapter 14   Review

12. Researcher Carol Gilligan states that, because femininity is defined through attachment, female gender is most threatened by
   a. divorce.
   b. personal loss.
   c. separation.
   d. dispassionate males.

13. Over the last two decades, one reason for the increase in the age of people at first marriage may be higher numbers of women
   a. entering the workforce.
   b. traveling alone.
   c. afraid of divorce.
   d. having children.

14. The term *biopsychosocial* refers to the interactions of biology, psychology, and _____ in relation to the individual.
   a. sociology
   b. theology
   c. environment
   d. heredity

15. Men are more likely to react to stress with a(n) _____ response, whereas women are more likely to react with a _____ response.
   a. assertive, subversive
   b. "bend-and-bond," "fight-or-flight"
   c. "fight-or-flight," "bend-and-bond"
   d. positive, negative

16. The person who used the term *validation* to describe our need, as humans, to feel loved and accepted is
   a. Fromm.
   b. Levinson.
   c. Bem.
   d. Erikson.

Answers

1. c 2. d 3. d 4. b 5. d 6. c 7. a 8. d 9. a 10. a 11. d 12. c 13. a 14. c 15. c 16. a

PHYSICAL AND COGNITIVE DEVELOPMENT IN MIDDLE ADULTHOOD

15

chapter

Chapter Objectives

After reading this chapter you should be able to answer the following questions.

- What kinds of physical changes affect people in middle adulthood?

- What are the main factors affecting a person's intellectual development in middle adulthood?

- What are the patterns of work that we most often see in this life stage?

The idea that there is a "middle" phase in adult life is a rather modern idea. Most non-Western and preindustrial cultures recognize only a mature stage of adulthood, from about 25 to about 60 years old, followed by a stage of old-age decline. Many Western scientists (including the authors of this book) now recognize four stages of adult life: young adulthood (approximate age range from 19 to 34); middle adulthood (approximate age range from 35 to 64); young elderly (approximate age range from 65 to 79); and old elderly (80+).

One non-Western country that does recognize middle adulthood is Japan. The Japanese word for middle age, *sonen,* refers to the "prime of life," the period between early adulthood and senility. Another quite positive word often used for the middle-adult years in Japan is *hataraki-zakari,* meaning the "full bloom of one's working ability."

Not all Japanese words for middle adulthood are quite so joyful. The word *kanroku* means "weightiness" or "fullness," both as in bearing a heavy load of authority and in being overweight.

Why do you suppose industrialized cultures such as North America and Japan have several words for middle adulthood, and other cultures have no words at all?

PHYSICAL DEVELOPMENT

"You're not getting older, you're getting better!"

You may hear middle-aged people saying this to each other. They hope that the changes they are experiencing are minor and not too negative, but let's face it, physical systems do decline with age. As you will see, biological forces greatly influence physical development, but be on the lookout for ways that psychological and social forces are at work as well. Now let us take a closer look at some of these functions.

Health

In general, concerns about health rise in the middle years. For example, a person's image of what he or she will be like in the future becomes increasingly health-related in midlife. This is not to say that middle-aged people are sickly. Their worries probably occur because they experience a greater number of serious illnesses and deaths of their loved ones than do younger people, and the changes in their bodies are more abrupt than in the bodies of young adults.

As one moves into middle adulthood, weight gain becomes a matter of concern. For example, about one-half of the United States adult population weighs over the upper limit of the "normal" weight range. For some, this is the result of genetic inheritance—about 40% of the people with one obese parent become obese, as compared with only 10% of those whose parents are not obese (CDC, 2000b). Others become overweight simply because they do not compensate for their lowering **basal metabolism rate (BMR).**

basal metabolism rate (BMR)
The minimum amount of energy an individual tends to use when in a resting state.

BMR is the minimum amount of energy an individual tends to use when in a resting state. As you can see from Figure 15.1, this rate varies with age and sex. Males have a slightly higher rate than females do. The rate drops most quickly during adolescence and then more slowly during adulthood. This is caused by a drop in the ratio of lean body mass to fat, thus lowering your BMR. Therefore, if you continue to eat at the same rate throughout your life, you will definitely gain weight. If you add to this a decreased rate of exercise, the weight gain (sometimes called "middle-age spread," referring to wider hips, thicker thighs, a "spare tire" around the waist, and a "beer belly") will be even greater. If you expect this to happen, it probably will (a **self-fulfilling prophecy**).

self-fulfilling prophecy
An idea that comes true simply because one believes that it will.

FIGURE 15.1

The decline of basal metabolism rate through the life cycle. BMR varies with age and sex. Rates are usually higher for males and decline proportionally with age for both sexes.

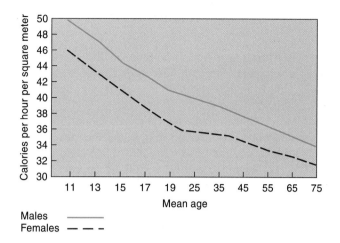

Males ——————
Females — — —

An interesting book on this topic is Janet Woititz's *Adult Children of Alcoholics* (1990). Lexington, MA: Health Communications. Woititz describes the characteristics of the adult children of alcoholics but insists that these are not character defects. This book provides readers with basic tools that will enable them to achieve greater self-knowledge and understanding.

Cardiovascular Health

Cardiovascular reaction to stressful challenges is normal (Kamarck et al., 2000; Manuck et al., 2000). Robinson & Cinciripini (2006) investigated reactions that are not typical. They examined the combined impact of smoking and stress on cardiovascular functioning, using a control group of nonsmokers. Not surprisingly, they concluded that smoking and stress contribute to increased risk of heart disease.

Effects of Alcohol

Even one or two drinks each day can be dangerous for anyone over the age of 50, because they can cause enlargement of the left ventricle of the heart. Such enlargement causes the heart to work harder and can often cause irregular heartbeats. If a person's heart is already enlarged, the danger is even greater. These data come from the Framingham (Massachusetts) Heart Study, which has furnished additional findings at www.framingham.com/heart/.

AN APPLIED VIEW

Food Imbalances

Since the beginning of human history, humans have tended to maintain a well-balanced diet. Only in the last century has this healthy balance been seriously tipped. An important example of this imbalance is the difference between omega-3 and omega-6 fatty acids. The first type is found in fish, nuts, and some vegetables. The second type is found in prepared foods, especially those made with corn and safflower oils. Whereas we used to eat as much fish as prepared foods, now most of us eat much more of the latter. Omega 6 acids can lead to clogged arteries.

In the chart below, the chief sources of the two fatty acids are listed. It is also possible to increase consumption of omega-3s by taking supplements in various forms.

Omega-3	*Omega-6*
salmon	Prepared foods made with
tuna	corn oil
herring	canola oil
sardines	cotton seed oil
mackerel	safflower oil
trout	soybeans in any form
halibut	

Source: U.S. Department of Agriculture, 2004.

Muscular Ability

Muscle growth is complete in the average person by age 17, but improvements in speed, strength, and skill can occur throughout the early adult years. In fact, most people reach their peak around age 25, depending on one's sex and the type of activity.

In the middle period of adulthood (35 to 64) there is a common but unnecessary decline in muscular ability, and the current popularity of aerobic activities may be reversing the trend in middle- age weight gain and muscle loss. Aerobic activity such as swimming and brisk walking appears to help maintain general health because it demands that the heart pump a great deal of blood to the large muscles of the legs.

Sensory Abilities

Although the stereotyped image of an older person losing hearing or vision is sometimes amusing, the gradual loss of function of one of the five physical senses—vision, hearing, smell, taste, and touch—is a serious concern for all of us. We often take everyday experiences such as reading, driving a car, enjoying a good meal, or holding a child in our arms for granted, yet all these experiences depend on one or more of the five senses. What changes in sensory ability can we expect as we pass through middle adulthood? The following trends are only general and vary widely among individuals.

Vision

Vision is the sense that we most depend on for information about what's going on around us. The eye begins to change physically at about age 40. The lens becomes less elastic and more yellow. At age 50 the cornea is increasing in curvature and thickness and the iris begins to respond less well to light (Whitbourne, 1999, 2000, 2001a, 2001b).

What happens as a result of these changes? In general, our eyes don't adapt to sudden, intense light or darkness as effectively as they once did. The ability to focus on nearby objects decreases, leading to a diagnosis of farsightedness and possibly a prescription for bifocals. The ability to detect certain colors can also be hampered as the lens yellows. For most people, these changes in visual ability pose a problem only when lighting is reduced, such as in night driving.

Hearing

Hearing also seems to be susceptible to decline at about age 40. This is when we begin to lose the ability to detect certain tones, particularly high frequencies (Whitbourne, 1999, 2000, 2001a, 2001b). Our ability to understand human speech also appears to decrease as we grow older, such as the inability to hear certain consonants. Cognitive capacity may play a role, because the ability to listen to speech in a crowded environment declines faster than the ability to listen to someone alone with no background noise.

It seems our visual system is a more reliable sense than our auditory system, as deafness in the United States appears to be increasing.In fact, the Centers for Disease Control (2001) reported that noise-induced hearing loss is the second most reported occupational illness or injury. Cross-cultural studies have shown that our relatively loud, high-tech culture contributes to our society's general loss of hearing.

Smell

Although not used as often as vision or hearing, the **olfactory sense** does more than just tell us when dinner is ready. First, the olfactory sense works closely with our taste buds to produce what we think of as the "taste" of a given food. In fact,

Because of changes in the eye that occur when we reach our 40s, glasses are often necessary. Why do you think adults put off getting sensory assistance, such as glasses or hearing aids, for as long as possible?

olfactory sense
Sense of smell, which uses the olfactory nerves in the nose and tongue.

TABLE 15.1	Major Causes of Abnormal Ability to Smell

Problems that prevent odors from reaching the sensory cells	Problems that involve the nervous system
allergies	diabetes
viral respiratory infections	Alzheimer's disease
sinusitis	Parkinson's disease
deviated nasal spectrum	Alcohol abuse
nasal polyps	AIDS
Problems that damage sensory cells	deficiencies of vitamin A, vitamin B12, zinc
	underactive thyroid gland
toxic chemicals, such as tobacco smoke	*Problems in multiple areas*
medications	
radiation treatment	head trauma or surgery
chemotherapy	tumors
	advancing age

Source: *Excerpted from the Harvard Men's Health Watch 2004.* © 2004 President and Fellows of Harvard College. For more information visit: http://www.health.harvard.edu/men. Harvard Health Publications does not endorse any products or medical procedures.

it is difficult in studies to separate which sense—taste or smell—actually contributes to the decline in performance on a certain task.

Studies of the brain have found that our sense of smell decreases as we age (Suzuki et al., 2001). Larsson and associates (2000) report that the sense of smell decreases for both men and women.

Table 15.1 cites the major causes of abnormal smell.

Taste

As we mentioned, our sense of taste is closely tied to our sense of smell, which makes studying age-related effects on taste very difficult. Recent studies have suggested that older adults may experience a decline in the ability to detect weak tastes but retain their ability to discriminate among those foods that have a strong taste, such as a spicy chicken curry (Kaneda et al., 2000; Mojet, Christ-Hazelhof, & Heidema, 2001). The decline in the ability to taste (and smell) may account in part for the decrease in weight that many elderly persons experience.

In general, we can say that, although our senses do decline somewhat throughout middle age, we are finding more and more ways to compensate for the losses, so they cause only slight changes in lifestyle. Another physical concern in our middle years is the climacteric.

The Climacteric

The word **climacteric** refers to a relatively abrupt change in the body, brought about by changes in hormonal balances. In women, this change is called **menopause.** It typically occurs over a four-year period during a woman's 40s or early 50s, and refers only to the cessation of menstruation. The *climacteric* also refers to the **male change of life.** The term **climacterium** refers to the loss of reproductive ability,

climacteric
Relatively abrupt change in the body, brought about by changes in hormonal balances.

menopause
Cessation of menstruation.

male change of life
Change in hormonal balance and sexual potency.

climacterium
Loss of reproductive ability.

which occurs at menopause for women, but tends to occur much later for men. In aging men there is a decline or loss of both libido (the part of sexuality involving conscious experience) and potency (the physical capacity to react to sexual stimuli), related to many biological factors (Gooren, 2006). Findings suggest that, although older adults may experience a decrease in physiological function, other factors are important to the overall satisfaction of one's sex life.

The Female Climacteric

The main physical change in menopause is that the ovaries cease to produce the hormones estrogen and progesterone, although the adrenal glands continue to produce some estrogen. At the onset of menopause, women's behavior is often affected by their attitudes toward sexuality, lifestyle, function within the family, and hormone levels (Avis, Crawford, & Johannes, 2002; Mansfield, Koch, and Voda, 2000; Wise et al., 2001). Kurpius and associates (2001) found that women who were satisfied with their marriage were less likely to report negative symptoms of menopause. Happily married women were angry or depressed less often than women in unhappy marriages. This suggests that contextual factors, such as the quality of the marital relationship, often influence the experience of menopause (Kurpius, Nicpon, & Maresh, 2001).

Furthermore, some menopausal women report an increase in sexual expression, such as cuddling and kissing. The researchers conjectured that this increase might be due, in part, to more comfort exploring different modes of sexual expression (Mansfield, Koch, and Voda, 2000). These factors interact as they impact a woman's life throughout the climacteric.

Some researchers feel that, because of a lack of communication, women are generally either unaware of or misinformed about menopause and its related issues. This misinformation concerning menopause may result in negative implications for women, their practitioners, and society (Buchanan, Villagran, & Ragan, 2002). It should be noted, however, that many women have positive feelings. For example, they no longer have to be concerned about becoming pregnant.

In one study, Mansfield, Koch, and Voda (2000) found that menopausal women were more likely to blame biological factors for negative situations, although they were more likely to think that positive events were caused by their lifestyle. For example, those women who experienced a decrease in sexual desire during menopause tended to think that this was due to hormonal changes. However, women who experienced increased interest in sex thought that this was because of factors in their lifestyle, such as good relationships with their spouses or feelings of professional pride.

For those women who experience serious problems with menopause, **hormone replacement therapy (HRT),** given at low levels for short periods of time, can offer relief. Recent studies, however, have shown that hormone replacement therapy may increase the chance of a heart attack, stroke, breast cancer, and blood clots (Nelson et al., 2002). Also, hormone replacement therapy is linked with serious increases in breast cancer (Ross et al., 2000; Schairer et al., 2000). Menopausal women are advised to consult with their gynecologists to weigh their risk factors for coronary heart disease, hip fracture, and breast cancer before deciding whether to undergo hormone replacement therapy or to consider **homeopathic treatment.**

The Male Climacteric

At one time, it was thought that the male hormone balance parallels that of the female. According to a well-designed study conducted by the National Institute on Aging (1998), however, the level of testosterone declines only very gradually with age. Dr. Mitchell Hermann, who conducted the study on men from age 25 to

---

Two works that include sections on middle-aged physical development are (1) The Boston Women's Book Collaborative (2005–2007). *Our Bodies, Growing Older.* Boston: Author. An excellent update of the popular *Our Bodies, Our Selves,* this book is for middle-aged and elderly women. (2) L. Nilsson and J. Lindberg. *Behold Man: A Photographic Journey of Discovery inside the Body* (1973). New York: Delacorte. This is a book of photographs, many of them pictures enlarged thousands of times. This is a magnificent description of the human body.

hormone replacement therapy (HRT)
Hormone therapy prescribed to treat the symptoms associated with menopause; it usually involves low-dose estrogen.

homeopathic treatments
Natural, alternative options for health care and management; remedies often include herbal supplements.

89, said that his findings contradict earlier results because most of those previous studies were of men in hospitals and in nursing homes who were afflicted with obesity, alcoholism, or chronic illness. All of his subjects were healthy, vigorous men.

Hermann suggested the decrease in sexual potency that men experience in later years is probably not the result of hormonal changes but, rather, slowing down in the central nervous system, together with a self-fulfilling prophecy (men expect to become impotent, so they do). There have been numerous speculations in the popular press about the nature of "male menopause" (for example, Margolese, 2000), but scientifically speaking the effects of hormonal changes on the appearance and emotional state of men are unclear at the present.

It seems likely that, as we better understand precisely how hormone balances change and how the different changes interact with one another, the impairments that have been attributed to these changes will decrease.

Although middle-aged people are generally healthier than the elderly, the chronic stress of poverty and prejudice is especially prevalent for African-Americans. Such stress can be linked to the deep-seated biases and discrimination African-Americans have faced throughout history in the United States (Shavers & Shavers, 2006). These socioeconomic and racial differences are a good place to see how the biopsychosocial model operates. What role would you say each of these three major forces plays in causing these differences?

Health also plays a role in the cognition of middle-aged adults. In the next section, we examine this important developmental capacity.

Guided Review

1. Adulthood has recently been thought of as having four stages: young adulthood (19 to 34 years of age), _____ _____ (35 to 64 years of age), _____ _____ (65 to 79 years of age), and old elderly (80+ years of age).

2. Basal metabolism rate is the _____ amount of energy an individual uses when in a resting state.

3. Our basal metabolism rate decreases with age, meaning that, if we eat the same amount all our lives, we will _____ weight.

4. According to recent research people over the age of 50 should be concerned about the effects of alcohol, as its use can result in enlargement of the _____, causing it to work harder.

5. All five senses decline during middle adulthood, but _____ loss has the greatest social stigma attached to it.

6. *Climacteric* is the term used for the abrupt change that occurs in the body owing to changes in _____ balances.

7. The term *menopause* refers to the _____ change of life, which includes the cessation of menstruation.

8. A number of women experience positive consequences from menopause, including a time of coalescence, integration, and _____.

9. _____ _____ therapy can be used to offer relief to women who are experiencing problems with regard to menopause.

Answers

1. middle adulthood, young elderly 2. minimum 3. gain 4. heart 5. hearing 6. hormonal 7. female 8. liberation 9. Hormone replacement

COGNITIVE DEVELOPMENT

I am all I ever was and much more, but an enemy has bound me and twisted me, so now I can plan and think as I never could, but no longer achieve all I plan and think.

—WILLIAM BUTLER YEATS

Of course, the "enemy" Yeats refers to is age. Was he right in believing he could think as well as ever, or was he just kidding himself? The question of declining intelligence across adulthood has long concerned humans.

Intelligence

Indeed, no aspect of adult functioning has received more research than intelligence. Most of the debate has been over whether intelligence declines with age, and if so, how much and in what ways. As a result of this considerable research, investigators have reached considerable agreement as to how cognition develops during adulthood. The leading theory is that of J. L. Horn, who argued that intelligence does decline in some ways, but in other ways it does not. The picture is quite complicated, and evidence indicates that:

- One type of intelligence declines, whereas another does not.
- Some individuals decline, whereas others do not.
- Although decline does eventually occur, it happens only late in life.

Horn has described two dimensions of intelligence: fluid and crystallized. The two can be distinguished as follows: **Fluid intelligence** depends on the proper functioning of the nervous system. It is measured by tasks that show age-related declines (speeded tasks, tests of reaction time). **Crystallized intelligence** demonstrates the cumulative effect of culture and learning of task performance and is measured by tests of verbal ability and cultural knowledge (Labouvie-Vief & Lawrence, 1985). Together they constitute what Horn calls "omnibus" intelligence.

Horn (1975, 1978) hypothesized that, whereas crystallized intelligence does not decline and may even increase, fluid intelligence probably does deteriorate, at least to some extent (see Figure 15.2). Horn and his colleagues (1981) found that this decline in fluid intelligence averages three to seven IQ points per decade for the three decades spanning the period from 30 to 60 years of age.

fluid intelligence
Involves perceiving relationships, educing correlates, maintaining span of immediate awareness in reasoning, abstracting, concept formation, and problem solving.

crystallized intelligence
Involves perceiving relationships, educing correlates, reasoning, abstracting, concept of attainment, and problem solving.

FIGURE 15.2

Horn's two types of intelligence

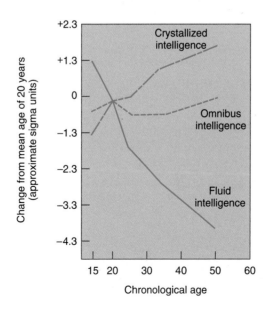

Some older research has suggested that certain achievement may involve more of one type of intelligence than the other (Lehman, 1964). For example, in fields such as mathematics, music, chemistry, and poetry, the best work is usually produced at a relatively young age and therefore may rely most on fluid intelligence. Other major achievements, such as in history, astronomy, philosophy, writing, and psychology, usually occur later in life, which may indicate greater reliance on crystallized intelligence.

A number of cross-sectional studies have attempted to validate Horn's theory. A good example is the work of Alan Kaufman and associates (1989). They studied groups of subjects ages 20 to 74 who were given the revised version of the WAIS-R. These researchers wanted to see whether the level of education subjects had completed would have any effect on their performance on the WAIS-R and the relationship those performance scores would have to the age of each subject group. Results of the study appear to support Horn's theory of fluid and crystallized intelligence. Test scores showed a decline in verbal IQ, performance, and full-scale IQ. However, when education was accounted for statistically, the decline in subjects' scores for verbal IQ disappeared yet remained for performance and full-scale IQs. A subsequent study showed that ethnic differences occur in tests of crystallized abilities, regardless of educational attainment (Kaufman et al., 1993). As was pointed out in Chapter 2, however, cross-sectional designs such as this may be flawed. The problem is that people of different ages, having grown up at different periods, have necessarily had different life experiences. Therefore, the results may be more due to this cohort effect than to aging.

A longitudinal study avoids this weakness because it looks at the same group of people over an interval of time. Schaie and Hertzog (1983) conducted a longitudinal study on cognitive abilities and found evidence that they decline as one ages. The evidence for a decline after the age of 60 was strong. They also found evidence that this process starts after the age of 50, although it is probably not observable in everyday life. Making the situation even more complex, Hertzog's latest research suggested that a decline in speed of performance makes declines in intelligence look worse than they are. "It may be the case that a sub stantial proportion of the age changes actually observed by Schaie in his longitudinal studies is not loss of thinking capacity per se but, rather, slowing in rate of intelligent thought" (Hertzog, 1989, p. 650). Perhaps you simply need more time to think and respond when you get older.

You should recall from Chapter 1, however, that longitudinal studies may suffer from the problem that studies done at different points in time may be distorted by historical effects. Only a sequential design can resolve this difficulty and, as of this time, no such study has been carried out.

The lifelong efforts of K. Warner Schaie (summarized in Schaie, 1994) are noteworthy; he has made powerful attempts to understand the adult life course of intellectual abilities. The Seattle Longitudinal Study examined, but was not limited to, the presence or absence of age-related changes and difference in individuals. Consequently, this study has provided data on the importance of age-related changes, variables that may explain such changes, and the basis for future interventions. By adopting the sequential format of studying a cross-sectional sample every seven years since 1956, Schaie has eliminated many limitations that accompany a strictly cross-sectional study or a longitudinal study.

New Views of Intelligence

In the valleys you've looked for the mountains. In the mountains you've searched for the rivers. There is nowhere to go. You are where you belong. You can live the life you dreamed.

—JUDY COLLINS

Part of the debate is a matter of definition. What, exactly, is intelligence? How is it measured? It is certainly composed of several different cognitive abilities, such as memory, language, reasoning, and the ability to manipulate numbers. Each of these mental processes can, in turn, be divided into various subprocesses.

Different definitions of intelligence lead to different measures of it. Each measure emphasizes different mental abilities. For example, if you define intelligence as rank in class or school achievement, then cognitive abilities such as verbal comprehension and general information may be much more important than rote memory and perceptual tasks. In fact, most of the commonly used IQ tests measure only a few of the cognitive abilities that could be measured. Under these circumstances, the question of whether intelligence declines with age becomes unanswerable. Furthermore, as cognitive expert Robert Sternberg asserts, "Intelligence cannot be fully or even meaningfully understood outside its cultural context" (2004, p. 325). Clearly, more specific questions must be asked.

Increasingly, general intelligence is being abandoned as a scientific concept and subject of study. More and more, researchers are proposing several quite distinct cognitive abilities. Horn has now added supporting abilities to the concepts of fluid and crystallized intelligence. These include short-term memory, long-term memory, visual processing, and auditory processing. Howard Gardner (1983) contended that there are eight different cognitive intelligences. His list includes linguistic, musical, logical-mathematical, spatial, bodily-kinesthetic, interpersonal and intrapersonal, and naturalistic intelligences.

Robert Sternberg has challenged traditional views of intelligence tests on the grounds that they measure only crystallized intelligence. He believes we should think of intelligence tests as measures of achievement; thus, a person's intelligence may change over the course of a lifetime. In his view (2002), successful intelligence consists of analytic components (solving problems), creative components (deciding what problems to solve), and practical components (devising effective solutions). He suggests that intelligence isn't so much a matter of quantity but, rather, a matter of balance, of knowing when and how to use the analytic, creative, and practical intelligence components. This ability peaks in the middle adult years. Because most people in these years have a better understanding of themselves, they can capitalize on their strengths and compensate for their weaknesses.

Baltes (1993) suggested another resolution to the question of how intelligence develops with age. He has proposed a **dual-process model** of intelligence. This model considers the interaction of the potential and the biological limits of the aging mind. Gains and losses are recognized as part of intellectual development. There is likely to be a decline in the mechanics of intelligence, such as classification skills and logical reasoning. These mechanics are largely dependent on genetics and are comparable to fluid intelligence. Clearly, variables such as memory play an important role in this. Pragmatics of intelligence remain stable or increase with age and include social wisdom, which is defined as good judgment about important but uncertain matters of life. Culture is the major influence on pragmatic intelligence.

This model seems to offer the most reasonable position. There are just too many famous people whose thinking obviously got better as they got older—to name a few, George Burns, Coco Chanel, Benjamin Franklin, Albert Einstein, Mahatma Gandhi, Helen Hayes, Michelangelo, Grandma Moses, Georgia O'Keefe, Pope John XXIII, Eleanor Roosevelt, Bertrand Russell, George Bernard Shaw, Sophocles, and Frank Lloyd Wright. It is no coincidence that these people also maintained their creative abilities well into old age.

Finally, intelligent mental operations may be broken down into subcategories, most of which appear to peak at the beginning of middle age. These categories are (Moshman, 1998) case-based reasoning (including analogical, precedent-based, and legal reasoning); law-based reasoning (including logical, rule-based, principal, and scientific reasoning); and dialectical reasoning (including dialectical reflection and argument reasoning).

As we have said, a key factor in the ability to continue to be productive well into the later years is creativity. Thus, an important question is "What is creativity?"

If you want to learn more on this subject, read Gardner's *Frames of Mind: The Theory of Multiple Intelligences* (1993). New York: Basic Books. It offers a comprehensive view of the numerous faces of intelligence.

dual-process model
Model of intelligence that says there may be a decline in the mechanics of intelligence, such as classification skills and logical reasoning, but that the pragmatics are likely to increase.

Certainly intelligence is related to creativity. Does creativity decline with age? Research indicates this is not the case.

The Development of Creativity

As the world changes more and more rapidly, it becomes more difficult to define creativity as a separate ability from originality, utility, and productivity (Aiken, 1998). At the same time, the role of creativity has become an even more important aspect of cognitive functioning. In this section, we explore the development of creative ability in the adult years. But first, the following is a description of the characteristics of creative adults.

Traits of the Highly Creative Adult

A number of studies (reviewed in Dacey, 1989a, 1989c; Dacey & Fiore, 2000; Dacey & Kenny, 1997; Dacey & Packer, 1992) have compared highly creative and average adults in a number of important traits. In general, highly creative adults

* Like to do their own planning, make their own decisions, and need the least training and experience in self-guidance.
* Do not like to work with others and prefer their own judgment of their work to the judgment of others. They therefore seldom ask others for opinions.
* Take a hopeful outlook when presented with complex, difficult tasks.
* Have the most ideas when a chance to express individual opinion is presented. These ideas frequently invoke the ridicule of others.
* Are most likely to stand their ground in the face of criticism.
* Are the most resourceful when unusual circumstances arise.
* Tolerate uncertainty and ambiguity better than others.
* Are not necessarily the "smartest" or "best" in competitions.

    In their compositions, creative adults typically

* Show an imaginative use of many different words.
* Are more flexible; for example, in a narrative they use more situations, characters, and settings. Rather than taking one clearly defined train of thought and pursuing it to its logical conclusion, creative adults tend to switch the main focus quickly and easily and often go off on tangents.
* Tend to elaborate on the topic assigned, taking a much broader connotation of it to begin with and then proceeding to embellish even that.
* Are more original. (This is the most important characteristic. The others need not be evidenced, but this one must be.) Their ideas are qualitatively different from those of the average person. Employers frequently react to the creative person's work in this way: "I know what most of my people will do in a particular situation, but I never know what to expect from this one!"

    Now let us turn to the research on the development of creativity.

Psychohistorical Studies of Creative Achievement

Lehman (1953) examined biographical accounts of the work of several thousand individuals born since 1774. He studied the ages at which these people made their creative contributions. He compared the contributions of deceased persons with those of people still living. On the basis of his study, he concluded that

> *on the whole it seems clear that both past and present generation scientists have produced more than their proportionate share of high-quality research not later than at ages 30 to 39, and it is useless to bemoan this fact or to deny it. (p. 26)*

As the "grande dame" of modern dance, Martha Graham's contributions to choreography made her one of the most creative adults in the 20th century. Why do you think some adults only become creatively productive in their later years?

A SOCIOCULTURAL VIEW | *Cultural Bias and Cognitive Decline*

A chief result of Schaie's studies (1994) has been the identification of variables that reduce the risk of cognitive decline. These are as follows:

- The absence of cardiovascular and other chronic diseases
- Living in favorable environmental circumstances, such as those who are above average in wealth tend to enjoy
- Substantial involvement in activities found in stimulating environments such as travel and extensive reading
- Having a flexible personality style
- Being married to a spouse who has a high cognitive functioning level
- Engaging in activities that require quick perception and thinking (such as verbal jousting with friends)
- Being satisfied with one's life accomplishments through midlife

No doubt all these variables are biopsychosocial in origin. We can probably do little about the biological factors involved. Now that these variables have been identified, however, there may be many actions we as a society could take to affect the psychological and environmental elements. Can you think of any?

Furthermore, some of these variables are particularly related to economic level, culture, and lifestyle. Two of the most important are rating oneself as being satisfied with one's life accomplishments and reporting a flexible personality style at midlife. These in turn tend to be related to having a high socioeconomic level, a complex and intellectually stimulating environment, being married to a spouse with high cognitive status, maintaining high levels of perceptual processing speed, and the absence of chronic diseases, especially cardiovascular disease. In summary, the richer you are and the higher your social class, the less your cognitive abilities decline.

These findings are strong evidence for a class bias in cognitive decline. What reasons can you give to explain the results?

Figure 15.3 portrays Lehman's general results.

In his report of his own research on this subject, Dennis (1966) criticized Lehman's work, stating that it included many individuals who died before they reached old age. Dennis points out that this biased the study statistically, because we cannot know what proportion of creative contributions these deceased people would have made, had they lived longer.

Dennis studied the biographies of 738 creative people, all of whom lived to age 79 or beyond and whose contributions were considered valuable enough to have been reported in biographical histories. He did this because he believed "that no valid statements can be made concerning age and productivity except from longitudinal data involving no dropouts due to death" (1966, p. 8).

He looked at the percentage of works done by these people in each of the decades among the ages of 20 and 80. When creative productivity is evaluated in this way, the results are quite different. Dennis found that scholars and scientists (with the exception of mathematicians and chemists) usually have little

FIGURE 15.3

Graph of Lehman's findings.

Data from H. C. Lehman, *Age and Achievement,* Princeton University Press, Princeton, NJ, 1953.

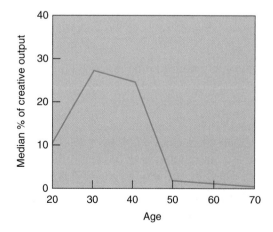

A growing number of middle-aged adults are choosing to express their creativity through playing an instrument. What do you suppose motivates them to do so?

creative output in their 20s. For most of them, the peak period is between their 40s and 60s, and most produce almost as much in their 70s as they did in their earlier years. The peak period for artists tended to be their 40s, but they were almost as productive in their 60s and 70s as they were in their 20s. Figure 15.4 depicts these relationships.

Dennis offered an interesting hypothesis to explain the difference in creative productivity among the three groups. The output curve of the arts rises earlier and declines earlier and more severely because productivity in the arts is primarily a matter of individual creativity. Scholars and scientists require a greater period of training and a greater accumulation of data than do others. The use of accumulated data and the possibility of receiving assistance from others cause the scholars and scientists to make more contributions in later years than people in art, music, and literature. Most of the individuals in Dennis's study were males. It would be interesting to investigate the patterns of productivity among a comparable all-female group.

FIGURE 15.4

Graph of Dennis's findings.

Data from W. Dennis, "Creative productivity between 20 and 80 years," in *Journal of Gerontology* 21:1–8, 1966.

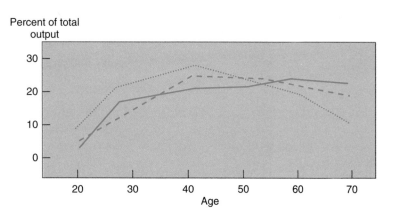

Percent of total output

Age

Key:
.... Artists
————— Scholars
– – – – Scientists

A highly respected source on the topic of creativity is *The Journal of Creative Behavior.* Pick up any volume of this fascinating journal at your library and browse through it. A wide variety of interesting topics is covered, and more often than not the articles are written creatively.

Studies by Simonton (1975, 1976, 1977a, 1977b) have attempted to resolve the differences between the Lehman and Dennis research. In general, Simonton found evidence that quantity declines with age, which favors Lehman, but that quality does not, which favors Dennis. Unfortunately, because of differences in design and criteria (for example, differing data sources, differing criteria for inclusion in the studies), it cannot be said that this issue is fully resolved at this time (Simonton, 1993).

We started this section on cognitive development by looking at the measurement of changes in intelligence over the adult years. Then we reviewed what we know about creative development. Now we will consider a third aspect, one that attempts to pull together a variety of intellectual factors.

Learning Ability

Is there a serious drop from early to late adulthood in the ability to learn? Despite some classic studies (for instance, Knowles, 1989; Taub, 1975), considerable disagreement over this matter still exists.

For example, many studies have shown a marked decline in paired associate learning (the ability to remember associations between two lists of words) (Kimmel, 1974). Obviously, memorizing pairs of words is itself of no great importance, but much essential learning is based on this skill. In most of these studies, however, the measure of how well the associations have been learned is speed of response. Do older persons perform poorly because they are slower to learn or only because they take longer to show what they have learned? As Botwinick (1977) reported:

The research strategy has been to vary both the amount of time the stimulus is available for study and the amount of time that is available for response. A general finding is that elderly people need more time for responding than typically is provided; they are at a disadvantage when this time is not available. When sufficient time for response is available, the performance of elderly people is only slightly inferior, or not inferior at all, to that of young people. (p. 278)

Does the apparent drop in learning ability from early to late adulthood occur strictly because of ability or because of factors such as motivation and dexterity?

Another factor in learning ability that has been studied is motivation to learn (Allen et al., 1999; Kinman & Kinman, 2001). It has been suggested that persons in middle and late adulthood are less motivated to learn than younger people are. For example, it often appears that they are anxious when placed in a laboratory situation for testing their learning ability. To the extent that this is true, their ability to learn is underestimated.

It has also been found in laboratory experiences that older adults are more likely than younger adults to make the "omission error." That is, when they suspect they may be wrong, they are more likely to refrain from responding at all and therefore are scored as having not learned the task. But when asked what they think the answer is, they are often right.

Also, the meaningfulness of the task affects motivation. It is clear that the motivation for middle-aged and elderly adults is different from that of younger adults, and many experiments have not taken this into consideration in studying learning ability.

Decline in cognitive ability due to aging can often be offset through motivation and new learning experiences. The growing number of adults who return to formal education in middle adulthood supports this idea. Education has also been linked to a greater sense of control among adults (Schieman, 2001).

Why are more and more adults going back to school? In the past, children could be educated to deal with a society and workplace that would remain essentially unchanged for their entire lives. Today the rate of change and innovation is too rapid. Fifty-year-old men and women were born while computers were being developed, and certainly didn't learn about computers in school as children Routinely asked to

AN APPLIED VIEW

Obstacles and AIDS to Creativity

We may agree that creativity is a valuable trait and should be fostered, but how? A number of theorists offered excellent suggestions (see, for example, Sternberg & Davidson, 1995), but educator Ralph Hallman's suggestions (1967) on the obstacles and aids to creativity are still classic. According to him, creativity has several persistent obstacles:

- *Pressures to conform.* The pressure on the individual to follow standardized routines and inflexible rules is probably the major inhibitor. Authoritarian parents, teachers, and managers who demand order are responsible for destroying a great deal of creative talent.
- *Ridicule of unusual ideas.* This destroys one's feelings of worth and makes one defensive and compulsive.
- *An excessive quest for success and the rewards it brings.* An overconcern with material success is often the result of trying to meet the standards and demands of others to obtain the rewards they have to give. In the long run, this distorts one's view of reality and robs one of the strength of character to be creative (Amabile et al., 1986).
- *Intolerance of a playful attitude.* Innovation calls for playing around with ideas, a willingness to fantasize and make believe, and a healthy disrespect for accepted concepts. Creative persons often are seen as childlike and silly and their activity wasteful, but these are only appearances. As Hallman remarks, "creativity is profound fun."

In addition to recommending that we avoid these obstacles, Hallman urges that we promote the following aids in ourselves and others:

- *Engage in self-initiated learning.* Most people who are in charge of others (managers, teachers, parents) find it hard to encourage others to initiate and direct their own learning. After all, this is certainly not the way most people were taught. They fear that, if their subordinates are given greater freedom to explore reality on their own, they will learn wrong things or will not learn the right things in the

proper sequence. We must put less emphasis on learning "the right facts" and more on learning how to learn. Even if we do temporarily mislearn a few things, in the long run the practice in experimentation and imagination will be greatly to our benefit.

- *Become deeply knowledgeable about your subject.* Only when people make themselves fully familiar with a particular situation can they detach themselves enough to get an original view of it.
- *Defer judgment.* It is important to make wild guesses, to juggle improbable relationships, to take intellectual risks, to take a chance on appearing ridiculous. Refrain from making judgments too early.
- *Be flexible.* Shift your point of view; to dream up new ideas for things, imagine as many possible solutions to a particular problem as possible.
- *Be self-evaluative.* When a person comes up with a creative idea, he or she is always a minority of one. History is replete with examples of ideas that were rejected for years before people began to realize their worth. Therefore, the creative person must be one who knows his or her own mind and is relatively independent of the judgment of others. To become a good judge of their own thinking, people must practice making many judgments.
- *Ask yourself lots of open-ended questions.* One extensive study showed that 90% of the time the average teacher asks questions to which there can be only one right answer, which the teacher already knows. Questions that pique curiosity and allow many possible right answers were asked only 10% of the time. Realize that you were probably taught that way, and take steps to rectify the tendency.
- *Learn to cope with frustration and failure.* Thomas Edison tried more than 2,000 combinations of metal before he found just the right kind for the electric element in his first lightbulb.

use computers at work, it is now commonplace for people to return to school in order to advance or even maintain their present career. Of course, sometimes an adult returns to school in order to learn a new skill or hobby for sheer enjoyment.

Women in particular are going back to school in large numbers. Many currently middle-aged women were not encouraged to pursue higher education when they were young. Some women are trying to catch up to be competitive with their male counterparts. Other women may return to school, not to study accounting or computer science but to study subjects not limited to a specific career path. Some pursue occupational training to support themselves and their families after a divorce.

The education system is adapting to this change. Most adults cannot afford to quit their current jobs to go back to school. More schools are now offering evening and part-time programs. Many schools offer courses that can be taken at home, on weekends, and online.

The beautiful thing about learning is that nobody can take it away from you.

—ANONYMOUS

Thus, new learning by middle-aged adults takes place in settings other than a formal school setting. Employees in many different types of work settings are asked to keep abreast of innovations. Other social experiences, such as practicing a religion, going to a library, watching television, and serving as a volunteer, involve new learning. Now more than ever, opportunities for lifelong learning are changing lives.

Guided Review

10. Despite extensive research on intelligence during adulthood, investigators do not agree on the state of intellectual ability. For instance, Terman's longitudinal study showed an increase in IQ scores with age among his gifted population. Horn's studies, however, show decline in _____ intelligence, with an increase in _____ intelligence.

11. According to Horn, fluid intelligence depends on the proper functioning of the nervous system. Crystallized intelligence indicates the cumulative effects of _____ and _____ on task performance.

12. Intelligent mental operations may be broken down into subcategories, most of which appear to _____ at the beginning of middle age.

13. Highly creative people like to do their own planning, are the most _____ when unusual circumstances arise, and can tolerate uncertainty and _____ better than others.

14. Today more adults are going back to school because the rate of change and _____ in our society is so rapid.

PATTERNS OF WORK

As the "baby-boom" generation enters middle age, many changes are occurring in the workplace. Fewer and fewer new young workers will be available to enter the workforce. Employers will find themselves with a larger number of older workers. This shrinking labor pool is leading many employers to pay more attention than ever to the welfare of their employees. Some of the new issues are family care, home-based work, nontraditional work schedules, and the spiraling cost of health-care benefits.

Answers

13. resourceful, ambiguity 14. innovation
10. fluid, crystallized 11. culture, learning 12. peak

Employees who feel trusted by their managers find their jobs more meaningful and empowering (Gomez & Rosen, 2001; Thompson & Bunderson, 2001). Individuals who feel that their work is an important, valuable part of their identity are more likely to have warmer, more caring interactions at work and at home (Gomez & Rosen, 2001; Thompson & Bunderson, 2001). When women work in jobs in which they have a lot of control, they are better able to handle the psychological stresses of a heavy workload (Bliese & Castro, 2000). A large percentage of women managers enjoy enhanced self-esteem and personal development as a result of working, and these qualities improved their marital relationships. However, a number of managers found that their husbands felt threatened by their successful careers and increased earning power, which caused more conflict in their marriages (Grant, 2000).

Employers are attempting more creative approaches to development and training. In the past, employers have tended to spend the majority of their training and development resources on younger employees. Perhaps this is just a matter of employers being unaware of the problems and concerns of their older employees, or perhaps money and time invested in younger employees were considered better spent. But in recent years, a trend has emerged among employers to recognize some of the concerns of middle-aged employees. Among them are the following:

- Awareness of advancing age and awareness of death
- Awareness of bodily changes related to aging
- Knowing how many career goals have been or will be attained
- Search for new life goals
- Marked change in family relationships
- Change in work relationships
- Sense of skills and abilities becoming outdated
- Feeling of decreased job mobility and increased concern for job security

Businesses have responded to these issues with continuing education, seminars, workshops, degree programs, and other forms of professional development. Employers are beginning to have a greater appreciation for the contribution of older workers. There is growing recognition that each individual has different career choices, patterns, and promotional opportunities (Collins & Collins, 2006). As the labor pool shrinks, the welfare of the older, established workforce becomes more valuable.

Special Challenges for the Working Woman

It is probably not news to you that challenges facing women in the workplace are different from those of men. But what actual difference does being a woman make? A review of the literature reveals the following four major challenges.

Sexual Harassment on the Job

Sexual harassment can take many forms (Looby, 2001), such as verbal sexual suggestions or jokes; leering; "accidentally" brushing against your body; a "friendly" pat, squeeze, or pinch or an arm around you; catching you alone for a quick kiss; explicit propositions backed by the threat of losing your job; and forced sexual relations.

Coping responses to sexual harassment vary across cultures and occupational classes, but they also share common themes. A study by Wasti and Cortina (2002) noted typical responses as avoidance, denial, and advocacy seeking.

DeJudicibus and McCabe (2001) reported that, in the workplace, females experience more sexual harassment than males. In addition, males and employees in general tend to blame the target of the sexual harassment, the women, more often than do nonworking people. Some women do not consider their personal experiences to be sexual harassment or sex discrimination (American Academy of Pediatrics, 2006). However, both sexual harassment and sexual discrimination result in negative work attitudes for women.

Equal Pay and Promotion Criteria

The Equal Pay Act was passed in 1963 and states that men and women in substantially similar jobs in the same company should get the same pay. Under this act, the complainant may remain anonymous while a complaint is being investigated.

In spite of these legal protections, women make less money on the average than men and are less often promoted to management-level jobs. Why? Male prejudice is one reason, no doubt, but there are probably others. Several explanations have been offered that have little current research evidence and support common stereotypes: (1) women may be absent more from work owing to illness of children and are much more likely to take parenting leave; (2) many women seem to have greater anxiety about using computers than males; and (3) women take less math in school.

Work–Family Conflict

work–family conflict
Phenomenon that occurs when a woman's roles as mother, wife, and worker spill over into one another.

Work–family conflict is defined as the phenomenon that occurs when demands of a woman's role as a wife and mother come into conflict or spill over into demands of her role as a worker. When this type of role overload or role conflict occurs, it often causes stress for the woman and the family. The role of family emotional support, leader–member exchange at work (that is, the quality of the employee–supervisor relationship), and the personality of the woman all influence her feelings of work–family conflict. For example, Bernas and Major (2000) found that higher levels of emotional support from a woman's family and her hardiness were associated with decreased work interference with the family and decreased reports of stress. The quality of the employee–supervisor relationship at work was another important factor in the woman's feelings of stress and conflict between home and work. Somewhat paradoxically, although a positive employee–supervisor relationship at work often resulted in lower feelings of stress in the women studied, it also resulted in an increased sense of work spillover into family life.

Travel Safety

Working women are exposed to a considerable number of hazards to which women who do not work outside the home are not subjected. Crimes against women are not limited to the inner city but occur in suburban and even rural areas with a high frequency.

These four problems are gradually being recognized in the workplace, and there is hope that they will be alleviated.

The Midcareer Crisis

midcareer crisis
Stage that some persons go through in middle age during which they come to question their career and personal goals and dreams.

Considerable attention is now being given to the crisis many people undergo in the middle of their careers. For some it is a problem of increasing anxiety, which is troublesome but no serious problem. For others a **midcareer crisis** is a reality, and it is truly threatening.

A number of changes in the middle years are not caused by work: the awareness of advancing age, the death of parents and other relatives, striking changes in family relationships, and a decrease in physical ability. Other changes are entirely work related.

Coming to Terms with Attainable Career Goals

By the time a person reaches the age of 40 in a professional or managerial career, it is pretty clear whether he or she will make it to the top of the field. If individuals haven't reached their goals by this time, most adjust their level of aspirations and, in some cases, start over in a new career. Many, however, are unable to recognize that they have unrealistic aspirations and thus suffer from considerable stress.

Even people whose career patterns are stable, such as doctors, often have a midcareer letdown. Nor is this crisis restricted to white-collar workers. Many blue-collar workers, realizing that they have gone about as far as they are going to go on their jobs, suffer from depression.

This is also the time when family expenses, such as college education for teenage children, become great. If family income does not rise, this obviously creates a conflict, especially if the husband is the sole provider for the family. If the wife goes back to work, other types of stress often occur. Nordblom (2004) argues that problems associated with work and finances affect married couples differently than cohabitating couples. Unmarried couples tend to save money (or not save) differently if they know a partner can bail them out financially. The author suggests that "mutual altruism" is key to prevention of some problems and encourages risk sharing between partners.

The Change in Work Relationships

Relationships with fellow employees obviously change when one has gone to the top of one's career. Some middle-aged adults take a mentoring attitude toward younger employees, but others feel resentful toward the young because they still have a chance to progress. When people reach their 40s and 50s, they often try to establish new relationships with fellow workers, and this contributes to the sense of conflict.

A Growing Sense of Outdatedness

In many cases, an individual has to work so hard just to stay in a job that it is impossible to keep up to date. Sometimes a younger person, fresh from an extensive education, joins the firm and knows more about modern techniques than the middle-aged person does. These circumstances usually cause feelings of anxiety and resentment in the older employee because he or she is afraid of being considered incompetent. A good example is society's heavy reliance on computers to help people manage many aspects of their business and personal lives. Today, very young children are taught how to use a computer in school and at home. Older adults did not have this training, and thus many feel challenged by the complexities of computers. Reed, Doty, and May (2005) found that confidence using computer technology, rather than chronological age, better explains age-related differences in computer abilities.

Inability to Change Jobs

Age discrimination in employment starts as early as age 35 in some industries and becomes pronounced by age 45. A federal law against age discrimination in employment was passed in 1968 to ease the burden on the older worker, but to date the law has been poorly enforced on both the federal and state levels. Many employers get around the law simply by telling older applicants that they are "overqualified" for the available position.

The Generativity Crisis

Erikson suggested that people in the middle years ought to be in the generativity stage. This is a time when they should be producing something of lasting value, making a gift to future generations. In fact, this is definitely a concern for middle-aged workers. The realization that the time left to make such a contribution is limited can come with shocking force. Braverman and Paris (1993) found that at mid-life, using work as a defense against dealing with emotional conflicts tends to break down, and problems of childhood can reemerge as midlife crises. However, for those out of work, receiving welfare can also have detrimental mental and physical effects (Ensminger & Juon, 2001).

The generativity crisis is similar to the identity crisis of late adolescence in many ways. Both often produce psychosomatic symptoms such as indigestion and extreme tiredness. Middle-aged persons often get chest pains at this time. These symptoms are rarely caused by organic diseases in people younger than 50 and usually are due to a depressed state associated with career problems.

The resolution of this crisis, and of other types of crises that occur during early and middle adulthood, depends on how the person's personality has developed during this period. In the following section, we continue our examination of this topic, which began in Chapter 14.

Culture

Diaz, Ayala, and Bein (2004) tested a "multivariate model of sexual risk including experiences of homophobia, racism, and poverty as predictors." Men who reported more instances of inequity and poverty were "more psychologically distressed and more likely to participate in 'difficult' sexual situations."

Pines (2004) proposes that "the root cause of burnout lies in people's need to believe that their lives are meaningful." In cultures such as Israel's, in which the population is constantly under threat, a strong conviction that life is meaningful seems to foster well-being and decreases levels of burnout.

Some Suggestions for Dealing with the Midcareer Crisis

Levinson and others found that a fair number of workers experience a stressful mid-life transition. One major way of dealing with it is for the middle-aged worker to help younger employees make significant contributions. Furthermore, companies are taking a greater responsibility for fostering continuing education of their employees. Advances in technology, for example, are creating more opportunities for women to develop their careers (Green, Felstead, & Gallie, 2003).

We should continue the type of job transfer programs for middle-aged people that we now have for newer employees. Although sometimes the changes can be threatening, the move to a new type of job and the requisite new learning experiences can bring back a zest for work.

Perhaps the federal government should consider starting midcareer clinics. Such clinics could help workers reexamine their goals, consider job changes, and provide information and guidance. Another solution might be the establishment of "portable pension plans" that would move with workers from one company to another so they would not lose all they have built up when they change jobs.

Can you imagine any other remedies?

Guided Review

15. A number of concerns face middle-aged employees. These concerns include knowing how many career goals have been or will be reached, changes in family relationships, change in work relationships, feelings of decreased job _____, and concern for job _____.

16. Some middle-aged workers may experience a _____ crisis on the realization that there may be limited time remaining for them to make contributions for future generations.

17. Some of the problems facing women in the workplace are _____ _____, equal pay, and travel safety.

18. Some women in the workplace experience _____, resulting in a questioning of competence, tougher job requirements, and blocks to career advancement.

CONCLUSION & SUMMARY

What is true of personality and social development appears to be true, though probably to a lesser extent, of physical and mental development: What you expect is what you get. If you expect

- your weight to go up,
- your muscles to grow flabby and weak,
- your senses to dull,
- your climacteric to be disruptive,
- your intelligence to drop,
- your creativity to plummet, and
- your sexual interest and ability to decline, they probably will.

This is called the self-fulfilling prophecy. People who take a positive outlook, who enthusiastically try to maintain their bodies and minds, have a much better chance at success. They are also better able to deal with the stresses that life naturally imposes on us all. This is not to say that we can completely overcome the effects of aging. It means that, through our attitudes, we can learn to deal with them more effectively.

This phenomenon is also seen in the world of work. There are, of course, major changes that occur to most workers as they age, but the disruption of these alterations will usually be more severe if the person is sure they are going to be. Many workplaces are establishing programs to help their employees deal with these stresses. Of particular concern are the special problems that afflict female but not male workers.

What kinds of physical changes affect people in middle adulthood?

- Health concerns in middle adulthood include increasing weight and lower metabolism.
- In the middle period of adulthood there is a common but often unnecessary decline in muscular ability, due in part to a decrease in exercise.
- Sensory abilities—vision, hearing, smell, and taste—begin to show slight declines in middle adulthood.
- The climacterium, the loss of reproductive ability, occurs at menopause for women but at much older ages for most men.

What are the main factors affecting a person's intellectual development in middle adulthood?

- Horn suggests that, although fluid intelligence deteriorates with age, crystallized intelligence does not.
- Sternberg suggests three types of intelligence: analytical, creative, and practical.

- Baltes has proposed a dual-process model of intelligence, which suggests a decline in the mechanics of intelligence (classification skills, logical reasoning) yet an increase in the pragmatics of intelligence (social wisdom).
- Creativity, important in a rapidly changing world, manifests itself at different peak periods throughout adulthood.
- Learning in middle adulthood can be enhanced through motivation, new learning experiences, and changes in education systems.

What are the patterns of work that we most often see in this life stage?

- In recent years, a trend has emerged among employers to recognize some of the concerns of middle-aged employees.
- Four major problem areas are related to working women: sexual harassment on the job, equal pay and promotion criteria, career and/ or family, and travel safety.
- Considerable attention is now being given to the crisis many people undergo in the middle of their careers.
- One major way of dealing with the midcareer crisis is for the middle-aged worker to help younger employees make significant contributions.

KEY TERMS

basal metabolism rate (BMR)
climacteric
climacterium
crystallized intelligence
dual-process model

fluid intelligence
homeopathic treatment
hormone replacement therapy (HRT)
male change of life
menopause

midcareer crisis
olfactory sense
self-fulfilling prophecy
work–family conflict

WHAT DO YOU THINK?

1. When you look at the physical shape your parents and grandparents are in, and their attitudes toward the subject, do you see evidence of the self- fulfilling prophecy?
2. If you are a female and have not yet gone through menopause, what do

you anticipate your feelings will be about it?
3. If you are a male, can you imagine what women facing menopause must be feeling?
4. What are some ways that our society might foster the

creative abilities of its adult citizens?
5. What are some ways that our society might foster the learning of its adult citizens?
6. What remedies can you think of for the midcareer crisis?

CHAPTER REVIEW TEST

1. **Basal metabolism rate refers to**
   a. the minimum amount of energy an individual tends to use after exercising.
   b. the minimum amount of energy an individual tends to use when in a resting state.
   c. the maximum amount of energy an individual tends to use after exercising.
   d. the maximum amount of energy an individual tends to use when in a resting state.

2. **For persons over age 50, even one or two drinks each day can be dangerous, because they can cause**
   a. permanent liver damage.
   b. irreversible kidney damage.
   c. clogged arteries.
   d. enlargement of the left ventricle of the heart.

3. **During middle adulthood, how does one's vision change?**
   a. The lens becomes more elastic.
   b. The cornea decreases in curvature and thickness.
   c. The iris responds less well to light.
   d. The ability to focus on nearby objects increases.

4. **Owing to physical changes in middle adulthood, our hearing can be affected in what way?**
   a. Certain frequencies are harder to hear.
   b. Sounds may need to be much louder.
   c. Human speech may be harder to understand.
   d. All of the answers are correct.

5. **During middle adulthood, how does hearing ability change?**
   a. Higher frequencies need to be louder to be heard.
   b. Lower frequencies need to be louder to be heard.
   c. The ability to hear human speech remains constant.
   d. The ability to listen to speech in a crowded environment declines, while the ability to listen to someone alone without background noise increases.

6. **Hormone replacement therapy has offered relief for women who experience serious problems with**
   a. mid-life crises.
   b. menopause.
   c. weight loss.
   d. fertility.

7. **What type of intelligence deteriorates with age, to some extent?**
   a. learned
   b. natural
   c. crystallized
   d. fluid

8. **What is an example of crystalized intelligence?**
   a. arithmetical reasoning
   b. letter grouping
   c. recalling paired associates
   d. dominoes

9. **People who like to do their own planning, make their own decisions, are flexible, and are able to stand their ground in the face of criticism demonstrate traits of a**
   a. highly creative person.
   b. career-oriented person.
   c. person with strong cognitive abilities.
   d. person who has successfully individuated himself or herself from significant others.

10. **An aid to creativity is**
    a. self-initiated learning.
    b. deferring judgment and being flexible.
    c. self-evaluation.
    d. all of these.

11. **While being tested on paired associate learning tasks the group most at a disadvantage if the amount of time available for response is not sufficient is the**
    a. group in early adulthood.
    b. group in middle adulthood.
    c. group in late adulthood.
    d. All groups would be at a disadvantage.

12. **Groups of middle-aged and elderly subjects are tested on their ability to remember associations between two lists of words.**

How are they most likely to respond when they suspect they may be wrong?
   a. take an educated guess
   b. refrain from responding
   c. confer with other group members
   d. state that they do not know the answer

13. **Research indicates that adults need to know why they need to learn something before undertaking it, that they have a self-concept of being responsible for their own decisions, and that they are life-centered in their orientation to learning. These findings highlight the difference between children and adults in**
    a. cognitive abilities.
    b. level of individuation.
    c. self-fulfillment.
    d. the learning process.

14. **A factor in learning ability during middle adulthood is motivation to learn. It is important for researchers to keep in mind that _____ affects an adult's level of motivation.**
    a. level of education
    b. meaningfulness of the task
    c. interest
    d. external distraction

15. **Consequences of discrimination against women in the workplace include**
    a. stiffer job requirements.
    b. inability to advance in their career.
    c. questioning of a woman's competence.
    d. all of these.

16. **When an accountant 20 years younger than Dan joined his marketing firm, Dan felt resentful and anxious because he feared he would be considered incompetent. Dan has a growing sense of**
    a. job distress.
    b. outdatedness.
    c. the "gold watch" syndrome.
    d. job reluctance.

Answers

PSYCHOSOCIAL DEVELOPMENT IN MIDDLE ADULTHOOD

16
chapter

Chapter Objectives

After reading this chapter you should be able to answer the following questions.

• **How do adults in general deal with stress?**

• **What are the typical patterns of marriage in the family during middle
adulthood?**

• **What are the main factors that affect sex and love among middle-aged
people?**

• **What happens to personality during the adult years: Does it typically
change or remain constant?**

Recently, a middle-aged woman friend shared some reflections with me: I remember walking to school one day in the second grade, chatting with my girlfriend's mother as she escorted us. I told her that I had noticed how much more quickly the day seemed to pass than it used to. Seven seemed a very advanced age to me then, so I was sure this phenomenon was related to being finally grown-up. Later that year we moved into a new house in a new community. Moving day was very exciting. The real grown-ups were very busy, so the most entertaining thing I had to do was to sit around and think about my life. Moving seemed to have wrapped up the first part of my life into a discrete little package. And it came to me that there I was, almost 8 years old, and I didn't have a feeling for all that time. I promised myself, as I sat in our old, soft maroon chair, holding some of my accumulated possessions dislocated by their recent journey, that five years later to the day I would sit again in the same spot, in the same position, holding the same objects. Then, I figured, with all the awareness born of old age, I would really know what five years would feel like. And five years later I did just that.

I am still trying to comprehend or capture a sense of time passing. Now only the units have changed. Every once in a while I hold very still and try to catch 20 years. Twenty years feel like those five did long ago. Twenty from now, if I'm lucky, I'll be staring my death in the face. It's all so odd. Somewhere inside I was all grown-up when I was 7. That "me" hasn't really aged or changed much, and it's still watching as the world wrinkles on the outside. Days are minutes, months are weeks, and years are months. I'll probably be menopausal in the morning! (Quoted by Lila Kalinich)

DEALING WITH THE STRESSES OF ADULTHOOD

What is to give light must endure burning.

VIKTOR FRANKL

We have included this section in the middle adult part of our book because the stresses of adulthood are different in one important way: More and more, adults are expected to deal with stress entirely on their own. True, adults can and should expect help from others, but an increasing number of crises call for independent decisions and actions. For example, many more families today exist in a state of perpetual crisis. These families often face challenges relating to work, poverty, safety, and children's behavior. Researchers have identified major causes of stress as well as specific strategies to reduce stress for families and loved ones (Dacey & Fiore, 2006).

Clearly, stress has many sources, regardless of age, and stress is mainly due to change. One consequence of human development is inexorable change in every aspect of our existence. This situation is difficult enough when we are young, but at least then we have the support of parents, teachers, and other adults, as well as a more resilient body. More stress does seem to occur as we get older. As we move from early to late adulthood, we must rely more and more on knowledge and insight to avoid having a stressful life.

The Chinese . . . are reported to have a way of writing the word "crisis" by two characters, one of which signifies danger, and the other opportunity.

LOUIS WIRTH

general adaptation syndrome
Set of reactions that occur in animals in response to all toxic substances; involves three stages: alarm, resistance, and exhaustion.

The General Adaptation Syndrome

In 1936 Hans Selye (the father of stress research) was studying a little-known ovarian hormone, which led to the discovery of the **general adaptation syndrome** (Selye,

1956, 1975). In one of the experiments, hormones from cattle ovaries were injected into rats to see what changes would occur. Selye was surprised to find that the rats had a broad range of reactions:

- The cortex became enlarged and hyperactive.
- A number of glands shrank.
- Deep bleeding ulcers occurred in both the stomach and upper intestines.

Further experiments showed that these reactions occurred in response to all toxic substances, regardless of their source. Later experiments also showed them occurring, although to a lesser degree, in response to a wide range of noxious stimuli, such as infections, hemorrhage, and nervous irritation.

Selye called the entire syndrome an **alarm reaction.** He referred to it as a generalized "call to arms" of the body's defensive forces. Seeking to gain a fuller understanding of the syndrome, he wondered how the reaction would be affected if stress were present for a longer period of time. He found that a rather amazing thing happens. If the organism survives the initial alarm, it enters a **stage of resistance.** In this second stage, an almost complete reversal of the alarm reaction occurs. Swelling and shrinkages are reversed; the adrenal cortex, which lost its secretions during the alarm stage, becomes unusually rich in these secretions; and a number of other shock-resisting forces are strengthened. During this stage, the organism appears to have adapted successfully to the stressor.

If the stressor continues, however, a gradual depletion of the organism's adaptational energy occurs (Selye, 1982). Eventually this leads to a **stage of exhaustion.** Now the physiological responses revert to their condition during the stage of alarm. The ability to handle the stress decreases, the level of resistance is lost, and the organism dies. Figure 16.1 portrays these three stages. Table 16.1 lists the physical and psychological manifestations of the three stages.

As you grow older, your ability to remain in the resistance stage decreases. Activity over the years gradually wears out your "machine," and the chances of sustaining life are reduced. As we will discuss in Chapter 17, no one dies of old age. Rather, people succumb to some stressor because their ability to resist it has become weakened through aging.

Selye compared his general adaptation stages with the three major stages of life. Childhood, he said, is characteristic of the alarm stage. Children respond excessively to any kind of stimulus and have not yet learned the basic ways to resist shock. In early adulthood, a great deal of learning has occurred, and the organism knows better how to handle the difficulties of life. In middle and old age, however, adaptability is gradually lost, and eventually the adaptation syndrome is exhausted, leading ultimately to death.

Selye suggested that all resistance to stress inevitably causes irreversible chemical scars that build up in the system. These scars are signs of aging. Thus, he said, the old adage that you shouldn't "burn the candle at both ends" is supported by the body's biology and chemistry. Selye's work with the general adaptation syndrome has also helped us to discover the relationship between disease and stress.

alarm reaction
Selye's term for a "call to arms" of the body's defensive forces.

stage of resistance
Selye's term for the body's reaction that is generally a reversal of the alarm reaction.

stage of exhaustion
Selye's term for the body's physiological responses that revert to their condition during the stage of alarm.

FIGURE 16.1

The general adaptation syndrome.

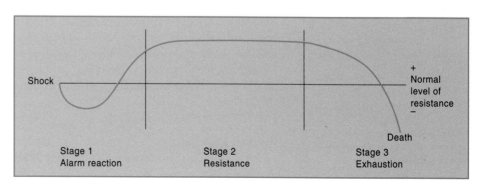

TABLE 16.1 Selye's Stress Adaptation Syndrome			
Stage	*Function*	*Physical Manifestations*	*Psychological Manifestations*
Stage I: Alarm reaction	Mobilization of the body's defensive forces.	Marked loss of body weight; increase in hormone levels; enlargement of the adrenal cortex and lymph glands.	Person is alerted to stress; level of anxiety increases; task-oriented and defense-oriented behavior; symptoms of maladjustment, such as anxiety and inefficient behaviors may appear.
Stage II: Stage of resistance	Optimal adaptation to stress.	Weight returns to normal; lymph glands return to normal size; reduction in size of adrenal cortex; constant hormonal levels.	Intensified use of coping mechanisms; person tends to use habitual defenses rather than problem-solving behavior; psychosomatic symptoms may appear.
Stage III: Stage of exhaustion	Body's resources are depleted and organism loses ability to resist stress.	Weight loss; enlargement and depletion of adrenal glands; enlargement of lymph glands and dysfunction of lymphatic system; increase in hormone levels and subsequent hormonal depletion; if excessive stress continues, person may die.	Personality disorganization and a tendency toward exaggerated and inappropriate use of defense mechanisms; increased disorganization of thoughts and perceptions; person may lose contact with reality, and delusions and hallucinations may appear; further exposure to stress may result in complete psychological disintegration involving violence or stupor.

Source: Adapted from *Adult Health Nursing* by Carol Ren Kneisl and SueAnn Wooster Ames. Addison-Wesley, Menlo Park, CA, 1986.

Risk and Resilience

resilience
Ability to recover from highly stressful situations.

risk factors
Stressors that individuals experience.

protective factors
Characteristics of resilient individuals that protect them from stress.

A relevant source on dealing with stress is the book by H. Benson and W. Proctor (1985). *Beyond the Relaxation Response.* New York: Berkeley. It outlines a stress reduction program that has helped millions of people live healthier lives. Another good book on this subject is *Flow* by M. Csikszentmihalyi (1990). New York: Harper & Row. "This book summarizes, for a general audience, decades of research on the positive aspects of human experience."

Individuals who deal well with stress and have few psychological, behavioral, or learning problems as a result of it are said to have **resilience** (see Chapter 10). In recent years, researchers have become interested in studying the characteristics of resilient individuals. The stressors that individuals experience are called **risk factors.** Risk factors include poverty, chronic illness, parental mental illness and drug abuse, exposure to violence through war or neighborhood tragedies, and the family experiences of divorce and teenage motherhood. Researchers have been interested in identifying **protective factors** (characteristics of resilient individuals that protect them from stress). Three kinds of protective factors have been found so far: family environments, support networks, and personality characteristics (Luthar & Cicchetti, 2000; Luthar, Cicchetti, & Becker, 2000). Recent research indicates that women tend to suffer more from domestic violence than men. Ball (2007) found that women around the world who suffered from domestic violence also experienced controlling behaviors by males in their lives. Domestic violence tended to occur less in industrialized areas than in less developed areas. Of course, a weakness of all self-report studies is the possibility that one group is unwilling to reveal their true feelings because of societal pressures. In addition, Fowler (2007) found that women also suffered from health problems if they developed psychopathology or drug addiction as a result of domestic abuse.

Prevention

Psychologists have been enthusiastic about identifying risk and protective factors in the hope that this knowledge will contribute to the prevention of psychological

AN APPLIED VIEW

Coping with Debilitating Anxiety

I know something about stress. Up until the last decade, I (John Dacey) spent most of my life struggling to overcome a group of phobias: irrational fears of situations such as traveling on buses, trains, and planes; going on bridges, elevators, and islands; and speaking in public. As a result, eventually I developed agoraphobia—the fear of leaving home. As you can imagine, these anxieties became a serious threat to my livelihood as a college teacher and researcher.

In desperation, I began studying the effects of a wide variety of antianxiety techniques on myself and others. This may seem like an obvious reaction, but anxious people try to avoid thinking about the circumstances that scare them, and this work was highly stressful for me. Nevertheless, the work bore fruit, and today my four-step COPE program is a mainstay for me as well as thousands of others who follow its recommendations. Briefly, here are the four steps.

1. *Calm your nervous system.* The first goal of the COPE method addresses the "fight-or-flight" response. This is the ancient human tendency to either attack or to run away when threatened. Today, however, most situations that scare us cannot be resolved either by running away or by attacking. For example, as you stand in front of our audience to make a presentation, you may feel like escaping, or you may feel angry with the people staring at you. However, what you really need to do is to quell these stress responses so that you can think clearly about what

it is you want to say and do. A calm nervous system, then, is an essential first step. Calming techniques that work best for women usually are not the same as those that work well for men.

2. *Originate a plan.* The second obstacle that anxious people often face is that even when calm, we are unable to think of really imaginative plans for dealing with our quandaries. Step two offers instruction on how to create your own special plan.

3. *Persist with your plan.* Most of the people I have studied started out well, but then they lost faith in their plans. The temptation to abandon their plans grew, and eventually they gave up. It became clear that a third step is almost always needed to encourage persistence in the face of adversity or "the wall," as marathon runners call it.

4. *Evaluate your progress.* Although having faith in your plan is important, knowing whether or not it really is working is also crucial to your success. Assessments must be performed while the plan is in operation, as well as after it has been carried out. This step describes how to do this.

You can learn more about COPE in the Jossey-Bass publications by Dacey and Fiore, *Your Anxious Child* (2000) and *The Safe Child Handbook* (2006).

The period in a marriage after which there is no longer a need to care for children is often a time for pursuing dreams that were previously impractical.

difficulties. Successful prevention programs reduce the occurrence of maladjustment and clinical dysfunction by reducing risk factors (when possible) and enhancing protective factors and effective coping strategies. Primary prevention programs try to eliminate problems before they begin. Secondary prevention programs intervene during the early stages of a problem to reduce its severity or the length of time it will last.

Prevention programs vary in whether they are directed toward all children and adolescents in a particular school or city, or whether only students identified to be at particular risk are invited. Among adolescents, prevention programs are most often delivered in the schools or in a community agency. School-based programs have been effective in building social skills and reducing at-risk behaviors. Effective programs have been developed for reducing the onset, use, and abuse of cigarettes, marijuana, and alcohol; reducing teen pregnancy; curbing dropout rates; improving academic performance; and reducing delinquent behavior (Algozzine & Kay, 2002; Wilson, Gottfredson, & Najaka, 2001).

Unfortunately, prevention programs are still limited and are not able to prevent the occurrence of mental disturbance. Psychotherapy, psychiatric hospitalization, and medications are needed to improve dysfunction for those individuals already suffering from mental disturbance.

A SOCIOCULTURAL VIEW

Cultural Stress: Membership in a Minority Group

Dave Mack, an urban worker in Chicago, observes that a variety of differences exist among Asian people living in America, and these differences can cause intense stress. Referring to someone as an "Asian" may be misleading. The Chinese are proud of their vast history and the cultures it has spawned. Koreans also possess a rich, though separate, history. Filipinos, Burmese, and Vietnamese, though possibly educated in Chinese schools, nevertheless associate with some Asians while dissociating with others. For instance, among Southeast Asian people, a great deal of animosity exists between Cambodians and the Hmong.

These attitudes of cultural pride provoke endless problems, especially in our large cities. Mack tells of a group of Vietnamese waiting for a bus in the rain after a basketball game. They got on the bus when it arrived, just as some Chinese people appeared at the bus stop. Since another bus was not immediately available to transport everyone, the Vietnamese bus driver ordered his riders off of the bus and into the rain so that the Chinese people could get onto the bus first.

Assimilation into urban American culture, itself a smorgasbord of ethnicities all within a few square miles, often proves immensely stressful for all involved. The tension also involves how far one should go in regard to becoming "American." Is there such a thing as an "ethnic American"? Should people who immigrate into America be expected to set aside cultural conflicts for the sake of their new home? Given the stress that is bound to result from such an acclimation, is it worth the cost? Is it harder if you are middle-aged or older than it would be for younger people?

Guided Review

1. Hans Selye outlined three stages of a general adaptation syndrome. These include alarm reaction, a stage of _____, and a stage of exhaustion.

2. Each of Selye's stages can be understood in terms of its _____, physical manifestations, and _____ manifestations.

3. The stressors that people feel are called risk factors, whereas the characteristics that increase resilience are called _____ factors.

4. _____ prevention programs try to eliminate problems before they begin.

MARRIAGE AND FAMILY RELATIONS

In this section, we consider four important aspects of middle-aged life today: relationships in marriage, relationships with aging parents, relationships with siblings, and divorce. Although not all would agree, we define this period of life as ages 35 to 64 years.

Marriage at Middle Age

mid-life transition
Levinson's term for the phase that usually lasts for five years and generally extends from age 40 to 45.

Middle age is often a time when husbands and wives reappraise their marriage. The **mid-life transition** (a period during which people seriously reevaluate their lives up to that time) often causes a person to simultaneously examine current relationships and consider changes for the future. Often, whatever tension exists in a marriage is suppressed while the children still live at home. As they leave to go off to college or to start families of their own, these tensions are openly expressed.

Sometimes partners learn to "withstand" each other rather than live with each other. The only activities and interests they share are ones that revolve around the children. When the children leave, they are forced to recognize how far apart they

Answers

1. resistance 2. function, psychological 3. protective 4. Primary

emotional divorce
Sometimes partners learn to "withstand" each other, rather than live with each other. The only activities and interests that they shared were ones that revolved around the children.

empty nest syndrome
Refers to the feelings parents may have as a result of their last child leaving home.

Three wonderful descriptions of middle-aged marriage are (1) Jimmy Breslin's *Table Money* (1986). New York: Ticknor & Fields. This is an empathetic tale of matrimony, alcoholism, and the struggle to attain maturity, focusing on a poor middle-aged Irish-American couple; (2) Judith Guest's *Ordinary People* (1976). New York: Viking Press. This is an evocative story of the relationships among a middle-aged couple, their teenage son, and his psychiatrist; (3) Lorraine Hansberry's *A Raisin in the Sun* (1995 [1959]). New York: Modern Library. This moving drama portrays the inner lives of an African-American family.

have drifted. In effect, they engage in **emotional divorce.** Often the experience of divorce can be thought of as a cluster of small divorces (Kaslow, 2000).

But most couples whose marriages have lasted this long have built the type of relationship that can withstand reappraisal, and they continue for the rest of their lives. U.S. Census data (1996) suggest that the highest rates for separation and divorce occur about five years after the beginning of the marriage. The period after the children leave home is like a second honeymoon for many. After the initial period of negative emotions that follows this disruption of the family, often called the **empty nest syndrome,** married couples can evaluate the job they have done with their children. They can pat themselves on the back for a job well done and then relax now that a major life goal has been accomplished. They then realize that they have more freedom and privacy and fewer worries. They usually have more money to spend on themselves. And this period after the children leave home is now much longer than it used to be. Husbands and wives now can look forward to spending 20 or 30 years together as a couple rather than as a large family.

The Happy Marriage

Bachand and Caron (2001) found, in a qualitative study of happy marriages of over 35 years, a wide range of unique factors. The most common reasons for happy marriages were friendship, love, and similar interests and backgrounds. There are many factors to consider, including the role of culture and gender on marriage and conflicts within a marriage (Mayer & Ziaian, 2002).

Another factor related to marital satisfaction is how well married couples can balance the different roles that they have within the family. Husbands and wives may need to balance the demands of their relationships with each other, their roles as a parent, and their work and leisure time (Marks, Johnson, & Mac Dermid, 2001). In addition, marital satisfaction can be affected when the wife earns more than the husband. Brennan and associates (2001) found that a husband has lower marital satisfaction if he has strong gender-role beliefs and his wife earns more than he does. The variation in income level does not appear to affect the wife's feeling of marital satisfaction. Rogers and White (1998) found that high marital satisfaction in couples was associated with significantly higher rates of parenting satisfaction. In other words, if a couple has a strong marriage, they are more likely to be content in their parenting roles. A strong marriage may also affect a couple's opinions on issues outside the parenting arena, for instance, in cases where religion plays a large role in the couple's lives (Jenks & Christiansen, 2002).

"Certain relationship skills—or the lack of them—can predict whether two people are headed for marital bliss or a painful breakup" (Doheny, 2004). One of the most important skills to develop is to handle conflicts constructively, by listening and remaining respectful of each other. If this does not happen, partners may express dissatisfaction with each other and begin to undermine or insult them. It is

AN APPLIED VIEW

Marriage Therapy in Middle Adulthood

Iwanir and Ayal (1991) suggest that the mid-life phase in the marital relationship is a complicated transition period, one that challenges the flexibility and coping skills of every couple. If a couple finds their marriage to be in trouble (the authors call this "Separation/Divorce Initiation," or S/DI), they recommend a three-step process to help. The steps include

(1) assessment of the relationship's stamina and the function of the S/DI; (2) treating symptoms and reactions to the traumatic event in an "emergency intervention" mode; and (3) steps and techniques to help the couple overcome the traumatic effects of the S/DI and to rebuild their relationship on a more appropriate basis (p. 609).

often evident early on in a couple's relationship whether or not the partners share this skill, and whether or not they do is a predictor of divorce. The good news about these early signs of turmoil is that they can be mediated; the way conflict is handled can often be relearned with the help of a marriage counselor.

The Unmarried Individual

About 1 in 20 people in middle age have never been married (U.S. Census Bureau, 1996). In general, a person who has never married by middle age will not get married. Such people tend to have either very low or very high education levels. As illustrated in Table 16.2, the number of persons who live together without marrying is steadily increasing.

Relationships with Aging Parents

Middle age is also a time when most people develop improved relationships with their parents. Middle-aged children, most of them parents themselves, gain a new perspective on parenthood and so reevaluate the actions taken by their own parents. Also, grandchildren can strengthen bonds that may have weakened when their parents left home as young adults.

In many cases, however, the relationship begins to reverse itself. As elderly parents grow older, they sometimes become as dependent on their middle-aged children as those children once were on them. Most people fail to anticipate the costs and emotional strains that the aging of their parents can engender. This can lead to new sources of tension and rancor in the relationship. Often, early family experiences may have a positive or negative effect on the later relationship between adult children and their aging parents (Whitbeck, Hoyt, & Huck, 1994). For example, young children who have close relationships with their parents, and whose parents provided consistent care, will have more positive later relationships.

The most frequently cited problem of middle-adult women is not menopause or aging but caring for their aging parents and parents-in-law (Singleton, 2000). Dautzenberg and associates (2000) point out that there is a sort of self-selection process that takes place among female siblings whereby the daughter living the closest with the fewest demands is most likely going to be the primary caregiver of aging

FIGURE 16.2

The number of unmarried people in the United States is climbing steadily.

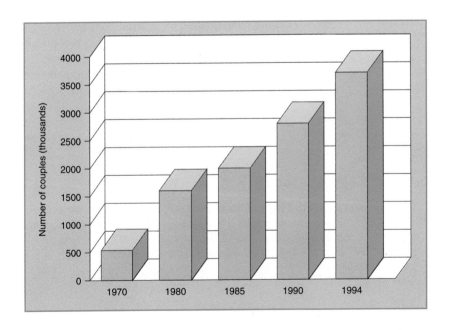

Relationships and roles among the generations are always changing. In what ways do the relationships and roles among the generations change as adults enter middle age?

parents. However, these caregivers face a number of issues in balancing the numerous roles they play, such as wife, homemaker, mother, and employee (Singleton, 2000).

Ducharme and others (2005) examined caring for elderly parents or in-laws and have proposed a "Taking Care of Myself" program. The authors determined several strategies to lessen the burdens associated with caregiving, such as consideration of cognitive stress, empowerment through caregivers' recognition of their own strengths and abilities to change or control their setting, and use of coping tools such as problem solving to deal with stressful factors. Because the stresses of caregiving are not easily measured, each dimension should be considered as having a possible effect on the critical relationship between caregiver and person receiving care.

There is an increasing amount of research on the effects on the caregiver when the elderly relative is gravely or terminally ill. In some cases, caring for a family member who is very sick can have negative effects on the mental health of the caregiver. For example, Beeson and colleagues (2000) found that caregivers for relatives with Alzheimer's disease were at higher risk for feelings of loneliness, since the disease causes the ailing relative to withdraw psychologically and emotionally from any relationship with the caregiver. The loneliness that results from the loss of companionship between the caregiver and the patient has been linked to higher levels of depression among caregiving wives, husbands, and daughters. The researchers also found that female caregivers experienced more depression than male caregivers, with caregiving wives experiencing the highest levels of depression.

We will turn next to two other features of family life in middle adulthood: relationships with siblings and the problems of divorce.

Relationships with Siblings

Developmental psychology has, for some time now, recognized the importance of sibling relationships for a child's cognitive and social growth. But do these special relationships stop contributing to a person's development after adolescence? Does the relationship decline in importance as one ages? Are characteristics of the relationship the same in middle adulthood as they were in childhood? Psychological research has recently begun to focus on some of these questions (see, for example, Lawson & Brossart, 2004).

Sibling relationships have the potential to be the most enduring that a person can have. You don't usually meet your spouse until young adulthood or at least adolescence. Your parents usually pass away before you do. You usually pass away before your children do. But most siblings are born within a few years of each other, and such a relationship can last 60, 80, or even 100 years!

One would hope that a growing maturity would lessen rivalry. Certainly adult siblings are faced with relatively more important tasks than are childhood siblings. For example, most middle-aged siblings must make mutual decisions concerning the care of their elderly parents and eventually deal with the aftermath of their death.

Another consideration is the effect of changing family patterns on sibling relationships. Couples now are having fewer or even no children. Children will therefore be less available to parents for companionship and psychological support. However, parents and their siblings will be living longer, more active lives. The obvious conclusion is that sibling relationships will become more and more important in the future.

Friendships

Middle age is a time when friendships become fewer and more precious. Actually, the findings of Fung, Cartensen, and Lang (2001) suggest that individuals begin narrowing their range of social partners long before middle age. The most dramatic decline occurs between the ages of 18 and 30. In early adulthood, interaction frequency with acquaintances and close friends begins to decline while at the same time it increases with spouses and siblings. It would seem that, at about age 30, individuals choose a select few relationships from which to derive support, self-definition, and a sense of stability. Emotional closeness, however, increases throughout adulthood in relationships with relatives and close friends. These relationships with a select few, then, become increasingly close and satisfying during the middle-adult years. Further, the idea that face-to-face contact is necessary for closeness cannot be supported. In fact, many parents report feeling close to their adult children after they have moved out of the house.

The Middle-Aged Divorced Person

Mid-life divorce has become an important focus of researchers. For example, several (Knoester & Booth, 2000; Smock, Manning, & Gupta, 1999) have found the relationship between divorce and economic status for women to be more complicated than had been thought. Whether or not a woman's financial status changes as a result of divorce depends on a number of factors.

The divorce rates are higher for second or subsequent marriages, for African-Americans, and for those who are less educated and who have lower earning ability. Mid-life is a time when a divorce is less likely to occur—most divorces take place during the first five years of marriage and the number tapers off rapidly after that (see Figure 16.3). Nevertheless, the proportion of divorced persons in mid-life is relatively high, because many who divorced earlier have never remarried. Research suggesting that men and women over 40 experience significantly more turmoil and unhappiness than do younger people at the same stage of divorce (Chiriboga, 1989) has been refuted (Marks & Lambert, 1998). The reasons are complex: length of time of marriage, economic and property linkages, social relationships, and different standards of living.

In respect to the last point, it should be noted that women, especially at mid-life, are often hard hit economically by divorce. The American Academy of Pediatrics (AAP) Task Force on the Family (2003) reported that "in 2000, the median income of female-headed households was only 47% of that of married-couple families and only 65% of that of families with two married parents in which the wife was not employed," (p. S1542). Furthermore, because most women who

FIGURE 16.3

This chart of divorces in the United States shows that most divorces occur within the first five years of marriage, with the peak at three years. Interestingly, the same pattern is found in most other societies, ranging from contemporary Sweden to the hunting and gathering groups of southwest Africa (U.S. Census Bureau, 2004).

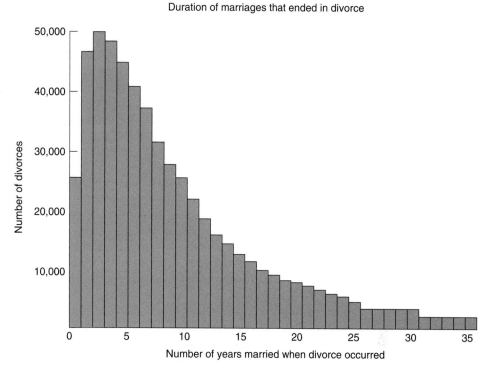

Duration of marriages that ended in divorce

divorce at mid-life are already working, they have little room to maneuver for more income after divorce. McKelvey and McKenry (2000) found that African-American mothers were better able to cope with divorce than white mothers. African-American mothers had higher levels of personal mastery, economic well-being, and formal support following divorce.

In a longitudinal study, Kinnunen and Pulkkinen (2003) examined childhood and adolescent variables that contributed to later marital stability. They found that those individuals who were divorced had generally been "more aggressive and less compliant" as well as "anxious and passive" as children (p. 223). They also found that "marriage at a young age in women and unstable careers and childlessness in men added to the explanation of divorce" (p. 237).

More and more children are living in homes without fathers. More than half of single-parent mothers are not receiving full child support, and half of those are not receiving any. Until recently, child support was awarded mainly because of the mother's limited income. Now, most states use a specific formula that relates child support to both parents' incomes. When both parents are actively involved in parenting their children, through physical or financial means, they tend to be more willing to pay child support (Roseman, 2007).

In general, new divorce laws were considered to have a liberating effect on women. Until the liberalization of divorce laws and attitudes, women usually had no choice but to endure a difficult and sometimes even abusive marriage. Cultural norms allowed men much more moral latitude, the so-called double standard. Women basically just had to put up with it.

Before liberalization, it was necessary to establish "reasonable grounds" for divorce, such as adultery or physical abuse. Women who were granted divorces were almost always awarded larger alimony settlements than they receive today, to make up for the loss of income. This was necessary because women lagged far behind men in their earning potential, and often women stayed at home to raise the children and run the household while the husband advanced a career. A woman could not survive a divorce if it left her and her family destitute.

In 1970, the divorce laws were liberalized in California; a change soon followed across the country. This was the introduction of a **no-fault divorce.** A major

no-fault divorce
The law that lets people get divorced without proving some atrocious act by one of the spouses. In legal language, this is known as an irretrievable breakdown of a marriage.

facet of the new laws was supposed to be gender neutrality. Men and women are treated equally under the divorce laws, and this includes the division of property and alimony. But perhaps these laws were premature. Men and women did not in 1970, and still do not today, live in an economically equitable system. Men still possess a competitive advantage in earning potential, and the dominant culture still holds women responsible for raising the children and running the household. When a divorce judge divides up the property equally, grants little or no alimony, and provides inadequate child support, it is the woman and children who suffer.

This is particularly true for middle-aged homemakers. The courts seldom give much recognition to the years spent running the household while the husband invested time in advancing a career. A woman coming out of this situation cannot reasonably be expected to compete with others who have been gaining experience in the marketplace while she stayed at home.

Another effect is that no-fault divorce laws mandate an even division of property. This often means that the family house must be sold. Before these laws, the house was almost always given to the woman and her children. Besides being an economic burden, the loss of the house has psychological consequences for the children's overall development. The dislocation often requires that the children leave their school, neighborhood, and friends, and this usually comes just after the divorce, a period of tremendous stress for any child.

Some indications show that reform is on the way. In California the rules for division of property and spousal support are being revised. More things are now being considered family assets to be divided equally, such as the major wage earner's salary, pension, medical insurance, and future earning power. In addition, some states have now become aggressive at pursuing husbands who are delinquent on child support payments. Their names are being published, and a part of their wages is being withheld and given to the ex-wife. Massachusetts is even considering paying spouses the money lost through delinquent payments and reimbursing the state through taxes and wage garnishments of the other spouse.

Divorce will probably never be the "civilized" process that the early proponents of no-fault divorce laws hoped it would become. At best, we can expect the suffering of spouses to become more equal and the suffering of the children to be reduced.

Marriage and family life are closely related to two other factors that play an important role in middle age: sex and love.

Guided Review

5. During middle age, marriage is sometimes affected by emotional _____ (which means drifting apart while still married).

6. After the initial period of negative emotions that follows after the children leave home, called the "_____ _____ syndrome," couples can evaluate the job they have done in raising their family.

7. Certain types of conflict in a marriage can be positive and are particularly beneficial if the _____ is willing to confront areas of disagreement.

8. It is unlikely that a middle-aged person who has never married will marry. Such people tend to have either very high or very low levels of _____.

9. One of the most challenging problems facing middle-adult women is that their parents or parents-in-law are now _____ on them.

10. New divorce laws were considered to have a _____ effect on women. These laws, however, have had the result of impoverishing many women.

Answers

SEX AND LOVE IN MIDDLE ADULTHOOD

Many couples find that, when they reach middle age, their relationship becomes more romantic. Can you think of any reasons why this might be so?

At mid-life, minor physiological changes occur in both male and female sexual systems. For the male, there may be lower levels of testosterone, fewer viable sperm, and slight changes in the testes and prostate gland (Beutel, Weidner, & Brahler, 2006). There is usually a need to spend more time and to give more direct stimulation to the penis to attain erection. Drugs such as Viagra and Levitra are prescribed to reduce erectile dysfunction (Wright, 2006) and have become part of the vernacular, owing to marketing campaigns that have brought much attention to male sexual behavior. None of the minor changes is sufficient to significantly alter men's interest and pleasure in a sexual and sensual life.

For the female, the reduction in estrogen occurring during and after menopause may cause changes, such as less vaginal lubrication and possible vaginal irritation at penetration, that can eventually affect the ease and comfort of sexual intercourse. Sexual arousal may be somewhat slower after the fifth decade, but orgasmic response is not impaired. As with the males, females may need more time and appropriate stimulation for vaginal lubrication and orgasmic response. Some studies have found a reduction of female interest and desire, whereas others have found a decrease in frequency of intercourse (Burgess, 2004).

A report on frequency of sexual activity among the adults of all ages, the Janus Report, gives a picture that weakens the stereotype that, as we grow older, we become more inactive sexually. As Table 16.3 illustrates, there is a small increase in sexual activity in the middle years, as compared with early adulthood. For men, middle age is a time when opportunity, if not desire, is at a peak. For women, age makes little difference across the adult lifespan. These findings are supported by Wallace (2000), who argues that physical and pathological changes associated with advancing age do not necessarily reduce the enjoyment of sex.

Generally speaking, attitudes toward love remain constant into middle age; however, Butler and associates (1995) learned that older adults differ in their conceptions of love from younger adults in several important ways: "Specifically,

TABLE 16.3 Frequency of Sexual Intercourse by Age

	AGES (YEARS)									
	18 to 26		*27 to 38*		*39 to 50*		*51 to 64*		*65+*	
	M	F	M	F	M	F	M	F	M	F
N =	254	268	353	380	282	295	227	230	212	221
a. Daily	15%	13%	16%	8%	15%	10%	12%	4%	14%	1%
b. A few times weekly	38	33	44	41	39	29	51	28	39	40
c. Weekly	19	22	23	27	29	29	18	33	16	33
d. Monthly	15	15	8	12	9	11	11	8	20	4
e. Rarely	13	17	9	12	8	21	8	27	11	22
Active = lines a + b	53%	46%	60%	49%	54%	39%	63%	32%	53%	41%
At least weekly = lines a through c	72%	68%	83%	76%	83%	68%	81%	65%	69%	74%

From *The Janus Report on Sexual Behavior* by S. Janus and C. Janus. Copyright ©1993 Wiley & Sons, New York. Reprinted with permission of the authors.

An award-winning novel that examines, among other aspects of middle age, several views of sexuality is Richard Russo's *Empire Falls* (2002). New York, Vintage.

greater age was related to lower agreement with items thought to reflect passive, dependent love (Mania) and all-giving, selfless love (Agape), and these tendencies were more pronounced in females than in males. Furthermore, the age-related decrease in agreement with Mania items was more pronounced among those who were currently in love" (p. 292).

The experts pretty well agree on the nature of physical alterations that occur through the middle years of adulthood. Much less agreement exists, however, on the course of personality development in these years.

Guided Review

11. Studies such as that conducted by Burgess (2004) claim that low _____ levels are associated with decreased sexual interest for women.

12. The Janus Report indicates that the stereotype that people become less _____ sexually as they age is not supported by the Januses' research.

13. Robert Sternberg has argued that the success of the adult intimate relationships depends on the level of compatibility of the partners' _____ _____.

PERSONALITY DEVELOPMENT: CONTINUOUS OR CHANGING?

In earlier chapters, we examined the controversy over whether personality is stable or changing. This debate is concerned with middle adulthood, too.

Continuity versus Change

Most of us have heard someone say, "Oh, he's been like that ever since he was a baby!" Such a comment doesn't sound like a philosophical statement, but think about what it implies. It implies that individuals can remain basically the same throughout their lifespan. This is the fundamental question that the issue of change versus continuity of development addresses. Do human beings really change very much over the course of their lives, or do we all stay pretty much the same? It is the focus of great debate by child-development and lifespan psychologists alike because of its implications.

The man who views the world at 50 the same as he did at 20 has wasted 30 years of his life.

—MUHAMMAD ALI

If we assume that people remain the same regardless of what happens to them as their life continues, then the period of early childhood takes on great meaning. Several of the developmental theorists we have discussed (for example, Freud and Piaget—see Chapter 2) have focused much of their attention on the early years of childhood in the belief that what happens to a person during childhood determines much of what will happen to him or her in the future.

Conversely, others (for instance, Erikson and other adult development theorists— See chapter 2) believe that because people are constantly changing and developing,

Answers   11. estrogen 12. active 13. love stories

all life experiences must be considered important. In that case, early childhood becomes a somewhat less significant period in the whole of development, and adolescence and adulthood come more into focus. It also implies that getting children "off on the right foot" is not enough to ensure positive development. These are just some of the implications of the debate about personality continuity versus change.

In the study of adulthood, the issue of continuity versus change gets even more complex. In general, two distinct theoretical positions influence the study of adult personality. Some theorists feel that adults remain basically the same—that the adult personality is stable. This is continuity in adult development. Other theorists view the adult as constantly in a process of change and evolution. That is what the position of change refers to.

The study of continuity versus change in adulthood is complicated by the many ways that the issue is studied. Use of the Internet allows for thousands of people to be reached quickly and cheaply and greatly facilitates data collection in studies addressing stability versus change (Srivastava et al., 2003). Some researchers look at pieces of the personality (personality traits) as measured by detailed questionnaires. They argue that the answers to such questionnaires assess adult personality. These researchers are known as **trait theorists.**

Others note that such questionnaires measure only parts of the personality. They argue that adult personality is much more complicated than any list of personality traits. What is interesting to them is how those traits fit with the whole of the person. Beyond that, they are also interested in how an adult's personality interacts with the world around him or her. They believe that research based on personality traits is too narrow in focus and that we must also look at the stages of change each person goes through. These researchers are known as **stage theorists.** The old saying "you can't see the forest for the trees" sums up their position—the parts prevent you from seeing the whole.

The differences in how to go about measuring adult personality complicate the study of continuity and change in adulthood. Researchers use extremely different methods of measuring adult personality and then relate their findings to support the position of either continuity or change. In general, trait theorists have found that the adult personality remains the same: Their work supports continuity.

The study of continuity versus change in adult psychology has important implications, just as it does in childhood psychology. The findings of personality studies add to our knowledge of what "normal" adult development means, yet, as we have seen, the studies vary in their definitions of what adult personality is and how it should be measured. Not surprisingly, studies also differ in what they tell us about normal adult development. Theorists have different answers to the question "If nothing very unusual happens (such as a catastrophe), how will the adult personality develop?"

Trait theorists such as McCrae and Costa (2000) might say: "If nothing unusual happens, then the adult personality will stay relatively the same. Normal adult personality development is really the maintenance of personality." Levinson, Vaillant, and Erikson, looking at the whole of the adult, would respond differently (see also Chapter 14). They might say: "The adult personality naturally and normally develops through change. Normal adult personality development is a continual process of growth and change."

Who is right? We suggest you read our summary of the studies that each camp provides and try to make up your own mind. We begin with Daniel Levinson's theory, as it applies to middle age.

Seasons of a Man's Life: Levinson

This section continues a discussion of Levinson's theory that was begun in Chapter 14. Figure 16.4 reproduces that part of his theory that applies to middle adulthood.

---

trait theorists
Researchers who look at pieces of the personality (personality traits), as measured by detailed questionnaires.

stage theorists
Researchers who believe that research based on personality traits is too narrow in focus and that we must also look at the stages of change each person goes through.

FIGURE 16.4

Levinson's theory—middle age.

From *The Seasons of a Man's Life* by Daniel Levinson. Copyright © 1975, 1978 by Daniel J. Levinson. Used by permission of Alfred A. Knopf, a division of Random House, Inc. and reprinted by permission of SLL/Sterling Lord Literistic, Inc.

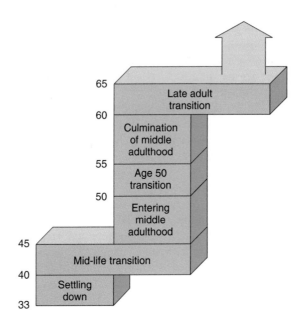

Settling Down

The settling down phase usually extends from age 33 to 40. At this time, most men have decided what occupation they choose to pursue. During this period, most men attempt to achieve two tasks: (1) establish a niche in society and (2) advance up the ladder of the occupational group. During this phase, the male attempts to overcome his dependency on his mentor and slowly is able to "become his own man." This is a step in the direction of greater individuation, in that the man thinks less and less as others want him to and more and more as his own views dictate. He is now ready to go into the third phase of his adulthood, the midlife transition.

The Mid-Life Transition

The mid-life transition, which usually lasts for five years, generally extends from age 40 to 45. It involves three major developmental tasks:

- The review, reappraisal, and termination of the early adult period.
- Decisions on how the period of middle adulthood should be conducted.
- Dealing with the polarities that are the source of deep division in the man's life at this stage. These polarities, which represent the continual struggle toward greater individuation, are (1) young/old, (2) destruction/creation, (3) masculinity/ femininity, and (4) attachment/separation.

Young/Old   Young/old is the major polarity to be dealt with during the mid-life transition. Levinson referred to Freud's disciple, Carl Jung (2001/1927), who suggested that the experience of thousands of generations of human beings has gradually produced deep-seated ideas that each of us must learn to deal with. The major one is that, although we begin to grow old even at birth, we are also interested in maintaining our youth, if only to avoid the ultimate consequence of our mortality: death.

In tribal symbolism, the word *young* represents fertility, growth, energy, potential, birth, and spring. *Old,* in contrast, encompasses termination, death, completion, ending, fruition, and winter. Until the age of 40, the man has been able to maintain his youthful self-image. Through producing and raising children, and in some cases through a creative product such as a book, an invention, or a painting, he has been able to see himself as part of a new and youthful recycling of life. Subconsciously, at least, he has been able to maintain the myth of immortality.

At about the time of his 40th birthday, he is confronted with evidence of his own declining powers. He is no longer able to run, play tennis, or shoot basketballs as effectively as he could in his 20s. He sometimes forgets things, and his eyesight may not be as good. Even more damaging to his hope for immortality is the illness of his friends. Heart attacks, strokes, and other serious illnesses are more frequent among people of his age. In many cases, his parents suffer serious illnesses or even die. These events lead to one inevitable realization: He is going to die, and perhaps in the not-too-distant future. Even the 32 years left him (on the average) do not seem like much, because over half of life is now already past.

A sense of wanting to leave a legacy now emerges. Most individuals want to feel that their life has made some difference, and they want to leave something behind them that can be remembered. Therefore, it is typical at this time that the individual becomes more creative and often works harder than he has in the past to make a contribution considered worthwhile by those who follow him.

Destruction/Creation The male going through a mid-life transition realizes not only the potential of the world to destroy but also his own capacity to be destructive. He recognizes the evil within himself and his own power to hurt, damage, and injure himself and others. He knows, if he is honest with himself, that he has hurt others not only inadvertently but sometimes with clear purpose. He sees himself as both victim and villain in the "continuing tale of man's inhumanity to man" (Levinson, 1978, p. 224).

The more honest he is with himself, the more he realizes how tremendous is his capacity to destroy. This honesty has a bonus, however: In recognizing his power to be destructive, he begins to realize how truly powerful he can be in creating new and useful forms of life. As with the young/old polarity, he now attempts to strike a new balance between his destructive and creative sides.

Masculinity/Femininity Levinson again borrowed from Jung, using his concept that all people have a masculine and a feminine side and that they emphasize one over the other because of the demands of society. This emphasis often costs us greatly. A rich adulthood can be achieved only by compensating for that part of us that was denied during our childhood. In most males, the feminine side has typically been undernourished and now must come to the fore if they are to be all they are capable of being.

According to Levinson, in early adulthood, femininity has a number of undesirable connotations for the male. To the young man, masculinity connotes bodily prowess and toughness, achievement and ambition, power, and intellect. Also to the young man, the feminine role represents physical weakness, lack of ambition, and emotionality. Now is the time when the polarity between these self-concepts must be acknowledged and reconciled.

The male who is to achieve greater individuation now recognizes that these dichotomies are false and that he does indeed have a feminine side that must also be nourished. The mature male is able to allow himself to indulge in what he before has disparaged as feminine aspects of his personality. Such a male feels secure enough in his masculinity to enjoy his ability to feel, to nurture, and be dependent. Levinson suggests such men are now freer to assume more independent relationships with their mothers, to develop more intimate love relationships with peer women, and to become mentors to younger men and women alike.

Attachment/Separation By the attachment/separation process, Levinson meant that each of us needs to be attached to our fellow members of society but also to be separate from them. As the human being develops, a fascinating vacillation occurs between each of these needs. In childhood a clear-cut attachment to mother and later to family exists. Children need support because of their developing abilities to deal with the complexity of the world around them. Nevertheless, children do begin the separation process by forming attachments to their peers.

You might enjoy reading the third in Updike's definitive series about the ordinary American male adult: *Rabbit Is Rich* (1981). New York: Knopf. In this volume, Rabbit reaches middle age.

During adolescence, this need switches toward an emphasis on separateness from family, as the individual proceeds through the identity moratorium. During this time, most adolescents need to separate themselves not only from their parents but also from the entire society around them in order to try out new ways of being. This need vacillates back toward attachment during early adulthood. The ultimate goal, of course, is interdependence (see Chapter 6).

Throughout their 20s and 30s, most men are involved in entering the world of work and in family and have a strong attachment to others who can help them be successful in these goals. Now, in the mid-life transition, a new separateness, perhaps a second adolescence, takes place. The man, especially the successful man, begins to look inside and gain greater awareness of his sensual and aesthetic feelings. He becomes more in touch with himself by being temporarily less in touch with the others around him.

Because Levinson and his colleagues extensively interviewed men between the ages of 35 and 45, their study of adult development ends at the mid-life transition. Levinson recognized, however, that a great deal is still to be learned about development after this stage. He ends his book by encouraging those who are attempting to develop theory and research on the periods following this stage of life.

Seasons of a Woman's Life: Levinson

More recently, Levinson (1990b) turned his attention to female progress toward maturity. For his research, he selected three groups of women between the ages of 35 and 45. One-third were homemakers whose lives had followed the traditional family-centered pattern, one-third were teachers at the college level, and one-third were businesswomen. He saw these women as representing a continuum from the domestic orientation to the public orientation, with the college teachers being somewhere in between. Each of the 45 women was interviewed 8 to 10 times by the research staff (half of whom were female) for a total of 15 to 20 hours.

Of greatest importance is the finding that females go through a sequence of stages very similar to the stages experienced by the males who were studied.

For women, an important transition appears to occur at about 30 years of age. What kinds of events are happening in middle age that might cause a transition to occur?

Each gender may be seen as going through an alternating series of structure-building and structure-changing stages. Levinson found, for example, that, men in their late 30s want to "become their own man." He also found that, at just this time, women desire to "become their own woman"; that is, they want greater affirmation both from the people in their world and from themselves.

Although male and female growth toward maturity may be in similar stages, Levinson and his associates also believed that major differences exist between the genders within these similar stages. Sociohistorical differences are important. For women, the central themes are gender splitting, the traditional marriage enterprise, and the emerging gender revolution.

Gender Splitting

gender splitting
Levinson's term; all societies support the idea that there should be a clear difference between what is considered appropriate for males and for females; gender splitting appears to be universal.

All societies support the idea that a clear difference should exist between what is considered appropriate for males and for females: **Gender splitting** appears to be universal. Women's lives have traditionally been devoted to the domestic sphere, men's to the public sphere. Human societies have seen a need for females to stay at home to protect the small number of offspring (compared with other species) while the male goes about being the "provider" (getting the resources the family needs outside of the home).

The Traditional Marriage Enterprise

traditional marriage enterprise
Levinson's term; the main goal of this type of marriage is to form and maintain a family.

In the final analysis, people get married because they believe they will have a better life by doing so. Some exceptions may occur, but they are probably rare. At any rate, the main goal of the **traditional marriage enterprise** is to form and maintain a family. Gender splitting is seen as contributing to this goal.

Being supportive of the husband's "public" role—that is, getting resources for the family—is traditionally seen by the wife as a significant part of her role. When she goes to work, this goal is not largely different. Levinson reported that it is still a source of conflict when a female does get to be the boss. Women have paid a heavy social and emotional price for the security this role affords. Many find it challenging to develop a strong sense of self.

However, with the increase of dual-career households over the past several years, husbands and wives have had to rework the idea of the traditional marriage enterprise. When both partners are employed outside of the home, gender splitting is no longer an effective way to balance the competing demands of home and work. Dual-career married couples must find other ways to satisfy these demands while maintaining an intimate and emotional relationship with each other. According to Perrone and Worthington (2001), the most important factors in marriage quality in a dual-career couple are love, sexual satisfaction, and communication. Many couples find that they are juggling too many roles and responsibilities, which leads to feeling strained. But those who incorporate coping behaviors into their lifestyle, such as organizational skills and leisure time, reported higher satisfaction with their marriage quality than those who did not.

The Gender Revolution

gender revolution
Levinson's term; the meanings of gender are changing and becoming more similar.

But the meanings of gender are changing and becoming more similar. This is because young and middle-aged adults have so much more work to do. The increase in life expectancy has created a large group, the elderly, who consume more than they produce. This, together with the decrease in birthrate, has brought many more women out of the home and into the workplace. Two other factors have also been at work in creating the **gender revolution:** the divorce rate and the increase in the educational levels of women. This has resulted in a "split dream" for women—to devote themselves to the nurturing of their children *and* to have a fulfilling career. For many women, the attempt to do both brings on role overload. At every transitional point—starting a career, becoming 30, the mid-life "correction"—this conflict arises. "Are the children old enough for me to go back to work?" "Do I stay at home so my husband can fulfill his dream?" It's a big concern for many women.

In his study of women, Levinson found support for the existence of the same stages and a similar midlife crisis as for men (Levinson, 1986). A major study of women's development (Reinke et al., 1985) used a methodology similar to Levinson's and found important transitions in the lives of women, but not exclusively clustered around the mid-life period (ages 40 to 45). Instead, women described important transitions in their lives at ages 30, 40, and 60.

We are, in Levinson's opinion, at a cultural crossroads. The old division of female homemakers and male providers is breaking down, but no clear new direction has yet appeared. Researchers will be watching this dramatic change closely.

Levinson operated from the viewpoint of psychology. The next theory is that of a psychiatrist, most of whom are trained in the Freudian tradition. As we shall see, that makes for a rather different view of adult personality development.

Generativity versus Stagnation: Erikson

The theory presented here is considered a classic. In this final section, we will put forth Erikson's explanation of personality development in middle adulthood: generativity versus stagnation.

generativity
Erikson's term for the ability to be useful to ourselves and to society.

Generativity means the ability to be useful to self and to society. As in the industry stage, the goal here is to be productive and creative. However, productivity in the industry stage is a means of obtaining recognition and material reward. In the generativity stage, which takes place during middle adulthood, one's productivity is aimed at being helpful to others. The act of being productive is itself rewarding, regardless of recognition or reward. Erikson added that generativity is

> that middle period of the life cycle when existence permits you and demands you to consider death as peripheral and to balance its certainty with the only happiness that is lasting: to increase, by whatever is yours to give, the good will and the higher order in your sector of the world. (1978, p. 124)

Although Erikson certainly approved of the procreation of children as an important part of generativity for many people, he did not believe people need to become parents in order to be generative. For example, some people, who from misfortune or because of special and genuine gifts in other directions, cannot apply this drive to offspring of their own and instead apply it to other forms of altruistic concern and creativity (Erikson, 1968).

A SOCIOCULTURAL VIEW | Does Having a "Midlife Crisis" Depend on Your Ethnic Background?

Over the years, a number of researchers have noticed that people of color are less likely to report having had a "mid-life crisis" than are whites. A number of hypotheses have been proposed as to why this might be so. (Can you guess what they might be?) In their extensive review of the literature, however, DeVries and Gallagher (1994) refuted this conclusion. They believed that encountering a mid-life crisis depends mainly on one's socioeconomic status, and the higher that is, the more likely is the individual to feel that he or she has been through such an experience. Because persons of color are more likely to be in the lower socioeconomic level, they are less likely to report the experience:

> Mid-life crises are an affliction of the relatively affluent: rosy illusions are easier to maintain when a person is already somewhat shielded from reality. Just as

childhood is often constricted among the poor, who early in life face adult realities and burdens, so middle age may be eclipsed by a premature old age brought on by poverty and poor health. Among working-class people, for whom strength and stamina may mean earning power, middle age may begin at 35 rather than the 45 often cited by respondents drawn from the sedentary middle class. (1994, p. 74)

In DeVries and Gallagher's view, then, just as "the moratorium of youth" we considered in Chapter 11 is mainly experienced by middle- and upper-class adolescents, the so-called mid-life crisis is primarily a problem for those who have the time and money to afford it. Can you think of any other life crises that may pertain only to one socioeconomic group? How about one ethnic group?

stagnation
According to Erikson, the seventh stage of life (middle-aged adulthood) tends to be marked either by generativity or by stagnation—boredom, self-indulgence, and the inability to contribute to society.

Generativity, Erikson's term for the major goal of the middle years of adulthood, includes coming to understand those who are different from you. How do you suppose this new understanding comes about?

At this stage of adulthood some people become bored, self-indulgent, and unable to contribute to society's welfare; they fall prey to **stagnation.** Such adults act as though they were their own only child. People who have given birth to children may fail to be generative in their parenthood and come to resent the neediness of their offspring.

Research examining generativity has found that adults in midlife may indeed be more psychologically mature and happier than younger people. Sheldon and Kasser (2001) report that, as adults age, their level of psychological maturity influences their level of well-being. Adults in mid-life with higher levels of maturity report higher levels of well-being than younger adults. Ackerman and associates (2000) found that higher levels of generativity for mid-life adults were associated with greater feelings of satisfaction with work and life. In addition, differences in the level of generativity for midlife adults were associated with the social support they receive from friends and family and their involvement in religious and political activities. In comparing the relationship between generativity and social involvement, Hart and associates (2001) found that African-Americans had higher levels of generative concerns and higher levels of social support and religious activity than did whites.

Although generativity may provide great satisfaction to those who reach it, theorists have suggested that the picture is not as clear as it might appear (McAdams, St. Aubin, & Logan, 1993). In a cross-sectional study that looked at generativity across age groups, McAdams and associates examined four different features of generativity: generative concern, commitments, action, and narration. They found some evidence for Erikson's hypothesis that generativity is relatively low in young adulthood, peaks at mid-life, and declines in the older years. These researchers reported that several studies have suggested differences between men and women. Most men appear to become fixed in the industry stage, doing work merely to obtain the social symbols of success. Most women, these studies suggested, become fixed in the identity stage, confused and conflicted about their proper role in life, which prevents them from achieving intimacy and reaching the stage of generativity. Is Erikson's more optimistic view correct or not? Only more sophisticated investigation of the question will resolve it.

Becoming generative is not easy. It depends on the successful resolution of the six preceding Eriksonian crises we have described in this book. People who are able to achieve generativity have a chance to reach the highest level of personhood in Erikson's hierarchy: integrity. We will examine that stage in Chapter 18.

As you can see, all the theories described thus far hold that as we age we go through many important changes. Let us turn now to the other side of the coin: the position that the adult personality is made up of traits that remain continuously stable, in most cases, throughout adulthood.

Continuous Traits Theory

five factor model (FFM) of personality
McCrae and Costa's theory that there are five major personality traits, which they believe govern the adult personality.

The origins of trait theories of personality can be traced back to the work of Allport and Odbert (1936), Cattell (1950), and Eysenck (1960) and, as we stated previously in this chapter, break down personality into individual traits. An individual trait can be thought of as an individual's tendency to have consistent patterns of thoughts, feelings, and behaviors (McCrae & Costa, 1990). Although there is debate within the field of personality on how many traits make up an individual's personality, recent studies have settled on five traits: neuroticism, extraversion, openness to experience, agreeableness, and conscientiousness. These five traits are referred to as the **five factor model (FFM) of personality** (McCrae and Costa, 1999). Each of these five traits is characterized by different tendencies, beliefs, and attitudes and can be broken down further into a number of subtraits or characteristics.

- *Neuroticism* is the tendency to experience some kind of breakdown under stress, such as sadness, depression, or guilt. An individual possesses a negative view of themselves, is a perfectionist, and/or is pessimistic about the future.

- *Extraversion* is the tendency to be outgoing and social, and seems to spill over into almost all aspects of the personality. An extraverted individual has an overriding interest in people and social connections.

- *Openness to experience* is exactly that, an openness to new ideas, fantasies, actions, feelings, and values. This type of individual demonstrates a lack of rigidity in regard to the unfamiliar characteristics openness to experience.

- *Agreeableness* is the willingness to cooperate and defer to others in social interactions. An individual may be forgiving and willing to comply with others' wishes in an effort to avoid interpersonal conflict.

- *Conscientiousness* is a strong sense of purpose with high expectations. An individual may possess strong leadership skills and have expertise directed at specific goals and expectations.

An extensive body of research has used the five factor model in an effort to understand the influence of personality traits on a wide range of issues. McCrae and Costa (1984, 1996, 1999) in their research of men at mid-life found that the five traits are stable throughout adulthood even though a person's habits, life events, opinions, and relationships constantly change over the course of their life. These authors also found no evidence for the existence of a mid-life crisis. They thought that people who experience a mid-life crisis probably have the personality makeup that biases them toward that behavior.

Other studies have found that one's personality traits may be influenced by one's culture (Katigak and others, 2002; McCrae, 2001) and may influence one's career success (Seibert & Kraimer, 2001), driving behavior (Cellar, Nelson, & Yorke, 2000), attraction to the opposite sex (Berry & Miller, 2001), and personality disorders (Clark, Vorhies, & McEwen, 2002). In addition, McCrae and Costa (1997) argue that the five factor model of personality is universal and can be applied across cultures. This claim is supported by a number of studies that have researched FFM in different countries and cultures such as Greece (Tsaousis & Nikolaou, 2001), China (Yang et al., 2002), and Pakistan (Aziz & Jackson, 2001).

AN INFORMED VIEW

Traits versus Stages

As you can see, a clear conflict exists between the trait researchers and the positions of the three stage theorists. It appears that they cannot both be correct, although the truth may lie somewhere in between. We have devoted much more space to the stage theories. In part this is because they have received so much attention in the popular press, as well as by scholars. It is also because we are biased toward them. (It is certainly obvious throughout this book that we have a great deal of admiration for the ideas of Erikson.)

Whatever the case may be, the important thing is that, through discussion, further reading, and observation, you try to come to your own opinion. What do you think? If you would like to have a more informed opinion on this issue, you might want to read one of the articles on the subject referenced in this chapter (for example, Levinson, 1990a and 1990b; McCrae & Costa, 1999).

However, there is criticism of the five factor model within the field of personality. Block (2001) raises several concerns about the usefulness of the FFM. The author points out that although there is agreement on what the five factors are, there is less agreement on what the five traits actually mean. He reported that studies exist that define the traits differently. In addition, the author reports that within personality assessment, traits not part of the FFM may need to be used to understand an individual's personality. Other criticisms of the FFM argue that the Costa and McCrae research lacks consideration of the reciprocal nature of influence of a person with his or her environment. Even so, the rigor of McCrae and Costa's work and the growing volume of research examining FFM warrants careful consideration from those interested in personality development across the lifespan.

Finally, in an article summarizing the best of previous research, Stewart and Ostrove (1998) surveyed what we know about college-educated women's personalities in middle age. They conclude that there are some important changes in personality that typically occur among these women from early adulthood, most significantly ". . . an increased sense of personal identity and confidence in personal efficacy, paralleled with somewhat increased preoccupation with aging itself" (p. 1191). They recommend that further study also look at changes in personality in poor women. As for men, they state: "Perhaps the early adoption of a confident and authoritative stance, associated with cultural expectations of men, means that middle age for men involves more acknowledgment of doubt and vulnerability. Perhaps, too, the social changes of recent years will mean that young men who make major investments in domestic life will experience middle age differently than their fathers did" (p. 1192).

Guided Review

14. Two theoretical positions influence the study of personality. Trait theorists believe that adults remain basically the same, and _____ theorists believe that the adult is constantly changing and evolving.

15. In his discussion on midlife transition, Daniel Levinson identifies four polarities that are a source of division in the life of a middle-adult man. These polarities are young/old, destruction/creation, masculinity/femininity, and _____.

16. From his studies on women, Levinson stated that the stages of women's development are similar to the stages for men, but he found three women's themes: _____ _____, the traditional marriage enterprise, and the emerging gender revolution.

17. McCrae and Costa refer to "an index of instability or a predisposition for some kind of breakdown under stress" as _____.

18. Erikson saw generativity (the ability to be useful to ourselves and society) versus _____ as the challenge for middle adulthood.

19. According to McCrae and Costa, _____, extroversion, and openness to experience are the three traits they found to be stable in middle-aged adult males.

Answers

14. stage 15. attachment/separation 16. gender splitting 17. neuroticism 18. stagnation 19. neuroticism

chapter 16 Review

CONCLUSION & SUMMARY

Dealing with change is as serious a challenge in mid-life as at any other time. Learning new ways to get along with one's spouse, parents, siblings, and children is necessary at this time of life. Considerable debate occurs over whether personality changes much during this period. Some think it goes through a series of predictable changes; others view it as continuous with earlier life. Workers often experience a "mid-life crisis" at this time, and women workers have an additional set of burdens to handle, yet with any luck, we make it safely through middle age and move on to late adulthood.

How do adults generally deal with stress?

- Many life events, including major events and daily hassles, contribute to stress in our lives.
- Selye's concept of the general adaptation syndrome includes the stages of alarm reaction, resistance, and exhaustion.
- It is not unusual for disease to result from stress.
- People who are exposed to many risk factors but develop few behavioral or psychological problems are called resilient.

What are the typical patterns of marriage in the family during middle adulthood?

- Middle age offers a time for marriage reappraisal, which proves positive for most couples.
- Middle age is also a time when most people develop improved relationships with their parents, though in some cases the relationship begins to reverse itself when those parents become dependent on their middle-aged children.
- Sibling relationships have the potential to be the most enduring that a person can have, with the relationship between sisters being strongest. It is usually one of these sisters who cares for the elderly parents.
- Reducing the number of one's friends begins in early adulthood. A deepening of the friendships that remain begins in middle age and goes on throughout the rest of life.
- Liberalization of divorce laws has improved the position of women following divorce; however, Weitzman argues that serious inequity still exists.

What are the main factors that affect sex and love among middle-aged people?

- Frequency of sexual intercourse as well as marital satisfaction appear to increase over the middle years.
- Some minor changes in sexual physiology occur for both sexes, but usually these need not hamper sexual satisfaction.
- Being a good lover is not a personality trait but, rather, the result of interaction with another person.

What happens to personality during the adult years: does it typically change or remain continuous?

- Research by trait theorists such as Kagan and McCrae and Costa generally supports the notion that human beings remain fairly stable throughout life.
- By contrast, theorists such as Erikson, Levinson, and Vaillant argue that human beings are best described as constantly changing and developing throughout life.
- Levinson suggested that most men go through a mid-life transition in which they must deal with the polarities between young and old, masculinity and femininity, destruction and creation, and attachment and separation.
- Levinson also suggested that females go through a similar experience to that of males, with some notably different influences.
- Erikson's theory placed middle adulthood within the stage labeled "generativity versus stagnation." Generativity means the ability to be useful to ourselves and to society without concern for material reward.
- McCrae and Costa defined three major personality traits that they believe govern the adult personality: neuroticism, extroversion, and openness to experience.
- In the study of college-educated women's personality by Stewart and Ostrove, sense of personal identity and confidence in personal efficacy increased with age.

KEY TERMS

alarm reaction
emotional divorce
empty nest syndrome
five factor model (FFM)
    of personality
gender revolution
gender splitting

general adaptation syndrome
generativity
mid-life transition
no-fault divorce
protective factors
resilience
risk factors

stage of exhaustion
stage of resistance
stage theorists
stagnation
traditional marriage enterprise
trait theorists

WHAT DO YOU THINK?

1. In what ways does Selye's concept for the general adaptation syndrome play a part in your life? In the lives of your friends?
2. What is the best way for middle-aged people to take care of their ailing, elderly parents?
3. What changes would you make in our divorce laws?
4. Why is the mid-life transition so stressful for some men and not for others?
5. What are the main differences between male and female personality development during the middle-adult years?
6. Who's right, the stage theorists or the trait theorists?

CHAPTER REVIEW TEST

1. If a person is alerted to stress, the level of anxiety increases, and task-oriented and defense-oriented behavior takes place, the person is experiencing the psychological manifestations of
   a. alarm reaction.
   b. an anxiety attack.
   c. defense mechanisms.
   d. denial.

2. According to Selye, your ability to remain in the resistance stage decreases when you are
   a. experiencing optimum drive.
   b. experiencing an alarm reaction.
   c. an adolescent.
   d. growing older.

3. Under continual stress, the gradual depletion of an organism's adaptational energy eventually leads to
   a. stage of resistance.
   b. stage of exhaustion.
   c. collapse of the nervous system.
   d. increased energy.

4. Francis and Joan have drifted apart over the years but remain married to each other because of their children. Their relationship illustrates the
   a. functional marriage.
   b. practical marriage.
   c. functional divorce.
   d. emotional divorce.

5. According to Gottman and Krokoff's longitudinal research on marital interactions, those who tend most to avoid relational confrontations are
   a. divorcing couples.
   b. couples married for more than 25 years.
   c. husbands.
   d. wives.

6. What is the most frequently cited problem of middle-aged adult women?
   a. aging
   b. menopause
   c. caring for their children
   d. caring for their aging parents

7. Research suggests that a typical characteristic of a sibling relationship in middle adulthood is
   a. growing distance.
   b. increased animosity.
   c. mutual caring for elderly parents.
   d. rivalry over the inheritance.

8. Because the no-fault divorce laws do not account for an inequitable economic system, who suffers most financially by divorce?
   a. the middle-aged homemaker
   b. the career-oriented woman
   c. the middle-aged father
   d. the adult children

9. The notion that adult personality changes over time is supported by
   a. stage theorists.
   b. transition theorists.
   c. trait theorists.
   d. lifespan theorists.

10. Trait theory is to _____ as stage theory is to _____.
    a. lifespan development; stair step transition
    b. continuity in adult development; change in adult development
    c. change in adult development; continuity in adult development
    d. stair step transition; lifespan development

11. The _____ that occur during Levinson's mid-life transition represent the continual struggle toward greater individuation.
    a. attachments
    b. separations
    c. levels of intimacy
    d. polarities

12. The idea that a clear difference exists between what is appropriate for males and for females is referred to as
    a. gender splitting.
    b. the gender revolution.
    c. role strain.
    d. the traditional marriage.

13. McCrae and Costa argued that, although habits, life events, opinions, and relationships may change over the lifespan, the basic _____ of an individual does not.
    a. value
    b. orientation
    c. personality
    d. coping mechanisms

14. **According to Erikson, during the generativity stage one's productivity is aimed at**
    a. career advancement.
    b. material rewards.
    c. being helpful to others.
    d. recognition.

15. **McCrae and Costa defined five major personality types** as neuroticism, extroversion, and
    a. agreeableness.
    b. openness to experience.
    c. conscientiousness.
    d. all of these.

16. **In the study of college-educated women's personality by Stewart and Ostrove, it was learned that** their sense of personal identity and their confidence in their personal efficacy
    a. decreased with age.
    b. increased with age.
    c. was unaffected by aging.
    d. was almost double that of men of the same age.

Answers

PHYSICAL AND COGNITIVE DEVELOPMENT IN LATE ADULTHOOD

17
chapter

Chapter Objectives

After reading this chapter you should be able to answer the following questions.

- Must we age and die?

- What are the key aspects of physical development among the elderly?

- How is cognitive development affected by old age?

*A*nd just as young people are all different, and middle-aged people are all different, so, too, are old people. We don't all have to be exactly alike. ... There are all kinds of old people coping with a common condition, just as kids in puberty when their voices start cracking. Every one of them is different. We old folks get arthritis, rheumatism, our teeth fall out, our feet hurt, our hair gets thin, we creak and groan. These are the physical changes, but all of us are different. And I personally feel that you follow pretty much the pattern of your younger years. I think that some people are born young and some people are born old and tired and gray and dull. ... You're either a nasty little boy turned old man or a mean little old witch turned old or an outgoing, free-loving person turned old. As for myself, I feel very excited about life and about people and color and books, and there is an excitement to everything that I guess some people never feel. ... I have a lot of friends who are 30-year-old clods. They were born that way and they'll die that way. ... But me, I'm happy, I'm alive, and I want to live with as much enjoyment and dignity and decency as I can, and do it gracefully and my way if possible, as long as possible. (M. F. K. Fisher)

A special session of the British House of Lords was being held to honor Winston Churchill on his 90th birthday. As he descended the stairs of the amphitheater, one member turned to another and said, "They say he's really getting senile." Churchill stopped, and leaning toward them, said in a stage whisper loud enough for many to hear, "They also say he's deaf!"

Although upbeat, these vignettes remind us of the stereotypes of old age as being a rather negative stage of life. Although sometimes difficult to notice, ageism fuels attitudes toward older people that maintain prejudices (Levy & Banaji, 2002). How much truth is there to them? Must growing old mean decline? Must the teeth and hair fall out, the eyes grow dim, the skin wrinkle and sag? Must intelligence, memory, and creativity falter? Must old age be awful?

Or is there actually only a relatively slight decline in capacity, a decline greatly exaggerated by our values and presumptions? Many elderly people seem to be having

Even when he was very old and ill, Winston Churchill's fabled sense of humor never left him. In addition, it was only in his later years that he found time to sharpen his artistic skills, which brought him world renown in that realm. What is there about individuals like Churchill that causes them to have such a prominent place in history?

the time of their lives! Could it be that the negative aspects of aging are largely the result of a self-fulfilling prophecy (people expect to deteriorate, so they stop trying to be fit, and then they do deteriorate)? Could most of us in our later years be as capable as those famous few who seem to have overcome age and remained vigorous into their nineties and beyond? In Chapter 17, we will investigate these questions.

The questions that introduced this chapter concern most of the 23 million men and women over 65 who constitute 12% of our population today. In 1900, the over-65 population was 3 million, only 3% of the total. By the year 2040, it will have reached 20% (see Figure 17.1). Such questions should also concern those of us who hope to join their ranks some day. In the next section we look at the answers to these questions, as revealed by considerable new research.

FIGURE 17.1

Age distribution of U.S. population, selected years.

Source: Social Security Administration.

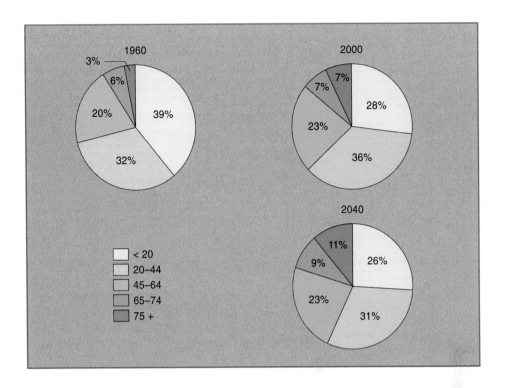

MUST WE AGE AND DIE?

It is never too late to be what you might have been.

—GEORGE ELIOT

"Nothing is inevitable except death and taxes," the old saying goes. But is death inevitable? True, no one so far has attained immortality; the oldest known person in the United States, as certified by the Social Security Administration, is 114 years old. And, of course, the vast majority of the people who have ever lived are dead.

But not all organisms die. Some trees alive today are known to be more than 2,500 years old; they have aged but show no sign of dying. Bacteria apparently are able to live indefinitely, as long as they have the requirements for their existence. The fact is, we are not sure why we age, and until we are, we cannot be certain that aging and death are absolutely inevitable. Nor can we overlook those who appear to age well, which is often referred to as "successful" (Vaillant & Mukamal, 2001; Westerhof et al., 2001). This uncertainty contributes to fears about adulthood that are felt by even the very young (Cummings, Kropf, & DeWeaver, 2000).

Physiological Theories of Aging

It is apparent that organisms inherit a tendency to live for a certain length of time. An animal's durability depends on the species it belongs to. The average human lifespan of approximately 70 years is the longest of any mammal. Elephants, horses, and hippopotamuses are known to live as long as 50 years, but most mammals die much sooner.

Some doctors are fond of stating that "no one ever died of old age." This is true. People die of some physiological failure that is more likely to occur the older one gets. One likely explanation of aging is that the various life-support systems gradually weaken. Illness and death come about as a cumulative result of these various weaknesses. Seven different physiological factors have been suggested as accounting for this process.

Wear and Tear Theory

wear and tear theory
Theory that aging is due to the cumulative effects of hard work and lifelong stress.

The **wear and tear theory** seems the most obvious explanation for aging, but there is actually little evidence for it. To date, no research has clearly linked early deterioration of organs with either hard work or increased stress alone.

A complex interaction, however, may be involved. It is known that lower rates of metabolism are linked to longer life and that certain conditions, such as absence of rich foods, cause a lower metabolism. Therefore, the lack of the "good life" may prolong life. However, it is also known that poor people, who seldom get to eat rich foods, tend to die at an earlier age than middle-class or wealthy people do. Therefore, the evidence on this theory is at best conflicting.

Aging by Program

aging by program
Theory that all animals seem to die when their "program" dictates.

homeostatic imbalance
Theory that aging is due to a failure in the systems that regulate the proper interaction of the organs.

collagen
Major connective tissue in the body; it provides the elasticity in our skin and blood vessels.

cross-linkage theory
Proteins that make up a large part of cells are composed of peptides. When cross-links are formed between peptides, the proteins are altered, often for the worse.

According to the **aging by program** theory, we age because it is programmed into us. It is hard to understand what evolutionary processes govern longevity (if any). For example, the vast majority of animals die at or before the end of their reproductive period, but human females live 20 to 30 years beyond the end of their reproductive cycles. This may be related to the capacities of the human brain. Mead (1972) argued that this extra period beyond the reproductive years has had the evolutionary value of helping to keep the children and grandchildren alive. For example, in times when food is scarce, older people may remember where it was obtained during the last period of scarcity. However, it may be that we humans have outwitted the evolutionary process and, owing to our medical achievements and improvements in lifestyle, are able to live on past our reproductive usefulness.

Another enduring hypothesis, originally proposed by Birren (1960), is known as the "counterpart" theory. According to this premise, factors in human existence that are useful in the earlier years become counterproductive in later years. An example is the mortality of most cells in the nervous system. The fact that brain cells are not constantly changing enhances memory and learning abilities in the earlier years, but it also allows the nervous system to weaken because dead cells are not replaced.

Homeostatic Imbalance

It may be a failure in the systems that regulate the proper interaction of the organs, rather than wear of the organs themselves, that causes aging and ultimately death. These homeostatic (feedback) systems are responsible, for example, for the regulation of the sugar and adrenaline levels in the blood. Apparently there is not a great deal of difference in the systems of the young and the old when they are in a quiet state. It is when stress is put on the systems (death of a spouse, loss of a job, a frightening experience) that we see the effects of the elderly **homeostatic imbalance.** The older body simply isn't as effective reacting to these stresses. Figure 17.2 shows graphically the relationship between problems with the homeostatic systems and the competence of the organism to react effectively to dangers in the environment.

Cross-Linkage Theory

The proteins that make up a large part of cells are composed of peptides. When cross-links are formed between peptides (a natural process of the body), the proteins are altered, often for the worse. For example, **collagen** is the major connective tissue in the body; it provides, for instance, the elasticity in our skin and blood vessels. When its proteins are altered, skin and vessels are adversely affected. This is known as the **cross-linkage theory.**

This olive tree found in Greece is more than 2,500 years old. Do you think it's possible that it will live forever?

FIGURE 17.2

Homeostasis and health; progressive stages of homeostasis from adjustment (health) to failure (death)

From Paola S. Timiras, *Developmental Physiology and Aging,* Figure 28.1, Macmillan Publishing Company, 1972. Used by permission of Paola S. Timiras.

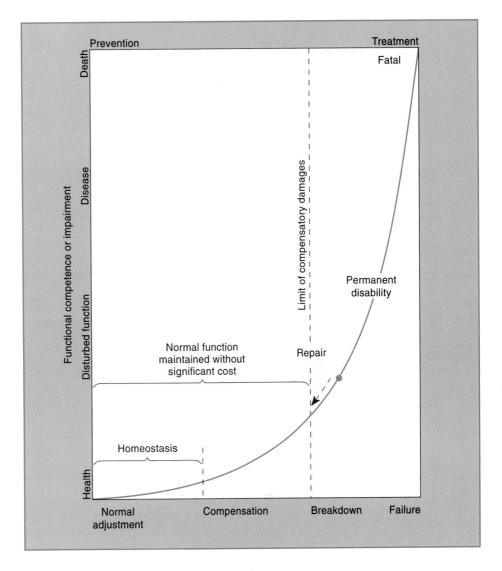

Accumulation of Metabolic Waste

Although the connection has not been clearly established as yet, it may be that waste products resulting from metabolism build up in various parts of the body and contribute to the decrease in competence of those parts. Examples of this effect of the **accumulation of metabolic waste** are cataracts on the eye, cholesterol in the arteries, and brittleness of bones.

Autoimmunity

With increasing age, there is increasing **autoimmunity,** the process by which the immune system in the body rejects the body's own tissue. Examples of this are rheumatoid arthritis, diabetes, vascular diseases, and hypertension. It may be that, with age, the body's tissues become more and more self-rejecting.

This may be the result of the production of new **antigens,** substances in the blood that produce antibodies, which in turn fight to kill them. An antigen may be a foreign substance such as bacteria, or formed within the body, such as a toxin. These new antigens may come about for one of two reasons:

- Mutations cause the formation of altered RNA or DNA.
- Some cells may be "hidden" in the body during the early part of life. When these cells appear later, the body does not recognize them as its own and forms new antibodies to kill them. This in turn may cause organ malfunction.

accumulation of metabolic waste Waste products resulting from metabolism build up in various parts of the body.

autoimmunity Process by which the immune system in the body rejects the body's own tissue.

antigens Substances in the blood that produce antibodies, which kill them.

Patients with a confirmed diagnosis of such ailments are usually instructed to begin drug therapy and change their lifestyles according to prescribed instructions (Clyman & Pompei, 1996a, 1996b). If patients continue to suffer from disabling pain, surgery is an alternative solution. However, elderly people who are bedridden, are wheelchair-bound, or have heart disease are not often candidates for surgery. Fortunately, doctors are considering alternate treatments that may be effective.

Accumulation of Errors

As cells die, they must synthesize new proteins to make new cells. As this is done, occasionally an error occurs. Over time these errors mount up. This **accumulation of errors** may finally grow serious enough to cause organ failure.

Genetic Theories of Aging

Gene theory also suggests that aging is programmed but says that the program exists in certain harmful genes. Whatever the reason, little doubt exists that genes affect how long we live. Kallman and Jarvik's (1959) research into identical twins still offers strong evidence of this. They found that monozygotic twins (those born from the same egg) have more similar lengths of life than do dizygotic twins (those born from two eggs). This effect is illustrated in Figures 17.3 and 17.4.

There is a distinct group of adults that does not fit neatly into any theory of aging. They are called the centenarians—those people 100 or older who do not succumb to common causes of death for persons their age. What factors contribute to the survival of these men and women? Smith's (1997) research suggested that, although these men and women are not necessarily more robust than their contemporaries (whom they've outlived), they are relatively resistant to illnesses such as cancer and circulatory diseases.

Effects of the Natural Environment on Aging

Our genes and the physiology of our organs greatly affect the length of our lives. This may be seen in the extreme accuracy with which insurance companies are able to predict the average number of deaths at a particular age. A mathematical formula to predict the number of deaths within a population was produced as early as 1825 by Gomertz. The formula is still quite accurate except for the early years of life.

accumulation of errors
As cells die, they must synthesize new proteins to make new cells. As this is done, occasionally an error occurs. Over time, these errors mount up and may finally grow serious enough to cause organ failure.

gene theory
Theory that aging is due to certain harmful genes.

FIGURE 17.3

One-egg twins at the ages of 12, 17, 67, and 91 years (note the long separation of these twins between the ages of 18 and 66).

FIGURE 17.4

One-egg twins at the ages of 5, 20, 55, and 86 years.

Today many fewer deaths occur in early childhood, because vaccines have eliminated much of the danger of diseases at this age. This shows that the natural environment is also an important factor in the mortality rate. Many of today's elderly would have died in childhood had they been born in the early part of the 19th century.

Considering mortality rates for specific cultures rather than world population shows the effects of the environment more specifically. Starvation in Africa and earthquakes in Guatemala obviously had a tragic effect on the mortality rates of those two regions. Some evidence indicates that the nuclear testing in the Pacific in the 1950s is affecting the aging process of some of the residents there. Little or no evidence exists, however, to suggest that the radiation we are all exposed to every day is having any impact on aging. It remains to be seen if events such as the nuclear accident at Three-Mile Island will have adverse effects.

Other Modifiers of Aging

In addition to genetic, physiological, and natural environmental factors that indirectly affect the individual's rate of aging, other factors can modify a person's level of ability more directly. Many of these modifiers interact with one another in complex ways. Some of the major modifiers are training, practice, motivation, nutrition, organic malfunction, illness, injury, stress level, educational level, occupation, personality type, and socioeconomic status.

For example, although it appears that social networks (the number and extent of friendships a person has) do not directly affect the survival of elderly people, they are related to their quality of life. Within nursing homes, those who tend to be aggressive and verbally agitated have poor social networks and generally lack intimacy with their fellow patients. Figure 17.5 summarizes the relationships among the hypothesized factors that affect aging of physical and mental systems. These include 2 genetic, 5 physiological, and 5 environmental factors, as well as 12 other modifiers of human abilities. You could find no clearer example of the biopsychosocial model at work!

It is a well-established fact that gender affects aging: Women live approximately seven years longer than men do (Kreeger, 2002). This is striking, given that women suffer from more sex-specific diseases and ailments than men do. For example, women

FIGURE 17.5

Influences on adult mental and physical systems.

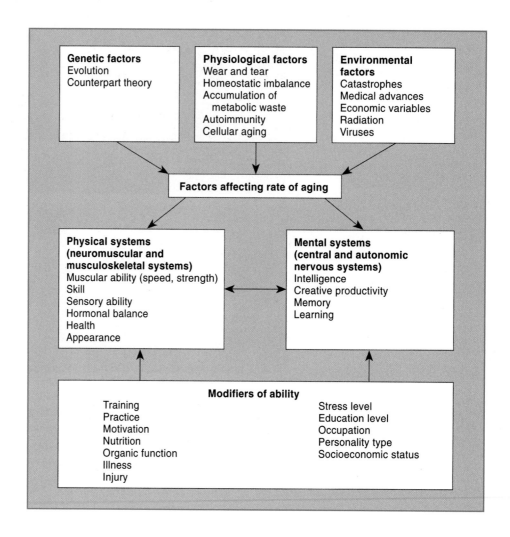

have higher incidences of autoimmune disease such as lupus, as well as more reported cases of multiple sclerosis, migraine headaches, osteoporosis, and colon cancer.

Before reading the next section, you might try your hand at the true-false test on the topic of aging in the box—An Applied View: The Facts on Aging Quiz.

Guided Review

1. Theorists have proposed three generic explanations for aging and death: physiological aspects, _____ aspects, and environmental aspects.
2. Within the physiological aspects, one of the explanations is called the _____ and _____ theory, meaning that hard work and stress gradually destroy body parts.
3. The other physiological aspects are aging by program, homeostatic imbalance, _____ theory, accumulation of metabolic waste, autoimmunity, and accumulation of errors.
4. The impact of the environment on aging and death helps us understand that our genes and the _____ of our organs affect the length of our lives.
5. Those people 100 years old or older are called _____.

Answers

AN APPLIED VIEW

The Facts on Aging Quiz

Mark the items T for true or F for false.

1. A person's height tends to decline in old age.
2. More older persons (over 65) have chronic illnesses that limit their activity more than younger persons.
3. Older persons have more acute (short-term) illnesses than persons under 65.
4. Older persons have more injuries in the home than persons under 65.
5. Older workers have less absenteeism than younger workers.
6. The life expectancy of African Americans at age 65 is about the same as whites.
7. The life expectancy of men at age 65 is about the same as women's.
8. Medicare pays over half of the medical expenses for the aged.
9. Social Security benefits automatically increase with inflation.
10. Supplemental Security Income guarantees a minimum income for needy aged.
11. The aged do not get their proportionate share (about 11%) of the nation's income.
12. The aged have higher rates of criminal victimization than persons under 65.
13. The aged are more fearful of crime than are persons under 65.

14. The aged are the most law abiding of all adult groups, according to official statistics.
15. There are two widows for each widower among the aged.
16. More of the aged vote than any other age group.
17. There are proportionately more older persons in public office than in the total population.
18. The proportion of African Americans among the aged is growing.
19. Participation in voluntary organizations (churches and clubs) tends to decline among the healthy aged.
20. The majority of the aged live alone.
21. About 3% less of the aged have incomes below the official poverty level than the rest of the population.
22. The rate of poverty among aged African-Americans is about three times as high as among aged whites.
23. Older persons who reduce their activity tend to be happier than those who remain active.
24. When the last child leaves home, the majority of parents have serious problems adjusting to their "empty nest."
25. The proportion of widowed is decreasing among the aged.

The key to the correct answers is simple: Alternating pairs of items are true or false (i.e., 1 and 2 are true, 3 and 4 are false, 5 and 6 are true, and so on; 25 is true).

PHYSICAL DEVELOPMENT

In this section, we consider development from the standpoints of reaction time, sensory abilities, other body systems, health, and appearance.

Reaction Time

Seniors usually find that their coordination declines with the years, so they often quit playing sports. What can they do, within reason, to reverse this trend?

It is obvious that physical skills decline as people grow older. This appears to be especially true of manual dexterity. Although older people are able to perform short, coordinated manual tasks, a long series of tasks such as playing a stringed instrument becomes increasingly difficult for them. Famed Spanish guitarist Andrés Segovia and pianist Vladimir Horowitz are notable exceptions.

Is this because the human nervous system deteriorates? To answer this question, psychologists have completed numerous studies of "reaction time," the time between the onset of a stimulus and the actual muscle activity that indicates a reaction to it. Studying reaction time is a scientific way of separating the effects of the central nervous system from the ability of the rest of the body to perform manual tasks.

We can conclude that variables other than sheer neural or motor activities account for most change in physical skills over time. One example of an alternative factor is ageism. Studies have found that younger people interact with older

ageism
Prejudice that the elderly are
inferior to those who are younger.

people in a manner that is depersonalized, discriminatory, and disrespectful (Levy & Banaji, 2002). This type of prejudice is known as **ageism.**

Because they are often treated in a condescending way, elderly persons sometimes behave in a less competent manner than they are capable of. Ageism is a prejudice that can seriously affect the elderly, lowering the quality of their lives. Furthermore, it robs our society of the diverse contributions that might otherwise be made by elderly persons, if their feelings of self-esteem and competence were not undermined by this prejudice.

What are some things you could do to fight this unfair attitude? For example, how might you help change the stereotype that senility is normal in the elderly?

Other factors that influence the reaction time of the elderly are motivation, depression, anxiety, response strategies, and response style. Older adults can improve their ability in these and other areas if they desire.

Sensory Abilities

Sensory functioning may be among the important determinants of individual differences in cognitive performance. Researchers have noted strong patterns of decline in the sensory systems—hearing, vision, and balance—of the elderly (Humes & Floyd, 2005; Wong, 2001). Lack of sensory stimulation is one of many factors that emerges during later phases of life and contributes to the aging process. Such late-life factors of development are powerful influences and may account for developmental changes in old age. We look at some of those changes in the following paragraphs.

We are always the same age inside.

—GERTRUDE STEIN

Vision

A number of problems may affect the eye as the adult ages. The lenses may become less transparent, thicker, and less elastic. This tends to result in farsightedness. The illumination required to perceive a stimulus also increases with age. Retina changes almost never occur before the age of 60; however, some have argued that conditions that affect the retina may occur without causing noticeable changes in the eye.

Increasing age often brings a heightened risk for vision problems (Learning to see, 2000). The main concerns are

- Floaters. These are particles suspended in the jelled substance that fills the eyeball. Floaters generally do not impair vision, but accompanied by flashes of light could indicate a more serious condition called retinal detachment.

- Dry eye. Stemming from diminished tear production, this can usually be eased with drops or minor surgical procedures.

- Age-related macular degeneration (AMD). Deposits form under the retina or tiny blood vessels rupture in this part of the eye, causing blurred central vision.

- Cataracts. The leading cause of blindness in people over 65, they occur when the eye lens clouds, impairing vision. They can often be removed, usually by laser surgery.

- Glaucoma. This disease results from increased pressure caused by fluid within the eye. Left untreated, it can damage the optic nerve and lead to blindness. Glaucoma usually has no symptoms and can be detected only through an eye exam.

Psychosocial adjustment to decline in vision, however, does not go unnoticed in late adulthood (Heyl & Wahl, 2001). Psychosocial factors such as depression, satisfaction with life, social support, self-esteem, stress, and motivation are all related to age-related decline in visual capabilities.

AN INFORMED VIEW | *When Should the Elderly Lose Their Licenses?*

By 2020, up to one out of every five Americans will be 65 or older, and the vast majority will possess a driver's license. This is of concern because statistics show that accidents caused by drivers over the age of 75 equal or surpass those of teenagers, who have been considered the most dangerous group of drivers. A number of states are moving to monitor older drivers more aggressively. However, in those cases where a license is denied or revoked, the drivers may find themselves stranded without crucial transportation (Harvard Health Letter, 1999).

If you would like to have a more informed opinion on this issue, you might want to read one of the articles on the subject referenced in this chapter (for example, Harvard Health Letter, 1999).

At any rate, with recent improvements in ophthalmology and optical surgery, the declining ability of the human eye need not greatly affect vision in older age, with the exception of visual challenges that hamper driving (Classen et al., 2006).

Hearing

Some regard decline in hearing ability as a more serious problem than decline in vision. However, we seem less willing to wear hearing aids than glasses, perhaps because of perceived weakness and age stereotypes.

Age-related hearing loss, called presbycusis, is one of the most common health problems of the elderly (Helzner et al., 2005). Research findings suggest that exposure to varying levels of noise affects older adults differently and may be linked to one's race, sex, and bone density.

Speech & Language

Perceptions about the elderly and the manner in which they communicate need to be reassessed in light of technological advances. As older adults gain greater access to the Internet, their abilities to initiate and sustain conversations across cultural and physical boundaries increase (O'Hara, 2004). Despite stereotypes, individual variation affects the complexity of our speech, regardless of age (Nippold et al., 2005).

Smell

Age does contribute to some atrophy of olfactory fibers in the nose (Harvard Men's Health Watch, 2004). When artificial amplifiers are added, however, the ability of the older people to recognize foods by smell is greatly improved.

Taste

Studying the effects of aging on the sense of taste is difficult because taste itself is so dependent on smell. About 95% of taste derives from olfactory nerves. It is clear, however, that there is decline in tasting ability among the elderly (Mojet, Christ-Hazelhof, & Heidema, 2001). Whereas young adults have an average of 250 taste buds, elderly adults have an average of no more than 100.

Other Body Systems

Included in the category of body systems are the skeletal system, skin, teeth, hair, and locomotion (ability to move about).

What are some of the factors that can cause a person's body to become shorter and stiffer with age?

Skeletal System

Although the skeleton is fully formed by age 24, changes in stature can occur for many reasons. Because the entire skeletal system becomes tighter and stiffer, the aged frequently have a small loss of height. Diseases of the bone system such as arthritis are probably the result of changes in the collagen in the bones with age.

Diseases such as osteoporosis can be crippling. In this regard there is good news. Studies provide strong evidence that if people over 50 (men as well as women) increase their daily intake of calcium to 1,200 milligrams and vitamin D intake to 400–800 international units, they can substantially decrease their risk of osteoporosis (Gruver, 2004).

Skin

Collagen also affects the skin because continuous stretching of collagen causes it to lengthen and the skin begins to lose its elasticity with age. The skin becomes coarser and darker, and wrinkles begin to appear. Darkness forms under the eyes, more because of a growing paleness of the skin than because of any change in the under-eye pigmentation. Years of exposure to the sun also contribute to these effects.

Another important cause of changes in skin texture has to do with typical weight loss among the elderly. They have a tendency to lose fat cells, which decreases the pressure against the skin itself. This tends to cause sagging, folds, and wrinkles in the skin.

Teeth

Loss of teeth may occur in older adults. Even when corrective measures are taken, the surgery involved or adjustment to dentures have a major impact on a person's self-image. In most cases, the loss of teeth is more the result of gum disease than decay of the teeth themselves. Education, the use of fluorides, the use of new brushing techniques, and daily flossing likely will make this aspect of aging less problematic in the future.

Hair

Probably the most significant signature of old age is the change in hair. Thinness, baldness, grayness, stiffness, and a growing amount of facial hair in women are all indications of growing old. Hormonal changes are undoubtedly the main culprit here. Improvements in hair coloring techniques and hair implants may make it possible to avoid having "old-looking" hair (for those who consider this important).

The Gastric System

For years doctors have assumed that digestive problems of the elderly have been linked to incidence of ulcers. The good news for older adults is that stress reduction plays a major role in ulcer prevention, among other concerns. Anxiety, tension, and depression are also affected by reducing stress (Kwong & Kwan, 2003), and alleviate pressure on the gastric system.

Locomotion

It is generally assumed that the decrease in locomotion by older adults is due to aging. However, physical activity interventions can increase one's ability to perform activities of daily living and general mobility (Brach & VanSwearingen, 2002). In fact, overall improvements in physical functioning contribute to greater independence among elderly people and overall well-being.

Health

Illness is not a major cause of death until one reaches the 30s, and only then among African-American females. This is probably because they generally receive fewer preventive health services and because medical treatment is frequently delayed until the later stages of disease. Not until adults reach the age of 40 does ill health, as opposed to accidents, homicide, and suicide, become the major cause of death. The major cause of death for all Americans is heart disease, followed by cancer, stroke, pulmonary disease, pneumonia and influenza, and diabetes (Guttman, 2000). However, the rates of health problems within different segments of the population vary greatly from group to group. For example, diabetes is ranked as the sixth leading cause of death in America but the third leading cause of death for Native-Americans and Native-Alaskans and the fourth leading cause of death for Hispanic-Americans (Guttman, 2000). The life expectancy and health of African-American and Latino-American adults is not as high as that of whites.

A critical factor affecting the health of older American adults is weight. Although 60% of American adults were found to be overweight in a recent poll (AAHPERD, 2007), only one-third were making an attempt to lose weight or exercise. Effective interventions for older Americans include a low-fat diet, a multivitamin, and increased exercise to reduce health risks.

Alcoholism

For adults aged 60 or older, both continuation of problem drinking and late-onset problem drinking are known to occur. Unfortunately, alcohol abuse is often difficult to recognize in elderly adults, who may exhibit conditions related to aging in general. For those taking medications, alcohol may cause them to suffer from negative reactions or may interfere in the aging process.

Prostate Cancer

Prostate cancer is the most common form of cancer in men and one of the leading causes of death among American men (Cohen & Jaskulsky, 2001; Harvard Men's Health Watch, 2004). Until recently, prostate cancer was seen as unrelated to lifestyle (Harvard Men's Health Watch, 2004). Related risk factors and behaviors include (Cohen & Jaskulsky, 2001):

- African-American males have a higher rate of prostate cancer than white males.
- Males over age 65 account for 80% of men diagnosed with prostate cancer.
- The larger the number of relatives with prostate cancer, the greater the risk to men.
- A diet containing excessive dietary fat or few fruits and vegetables.
- Excessive alcohol use (heavy drinkers, more than 22 drinks a week, had a 40% greater risk than light drinkers) and/or smoking (even light smoking is risky).
- Too little exercise (those who burn 4,000 calories per week cut their risk in half).

Alzheimer's Disease

The two most common forms of dementia that affect the elderly are Alzheimer's disease and vascular dementia (decreased blood flow to the brain). Older women (aged 65 or older) are at greater risk for developing Alzheimer's disease than men but have similar rates of vascular dementia in general as older men (Dilworth-Anderson, 1999). The risk of developing both kinds of dementia increases moderately for both sexes. However, the risk of developing Alzheimer's disease increases more significantly for women than men after age 75.

The German neurologist Alois Alzheimer discovered the disease in 1906, but it did not gain attention until the 1970s. Researchers have announced that they have found a gene that is implicated in the cause. This does not, however, mean they have found a cure for it. Alzheimer's is difficult to diagnose and even more difficult to treat. Relatively few of its symptoms respond to any type of treatment, and then only in the earliest stages. Alzheimer's disease usually follows a 6- to 20-year course (Eastman, 1997). Symptoms include the deterioration of abilities relating to learning, memory, and behavior. These symptoms tend to begin slowly and become steadily worse.

The normal brain consists of billions of nerve cells (neurons), which convey messages to one another chemically by way of branchlike structures called dendrites and axons. Neuron groups generate specific chemical transmitters that travel between cells at the synapses. Although Alzheimer's victims appear normal, their brains are undergoing severe changes. Brain autopsies unmask severe damage, abnormalities, and even death of neurons. Once neurons die, they can never be replaced. Current research on Alzheimer's, however, is developing medications that might actually preserve the health of nerve cells before they die.

Several theories have been put forth to explain the causes of Alzheimer's. Some theorists believe that a virus causes the disease, whereas others think that environmental factors are involved. A popular theory is that an overabundance of metal accumulation in the neurons, mainly aluminum, causes it. Some dispute this theory because, although we all ingest aluminum, our bodies reject it by refusing to digest it. There is also some indication that Alzheimer's burns holes in the cells, thus impairing their function. Administering large doses of vitamin E may help prevent the disease and may slow its progress. All these possibilities are currently being studied scientifically.

It now appears that Alzheimer's may be transmitted genetically, because we know that a sibling of an Alzheimer's patient has a 50% chance of contracting the disorder. Almost all persons with Down syndrome, a genetic disorder, will develop Alzheimer's disease if they live long enough. It may be that a defective gene makes a person likely to get it if environmental conditions are present.

It is also known that Alzheimer's does not discriminate on the basis of ethnicity (Yeo & Gallagher-Thompson, 2006). Women are somewhat more likely to contract the disease, but to date it is not known why, and some research has shown that being female is not a risk factor.

The Alzheimer's Association reports that the average lifetime cost of caring for an Alzheimer's patient is $174,000 (Alzheimer's Association, 2005). The financial burden is usually placed on the patient's family, because neither Medicare nor most private health care insurance covers the cost of the long-term care these patients need. As a result, nearly 75% of homecare is provided by family and friends (Alzheimer's Association, 2005). Another alternative to chronic care is the adult-care facility. These programs provide help with daily tasks such as feeding, washing, toileting, and exercising.

Until recently the outlook has been bleak for patients and families suffering with Alzheimer's. Breakthroughs appear to be on the horizon on four fronts (Eastman, 2000):

1. New ways to combat key enzymes that contribute to Alzheimer's.
2. New understanding of how to immunize people against a protein that becomes abnormal.
3. The emergence of human gene therapy capable of vitalizing damaged brain cells.
4. New educational techniques.

New research suggests that "some people with early cognitive impairment can still be taught to recall important information and to better perform daily tasks" (Alzheimers.org, 2004). Research conducted in Miami, Florida, sought to improve

Two books that offer many suggestions on how to care for Alzheimer's patients at home are (1) Carly Hellen's *Alzheimer's Disease: Activity-Focused Care* (1992). Boston: Andover Medical Publishers. (2) The Alzheimer's Association's *Activity Programming for Persons with Dementia*, Chicago, IL.

targeted skills in mildly impaired Alzheimer's disease patients. By participating in cognitive rehabilitation therapy, these patients experienced a "170% improvement, on average, in their ability to recall faces and names and a 71% improvement in their ability to provide proper change for a purchase." These improvements were not transient; patients maintained these skills three months after their therapy had ended. This offers hope for people with early cognitive impairment by suggesting that there are ways for those with "early stages of AD to be taught techniques to help stay engaged in everyday life." With the help of cognitive rehabilitation therapy, patients may be able to retain a higher level of functioning well into the disease.

Not all the news is good, however. A recent study (NIA News, 2000) found that low-dose regimen of the steroid prednisone, an anti-inflammatory drug, is not effective in the treatment of Alzheimer's disease. The study, one of the first from a number of clinical trials trying to determine the usefulness of anti-inflammatory agents to prevent or treat Alzheimer's, suggests that not all classes of such drugs may slow the rate at which people develop the disease or suffer cognitive decline.

If you desire further information on what is known about the disease, write to the Alzheimer's Association, 70 East Lake Street, Suite 600, Chicago, Illinois, 60601, or go to www.alzheimers.org.

The Relationship between Physical and Mental Health

The reciprocal link between physical and mental health means that as one is affected, so is the other. Examples include stress and depression, in that physical symptoms such as stomachaches, headaches, and sleep disturbances accompany mental issues that can range from minor to severe. In addition, men and women in late adulthood are at increased risk for suicide. The literature reports that the group at greatest risk for suicide in America are older white men who live by themselves and are socially isolated, use alcohol, and have a history of depression (Lantz, 2001). Older women who have recently become single because of separation, divorce, or death of a spouse and have a number of medical problems are also at greater risk for suicide (Lantz, 2001). In addition, older depressed adults are also at higher risk for poor health and cognitive functioning and physical disability (Huang et al., 2000).

AN APPLIED VIEW | *New Research Shatters a Long-Standing Belief about Neurons*

According to the National Institute on Aging (NIA, 1999), scientists have always thought that neurons were formed only during the fetal period and for a short time after birth. Once a person had his or her full complement of neurons, that was that—the adult human body could not create new ones.

However, that belief has changed dramatically. Researchers have discovered that the human brain does indeed retain the ability to generate neurons throughout life (Eriksson, 1998). In this study, cancer patients received injections of a compound called BrdU, which was used for diagnostic purposes. The BrdU was incorporated into the cells' DNA as they divided. Upon examining brain tissue from the patients after death, the investigators found that these adult brains contained dividing neuronal stem cells. By demonstrating that new neurons can be generated in the adult brain, it may now be possible to stimulate intrinsic brain repair mechanisms to replace neurons and glial cells lost through age, trauma, and disease. Alzheimer's and Parkinson's diseases, strokes, and spinal cord injuries are all characterized by neuronal dysfunction and death. Finding ways to stimulate the formation of new brain and spinal cord neurons may one day lead to novel therapeutic approaches for these and other conditions.

Source: NIA (1999). *Progress Report and Alzheimer's Disease.* Washington, D.C.: United States Department of Health and Human Services, NIH Publication No. 99-4664.

A SOCIOCULTURAL VIEW | Gateball and the Japanese Elderly

Gateball, developed in post–World War II Japan, is a team sport combining elements of golf and croquet. It employs strategies that exercise both mind and body. Although the object is to score the most points, a great deal of emphasis is placed on the individual's contributions to the team as opposed to individual achievement.

In addition to these benefits, gateball also provides a social outlet, building relationships around a common interest. Gateball has become immensely popular among "silver agers," as older people are called by the Japanese. In a modern, crowded, industrial country such as Japan, with early retirement and the highest life expectancy in the world, gateball provides a way for seniors to continue their lifelong pattern of group participation in something worthwhile.

Observations of gateball players in action found people who share information, laughter, and a relaxed sense of belonging. When a player who hadn't been there for some time reappeared, he or she was warmly welcomed back. Exchange of food occurs routinely on the break, and people often encourage others to take some home with them.

In America, this kind of community spirit among seniors is evidenced in some sports (such as golf and bowling), but the stereotype of the elderly person in the rocking chair remains pervasive. Sports provide a means by which older people can remain healthy as well as connected to other people. It is another important lesson we might glean from Japanese culture.

Health and Retirement

Dychtwald (2005) argues that increased life expectancy and potential for high creativity will usher in a new era of retirement, better termed "rehirement." Many people desire a change or turning point in their lives, or simply part-time employment, and feel "youthful and active." Research indicates that the decision to retire is influenced by the retiree's desire to reinvent herself, physically or mentally.

Health unquestionably affects the physical abilities of adults across the age range, yet it is also clear that social circumstances are the main factor in health in the older years. Thus, the healthiness of adults appears to be more a result of the cultural conditions in which they find themselves than of their age.

Appearance

All the physical factors treated earlier have an effect on the person's self-concept, but none has a stronger impact than physical appearance. Appearance is of great importance in the United States. A youthful appearance matters a great deal and to women more than to men. Females are affected by the "double standard" of aging—a somewhat overweight, greying man is "distinguished-looking," whereas a woman with the same traits is "growing old." Thus, women are more likely to use diet, exercise, clothing, and cosmetics to maintain their youthful appearance. Nevertheless, significant changes in physical appearance occur with age that cannot be avoided. Perhaps in today's society, a decline in female self-concept is also inevitable as the woman ages (Pinquart & Sorensen, 2001).

As you can see from the data presented in this chapter, a certain amount of physical decline happens in later life, but it does not occur until most people are quite advanced in age. And with the new medical technologies and marked trend toward adopting more healthy living styles, you can expect to see a much more capable elderly population. Will this happy news also be true for cognitive development?

Guided Review

6. Physical abilities such as reaction time are not only affected by the aging process but also by motivations, depression, anxiety, _____ _____, response style, and ageism.

7. All five senses decline with age, but hearing ability may be a more serious problem than _____, because people are less likely to wear a hearing aid than they are _____.

8. Because of continuous stretching of _____, the skin begins to lengthen and lose its elasticity with age.

9. One developing breakthrough in treatments for Alzheimer's disease, a serious mental loss in some elderly persons, is in the discovery of new ways to combat key (germs, enzymes).

10. Research indicates that Alzheimer's disease may be transmitted (genetically, socially), because we know that a (grandparent, sibling) of an Alzheimer's patient has a 50% chance of contracting the disorder.

11. When it comes to appearance in aging, there is a _____ _____ for men and for women.

COGNITIVE DEVELOPMENT

In Chapter 15, we described the changes in intelligence that develop across the adult lifespan, focusing on middle age. In this chapter, we take a closer look at old age.

The effect of aging on mental ability has been the subject of many studies. It has been concluded that some mental deficits do occur with old age. For instance, elderly people take longer to learn new information such as a different language. Seniors have greater difficulty completing multiple mental tasks at once. In addition, mental illnesses such as dementia or untreated diabetes can greatly limit the mental capacity of older adults.

However, new research suggests that the effects of aging on the human brain are not all bad (Finch, 2003; Hess et al., 2003; Pitkin & Savage, 2004; Söderlund et al., 2003; Toussaint, 2003; Tremblay, Piskosz, & Souza, 2003). For example, research by Hess and associates (2003) determined that elders make up for most intellectual limitations with better mental abilities in other areas such as an increased vocabulary and a greater global awareness. These researchers concluded that the extreme differences between the intelligence of younger and older adults as found in previous research was due to biases within the studies. It turns out that some aspects of the testing processes greatly affected the results. For instance, and not surprisingly, elders performed better when they were tested in the morning and on material that was important in their lives.

Other studies show that the brain will make up for much of the cell loss that happens with age by growing new cells and building new connections among those cells. Molly Wagster of the National Institute on Aging suggests that there are ways to increase this process of cell growth (cited in Dembner, 2003). According to Wagster, mental exercises, aerobic physical exercise, and good nutrition can lessen the effects of old age on mental competence.

Answers

6. response strategies 7. vision, glasses 8. collagen 9. enzymes 10. genetically, sibling 11. double standard

AN APPLIED VIEW

A Comparison of Physical Abilities

One of the best ways of comprehending adult development is to do a miniseries of experiments of your own. In this activity, you can compare the physical development of friends and relatives with just a few simple pieces of equipment. Pick at least three people in at least two age groups. The results might surprise you. You may find that you need to alter the instructions of the following experiments to make it more convenient for you to do the study. This is perfectly all right, as long as you make sure that each test is the same for every person who takes it. The greater the variety of the adults you enlist in the study, in factors such as age, sex, and religion, the more interesting your results will be.

Muscular Strength. Several of the following tests require a heavy table. Simply have each subject grasp a leg of the table with one hand and raise the leg off the ground 3 inches. Subjects who can hold it up 3 inches for 30 seconds have succeeded in step 1. Now have them try to hold it up another 3 inches, and if they succeed they get credit for step 2 (each step must be done for 30 seconds). In step 3 they must hold it at a height of 1 foot, in step 4 they must hold it at a height of 1½ feet, and in step 5 at a height of 2 feet. Record one point for each step successfully completed.

Vision. The subject should be seated at the table with chin resting on forearms and forearms resting on the table. Set a magazine at a distance of 2 feet and ask the subject to read two lines—next 3 feet, then 4 feet, then 5 feet, and finally at 6 feet. One point is given for each step.

Hearing. The subject is seated with his or her back to the table. You will need some instrument that makes the same level of noise for the same period of time. For example, a portable radio might be turned on a brief moment and turned back off, each time at the same volume. A clicker might be used. Whatever you use, make the standard noise at 2 feet behind the subject and have him or her raise a hand when the sound is heard. Then make the sound at 4 feet, 6 feet, 10 feet, and 20 feet. You may need to vary these distances, depending on the volume of the instrument you are using.

Be sure to vary the intervals between the noises that you make, so that you can be sure the subject is really hearing the noise when you make it. Give points for each appropriate response.

Smell, Taste, and Touch. For these three tests, you will need five cups of equal size. The cups should hold milk, cola, soft ice cream, yogurt, and applesauce. Each food should be chilled to approximately the same temperature. Blindfold subjects and ask them to tell you what the five substances are.

Reaction Time. For this test you will need three squares, three circles, three triangles; one of each is 1 inch high, 2 inches high, and 3 inches high. Make them of cardboard, plastic, or wood. Arrange the nine figures in random order in front of the subject. Tell the subject that when you call out the name of one of the figures (for example, a large square), he or she is to put a finger on it as quickly as possible. Call out the name of one of the figures and time the response. Repeat this test five times, calling out a different figure each time, and compute the total time required for the five trials.

Reaction Time. Again arrange the nine pieces randomly in front of the subject. You will call out either the shape ("circle") or a size ("middle-size"). The subject puts the three circles or the three middle-size pieces in a pile as quickly as possible. Repeat this experiment five times, using a different designator each time, and compute the total time the task requires.

Health. Ask subjects to carefully count the number of times they have been in the hospital. Give them one point if they have been hospitalized 10 times or more, two points for 5 through 9 times, three points for 3 times, four points for no more than 1 time, five points if they have never been hospitalized for any reason (pregnancy should not be counted).

Health. Ask subjects to carefully remember how many times they have visited a doctor within the past year. Give one point for 4 or more times, two points for 3 times, three points for 2 times, four points for 1 time, five points for no visits at all.

Compare the scores for each test for persons within the age groups you have chosen. Do you see any patterns? Are the results of aging evident? What other conclusions can you draw?

Cognitive Ability in the Elderly: Tests versus Observations

So wherein lies the truth—in the results of tests or in our observations of actual performance? As we said, the answer is not simple. What factors could account for this discrepancy? Currently there are four hypotheses, each of which plays a part (Salthouse, 2001):

1. *Differences in type of cognition.* Intelligence tests tend to measure specific bands of cognitive ability, whereas assessments of real-life activities probably also include noncognitive capacities, such as personality traits. Thus, some aspects of IQ may decline without causing lowered performance on the job, for example.

Researchers have come to several different conclusions concerning the effect of age on intelligence level. In the final analysis, what do you believe is the effect of age on a person's intelligence level?

2. *Differences in the representativeness of the individuals or observations.* Many examples exist of elderly persons who can perform admirably even into their nineties, but do these individuals really represent the average elderly person? Probably not. It is also probable that only the most competent individuals are able to survive in such demanding situations. Those who are less competent will have dropped out of the competition at an earlier age. Therefore, when we examine the abilities of successful older persons, we may be studying only the "cream of the crop." Finally, it seems likely that observed competence represents only one type of cognitive ability (balancing the company's books, reading music), whereas intelligence testing involves several (verbal, math, reasoning, and other abilities).

3. *Different standards of evaluation.* Most cognitive tests tend to push individuals to their limits of ability. Assessments of real-life tasks, those with which people are quite familiar (such as reading the newspaper), may require a lower standard of testing.

4. *Different amounts of experience.* Doing well on an intelligence test requires one to employ traits that are not used every day, such as assembling blocks so that they resemble certain patterns. The skills assessed in real-life situations are more likely to be those the individual has practiced for years. For example, driving ability may remain high if the person continues to drive regularly as he or she ages. Young adults may type well because they have greater dexterity, but older typists may do just as well because they are better able to anticipate the text they are typing.

Each of these hypotheses seeks to explain the discrepancy between tested ability and actual performance as being the result of faulty research techniques. Although virtually all studies described here use IQ tests to measure intelligence, the two are not identical. IQ involves school-related abilities, whereas intelligence is made up of these and many other abilities (for instance, spatial ability and "street smarts"). It is not possible at present to discern how much this discrepancy affects the research. Another mental trait that is hard to study, but is even more vital to understand and cultivate, is creativity.

Creativity

In Chapter 15, we concluded that quantity of creative production probably drops in old age but that quality of production may not. This is based on studies of actual productivity. But what about potential for production? Might it be that the elderly are capable of great creativity but that, as with IQ, factors such as motivation and opportunity prevent them from fulfilling this ability? That is the question addressed by the next set of studies presented.

Cross-Sectional Studies of Creative Productivity

The first large-scale study to look at the creative productivity of typical, living people at various ages was completed by Alpaugh and associates (Alpaugh & Birren, 1977). They administered two sets of creativity tests to 111 schoolteachers aged 20 to 83. Their findings supported the idea that creativity does decline with age. One major criticism of their research is that the tests they used are probably not equally valid for all age groups. The younger subjects are more likely to have had practice with these types of materials than the older ones. For example, the study of creativity is relatively new, so the tests used to measure it have been designed recently. Thus, those who attended school more recently are more likely to have encountered such tests than those who graduated many years ago. Such familiarity would provide an advantage to the younger subjects in the study.

Jaquish and Ripple (1980) attempted to evaluate the effects of aging while avoiding the problem of using age-related materials. These researchers gathered data on six age groups across the lifespan: 10 to 12 years (61 people); 13 to 17 years (71 people);

AN APPLIED VIEW

Ways to Keep Memory Functioning

Memory loss is one of the signs of aging that causes people the most concern. A 50-year-old may worry about forgetfulness, whereas a 70-year-old may fear that this forgetfulness is actually a sign of Alzheimer's disease. In a society that is full of information, such as written words, television, and computer technology, it is not surprising that people feel a sense of overload, and a sense of fear when they can't remember where they parked their car. What may be surprising, however, are the recent findings that memory doesn't really diminish over the years.

Although brain changes do occur with age, these changes do not necessarily mean that memory loss will be the result. Rather, it simply takes older people longer to learn, and it requires more effort to store memory for quick recall later. It is the stresses and distractions in the environment that keep people from retrieving details more easily. In the right environment, one that includes physical and mind-stimulating activities and reduced stress, the memory of healthy people in their 70s and 80s can expand.

Photographs can aid memory but also can induce false memory in older adults (ages 60 to 75). Angell and associates (1997) found that viewing photographs can prompt better recall in both older and younger adults (ages 16 to 22). However, older adults are more likely to "remember" an event in which they had not participated but only had viewed in a photograph.

Studies have shown that people who feel good about themselves and who feel a sense of control in their lives are better prepared to maintain their mental abilities. Self-help classes for memory improvement are one way in which older people can take an active role in strengthening their memory capacities. Although some people believe that drugs or herbs can improve memory, there is no convincing proof that substances work. Taking the initiative to exercise their minds, older people may still occasionally forget where they put their slippers, but they won't soon forget the essentials.

18 to 25 years (70 people); 26 to 39 years (58 people); 40 to 60 years (51 people); and 61 to 84 years (39 people). The study had a total of 350 subjects.

The definition of creativity in this study was restricted to the concepts of fluency, flexibility, and originality; these are collectively known as divergent thinking abilities (see Parkhurst, 1999, for a discussion of definitions of creativity). These three traits were measured through the use of an auditory exercise. Known as the Sounds and Images Test, it elicits responses to the "weird" sounds presented on a cassette. Responses are then scored according to the three traits of divergent thinking. The researchers believe that this test is so unusual that no age group is likely to have had more experience with it than any other.

Research indicates that the time right after retirement can be a period of creative growth, as the individual turns from the demands of a work schedule to the opportunities offered by an artistic endeavor.

A number of interesting findings have resulted from this study, as you can see in Table 17.1. On all three measures of divergent thinking, the scores generally increased slightly across the first five age groups. Scores for the 40- to 60-year-old group increased significantly, whereas scores for the 61- to 84-year-old group decreased significantly below the scores of any of the younger age groups. Furthermore, when decline in divergent thinking did occur, it was more pronounced in quantity than in quality. That is, greater age differences occurred in fluency (a measure of quantity) than in originality (a measure of quality). Finally, it is not known to what

TABLE 17.1	Means for Divergent Thinking and Self-Esteem Scores			
Age Group	Fluency Mean	Flexibility Mean	Originality Mean	Self-Esteem Mean
18–25	31	19	19	34
26–39	30	18	19	37
40–60	36	21	20	38
61–84	22	15	15	32

From G. Jaquish and R.E. Ripple "Cognitive Creative Abilities Across the Adult Life Span" in *Human Development*. Copyright ©1980 S. Karger AG, Basel, Switzerland. Reprinted by permission of the publisher.

extent the oldest subjects were affected by hearing loss, particularly of high and low tones. This could be an alternative explanation of the findings for this oldest group.

Probably the most important finding of the study had to do with the relationship between divergent thinking and self-esteem, which was measured by the Coopersmith Self-Esteem Inventory. Table 17.1 indicates that self-esteem follows a pattern quite similar to the other three traits.

Of special interest is the relationship between self-esteem and divergent thinking for the oldest group: The correlations were moderately high in every case. This indicates that self-esteem may have a positive effect on creative abilities over the years, that creativity may enhance self-esteem, or both. Jaquish and Ripple (1980) concluded that

> there is much more plasticity in adult development than has been traditionally assumed. Such an interpretation should find a hospitable audience among those people concerned with educational intervention. If the creative abilities of older adults were to be realized in productivity, it would be difficult to overestimate the importance of the formation of new attitudes of society, teachers in continuing adult education programs, and in the older adults themselves. (p. 152)

The Stages of Life during Which Creativity May Best Be Cultivated

In this section we present Dacey's theory (1989b) that there are certain critical periods in life during which creative ability can be cultivated most effectively. Its relevance to the study of late adulthood will be obvious. Table 17.2 presents a list of these periods for males and females.

The basic premise of this theory is that a person's inherent creativity can blossom best during a period of crisis and change. The six periods chosen in Table 17.2 are ages at which most people experience stress owing to life changes.

The table presents a new theory, and thus it must be considered speculative. Nevertheless, some direct evidence supports it (Esquivel, 1995; Hennessey, 1995). Some excellent research from the fields of personality and cognitive development also indicates that these periods are more volatile than any others.

Included in the theory is the concept that major gains in creative performance are less likely with each succeeding period. That is, what happens to the person in the early years is far more influential than what happens in the later years. The older people become, the less likely they are to have a sudden burst of highly creative production.

TABLE 17.2	Peak Periods of Life during Which Creativity May Most Readily Be Cultivated

For Males	For Females
1. 0–5 years old	0–5 years old
2. 11–14 years old	10–13 years old
3. 18–20 years old	18–20 years old
4. 29–31 years old	29–31 years old
5. 40–45 years old	40 (37?)–45 years old
6. 60–65 years old	60–65 years old

Reprinted with the permission of Lexington Books, an imprint of The Free Press, a division of Simon & Schuster, Inc., from *Fundamentals of Creative Thinking* by John S. Dacey. Copyright ©1989 by Lexington Books.

The Sixth Peak Period   Evidence for the first five peak periods has been presented earlier in this book. The first period is mentioned in Chapter 7 (although not called creativity per se), the second and third in Chapter 12, the fourth in Chapter 14, and the fifth in Chapter 16. The rationale for the sixth period, from 60 to 65, is reviewed here.

For most men and for a growing number of women, this is the period in which retirement occurs. Even if a woman has not been active in the labor force, she has many adjustments to make because of her husband's retirement. Thus, most adults are faced with a major adjustment of self-concept at this time in their lives.

Although some do not adjust well and begin withdrawing from society, others take advantage of the change to pursue creative goals that had previously been impossible for them. Obviously a majority of the "young old" (the new term for those who are aged 60 to 70) do not suddenly become creative, but a substantial number do. Of the several thousand highly productive people he studied, Lehman (1953, 1962) found more than 100, or almost 5%, whose major productivity began in the years after 60.

This is not to say that maintaining or increasing creative performance in one's later years is easy. Psychologist B. F. Skinner (1983), who had a 60-year-long career of highly creative achievement, stated that productivity is difficult for the elderly because they tend to lose interest in work, find it hard to start working, and work more slowly:

> *It is easy to attribute this change to them, but we should not overlook a change in their world. For motivation, read reinforcement. In old age, behavior is not so strongly reinforced. Biological aging weakens reinforcing consequences. Behavior is more and more likely to be followed by aches and pains and quick fatigue. Things tend to become "not worth doing" in the sense that the aversive consequences exact too high a price. Positive reinforcers become less common and less powerful. Poor vision closes off the world of art, faulty hearing the enjoyment of highly fidelitous music. Foods do not taste as good, and erogenous tissues grow less sensitive. Social reinforcers are attenuated. Interests and tastes are shared with a smaller number of people. (p. 28)*

It is increasingly clear that creativity may blossom at any age. This theory of "the peak periods of creative growth" is not meant to disparage that fact. Solid evidence indicates, however, that the best opportunities lie in the six periods identified by the theory. Are there also periods in the development of gender roles in later life that have special importance? Of sexuality? Of family relations? Of work and retirement? We'll examine these questions in the next chapter.

Wisdom

What is the relationship between intelligence and creativity, and how do they relate to the highest level of human cognition, **wisdom?** In Table 17.3, Robert Sternberg's (1990) comparison of the three is presented. He makes a fascinating comparison of wisdom, intelligence, and creativity, for each of the relevant aspects of life: knowledge; mental processes; intellectual styles; personality; motivation; and environmental context (see Chapter 2).

As you can see in Table 17.3, the phrase "going beyond" typifies the concept of creativity. Robert Kegan, in his groundbreaking book *In Over Our Heads* (1994), suggests that, as the average lifespan continues to increase, we will be "going beyond" more and more, simply because more people live to old age:

> *A hundred years ago the average American lived to the middle 40s. Today the average American lives more than 20 years longer, an entire generation longer for each individual life. What might the individual generate given an additional generation to live? My candidate: a qualitatively new order of consciousness. I suggest we are gradually seeing more adults working on a qualitatively different order of consciousness than did adults 100 years ago because we live 20 or more years longer than we used to. (p. 352)*

Baltes and Staudinger (2000) offer a somewhat different view of the concept of wisdom; they find it to be "an expert knowledge system concerning the fundamental pragmatics of life. These include knowledge and judgment about the meaning and conduct of life and the orchestration of human development toward excellence while attending conjointly to personal and collective well-being" (p. 122). The phrase "tend jointly to personal and collective well-being" really means the same thing as the concept of "going beyond" employed by Sternberg and Kegan. Baltes and Staudinger suggested that wisdom is the result of five factors:

1. Intelligence, including both fluid and crystallized types.
2. Personality traits, such as openness to experience, generativity (see Erikson's theory in Chapter 16), and a continuing willingness to meet life's challenges (Bandura, 1997).

Two books that delve into cognitive functioning in old age are (1) May Sarton's *As We Are Now* (1992 [1973]). New York: Norton, which is a novel in the form of the diary of a retired schoolteacher. (2) B. F. Skinner and M. E. Vaughan's *Enjoy Old Age: A Program of Self-Management* (1997 [1983]). New York: Norton. In this book, the grandfather of behaviorism explains how to use behavior modification to better handle the problems of aging.

TABLE 17.3 Summary, Simplified Comparison among Wisdom, Intelligence, and Creativity

	CONSTRUCT		
Aspect	*Wisdom*	*Intelligence*	*Creativity*
Knowledge	Understanding of its presuppositions and meanings as well as its limitations	Recall, analysis, and use	Going beyond what is available
Processes	Understanding of what is automatic and why	Automatization of procedures	Applied to novel tasks
Primary intellectual style	Judicial	Executive	Legislative
Personality	Understanding of ambiguity and obstacles	Eliminating ambiguity and overcoming obstacles within conventional framework	Tolerance of ambiguity and redefinition of obstacles
Motivation known	To understand what is known and what it means	To know and to use what is known	To go beyond what is
Environmental context	Appreciation in environment of depth of understanding	Appreciation in environment of extent and breadth of understanding	Appreciation in environment of going beyond what is currently understood

From *Wisdom* by R.J. Sternberg. Copyright © 1990 Cambridge University Press, New York. Reprinted with the permission of Cambridge University Press.

3. The personality-intelligence interface, which includes creativity and social intelligence.

4. Life experience.

5. Age (by and large, the older the person, the greater the wisdom).

Guided Review

12. Discrepancies between the results of tests and our observations of cognitive abilities may be due to differences in type of cognition, differences in the representation of the individuals or observations, different standards of _____, and different amounts of experience.

13. It is suggested that a decline in intelligence in the later years may be caused by the person's _____ of impending death.

14. Jaquish and Ripple found in their studies on creativity that there is a correlation between _____ and creativity.

15. Dacey sees creativity as blossoming during periods of _____ and _____.

16. Wisdom is different from both creativity and intelligence, in that it has a focus on _____.

17. Baltes and Staudinger suggest that wisdom is the result of intelligence, personality, the intelligence-personality interaction, life experience, and _____.

Answers   12. evaluation (or testing) 13. perception 14. self-esteem 15. crisis, change 16. understanding 17. age

CONCLUSION & SUMMARY

At the beginning of this chapter we asked, "Must growing old mean decline?" The answer is that some decline is inevitable, but the picture is much less gloomy than we have been led to believe. The loss of mental and physical abilities is, on the average, relatively slight; some individuals experience only moderate physical loss and no cognitive loss at all. For many older adults, compensatory skills and abilities may replace lost capacities. The same is true for personal and social development.

Here once again we run into the bugaboo of all human development: the self-fulfilling prophecy. Because American society has been changing rapidly for many decades, older adults are frequently viewed as incompetent—their experience appears to have little relevance in "modern times," yet carefully controlled laboratory measurements of their abilities make clear that their losses may be relatively slight.

Perhaps as we learn to understand the aging process, and as the process is better understood by the public in general, the majority of adults will not assume that their abilities must undergo severe decline. In such a situation, the quality of life of the elderly surely will improve greatly, and because we could reasonably expect an increase in the productive contributions of seniors, all of society would benefit!

Must we age and die?

- A variety of physiological theories regarding aging and death exist. These include aging by program, homeostatic imbalance, and cross-linkage theories.

- Gene theory also suggests that aging is programmed but says that the program exists in certain harmful genes.

- The natural environment is also an important factor in mortality (for example, now fewer elderly mortalities are due to the spread of influenza).

- Major modifiers of ability such as training, nutrition, illness, stress level, and personality type also affect one's rate of aging.

What are the key aspects of physical development among elderly?

- Although reaction time appears to decline with age, Elias and others have pointed to several reasons for this decline.

- We may conclude that variables other than sheer neural or motor activities account for most change in physical skills over time. These include ageism, motivation, depression, anxiety, response strategies, and response style.

- Changes in sensory abilities, the skeletal system, skin, teeth, hair, and locomotion are noticeable in late adulthood.
- Even though hormone production slows down during late adulthood, a detriment in one area is often compensated for by some other gland.
- Probably the single greatest scourge of the elderly, and in many ways the most debilitating, is Alzheimer's disease.

- A strong relationship exists between physical and mental health.

How is cognitive development affected by old age?

- A number of factors have been suggested as explaining the difference between tested and observed changes in elderly cognition. These include differences in type of cognition, the representativeness of the individuals or observations, standards of evaluation, and amounts of experience.

- Creativity is evidenced in late adulthood and in some cases may be strongest during this time. Although quantity of creative production probably drops in old age, the quality of creative production and potential ability probably do not.
- Wisdom refers to going beyond what is known to an understanding of the implication of things. It is the result of intelligence, personality, the intelligence-personality interaction, life experience, and age.

 ## KEY TERMS

accumulation of errors
accumulation of metabolic waste
ageism
aging by program

antigens
autoimmunity
collagen
cross-linkage theory

gene theory
homeostatic imbalance
wear and tear theory
wisdom

 ## WHAT DO YOU THINK?

1. Which of the explanations of why we age and die do you find most persuasive?
2. Which factors do you believe most strongly affect aging: physiological, genetic, environmental, or some others?
3. Regarding the decline of physical systems, which has the greatest impact on the person's life: reaction time, sensory abilities, other body systems, hormonal balance, health, or appearance? Why?
4. Johnny Kelly of Boston ran the Boston Marathon every year until he was well into his 80s. Why do some people seem to age so much better than others?
5. Regarding the decline of cognitive systems, which has the greatest impact on the person's life: intelligence, creativity, memory, or learning? Why?
6. Programs in which young people meet regularly with elderly adults seem to have rewards for all involved. By what other means might we better tap the knowledge and creativity of the elderly?
7. Which is more important to society, intelligence, creativity, or wisdom?

 ## CHAPTER REVIEW TEST

1. **The counterpart theory holds that**
   a. the aging process is programmed.
   b. factors that are useful in the earlier years become counterproductive in later years.
   c. early deterioration is due to hard work and a stressful lifestyle.
   d. the aging process is due to alterations in cell proteins.

2. **One explanation of aging is that the various life-support systems gradually weaken and that death comes about as a cumulative result of these various weaknesses. This refers to which aspect of aging?**
   a. genetic
   b. environmental
   c. physiological
   d. human abilities

3. **According to the cross-linkage theory, what happens to collagen, the major connective tissue in the body that provides elasticity in our skin, as we grow older?**
   a. It becomes a waste product as a result of a metabolism build-up in the body.
   b. It causes early aging.

chapter 17 Review

c. It contributes to our body's tissues becoming more self-rejecting.

d. Our skin wrinkles because the proteins of collagen are altered.

4. **A failure in the body's systems to regulate the proper interaction of organs is known as**
   a. cross-linkage theory.
   b. autoimmunity.
   c. homeostatic imbalance.
   d. counterpart theory.

5. **Studies of monozygotic twins showing that they have more similar lengths of life than do dizygotic twins are evidence of which aspect of aging?**
   a. human ability
   b. environmental
   c. physiological
   d. genetic

6. **In examining the effects of the environment on aging, one factor that has contributed to lower mortality rates in Western culture is**
   a. better diet.
   b. changes in the evolutionary process.
   c. the increased use of vaccines in early childhood.
   d. none of these.

7. **Stress level, educational level, motivation, and personality type are examples of**
   a. genetic factors.
   b. physiological factors.
   c. environmental factors.
   d. modifiers of ability.

8. **Ageism can be defined as**
   a. the study of late adulthood.
   b. the study of human development as one ages.
   c. a type of prejudice toward older adults.
   d. physical changes from middle to older adulthood.

9. **Breakthroughs that appear to be on the horizon for combating Alzheimer's include**
   a. new ways to combat key enzymes that contribute to cell damage.
   b. new understanding of how to immunize people against a protein that becomes abnormal.
   c. the emergence of human gene therapy.
   d. all of these.

10. **Alzheimer's disease is**
    a. one of the two most common forms of dementia that affect the elderly and is probably the single greatest source of affliction and debilitation.
    b. caused largely by bacteria.
    c. suffered most by people whose IQ is the top third of the population.
    d. strongly regressive.

11. **According to the research of Salthouse, _____ accounts for the differences between tests of cognitive ability and actual performance of the elderly.**
    a. different types of cognition
    b. different standards of evaluation
    c. different amount of experience
    d. all of these

12. **Probably the strongest influence on an elder's self-concept is**
    a. wealth.
    b. appearance.
    c. skeletal integrity.
    d. social ability.

13. **Jaquish and Ripple (1980) found a positive relationship between self-esteem and _____ for the oldest group of subjects.**
    a. divergent thinking
    b. originality
    c. flexibility
    d. fluency

14. **According to the theory of Baltes and Staudinger, wisdom is the result of**
    a. life experience.
    b. age.
    c. personality and intelligence.
    d. all of these.

15. **Dacey (1989b) proposed that there are certain _____ in life during which creative ability can be cultivated most effectively.**
    a. work-related experiences
    b. critical periods
    c. ages
    d. educational experiences

16. **According to Dacey's research, a peak period during life in which female creativity may most readily be cultivated is**
    a. 10 to 13 years old.
    b. 18 to 20 years old.
    c. 29 to 31 years old.
    d. all of these.

Answers

1. b 2. c 3. d 4. c 5. d 6. c 7. d 8. c 9. d 10. a 11. a 12. b 13. a 14. d 15. b 16. d

PSYCHOSOCIAL DEVELOPMENT IN LATE ADULTHOOD

18
chapter

Chapter Objectives

After reading this chapter you should be able to answer the following questions.

- How do social relationships develop during late adulthood?

- What are major factors affecting the older worker?

- Is personality development any different among older adults?

etting married in 1948 I married into a world that had a very definite definition of marriage. I married into a man-oriented society, where the man was the provider, the center, the whatnot, and the woman circled around the man. But I married Ruby Dee; Ruby had some other ideas about marriage. [Laughs.] There were one or two other extra things on her agenda that I didn't know about, but when they came up I saw no reason to challenge her. For example, after our first baby was born and we moved down to Mount Vernon, New York, I remember Ruby standing washing dishes one day and saying to me, quite confidently, "You know, I'm not going to do this the rest of my life." I said, "No? What are you going to do?" She said, "Well, I'm going to be an actor. I'm still going to act." I said, "Yes." She said, "I'm going to go to acting school." And I said, "Well, okay." And at that time we didn't have much money, so we decided that Ruby would go to acting school and I would stay home and sometimes wash the dishes and take care of the baby. And when Ruby came home she would teach me what she learned at the acting class.

Now, when I stepped into the marriage I didn't think of that, but that happened. And over the years I think the central thing that I've learned is how to more easily open my life and let Ruby in. I think women are much more generous in letting people into their lives than men—although I might be wrong. I think that men come with a sense that they are the complete embodiment of what God intended should represent value, virtue, power, and all that sort of thing, and that women, to some degree, are there to service and serve them—that's how women fulfill themselves. Gradually my wife and the circumstances of the time led me to a different understanding, and I'm glad for that, because it made me a broader and a deeper and a much richer person. It has enriched my spirit, my spirituality. It means also—and this is the best part of it all—that I learned a lesson a long time ago, and the lesson is, "The way to make a man rich is to decrease his wants." I learn more and more every day what not to want and how not to want it. To me that is the regimen of the spirit. (Actor, writer, and social activist Ossie Davis [1917–2005], age 78)

Recently, research on the aging process has gotten an encouraging boost from the American Psychological Association (APA), a parent organization for

Actor, writer, and social activist Ossie Davis, age 78, and wife, Ruby Dee

The "crossover effect" concerns the tendency of men to do more things that are considered feminine, such as washing the dishes, and for women to do more things that are considered masculine, such as taking charge of repairs to the home.

psychologists. Continuing the work of the Committee on Aging (CONA) begun in 1997, the APA's efforts focus on education and advocacy. Recognizing a gap between need and accessibility of psychological services for older adults (Quall et al., 2002), APA projects include the Preparing Psychology for an Aging World Initiative (DiGilio & Levitt, 2002). This initiative aims to build interest in the field of geropsychology among undergraduates, who may enter the workforce and have direct impact on the elderly population. In his 1997 keynote address to the APA annual convention, Nobel Laureate Elie Wiesel emphasized the need for gratitude to the elderly for their role in helping us remember the lessons of the past (Abeles, 1997) as has been the case with the Holocaust. He defended the right of the elderly and other often-victimized populations. Efforts by the APA to focus on elderly issues should help us deal with problems caused by increasing numbers of those in this age group, particularly in the area of social development.

SOCIAL DEVELOPMENT

You shall more command with your years than with your weapons.

—*OTHELLO*, SHAKESPEARE

This section is devoted to five aspects of social development: gender roles, sexuality, families, the older worker, and retirement.

Gender Roles

You might think that, when people reach old age, their gender roles have become pretty well fixed. In fact, researchers generally agree with the statement by Sales (1978) that this is not so:

> When people enter their 60s, they enter a new and final stage in the life cycle. At this point they confront the loss of many highly valued roles, the need to establish a new life structure for the remaining years, and the undeniable fact of life's termination. Widowhood and retirement are the central role transitions likely to occur at this time, but the death of friends and relatives also diminishes one's social network. Although people are aware of the inevitability of these role losses as they enter old age, their often abrupt reality may result in severe role discontinuity. (p. 185)

role discontinuity
Abrupt and disruptive change caused by conflicts among one's various roles in life.

crossover
Older men become more like women, and older women become more like men.

To sum up, the major concern for gender roles among the elderly is **role discontinuity.** See the accompanying box for several questions you should keep in mind as you read the theories and research summaries that follow.

A number of gerontologists have noted that people in late adulthood experience a **crossover** in gender roles. Older men become more like women, and older women become more like men. They do not actually cross over—they just become more like each other. For example, this is what Neugarten (1968) found in her groundbreaking studies of aging men and women. She stated that "women, as they age, seem to become more tolerant of their own aggressive, egocentric impulses; whereas men, as they age, [become more tolerant] of their own nurturative and affiliative impulses" (p. 71).

The differences between men and women, many of which seem to be based on sexuality, are no longer as important. With the barriers breaking down, older men and women seem to have more in common with each other and thus may be more of a solace to each other as they deal with the disruptive changes of growing

AN INFORMED VIEW | Is Role Discontinuity Inherent in Growing Old?

Role discontinuity occurs when people experience an abrupt change in their style of life and their role in it. Is this a natural part of growing old? Should we expect our world to shrink and our power to erode? Or is this just a stereotype of old age? Is role discontinuity a problem only for the poor, who have less control over their lives than the wealthy? Does high intelligence make a difference? How about gender? What's your view?

If you would like to have a more informed opinion on this issue, you might want to read one of the articles on the subject referenced in this chapter (for example, Haan, 1989; AARP, 2000).

old. This is not to say that men and women reverse gender roles. Rather, they move toward androgyny (see Chapter 14), accepting whatever role, male or female, is appropriate in the situation.

On the basis of data obtained by University of California at Berkeley, Norma Haan (1989) concluded that the gender-role changes that result from aging generally lead toward greater candor with others and comfort with oneself. For the most part, she said, "people change, but slowly, while maintaining some continuity" (p. 25). Gender differences were also evident in the work of Kulik (2001, 2002), who found that marital relations are affected by distribution and perception of power, as well as by tangible concepts such as retirement.

Friendships among the elderly also show gender-role differences (AARP, 1997). For example:

- Men tend to trust their best friends more.
- However, men have less personal conversations with their male friends than do women with their female friends.
- Women place relationships at the top of their list, whereas for men, topical subjects such as sports, politics, and career are most important.

Sexuality

Recent studies suggest that older adults might feel uncomfortable expressing their sexuality, for a number of reasons. However, older individuals often still feel that talking about sexual matters is taboo, and they hesitate to discuss their questions or concerns with someone (Blank, 2000). Another issue is that society sends men and women the message that they are less sexually attractive as they get older. Elderly adults who have a negative physical self-image might not be as likely to initiate sexual activity as when they were younger (Blank,

What would you say would be a reasonable resolution of the conflict concerning residents in nursing homes engaging in sex?

2000). Furthermore, the fears about sexual performance, such as impotence, that accompany old age create doubts about their sexual desirability.

According to one study of sexual behaviors, 75% of 65- to 75-year-old men and women reported that they were satisfied with their sex lives (Dunn et al., 2000). While men (30%) tended to report more dissatisfaction with the frequency of sex than women (20%), overall sexual satisfaction did not decline with age. In fact, people over age 65 were just as satisfied with their sexual activity as people under 65.

A study conducted by Hillman and Stricker (1996) revealed another factor that influences attitudes toward elderly sexuality. People with close contact to their grandparents tend to have a more permissive attitude toward elderly sexuality than those who are less involved with their grandparents. Close contact with elderly relatives and others may disprove commonly held assumptions about sex and aging.

Widowhood and Sexuality

A number of factors account for gender differences in attitudes and interest in sex. For example, women outlive men by approximately seven years. Most married women will become widows because they marry men nearly four years older than themselves. In contrast, most men in society will not become widowers unless they reach age 85. Because of this imbalance of elderly males and females, it is more difficult for women to find sexual partners in their aging years.

Social networking online creates new opportunities for women and men to communicate with people they might not meet otherwise, owing to geographic or physical limitations. Clearly, technology has had a major impact on relationships, and raises some interesting questions about friendship and intimacy, and related boundaries.

Impotency

impotency
Inability to engage in the sexual act.

One of the biggest fears in males of increasing age is **impotency.** Physical changes, nonsupportive partners and peers, and internal fears may be enough to inhibit or terminate sexual activity in males. It may become a self-fulfilling prophecy (if you think something is going to happen, there is a greater likelihood that it will).

Sleep laboratory experiments have shown that many men in their 60s to 80s who have labeled themselves as impotent regularly experience erections in their sleep. In many cases a man is capable of having intercourse, but a physical condition such as diabetes impedes it. New types of prosthetic devices can remedy a variety of psychological and physical problems, and drugs such as Viagra, have changed the perception of prosthetics as the only solution.

prostatectomy
Removal of all or part of the male prostate gland.

One pervading myth is that surgery of the prostate gland inevitably leads to impotency. Many elderly men experience pain and swelling of this small gland, and a **prostatectomy** (removal of all or a part of this gland) is sometimes necessary. Most impotency that results from the removal of this gland is psychological rather than physical.

Most sexual problems that women experience are due to hormonal changes. The vaginal walls begin to thin, and intercourse may become painful, with itching and burning sensations. Estrogen pills and hormone creams relieve many of these symptoms. Further, if women believe that sexual activity ceases with menopause and aging, it probably will. Although women have fewer concerns about sex, they are often worried about losing their attractiveness, which can also have a negative effect on their sex lives.

Two Kinds of Love

At any rate, it is quite likely that there is a real decline in sexual activity as people age. Men are often concerned about their ability to consummate intercourse. They also worry about their loss of masculinity, in terms of looks and strength. The literature on sex among the elderly, however, shows a new attitude emerging. Datan

A substantial number of older men find it difficult to achieve or maintain an erection, at least occasionally. This is known as erectile dysfunction, a medical condition with many possible causes. The first step in treatment is to look for an underlying problem that can be corrected. That means a medical checkup, paying particular attention to medications that may be hampering sexual function.

Because the oral PDE-5 inhibitors are convenient, effective, and generally safe, many doctors start with a prescription for sildenafil (Viagra) or one of its two new rivals (Levitra and Cialis). But about a third of men don't respond well, others develop side effects, and some can't even try these medications because they take nitroglycerin or other nitrates. Fortunately there are alternatives.

Alprostadil is a potent vasodilator that increases penile blood flow. But it must be administered directly into the obstinate organ. Men can learn to do this themselves using injections (Caverject, Edex) or soft urethral pellets (MUSE). Many men find the idea unpleasant, but most who learn the technique find it acceptable. About 80% respond to injections, and about 50% get erections from the pellets.

Vacuum pumps are available without a prescription. When the time is right, the penis is placed in an airtight plastic cylinder. As a hand pump removes the air, blood is pulled into the blood vessels of the penis. A special band is then applied to the base of the penis to keep it erect after the pump is removed. It's a bit cumbersome, but no treatment is more effective or safer.

Penile implants have declined in popularity in the Viagra era. Still, some men prefer surgical treatment with silicone rods, which produce permanent erections, or inflatable devices, which can be pumped up with fluid on demand.

Counseling and sex therapy may be the best choices for the 15% of men whose erectile dysfunction stems from psychological issues.

Despite the availability of all these good treatments, many men still succumb to temptation and attempt to treat themselves with "dietary supplements" that promise miraculous results. The ineffective remedies include yohimbine, ginseng, DHEA, Andro, and a bewildering array of vitamins and herbs. Save your money.

Source: From Datan, N., Rodeheaver, D. and Hughes, F., "Adult Development and Aging." *Annual Review of Psychology,* 38, 1987, 153-180. © Annual Reviews. Reprinted with permission.

generative love
Most characteristic of parenthood, a time during which sacrifices are gladly made for the sake of the children.

existential love
The capacity to cherish the present moment, perhaps first learned when we confront the certainty of our own personal death.

and colleagues (1987) described well the difference between **generative love** and **existential love***:*

> *We believe that existential love, the capacity to cherish the present moment, is one of the greatest gifts of maturity. Perhaps we first learn this love when we first confront the certainty of our own personal death, most often in middle adulthood. Generative love is most characteristic of parenthood, a time during which sacrifices are gladly made for the sake of the children. However, it is existential love, we feel, that creates the unique patience and tenderness so often seen in grandparents, who know how brief the period of childhood is, since they have seen their own children leave childhood behind them.*
>
> *We have not yet awakened to the potential for existential love between old women and old men, just as we are not yet prepared to recognize the pleasures of sexuality as natural to the life span, particularly to the post-parental period.*
>
> *Those old people who have had the misfortune of spending their last days in nursing homes may learn that love can be lethal. We have been told of an old woman and an old man who fell in love. The old man's children thought this late flowering was "cute"; however, the old woman's children thought it was disgraceful, and over her protests, they removed her from the nursing home. One month later she registered her final protest: she died. (p. 287)*

It is worth considering a new definition of "touch"—one that extends beyond the physical to the social and emotional contact elderly people have with others. ALL people desire to be touched, but the elderly population may need it for very distinct, human reasons.

The Elderly and Their Families

The familial relationship undergoes changes in membership, organization, and role during the aging process. With the elderly living longer, married couples are finding that they have more years together after their children leave home, and they are having longer relationships with generations of their kin (Bengtson, 2001). Bengtson also finds that these relationships remain strong, despite the tremendous diversity of the makeup of families. Most couples go through similar stages in the life cycle. Following are the four basic phases:

1. The child-rearing stage.
2. The stage of childlessness before retirement.
3. The retirement stage.
4. Widowhood and widowerhood.

The duration of each stage in the life cycle and the ages of the family members for each stage vary from family to family. Childbearing patterns have a lot to do with life in the late stages of life. Couples who raise children early in their marriage will have a different lifestyle when their last child leaves home than couples with "change of life" babies, who may have a dependent child at home when they are ready to retire. This can pose serious economic problems for retirees on fixed incomes, trying to meet the staggering costs of education. In addition, with children in the home, saving for retirement is difficult.

In one study, partners in long-standing marriages (between 20 and 29 years) showed lower levels of disease and disability, such as hypertension, arthritis, and functional limitations, than did their counterparts in marriages of shorter length (Pienta, Hayward, & Jenkins, 2000). However, widows and divorcees tended to report higher levels of these types of health problems than people of any other marital status.

It has been found, however, that those situations in which one spouse suffers a long-term illness do tend to have more problems (Leinonen & others, 2001). As couples change over time, it will be interesting to see whether interactions in a long-term marriage also change, or if they remain stable despite individual development.

Conflict is an inevitable part of any relationship that lasts over time. The relationship between elderly parents and their adult children is no exception. Clarke and associates (1999) conducted a study of aging parents and their middle-aged children. They were specifically interested in the emergence of common conflict themes. They found six types of conflict:

1. Communication and style of interaction.
2. Lifestyle choices and habits.
3. Parenting practices and values.
4. Religion, ideology, and politics.
5. Work habits.
6. Standards of household maintenance.

Interesting generational differences were found. For example, older parents more often reported conflicts over habits and lifestyle choices than their adult children did. The children more often reported communication conflicts and interaction style conflicts. Regardless of the source of conflict, relationships also provide a tremendous source of strength, which is greatly needed in times of loss.

Widowhood

In the lives of older adults, widowhood is a tremendously stressful and life-altering event. Carr and associates (2001) report that people who experience the sudden death of a spouse have a more difficult time coping than those who anticipate the death of their spouse. However, these researchers found that there is no significant difference between spouses' experiencing sudden death or who anticipated it in terms of their feelings of depression, anger, shock, and grief.

The surviving spouse, male or female, faces a number of life changes, from shifting social relationships with family and friends to the demands of new responsibilities, such as cleaning, cooking, managing household finances, and even needing to find work. Lee and associates (2001) have found that men and women experience similar levels of depression at the loss of a spouse. However, these researchers also report that men have a harder time than women in coping with widowhood. Because married men are typically less depressed than married women, the men's expression of the loss of a spouse is seen as being a greater change for men than for women. Additional factors that make the death of a spouse harder for men are less involvement in church and children and dislike of household tasks. However, women are more likely to be the surviving spouse because they outlive men by large margins. Only half of women over 65 are living with a partner. Lee and associates (2001) report that women tend to adapt relatively well in the long run. Perhaps, as society's attitude toward death has changed over time, our attitudes about death, sex, and relationships have been influenced in kind (Lovibond, 2004).

Seniors who choose to remarry enjoy much success if the ingredients of love, companionship, financial security, and offspring consent are present. Accepting the remarriage of a parent can be difficult, even for adult children of older parents. Ganong and associates (1998) studied the responses of adult children to vignettes portraying the later life remarriage of an older parent. The vignettes described situations in which either the parent or the stepparent needed help. Overall, Ganong and associates found that the adult children felt an obligation to help either their parent or their stepparent, but the obligation felt toward stepparents was not as great.

Care of Elderly Parents

Developmental psychologists have become much more interested in caregiving to elders in recent years. Variables studied have included stress caused by living alone or in nursing homes (Gordon & Brill, 2001; Liu & Gong, 2001; McAuley & Travis, 2000), abuse (Jogerst et al., 2000; Wilbur & McNeilly, 2001; Wolf & Pillemeer, 2000), and coping strategies (Kramer & Lambert, 1999; Mui, 2001; Perodeau et al., 2001).

Elderly people identify their adult children, when they have them, as the primary helpers in their lives. When these people have both an adult son and an adult daughter, tasks often fall into gender-stereotyped categories, with women attending to housework and personal needs and men handling yardwork, general home repair, and finances (Mosher & Danoff-Burg, 2004).

In the past, elder care was most often done by unmarried daughters, if there were any. They were expected to do this because it was assumed that the work would be easier for them, as they had no responsibilities for husbands or children. Research by Mosher and Danoff-Burg (2004) revealed that whether or not the elderly person was employed or retired affected the levels of support that male and female caregivers would offer, regardless of their own employment status. Women also reported more emphasis on emotional support.

Support for the caregivers involved in caring for the elderly is critical. Depression and stress are two of the most common risk factors cited in the literature. The degree of stress and depression experienced has been associated with specific caregiver characteristics. For example, Meshefedjian and associates (1998) found that, the closer the relationship of the caregiver to the elderly person, the higher the caregiver scored on a test of depression. In addition, the less education caregivers have, the more likely they are to be depressed. Lawrence and associates (1998) also found that having a close relationship with the elderly person resulted in increased perceptions of overload by the caregiver. Not only is the closeness of the relationship

For those who want to work with older adults, put *Promoting Successful Aging* (1989). New York: Burnham at the top of your reading list. Roff and Atherton have written a readable book that is half about theory and research and half about the specific strategies for dealing with the needs of the elderly.

A SOCIOCULTURAL VIEW | *Caregiving for the Elderly in Two Cultures*

Draper and Keith (1992) were perplexed by the question "Why is care for the elderly such a problem for Americans?" Draper had recently returned from studying the lifestyle of the !Kung people of Botswana and decided to do a comparison study with Keith of elder care in Swarthmore, a Philadelphia suburb.

Older residents of Swarthmore are extremely worried about their care, especially with regard to loss of health, which generates feelings of fear. The researchers learned that, for many of the elders, need for care is a primary reason for moving into Swarthmore. They do so to be near a child or relative who could supervise their eventual move into a retirement home should professional care prove necessary. The problem is that, whether they moved into Swarthmore (to be near relatives) or moved out of Swarthmore (to enter a retirement community),

the costs to the older person usually involve loss of ties to their communities.

In contrast, elders of the !Kung villages "age in place." They do not retire, relocate, or enter age-graded elder care institutions. Indeed, they have no other place to go. The !Kung were asked, "For an old person, what makes a good life?" One-third responded, "If you have a child to take care of you, you have a good life." Care is almost always provided by one's children and community.

For the people of Swarthmore, technologically superb care is available, but its benefits must be weighed against the loss of community ties and personal autonomy. For the !Kung, social needs and physical care are compatible.

(that is, parent/child) a factor in caregiver mental health, but the quality of these associations between them is also important. Poor interactions between caregivers and those in their care even result in verbally and physically aggressive behaviors in adults (Cohen-Mansfield & Werner, 1998). Researchers have also found that the number of difficulties encountered in one's role as a caregiver is related to stress and burden. For example, Riedel and associates (1998) found that caregivers who reported many types of difficulty in their role experienced higher levels of burden than caregivers who reported only one type of difficulty.

As indicated, there are clear risks of stress and depression for the caregiver when placed in this role. David Guia (2003) has defined Caregiver Stress Syndrome as including "pathological, morbid changes in physiological and psychological function. This syndrome can be the result of acute or chronic stress, directly as a result of caregiving activities" (p. 144). Many researchers have studied the caregiver role to find ways in which to ease the burden of caregiving responsibilities. Religious and spiritual beliefs, shared caregiving responsibility, and adult day care facilities have been useful in reducing caregiver stress levels.

What about the situation in which the elders have no children, or at least none who are willing or able to care for them? Research indicates that elderly individuals who have no kin tend to substitute a close friend whom they persuade to take the place of the absent relative. Most family and close friends still feel that they ought to take care of the elderly in their own homes if possible. Racial and ethnic variations play a role in who should be responsible for caring for the older generation; however, Lee and associates (1998) found that African-American elderly were more likely to expect to be cared for by their children than were elderly white parents. Burr and Mutchler (1999) found that elderly Latinos were also more likely to agree that the younger generation should care for them.

It is not always the younger generation that provides caretaking for elderly persons. Often this role is taken by the spouse of the elderly person. Kramer and Lambert (1999) studied older husbands who cared for their ailing wives. They found that these men did less well than men married to healthy wives in the following areas: marital interactions, social integration, household responsibilities, and well-being. These findings confirm that it is more stressful to be in a relationship with an ailing person than with a healthy person. Caring for an elderly person with dementia has been found to be the most stressful situation of all. Ory and associates

AN APPLIED VIEW

Abuse and Older Adults

On June 15, 2006, events around the United States were held in honor of World Elder Abuse Awareness Day. Health professionals, lawyers, social workers, members of the media, and community members participated in various programs with the goal of raising both awareness and prevention efforts. What exactly is elder abuse? The National Center on Elder Abuse defines it as: "Any knowing, intentional, or negligent act by a caregiver or any other person that causes harm or a serious risk of harm to a vulnerable adult." Such abuse may be physical, emotional, or sexual, and can include exploitation, neglect, or abandonment. Strangers or hired caregivers can commit elder abuse, but more often it is committed by family members of the elderly victim.

How can you help? The good news is that reports of elder abuse have increased steadily in recent years. If you suspect someone is being abused, you can contact Eldercare Locator services at (800) 677-1116. Trained professionals are able to direct callers to local agencies in an effort to help elderly citizens, and callers may remain anonymous. One of the most important steps in prevention is speaking up. You might investigate volunteer opportunities in your area so you can join the effort to support elders.

(1999) found that caregivers of dementia patients spend significantly more time each week in their role than other types of caregivers. Dementia caregivers experience more caregiver strain and report higher levels of physical and mental health problems.

Another option for elderly care is a nursing home facility. If a family does choose long-term care for an elderly parent, how do they choose the right nursing home for that parent? The US department of Health and Human services has a listing available at www.medicare.gov that provides information on over 17,000 nursing homes nationwide. This information, while useful, does not change the fact that funding for such facilities is the best way to maintain or improve quality (McCarthy, 2002).

The Changing Role of the Grandparent

In today's world, with increased life expectancy, grandparenthood has become a unique, often rewarding, experience within the family system (Drew & Smith, 1999; King & Elder, 1998; Giarrusso, Silverstein, & Feng, 2000). Grandparenthood is positively linked to the mental health and morale of elderly persons. For example, in a classic study, Neugarten and Weinstein (1964) examined styles of grandparenting and created categories for five general styles: "formal," "the fun seeker," "the surrogate parent," "the reservoir of family wisdom," and "the distant figure." An interesting finding was that the fun seeker and the distant figure emerged as the most popular styles of grandparenting. Both exclude an emphasis on authority. Many grandparents preferred a grandparent–grandchild relationship in which their role was simply to enjoy being with their grandchildren rather than feeling responsible as coparents with their adult children.

Today, however, many grandparents play a more integral part in the lives of their grandchildren. A survey completed by the American Association of Retired Persons (A.A.R.P., 2000) concluded that the state of American grandparenting is strong. A 2002 report of the US Census Bureau stated that over 2,400,000 grandparents were raising their grandchildren in the United States, and the numbers today are likely higher.

Research by Pruchno (1999) revealed that many grandparents are raising their grandchildren alone. The parents of these children, the middle generation, are usually absent. This absence is due to many reasons such as parental death, substance abuse, or incarceration. Pruchno found that African-American and white grandmothers differed in two important ways. First, it is more common

AN APPLIED VIEW

Do You Know Your Grandparents?

Are your grandparents still alive? Even though you have probably known them for many years, you may not know them very well. Try answering the following questions for one set of your grandparents, and if possible, check your answers with them to get your GKQ (Grandparent Knowledge Quotient).

1. What's your grandmother's favorite activity?
2. In total, how many rings do your grandparents wear?
3. What color are your grandfather's eyes?
4. Where does your grandfather eat lunch?
5. What is your grandmother's favorite TV show?

6. In what year did your grandparents meet?
7. For whom did your grandmother vote for president in 2000?
8. Does your grandfather know how to prepare asparagus?
9. Who is your grandfather's favorite relative?
10. Name some of either of your grandparents' favorite movie stars.

You might try making up a test like this about yourself and asking your grandparents, parents, siblings, and friends to respond to it. It should be interesting to see which of them knows you best.

---

for African-American grandmothers to have peers who are also raising grandchildren alone. Second, a household containing multiple generations living together is not an uncommon condition for black grandmothers. These two findings may explain why black grandmothers experienced fewer emotional burdens from their caregiving role than did white grandparents.

Grandparents are also playing a bigger role as day-care providers for their grandchildren. While most grandparents hope to have a positive effect on their grandchildren, it is critical that social and financial supports are available to ease the challenges associated with such care arrangements and contribute to grandparents' well-being (Gerard, Landry-Meyer, & Roe, 2006).

Erikson (1963) explained, in his stage of generativity, the significance of grandchildren to grandparents. Erikson believed that generativity referred to providing a better life for future generations and that not having reached the stage of generativity would cause stagnation and self-absorption in the individual (see Chapter 16). The personal development of grandparents is furthered by their close rapport with younger generations and vice versa, and deserves further investigation (Thiele & Whelan, 2006). The term "generative" refers to producing and contributing to family and society, but to the work force as well.

THE OLDER WORKER

Only a small percentage of all older adults are in the labor force—about 11%. Many retirements were due to forced retirement. Today, only airline pilots and public safety workers such as firefighters and police can be forced to retire because of their age. However, there is a growing trend toward staying in the workforce that has been the focus of recent research (Finch & Robinson, 2003). Economists' theories on why people choose to remain in the work force include: Social Security reforms, increased opportunities in the workplace, and freedom from pension constraints (Johnson, 2002). Individuals have their own reasons for seeking personal and professional rewards.

Performance

As this society ages through greater longevity, the aging of the baby-boom generation, and decreased birthrates, some of the stereotypes about aging are coming under closer scrutiny. An excellent series of longitudinal studies performed by Palmore and associates (1985), which yielded a sample of more than 7,000 subjects, has provided an in-depth look at this and other aspects of the relationships between old age and work. The stereotype that age equals declining performance is getting more research attention because by 2012 over 29% of men and 20% of women ages 65–74 will be in the workforce, and over 8% of men over age 75 as well (Phillips, 2004).

The stereotype is bolstered by research on aging that demonstrates a decline in abilities such as dexterity, speed of response, agility, hearing, and vision. If all these abilities decline, then one may conclude that job performance must decline with age. McEvoy and Cascio (1989) conducted an extensive meta-analysis (a study that compiles the results of many other studies) of 96 studies and found no relationship between age and job performance. It made no difference whether the performance measure was ratings or productivity measures, or whether the type of job was professional or nonprofessional.

What explanation is there for these results? How does the older worker deal with the mild decline of physical abilities that affects most elderly persons? Experience is one answer. There is said to be no substitute for it, and it is certainly valued by employers. Other reasons cited are that older workers have lower absenteeism, turnover, illness, and accident rates (Kacmar & Ferris, 1989; Martocchio, 1989). They also tend to have higher job satisfaction and more positive work values than younger workers. These qualifications seem to offset any decreases in physical ability that increasing age causes.

Retirement

The path to retirement for older adults and the decision can take many different forms. Flippen and Tienda (2000) found that Black, Latino, and white female older workers had the highest rates of job loss before they decided to retire. "Minority disadvantages in human capital, health, and employment characteristics accounts for a large part of racial and ethnic differences in labor force withdrawal" (Flippen & Tienda, 2000, p. 514).

For many people, retirement is a welcome relief from a frustrating and boring job. For others, it is just as difficult as being unemployed. Retirement requires changing the habits of an adult lifetime. This probably explains why more than 11% of those 65 and over are employed. Nearly 80% of baby-boomers say they plan to work after 65 (www.boston.com, June 5, 2002).

Nevertheless, the great majority of the elderly choose not to work. The decision is a complicated one, but many people feel they have enough financial security so that they need not work. Health may be the biggest factor. Morris (2006) sums up retirement, stating:

The best is yet to come? That's a falsehood of governmental proportions, absurd on its smiling face and no more plausible after the smile contracts. But it has become one of the lies we live by . . . The "senior citizens" who have replaced the former "old" in a powerful national myth are curious and adventurous, well-heeled and free—but for the doctors' appointments and hospital stays around which they have to schedule their adventures . . . They've no strings attached, though they may sport an array of other medically mandated paper, plastic, or metal products. (p. 72)

Retirement and Leisure

How you view retirement depends on the work and leisure experiences you have had up to the point of retirement. The leisure activities pursued throughout life play a crucial role in your social adjustment later on.

The type of work you do directly affects how you spend leisure time, in two ways. The scheduling of work affects when leisure time is available. A person who works second or third shift might be unable to take part in activities that are often thought of as evening activities, such as dining and dancing. Second, the content of work may influence how much time will be left over for leisure activities. Persons with physically draining positions may be too tired to do anything but nap after work. On the other hand, a person with a desk job may choose physically challenging activities during leisure hours.

When leisure is no more than an extension of work experiences and attitudes, it performs what leisure theorists call a spillover function. For example, some people try to relax by performing some of their easier tasks at home. Conversely, when leisure time is engaged in to make up for disappointment and stress at work, it is viewed as a compensatory function. An example is excessive partying at the end of the week in an attempt to achieve happiness, however fleeting.

Making Retirement More Enjoyable

The belief is growing that retired persons are an important resource to the community. Numerous efforts have been made in recent years to tap this powerful resource. A number of national programs now make an effort to involve retired persons in volunteer and paid work as service to society.

Recent surveys seem to indicate that the "golden years" are not so golden for many retired persons. But with improving health conditions (see Chapter 17), improved understanding of the nature of life after 65, and a considerable increase in government involvement, the lives of retirees have a far better chance of being fruitful.

Contrary to the stereotype, getting old need not, and usually does not, mean being lonely. In fact, the elderly, most of whom have a good deal of free time, often use it to develop their social lives. For example, older adults are the fastest-growing group of Internet users, and are accessing technology through various venues (Czaja et al., 2006). We now move to a discussion about their personal development.

An excellent source of information on the elderly is the American Association of Retired Persons (AARP). With about 30 million members, this powerful group publishes materials that may interest you. Write to National Headquarters, 601 E Street NW, Washington, D.C. 20049.

Guided Review

1. Many changes occur in late adulthood, including role _____ (an abrupt and disruptive change in role) and "crossover" of sex roles.

2. In late adulthood, the gender role of older men becomes (more, less) like that of women, and women's role becomes (more, less) like that of men.

3. The child-rearing phase, the childless preretirement period, the retirement phase, and _____ are stages most middle-aged and aged couples can anticipate.

4. Most family and close friends feel that the best place to take care of the elderly is (in a hospital, in a nursing home, in their own homes).

5. Five general styles of grandparenting have been identified by Neugarten and Weinstein (1964): formal, fun seeker, _____ _____, reservoir of family wisdom, and distant figure.

6. Although some decline in dexterity, speed, and agility occurs in older workers, _____ may be one of the reasons that job performance does not generally decline among these workers.

7. Leisure theorists write about two functions for leisure: a spillover function and a _____ function.

8. Retirement is generally (more, less) difficult for females than for males.

Answers

1. discontinuity 2. more, more 3. widowhood/widowerhood 4. in their own homes 5. surrogate parent 6. experience 7. compensatory 8. less

PERSONAL DEVELOPMENT

Two points of view have received most interest in the field of personality development in the elderly: those of the Committee on Human Development and those of Erik Erikson. Although dated, these two bodies of research are still respected by personality experts.

The Committee on Human Development

What are the effects of aging on personal development? The Committee on Human Development, consisting of gerontologist Bernice Neugarten and her associates at the University of Chicago, has been responsible for some of the most highly respected research on this topic (for example, Havighurst, Neugarten, & Tobin, 1968; Neugarten, 1968).

Adults between the ages of 54 and 94 who were residents of Kansas City were asked to participate in a study of change across the adult lifespan. The sample was somewhat biased in that it represented only white persons who were living on their own (that is, not institutionalized) at the time of the study. They were somewhat better educated and of a higher socioeconomic group than is typical for this age group. Nevertheless, the sample was reasonably well balanced, and because of the thoroughness with which these persons were studied, this research has become a classic in the field of adult psychology. Neugarten summarized the findings:

- In the middle years (especially the 50s), a change occurs in the perception of time and death and the relationship of the self to them. Introspection, contemplation, reflection, and self-evaluation become important aspects of life. People at this age become more interested in their "inner selves."

- Perception of how well one can control the environment undergoes a marked change: Forty-year-olds, for example, seem to see the environment as one that rewards boldness and risk-taking, and to see themselves as possessing energy congruent with the opportunities perceived in the outer world. Sixty-year-olds, however, perceive the world as complex and dangerous, no longer to be reformed in line with one's wishes, and the individual as conforming and accommodating to outer-world demands. (1968, p. 140)

- *Emotional energy* declines with age. Tests showed that intensity of emotion invested in tasks undergoes a definite decline in the later years.

- *Gender-role reversals* also occur with age (discussed earlier in this chapter).

- *Age-status* becomes more rigid with development. *Age-status* refers to society's expectations about what is normal at various ages. These expectations change not only with advancing years but also according to the particular society and to the historical context. For example, in 1940 a woman who was not married by age 22 was not considered unusual, but if she had not married by the time she was 27, people began to worry. Fifty years later, the expected age of marriage was much less rigid. This holds only for the United States; in Samoa, for example, concern arises if a person is not married by age 15.

What is the optimum pattern of aging in terms of our relationships with other people? The Committee on Human Development has also investigated this question. For many years, there have been two different positions on this question, known as the activity theory and the disengagement theory.

According to the **activity theory,** human beings flourish through interaction with other people and physical activity. They are unhappy when, as they reach the older years, their contacts with others shrink as a result of death, illness, and societal

activity theory
Human beings who are able to keep up the social activity of their middle years are considered the most successful.

disengagement theory
The most mature adults are likely to gradually disengage themselves from their fellow human beings in preparation for death.

limitations. Those who are able to keep up the social activity of their middle years are considered the most successful.

Disengagement theory contradicts this idea. According to this position, the belief that activity is better than passivity is a bias of the Western world. This was not always so; the Greeks, for example, valued their warriors and athletes but reserved the highest distinction for such contemplative philosophers as Sophocles, Plato, and Aristotle. Many people in the countries of the Eastern Hemisphere also hold this view. According to disengagement theory, the most mature adults are likely to gradually disengage themselves from their fellow human beings in preparation for death. They become less interested in their interactions with others and more absorbed in internal concerns. They accept the decreasing attention of a society that views them as losing power.

Does this mean that the tendency toward disengagement is more normal than the tendency toward activity? It is now believed that what has appeared to be disengagement is instead a temporary transition from the highly active role of the middle-aged adult to the more sedate, spiritually oriented role of the elderly person. Most humans truly enjoy social contact, so disengagement from one's fellows may be the result of traumatic experience or a physiologically caused mental disturbance such as clinical depression. However, activity theory, with its emphasis on social involvement, is now considered too general (Marshall, 1994). For example, many people may reduce social contacts but keep active with solitary hobbies. Activity per se has not been found to correlate with a personal sense of satisfaction with life. Carstensen (1995, 1996) offered a resolution of the debate with her **socioemotional selectivity theory.** She suggested that humans use social contact to obtain physical survival, to get information they need, to maintain a sense of self, and to acquire pleasure and comfort. These goals exist throughout life, but the importance of each shifts with age. For the elderly, the need for physical survival so important in infancy and the need for information from others in younger adulthood become less important. The need for emotional support grows. They tend to get this support from relatives and close friends (their "social convoys," as they have been called) more and more, and less and less from casual acquaintances such as coworkers. In fact, this is true of anyone who is threatened, such as terminally ill young people. Joseph Cardinal Bernardin, when dying of cancer, expressed it this way (Time, 1996):

socioemotional selectivity theory
According to this theory, humans use social contact for four reasons: to obtain physical survival, to get information they need, to maintain a sense of self, and to acquire pleasure and comfort.

One of the things I have noticed about illness is that it draws you inside yourself. When we are ill, we tend to focus on our own pain and suffering. We may feel sorry for ourselves or become depressed. (p. 21)

In three words I can sum up everything I've learned about life. It goes on.

—Anonymous

Further, the challenges faced in later life can be quite different. For example, Lang (2001) found that older adults who are able to maintain their close emotional relationships and let other, less important relationships go have a greater sense of well-being. In addition, older African-Americans and whites are more likely to have similar small, close social networks made up mainly of kin (Ajrouch, Antonucci, & Janevic, 2001). Thus, the elderly appear to be disengaging, but, in fact, perhaps they are simply becoming more selective about with whom they wish to spend their social time. Carstensen's socioemotional selectivity theory appears to explain the changes that occur better than either disengagement or activity theory.

Erikson

integrity
The resolution of each of the first seven crises in Erikson's theory should lead us to achieve a sense of personal integrity. Older adults who have a sense of integrity feel their lives have been well spent.

Erikson believed that the resolution of each of the first seven crises in his theory should lead us to achieve a sense of personal **integrity.** Older adults who have a

Clearly the group on the left is enjoying itself more than the woman on the right, but does that mean that the disengagement theory is wrong?

sense of integrity feel their lives have been well spent. The decisions and actions they have taken seem to them to fit together—their lives are integrated. They are saddened by the sense that time is running out and that they will not get many more chances to make an impact, but they feel reasonably well satisfied with their achievements. They usually have a sense of having helped to achieve a more dignified life for humankind.

Sheldon and Kasser (2001) found that older adults develop a sense of responsibility for their behavior, and they are increasingly motivated by personal values of self-acceptance, emotional intimacy, and common contribution. In addition, the authors found that growing older is associated with a greater sense of well-being.

When people look back over their lives and feel that they have made many wrong decisions or, more commonly, that they have frequently not made any decisions at all, they tend to see life as lacking integrity. They feel **despair,** which is the second half of this last stage of crisis. They are angry that there can never be another chance to make their lives make sense. They often hide their fear of death by appearing contemptuous of humanity in general and those of other religions and races in particular. As Erikson put it: "Such despair is often hidden behind a show of disgust" (1968, p. 140).

despair
When people look back over their lives and feel that they have made many wrong decisions or, more commonly, that they have not made any decisions at all.

AN APPLIED VIEW

Getting Perspective on Your Thinking

If you hope to be the kind of person who ends his or her life with a sense of integrity, the time to begin is right now. You don't get to be a happy elderly person unless you plan and work for it. You can do this in many ways, but we have some suggestions to pass along to you.

Whenever you are about to make an important decision, follow these four steps:

1. Come to some tentative conclusion about what you should do.
2. Close your eyes and picture yourself as a 75-year-old woman or man.

3. Imagine yourself explaining your decision to that old person, and try to picture her or him telling you what she or he thinks about what you have decided.
4. If you don't like what you hear, rethink the decision and go through this process again.

Use this technique to get a better perspective on your thinking; you will be surprised by how much wisdom you already have.

Would you agree that the old Swedish doctor in Bergman's famous film, *Wild Strawberries*, represents a good portrayal of the concept of integrity?

To better understand what it feels like for an individual to reach late adulthood, you may want to read the following books: (1) Malcolm Cowley's *The View from 80* (1980). New York: Viking Press, a personal account the author wrote when he was 82 years old. Critic Donald Hall describes this book as "eloquent on the felt disparity between an unchanged self and the costume of altered flesh"; (2) *The Coming of Age* (1972). New York: Putnam, written by Simone de Beauvoir, is a magnificent psychological study that provides an intense look at what it means, rather than how it feels, to become old.

Erikson (1978) provided a panoramic view of his life-cycle theory in an analysis of Swedish film director Ingmar Bergman's famous film *Wild Strawberries*. In this picture, an elderly Swedish doctor goes from his hometown to a large city, where he is to be honored for 50 years of service to the medical profession. On the way, he stops by his childhood home and, resting in an old strawberry patch, begins an imaginary journey through his entire life, starting with his earliest memories. In the ruminations of this old man, Erikson saw clear and specific reflections of the eight stages he proposed. Erikson demonstrated through Bergman's words that, like his other seven stages, this last stage involves a life crisis. Poignantly, the old doctor struggles to make sense out of the events of his life. He is ultimately successful in achieving a sense of integrity. The film is well worth seeing, and Erikson's analysis makes it an even more meaningful experience.

Guided Review

9. Researchers with the Committee on Human Development found that adults between the ages of 54 and 94 changed their perception of how well they could control the environment and that there was a marked decline in the _____ _____ they invested in tasks as they aged.

10. _____ theory and _____ theory offer explanations of ways in which people cope with aging.

11. According to the disengagement theory, most adults will disengage themselves from their fellow human beings in preparation for _____.

12. According to Carstensen's socioemotional selectivity theory, humans use social contact for four reasons: to obtain physical survival, to get information they need, to maintain a ____ ____ ____, and to acquire pleasure and comfort.

13. Erikson suggested that, as we look back over our lives, if we see our lives as having been _____, we have achieved the goal of the final stage of life.

Answers

CONCLUSION & SUMMARY

Many changes happen during later adulthood. A crossover effect in gender roles occurs, sexual activity changes, and the nature of family relationships undergoes several alterations.

As we leave the industrial age and enter the age of information processing, the nation's older workers experience an incredibly different environment from that of their predecessors of 50 years ago. Even retirement is a much-changed adventure. As in each of the preceding chapters, life appears as never-ending change, but change with discernible patterns. Perhaps more stress takes place in old age than before, but more effective techniques are also available for dealing with it.

How do social relationships develop during late adulthood?

- A number of gerontologists have noted that people in late adulthood experience a crossover in gender roles: Older men become more like women, and older women become more like men.

- White summarizes that in late adulthood males are generally more sexually active than females but that declining activity in the female is usually attributable to declining interest or illness in the male partner.
- Elderly people identify their adult children, when they have them, as the primary helpers in their lives. When these people have both an adult son and an adult daughter, elderly people most often name the son as the primary helper, although the daughter usually does most of the caregiving.

What are major factors affecting the older worker?

- Research suggests four basic phases through which most middle-aged and aged couples pass: child rearing, childless preretirement, retirement, and widowhood/widowerhood.
- Although older people show less interest in working than younger people, discrimination and stereotypes about older workers underestimate their desire to help.

- Men usually find retirement more difficult than do women.

Is personality development any different among older adults?

- Neugarten's work on the effects of aging on personal development reveals that elderly people become more interested in their "inner selves," perceptions of the environment change, psychic energy declines, gender-role reversals occur, and age-status becomes more rigid.
- The Committee on Human Development investigated patterns of aging, including activity theory and disengagement theory. Today, the more accepted explanation of elderly social behavior is Carstensen's socioemotional selectivity theory.
- For Erikson, the resolution of each of the first seven stages in his eight-stage theory should lead people to achieve a sense of integrity in the last stage. If not, they experience despair.

KEY TERMS

activity theory
crossover
despair
disengagement theory

existential love
generative love
impotency
integrity

prostatectomy
role discontinuity
socioemotional selectivity theory

WHAT DO YOU THINK?

1. Traditionally in Western society, elderly men marrying young women has been more accepted than elderly women marrying young men. Why do you believe these attitudinal differences arose?

2. What is your position on sex in old-age institutions? Should there be any restrictions at all?

3. Which aspect of your family life do you most fear facing a change with as you get old?

4. What are some ways that the experience of older workers facing mandatory retirement could best be used in our society?

5. Some have said that, whereas Erikson's first seven stages describe

crises in which action should be taken, the last stage, integrity versus despair, is merely reactive. All he has the elderly doing is sitting in a rocking chair and looking back over their lives. Do you believe that this criticism is valid?

CHAPTER REVIEW TEST

1. **In late adulthood, crossover in sex roles means that**
   a. older men and women identify with each other more.
   b. older men become more like women and older women become more like men.
   c. older men take on roles most often associated with women.
   d. older women take on roles most often associated with men.

2. **Whether or not an older woman is sexually active depends mainly on her**
   a. level of interest.
   b. marital status.
   c. perception of her children's attitudes.
   d. number of interpersonal relationships.

3. **Examples of experiences that may inhibit or terminate sexual activity in adult men include**
   a. physical changes.
   b. nonsupportive partners and peers.
   c. internal fears.
   d. all of these.

4. **What is the first phase of the life cycle most middle-aged couples go through?**
   a. widowhood/widowerhood
   b. the retirement phase
   c. the child-rearing phase
   d. the childless preretirement period

5. **John and Sarah are the parents of three children and provide an example of generative love. They**
   a. gladly make many sacrifices for the sake of the children.
   b. cherish the time they have with their children at present.
   c. expose their children to the culture and traditions of their ancestry.
   d. are committed to spending all their time with the children.

6. **The reason most widowers do not remarry is that**
   a. many widows view remarriage as improper.
   b. children may oppose remarriage.
   c. there are three single women for every single man over age 65.
   d. all of these.

7. **Ganong and associates found that the obligation adult children feel toward helping either their parent or their stepparent**
   a. is much greater toward the parent.
   b. is about equal.
   c. is somewhat greater toward the parent.
   d. is usually greater toward the stepparent.

8. **Older workers make valued employees for all of the following reasons, except lower**
   a. absenteeism.
   b. turnover.
   c. accident rates.
   d. job skills.

9. **Research conducted by Smith and Moen (1998) indicates that the decision to retire is primarily influenced by the retiree's**
   a. spouse.
   b. job expectancies.
   c. sense of well-being.
   d. level of education.

10. **Retirement may be most stressful for men because**
    a. they wish they could stay working.
    b. they feel they now have nothing to do.
    c. they worry over Social Security benefits.
    d. none of the above.

11. **According to leisure theorists, a spillover function is**
    a. when leisure is no more than an extension of work experiences and attitudes.

    b. when leisure time is engaged in to make up for disappointment and stress at work.
    c. when leisure time is spent worrying about stressful events at work.
    d. when leisure time takes away from time to be spent at work.

12. **The idea that there are societal expectations about what is normal at various stages refers to**
    a. gender roles.
    b. socialization.
    c. age status.
    d. role continuity.

13. **According to Carstensen's socio-emotional selectivity theory, humans use _____ to obtain physical survival, information they need, the maintenance of a sense of self, and pleasure and comfort.**
    a. psychological engagement
    b. social contact
    c. emotional reflection
    d. social love

14. **When adults distance themselves from other human beings in preparation for death and become less interested in their interactions with others, it is referred to as**
    a. disengagement theory.
    b. separation theory.
    c. distantiation.
    d. personal engagement theory.

15. **For Erik Erikson, we are led to a sense of personal integrity by**
    a. personal well-being.
    b. a sense of self-control.
    c. achievement.
    d. a sense that life has been well spent.

16. **According to Erikson, people who are contemptuous of humanity**
    a. have psychologically disengaged.
    b. have been socially rejected.
    c. are preparing for an attack.
    d. are looking back over their lives and hiding their fear of death.

Answers   1. b 2. b 3. d 4. c 5. a 6. d 7. c 8. d 9. a 10. b 11. a 12. c 13. b 14. a 15. d 16. d

19 chapter

DYING AND SPIRITUALITY

Chapter Objectives

After reading this chapter you should be able to answer the following questions.

- What is the role of death in life?

- What is the purpose of "grief work"?

- What are the factors that cause and determine the nature of suicide?

- What is the meaning of "successful dying"?

- How do psychologists define the nature of spirituality?

As I said, you got to check out some time; you can't stay here forever.... Well, you just hope you go with a little dignity, that you don't have to suffer from Alzheimer's or die slowly in a rest home alone somewhere. I thought it was very interesting when I was in Bora Bora for six months. I was down there making a movie.... I did not live with the company, but found a house by myself up a road. There was a family next door—Polynesian natives—and the old lady of the house was there and she was dying. She suddenly said, "I'm going to die," and went to bed for three days and died. I remember at her funeral that everybody was dressed in white; it was like a wedding almost. And I was talking to them about it and they said, "Oh, yes, the fathers and the mothers are the most respected. They just go and die when they're ready." I said, "Geez, does that really go on like this all the time?" They said, "That's the way this society works." There are no old age homes, no old people wandering around, you know, suffering to death. Isn't it a strange thing, I thought to myself. What a respect for age that we don't have.... Like I say, life is like a hotel. We all check in and we all check out. Seems to me that the Polynesian approach to checking out is a great deal better than ours. (Actor Jason Robards [1922–2000])

THE ROLE OF DEATH IN LIFE

When your time comes to die, be not like those whose hearts are filled with fear of death, so that when their time comes they weep and pray for a little more time to live their lives over again in a different way. Sing your death song, and die like a hero going home.

TECUMSEH, NATIVE-AMERICAN SAGE

Americans, who have long been accused of abhorring the subject of death, are now giving it considerable attention.

In this section, we review research and theory from the social and physical sciences to examine three major concerns: What is death? How do we deal with the death of others? How do we deal with our own death?

What Is Death?

The matter of my friend rests heavy upon me.
How can I be salved?
How can I be stilled?
My friend, who I loved, has turned to clay.
Must I, too, lie me down
Not to rise again for ever and ever? (Epic of Gilgamesh, c. 2000 B.C.E.)

In the movies, death is almost invariably portrayed in the same sequence: Dying people make a final statement, close their eyes, fall back on the pillow or into the arms of a loved one, and are pronounced dead. In fact, death rarely occurs that way. In most cases, the person dies gradually. Death is a state, but dying is a process.

Ascertaining when people are truly and finally dead has been a medical problem for centuries. For example, in the early 1900s, Franz Hartmann claimed to have collected approximately 700 cases of premature burial or "close calls." In 1896 the "Society for the Prevention of Premature Burial" was founded. Fear of premature burial was so strong that, in 1897 in Berlin, a patent was granted for a life signal device that sent up a warning flag and turned on a light if movement was detected inside a coffin.

FIGURE 19.1

Death rates by cause and sex, United States.

Statistics from *Statistical Abstract of the United States* (2006) by U.S. Census Bureau, Washington, DC: U.S. Government Printing Office.

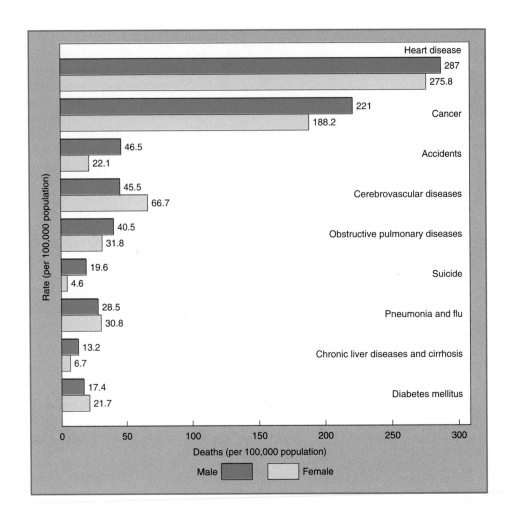

The more absolute death seems, the more authentic life becomes.

—JOHN FOWLES

We no longer have any serious problem in determining whether a person is dead. But determining exactly when death occurs has come to be of even greater importance because of organ donations. All the body's systems do not cease simultaneously, so disagreements exist over which system is most significant in judging whether a person is dead.

The Leading Causes of Death in the United States

In Figure 19.1 we see the 10 major causes of death for people of all ages. The rates are given for males and females, and some of the differences in rates between the two are interesting. (Cerebrovascular diseases pertain to the heart and blood vessels; pulmonary diseases have to do with the lungs.)

Four Types of Death

Today, four types of death are recognized: clinical death, brain death, biological or cellular death, and social death.

Clinical Death

In one sense, the individual is dead when his or her respiration and heartbeat have stopped. This is the aspect of dying referred to in the movies when the doctor turns

Since before the first historian, Herodotus, began describing the people and places he saw in Greece and the Mediterranean area in the 5th century B.C.E., the meaning of death has been a central issue.

clinical death
The individual is dead when his or her respiration and heartbeat have stopped.

cardiopulmonary resuscitation (CPR)
Technique for reviving an individual's lungs and heart that have ceased to function.

brain death
Occurs when the brain fails to receive a sufficient supply of oxygen for a short period of time (usually 8 to 10 minutes).

biological death
Occurs when it is no longer possible to discern an electrical charge in the tissues of the heart and lungs.

social death
Point at which a patient is treated essentially as a corpse, although perhaps still "clinically" or "biologically" alive.

and sadly announces, "I'm sorry, but he's gone." Actually, **clinical death** is the least useful to the medical profession and to society at large because it is unreliable. Owing to the advent of **cardiopulmonary resuscitation (CPR),** many individuals whose lungs and heart had ceased to function have been saved. In other cases, spontaneous restarting of the heart and lungs has occurred after failure.

Brain Death

Death of the brain occurs when it fails to receive a sufficient supply of oxygen for a short period of time (usually 8 to 10 minutes). The cessation of brain function occurs in three stages: First the cortex stops, then the midbrain fails, and finally the brain stem ceases to function. When the cortex, midbrain, and brainstem stop operating, **brain death** has occurred, and the person enters an irreversible coma. The body can remain alive in this condition for a long time, because the autonomic processes such as breathing and heartbeat are governed by the brain stem. Consciousness and alertness, however, will never be regained (Sullivan, Seem, & Chabalewski, 1999).

Biological Death

The cells and the organs of the body can remain in a functioning condition long after the failure of the heart and lungs. **Biological death** occurs when it is no longer possible to discern an electrical charge in the tissues of the heart and lungs, thus signaling the cessastion of all life functions.

Social Death

Sudnow (1967) was the first to suggest the concept of **social death,** which, "within the hospital setting, is marked at that point at which a patient is treated essentially as a corpse although perhaps still 'clinically' or 'biologically' alive" (p. 74). He cites cases in which body preparation (for instance, closing the eyes, binding the feet) were started while the patient was still alive, to make things easier for the staff. Also, in some cases, family members have signed autopsy permissions while the patient was still alive.

So when is a person really dead? If a person has suffered brain death but the heart is still beating, should the heart be removed and used for a transplant operation?

One complex case (Goldsmith, 1988) involved the Loma Linda University Medical Center, famous for its work in the area of organ transplants. It attempted to

It is possible to ensure that all or part of your body will be donated for use after your death, usually by a designation on your driver's license. Have you done this? If not, what are your reasons for refraining?

legal death
Condition defined as "unreceptivity and unresponsivity, no movements or breathing, no reflexes, and a flat electroencephalogram (EEG) reading that remains flat for 24 hours."

electroencephalogram (EEG)
Graphic record of the electrical activity of the brain.

initiate a program that would provide scarce organs for transplants. In this program, healthy hearts and other organs would be taken from babies born with anencephaly, a condition in which part or all of the brain is missing at birth. Ninety-five percent of these babies die within one week. When the anencephalic infants were born, they were flown to Loma Linda and given traditional "comfort care" (warmth, nutrition, and hydration). In addition, they were put on artificial breathing support for a maximum of seven days. The hospital maintained that they were put on respirators until a technical definition of brain death could be ascertained. But critics contended that this was done because the organs needed the time to mature for a successful transplant to occur. A storm of controversy ended the program before any donations could be made. Critics accused the hospital of "organ farming." The hospital argued that it was not only trying to increase the number of organ donors for infants but also giving the families of anencephalic babies an opportunity to "turn their tragedy into something good." With the advent of more advanced technology, the distinction between life and death becomes blurred, and the ethical considerations grow increasingly complex.

The Legal Definition of Death

In 1968 the Harvard Ad Hoc Committee to Examine the Criteria of Brain Death suggested the following criteria for **legal death:** "unreceptivity and unresponsivity, no movements or breathing, no reflexes, and a flat **electroencephalogram (EEG)** reading that remains flat for 24 hours."

Such criteria preclude the donation of organs in most cases, because the organs would probably suffer irreparable damage in the 24 hours needed to check the EEG. Others have suggested that the time at which the cerebral cortex has been irreparably damaged should be accepted as the time when organs can be removed from the body (Jefko, 1980).

Organ donation is not the only difficulty involved. An increasing number of cases, such as the recent Terri Schiavo case (see http://en.wikipedia.org/wiki/Terri_Schiavo), illustrate the ethical problems created by maintaining the life of individuals with the support of technical equipment. A number of medical personnel, philosophers, and theorists have suggested that maintaining life under these conditions is wrong. What do you think?

Although scientists may disagree on the exact nature of death itself, we have been learning much about how people deal, and how they should deal, with the death of their loved ones. We turn to that subject now.

Dealing Successfully with the Death of Others

Prior to the 20th century, people were used to seeing death. It was considered a normal part of life. Half of all children died before their tenth birthday, one-third within their first year. Only in recent decades have the rates of death from all causes declined so much. Even the number of deaths from the scourge of AIDS is decreasing (CDC, 2007).

In modern Western societies, death comes mostly to the old. For example, 55% of all males are age 65 or over when they die, and almost a third are past 75. The mortality rate has declined in our country from 17 per 1,000 population in 1900 to 8 per 1,000 in 2004 (Mininno et al., 2006). A family may expect to live 20 years (on the average) without one of its members dying.

An important exception should be noted: the huge number of children who are losing their parents to AIDS (UNICEF, 2005). In 2001 approximately 14 million children had lost one or both parents to AIDS. The greatest proportion and actual number of AIDS orphans, respectively, are sub-Saharan Africa and Asia.

The causes of overall lower mortality are clear: virtual elimination of infant and child mortality and increasing control over the diseases of youth and middle age. In the first half of the 20th century, when these goals were unattainable, the subject of death became more and more taboo. Probably as a result, social scientists spent little time studying our reactions to it or trying to find better ways to help us deal with it. Fortunately, in recent decades, this has changed.

GRIEF WORK

No one ever told me that grief felt so like fear. I am not afraid, but the sensation is like being afraid. The same fluttering in the stomach, the same restlessness, the yawning. I keep on swallowing.

—C. S. Lewis

Grief has a great deal in common with fear, and most grieving people really are afraid, at least unconsciously. They are frightened by the strength of their feelings and they often fear that they are losing their sanity. They feel that they cannot go on, that their loss is so great that their own lives are in danger.

Grief not only follows death; when there is advance warning, it frequently precedes it. Fulton (1977) found that anticipatory grief has four phases: depression, a heightened concern for the ill person, a rehearsal of death, and finally an attempt to adjust to the consequences that are likely to occur after the death.

The topic of grief has received increasing attention lately, with particular emphasis on the role of culture in the grieving process. Numerous factors are involved in how one processes grief, such as personality, religion, and family dynamics (Dunne, 2004). Therefore, people experience grief differently (Matzo et al., 2003), and these differences reflect cultural beliefs and practices (Haas, 2003).

Pathological Grieving

The process of grieving, painful as it is, is experienced and resolved by most individuals. In some cases, however, morbid grief reactions occur that prevent the successful conclusion of this life crisis. Three types of these grief reactions are delayed reaction, distorted reaction, and complicated grief.

Anticipatory grief, which precedes the sick person's death, is usually very difficult. Can you think of any benefits of grieving?

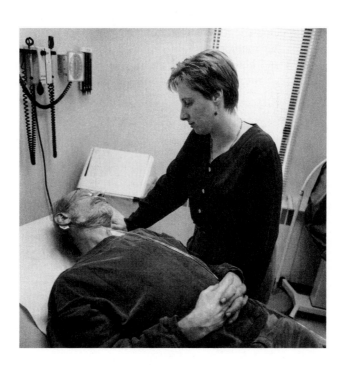

Delayed Reaction

In some cases, the intense reaction of the first stage is postponed for days, months, and in some cases years. In these cases, it is common for some seemingly unrelated incident to bring to the surface an intense grieving, which the individual does not even recognize as grief. Take, for example, the case of a 42-year-old man who underwent therapy to deal with an unaccountable depression. During conversation he disclosed that, when he was 22, his 42-year-old mother committed suicide. Apparently, the occurrence of his own 42nd birthday brought to the surface all the feelings that he had managed to repress since that time.

Distorted Reactions

In most cases, distorted reactions are normal symptoms carried to an extreme degree. They include adopting the behavior traits of the deceased, such as aspects of the deceased's fatal illness and other types of psychosomatic ailments, particularly colitis, arthritis, and asthma.

One example is a young man whose mother died of lymphomic cancer. At her death, she had large boils on her neck. Some weeks after she died, her son discovered lumps on his neck that quickly developed into boils. On examination, they were found to be benign. In fact, it was determined that they were entirely psychosomatic. That is, the doctors decided that the only explanation of their existence was the great stress in the young man's mind over the loss of his mother.

The ultimate distorted reaction is depression so deep that it causes the death of a surviving loved one. This is especially likely to happen to widowers (Asch-Goodkin & Kaplan, 2006).

Pathological Mourning

With complicated grief the mourning process is not skipped but is prolonged and intensified to an abnormal degree (disabling distress is experienced for at least six months) (Wellbery, 2005; Wortman & Boerner, 2007). Frequently, the person suffers from impaired physical and/or mental health.

An example of this illness is a man who worked hard with his wife to renovate an old cottage they had bought in order to live by a lake not far from their home. A few days before they were going to move in, she died of a heart attack. Many months later, friends noticed that he would disappear for several days at a time. One friend followed him to the cottage and found that he had created a shrine to her memory in it. Her clothes and other possessions were laid out in all the rooms, and her picture was on all the walls. Only after extensive therapy was he able to go through a more normal grief, give up the shrine, and move on with his life.

The Role of Grief

Most psychologists who have examined the role of grief have concluded that it is an essential aspect of a healthy encounter with the crisis of death. They believe that open confrontation with the loss of a loved one is essential to accepting the reality of a world in which the deceased is no longer present. Attempts to repress or avoid thoughts about the loss are only going to push them into the subconscious, where they will continue to cause problems until they are dragged out and fully accepted. And yet dealing with grief is also costly. For example, the mortality rate among grieving persons is seven times higher than a matched sample of nongrieving persons. However, the Japanese are most reticent about public grief and yet seem to suffer no ill effects from this reticence. The Balinese frequently laugh at the time of death, because, they say, they are trying to avoid crying, yet they seem to be psychologically healthy. Some cultures employ "keeners," who wail loudly so that the bereaved will not have to do so themselves.

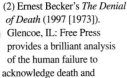

To learn more about dealing with death, you may want to read one of the following books: (1) A Pulitzer Prize–winning novel related to this topic is James Agee's *A Death in the Family* (1957 [1998]). New York: Vintage. This novel focuses on the effect of a man's death on his young son; (2) Ernest Becker's *The Denial of Death* (1997 [1973]). Glencoe, IL: Free Press provides a brilliant analysis of the human failure to acknowledge death and explores the theories of Freud, Rank, Jung, Fromm, and others. Becker was awarded the Pulitzer Prize for this work; (3) One of Freud's most famous works, *Totem and Taboo* (1998 [1913]). New York: Vintage, explains how psychoanalysis looks at death and dying.

AN APPLIED VIEW | A Personal Experience of One of the Authors with Delayed Reaction

I am stepping out of my role as an author to relate an experience of mine that is relevant to this discussion of the function of grief. In April 1957 I joined the U.S. Navy and sailed to the Mediterranean for a 6-month tour of duty on an oil supply ship. In early November I returned home to a joyful reunion with my family. After this wonderful weekend at home, I returned to my ship. Two days later I received a telegram informing me of a tragedy: My mother, two younger brothers, and two younger sisters had been killed in a fire that had destroyed our house. My father and three younger brothers and a sister had escaped with serious burns.

On the long train ride home from the naval port, I recall thinking that, as the oldest, I should be especially helpful to my father in the terrible time ahead. I was also aware of a curious absence of dismay in myself.

In our medium-sized upstate New York town, the catastrophe was unprecedented, and expressions of grief and condolences were myriad. People kept saying to me, "Don't try to be so brave. It's good for you to let yourself cry." And I tried to, but tears just wouldn't come.

At the funeral, the caskets were closed, and I can remember thinking that maybe, just maybe, this was all just a horrible dream. I distinctly remember one fantasy about my brother Mike. He was born on my first birthday and in the several years before the fire, I had become especially close to him. I imagined that he had actually hit his head trying to escape and had wandered off to Chicago with a case of amnesia and that no one was willing to admit that they didn't know where he was. I knew this wasn't true, yet I secretly clung to the possibility. After a very difficult period of time, our family gradually began a new life. Many people generously helped us, and eventually the memories faded.

Several times in the years that followed, I went to doctors because of a stomachache, a painful stiff neck, or some other malady that couldn't be diagnosed physically. One doctor suggested that I might be suffering from an unresolved subconscious problem, but I doubted it.

Then one night in 1972, 15 years after the fire, I was watching *The Waltons' Christmas,* a television show in which the father of a close family is lost and feared dead. Although dissimilar from my own experience, this tragedy triggered an incredible response in me. Suddenly and finally it occurred to me: "My God, half my family is really gone forever!" I began sobbing and could not stop for more than 3 hours. When I finally stopped, I felt weak and empty, relieved of an awful burden. In the days that followed I believe I went through a clear-cut "delayed grief" reaction.

Therefore, the answer to the question, at least in my experience, is clear: Grief work really is essential, and we avoid it only at the cost of even greater pain. My father died some years ago, and my grief was immediate and intense. I cannot help but feel that my emotional response that time was considerably more appropriate and healthy. (John Dacey)

AN APPLIED VIEW | Dealing with Grief and Associated Anger

Many people suffering from grief and the anger that often accompanies it believe that their only option is to "wait it out" and "just get through it." As one person put it, "I can't believe I'm so weak that I can't get past this!" In fact, grief sufferers have a number of options; most of these activities can provide relief from their pain, often by turning it to some good:

- Join a volunteer program. For example, those who have lost a loved one in a drunk driving incident can join Mothers Against Drunk Driving.
- Volunteer to do work for a friend or neighbor who needs the help.
- Find physical outlets for painful feelings—anything from joining an exercise club to beating the carpets with a broom.

- Talk about feelings with a trusted friend or relative.
- Seek psychotherapeutic help. There are specialists who are trained to help with grief and anger.
- Join a support group. In addition to groups that deal generally with grief or anger, there are specialty groups such as groups for those who have lost a child or are related to a suicide victim.
- Work for a hotline such as those operated by the Good Samaritans.
- Learn to meditate.
- Join a yoga class.

In your opinion, what are the appropriate arrangements for a funeral? Are you in favor of formal religious services? Why or why not?

Research by Clements and associates (2004) on the grief response found that a number of widely held beliefs are not supported by the evidence. They concluded that

- Crying during the grief process does not mean successful resolution of the crisis of death. Likewise, not crying does not signal improper grieving. Culturally sensitive assessments are warranted.
- The true experts on grief are the surviving family members, who often seek the expertise of a therapist during the painful mourning process.
- The use of drugs, alcohol, and violence should not be considered a normal part of the grieving process.
- The idea that grieving normally ends after one year is false; there is wide variation in the length of time people need to recover from loss.
- People often feel worse as the one-year anniversary of death approaches, since they are reminded of the traumatic event.

The Role of the Funeral

One of the hardest aspects of dealing with the death of a loved one is deciding how the funeral (if there is to be one) is to be conducted. Funerals have always been an important part of American life, whether the elaborate burial rituals practiced by Native-Americans or the simple funerals of our colonial forebears.

Once the intimate responsibility of each family, care for the dead in the United States has been transferred to a paid service industry. The need for this new service was brought about by changes in society during the first part of the 20th century. The more mobile, urbanized workforce had less family support and less time to devote to the task of caring for the dead. In a relatively short time, funeral homes and funeral directors became the accepted form of care for one's dead relatives.

This commercialization of care for the dead has had mixed results. During the 1950s and 1960s, funeral homes came under stinging criticism for their expense and their lack of sensitivity to the needs of the surviving family members. In recent years, coffins have become available for purchase in warehouse stores, such as Costco. Picking up on an opportunity to explore and humanize the commercial and personal sides of the "death business," the television series "Six Feet Under" on HBO became highly acclaimed. In this program, the Fisher family comes to terms with its own family grief against the backdrop of their family business: a funeral home.

Dealing Successfully with One's Own Death

Having nearly died, I've found death like that sweet feeling that people have that let themselves slide into sleep. I believe that this is the same feeling that people find themselves in whom we see fainting in the agony of death, and I maintain that we pity them without cause. If you know not how to die, never trouble yourself. Nature will in a moment fully and sufficiently instruct you; she will exactly do that business for you; take you no care for it. (Michel de Montaigne)

Why is the acceptance of death so painful to so many of us? Why does it come up in every developmental stage, only to be partially resolved and partially denied?

Many people find dying a much harder experience than Montaigne would have us believe it is. Many dying patients feel seriously depressed before their deaths,

A SOCIOCULTURAL VIEW | The Funeral in Other Times and Countries

Looking at the funeral practices of former cultures shows us not only how they buried their dead but also something about their values.

Ancient Egypt

Upon the death of the head of the house in ancient Egypt, women would rush through the streets, beating their breasts and clutching their hair. The body of the deceased was removed to the embalming chambers, where a team proceeded with the embalming operation. (The Egyptians believed in the life beyond; embalming was intended to protect the body for this journey.) While the body was being embalmed, arrangements for the final entombment began. When the mummified corpse was ready, it was placed on a sledge drawn by oxen or men and accompanied by wailing servants, professional mourners simulating anguished grief, and relatives. It was believed that when the body was placed in an elaborate tomb (family wealth and prestige exerted an obvious influence on tomb size), its spirits would depart and later return through a series of ritualistic actions.

Ancient Greece

Reverence for the dead permeated burial customs during all phases of ancient Greek civilization. Within a day after death the body was washed, anointed, dressed in white, and laid out in state for one to seven days, depending on the social prestige of the deceased. For the funeral procession, the body was carried by friends and relatives and followed by female mourners, fraternity members, and hired dirge singers. Inside the tomb were artistic ornaments, jewels, vases, and articles of play and war. Like the Egyptians, the ancient Greeks prepared their tombs and arranged for subsequent care while they were still alive. About 1000 B.C.E. the Greeks began to cremate their dead. Although earth burial was never entirely superseded, the belief in the power of the flame to free the soul acted as a strong impetus to the practice of cremation.

The Roman Empire

Generally speaking, the Romans envisioned some type of afterlife and, like the Greeks, practiced both cremation and earth burial. When a wealthy person died, the body was dressed in a white toga and placed on a funeral couch, feet to the door, to lie in state for several days. For reasons of sanitation, burial within the walls of Rome was prohibited; consequently, great roads outside the city were lined with elaborate tombs erected for the well-to-do. For the poor, there was no such magnificence; for slaves and aliens, there was a common burial pit outside the city walls.

Anglo-Saxon England

In 5th-century Anglo-Saxon England, the body of the deceased was placed on a bier or in a hearse. On the corpse was laid the book of the Gospels as a symbol of faith and the cross as a symbol of hope. The funeral procession included priests, friends, relatives, and strangers who deemed it their duty to join the party. Mass was then sung for the dead, the body was solemnly laid in the grave (generally without a coffin), the mortuary fee was paid from the estate of the deceased, and liberal alms were given to the poor.

Colonial New England

Christian burials and funeral practices were models of simplicity and quiet dignity in 18th-century New England. Upon death, neighbors or a nurse would wash and lay out the body. The local woodworker would build the coffin, selecting a quality of wood to fit the social position of the deceased. In special cases, metal decorations imported from England were used on the coffin. Funeral services consisted of prayers and sermons said over the pall-covered bier. Funeral sermons often were printed (with skull and crossbones prominently displayed) and circulated among the public. The service at the grave was simple, primarily a brief prayer followed by the ritual commitment of the body to the earth.

Let's hope it won't happen, but what would you do if you were called on to organize a funeral tomorrow? Would you know whom to notify? How would you arrange for the preparation and disposition of the body? What kind of ceremony, religious or otherwise, would you ask for? What would you do about a funeral home, a cemetery plot, and the will and death benefits of the deceased?

Perhaps you could discuss this with some of your friends or classmates, to see how they would feel. Note how you feel about opinions that differ from yours.

Source: Turner & Helms (1989, pp. 492–493).

and a large number have suicidal feelings. Among the reasons for these depressions are the following:

- Medication-induced mood alterations.
- Awareness of how little time is left.
- Feelings of isolation from relatives and friends who are withdrawing.
- Feelings of grief for the losses that are close at hand.
- Feelings of disillusion and resentment over injustice.

FIGURE 19.2

Kübler-Ross's stages of dying

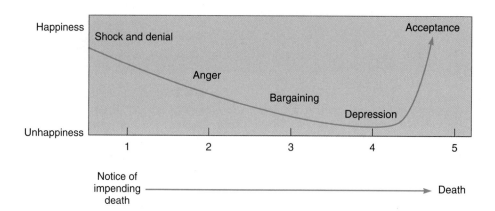

Depression is sometimes described as cognitive withdrawal because many patients have a decreasing ability and motivation to process stimuli as death nears.

Must dying, then, always be such an unhappy experience? European psychiatrist Elisabeth Kübler-Ross is the most famous student of the process of death. Her three books on the subject have all been best-sellers: *On Death and Dying* (1969), *Death—the Final Stage of Growth* (1975), and *To Live until We Say Good-Bye* (1978). Kübler-Ross discovered that, far from wanting to avoid the topic of death, many dying patients have a strong urge to discuss it. She interviewed hundreds of terminally ill people. On the basis of these interviews, she developed a five-stage theory describing the emotions that underlie the process of dying. The stages in her theory are flexible, in that people can move through them quickly, slowly, or not at all. Some fluctuation occurs between the stages, but by and large people tend to move through them in sequential order. They are portrayed in Figure 19.2.

Kübler-Ross's stage theory was the first to counter the common assumption that it is abnormal to have strong emotions during the dying process. However, no empirical confirmation that this particular sequence of stages is universal exists. Her theory overlooks the effects of personality, ethnic, or religious factors. For example, people in some cultures such as some Native-American and Asian ethnic groups view death as just another stage of existence and do not encourage dread of it. So should we accept Kübler-Ross's model or not? The biological, psychological, and social aspects of the process of dying are obviously very complex. We will need to know much more—knowledge gained through careful research—before we can answer this question. We can say that her theory, like all good theories, has at least provided us with constructs (the five stages) to help guide future research.

Another theory, also based on observation and describing five stages, is that of Saunders (1989). Her suggested stages are shock, awareness of loss, withdrawal, healing, and renewal. The similarities with Kübler-Ross's stages are noteworthy. Wortman and Silver (1989) agree with the themes presented by Kübler-Ross and Saunders but urge that they do not occur in set stages in all individuals. Rather, these studies find that the themes are intermingled, ending with some people on a positive note and others react finally with anger and/or depression. As to the latter, some have urged that it is the right reaction. We are reminded of Dylan Thomas's famous lines of poetry (*Collected Poems,* 1971), addressed to his father:

Do not go gentle into that dark night—
Rage, rage against the dying of the light!

No matter how well prepared we are, death is usually sad and stressful. Most of the time, though, we know that we can do nothing about it, and so we must accept the inevitable. How different it is when the death was not inevitable but was chosen by a person because he or she believes life is no longer worth living.

Guided Review

1. Currently four different definitions of death exist: clinical death (stoppage of respiration and heart), brain death (cessation of cortex and midbrain activity), _____ death (not possible to discern electrical changes in the tissues of heart and lungs), and _____ death (person treated essentially as dead).

2. The criteria for legal death is unreceptivity, no movements or breathing, no reflexes, and a flat _____ reading that remains flat for 24 hours.

3. The causes in Western society for lower mortality rates are the reduction of infant and child mortality and increasing control over the _____ of youth and middle age.

4. In addition to normal grief, there are three types of morbid grief reactions: _____ grief, distorted reactions, and _____ mourning.

5. Anticipatory grief is characterized by four phases: _____, a heightened concern for the ill person, _____ of death, and an attempt to adjust to the consequences that will occur after death.

6. Most psychologists believe that grief is essential as a part of a _____ encounter with death, but the forms that healthy grief might take have not yet been studied well empirically.

7. People may feel depressed before their own death because they are experiencing feelings of loss for friends and family, as well as feeling a sense of _____ over injustice.

8. Elisabeth Kübler-Ross argues that dying has five stages. These stages are shock and denial, anger, _____, depression, and acceptance.

SUICIDE: THE REJECTION OF LIFE

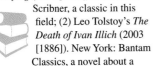

To better understand how we, as individuals, handle our own death, read: (1) Elisabeth Kübler-Ross's *On Death and Dying* (1997 [1969]). New York: Scribner, a classic in this field; (2) Leo Tolstoy's *The Death of Ivan Illich* (2003 [1886]). New York: Bantam Classics, a novel about a man who learns that he has terminal cancer, and his lonely journey into understanding the meaning of life and the ability to accept his own death.

As you will see, we are beginning to learn more about how and why suicides happen. This information will surely help us in our efforts to prevent such unfortunate deaths.

The Overall Picture

Suicide and attempted suicide among adolescents is a national problem that has declined in recent years, after reaching high numbers in the 1990s (Gould et al., 2003). Suicide now ranks as the third leading cause of death among persons age 13 to 19 (National Center for Health Statistics, 2004), and some experts believe that, if no suicides were "covered up," it would be the leading cause. The rates are higher for whites than for nonwhites (CDC, 2006).

Two other groups are much more prone to suicide, however: the so-called middle-old and old-old groups. Although the suicide rate for 15- to 24-year-olds is high, the rate for those 65 and older is higher, with non-Hispanic males at 17.4 per 100,000 people (CDC, 2006a). Roff (2001) reported that suicide among the elderly is a significant public health problem, with the elderly accounting for 20% of the nation's suicides, despite accounting for only 13% of the population.

Answers
1. biological, social 2. electroencephalogram (EEG) 3. diseases 4. delayed, pathological 5. depression, rehearsal 6. healthy 7. resentment 8. bargaining

For the elderly, poor health is often a cause of suicide because it is linked to depression. Poor health is used as a way of justifying suicide. Furthermore, Leibson and associates (1999) warn that older people with serious depression often do not provide accurate health information when questioned in research studies. It was found that illnesses reported by doctors' records were more accurate in describing a depressed state than the person's self-report. Loneliness is a second major factor. Effects of factors and forces on the behavior of people are critical in understanding the causes leading to suicide (Stravynski & Boyer, 2001). It should be noted that, for unstable individuals, even minor changes in their life patterns can push them toward committing suicide or inhibit their tendency to do so.

There is a story of an elderly retiree from the police force who had made an excellent adjustment to leaving the force. When he discovered that he had a large brain tumor, however, he became very depressed at the thought of leaving his wife, children, and nine grandchildren, to all of whom he was deeply attached. One day, after asking his wife to go to the store for his favorite candy, he shot himself. His wife discovered him and threw away his pistol. She told the paramedics she saw a man fleeing from her house. The "case" remained unsolved, and she was able to bury her husband in a Catholic cemetery.

The Influence of Gender on Suicide

At all ages, major gender differences in suicide exist. The rate for males is much higher, owing to the type of suicidal behavior engaged in, the methods used, the lethality of the attempt, and the degree of psychiatric disturbance present. Males and females are two very different suicidal types. Universally, males are about four times more likely to die of suicide than females (CDC, 2006a). Attempt rates show even more dramatic gender differences, but in the opposite direction. Failed attempts at suicide among females are much higher than for males (Curran, 2006). A major reason for the high survival rate among females is the method used. Whereas males often resort to such violent and effective means as firearms and hanging, females tend to choose less violent and less deadly means, such as pills. Male suicide attempts may be influenced by factors such as alcohol and drug use, unemployment, and divorce (Appleby, 2000). Males are usually more committed to dying and therefore succeed far more often.

In their study of suicide attempts among low-income, African-American adults, Kaslow and associates (2004) found that "attempters reported more psychological distress, aggression, substance use, and maladaptive coping strategies" than blacks who had never attempted suicide (p. 5). Attempters were also less religious and low in spirituality, and were less likely to identify with being black.

Males are about four times more likely to die of suicide attempts than are females.

In light of the increase of suicides among the elderly, the prevention of suicide is gaining more attention (Hyman, 2001; Pearson & Brown, 2000). Health care professionals can play an important role in suicide prevention. Examining the practical role of the community in the lives of the elderly is a good beginning in these prevention efforts.

It should be noted, however, that although some elderly people may contemplate suicide, many have successfully resisted the urge to commit it. Older adults have certain coping

AN APPLIED VIEW

The Danger Signs of Suicide

- Sudden changes in mood or behavior.
- Pulling away from family and friends.
- Marked increase or decrease in sleeping.
- Becoming "accident prone."
- Talking about death or suicide or heightened interest in reading about them.
- Heightened interest in music or art that deals with death.
- Giving away favorite possessions.
- Impetuous desire to get affairs in order.
- Abrupt drop in school or work performance.
- Impulsive drug and alcohol abuse.
- Changes in personal hygiene.

- Lack of interest in food.
- Unusual anger, anxiety, or apathy.
- Hypochondria.
- Inability to concentrate.
- Experience of serious personal loss.
- Previous history of suicide attempts.

No single one of these signs is in itself a clear indication of suicidal ideation. Several of them, however, are cause for concern. Anyone talking about committing suicide should be taken seriously and a mental health professional should be consulted, even when you feel sure the person is "only talking about it to get attention or sympathy."

abilities and reasons for living that enable them to face many demands of advanced age (Range & Stringer, 1996). One possible reason that more men than women die by their own hands is that older women are able to list more reasons for living than are men. In fact, Range and Stringer reported that older women often have greater ability to cope than they even realize. The authors suggest that suicide prevention strategies target men and encourage the development of deterrents to suicide.

Guided Review

9. Suicide and attempted suicide are increasingly common responses to _____ and depression among young people.

10. The suicide rate for men and women over 70 years of age is almost _____ as high as for men and women between the ages of 15 and 24 years.

11. Younger adults today have generally (lower, higher) rates of suicide than their grandparents did at that age.

12. For the elderly, _____ _____, depression, and _____ are some of the major factors of suicide.

"SUCCESSFUL" DYING

Death and dying, by whatever means, are not one of our favorite topics, but they do have an important place in our study of life. In the next section of this chapter, we will discuss two of the ways we humans have to deal with death in a mature and satisfying way.

Answers

9. stress 10. twice 11. higher 12. poor health, loneliness

Death with Dignity

So, my judges, face death with good hope, and know for certain that no evil can happen to a good man, either in life or after death.

—SOCRATES

euthanasia
A "good death"; there are two types: passive euthanasia, in which the patient's legal instructions are carried out by the medical team, and active euthanasia, in which the patient's life is ended in ways that are now illegal.

physician-assisted suicide (PAS)
Doctors give patients death-inducing drugs.

No doubt most people would rather not suffer serious physical pain when they die, and many would prefer to avoid the emotional pain that often attends death. Until recently, however, only a few had any choice. Today, great debates have formed around two alternatives, both of them a form of **euthanasia.** There are two types of euthanasia (which means a "good death" in Greek). Passive euthanasia refers to refraining from continuing efforts to sustain a faltering life, such as turning off life-support systems. These methods either are covered by a living will or are determined by the patient's legal representative. *Active euthanasia* means actively ending a life, either through directly killing the patient or by **physician-assisted suicide (PAS).** In PAS, it is against the law everywhere for the physician to actually give the patient a death-inducing drug. In Holland doctors do administer such drugs, but with strict guidelines under the law. In Oregon, there is a law allowing doctors to prescribe such drugs, but the patients must take it themselves.

On 30 September 1976, Governor Edmund Brown, Jr., of California signed the "Natural Death Act," the first death with dignity law in the nation. The statute states the right of an adult to sign a written directive instructing his or her physician to withhold or withdraw life-sustaining procedures in the event of a terminal condition. The law contains specific definitions for "terminal condition," "life-sustaining procedure," and "qualified patient." The directive must be drawn up in the form set forth by the statute. It must be signed and dated by an adult of sound mind and witnessed by two people not related by blood or entitled to the estate of the declarant.

Since then all but 10 states have established such procedures. In June 1990 the Supreme Court ruled that, because the desires of a Missouri woman who had been lying in a coma since 1983 had not been made explicit through a living will, she could not be allowed to die despite her parents' wishes. However, the Court has ruled that, when procedures established within each state are followed, the "right to die" is constitutional.

Almost 80% of Americans die in hospitals, and 70% of those deaths involve some aspect of medical technology such as breathing, feeding, and waste-elimination equipment. Hence, it is essential that those who do not want to be maintained on life-support systems if they become terminal put their wishes in writing according to their state's laws. Open communication with one's doctor is also essential (Henden, 1999; von Gunten, Ferris, & Emanuel, 2000). This type of decision making before the end of one's life seems to be increasing, and is practiced in many European countries (van der Heide et al., 2003).

Whatever you want to do, do it now. There are only so many tomorrows.

—ANNE MORROW LINDBERGH

Today there is a serious debate over the appropriateness of physician-assisted suicide (Bernat, 2001; DiPasquale & Gluck, 2001; Ganzini et al., 2001; Kaldijian, 2001). In this case, someone on the medical team typically injects an overdose of morphine, which quickly brings on unconsciousness and death. Those who support it claim a number of advantages for it: Time of death is up to the patient; it can be used by those for whom the hospice or hospital is inappropriate; and death is painless if the patient is given a high enough dose of morphine. Shapiro (2000) describes the experience of a Dutch doctor, Dr. Herbert Cohen:

He performed euthanasia between 50 and 100 times until he gave up his family practice a few years ago. Sometimes, he brought flowers.

Sometimes his patient gave him a bottle of wine and they toasted death together. Often, a minister present read the 23rd Psalm. Yet each time, Cohen says about helping the patient die, "it is a mountain you have to climb" (p. 148).

Others suggest that its limitations are that it is an extreme way to end suffering; some family members may be made to feel guilty; it may interfere with healing in relationships; it is opposed by most major religions; and it could be abused in order to save money. In a letter to the Supreme Court from his deathbed (Woodward & McCormick, 1996, p. 62), Cardinal Bernardin wrote, "As one who is dying, I have especially come to appreciate the gift of life. Creating a new right to assisted suicide will endanger society and send a false signal that a less than 'perfect' life is not worth living."

At this time, the American public seems to favor physician-assisted suicide. A recent Harris Poll found that two-thirds of the American public wants legislation permitting some form of the practice (The Harris Poll, 2005). The American Medical Association's Council of Ethical and Judicial Affairs (Goodman, 1998) has proposed new guidelines for the optimal use of directives. The guidelines urge the use of detailed worksheets in tailoring end-of-life care to the specific preferences of the patient. They proposed a process that physicians should be required to follow when educating their patients about death and dying. It remains to be seen whether or not these directives will be enacted.

The Hospice: "A Better Way of Dying"

The "death ward" in most hospitals is not a nice place to be. The atmosphere is one of hushed whispers and fake smiles. No children below the age of 12 are allowed. Medications to control the pain are usually given on a schedule rather than as needed. Machines are used to continue life at all costs, though the patient may desire death. Viewing a typical American death ward made British historian Toynbee conclude, "death is un-American."

In reaction to this, some have reached back to the Middle Ages, when religious orders set up havens in which dying pilgrims could go to spend their last days. The modern **hospice** was established to provide for a more "natural" death for those who are terminally ill. The first U.S. hospice opened in New Haven, Connecticut, in 1971. Since then the National Hospice Organization has been formed to help promulgate this movement.

hospice
Services aimed at relieving suffering of terminally ill patients.

The hospice is not a new type of facility; it is a new philosophy of patient care in the United States (although not new in Europe). Hospices do pioneering work in such neglected areas as the easing of pain and psychological counseling of patients and their families. Even before patients begin to suffer pain, which in diseases such as cancer can be excruciating, they are given a mixture of morphine, cocaine, alcohol, and syrup so they come to realize that pain can be controlled. Known as "Brompton's Mixture," this concoction is used only when the patient's need is severe; it is very effective in alleviating both pain and the fear accompanying it. A major goal of the hospice is to keep the person's mind as clear as possible at all times. A person whose mind is clear can think more cogently about the dying process and to explore the feelings associated with death and the meaning of dying (Dobratz, 2003).

The hospice program movement has now grown to the point that it supports its own journal. Articles in the Hospice Journal often provide supplementary information about special issues concerning the terminally ill. For example, a recent issue of the Hospice Journal included articles investigating the well-being of the spouses of hospice patients (Haley et al., 2001), medical students' views of hospice care (Plymale et al., 2001), and a home-based family caregiver cancer education program (Pickett, Barg, & Lynch, 2001).

The modern hospice is organized to afford a more "natural death" to the dying. What is your opinion of this process?

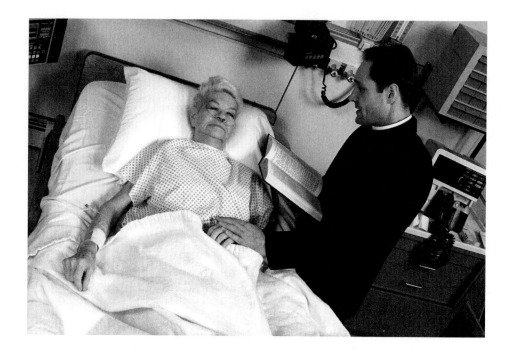

One of the major questions now being considered is whether the hospice should continue as a separate facility run solely for that purpose or become a standard part of all major hospitals. Currently, hospice programs in the United States are primarily home-based care, with the sponsorship of such programs evenly divided between hospitals and community agencies. Many insurance programs now cover hospice care. Although many assume hospices deal only with the elderly, as can be seen in Figure 19.3, nearly one-third of the patients are younger than 65. Whatever the case, dying is frightening for most of us, and ultimately very hard to understand. To come to terms with it, we almost always rely on our spiritual rather than our cognitive powers.

FIGURE 19.3

Growth of hospices in the United States.

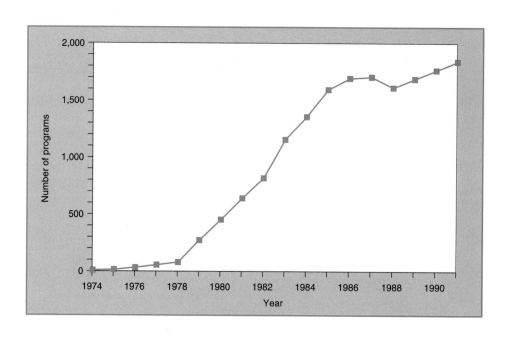

Guided Review

13. A law was passed in California in 1976 that allows death with dignity, which means that adults have the right to legally state their rejection of _____ procedures when they are in a terminal condition.

14. The hospice was established to provide a more _____ death for people who are terminally ill.

15. The hospice movement contributes to the death with dignity movement by providing relief from distressing symptoms and providing a _____ _____ for the terminal patient.

16. One of the major goals of the hospice is to keep the patient's _____ as clear as possible.

SPIRITUALITY

There is but one true philosophical problem, and this is suicide: Judging whether life is or is not worth living amounts to answering the fundamental question of philosophy.

—ALBERT CAMUS

Spirituality is concerned not only with whether life is worth living but also with why it is worth living. It may involve the attempt to better understand the reasons for living through striving to know the intentions of a Supreme Being. An example is reading inspired books such as the Bible, the Koran, and Native-American writings. Another is trying to discern the purposes and goals of some universal life force by, for example, examining historical trends in biological changes of species. In any case, spirituality includes all of our efforts to gain insight into the underlying, overriding forces of life. For many, it is the only justification for morality. How important a role does spirituality play in the lives of typical American adults? One way this question has been investigated is through looking at religious participation and at religious attitudes. These factors are sometimes misleading, but together they offer one part of the answer to the question.

Religious Participation

Americans have always been highly religious. This statement is supported by recent Gallup polls (Harper, 2004). A majority of elderly people consider religious practice to be of major importance in their lives. According to surveys, 96% of those over 65 believe in God, and 82% report that religion plays a significant role in their lives.

Religious values become stronger with age. For example, the percentage of people who express strong religious beliefs increases from 35% among young adults to 47% in middle age to 66% among the elderly. Attending services once or more each month grows among these three age groups from 50% to 67% to nearly 75% (Russell, 1989). Furthermore, the influence of religion appears to be highly related to a sense of well-being in elderly persons.

Using data from a sample of 2,812 men and women ages 65 and older, Van Ness and Kasl (2003) attempted to clarify factors. They looked at demographic variables, cognitive functioning, and social commitments, as well as organized religious practices. They found that religious attendance, not religious identity, was associated with less cognitive decline in old age.

Answers 13. life-sustaining 14. natural 15. caring environment 16. mind

AN APPLIED VIEW

If You Had Your Life to Live Over Again, What Would You Do Differently?

This question was asked of 122 retired persons by DeGenova (1992). She discovered that her sample chose the pursuit of education more than any other area. This emphasis on education among retirees may be because they feel their lack of education led to missed or limited opportunities. Although these people indicated they would have spent more time doing a variety of things, they said that they would have spent less time worrying about work.

This poem describes the feelings of one 81-year-old lady, Nadine Stair, on the topic:

If I had my life to live over,
I'd like to make more mistakes next time.
I'd relax, I would limber up. I would be sillier
than I have been this trip. I would take fewer
things seriously. I would take more chances.
I would climb more mountains and swim more
rivers. I would eat more ice cream and less
beans. I would perhaps have more actual troubles,

but I'd have fewer imaginary ones.
You see, I'm one of those people who live sensibly
and sanely hour after hour, day after day. Oh, I've
had my moments, and if I had it to do over again,
I'd have more of them. In fact, I'd try to have
nothing else. Just moments, one after another,
instead of living so many years ahead of each day.
I've been one of those persons who never goes
anywhere without a thermometer, a hot water
bottle, a raincoat, and a parachute. If I had to do
it again, I would travel lighter than I have.
If I had my life to live over, I would start
barefoot earlier in the spring and stay that way later
in the fall.
I would go to more dances.
I would ride more merry-go-rounds.
I would pick more daisies!

Spirituality does appear to develop with age. A number of theories have been offered as to how and why this is so. Among them, four views have come to receive highest regard: those of Viennese psychoanalysts Viktor Frankl and Carl Jung, sociobiologist E. O. Wilson, and theologian James Fowler.

Frankl's Theory of Spirituality

Frankl (1967) described human life as developing in three interdependent stages, according to the predominant dimension of each stage.

1. *The somatic (physical) dimension.* According to the somatic dimension, all people are motivated by the struggle to keep themselves alive and to help the species survive. This intention is motivated entirely by instincts. It exists at birth and continues throughout life.

2. *The psychological dimension.* Personality begins to form at birth and develops as a result of instincts, drives, capacities, and interactions with the environment. The psychological dimension and the somatic dimension are highly developed by the time the individual reaches early adulthood.

3. *The noetic dimension.* The noetic dimension has roots in childhood but primarily develops in late adolescence. It is spiritual not only in the religious sense but also in the totality of the search for the meaningfulness of life. This aspect distinguishes humans from all other species. The freedom to make choices is the basis of responsibility. Reason exists in the noetic realm. Conscience, which greatly affects the meaningfulness that we discover in life, resides in the noetic.

Frankl believed that development in the physical and personality dimensions results from the total sum of the influences bearing upon an individual. The noetic,

Dr. Carl Jung, a student of Freud's, introduced many concepts into psychology, including the anima and animus (his concepts of the female and male soul).

Wilson's Theory of Spirituality

The predisposition to religious belief is the most complex and powerful force in the human mind and in all probability an ineradicable part of human nature.

—EDWARD WILSON

Harvard sociobiologist Edward O. Wilson, the leading spokesperson for the sociobiological point of view (see Chapter 13), argued that religion and spirituality are inseparable. Together they grant essential benefits to believers. He argued that all societies, from hunter-gatherer bands to socialist republics, have religious practices with roots that go back at least as far as the Neanderthal period. Wilson argued that humans have a need to develop simple rules for handling complex problems. We also have a strong need for an unconscious sense of order in our daily lives. We strongly resist attempts to disrupt this order, which religion almost always protects.

Once we truly know that life is difficult—once we truly understand and accept it— then life is no longer difficult. Because once it is accepted, the fact that life is difficult no longer matters.

—M. S. PECK

Religion is one of the few uniquely human behaviors. Rituals and beliefs that make up religious life are not seen among any other animals. Some scientists, notably Lorenz and Tinbergen, argued that animal displays, dances, and rituals are similar to human religious ceremonies. Wilson believed this comparison was wrong; animal displays are for the purpose of communicating (sexual desire, and so on), but religious ceremonies intend far more than mere communication.

Their goal is to "reaffirm and rejuvenate the moral values of the community" (Wilson, 1978, p. 179). Furthermore, religious learning is almost entirely unconscious. Most religious tenets are taught and deeply internalized early in life. Early teaching is beneficial if children are to learn to consider their natural self-interests in relation to the larger society.

The sociobiological explanation of spirituality, then, is that, through religious practice, the survival of practitioners is enhanced. Those who practice religion are more likely to stay alive (or at least they were in the past) than those who do not practice religion.

Wilson believed that even a person's willingness to be controlled may be genetic. Although all societies need some rebels, they also require that the vast majority of people be controllable, typically through religious and political beliefs. Therefore, Wilson believed that, over time, genes that favor willingness to be controlled have been favored by natural selection.

The potential for self-sacrifice can be strengthened in this manner because the willingness of individuals to relinquish rewards or even surrender their own lives will favor group survival. The Jonestown mass suicide, for example, appears to have occurred because of the group's hope to remain united in afterlife.

Religions usually favor survival of their believers. This is not always true, though, and is true to differing degrees. It has been estimated that there have been more than 100,000 different religious faiths since humankind began. Obviously most have vanished.

Some religions are even contrary to the survival needs of their believers. The Shaker religion, which disallows sexual intercourse to any of its participants, is an example. Shakerism lasted in this country for no more than two centuries. It flourished in the 19th century, but only a very few believers exist today. With no new recruits, it seems doomed to extinction. This, Wilson argued, is always the case for those religions that do not somehow enhance the vitality and hardiness of the groups that support them. The constant pursuit of a better chance for survival is why new ones are started.

Religions, according to the sociobiological point of view, develop through three steps:

objectification
Wilson's term for the person's perception of reality.

1. **Objectification.** First, a perception of reality is described. Objectification occurs, which includes images and definitions that are easy to understand. Examples are good versus evil, heaven versus hell, and the control of the forces of nature by a god or gods.

commitment
According to Wilson, people devote their lives to objectified ideas; they are willing under any circumstances to help those who have done the same.

2. **Commitment.** People devote their lives to these objectified ideas. Out of this commitment, they are willing under any circumstances to help those who have done the same.

mythification
According to Wilson, stories are developed that tell why members of a religion have a special place in the world. These stories are rational and enhance the person's understanding of the physical as well as the spiritual world.

3. **Mythification.** In mythification, stories are developed that tell why the members of the religion have a special place in the world. These stories are rational and enhance the person's understanding of the physical as well as spiritual world. The stories include explanations of how and why the world, as well as the religion, came to be. In earlier, less sophisticated religions, the faith is said to have been founded at the same time as the beginning of the race. These rarely include all-powerful or all-knowing gods. In less than one-third of the known religions is there a highly placed god, and in even fewer is there a notion of a moral god who has created the world. In the later religions, God is always seen as male, and almost always as the shepherd of a flock.

Not surprisingly, Wilson saw science as taking the place of theology today, because science has explained natural forces more effectively than theology. In fact, he asserted that science has explained theology itself. Although he saw theology as being phased out, he argued that the demise of religion is not at all likely. As long as religions make people more likely to survive and propagate themselves, Wilson suggested, they will enjoy worldwide popularity.

Wilson's theory attempted to explain spiritual development within societies. Theologian James Fowler has offered a description of the development of faith throughout the life cycle of individuals without regard to the culture in which faith forms.

Fowler's Theory of Spirituality

James Fowler (1993, 2000) offered a theoretical framework built on the ideas of Piaget, Erikson, and Kohlberg. He believed strongly that cognitive and emotional needs are inseparable in the development of spirituality. Spirituality cannot develop faster than intellectual ability and depends on the development of personality. Thus, Fowler's theory of faith development integrates the role of the unconscious, of needs, of personal strivings, and of cognitive growth. As he described it (1993),

> *Faith develops with the establishment of new centers of value, new images of power, and new master stories that coalesce in stages and advance toward a point where there is maximal individuation of the self and corresponding minimization of the personal ego as the point from which evaluations are made.* (p. 27)

Fowler saw faith developing in six steps. He said that the stages in faith development can be delayed indefinitely, but the person must have reached at least a certain minimal age at each stage in order to move on to a succeeding stage. His six stages are as follows:

1. **Intuitive-projective faith.** For intuitive-projective faith, the minimal age is 4 years. In this stage, the individual focuses on surface qualities, as portrayed by adult models. This stage depends to a great extent on fantasy. Conceptions of God or another Supreme Being reflect a belief in magic.

2. **Mythical-literal faith.** For mythical-literal faith, minimal age is 5 to 6 years. Fantasy ceases to be a primary source of knowledge at this stage, and verification of facts becomes necessary. Verification of truth comes not from actual experience but from such authorities as teachers, parents, books, and tradition. Faith in this stage is mainly concrete and depends heavily on stories told by highly credible storytellers. For example, the traditional story of Adam and Eve is taken quite literally.

3. **Poetic-conventional faith.** For poetic-conventional faith, minimal age is 12 to 13 years. The child is entering Piaget's codification stage. Faith is still conventional and depends on a consensus of opinion of other, more authoritative persons. Now the person moves away from family influence and into new relationships. Faith begins to provide a coherent and meaningful synthesis of these relationships.

   Individuals become aware of symbolism and realize that there is more than one way of knowing truth. Learned facts are still taken as the main source of information, but individuals in stage 3 begin to trust their own judgment and the quality of selected authorities. Nevertheless, they do not yet place full confidence in their own judgment.

4. **Individuating-reflective faith.** For individuating-reflective faith, minimal age is 18 to 19 years. Youths in stage 3 are unable to synthesize new areas of experience because depending on others in the community does not always solve problems. Individuals in stage 4 begin to assume responsibility for their own beliefs, attitudes, commitments, and lifestyle. The faith learned in earlier stages is now disregarded, and greater attention is paid to one's own experience. Those individuals who still need authority figures have a tendency to join and become completely devoted to clubs and cults.

5. **Paradoxical-consolidation faith.** For paradoxical-consolidation faith, minimal age is 30. In this stage such elements of faith as symbols, rituals, and beliefs start to become understood and consolidated. The person begins to realize that other approaches to dealing with such complex questions as the supernatural and Supreme Being can be as valid as his or her own. The individual at this stage considers all people to belong to the same universal community and has a true regard for the kinship of all people.

6. **Universalizing faith.** For universalizing faith, minimal age is 40 years. As with Kohlberg's final stage, very few people ever reach this level. Here the individual lives in the real world but is not of it. Such persons do not merely

intuitive-projective faith
First developmental stage of Fowler's theory of faith. In this stage, the individual focuses on surface qualities, as portrayed by adult models.

mythical-literal faith
Second developmental stage of Fowler's theory of faith. Fantasy ceases to be a primary source of knowledge at this stage, and verification of facts becomes necessary.

poetic-conventional faith
Third developmental stage of Fowler's theory of faith. Faith is still conventional and depends on a consensus of opinion of other, more authoritative persons.

individuating-reflective faith
Fourth developmental stage of Fowler's theory of faith. Individuals in stage 4 begin to assume responsibility for their own beliefs, attitudes, commitments, and lifestyle.

paradoxical-consolidation faith
Fifth developmental stage of Fowler's theory of faith. In this stage, such elements of faith as symbols, rituals, and beliefs start to become understood and consolidated.

universalizing faith
Sixth developmental stage of Fowler's theory of faith. Final developmental step of Fowler's theory of faith. Here the individual lives in the real world but is not of it. Such persons do not merely recognize the mutuality of existence; they act on the basis of it.

recognize the mutuality of existence; they act on the basis of it. People at this stage appear to be truly genuine and lack the need to "save face" that exists at the lower stages.

Stage 6, as described by Fowler, compares closely with a hypothetical stage 7 of morality proposed by Kohlberg (see Chapter 9). Although he never found anyone at a stage 7 level of morality, Kohlberg believed that theoretically there should be a stage for those few persons who rise above the purely cognitive and achieve a place where they transcend logic. These individuals, who are rare indeed, come to understand why one should be just and ethical in a world that is unjust. A burning love of universal humankind presses them always to act in truly moral ways.

The development of spirituality and morality appears to be parallel all along the sequence, especially in the Kohlberg and Fowler models. At the early levels, the orientation is basically selfish; ethical thinking and behavior are virtually non-existent. The child is "good" only to please more powerful persons.

At the second two levels, concern for the opinion of the community in general takes over. "What will people think?" is uppermost in religion as well as in moral decisions. Only if and when the highest levels are reached do true spirituality and morality emerge. And for a few individuals at the highest level, the distinction between the moral and the spiritual no longer exists.

Why do people vary so much in level of spirituality? Can the biopsychosocial model help us answer this question? Do you believe that Fowler's ideas would apply to Eastern cultures? What's your opinion?

Religion is for those who are afraid to go to Hell. Spirituality is for those who have already been there.

—AN ELDERLY RECOVERING ALCOHOLIC

Guided Review

17. _____ is concerned with whether life is worth living and why it is worth living.

18. For many Americans, religion is connected to spirituality. The influence of religion appears to be highly related to a sense of _____ in elderly persons.

19. Victor Frankl looked at spirituality, and especially the third, or _____, dimension, as directed toward transcending training and aspiring to higher levels of thought and behavior.

20. Carl Jung saw life in two halves, with the _____ second half of life directed toward finding meaning and _____, as well as preparing for death.

21. Wilson argues that the evolutionary, or survival, value of spirituality develops in three stages. These stages are objectification, commitment, and _____.

22. Fowler, like Piaget, Erikson, and Kohlberg, included stages of development and a _____ age for each stage in his theory of faith development.

23. Fowler sees faith developing in six stages: intuitive-projective, _____, poetic-conventional, individuating-reflective, paradoxical-consolidation, and _____.

Answers

CONCLUSION & SUMMARY

"The distinction between the moral and the spiritual no longer exists." What a wonderful goal to choose as a means of living the good life. It is probably also the best way to ensure a successful death. We sincerely hope that having read this book will contribute in some small way to your achievement of those two preeminent goals!

What is the role of death in life?

- Today, four types of death are recognized: clinical death, brain death, biological or cellular death, and social death.
- In modern Western societies, death comes mostly to the old.

What is the purpose of "grief work"?

- Grief both follows and can precede the death of a loved one.
- In some cases, morbid grief reactions occur that prevent the successful conclusion of the life crisis. These are known as delayed reactions, distorted reactions, and pathological reactions.
- Most psychologists who have examined the role of grief have concluded that it is a healthy aspect of the crisis of death.
- Funerals have always been an important part of American life. Research has indicated that the rituals surrounding funerals have therapeutic benefits that facilitate the grieving process.
- Kübler-Ross has offered five stages of dying: shock and denial, anger, bargaining, depression, and acceptance.

What are the factors that cause and determine the nature of suicide?

- Suicide rates for those over 75 is double that of adolescents, with older white males most likely to take their lives.
- Males and females are very different regarding suicide, with men being more likely to die than women.

What is the meaning of "successful dying"?

- The hospice movement and death with dignity legislation have provided people with more control over their own death, making it a bit easier to accept.

How do psychologists define the nature of spirituality?

- In recent decades, participation in religious activities has been changing in a number of ways.
- The elderly practice their religions to a greater degree than other adults.
- Theories of spirituality have been presented by Frankl, Jung, Wilson, and Fowler.
- Fowler has incorporated the work of Erikson, Piaget, and Kohlberg in his theory of the development of faith, which proceeds through six stages.

KEY TERMS

anima
animus
biological death
brain death
cardiopulmonary resuscitation (CPR)
clinical death
commitment

electroencephalogram (EEG)
euthanasia
hospice
individuating-reflective faith
intuitive-projective faith
legal death
mythical-literal faith

mythification
objectification
paradoxical-consolidation faith
physician-assisted suicide (PAS)
poetic-conventional faith
social death
universalizing faith

WHAT DO YOU THINK?

1. It has been suggested that people in Western society typically are more fearful of death than are members of Eastern cultures. If so, what factors contribute to our more frightened attitude?

2. Most of us think of grief as something that happens to us. Do you think it makes sense to describe it as "work"?

3. How do you feel about the idea of "successful death"?

4. Are there some old people—those who have lost their spouse and all their friends or those who are undeniably terminal—who should be allowed to take their own lives? Should these people be helped to have a "ceremony of death"?

5. In this chapter we have suggested two ways of making death more dignified. Can you think of any others?

6. Are you satisfied with your own level of religious participation? What do you think you should do differently?

7. How would you define your own spirituality?

8. Fowler states that there is a certain minimal age for each of his stages of spiritual development. What kinds of experience do you think would move a person from one stage to the next?

CHAPTER REVIEW TEST

1. **If brain death occurs, a person still remains alive in this condition because**
   a. autoplasia stimulates the autonomic processes.
   b. neuroplasia stimulates the autonomic processes.
   c. the autonomic processes are governed by the brain stem.
   d. the autonomic processes are governed by the cortex.

2. **Legal death occurs when**
   a. respiration and heartbeat have stopped.
   b. the brain fails to receive sufficient amount of oxygen.
   c. there is an unreceptivity and unresponsivity, no movements or breathing, no reflexes, and a flat electroencephalogram reading that remains flat for 24 hours.
   d. it is no longer possible to discern an electrical charge in the tissues of the heart and lung.

3. **The phases of anticipatory grief are**
   a. depression, a heightened concern for the ill person, a rehearsal of death, and an attempt to adjust to the consequences that are likely to occur after the death.
   b. depression and rehearsal of death.
   c. a heightened concern for the ill person, a rehearsal of death, and an attempt to adjust to the consequences that are likely to occur after the death.
   d. depression, a heightened concern for the ill person, and a rehearsal of death.

4. **Knowledge of the impending death of a loved one can have which therapeutic consequence?**
   a. avoidance of shock
   b. ability to plan for the future
   c. time to prepare for impending changes
   d. all of the answers are correct.

5. **According to Kübler-Ross's theory, dying need not be a(n) _____ experience.**
   a. religious
   b. unexpected

   c. unhappy
   d. expensive

6. **A young man, whose father died from lung cancer, is displaying grief known as distorted reaction. He has**
   a. experienced grieving stages that are prolonged and intensified to an abnormal degree.
   b. developed some of the same symptoms his father had, which his doctor determined were entirely psychosomatic.
   c. created a shrine in memory of his father.
   d. experienced anticipatory grief.

7. **Why do many dying patients feel depressed before their deaths?**
   a. medication-induced mood alterations
   b. feelings of isolation from relatives and friends who are withdrawing
   c. awareness of how little time is left
   d. all the answers are correct.

8. **Of all adult groups, older single white males are the most likely to die of**
   a. cancer.
   b. heart disease.
   c. accident.
   d. suicide.

9. **The law that grants an adult the right to instruct his or her physician to withhold or withdraw life-sustaining procedures in the event of a terminal condition is known as a**
   a. "right to life" law.
   b. "living will" law.
   c. "death with dignity" law.
   d. None of the answers is correct.

10. **Home-based care for the dying is known as the**
    a. Visiting Nurses program.
    b. hospice program.
    c. behavioral medicine program.
    d. home-health program.

11. **Whether life is worth living and why it is worth living are the major premises of**
    a. spirituality.
    b. religion.
    c. separation anxiety.
    d. None of the answers is correct.

12. **In what stage in Frankl's theory of spirituality are persons motivated by the struggle to keep themselves alive and to help the species survive?**
    a. somatic dimension
    b. psychological dimension
    c. noetic dimension
    d. none of the answers is correct.

13. **In Fowler's theory of spirituality, stages in _____ can be delayed indefinitely, but the person must have reached a certain minimal age at each stage to move on to a succeeding stage.**
    a. psychological growth
    b. spiritual belief
    c. faith development
    d. commitment

14. **According to Fowler, what is the minimal age at which a person can gain universalizing faith?**
    a. 12 to 13 years old
    b. 18 to 19 years old
    c. 30 years old
    d. 40 years old

15. **According to Jung, by the age of 35, most people are well**
    a. established.
    b. prepared for life's work.
    c. individuated.
    d. on their way to developing a wholeness of personality.

16. **The sociobiological point of view states that we develop religion through what steps?**
    a. objectification, commitment, mythification
    b. commitment and mythification
    c. objectification and mythification
    d. objection and commitment

Answers

Glossary

A

absorbent mind   Montessori's term for a child's ability to absorb experiences from the environment (0–6 years).

accommodation   Piaget's term to describe the manner by which cognitive structures change.

accumulation of errors   As cells die, they must synthesize new proteins to make new cells. As this is done, occasionally an error occurs. Over time, these errors mount up and may finally grow serious enough to cause organ failure.

accumulation of metabolic waste   Waste products resulting from metabolism build up in various parts of the body.

activity theory   Human beings who are able to keep up the social activity of their middle years are considered the most successful.

adaptation   One of the two functional in-variants in Piaget's theory.

adolescent egocentrism   Reversion to the self-centered thinking patterns of childhood that sometimes occurs in the teen years.

adoption   To take a child of other parents voluntarily as one's own.

Adult Attachment Interview (AAI) Evaluates adults' responses to questions about attachment.

afterbirth   Stage three of the birth process, during which the placenta and other membranes are discharged.

ageism   Prejudice that the elderly are inferior to those who are younger.

aggression   Hostile or destructive behavior directed at another person.

aging by program   Theory that all animals seem to die when their "program" dictates.

AIDS (Acquired Immune Deficiency Syndrome)   Condition caused by the HIV virus, which can invade a newborn baby's immune system, thus making it vulnerable to infections and life-threatening illnesses.

alarm reaction   Selye's term for a "call to arms" of the body's defensive forces.

alleles   Different forms of a gene.

amniocentesis   Process of fetal testing that entails inserting a needle through the mother's abdomen, piercing the amniotic sac, and withdrawing a sample of the amniotic fluid.

amniotic sac   Fluid-filled uterine sac that surrounds the embryo/fetus.

anal stage   Freud's belief that the anus is the main source of pleasure during the years 1 1/2 to 3 years.

androgyny   Functional level of gender-role identifications that incorporates male and female qualities.

anima   Female side of the personality; males tend to repress it until later in life.

animism   Children consider inert objects as alive and conscious; a form of Piagetian preoperational thinking.

animus   Male side of the personality; females tend to repress it until later in life.

anorexia nervosa   Syndrome of self-starvation that mainly affects adolescent and young adult females.

anoxia (lack of oxygen)   Condition involving lack of oxygen, which possibly can cause fetal brain damage or death, even during birth.

anticipatory images   Piaget's term for images (which include movements and transformation) that enable the child to anticipate change.

antigens   Substances in the blood that produce antibodies, which kill them.

apgar   A scale to evaluate a newborn's basic life signs administered 1 minute after birth and repeated at 3-, 5-, and 10-minute intervals; it uses five life signs: heart rate, respiratory effort, muscle tone, reflex irritability, skin color

apnea   Brief periods when breathing is suspended.

artificial insemination by donor (AID) Injection of sperm into woman.

artificialism   Children attribute human life to inanimate objects; a form of Piagetian preoperational thinking.

assimilation   Piaget's term to describe the manner in which we incorporate data into our cognitive structures.

assisted reproduction technologies (ART) Fertilization occurs with help and outside the woman's body.

attachment   Behavior intended to keep a child (or adult) in close proximity to a significant other.

au pair   Young woman from another country who provides child care services.

authoritarian parenting   Parents strive for complete control over their children's behavior by establishing complex sets of rules.

authoritarian parents   Baumrind's term for parents are who demanding and want instant obedience as the most desirable child trait

authoritative parents   Baumrind's term for parents who respond to their children's needs and wishes; believing in parental control, they attempt to explain the reasons for it to their children.

autoimmunity   Process by which the immune system in the body rejects the body's own tissue.

autonomy   Infants' realization that they have a share in controlling their interactions with others.

autosexuality   Stage at which the child becomes aware of sexual pleasure and consciously experiments with masturbation.

B

babbling   Infant produces sounds approximating speech between 5 and 6 months.

basal metabolism rate (BMR)   The minimum amount of energy an individual tends to use when in a resting state.

battered child syndrome   Kempe and associates' term for classic physical abuse of children.

bend-and-bond response   The more typically female response to threats is to seek a compromise, rather than the male response of "fight-or-flight."

bilingual immersion   Students are taught partly in English and partly in their own language.

bioecological model   The belief that the interactions between person and environment are best explained by systems analysis.

biological death   Occurs when it is no longer possible to discern an electrical charge in the tissues of the heart and lungs.

biopsychosocial interactions   The idea that development proceeds by the interaction of biological, psychological, and social forces.

biopsychosocial theory of homosexuality   Theory that some factor in a person's DNA affects temperament, which affects sexual orientation.

blastocyst   The fertilized egg when it reaches the uterus (about 7 days after conception).

brain death   Occurs when the brain fails to receive a sufficient supply of oxygen for a short period of time (usually 8 to 10 minutes).

Brazelton Neonatal Assessment Scale   Device to assess an infant's behavior; examines both neurological and psychological responses.

breech birth   Birth in which the baby is born feet first, buttocks first, or in a crosswise position (transverse presentation).

bulimia nervosa   Disorder is characterized by "episodic binge eating accompanied by an awareness that the eating pattern is abnormal, fear of not being able to stop eating voluntarily, and depressed mood and self-deprecating thoughts following the eating binges."

bully   Cruel, bossy person who has aggressive reaction patterns and considerable physical strength.

C

capacitation   Removal of layer surrounding sperm.

cardiopulmonary resuscitation (CPR)   Technique for reviving an individual's lungs and heart that have ceased to function.

cellular differentiation   Embryonic cells are destined for specific functions and thus differentiate themselves.

centration   Feature of preoperational thought—the centering of attention on one aspect of an object and the neglecting of any other features.

cesarean section   Surgery performed to deliver the baby through the abdomen if for some reason the child cannot come through the birth canal.

child abuse   Infliction of injury to a child; commonly includes physical abuse, sexual abuse, emotional maltreatment, and neglect.

chlamydia   Bacterial infection that may cause infertility; now the most common STI, there often are no symptoms.

cholesterol   Substance in the blood (including HDLs and LDLs) that may adhere to the walls of the blood vessels, restricting the flow of blood and causing strokes and heart attacks.

chorionic villi sampling (CVS)   Fetal-testing procedure in which a catheter (small tube) is inserted through the vagina to the uterine villi, and a small section is suctioned into the tube.

chromosome failure   Biological changes such as enlarged breasts in males and abnormal body hair in females.

chromosomes   Stringlike bodies that carry the genes; they are present in all body cells.

classification   Process by which children in the concrete operational period can group objects with some similarities within a larger category.

climacteric   Relatively abrupt change in the body, brought about by changes in hormonal balances.

climacterium   Loss of reproductive ability.

clinical death   The individual is dead when his or her respiration and heartbeat have stopped.

closed adoption   Natural parents knew nothing about the adopting parents.

cognitive structures   Piaget's term to describe the basic tools of cognitive development.

collagen   Major connective tissue in the body; it provides the elasticity in our skin and blood vessels.

color blindness   Usually X-linked red/green color blindness.

commitment   (1) According to Wilson, people devote their lives to objectified ideas; they are willing under any circumstances to help those who have done the same; (2) Sternberg's term for the strongly held conviction that one will stay with another, regardless of the cost. (3) Third phase in Perry's theory, in which the individual realizes that certainty is impossible but that commitment to a certain position is necessary, even without certainty.

competence   Measure of children's level of self-esteem; related to scholastic competence, athletic competence, peer popularity, physical appearance, and behavior.

concrete operational period   Piaget's third stage of cognitive development, during which children begin to employ logical thought processes with concrete material.

conservation   The understanding that an object retains certain properties, no matter how its form changes.

constructed knowledge   Belenky's fifth phase of women's thinking; characterized by an integration of the subjective and procedural ways of knowing (Perry's types 3 and 4).

continuity   The lasting quality of experiences; development proceeds steadily and sequentially.

controlled scribbling   Drawing in which children carefully watch what they are doing, when before they looked away (random scribbling).

convergent thinking   Thinking used to find one correct answer.

cooing   Early language sounds that resemble vowels.

coordination of secondary schemes Infants combine secondary schemes to obtain a goal; term associated with Piaget's theory.

crawling Locomotion whereby the infant's abdomen touches the floor and the weight of the head and shoulders rests on the elbows.

creeping Movement on hands and knees; the trunk does not touch the ground; creeping appears from 9 months in most youngsters.

cross-linkage theory Proteins that make up a large part of cells are composed of peptides. When cross-links are formed between peptides, the proteins are altered, often for the worse.

crossover Older men become more like women, and older women become more like men.

cross-sectional studies Compares groups of individuals of various ages at the same time in order to investigate the effects of aging.

crowds Groups known for certain values, attitudes, or activities.

cryopreservation Freezing embryos for future use.

crystallized intelligence Involves perceiving relationships, educing correlates, reasoning, abstracting, concept of attainment, and problem solving.

culture The values, beliefs, and behaviors characteristic of a large group of people—for example, those of Hispanic origin.

cystic fibrosis Chromosomal disorder producing a malfunction of the exocrine glands.

cytogenetics The study of chromosomes.

cytomegalovirus (CMV) Virus that can cause fetal damage ranging from mental retardation, blindness, deafness, and even death. One of the major difficulties in combating this disease is that it remains unrecognized in pregnant women.

D

day care Location providing services and care for children.

decentering Process by which children in the concrete operational period can concentrate on more than one aspect of a situation.

deferred imitation Imitative behavior that continues after the disappearance of the model to be imitated; a form of Piagetian preoperational thinking.

DES (diethylstilbestrol) In the late 1940s and 1950s, DES (a synthetic hormone) was administered to pregnant women supposedly to prevent miscarriage. It was later found that the daughters of the women who had received this treatment were more susceptible to vaginal and cervical cancer.

descriptive studies Gathered information on subjects without manipulating them in any way.

despair When people look back over their lives and feel that they have made many wrong decisions or, more commonly, that they have not made any decisions at all.

developing readers Children who are beginning to understand the relationship between sound and symbol and pay close attention to the print in their efforts at decoding.

development The changes that occur in the lifespan.

developmental risk Threat to children who may be susceptible to problems because of some physical or psychological difficulty ("at-risk" children).

developmental systems theory Set of beliefs leading to the conclusion that we construct our own views of the world.

developmentally delayed Term that describes children who experience a developmental lag because of either physical or psychological causes; these children usually "catch up."

diethylstilbestrol Drug earlier administered to pregnant women to help them hold embryo or fetus; later found to increase the risk of genital cancer in the daughters of these women.

difficult children Restless, irritable children; term associated with Chess and Thomas.

dilation Stage one of the birth process during which the cervix dilates to about 4 inches in diameter.

discontinuity Behaviors that are apparently unrelated to earlier aspects of development.

disengagement theory The most mature adults are likely to gradually disengage themselves from their fellow human beings in preparation for death.

distantiation The readiness of all of us to distance ourselves from others when we feel threatened by their behavior.

divergent thinking Thinking used when a problem to be solved has many possible answers.

dizygotic twin Nonidentical twin.

DNA Deoxyribonucleic acid; the chemical structure of the gene that accounts for our inherited characteristics.

dominance Phenotypes of both alleles.

dominant Tendency of a gene to be expressed in a trait.

Down syndrome Genetic abnormality caused by a deviation on the twenty-first pair of chromosomes.

drawing According to Piaget, a skill that indicates a growing symbolic ability.

dual-career family Family in which both the mother and the father are working, usually full time.

dualism Perry's initial phase of ethical development, in which "things are either absolutely right or absolutely wrong."

dual-process model Model of intelligence that says there may be a decline in the mechanics of intelligence, such as classification skills and logical reasoning, but that the pragmatics are likely to increase.

DUPE Problem-solving model (**D**etermine a problem exists, **U**nderstand its nature, **P**lan for its solution, and **E**valuate the solution).

E

early-onset trajectory Refers to criminal behavior that begins before puberty.

easy children Calm, relaxed children; term associated with Chess and Thomas.

ectoderm Outer layer of the embryo that gives rise to the nervous system, among other developmental features.

ectopic pregnancy Pregnancy in which the fertilized egg attempts to develop in one of the fallopian tubes (outside the uterus); this is sometimes referred to as a *tubal pregnancy*.

egg donation Woman either donates or sells eggs.

ego One of the three structures of the psyche according to Freud; mediates between the id and the superego.

egocentric speech Piaget's term to describe children's speech when they do not care to whom they speak or whether a listener is even present.

egocentrism Child focuses on self in early phases of cognitive development; term associated with Piaget.

electroencephalogram (EEG) Graphic record of the electrical activity of the brain.

ELSI (Ethical, Legal, and Social Implications) Program designed to study the ethical, social, and legal implications of the Human Genome Project.

embryo transfer Form of assisted reproduction (GIFT).

embryonic period Third through the eighth week following fertilization.

embryonic stem cells Cells from the inner cell mass that have the potential to become any cell in the body.

emergent readers Children who can identify letters and recognize some common words; they know what books "do," and they attempt to read by using semantic and syntactic cues.

emotional divorce Sometimes partners learn to "withstand" each other, rather than live with each other. The only activities and interests that they shared were ones that revolved around the children.

emotional maltreatment Emotional ill-treatment; a form of child abuse.

empty nest syndrome Refers to the feelings parents may have as a result of their last child leaving home.

endoderm Inner layer of the embryo that gives rise to the lungs, liver, and pancreas, among other developmental features.

entrainment Term used to describe the rhythm that is established between a parent's and an infant's behavior.

equilibration Piaget's term to describe the balance between assimilation and accommodation.

escape Others refuse responsibility for making any commitments because everyone's opinion is "equally right."

ESL English as a Second Language.

ethology Study of behavior in natural settings.

euthanasia A "good death"; there are two types: passive euthanasia, in which the patient's legal instructions are carried out by the medical team, and active euthanasia, in which the patient's life is ended in ways that are now illegal.

evolutionary psychology Explanation of development that rests on the assumption that our physiological and psychological systems resulted from evolution by selection.

existential love The capacity to cherish the present moment, perhaps first learned when we confront the certainty of our own personal death.

exosystem Environment in which the developing person is not present but that nevertheless affects the person's development.

expressive language Language that children use to express their own ideas and needs.

expulsion Stage two of the birth process, during which the baby passes through the birth canal.

extinction Refers to the process by which conditioned responses are lost.

F

failure-To-Thrive (FTT) Condition in which the weight and height of infants consistently remain far below normal (the bottom 3% of height and weight measures).

fallopian tubes Passageway for the egg once it is discharged from the ovary's surface.

fast mapping Mental process whereby children use context to detect word meanings.

feminist movement The efforts of some women to secure more equitable standards in workplace, society, and home.

fetal alcohol syndrome (FAS) Refers to condition of babies whose mothers drank alcohol during pregnancy; babies manifest four clusters of symptoms: psychological functioning, growth factors, physical features, and structural effects.

fetal period Period extending from the beginning of the third gestational month to birth.

fetoscopy Procedure in which a tiny viewing instrument called a *fetoscope* is inserted into the amniotic cavity making it possible to see the fetus.

five factor model (FFM) of personality McCrae and Costa's theory that there are five major personality traits, which they believe govern the adult personality.

fluid intelligence Involves perceiving relationships, educing correlates, maintaining span of immediate awareness in reasoning, abstracting, concept formation, and problem solving.

forceps delivery Procedure in which the physician, for safety, withdraws the baby with forceps during the first phase of birth.

fragile X syndrome Sex-linked inheritance disorder in which the bottom half of the X chromosome looks as if it is ready to fall off; causes mental retardation in 80% of the cases.

friend Nonfamilial relationship that offers feelings of warmth and support.

functional invariants In Piaget's theory, the psychological mechanisms of adaptation and organization.

G

games with rules According to Piaget, games typical of the 7–11-year period.

gamete intrafallopian transfer (GIFT) Sperm and egg are placed in fallopian tube.

gender identity The conviction that one is either male or female.

gender revolution Levinson's term; the meanings of gender are changing and becoming more similar.

gender role Sexual behavior acceptable within one's culture.

gender splitting Levinson's term; all societies support the idea that there should be a clear difference between what is considered appropriate for males and for females; gender splitting appears to be universal.

gender stereotype Narrow beliefs about the characteristics associated with being male or female.

gene Inherited trait determined by the elements of heredity that are transmitted from parents to offspring in reproduction.

gene theory Theory that aging is due to certain harmful genes.

general adaptation syndrome Set of reactions that occur in animals in response to all toxic substances; involves three stages: alarm, resistance, and exhaustion.

generative love Most characteristic of parenthood, a time during which sacrifices are gladly made for the sake of the children.

generativity Erikson's term for the ability to be useful to ourselves and to society.

genital herpes Incurable sexually transmitted infection, with about 500,000 new cases every year.

genital stage According to Freud, the belief in a resurgence of a strong sex drive from 12 years and beyond.

genotype Individual's genetic composition.

germinal period First two weeks following fertilization.

gonorrhea Well-known venereal infection accounting for between 1.5 and 2 million cases per year.

goodness of fit   Compatibility between parental and child behavior; how well parents and their children get along.

group marriage   Marriage that includes two or more of both husbands and wives, who all exercise common privileges and responsibilities.

H

habituation   Process in which stimuli that are presented frequently cause a decrease in an infant's attention.

halo effect   Assigning a high grade to students because of their appearance (neat, attractive).

hazing   The practice of initiating individuals into group membership through arduous and demeaning tasks.

head start   Early intervention program intended to provide educational and developmental services to disadvantaged children.

hemophilia   Genetic condition causing incorrect blood clotting; called the "bleeder's disease."

hepatitis B   Viral infection transmitted through sex or shared needles.

herpes simplex   Infection that can be contracted by a child during birth; the child can develop the symptoms during the first week following the birth. The eyes and the nervous system are most susceptible to this disease.

heterosexuality   Love of members of the opposite sex.

holophrase   Children's first words, which usually carry multiple meanings.

holophrastic speech   Use of one word to communicate many meanings and ideas.

homelessness   Those who live in shelters, or on the street, or in parks.

homeopathic treatments   Natural, alternative options for health care and management. Remedies often include herbal supplements.

homeostatic imbalance   Theory that aging is due to a failure in the systems that regulate the proper interaction of the organs.

homosexual marriages   Though not accepted legally everywhere, the weddings of homosexuals are now accepted by some religions.

homosexuality   Love of members of one's own sex.

hormonal balance   One of the triggering mechanisms of puberty that may be used to indicate the onset of adolescence.

hormone replacement therapy (HRT)   Hormone therapy prescribed to treat the symptoms associated with menopause; it usually involves low-dose estrogen.

hospice   Services aimed at relieving suffering of terminally ill patients.

Human Genome Project   Process of identifying and mapping the 50,000 to 100,000 genes that constitute the human genetic endowment.

human immunodeficiency virus (HIV)   Virus that leads to AIDS.

I

id   One of the three structures of the psyche according to Freud; the source of our instinctive desires.

identity crisis   Erikson's term for those situations, usually in adolescence, that cause us to make major decisions about our identity.

identity status   Marcia's four aspects of identity formation.

imaginary audience   Adolescents' perception that the world is constantly scrutinizing their behavior and physical appearance.

imitative behavior   The tendency of infants to mimic the behavior of others.

implantation   Fertilized egg attaches and secures itself to uterine wall.

impotency   Inability to engage in the sexual act.

impulsivity   Child's lack of ability to delay gratification.

in vitro fertilization   Fertilization that occurs "in the dish"; an assisted fertilization technique.

incomplete dominance   A genetic trait is not fully expressed.

independent readers   Children who can read ably and without assistance using all the cueing systems.

individuating-reflective faith   Fourth developmental stage of Fowler's theory of faith; individuals in stage 4 begin to assume responsibility for their own beliefs, attitudes, commitments, and lifestyle.

individuation   Refers to our becoming more individual; we develop a separate and special personality, derived less and less from our parents and teachers and more from our own behavior.

infantile amnesia   Our inability to recall events from early in life.

infertility   Inability to achieve pregnancy after two years.

inner speech   Serves to guide and plan behavior; plays a critical role in Vygotsky's interpretation of cognitive developments.

instrumental conditioning   Skinner's form of conditioning, in which a reinforcement follows the desired response; also known as *operant conditioning*.

integrity   The resolution of each of the first seven crises in Erikson's theory should lead us to achieve a sense of personal integrity. Older adults who have a sense of integrity feel their lives have been well spent.

interindividual differences   Differences among individuals.

internal fertilization   Natural process in which fertilization occurs within the woman.

intimacy   (1) Erikson's stage that represents the ability to relate one's deepest hopes and fears to another person and to accept another's need for intimacy in turn. (2) Sternberg's term for the ability to share one's deepest and most secret feelings and thoughts with another.

intracytoplasmic sperm injection (ICSI)   Sperm is injected directly into egg.

intraindividual   Differences in the potential for change within an individual.

intrauterine device   Usually a plastic loop inserted into the uterus as a contraceptive device.

intuitive-projective faith   First developmental stage of Fowler's theory of faith. In this stage, the individual focuses on surface qualities, as portrayed by adult models.

irreversibility   Inability to reverse thinking, that is, to solve a problem and then proceed in reverse, tracing the steps back to the original question or premise.

isolation   The readiness all of us have to isolate ourselves from others when we feel threatened by their behavior.

K

Klinefelter syndrome   XXY chromosomal pattern in males.

knowledge-acquisition components   Sternberg's term for intelligence components that help us to learn how to solve problems in the first place.

L

language   According to Piaget, a vehicle for thought for preoperational children.

latency stage   Freud's belief that the sex drive becomes dormant from age 5 to 12.

late-onset trajectory   Refers to criminal behavior that begins after puberty.

learning   Process that results in the modification of behavior.

learning theory of homosexuality   Belief that homosexuality is the result of learned experiences from significant others.

legal death   Condition defined as "unreceptivity and unresponsivity, no movements or breathing, no reflexes, and a flat electroencephalogram (EEG) reading that remains flat for 24 hours."

life course   Levinson's term; life refers to all aspects of living—everything that has significance in a life; course refers to the flow or unfolding of an individual's life.

Life Course Theory   Theory referring to a sequence of socially defined, age-graded events and roles that individuals enact over time.

life cycle   Levinson's term; the life cycle is a general pattern of adult development, whereas the life course is the unique embodiment of the life cycle by an individual.

life structure   The underlying pattern or design of a person's life at a given time.

lifespan psychology   Study of human development from conception to death.

longitudinal studies   Studies whereby the experimenter makes several observations of the same individuals at two or more times in their lives. Examples are determining the long-term effects of learning on behavior; the stability of habits and intelligence; and the factors involved in memory.

M

macrosystem   The blueprint of any society.

manipulative experiments   The experimenter attempts to keep all variables (all the factors that can affect a particular outcome) constant except one, which is carefully manipulated.

meiosis   Cell division in which the number of chromosomes is halved.

menarche   Onset of menstruation.

menopause   Cessation of menstruation.

mental images   Internal representation of people, objects, or events.

mesoderm   Middle layer of the embryo that gives rise to muscles, skeleton, excretory system.

mesosystem   Relationship among microsystems.

metacomponents   Sternberg's term for intelligence components that help us to plan, monitor, and evaluate our problem-solving strategies.

microsystem   Home or school.

mid-life transition   Levinson's term for the phase that usually lasts for five years and generally extends from age 40 to 45.

mid-career crisis   Stage that some persons go through in middle age during which they come to question their career and personal goals and dreams.

miscarriage   Term that describes the spontaneous ending of a pregnancy before the 20th week.

mitosis   Cell division in which the number of chromosomes remains the same.

modeling   Bandura's term for observational learning.

monogamy   Standard marriage form in the United States and most other nations, in which there is one husband and one wife.

monozygotic twin   Identical twin.

moral dilemma   Modified clinical technique used by Kohlberg whereby a conflict is posed for which subjects justify the morality of their choices.

motherese   Using simplified vocabulary and a high-pitched voice with young children.

motor skills   Skills (both gross and fine) resulting from physical development enabling children to perform smooth and coordinated physical acts.

multiple intelligences   Gardner's theory that attributes eight types of intelligence to humans.

mutations   Abrupt hereditary changes.

mythical-literal faith   Second development stage of Fowler's theory of faith; fantasy ceases to be a primary source of knowledge at this stage, and verification of facts becomes necessary.

mythification   According to Wilson, stories are developed that tell why members of a religion have a special place in the world. These stories are rational and enhance the person's understanding of the physical as well as the spiritual world.

N

nanny   Professional child care provider, frequently a former nurse.

naturalistic experiments   The reseacher acts solely as an observer and does as little as possible to disturb the environment. "Nature" performs the experiment, and the researcher acts as a recorder of the results.

negative reinforcement   Refers to stimuli whose withdrawal strengthens behavior.

neglect   Lack of care; a form of child abuse.

neonate   Term for an infant in the first days and weeks after birth.

neurological assessment   Identifies any neurological problem, suggests means of monitoring.

New York Longitudinal Study   Long-term study by Chess and Thomas of the personality characteristics of children.

no-fault divorce   The law that lets people get divorced without proving some atrocious act by one of the spouses. In legal language, this is known as an irretrievable breakdown of a marriage.

nonstage theorists   Those who believe that children's reading should unfold naturally, similar to language development.

novice phase   Period of ages 17–33 that includes early adult transition, according to Levinson.

numeration   Process by which children in the concrete operational period grasp the meaning of number, the oneness of one.

nurturing parenting style   Parents use indirect methods and modeling to influence their child's behavior.

O

object permanence   Refers to children gradually realizing that there are permanent objects around them, even when these objects are out of sight.

objectification   Wilson's term for the person's perception of reality.

olfactory sense   Sense of smell, which uses the olfactory nerves in the nose and tongue.

one-time, one-group studies Studies carried out only once on one group of studies.

open adoption Natural parents have considerable input into the adoption process.

operant conditioning Skinner's form of conditioning, in which a reinforcement follows the desired response; also known as instrumental conditioning.

oral stage According to Freud, the period when the mouth is the main source of pleasure 0–1 1/2 years).

organ reserve That part of the total capacity of our body's organs that we do not normally need to use.

organization (1) One of the two functional invariants in Piaget's theory. (2) Memory strategy that entails discovering and imposing an easy-to-remember structure on items to be memorized.

organogenesis Formation of organs during the embryonic period.

overextensions Children's over-broad applications of words.

overregulation Children's inappropriate use of language rules they have learned.

ovulation Egg bursts from the surface of the ovary.

P

paradoxical-consolidation faith Fifth development stage of Fowler's theory of faith; in this stage, such elements of faith as symbols, rituals, and beliefs start to become understood and consolidated.

passion Sternberg's term for a strong desire for another person and the expectation that sex with them will prove physiologically rewarding.

peers Youngsters who are similar in age, usually within 12 months of one another.

pelvic inflammatory disease (PID) Infection that often results from chlamydia or gonorrhea and frequently causes prolonged problems, including infertility.

perception Obtaining and interpreting information from stimuli.

performance components Sternberg's term for intelligence components that help us to execute the instructions of the metacomponents.

permissive parents Baumrind's term for parents who take a tolerant, accepting view of their children's behavior; they rarely make demands or use punishment and may have little or no control over their children.

personal fable Adolescents' tendency to think of themselves in heroic or mythical terms.

phallic stage According to Freud, the period when the sex organs become the main source of pleasure (3–5 years).

phenotype The observable expression of gene action.

phenylketonuria (PKU) Chromosomal disorder resulting in a failure of the body to break down the amino acid phenylalanine.

phonology A language's sound system.

physical abuse Nonaccidental physical injury to a child.

physician-assisted suicide (PAS) Doctors give patients death-inducing drugs.

placenta Uterine tissue that supplies the embryo with all its needs, carries off all its wastes, and protects it from danger.

play Activity that children engage in because they enjoy it for its own sake.

poetic-conventional faith Third development stage of Fowler's theory of faith; faith is still conventional and depends on a consensus of opinion of other, more authoritative persons.

polyandry Marriage in which there is one wife but two or more husbands.

polygamy Marriage in which there is one husband but two or more wives.

polygenic inheritance Many genes contribute to the formation of a particular trait.

positive reinforcement Process whereby stimuli whose presentation as a consequence of a response strengthens or increases the rate of the response.

postnatal period The time immediately following birth when women must adjust physically and psychologically to pregnancy and birth.

practice games According to Piaget, games that are characteristic of the sensorimotor period.

pragmatics Rules that describe how people converse.

precociousness Ability to do what others are able to do, but at a younger age.

preintellectual speech Vygotsky's expression for crying, cooing, and babbling, which lead to more sophisticated forms of speech.

prematurity Early birth; condition that occurs less than 37 weeks after conception and is defined by low birth weight and immaturity.

preoperational Piaget's second stage of cognitive development, extending from about 2 to 7 years.

prepared childbirth Combination of relaxation techniques and information about the birth process; sometimes called the *Lamaze method,* after its founder.

prepared environment Montessori's term for use of age-appropriate materials to further cognitive development.

primary circular reactions Infants repeat some act involving their bodies; term associated with Piaget's theory.

procedural knowledge Belenky's fourth phase of women's thinking; characterized by a distrust of both knowledge from authority and the female thinker's own inner authority, or "gut."

prodigiousness Ability to do qualitatively better than the rest of us are able to do; such a person is referred to as a prodigy.

Project Head Start Programs intended to provide educational and developmental services to preschool children from low-income families.

prosocial behavior Socially supportive behaviors such as friendliness, self-control, and being helpful.

prostatectomy Removal of all or part of the male prostate gland.

protective factors Characteristics of resilient individuals that protect them from stress.

proximal processes Bronfenbrenner's term for the reciprocal interactions between a person and the environment.

psychoanalytic theory Freud's theory of the development of personality.

psychoanalytic theory of homosexuality Freud's theory that if the child's first sexual feelings about the parent of the opposite sex are strongly punished, the child may develop a permanent homosexual orientation.

puberty Relatively abrupt and qualitatively different set of physical changes that normally occur at the beginning of the teen years.

punishment Usually refers to an decrease in the frequency of a response when certain unpleasant consequences immediately follow it.

R

random scribbling Drawing in which children use dots and lines with simple arm movements.

realism   Refers to when children learn to distinguish and accept the real world; a form of Piagetian preoperational thinking.

received knowledge   Belenky's second phase of women's thinking; characterized by being awed by the authorities but far less affiliated with them than in the first phase.

received knowledge   Belenky's second phase of women's thinking; characterized by being awed by the authorities but far less affiliated with them then in the first phase.

receptive language   Children's indication that they understand words without necessarily producing them.

recessive   Gene whose trait is not expressed unless paired with another recessive gene; for example, both parents contribute genes for blue eyes.

reciprocal interactions   Similar to transactional model; recognizes the child's active role in its development: I do something to the child, the child changes; as a result of the changes in the child, I change; interactions that result in mutual changes.

reflex   When a stimulus repeatedly elicits the same response.

rehearsal   Mnemonic strategy that describes a person repeating target information.

reinforcement   Usually refers to an increase in the frequency of a response when certain pleasant consequences immediately follow it.

relativism   Second phase in Perry's theory; attitude or a philosophy that says anything can be right or wrong depending on the situation; all views are equally right.

representation   Child's application of abstract thinking during Piaget's preoperational period.

reproductive images   Mental images that are faithful to the original object or event being represented; Piaget's term for images that are restricted to those sights previously perceived.

repudiation   Striving toward a state of identity means committing to one lifestyle and repudiating (giving up) all the other possibilities, at least for the present.

resilience   Ability to recover from highly stressful situations.

resilient children   Children who sustain some type of physiological or psychological trauma yet remain on a normal developmental path.

respiratory distress syndrome (RDS)   Problem common with premature babies that is caused by the lack of a substance called *surfactant,* which keeps the air sacs in the lungs open.

reticular activation system (RAS)   Complex sub-cortical system that protects the brain from being overwhelmed.

retreat   According to Perry's theory of ethical development, when someone retreats to an earlier ethical position.

retrieval   The obtaining of information from memory.

reversibility   A thought that can be retraced by an opposite action (2 + 2 = 4; 4 − 2 = 2).

Rh factor   Involves possible incompatibility between the blood types of mother and child; if the mother is Rh-negative and the child Rh-positive, miscarriage or even infant death can result.

risk factors   Stressors that individuals experience.

RNA (ribonucleic acid)   Nucleic acid similar to DNA.

role discontinuity   Abrupt and disruptive change caused by conflicts among one's various roles in life.

rubella (German measles)   Typically mild childhood disease caused by a virus; pregnant women who contract this disease may give birth to a baby with a defect: congenital heart disorder, cataracts, deafness, mental retardation. The risk is especially high if the disease appears early in the pregnancy.

S

scaffolding   Helping children move from initial difficulties with a topic to a point where, with help, they gradually learn to perform the task independently.

scheme   Piaget's term to describe the patterns of behavior that infants use to interact with their environment.

secondary circular reactions   Infants direct their activities toward objects and events outside themselves; term associated with Piaget's theory.

secular trend   Phenomenon (in recent centuries) of adolescents entering puberty sooner and growing taller and heavier.

self-concept   Person's evaluation of his/her self.

self-control   Self-restraint exercised over impulses, emotions, and desires.

self-esteem   How children rank themselves compared to others (self-worth).

self-fulfilling prophecy   An idea that comes true simply because one believes that it will.

semantics   Rules that describe how to interpret the meaning of words.

sensitive periods   Montessori's term for ideal times of readiness for learning.

sensitive responsiveness   Refers to the ability to recognize the meaning of a child's behavior.

sensorimotor period   Piaget's term for the first of his cognitive stages of development (0–2 years).

sequential (longitudinal/cross-sectional) studies   Cross-sectional studies done at several times with the same groups of individuals.

seriation   Process by which children in the concrete operational period can arrange objects by increasing or decreasing size.

sperm   Germ cell that carries the male's 23 chromosomes.

sex cleavage   Youngsters of the same sex tend to play and do things together.

sex-linked inheritance   Genes on the sex chromosome that produce traits other than sex.

sexual abuse   Any sexual activity between a child and adult, whether by force or consent.

sexually transmitted infections (STIs)   Class of infections that are transmitted through sexual behavior.

sibling underworld   Familial subsystem, or coalition, of brothers and sisters.

siblings   Brothers and/or sisters.

sickle-cell anemia   Chromosomal disorder resulting in abnormal hemoglobin.

silence   Belenky's first phase of women's thinking, characterized by concepts of right and wrong.

slow-to-warm-up children   Children with low intensity of reactions; may be rather negative when encountering anything new; term associated with Chess and Thomas.

social (cognitive) learning theory   Bandura's theory that refers to the process whereby the information we glean from observing others influences our behavior.

social death   Point at which a patient is treated essentially as a corpse, although perhaps still "clinically" or "biologically" alive.

social perspective taking   The idea that children's views on how to relate to others emerge from their personal theories about the traits of others.

socialization   Refers to the need to establish and maintain relations with others and to regulate behavior according to society's demands.

socioemotional selectivity theory   According to this theory, humans use social contact for four reasons: to obtain physical survival, to get information they need, to maintain a sense of self, and to acquire pleasure and comfort.

solidarity   Erikson's term for the personality style of persons who are able to commit themselves in concrete affiliations and partnerships.

span of apprehension   The amount of information a person can attend to at one time.

sperm donor   Male who either donates or sells sperm.

spina bifida   Genetic disorder resulting in the failure of the neural tube to close.

spindle cell   Neurons that play a large role in emotion.

stability   Belief that children's early experiences affect them for life.

stage of exhaustion   Selye's term for the body's physiological responses that revert to their condition during the stage of alarm.

stage of resistance   Selye's term for the body's reaction that is generally a reversal of the alarm reaction.

stage theorists   Those who believe that children's abilities and reading tasks change qualitatively over time; also researchers who believe that research based on personality traits is too narrow in focus and that one must also look at the stages of change each person goes through.

stagnation   According to Erikson, the seventh stage of life (middle-aged adulthood) tends to be marked either by generativity or by stagnation—boredom, self-indulgence, and the inability to contribute to society.

state of identity   If individuals were in a state of identity (an ideal circumstance), the various aspects of their self-image would be in agreement with each other; they would be identical.

stillbirth   Term that describes the spontaneous end of a pregnancy after the 20th week; called a stillbirth if the baby is born dead.

STORCH diseases   **S**yphilis, **t**oxoplasmosis, **o**ther infections, **r**ubella, **c**ytomegalovirus, **h**erpes.

strange situation   Measure designed to assess the quality of attachment.

stress   Anything that upsets a person's equilibrium—psychologically and physiologically.

structure-building   During structure-building periods, individuals face the task of building a stable structure around choices they have made.

structure-changing   Process of reappraising the existing life structure and exploring the possibilities for new life structures characterizes the structure-changing period.

subculture   A subgroup within a culture, in this case a social culture.

subjective knowledge   Belenky's third phase of women's thinking; characterized by some crisis of male authority that sparked a distrust of outside sources of knowledge and some experience that confirmed a trust in women thinkers themselves.

sudden infant death syndrome (SIDS)   Death of an apparently healthy infant, usually between 2 and 4 months of age; thought to be a brain-related respiratory problem.

superego   One of the three structures of the psyche according to Freud; acts as a conscience.

surrogate motherhood   One woman carries another woman's embryo.

symbolic games   According to Piaget, games that begin at 18–24 months.

symbolic play   The game of pretending; one of five Piagetian preoperational behavior patterns.

symmetry   Infant's capacity for attention; style of responding influences interactions.

synchrony   Ability of parents to adjust their behavior to that of an infant.

syntax   Rules of sentence structure.

syphilis   Sexually transmitted infection that presents a great danger in that in its early stage there are no symptoms; if untreated, it can be fatal; it can also affect the fetus.

T

Tay-Sachs disease   Failure to break down fatty materials in the CNS.

telegraphic Speech   Initial multiple-word utterances, usually two or three words.

temperament   (1) The manner of interacting with the environment. (2) A child's basic personality; technically refers to constitutionally based individual differences in emotional, motor, and attentional reactivity and self-regulation.

temporizing   Some people remain in one position for a year or more, exploring its implications but hesitating to make any further progress.

teratogens   Any agents that can cause abnormalities, for example, drugs, chemicals, infections, pollutants.

tertiary circular reaction   Repetition with variation; the infant is exploring the world's possibilities; term associated with Piaget's theory.

thalidomide   Popular drug prescribed during the early 1960s that was later found to cause a variety of birth defects when taken by women early in their pregnancy.

theory of mind   Children's understanding of others' thoughts, desires, and emotional states; emerges at about 2-years of age.

toxoplasmosis   Infection caused by a protozoan; may cause damage to the nervous system; transmitted by animals, especially cats.

traditional marriage enterprise   Levinson's term; the main goal of this type of marriage is to form and maintain a family.

trait theorists   Researchers who look at pieces of the personality (personality traits), as measured by detailed questionnaires.

transition   Levinson's concept that each new era begins as an old era is approaching its end; that "in-between" time is a transition.

transition-linked turning points   Constellation of events that define the transition period or the timing and sequence of events that occur within a transitional period.

treatment   The variable that the experimenter manipulates.

Triarchic Model of Intelligence   Three-tier explanation of intelligence proposed by Robert Sternberg.

trophoblast   Outer surface of the fertilized egg.

Turner syndrome   XO chromosomal pattern in females.

U

ultrasound   Use of sound waves and special equipment to produce an image that enables a physician to detect internal structural abnormalities.

umbilical cord   Contains blood vessels that go to and from the mother through the arteries and veins supplying the placenta.

uniform growth   Montessori's term to describe the developmental period in which children show considerable stability.

universalizing faith   Sixth development stage of Fowler's theory of faith; final developmental step of Fowler's theory of faith. Here the individual lives in the real world but is not of it. Such persons do not merely recognize the mutuality of existence; they act on the basis of it.

V

validation   Fromm's term for the reciprocal sharing of deep secrets and feelings that allows people to feel loved and accepted.

vocables   Consistent sound patterns referring to objects and events.

W

wear and tear theory   Theory that aging is due to the cumulative effects of hard work and lifelong stress.

wisdom   Superior insight and judgment that can come only from experience.

word spurt   Rapid increase of vocabulary from 18 months to 3 years.

work–family conflict   Phenomenon that occurs when a woman's roles as mother, wife, and worker spill over into one another.

Z

zygote   Fertilized egg.

zygote intrafallopian transfer (ZIFT)   Fertilized egg (zygote) is transferred to the fallopian tube.

Bibliography

A.A.R.P. (1997, September–October). Friendship facts. *Modern Maturity,* 41.

———. (2000, February). Grandparents and kids: Getting along fine. Washington, D.C.: *AARP Bulletin,* 21.

———. (2004, February). Guess who are the big gun owners now? *American Association of Retired Persons,* 1.

Aalto-Setala, T., Marttunen, M., & Tuulio-Henriksson, A. (2003). Depressive symptoms in adolescence may increase the risk of psychiatric disorders in early adulthood. *Evidence-Based Mental Health, 6,* 60–63.

Abeles, N. (1997). A victory for the aging community. *APA Monitor, 28* (10), 2.

Ackerman, S., Zuroff, D., & Moskowitz, D. (2000). Generativity in midlife and young adults: Links to agency, communion, and subjective well-being. *International Journal of Aging & Human Development, 50,* 17–41.

Adam, E., Gunnar, M., & Tanaka, A. (2004). Adult attachment, parent emotion, and observed parenting behavior: Mediator and moderator models. *Child Development, 75* (1), 110–122.

Adams, G., Montemayor, R., & Gullotta, T. (1996). Psychosocial development during adolescence: The legacy of John Hill. In G. Adams, R. Montemayor, & T. Gullotta (Eds.), *Psychosocial development during adolescence.* Thousand Oaks, CA: Sage.

Adolph, K. (1997). Learning in the development of infant locomotion. *Monographs of the Society for Research in Child Development, 262* (3).

Ahnert, L., & Lamb, M. (2003). Shared care: Establishing a balance between home and child care settings. *Child Development, 74* (4), 1044–1049.

Aiken, L. (1998). *Human development in adulthood.* NY: Plenum.

Ainsworth, M. (1973). The development of infant-mother attachment. In B. Caldwell & H. Riccuti (Eds.), *Review of child development research.* Chicago: University of Chicago Press.

———. (1979). Infant-mother attachment. *American Psychologist, 34,* 932–937.

Ainsworth, M., & Bowlby, J. (1991). An ethological approach to personality. *American Psychologist, 46,* 333–341.

Ajrouch, K., Antonucci, T., & Janevic, M. (2001). Social networks among blacks and whites: The interaction between race and age. *Journal of Gerontology, 56B,* S112–S118.

Alexander, G., & Korenbrot, C. (1995). The role of prenatal care in preventing low birth weight. *The Future of Children, 5* (1), 103–120.

Algozzine, B. & Kay, P. (2002). *Preventing problem behaviors: A handbook of successful prevention strategies.* Thousand Oaks, CA: Corwin Press.

Allen, T., Russell, J., Poteet, M., & Dobbins, G. (1999). Learning and development factors related to perceptions of job content and hierarchical plateauing. *Journal of Organizational Behavior, 20,* 1113–1137.

Allport, G., & Odbert, H. (1936). Trait names: A psycho-lexical study. *Psychological Monographs, 47* (1, whole No. 211).

Al-Mateen, C. S., Brookman, R., Best, A. M., & Singh, N. N. (1996). Inquiring about sexual abuse. *Journal of the American Academy of Child & Adolescent Psychiatry, 35* (4), 407–408.

Alpaugh, P. K., & Birren, J. E. (1977). Variables affecting creative contributions across the adult life span. *Human Development, 20* (4), 240–248.

Als, H., Duffy, F., & McAnulty, G. (1996). Effectiveness of individualized neuro-developmental care in the neonatal intensive care unit (NICU). *Acta Pediatrica, 416,* 21–30.

Als, H., Lawhorn, G., Brown, E., Gibes, R., Duffy, F., McAnulty, G., & Blickman, J. (1986). Individualized behavioral and environmental care for the very low birthweight preterm infant at high risk for bronchopulmonary dysplasia: Neonatal intensive care unit and developmental outcome. *Pediatrics, 78,* 1123–1132.

Alsaker, F. (1996). Annotation: The impact of puberty. *Journal of Child Psychology and Psychiatry and Allied Disciplines, 37* (3), 249–258.

Altman, L. (1994, August 17). High H.I.V. levels raise risks to newborns. *New York Times,* 22–27.

Alzheimer's Association. (1999). *President's report.* Silver Springs, MD: Alzheimer's Disease Education.

Alzheimers.org. (2003). www.alzheimers. org.

———. (2004). Studies suggest people with early AD can still learn. www. alzheimers.org/nianews/nianews67.html.

Amabile, T. M., Hennessey, B. A., & Grossman, B. S. (1986). Social influence on creativity: The effects of contracted-for reward. *Journal of Personality & Social Psychology, 50* (1), 14–23.

American Academy of Pediatrics. (1997). Human milk. In G. Peter (Ed.), *Red Book: Report of the committee on infectious diseases*. Elk Grove Village, Illinois: American Academy of Pediatrics.

———. (2000). Fetal alcohol syndrome and alcohol-related neurodevelopmental disorders. *Pediatrics, 106* (2), 358–361.

———. (2001). Media violence. *Pediatrics, 108* (5), 1222–1226.

———. (2003). Family pediatrics: Report of the Task Force on the Family. *Pediatrics*, 111(6), S1541–S1572.

———. (2006a). Prevention of sexual harassment in the workplace and educational settings. *Pediatrics*, 118(4), 1752–1777.

———. (2006b).The secrets of successful aging. *Pediatrics*, 117(4), p. 1183.

American Alliance for Health, Physical Education, Recreation, and Dance. (2007). Accepting overweight. *Journal of Physical Education, Recreation, and Dance*, 78(1), p. 3.

American Community Survey (2005). ch 14, p. 877

American Heart Association. (1998). *Diet and the heart*. Washington, D.C.: Author.

American Psychiatric Association. (2000). *The diagnostic and statistical manual of mental disorders* (4th edition, text revised). Washington, D.C.: Author.

Anderson, A., & Middleton, L. (2006). What is this thing called love? Euphoria, peace, obsession, reassurance . . . We have all experienced love's kaleidoscope of feelings. Can science help us understand the origins of love or should we leave it to the poets? *New Scientist*, 190(2549), 32–36.

Anderson, L. (1998, June 5). Prodding teenagers into action: Programs try to boost level of fitness, exercise. Boston: *Boston Globe*, 1.

Anderson, L., & Krathwohl, D. (2002). *A taxonomy for learning, teaching, & assessing: A revision of Bloom's taxonomy of educational objectives*. Chicago: University of Chicago Press.

Anderson, M., Kaufman, J., Simon, T., Barrios, L., Paulozzi, L., Ryan, G., Hammond, R., Modzeleski, W., Feucht, T., & Potter, L. (2001). School-associated violent deaths in the United States, 1994–1999. *Journal of the American Medical Association, 286*, 2695–2702.

Anderson, R., Elfreida H., Scott, J., & Wilkinson, Ian. (1985). *Becoming a nation of readers: The Report of the Commission on Reading*. Center for the Study of Reading. Champaign, IL.

Anderson, S. E., Dallal, G. E., & Must, A. (2003). Relative weight and race influence average age at menarche: Results from two nationally representative surveys of US girls studied 25 years apart. *Pediatrics*, 111(4), 844–850.

Andreasen, N. (2001). *Brave new brain*. New York: Oxford University Press.

Angell, K. E., Gross, W., Johnson, M. S., Koutstaal, W., & Schacter, D. L. (1997). False recollection induced by photographs: A comparison of older and younger adults. *Psychology and Aging, 12* (2) 203–215.

Angie, W., & Giles, H. (1998). *Communication of ageism*, in M. Hecht (Ed.). Thousand Oaks, CA, US: Sage Publications.

Apgar, V. (1953). A proposal for a new method of evaluation of the newborn infant. *Anesthesia and Analgesia, 32,* 260–267.

Appleby, L. (2000). Suicide in women. *The Lancet, 355* (211), 1203.

Arenson, J., & Drake, P. (2007). *Maternal and newborn health*. Sudbury, MA: Jones and Bartlett.

Aristotle. (1926). *The nicomachean ethics* (H. Rackmam, Trans.). Cambridge, MA: Harvard University Press.

Arnett, J. J. (2000). Emerging adulthood: A theory of development from the late teens through the twenties. *American Psychologist* (55), 469–480.

Arnold, R. (2005). Charming the next generation. *School Library Journal*, July, 30–32.

Arnsten, A. & Shansky, S. (2004). Adolescence: vulnerable period for stress-induced prefrontal cortical function? Introduction to part IV. *Academy of Sciences, 1021,* 143–147.

Arsenault, L., Walsh, E., Trzesniewski, k., Newcombe, R., Caspi, A., & Moffitt, T. (2006). Bullying victimization uniquely contributes to adjustment problems in young children. *Pediatrics, 118* (1), 130–138.

Asch-Goodkin, J., & Kaplan, D. (2006). When a spouse is hospitalized (bereavement effect in spouse death).

Patient Care for the Nurse Practitioner.

Ascribe Newswire. (2003, November 12). Sexual orientation among men is connected with brain metabolism. University of Chicago Research. PsycPort. com, 1–2.

Astington, J. (2001). The future of theory-of-mind research: Understanding motivational states, the role of language, and real-world consequences. *Child Development, 72* (3), 685–687.

Atkinson, D. (1999). The three R's of children of alcoholics: Rules, roles, roads. *Journal of Health Education., 30* (4), 254–255.

Averett, S. L., Gennetian, L. A., & Peters, H. E. (2000). Patterns and determinants of paternal child care during a child's first three years of life. *Marriage and Family Review, 29* (2/3), 115–136.

Avery, M. E., & Litwack, G. (1983). *Born early*. New York: Little, Brown.

Avis, N., Crawford, S., & Johannes, C. (2002). Menopause. In G. M. Wingood & R. J. DiClemente (Eds.), *Handbook of women's sexual and reproductive health. Issues in women health*. New York: Kluwer/Plenum, 367–391.

Azar, B. (1999a). E. O. Wilson to speak at APA's convention. *APA Monitor, 30* (4), 17.

———. (1999b). Mom's stress may affect early child development. *APA Monitor, 30*, 20.

Aziz, S., & Jackson, C. (2001). A comparison between three and five factor models of Pakistani personality data. *Personality & Individual Differences, 31*, 1311–1319.

Bachand, L.,and Caron, S. (March 2001). Ties that bind: A qualitative study of happy long-term marriages. *Contemporary Family Therapy: An International Journal, 23* (1), 105–121.

Baillargeon, R. (1987). Object permanence in $3\frac{1}{2}$ and $4\frac{1}{2}$ month old infants. *Developmental Psychology, 23*, 655–664.

Baird, A., & others. (1999). Functional magnetic resonance imaging of facial affect recognition in children and adolescents. *Journal of the American Academy of Child & Adolescent Psychiatry, 38*, 195–199.

Baker, K. (1999). How can we best serve LEP students? A reply to Nicholas Meier and Stephen Krashen. *Phi Delta Kappan, 80* (9), 707–710.

Balcazar, H., & Mattson, S. (2000). Nutrition. In S. Mattson & J. Smith (Eds.), *Core curriculum for maternal-newborn nursing.* Philadelphia: W. B. Saunders.

Balch, G. I. (1998). Exploring perceptions of smoking cessation among high school smokers: Input and feedback from focus groups. *Preventive Medicine: An International Devoted to Practice and Theory, 27* (5), A55–A63.

Baldwin, N. (1995). *Edison: Inventing the century.* New York: Hyperion.

Ball, H. (2007). Levels of intimate partner violence vary greatly according to country and rural or urban setting. *International Family Planning Perspectives, 33* (1), 40–42.

Ball, J., & Bindler, R. (2006). *Child health nursing: Partnering with children and families.* Upper Saddle River, NJ: Prentice Hall.

Baltes, P., Lindenberger, U., & Staudinger, U. (1998). Lifespan theory in developmental psychology. In R. M. Lerner (Ed.), *Handbook of child psychology: Volume 1. Theoretical models of human development.* New York: John Wiley.

———. (2006). Lifespan theory in developmental psychology. In W. Damon & R. Lerner (Series Eds.) & R. Lerner (Volume Ed.), *Handbook of child psychology: Volume 1. Theoretical models of human development.* New York: John Wiley.

Baltes, P. B., & Shaire, K. (1993). The aging mind: Potential and limits. *The Gerontologist, 33* (5), 580–594.

Baltes, P. B., & Staudinger, U. M. (2000). Wisdom: A metaheuristic (pragmatic) to orchestrate mind and virtue toward excellence. *American Psychologist, 55* (1), 122–136.

Bandura, A. (1997). *Self-efficacy: The exercise of control.* New York: Freeman.

Bandura, A., Barbaranelli, C., Caprara, G., & Pastorelli, C. (2001). Self-efficacy beliefs as shapers of children's aspirations and career trajectories. *Child Development, 72* (1), 187–206.

Bandura, A., Ross, D., & Ross, S. (1963). Imitation of film-mediated aggressive models. *Journal of Abnormal and Social Psychology, 66,* 3–11.

Bandura, A. & Walters, R. (1963). *Social learning and personality development.* New York: Holt, Rinehart & Winston.

Banks, J., & Banks, C. A. (Eds.). (1993). *Multicultural education: Issues and perspectives.* Boston: Allyn & Bacon.

Bankston, C. L., & Caldas, S. J. (1998). Family structure, schoolmates, and racial inequalities in school achievement. *Journal of Marriage and the Family, 60,* 715–723.

Barkley, R. (2003). Attention-deficit/hyperactivity disorder. In E. Mash & R. Barkley (Eds.), *Child Psychopathology.* New York: Guilford Press.

Barkley, R., Connor, D., & Kwasnik, D. (2000). Challenges to determining adolescent medication response in an outpatient clinical setting: Comparing Adderall and methylphenidate for ADHD. *Journal of Attention Disorders, 4,* 102–113.

Barnard, K., & Solchany, J. (2002). Mothering. In M. Bornstein (Ed.), *Handbook of parenting.* Mahwah, NJ: Lawrence Erlbaum.

Barnett, R. C. (2001). Work-family balance. In J. Worell (Ed.), *Encyclopedia of women and gender.* San Diego: Academic Press.

Baron-Cohen, S. (2005). The male condition. *New York Times,* August 8, Op Ed Contribution.

Barton, L., Hodgman, J., & Pavlova, Z. (1999). Causes of death in the extremely low birth weight infant. *Pediatrics, 103* (2), 446–451.

Bartsch, K., & Wellman, H. (1995). *Children talk about the mind.* New York: Oxford University Press.

Barzun, J. (1954). *The teacher in America.* Boston: Little, Brown.

Baumeister, R., Campbell, J., Krueger, J., & Vohs, K. (2007). Exploding the self-esteem myth. *Scientific American,* January, 84–91.

Baumrind, D. (1967). Child-care practices anteceding three patterns of preschool behavior. *Genetic Psychology Monographs, 75,* 43–88.

———. (1971). Current patterns of parental authority. *Developmental Psychology Monographs, 4,* 1–103.

———. (1986). *Familial antecedents of social competence in middle childhood.* Unpublished manuscript.

———. (1991a). The influence of parenting style on adolescent competence and substance use. Special Issue: The work of John P. Hill: I. Theoretical, instructional, and policy contributions. *Journal of Early Adolescence, 11* (1), 56–95.

———. (1991b). To nurture nature. *Behavioral and Brain Sciences,* XIV, 386.

———. (1991c). Parenting styles and adolescent. In R. Lerner, A. Peterson, & J. Brooks-Gunn (Eds.), *The encyclopedia of adolescence.* New York: Garland.

Bear, M., Connors, B., & Paradiso, M. (2007). *Neuroscience: Exploring the brain.* Baltimore: Lippincott Williams & Wilkins.

Beausang, C. C., & Razor, A. G. (2000). Young Western women's experiences of menarche and menstruation. *Health Care for Women International, 21,* 517–528.

Bebbington, P., & others. (1998). The influence of age and sex on the prevalence of depression conditions. *Psychological Medicine, 28* (1), 9–19.

Beeson, R., Horton-Deutsch, S., Farran, C., & Neundorfer, M. (2000). Loneliness and depression in caregivers of persons with Alzheimer's disease or related disorders. *Issues in Mental Health Nursing, 21,* 779–806.

Belenky, M. F., Bond, L. A., & Weinstock, J. S. (1997). *A tradition that has no name: Nurturing the development of people, families, and communities.* New York: Basic Books, Inc.

Belenky, M., Clinchy, B., Goldberger, N., & Tarule, J. (1986). *Women's ways of knowing.* New York: Basic Books.

Belsky, J. (1996). Parent, infant, and social-contextual antecedents of father-son attachment security. *Developmental Psychology, 32* (5), 905–913.

Bem, S. (1996). Exotic becomes erotic. *Psychological Review, 103* (2), 320–335.

———. (1999). *An unconventional family.* New Haven, CT: Yale University Press.

———. (2001). Exotic becomes erotic: Integrating biological and experiential antecedents of sexual orientation. In A. D'Augelli & C. Patterson (Eds.), *Lesbian, gay, and bisexual identities and youth: Psychological perspectives.* London: Oxford University Press, 52–68.

Bengtson, V. (2001). Beyond the nuclear family: The increasing importance of multigenerational bonds. *Journal of Marriage and the Family, 63,* 1–16.

Benson, E. (2003). Study finds sex differences in relationship between arousal and orientation. *Monitor on Psychology, 34* (4), 51.

Benson, G. S. (1996). Editorial: Male sexual dysfunction—Pitfalls, pills and prostheses. *The Journal of Urology, 156,* 1636.

Bergh, S., & Erling, A. (2005). Adolescent identity formation: A Swedish study of identity status using the EOM-EIS-II. *Adolescence, 40* (158), 377–397.

Berliner, D. (2006). Educational psychology: Searching for essence throughout a century of influence. In Patricia Alexander and Philip Winne (Eds.), *Handbook of educational psychology.* Mahwah, NJ: Lawrence Erlbaum.

Berliner, D., & Calfee, R. (Eds.) (1996). *Handbook of educational psychology.* New York: Macmillan.

Bernas, K. H., & Major, D. A. (2000). Contributors to stress resistance: Testing a model of women's work-family conflict. *Psychology of Women Quarterly, 24,* 170–178.

Bernat, J. (2001). Ethical and legal issues in palliative care. *Neurologic Clinics, 19,* 969–987.

Berninger. V. (2006). A developmental approach to learning disabilities. In W. Damon & R. Lerner (Series Eds.) & K. Renninger & I. Sigel (Volume Eds.), *Handbook of child psychology: Volume 4. Child psychology in practice.* New York: John Wiley.

Berry, D., & Miller, K. (2001). When boy meets girl: Attractiveness and the five factor model in opposite-sex interactions. *Journal of Research in Personality, 36,* 62–77.

Berstein, L., Beig, S., Siegenthaler, A., & Grady, C. (2002). The effect of encoding strategy on the neural correlates of memory for faces. *Neuropsychologia, 40,* 86–98.

Berzonsky, M., & Kuk, L. (2000). Identity status, identity processing style and transition to university. *Journal of Adolescent Research, 15* (1), 81–98.

Beutel, M. E., Weidner, W., & Brahler, E. (2006). Epidemiology of sexual dysfunction in

Bezdek, M., Croy, C., & Spicer, P. (July 2004). Documenting natural recovery in American-Indian drinking behavior: A coding scheme. *Journal of Studies on Alcohol, 65* (4), 428–435.

Bingham, C. R., & Crockett, L. J. (1996). Longitudinal adjustment patterns of boys and girls experiencing early, middle, and late sexual intercourse. *Developmental Psychology, 32* (4), 647–658.

Birren, J. (1960). Behavioral theories of aging. In N. Shock (Ed.), *Aging.* Washington, D.C.: American Association for the Advancement of Science.

Birren, J. & Fisher, L. (1992). Aging and slowing of behavior. In John Berman & Theo Sonderegger (Eds.), *Psychology and aging: Nebraska Symposium on Motivation 1991.* Lincoln: The University of Nebraska.

Bishop, D. (2006). Speech and language difficulties. In M. Rutter and E. Taylor (Eds.). *Child and adolescent psychiatry.* London: Blackwell.

Bishop, R. S. (1997). Selecting literature for a multicultural curriculum. In V. Harris (Ed.), *Using multiethnic literature in the K-8 classroom.* Norwood, MA: Christopher-Gordon Publishers.

Bjorklund, D. (1997). In search for a metatheory for cognitive development (or, Piaget is dead and I don't feel so good myself). *Child Development, 68* (1), 144–148.

———. (2000). *Children's thinking: Developmental function and individual differences.* Belmont, CA: Wadsworth.

———. (2005). *Children's thinking.* Belmont, CA: Wadsworth.

Bjorklund, D. & Pellegrini, A. (2000). Child development and evolutionary psychology. *Child Development, 71* (6), 1687–1708.

Black, M., Dubowitz, H., Krishnakumar, A., & Starr, R. (2007). Early intervention

Blackman, J. (1997). *Medical aspects of developmental disabilities in children birth to three.* Gaithersburg, MD: Aspen.

Blair, R., & others (2002). Fractionation of visual memory: Agency detection and its impairment in autism. *Neuropsychologia, 40,* 108–118.

Blakeslee, S. (2003, December). Humanity? Maybe it's in the wiring. *The Miracle of Consciousness—New York Times,* A23–24.

Blank, J. (2000). *Still doing it: Women and men over sixty write about their sexuality.* New York: Down There Press.

Bliese, P. D., & Castro, C. A. (2000). Role clarity, work overload, and organizational support: Multilevel evidence of the importance of support. *Work & Stress, 14* (1), 65–73.

Block, J. (2001). Millennial contrarianism: The five factor approach to personality description 5 years later. *Journal of Research in Personality, 35,* 98–107.

Block, R., Krebs, N., and the Committee on Child Abuse and Neglect, and the Committee on Nutrition. (2005). Failure to thrive as a manifestation of child neglect. *Pediatrics, 116* (5), 1234–1237.

Bloom, B. (1956). Taxonomy of educational objectives. *Handbook I: Cognitive domain.* New York: McKay.

Bloom, L. (1998). Language acquisition in its developmental context. In D. Kuhn & R. Siegler (Eds.), *Handbook of child psychology: Volume 5.* New York: John Wiley.

———. (2000). Language acquisition in its developmental context. In W. Damon (Series Ed.) & D. Kuhn & R. Siegler (Volume Eds.), *Handbook of child psychology: Volume 2, Cognition, perception, and language.* New York: John Wiley.

Blum, R. W., Harmon, B., Harris, L., Bergeisen, L., & Resnick, M. (1992). American-Indian-Alaska native youth health. *Journal of the American Medical Association, 267,* 1637–1644.

Blumstein Posner, R. (2006). Early menarche: A review of research on trends in timing, racial differences, etiology and psychosocial consequences. *Sex Roles, 54,* 315–323.

Blustein, D. (2000–2001). The interface of work and relationships. *The Counseling Psychologist, 29* (2), 261–272.

Bock, R. (1993). *Understanding Klinefelter syndrome.* Washington, D.C.: U.S. Department of Health and Human Services.

Bohannon, J. R. & Blanton, P. W. (1999). Gender role attitudes of American mothers and daughters over time. *The Journal of Social Psychology, 139* (2), 173–179.

Borko, H., & Putnam, R. (1996). Learning to teach. In D. Berliner and R. Calfee (Eds.), *Handbook of educational psychology.* Mahwah, NJ: Lawrence Erlbaum.

Bornstein, M. (1995). Parenting infants. In M. Bornstein (Ed.), *Handbook of parenting: Volume 3.* Hillsdale, NJ: Erlbaum.

———. (2002). Parenting Infants. In M. Bornstein, (Ed.) *Handbook of parenting: Volume 1.* Mahwah, NJ: Lawrence Erlbaum Associates.

———. (2006). Parenting science and practice. In W. Damon & R. Lerner (Series Eds.) & K. Renninger & I. Sigel (Volume Eds.), *Handbook of child psychology: Volume 4. Child psychology in practice.* New York: John Wiley.

Bornstein, M. (Ed.). (2002). *Handbook of parenting* (2nd edition). Mahwah, NJ: Erlbaum.

Bornstein, M., & Arterberry, M. (1999). Perceptual development. In M. Bornstein & M. Lamb (Eds.), *Developmental psychology: An advanced textbook.* Mahwah, NJ: Erlbaum.

Borstelman, L. (1983). Children before psychology: Ideas about children from antiquity to the late 1800s. In Paul Mussen (Ed.), *Handbook of child psychology.* New York: John Wiley.

Borum, R. (1996). Improving the clinical practice of violence risk assessment. *American Psychologist, 51,* 945–956.

Botwinick, J. (1977). Intellectual abilities. In J. E. Birren & K. W. Schaie (Eds.), *Handbook of the psychology of aging.* New York: Van Nostrand Reinhold.

Bouchard, T. (1994). Genes, environment, and personality. *Science, 264,* 1700–1791.

Bowker, A., Gadbois, S., & Cornock, B. (2003). Sports participation and self-esteem: Variations as a function of gender and gender role orientation (1). *Sex Roles: A Journal of Research, 12,* 47–69.

Bowlby, J. (1969). *Attachment.* New York: Basic Books.

———. (1982). Attachment and loss: Retrospect and prospect. *American Journal of Orthopsychiatry, 52,* 664–678.

———. (1988). *A secure base.* New York: Basic Books.

Brach, J. S., & VanSwearingen, J. M. (2002). Physical impairment and disability: Relationship to performance of activities of daily living in community-dwelling older men. *Physical Therapy, 82* (8), 752–762.

Brady, S. S., & Halpern-Fisher, B. L. (2007). Adolescents' reported consequences of having oral sex versus vaginal sex. *Pediatrics, 119* (2), 229–237.

Bransford, J., & Stein, B. (1993). *The IDEAL problem solver.* New York: Freeman.

Bransford, J., Stevens, R., Schwartz, D., Meltzoff, A., Pea, R., Roschele, J., Vye, N., Kuhl, P. Bell. P., Barron, B., Reeves, B., and Sabelli, N. (2006). Learning theories and education: Toward a decade of synergy. In Patricia Alexander and Philip Winne (Eds.), *Handbook of educational psychology.* Mahwah, NJ: Lawrence Erlbaum.

Braverman, S., & Paris, J. (1993). The male mid-life crisis in the grown-up resilient child. *Psychotherapy, 30,* 651–656.

Brazelton, T., & Cramer, B. (1990). *The earliest relationship.* Reading, MA: Addison-Wesley.

Brazelton, T., Christophersen, E., Frauman, A., Gorski, P., Poole, J., Stadtler, A., & Wright, C. (1999). Instruction, timeliness, and medical influences affecting toilet training. *Pediatrics, 103* (6), 1353–1358.

Brazelton, T., & Nugent, K. (1995). *Neonatal behavioral assessment scale.* London: MacKeith Press.

Brazelton, T., & Sparrow, J. (2001). *Touchpoints three to six.* Cambridge, MA: Perseus.

Bredekamp, S., & Copple, C. (Eds.). (1997). *Developmentally appropriate practice in early childhood programs.* Washington, D.C.: National Association for the Education of Young People.

Brelis, M. (1998, July 3). Lewd hazing on cutter detailed. *Boston Globe,* B1, C3, 4.

Brennan, R., Barnett, R., & Gares, K. (2001). When she earns more than he does: A longitudinal study of dual-earner couples. *Journal of Marriage and the Family, 62,* 168–182.

Brenner, A. (1984). *Helping children cope with stress.* San Diego, CA: Lexington Books.

Brim, O., & J. Kagan (1980). *Constancy and change in human development.* Cambridge, MA: Harvard University Press.

Brindle, M. & Salancik, G. (1999). The social construction of an institution: The case of brain death and the organ transplant industry, 1968–1992. In J. Wagner (Ed.), *Advances in qualitative organization research: Volume 2.* Stamford, CT: JAI Press, 1–35.

Brisk, M. (1998). *Bilingual education.* Mahwah, NJ: Erlbaum.

———. (2005). Bilingual education. In E. Hinkel (Ed.), *Handbook of research in second language teaching and learning.* Mahwah, NJ: Erlbaum.

Brody, G. H., Stoneman, Z., & Flor, D. (1996). Parental religiosity, family processes, and youth competence in rural, two-parent African American families. *Developmental Psychology, 32* (4), 696–706.

Brody, J. (2000, June 6). What could be good about morning sickness? Plenty, *New York Times,* p. D7.

Brodzinsky, D., Lang, R., & Smith, D. (1995). Parenting adopted children. In M. Bornstein (Ed.), *Handbook of parenting: Volume 3.* Hillsdale, NJ: Erlbaum.

Brodzinsky, D., & Pinderhughes, E. (2002). Parenting and child development in adoptive families. In M. Bornstein (Ed.), *Handbook of parenting* (2nd edition). Mahwah, NJ: Erlbaum.

Bronfenbrenner, U. (1978). *The ecology of human development.* Cambridge, MA: Harvard University Press.

———. (1989). Ecological systems theory. *Annals of Child Development, 6,* 187–249.

Bronfenbrenner, U., & Morris, P. (1998). The ecology of developmental processes. In R. M. Lerner (Ed.), *Handbook of child psychology: Volume 1. Theoretical models of human development.* New York: John Wiley.

Bronson, M. (1995). *The right stuff for children birth to 8.* Washington, D.C.: National Association for the Education of Young People.

———. (2000). *Self-regulation in early childhood.* New York: Guilford.

Brooks, J., & Lewis, M. (1976). Midget, adult and child: Infants' responses to strangers. *Child Development, 47,* 323–332.

Brooks-Gunn, J., Han, W., & Waldfogel, J. (2002). Maternal employment and child cognitive outcomes in the first three years of life: The NICHD study of early child care. *Child Development, 74* (4), 1052–1072.

Brooks-Gunn, J., & Paikoff, R. (1997). Sexuality and developmental transitions during adolescence. In J. Schulenberg, & J. L. Maggs (Eds.), *Health risks and developmental transitions during adolescence.* New York, NY: Cambridge University Press, 190– 219.

Brown, B. B. (1990). Peer groups and peer cultures. In S. Feldman & G. Elliot (Eds.), *At the threshold: The developing adolescent.* Cambridge, MA: Harvard University Press.

Brown, B., Dolcini, M., & Leventhal, A. (1997). Transformations in peer relationships at adolescence: Implications for health-related behavior. In J. Schulenberg & J. L. Maggs (Eds.), *Health risks and developmental transitions during adolescence.* New York: Cambridge University Press, 161–189.

Brown, R. (1973). *A first language: The early stages.* Cambridge, MA: Harvard University Press.

Brunstein, J. C., Dangelmayer, G., & Schultheiss, O. C. (1996). Personal goals and social support in close relationships: Effects on relationship mood and marital satisfaction. *Journal of Personality and Social Psychology, 71* (5), 1006–1019.

Buchanan, M., Villagran, M., & Ragan, S. (2002). Women, menopause, and (Ms.) information: Communication about the climacteric. *Health Communication, 14,* 99–119.

Buhs, E., & Ladd, G. (2001). Peer rejections as an antecedent of young children's school adjustment: An examination of mediating processes. *Developmental Psychology, 37* (4), 550–560.

Burchinal, M., Roberts, J., Riggins, R., Zeisel, S., Neebe, E., & Bryant, D. (2000). Relating quality of center-based child care to early cognitive and language development longitudinally. *Child Development, 71* (2), 339–357.

Burgess, E. O. (2004). Sexuality in midlife and later life couples. In J. H. Harvey & A. Wetzel (Eds.), *The handbook of sexuality in close relationships.* Mahwah, NJ: Erlbaum.

Burkhardt, S., & Rotatori, A. (1995). *Treatment and prevention of childhood sexual abuse.* Washington, D.C.: Taylto & Francis.

Burr, J. A., & Mutchler, J. E. (1999). Race and ethnic variation in norms of filial responsibility among older persons. *Journal of Marriage and the Family, 61* (3), 674–687.

Burton, S., & Mitchell, P. (2003). Judging who knows best about yourself: Developmental change in citing the self across middle childhood. *Child Development, 74* (2), 426–443.

Business Week Online (July 14, 2006). The Dyson school: Feel free to fail.

Buss, D. (2001). Cognitive biases and emotional wisdom in the evolution of conflict between the sexes. *Current Directions in Psychological Science, 10,* 219–223.

Bussey, K., & Bandura, A. (1999). Social cognitive theory of gender development and differentiation. *Psychological Review, 106* (4), October, 676–713.

Butler, R., Walker, W., Skowronski, J., & Shannon, L. (1995). Age responses to the love structures scale. *International Journal of Aging and Human Development, 40* (4), 281–296.

Cabrera, N., Tamis-LeMonda, C., Bradley, R., Hofferth, S., & Lamb, M. (2000). Fatherhood in the twenty-first century. *Child Development, 71* (1), 127–136.

Cairns, R. (1998). The making of developmental psychology. In R. M. Lerner (Ed.), *Handbook of child psychology: Volume 1. Theoretical models of human development.* New York: John Wiley.

Cairns, R., & Cairns, B. (2006) The Making of Developmental Psychology. In W. Damon & R. Lerner (Series Eds.) & R. Lerner (Volume Ed.), *Handbook of child Psychology: Volume 1. Theoretical models of human development.* New York: John Wiley.

Calhoun. K., & Wilson, A. (2000). In L. Szuchman & F. Muscarella (Eds.), *Psychological perspectives on human sexuality.* New York: Wiley.

Calkins, L. (1997). *Raising lifelong learners.* Reading, MA: Perseus Books.

Campbell, F., Pungello, E., Miller-Johnson, S, Burchinal, M., & Ramey, C. (2001). The development of cognitive and academic abilities: Growth curves from an early childhood educational experiment. *Developmental Psychology, 37* (2), 231–242.

Campbell, F., & Ramey, C. (1994). Effects of early intervention on intellectual and academic achievement: A follow-up study of children from low-income families. *Child Development, 65,* 684–698.

Campbell, N., & Reece, J. (2005). *Biology.* New York: Pearson/Cummings.

Campos, J., Frankel, C., & Camras, L. (2004). On the nature of emotion regulation. *Child Development, 75,* 377–394.

Campos, S., Poulos, G., & Sipple, J. (2005). Prevalence and profiling: Hazing among college students and points of

intervention. *American Journal of Health Behavior, 29* (2), 137–149.

Cancian, M., & Meyer, D. R. (1996). Changing policy, changing practice: Mothers' incomes and child support orders. *Journal of Marriage and the Family, 58* (8), 618–627.

Cannister, M. W. (1999). Mentoring and the spiritual well-being of late adolescents. *Adolescence, 34* (136), 769–779.

Carlson, B. (2004). *Human embryology and developmental biology.* Philadelphia: Mosby.

Carr, D., House, J., Wortman, C., Nesse, R., & Kessler, R. (2001). Psychological adjustment to sudden and anticipated spousal loss among older widowed persons. *Journal of Gerontology, 56B,* S237–S248.

Carrioin, V., Weems, W., & Reiss, A. (2007). Stress predicts brain changes in children: A pilot longitudinal study on youth stress, posttraumatic stress disorder, and the hippocampus. *Pediatrics, 119* (3), 509–516.

Carstensen, L. L. (1995). Evidence for a lifespan theory of socioemotional selectivity. *Current Directions in Psychological Science, 4* (5), 151–156.

Carstensen, L. L., Edelstein, B. A., & Dornbrand, L. (1996). *The practical handbook of clinical gerontology.* Thousand Oaks, CA, US: Sage Publications, Inc.

Casas, J., & Pytluk, S. (1995). Hispanic identity development: Implications for research and practice. In J. Ponterotto, J. Casas, L. Suzuki, & C. Alexander (Ed.), *Handbook of multicultural counseling.* Thousand Oaks, CA: Sage.

Case, R. (1998). The development of conceptual structures. In W. Damon (Series Ed.) & D. Kuhn & R. Siegler (Volume Eds.), *Handbook of child psychology: Volume 4.* New York: John Wiley.

Caserta, M. S., Lund, D. A., & Wright, S. D. (1996). Exploring the caregiver burden inventory (CBI): Further evidence for a multidimensional view of burden. *International Journal of Aging and Human Development, 43* (43), 21–34.

Casey, M. B., Nuttall, R., & Pezaris, E. (1997). Mediators of gender differences in mathematics college entrance test scores. *Developmental Psychology, 33* (4), 669–680.

Casper, L., & Bryson, K. (1999). Growth in single father's outpace this growth and single mothers. *United States Department of Commerce News.* Washington, D.C.: Department of Commerce.

Caspi, A. (1998). Personality development across the life-course. In W. Damon (Series Ed.) & N. Eisenberg (Volume Ed.), *Handbook of child psychology: Volume 3. Social, emotional, and personality development.* New York: John Wiley.

Castle, N. G., & Fogel, B. (1998). Characteristics of nursing homes that are restraint free. *The Gerontologist, 38* (2), 181–188.

Cates, W. (1999). Estimates of the incidence and prevalence of sexually transmitted diseases in the United States. *Sexually Transmitted Diseases, 26,* 2–7.

Cattell, R. (1950). *Personality: A Systematic Theoretical Factual Study.* New York: McGraw-Hill.

Ceci, S. (1996). *On intelligence.* Cambridge, MA: Harvard University Press.

Cellar, D., Nelson, Z., & Yorke, C. (2000). The five-factor model and driving behavior: Personality and involvement in vehicular accidents. *Psychological Reports, 86,* 454–456.

Centers for Disease Control and Prevention (CDC). (1996). *Teenage suicide.* Atlanta: Author.

————. (2000). *Sexually transmitted diseases sourcebook.* Atlanta: Author.

————. (2001a). *Women and Smoking.* Atlanta: CDC.

————. (2001b). *Work-related hearing loss* [online]: www.cdc.gov/niosh/hp-workrel.html.

————. (2002). *Magnitude of the epidemic overall.* Washington, D.C.

————. (2003). *Reproductive health.* Washington, D.C.

————. (2004a). National Center for Inquiry Prevention and Control. Web-based Inquiry Statistics and Query Reporting System (WISQARS). www.cdc.gov/ncipc/wisqars/default.htm.

————. (2004b). Persons with HIV/AIDS over the age of 13. Atlanta: Centers for Disease ? Control.

————. (2006a). National Center for Inquiry Prevention and Control. Web-based Inquiry Statistics. Query and Reporting System (WISQARS) *Suicide in the U.S.: Statistics and prevention.* www.cdc.gov/ncipc/wisqars.

————. (2000b). Tobacco use among middle and high school students–United States, 1999. *Morbidity and Mortality Weekly Report* (Washington, D.C.), 49–53.

————. (2006c). State-specific prevalence of obesity among adults–United States, 2005. Sept. 2006/55 (36), 985–988.

————. (2007). *A glance at the HIV/AIDS Epidemic.* Washington, D.C.

Chall, J. (1983). *Stages of reading development.* New York: McGraw-Hill.

Chall, J., Jacobs, V., & Baldwin, L. (1990). *The reading crisis: Why poor children fall behind.* Cambridge, MA: Harvard University Press.

Chandler, M., Sokol, B., & Wainryb, C. (2000). Beliefs about truth and beliefs about rightness. *Child Development, 71* (1), 91–97.

Chang, B. H., Noonan, A. E., & Tennstedt, S. L. (1998). The role of religion/spirituality in coping with caregiving for disabled elders. *The Gerontologist, 38* (4), 463–470.

Chao, R. (2001). Extending research on the consequences of parenting style for Chinese Americans and European Americans. *Child Development, 72,* 1832–1843.

Chavous, T., Bernat, D., Schmeelk-Cone, K., Caldwell, C., Kohn-Wood, L., & Zimmerman, M. (2003, July/August). Racial identity and academic attainment among African American adolescents. *Child Development, 74* (4), 1076–1090.

Chen, X., Rubin, K., & Li, D. (1997). Relation between academic achievement and social adjustment: Evidence from Chinese children. *Developmental Psychology, 33* (3), 518–525.

Chen, Z., & Kaplan, H. (2003). School failure in early adolescence and status attainment in middle adulthood: A longitudinal study. *Sociology of Education, 76,* 110–118.

Chen, Z., & Siegler, R. (2000). Across the great divide: Bridging the gap between understanding of toddlers' and older children's thinking. *Monographs of the Society for Research in Child Development, 65* (2), Serial No. 261.

Chess, S., & Thomas, A. (1987). *Know your child.* New York: Basic Books.

————. (1999). *Goodness of fit.* Philadelphia: Brunner/Mazel.

Child and Adolescent Mental Health Government Guide. Retrieved June 30, 2002, from www.nih.gov/&CID=16101830/.

Child Neglect. *Pediatrics, 116* (5), 1234–1237.

Children's Foundation (2003). *The 2003 child care center licensing study.* Washington, D.C.: The Children's Foundation.

Chiriboga, D. A. (1989). Mental health at the midpoint. In S. Hunter & M. Sundel (Eds.), *Midlife myths.* Newbury Park, CA: Sage.

Chomsky, N. (1957). *Syntactic structure.* The Hague: Mouton.

Christ, G. (2000). *Healing children's grief: Surviving a parent's death from cancer.* New York: Oxford University Press.

Chumlea, A. C., C. M. Schubert, A. F. Roche, H. F. Kulin, P. A. Lee, J. H. Himes, et al. (2003). Age at menarche and racial comparisons in U.S. girls. *Pediatrics, 111* (1), 110–113.

Cicchetti, D., & Toth, S. (1998). Perspectives on research and practice in developmental psychopathology. In W. Damon (Series Ed.) & I. Sigel & K. Renninger (Volume Eds.), *Handbook of child psychology: Volume 4. Child psychology in practice.* New York: John Wiley.

Cillessen, A., & Bukowski, W. (Eds.). (2000, Summer). Recent advances in the measurement of acceptance and rejection in the peer system. *New Directions for Child and Adolescent Development, 88,* 201–208.

Clark, L., Vorhies, L., & McEwen, J. (2002). Personality disorder symptomatology from the five-factor model perspective. In P. T. Costa, Jr. & T. A. Widiger (Eds.), *Personality disorders and the five-factor model of personality* (2nd edition) Washington, D.C.: American Psychological Association, 125–147.

Clarke, E., Preston, M., Raksin, J., & Bengtson, V. (1999). Types of conflicts and tensions between older parents and adult children. *The Gerontologist, 39* (3), 261–270.

Clarke-Stewart, K., & Allhusen, V. (2002). Nonparental caregiving. In M. Bornstein (Ed.), *Handbook of parenting.* Mahwah, NJ: Lawrence Erlbaum.

————. (2005). *What we know about child care.* Cambridge, MA: Harvard University Press.

Clarke-Stewart, K., Allhusen, V., & Clements, D. (1995). Nonparental caregiving. In M. Bornstein (Ed.), *Handbook of parenting*. Hillsdale, NJ: Erlbaum.

Classen, S., C. W. Garvan, K. Awadzi, S. Sundaram, S. Winter, E. D. S. Lopez, & N. Ferree (2006). Systematic literature review and model for older driver safety. *Topics in Geriatric Rehabilitation, 22* (2), 87–99.

Clay, R. (1996). Some elders thrive on working into late life. *APA Monitor, 35,* 12.

———. (1997). Laughter may be no laughing matter. *APA Monitor, 28* (9), 18.

Clements, P. T., DeRanieri, J. T., Vigil, G. J., & Benasutti, K. M. (2004). Life after death: Grief therapy after the sudden traumatic death of a family member. *Perspectives in Psychiatric Care, 40* (4), 149–155.

Cleveland, H., & Wiebe, R. (2003, January/February). The moderation of adolescent-to-peer similarity in tobacco and alcohol use by school levels of substance use. *Child Development, 74* (1), 279–291.

Clifford, B., Gunter, B., & McAleer, J. (1995). *Television and children.* Hillsdale, NJ: Erlbaum.

Cloherty, J. P. (1998). Syphilis. In J. Cloherty and A. Stark (Eds.), *Manual of neonatal care*. Philadelphia: Lippincott-Raven.

Clyman, B. B., & Pompei, P. (1996a). Osteoarthritis: New roles for drug therapy and surgery. *Geriatrics, 51* (9), 32–36.

———. (1996b). Osteoarthritis: What to look for, and when to treat it. *Geriatrics, 51* (8), 36–41.

Cohall, A., Kassotis, J., Parks, R., Vaughan, R., Bannister, H., & Northridge, M. (2001). Adolescents in the age of AIDS: Myths, misconceptions, and misunderstandings regarding sexually transmitted diseases. *Journal of the National Medical Association, 93,* 64–69.

Cohen, J. (1997, February 7). The genomics gamble. *Science, 275,* 767–772.

Cohen, L. (2001). *Playful parenting.* New York: Ballantine.

Cohen, S., & Jaskulsky, S. (2001). Prostate cancer: Therapeutic options based on tumor grade, life expectancy, and patient preferences. *Geriatrics, 56,* 39–52.

Cohen-Mansfield, J., & Werner, P. (1998). Predictors of aggressive behaviors: A longitudinal study in senior day care centers. *Journal of Gerontology, 53B* (5), P300–P310.

Coie, J., & Dodge, K. (1998). Aggression and antisocial behavior. In W. Damon (Series Ed.) & N. Eisenberg (Volume Ed.), *Handbook of child psychology: Volume 3. Child psychology in practice.* New York: John Wiley.

Coie, J., Dodge, K., Schwartz, D., Cillessen, A., Hubbard, J., & Lemerise, E. (2002). It takes two to fight: A test of relational factors and a method for assessing aggressive dyads. *Developmental Psychology, 35* (5), 1179–1188.

Colditz, G. A., & Stein, C. (2005). Smoking cessation, weight gain, and lung function (risk of smoking cessation). *The Lancet, 365* (9471), 1600–1602.

Cole, M. (1996). *Cultural psychology.* Cambridge, MA: Harvard University Press.

———. (1999). Culture in development. In M. Bornstein & M. Lamb (Eds.), *Developmental psychology: An advanced textbook.* Mahwah, NJ: Erlbaum.

———. (2006). Culture and cognitive development in phylogenetic, historical, and ontogenetic perspective. In W. Damon & R. Lerner (Series Eds.) & D. Kuhn & R. Siegler (Volume Eds.), *Handbook of child psychology: Volume 2. Cognition, perception, and language.* New York: John Wiley.

Cole, M., & Cole, S. (1996). *The development of children.* New York: Freeman.

Cole, N. F., Eckman, M. H., Kara, R. H., Pauker, S. G., Goldberg, R. J., Ross, E. M., Orr, R. K., & Wong, J. B. (1997, April 9). Patient-specific decisions about hormone replacement therapy in postmenopausal women. *Journal of the American Medical Association 277* (14), 1140–1147.

Cole, P., Bruschi, C., & Tamang, B. (2002). Cultural differences in children's emotional reactions to difficult situations. *Child Development, 73* (3), 983–996.

Cole, P., Martin, S., & Dennis, T. (2004). Emotion regulation as a scientific construct: Methodological challenges and directions for child development research. *Child Development, 75* (2), 317–333.

Cole, R. (1998).The genome and the human genome project. In T. Peters (Ed.), *Genetics: Issues of social justice.* Cleveland, OH: Pilgrim Press.

Coleman, J., & Roker, D. (1998). *Adolescence. Psychologist, 11,* 593–598.

Collins, S. K., & K. S. Collins (2006). Valuable human capital: the aging health care worker. *The Health Care Manager, 25* (3), 213–221.

Collins, W., Harris, M., & Susman, A. (1995). Parenting during middle childhood. In M. Bornstein (Ed.), *Handbook of parenting: Volume 1. Applied and practical parenting.* Mahwah, NJ: Erlbaum.

Coltrane, S., & Ishii-Kuntz, M. (1992). Men's housework: A life course perspective. *Journal of Marriage and the Family, 54,* 43–57.

Committee on Nutrition. (2005). Failure to thrive as a manifestation of child neglect, *Pediatrics, 116*(5), 1234–1237.

Compas, B., Benson, M., Boyer, M., Hocks, T., & Konik, B. (2002). Problem-solving and problem-solving therapies. In M. Rutter and E. Taylor (Eds.). *Child and adolescent psychiatry.* London: Blackwell.

Comstock, G. (1993). The medium and society: The role of television in American society. In G. Berry & J. Asamen (Eds.), *Children and television.* Newbury Park, CA: Sage.

Comstock, G., & Paik, H. (1994). The effects of television violence on antisocial behavior: A meta-analysis. *Communication Research, 21,* 269–277.

Comstock, G., & Scharrar, E. (1999). *Television.* San Diego: Academic Press.

Connors, M. (2001). Relationship of sexual abuse to body image and eating problems. In J. K. Thompson & L. Smolak (Eds.), *Body image, eating disorders, and obesity in youth: Assessment, prevention, and treatment,* Washington, D.C.: American Psychological Association, 149–167.

Conwell, Y. (1995). Suicide among elderly persons. *Psychiatric Services, 46* (6), 563–572.

Cooney, T., & Mortimer, J. (1999). Family structure differences the timing of leaving home: Exploring mediating factors. *Journal of Research on Adolescence, 9* (4), 367–393.

Cooper, H. (2006). Research questions and research designs. In P. Alexander & P. Winne, Eds.). *Handbook of educational psychology*. Mahwah, NJ: Lawrence Erlbaum.

Cooper, T., Berseth, C., Adams, J., & Weisman, L. (1998). Actuarial survival in the premature infant less than 30 weeks' gestation. *Pediatrics, 101* (6), 975–978.

Costa, P. T. J., & McCrae, R. R. (1996). Mood and personality in adulthood. In C. Magai, & S. H. McFadden (Eds.), *Handbook of emotion, adult development, and aging*. San Diego, CA: Academic Press, 369–383.

Cowan, N., Nugent, L., Elliott, E., Ponomarev, I., & Saults, J. (1999). The role of attention in the development of short-term memory: Age differences in the verbal span of apprehension. *Child Development, 70* (5), 1082–1097.

Cox, M., & Paley, B. (2004). Understanding families as systems. In J. Lerner & A. Alberts (Eds.), *Current directions in developmental psychology*. Prentice Hall: New Jersey, 92–98.

Cox, M., Paley, B., Burchinal, M., & Payne, C. (1999). Marital perceptions and interactions across the transition to parenthood. *Journal of Marriage and the Family, 61,* 611–625.

Crain, W. (2005). *Theories of development*. Upper Saddle River, NJ: Pearson/ Prentice Hall.

Crick, N. (1996). The role of overt aggression, relational aggression, and prosocial behavior in the prediction of children's future social adjustment. *Child Development, 67,* 2317–2327.

Crick, N., Casas, J., & Ku, H. (1999). Relational and physical forms of peer victimization in preschool. *Developmental Psychology, 35* (2), 376–385.

Crick, N., Casas, J., & Mosher, M. (1997). Relational and overt aggression in preschool. *Developmental Psychology, 33* (4), 579–588.

Criss, M., Pettit, G., Bates, J., Dodge, K., & Lapp, A. (2002). Family adversity, positive peer relationships, and children's externalizing behavior: A longitudinal perspective on risk and resilience. *Child Development, 73* (4), 1220–1237.

Cruickshank, D., Bainer, D., & Metcalf, K. (1995). *The act of teaching*. New York: McGraw-Hill.

Csikszentmihalyi, M., & Rathunde, K. (1998). In R. M. Lerner (Ed.), *Handbook of child psychology: Volume 1. Theoretical models of human development*. New York: John Wiley.

Cummings, S. M., Knopf, N. P., & DeWeaver, K. L. (2000). Knowledge of and attitudes toward aging among nonelders: Gender and race differences. *Journal of Women & Aging, 12,* 77–87.

Curran, J. (2006). Deliberate self-harm in the over 60s. *Mental Health Practice, 10* (1), 29–30.

Curtis, H., & Barnes, N. S. (1998). *Invitation to biology*. New York: Worth.

Curtis, J. M., & Curtis, M. J. (1993). Factors related to susceptibility and recruitment by cults. *Psychological Reports, 73,* 451–460.

Cutler, W., Schleidt, W., & Friedmann, E. (1987). Lunar influences on the reproductive cycle in women. *Human Biology, 59,* 959–972.

Czaja, S., & Sharit, J. (1998). Age differences in attitudes toward computers. *Journal of Gerontology, 53B* (5), 329–340.

Czaja, S. J., Charness, N., Fisk, A. D., Hertzog, C., Nair, S. N., Rogers, W. A., & Sharit, J. (2006). Factors predicting the use of technology: Findings from the Center for Research and Education on Aging and Technology (CREATE). *Psychology and Aging, 21,* 333–352.

D'Augelli, A., & Patterson, C. (1995). *Lesbian, gay, and bisexual identities over the lifespan*. New York: Oxford University Press.

Dacey, J. S. (1998). A history of the concept of creativity. In H. Gardner & R. Sternberg (Eds.), *Encyclopedia of creativity*. San Francisco: Academic Press.

———. (1989a). Discriminating characteristics of the families of highly creative adolescents. *The Journal of Creative Behavior, 24* (4), 263–271.

———. (1989b). *Fundamentals of creative thinking*. Lexington, MA: D. C. Heath/ Lexington Books.

———. (1989c). Peak periods of creative growth across the life span. *The Journal of Creative Behavior, 24* (4), 224–247.

Dacey, J. S., deSalvatore, L., & Robinson, J. (1997, Winter). The results of teaching middle school students two relaxation techniques as part of a conflict prevention program. *Research in Middle Level Education, 20* (2), 91–102.

Dacey, J. S., & Fiore, L. (2000). *Your anxious child*. San Francisco: Jossey-Bass.

Dacey, J. S., & Kenny, M. (1997). *Adolescent development* (2nd edition). Boston: McGraw-Hill.

Dacey, J. S., Kenny, M., & Margolis, D. (2002). *Adolescent development,* Houston, TX: Thompson.

Dacey, J. S., & Lennon, K. (1998). *Understanding creativity: The interplay of biological, psychological and social forces*. San Francisco: Jossey-Bass.

Dacey, J. S., & Packer, A. (1992). *The nurturing parent: How to raise a creative, loving, responsible child*. New York: Fireside/Simon & Schuster.

Damasio, A. (1999). *The feeling of what happens*. New York: Harcourt Brace & Company.

Dancer, L., & Gilbert, L. (1993). Spouses' family work participation and its relation to wives' occupational level. *Sex Roles, 28* (3/4), 127–145.

Darkenwald, G., & Novak, R. (1997). Classroom age competition and academic achievement in college. *Adult Education Quarterly, 47* (3/4), 108.

Darley, J., & Foss, D. (2004). *Annual Review of Psychology*. Palo Alto, CA: Annual Reviews.

Darwin, C. (1877). Biographical sketch of an infant. *Mind, 2,* 285–294.

Datan, N. (1995). Corpses, lepers, and menstruating women: Tradition, transition, and the sociology of knowledge. *Feminism & Psychology, 5* (4), 449–459.

Datan, N., Rodeheaver, D., & Hughes, F. (1987). Adult development and aging. *Annual Review of Psychology, 38,* 153–180.

Dautzenberg, M., & others. (March 2000). The competing demands of paid work and parent care: Middle-aged daughter providing assistance to elderly parents. *Research on Aging, 22*(2), 165–187.

Davidson, J. M. (1989). Sexual emotions, hormones, and behavior. *Advances, 6* (2), 56–58.

Davis, C., Woodside, D., Olmsted, M., & Kaptein, S. (1999). Psychopathology in the eating disorders: The influence of physical activity. *Journal of Applied Biobehavioral Research, 4* (2), 139–156.

Davis, K. J., Sloane, P. D., Mitchell, C. M., Pressier, J., Grant, L., Hawes, M. C., Lindeman, D., Montgomery, R., Long,

K., Phillips, C., & Koch, G. (2000). Specialized dementia programs in residential care settings. *Gerontologist, 40* (1), 32–42.

Dawood, K., & others. (2000). Familial aspects of male homosexuality. *Archives of Sexual Behavior, 29,* 155–163.

Dawson, G., & Fischer, K. (Eds.). (1995). *Human behavior and the developing brain.* New York: Guilford.

Deacon, S., Minichiello, V., & Plummer, D. (1995). Sexuality and older people: Revisiting the assumptions. *Educational Gerontology, 21* (5), 497–513.

DeAngelis, T. (1997). Elderly may be less depressed than the young. *APA Monitor, 28* (10), 25.

Deblinger, E., Mannarino, A. P., Cohen, J. A., & Steer, R. A. (2006). A follow-up study of a multisite, randomized, controlled trial for children with sexual abuse-related PTSD symptoms. *Journal of the American Academy of Child and Adolescent Psychiatry, 45* (12), 1474–1485.

DeCasper, A., & Spence, M. (1986). Prenatal maternal speech influences newborn's perception of speech sounds. *Infant behavior and development, 9,* 133–170.

DeGenova, M. K. (1992). If you had your life to live over again, what would you do differently? *International Journal of Aging and Human Development, 34* (2), 135–143.

DeGenova, M. K., & F. P. Rice (2005). *Intimate relationships, marriages, and families* (6th edition) Boston, MA: McGraw-Hill Higher Education.

DeJudicibus, M., & McCabe, M. (2001). Blaming the target of sexual harassment: Impact of gender role, sexist attitudes, and work role. *Sex Roles, 44,* 401–417.

Dekovic, M. (1999). Parent-adolescent conflict: Possible determinants and consequences. *International Journal of Behavioral Development, 23,* 977–1000.

DeLamater, J., & Friedrich, W. N. (2002). Human sexual development. *The Journal of Sex Research, 39,* 10–15.

Delancy, C. H. (1995). Rites of passage in adolescence. *Adolescence, 30,* 89–93.

Dembner, A. (December, 2003). New research affirms seniors' mental abilities. *Boston Globe,* B12.

Demick, J. (2002). Stages of parental development. In M. Bornstein (Ed.), *Handbook of parenting* (2nd edition). Mahwah, NJ: Erlbaum.

Dempsey, C. L. (1994). Health and social issues of gay, lesbian, and bisexual adolescents. *Families in Society, 75* (3), 160–167.

Denham, S., Blair, K., DeMulder, E., Levitas, J., Sawyer, K., Auerbach-Major, S., & Queenan, P. (2003). Preschool emotional competence: pathway to social competence? *Child Development, 74* (1), 238–256.

Dennis, W. (1966). Creative productivity. *J. Gerontology, 21,* 1–8.

DeVries, B., Davis, C. G., Wortman, C. B., & Lehman, D. R. (1997). Long-term psychological and somatic consequences of later life parental bereavement. *Omega: Journal of Death & Dying, 35* (1), 97–117.

DeVries, H. M., & Gallagher-Thompson, D. (1994). Older adults. In F. M. Dattilio & A. M. Freeman (Eds.), *Cognitive-behavioral strategies in crisis intervention.* New York: Guilford Press, 200–218.

Diamond, A. (2000). Close interrelation of motor development and cognitive development and of the cerebellum and prefrontal cortex. *Child Development, 71* (1), 44–56.

Diamond, M. (1999). *Magic trees of the mind.* New York: Penguin.

Diaz, R., Ayala, G., & Bein, E. (2004). Sexual risk as an outcome of social oppression: Data from a probability sample of Latino gay men in three U.S. cities. *Cultural Diversity & Ethnic Minority Psychology, 10* (3), 255–267.

Dickson, N., Paul, C., & Herbison, P. (2003). Same-sex attraction in a birth cohort: Prevalence and persistence in early adulthood. *Social Science & Medicine, 56,* 1607–1617.

DiGilio, D., & N. G. Levitt (2002). APA bridging the gap on aging-related issues. *Professional Psychology: Research & Practice, 33* (5), 443–445.

Dilworth-Anderson, P., & Gibson, B. E. (1999). Ethnic minority perspectives on dementia, family caregiving, and interventions. *Generations, 23* (3), 40–45.

DiPasquale, T., & Gluck, J. (2001). Psychologists, psychiatrists, and physician-assisted suicide: The relationship between underlying beliefs and

professional behavior. *Professional Psychology: Research & Practice, 32,* 501–506.

Dixon, R., & Lerner, R. (1999). History and systems in developmental psychology. In M. Bornstein & M. Lamb (Eds.), *Developmental psychology: An advanced textbook.* Mahwah, NJ: Erlbaum.

Dobratz, M. C. (2003). The self-transacting dying: Patterns of social-psychological adaptation in home hospice patients. *The Journal of Death & Dying, 46,* 151–163.

Dodge, K., Lansford, J., Burks, V., Bates, J., Pettit, G., Fontaine, R., & Price, J. (2003). Peer rejection and social information-processing factors in the development of aggressive behavior problems in children. *Child Development, 74* (2), 374–393.

Doheny, K. (2004). "We're done" can be predicted before "I do." *HealthDay, 1.*

Donner, M. (1997, February). A genetic basis for the sudden infant death sex ratio. *Medical Hypotheses, 2,* 137–142.

Dori, G. A., & Overholser, J. C. (1999). Depression, hopelessness, and self-esteem: Accounting for suicidality in adolescent psychiatric inpatients. *Suicide & Life-Threatening Behavior, 29* (4), 309–318.

Dorn, L. D., Dahl, R. E., Williamson, D.E., Birmaher, B., Axelson, D., Perel, J., Stull, S. D., & Ryan, N. D. (1990). Developmental markers in adolescence: Implications for studies of pubertal processes. *Journal of Youth and Adolescence, 32* (5), 315–325.

Dorn, L. D., Nottelmann, E. D., Susman, E. J., & Inoff-Germain, G. (1999). Variability in hormone concentrations. *Journal of Youth and Adolescence, 12* (4), 343–350.

Douglas, A., Johnstone, H., & Russell, J. (2000). Sex-steroid induction of endogenous opoid inhibition on oxytocin secretory responses to stress. *Journal of Neuroendocrinology, 12* (4), 343–350.

Dragoi, V., & Staddon, J. (1999). The dynamics of operant conditioning. *Psychological Review, 106* (1), 20–61.

Draper, P., & Keith, J. (1992). Cultural contexts of care: Family caregiving for elderly in America and Africa. *Journal of Aging Studies, 6* (2), 113–134.

Drew, L., & Smith, P. (1999). The impact of parental separation/divorce on grandparent-grandchild relationships. *International Journal of Aging and Human Development, 49* (1), 61–78.

Ducharme, F., Levesque, L., Lachance, L., Giroux, F., Legault, A., & Preville, M. (2005). "Taking care of myself": Efficacy of an intervention programme for caregivers of a relative with dementia living in a long-term care setting. *Dementia, 4* (1), 23–48.

Dumont, M., & Provost, M. A. (1999). Resilience in adolescents: Protective role of social support, coping strategies, self-esteem, and social activities on experience of stress and depression. *Journal of Youth and Adolescence, 28* (3), 343–363.

Duncan, G., & Brooks-Gunn, J. (2000). Family poverty, welfare reform, & child development. *Child Development, 71* (1), 188–196.

Dunn, J. (1994). Experience and understanding of emotions, relationships, and membership in a particular culture. In P. Ekman & R. Davidson (Eds.), *The nature of emotion.* New York: Oxford University Press.

Dunn, J., Brown, J., & Maguire, M. (1995). The development of children's moral sensibility: Individual differences and emotion understanding. *Developmental Psychology, 31,* 649–659.

Dunn, J., Cutting, A., & Fisher, N. (2002). Old friends, new friends: Predictors of children's perspective on their friends at school. *Child Development, 73* (2), 621–635.

Dunn, J., Slomkowski, C., & Beardsall, L. (1994). Sibling relationships from the preschool period through middle childhood and early adolescence. *Developmental Psychology, 30* (3), 315–324.

Dunn, K. M., Croft, P. R., & Hackett, G. I. (2000). Satisfaction in the sex life of a general population sample. *Journal of Sex and Marital Therapy, 26,* 141–151.

Dunne, K. (2004). Grief and its manifestations (Bereavement). *Nursing Standard, 18* (45), 45–54.

Durham, M. G. (1998). Dilemmas of desire: Representations of adolescent sexuality in two teen magazines. *Youth and Society, 29* (3), 369–389.

Dychtwald, K. (2005). Ageless aging: The next era of retirement; "Old age" and "retirement" must be rethought and redefined as the baby boomers surge through the later stages of life, according to a renowned authority on aging. *The Futurist, 39* (4), 16–22.

Eagle, M. (2000). Psychoanalytic theory: History of the field. In A. Kazdin (Ed.), *Encyclopedia of psychology.* Washington, D.C.: American Psychological Association.

Eastman, P. (1997). Slowing down Alzheimer's. *American Association of Retired Persons Bulletin, 38,* 1–6.

———. (2000, January). Scientists piecing Alzheimer's puzzle. *AARP Bulletin, 41* (1), 18–19.

Eccles, J., & Roeser, R. (1999). School and community influences on human development. In M. Bornstein & M. Lamb (Eds.), *Developmental psychology: An advanced textbook.* Mahwah, NJ: Erlbaum.

Eccles, J. (2003). Education: Junior and high school. In G. Adams & M. Berzonsky (Eds.), *Blackwell handbook of adolescence.* Malden, MA: Blackwell.

Edwards, C. P., Gandini, L., & Forman, G. E. (Eds.) (1998). *The hundred languages of children: The Reggio Emilia approach–Advanced reflections* (2nd edition). Greenwich, CT: Ablex.

Edwards, R., & Usher, R. (1997). University adult education in the postmodern moment. *Adult Education Quarterly, 47,* (3/4), 153.

Eiger, M., & Olds, S. (1999). *The complete book of breastfeeding.* New York: Workman Publishing.

Eisenberg, B., & Berkowitz, R. (2003). *The Big6 workshop handbook.* Columbus, Ohio: Linworth Publishing.

Eisenberg, N. (1992). *The caring child.* Cambridge, MA: Harvard University Press.

———. (2006). Introduction. In W. Damon & R. Lerner (Series Eds.) & N. Eisenberg (Volume Ed.), *Handbook of child psychology: Volume 3. Social, emotional, and personality development.* New York: John Wiley.

Eisenberg, N., & Fabes, R. (1998). Prosocial development. In W. Damon (Series Ed.) & N. Eisenberg (Volume Ed.), *Handbook of child psychology: Volume 3, Social, emotional, and personality development.* New York: John Wiley.

Eisenberg, N., Fabes, R., & Spinrad, T. (2006). *Prosocial behavior.* In W. Damon & R. Lerner (Series Eds.) & N. Eisenberg (Volume Ed.), *Handbook of child psychology: Volume 3. Social, emotional, and personality development.* New York: John Wiley.

Eisenberg, N., Martin, C., & Fabes, R. (1996). Gender development and gender effects. In D. Berliner & R. Calfee (Eds.), *Handbook of educational psychology.* New York: Macmillan.

Eisler, I. (2002). Family interviewing: Issues of theory and practice. In M. Rutter and E. Taylor (Eds.). *Child and adolescent psychiatry.* London: Blackwell.

Ekman, P. (2003). *Emotions revealed.* New York: Henry Holt & Co.

Ekman, P., & Davidson, R. (Eds.). (1994). *The nature of emotions.* New York: Oxford University Press.

Elder, G. (1998). Theories of human development: Contemporary perspectives. In R. M. Lerner (Ed.), *Handbook of child psychology: Volume 1. Theoretical models of human development.* New York: John Wiley.

Elder, G., & Shanahan, M. (2006). The life course and human development. In W. Damon & R. Lerner (Series Eds.) & R. Lerner (Volume Ed.), *Handbook of child psychology: Volume 1.Theoretical models of human development.* New York: John Wiley.

Eliason, M. J. (1995). Accounts of sexual identity formation in heterosexual students. *Sex Roles, 32* (11/12), 821–834.

Eliot, E. (2000). *What's going on in there?* New York: Bantam.

Elkind, D. (1978). *The child's reality: Three developmental themes.* Hillsdale, NJ: Erlbaum.

Elkind, D., & Bowen, R. (1979). Imaginary audience behavior in children and adolescents. *Developmental Psychology, 15,* 38–44.

Elliott, S., Kratochwill, T., Littlefield, J., & Travers, J. (2000). *Educational psychology: Effective teaching, effective learning.* Dubuque, IA: Brown & Benchmark.

Ellis, B., Bates, J., Dodge, K., Fergusson, D., Horwood, L., Pettit, G., & Woodward, L. (2003, May/June). Does father absence place daughters at special risk for early sexual activity and teenage pregnancy? *Child Development, 74* (3), 801–821.

Ellis, B. J., McFadyen-Ketchum, S., Dodge, K. A., Pettit, G. S., & Bates, J. E. (1999). Quality of early family relationships and individual differences in the timing of pubertal maturation in girls: A longitudinal test of an evolutionary model. *Journal of Personality & Social Psychology, 77* (2), 387–401.

Ely, R. (1997). Language and literacy in the school years. In J. Gleason (Ed.), *The development of language*. Needham, MA: Allyn & Bacon.

Emde, R. (1998). Early emotional development: New modes of thinking for research and intervention. In J. Warhol & S. Shelov (Eds.), *New perspectives in early emotional development*. New York: Johnson & Johnson Pediatric Institute.

Emde, R., Plomin, R., Robinson, J., Corley, R., DeFries, J., Fulker, D., Reznick, J., Campos, J., Kagan, J., & Zahn-Waxler, C. (1992). Temperament, emotions, and cognition at fourteen months: The MacArthur, Longitudinal Twin Study. *Child Development, 63* (6), 1437–1455.

Emery, R., & Laumann-Billings, L. (2002). Child abuse. In M. Rutter and E. Taylor (Eds.), *Child and adolescent psychiatry*. London: Blackwell.

Enright, R. D., Levy, V. M., Harris, D., & Lapsley, D. K. (1987). Do economic conditions influence how theorists view adolescents? *Journal of Youth and Adolescence, 16* (6), 541–560.

Ensminger, M. E., & Ju'on, H. (2001). The influence of patterns of welfare receipt during the child-rearing years on later physical and psychological health. *Women & Health, 1,* 25–32.

Erikson, E. (1958). *Young man Luther: A study in psychoanalysis and history.* New York: Norton.

———. (1959). Growth and crises of the healthy personality. *Psychological Issues, 1,* 40–52.

———. (1963). *Childhood and society* (2nd edition). New York: Norton.

———. (1968). *Identity: Youth and crisis.* New York: Norton.

———. (1969). *Gandhi's truth: On the origins of militant nonviolence.* New York: Norton.

———. (1978). *Adulthood.* New York: Norton.

———. (1998). Adrenal responsivity in normal aging and mild to moderate Alzheimer's disease. *Biological Psychiatry, 43* (6), 401–407.

Eskilson, A., & Wiley, M. (1999). Solving for the X: Aspirations and expectations of college students. *Journal of Youth and Adolescence, 28,* (1), 51–57.

Esquivel, G. B. (1995). Teacher behaviors that foster creativity. Special Issue: Toward an educational psychology of creativity: I. *Educational Psychology Review, 7* (2), 185–202.

Etounga-Manguelle, D. (2000). Does Africa need a cultural adjustment program? In L. Harrison & S. Huntington (Eds.), *Culture matters.* New York: Basic Books.

Evans, G. (2004). The environment of childhood poverty. *American Psychologist, 59* (2), 77–92.

Evans, G., & English, K. (2002). The environment of poverty: Multiple stressor exposure, psychophysiological stress, and socioemotional adjustment. *Child Development, 73* (4), 1238–1248.

Everaerd, W., Laan, E., & Spiering, M. (2000). Male sexuality. In L. Szuchman & F. Muscarella (Eds.), *Psychological perspectives on human sexuality.* New York: Wiley.

Eysenck, H. (1960). *The Structure of Human Personality.* London: Methuen.

Ezzo, A., Dirks, D., Auguston, S., Nelson, S., Harer, P., & Hoefke, K. (2003). *On becoming birthwise.* Charleston, SC: Charleston Publishing.

Fagot, B. (1995). Parenting boys and girls. In M. Bornstein (Ed.), *Handbook of parenting.* Hillsdale, NJ: Erlbaum.

Fantz, R. (1961). The origin of form perception. *Scientific American, 204,* 66–72.

Farrell, M., & Nicoteri, J. (2007). *Nutrition.* Sudbury, MA: Jones & Bartlett.

Federal Bureau of Investigation (FBI). (2000). *Uniform crime reports for the U.S.* Washington, D.C.: Author.

Feinbloom, R. (1993). *Pregnancy, birth, and the early months* (2nd. edition). Reading, MA: Addison-Wesley.

Feiring, C., Deblinger, E., Hoch-Espada, A. & Haworth, T. (2002). Romantic relationship aggression and attitudes in high school students: The role of gender, grade, and attachment and emotional styles. *Journal of Youth and Adolescence, 31,* 373–388.

Feiring, C., Taska, I., & Lewis, M. (2002). Adjustment following sexual abuse discovery: The role of shame and attributional style. *Developmental Psychology, 38* (1), 79–92.

Feldman, D. (1979). The mysterious case of extreme giftedness. In A. H. Passow (Ed.), *The gifted and the talented: Their education and development.* Chicago: University of Chicago Press (NSSE).

———. (1994). *Beyond universals in cognitive development* (2nd edition). Norwood, NJ: Ablex.

Feldman, R., Weller, A., Sirota, L., & Eidelman, A. (2002). Skin-to-skin contact (kangaroo care) promotes self-regulation in premature infants: Sleep-wake cyclicity, arousal modulation, and sustained exploration. *Developmental Psychology, 38* (2), 194–207.

Ferber, R. (1985). *Solve your child's sleep problems.* New York: Simon & Schuster.

———. (2006). *Solve your child's sleep problems.* New York: Simon & Schuster.

Ferguson, T., Stegge, H., Miller, E., & Olsen, M. (1999). Guilt, shame, and symptoms in children. *Developmental Psychology, 35* (2), 347–357.

Fergusson, D. M., & Lynskey, M. T. (1996). Adolescent resiliency to family adversity. *Journal of Child Psychology and Psychiatry and Allied Disciplines, 37* (3), 281–292.

Ferris, P. (1997). *Dr. Freud: A life.* Washington, D.C.: Counterpoint.

Field, T. (1990). *Infancy.* Cambridge, MA: Harvard University Press.

———. (2002). Violence and touch deprivation in adolescents. *Adolescence, 37,* 735–745.

Field, T., Hernandez-Reif, M., & Freedman, J. (2004). Stimulation programs for preterm infants. *Social Policy Report: Society for Research in Child Development, XVIII* (1), 3–13.

Fields, R. (2004). The other half of the brain. *Scientific American, 290* (4), 55–61.

Finch, C. (2003). Neurons, glia, and plasticity in normal brain aging. *Neurobiology of Aging, 24* (Suppl 1), S123–S127.

Finch, J., & Robinson, M. (2003). Aging and late-onset disability: addressing workplace accommodation. (Aging and Late-Onset Disability). *The Journal of Rehabilitation, 69* (2), 38-43.

Fincham, F. (2004). Marital conflict: Correlates, structure, and context. In J. Lerner & A. Alberts (Eds.), *Current directions in developmental psychology.* New Jersey: Prentice Hall, 63–70.

Findling, R., & others. (2001). Psychotic disorders in children and adolescents. *Developmental Clinical Psychology Psychiatry, 44.* Thousand Oaks, CA: Sage.

Finkelhor, D. (1996, August). *Keynote address.* Presented at the International Congress on Child Abuse and Neglect. Dublin, Ireland.

Fischer, K., & Rose, S. (Eds.). (1994). Dynamic development of coordination of components in brain and behavior. In G. Dawson & K. Fischer (Eds.), *Human behavior and the developing brain.* New York: Guilford.

Fitzgerald, J. (2004). *The great brain.* New York: Dell.

Fitzpatrick, M. (2003). Women on the treadmill (doctoring the risk society). *The Lancet, 361*(9361), p. 976.

Flannery, D. (1998). Youth gangs: A developmental perspective. In T. P. Gullotta & G. R. Adams et al. (Eds.), *Delinquent violent youth: Theory and interventions. Advances in adolescent development: An annual book series: Voulme 1.* Thousand Oaks, CA: Sage. 175–204.

Flavell, J. (1963). *The developmental psychology of Jean Piaget.* New York: Van Nostrand.

———. (1998). Social cognition. In W. Damon (Series Ed.) & D. Kuhn & R. Siegler (Volume Eds.), *Handbook of child psychology: Volume 2. Cognition, perception, and language.* New York: John Wiley.

———. (1999). Cognitive development: Children's knowledge about the mind. In J. Spence, J. Darley, & D. Foss (Eds.), *Annual Review of Psychology.* Palo Alto, CA: Annual Reviews.

Flavell, J., Beach, D., & Chinsky, J. (1966). Spontaneous verbal rehearsal in a memory task as a function of age. *Child Development, 37,* 282–299.

Fleming, D., McQuillian, G., & Johnson, R. (1997). Herpes simplex virus type 2 in the United States, 1976 to 1994. New England *Journal of Medicine, 337,* 1105–1111.

Flippen, C., & Tienda, M. (2000). Pathways to retirement: Patterns of labor force participation and labor market exit among the pre-retirement population by race, Hispanic origin, and sex. *Journal of Gerontology, 55B,* S14–S27.

Floyd, F., Stein, T., Harter, K., Allison, A., & Nye, C. (1999). Gay, lesbian, and bisexual youths: Separation-Individuation, parental attitudes, identity consolidation, and well-being. *Journal of Youth and Adolescence, 28* (6), 719–725.

Flum, H. (March 2001). Dialogues and challenges: The interface between work and relationships. *Counseling Psychologist, 29* (2), 259–270.

Foreman, J. (1999, August 2). Miracle before birth. *The Boston Globe,* C1, 4.

———. (2000, September 10). Two tongues better than one. *The Boston Globe,* G1, G3.

Forthofer, M. S., Markman, H. J., Cox, M., Stanley, S., & Kessler, R. C. (1996). Associations between marital distress and work loss in a national sample. *Journal of Marriage and the Family, 58* (8), 597–605.

Fouad, N., & Brown, M. (2000). The role of race and social class in development. In S. Brown & R. Lent (Eds.), *Handbook of counseling psychology.* New York: Wiley.

Fowler, D. (2007). The extent of substance use problems among women partner abuse survivors residing in a domestic violence shelter. *Family and Community Health,* 30(1), S106-109.

Fowler, J. (1993). Response to Helmut Reich: Overview or apologetic? *International Journal for the Psychology of Religion, 3* (3), 173–179.

———. (2000). *Becoming adult, becoming Christian.* San Francisco: Jossey-Bass.

Fox, J. (1997). *Primary health care of children.* St. Louis: Mosby.

———. (2003, December). Ganging up. *The Boston Globe,* A17.

Fraiberg, S. (1959). *The magic years.* New York: Charles Scribner's Sons.

Fraiberg, S., Adelson, E., & Shapiro, V. (1987). Ghosts in the nursery: A psychoanalytic approach to the problems of impaired mother-infant relationships. In L. Fraiberg (Ed.), *Selected writings of Selma.* Columbus: Ohio State University Press, 100–136.

Frankenberger, K. (2000). Adolescent egocentrism: A comparison among adolescents and adults. *Journal of Adolescence, 23,* 343–354.

Frankl, V. (1967). *Psychotherapy and existentialism.* New York: Simon & Schuster.

Frankland, P. W., Blendy, J. A., Coblentz, J., Marowitz, Z., Scheutz, G., Silva, A. J., & Kogan, J. H. (1997). Spaced training induces normal long-term memory in CREB mutant mice. *Current Biology, 17* (1), 1–11.

Franzini, L. (2002). *Kids who laugh: How to develop your child's sense of humor.* New York: Square One Press.

Freitag, M., Belsky, J., Grossman, K., Grossman, K., & Scheueerer, H. (1996). Continuity in parent-child relationships from infancy to middle childhood and relationships with friendship competence. *Child Development, 67,* 1437–1454.

Freud, A., & Dann, S. (1951). An experiment in group upbringing. *Psychoanalytic Study of the Child, 6,* 127–168.

Freud, S. (1949). *An outline of psychoanalysis.* New York: Norton.

———. (1996). Obsession and phobias: Their psychic mechanism and their etiology/Zwangsvortellungen und Phobien: Ihr psychischer Mechanismus und ihre Aetiologie. (trans. from the *Revue neurologique* by Dr. A. Schiff). Herausgegeben von Michael Schröter). *Jahrbuch der Psychoanalyse, 37,* 196–205.

Friedan, B. (1963). *The feminine mystique.* New York: Norton.

Friedman, R., & P. Lindsay Chase-Lansdale. (2002). Chronic adversities. In M. Rutter and E. Taylor (Eds.). *Child and adolescent psychiatry.* London: Blackwell.

Friedman, S. R., & Weissbrod, C.S. (2005). Work and family commitment and decision-making status among emerging adults. *Sex Roles: A Journal of Research* 53(5-6), p. 317.

Fromm, E. (1955). *The sane society.* New York: Holt, Rinehart & Winston.

———. (1968 [1956]). *The art of loving.* New York: Harper & Row.

Fulton, R. (1977). General aspects. In N. Linzer (Ed.), *Understanding bereavement and grief.* New York: Yeshiva University Press.

Fung, H., Cartensen, L., & Lang, F. (2001). Age-related patterns in social networks among European Americans and African Americans: Implications for socioemotional selectivity across the life span. *International Journal of Aging & Human Development, 52,* 185–206.

Furman, W., & Lanthier, R. (2002). Parenting siblings. In M. Bornstein (Ed.), *Handbook of parenting: Volume 1.* (2nd edition). Mahwah, NJ: Erlbaum.

Gabriel, T. (1997, January 5). Pack dating: For a good time, call a crowd [New York Times Magazine]. *The New York Times,* 22–23, 38.

Galambos, N., & Tilton-Weaver, L. C. (2000). Adolescents' psychosocial maturity, problem, behavior, and subjective age: In search of the adultoid. *Applied Developmental Science, 4* (4), 178–192.

Galambos, N., Barker, E., Almeida, D. (2003, March/April). Parents do matter: Trajectories of change in externalizing and internalizing problems in early adolescence. *Child Development, 74* (2), 578–594.

Galdone, P. (1975). *The gingerbread boy.* New York: Clarion Books.

———. (1998). *The three little pigs.* New York: Clarion Books.

Galen, B., & Underwood, M. (1996). A developmental investigation of social aggression among children. *Developmental Psychology, 33* (4), 589–600.

Gallup, G. (1988). *The Gallup poll.* New York: Random House.

Galton, F. (1870). *Hereditary genius.* New York: Appleton.

———. (1879). Psychometric experiments, *Brain, 2,* 148–162.

Ganong, L., Coleman, M., McDaniel, A. K., & Killian, T. (1998). Attitudes regarding obligations to assist an older parent or stepparent following later-life remarriage. *Journal of Marriage and the Family, 60,* 595–610.

Ganzel, A. (1999). Adolescent decision making: The influence of mood, age, and gender on the consideration of information. *Journal of Adolescent Research, 14* (3), 289–295.

Ganzini, L., Kraemer, D., Lee, M., & Schmidt, T. (2001). "Patient-physician discussions about physician–assisted suicide": Reply. *Journal of the American Medical Association, 286,* 789.

Garbarino, J. (1999). *Lost boys: Why our sons turn violent and how we can save them.* New York: The Free Press.

Garbarino, J., & Bedard, C. (2001). *Parents under siege.* New York: The Free Press.

Garbarino, J., & Benn, J. (1992). The ecology of childbearing and childrearing. In J. Garbarino (Ed.), *Children and families in the social environment.* New York: Aldine.

Garcia, M., Shaw, D., Winslow, E., & Yaggi, K. (2000). Destructive sibling conflict and the development of conduct problems in young boys. *Developmental Psychology, 36* (1), 44–53.

Garcia Coll, C., Lamberty, G., Jenkins, R., McAdoo, H., Crnic, K., Wasik, B., & Garcia, H. (1996). An integrative model for the study of developmental competencies in minority children. *Child Development, 67,* 1891–1914.

Gardner, D., Weissman, A., Howles, C., & Shoham, Z. (2004) *Textbook of assisted reproductive techniques.* Oxford (UK): Taylor & Francis.

Gardner, H. (1983). *Frames of mind: The theory of multiple intelligences.* New York: Basic Books.

Gardner, H. (1991). *The unschooled mind.* New York: Basic Books.

———. (1993a). *Creating minds.* New York: Basic Books.

———. (1993b). *Multiple intelligences: The theory in practice.* New York: Basic Books.

———. (1995). *Leading minds: An anatomy of leadership.* New York: Basic Books.

———. (1997). *Extraordinary minds.* New York: Basic Books.

———. (1999a). *The disciplined mind.* New York: Simon & Schuster.

———. (1999b). *Intelligence reframed.* New York: Basic Books.

———. (2003). *The real head start.* Boston Globe, September 7, D1, D2.

Gardner, H., & Moran, S. (2006). The science of multiple intelligences theory. *Educational Psychologist, 41* (4), 227–232.

Garmazy, N., & Rutter, M. (1983). *Stress coping, and development.* NY: McGraw-Hill.

———. (1985). Acute reactions to stress. In *Child and adolescent psychiatry.* Blackwell: Oxford, England.

Garnier, H., & Stein, J. (1998). Values and the family: Risk and protective factors for adolescent problem behaviors. *Youth and Society, 30* (1), 89–120.

Garratt, D., Roche, J., & Tucker, S. (1997). *Changing experiences of youth.* London: Sage.

Garrod, A., Smulyan, L., Power, S., & Kilkenny, R. (1995). *Adolescent portraits.* Needham Heights, MA: Allyn & Bacon.

Garvey, C. (1990). *Play.* Cambridge, MA: Harvard University Press.

Gary, F., Moorhead, J., & Warren, J. (1996). Characteristics of troubled youths in a shelter. *Archives of Psychiatric Nursing, 10* (1), 41–48.

Gazzaniga, M., Ivry, R., & Mangun, G. (1998). *Cognitive neuroscience.* New York: Norton.

Ge, X., Best, K. M., Conger, R. D., & Simons, R. L. (1996a). Parenting behaviors and the occurrence and co-occurrence of adolescent depressive symptoms and conduct problems. *Developmental Psychology, 32* (4), 717–731.

Ge, X., Conger, R. D., Cadoret, R. J., Neiderhiser, J. N., Yates, W., Troughton, E., & Stewart, M. A. (1996b). The developmental interface between nature and nurture: A mutual influence model of child antisocial behavior and parent behaviors. *Developmental Psychology, 32* (4), 574–589.

Ge, X., Conger, R., & Elder, G. (2001). The relation between puberty and psychological distress in adolescent boys. *Journal of Research on Adolescence, 11,* 49–70.

Geary, D., & Bjorklund, D. (2000). Evolutionary developmental psychology. *Child Development, 71* (1), 57–65.

Gebhardt, W. A., Kuyper, L., & Dusseldorp, E. (2006). Condom use at first intercourse with a new partner in female adolescents and young adults: The role of cognitive planning and motives for having sex. *Archives of Sexual Behavior, 35* (2), 217-224.

Gelb, M. (1996). *Thinking for a change.* London: Aurum Press.

Gelman, R., & Baillargeon, R. (1983). A review of some Piagetian concepts. In P. Mussen (Ed.), *Handbook of child psychology: Volume 3.* New York: Wiley.

Gerard, J. M., Landry-Meyer, L., & Roe, J. G. (2006). Grandparents raising grandchildren: The role of social support in coping with caregiving challenges.(Author abstract). *International Journal of Aging & Human Development, 62* (4), 359–384.

Gerhardt, C. A., Compas, B. E., Connor, J. K., & Achenbach, T. M. (1999). Association of a mixed anxiety-depression syndrome and symptoms of major depressive disorder during adolescence. *Journal of Youth & Adolescence, 28* (3), 305–323.

Gerson, L. W., Jarjoura, D., & McCord, G. (1987). Factors related to impaired mental health in urban elderly. *Research on Aging, 9* (3), 356–371.

Gerstner, L. V. (1994). *Reinventing education*. New York: Dutton.

Gfellner, B. B. (1994). A matched group comparison of drug use and problem behavior among Canadian Indian and white adolescents. Special Issue: Canadian research on early adolescence. *Journal of Early Adolescence, 14*, 24–48.

Gfroerer, J., Wright, D., & Kopstein, A. (1997). Prevalence of youth substance abuse: The impact of methodological differences between two national surveys. *Drug & Alcohol Dependence, 47* (1), 19–30.

Giarrusso, R., Silverstein, M., & Feng, D. (2000). Psychological costs and benefits of raising children: Evidence from a national survey of grandparents. In C.B. Cox (Ed.), *To grandmother's house we go and stay: Perspectives on custodial grandparents*. New York: Springer, 71–90.

Gibbs, W. (2004). The unseen genome: Beyond DNA. *Scientific American, 289* (6), 106–113.

Gibson, E., & Walk, R. (1960). The visual cliff. *Scientific American, 202,* 64–71.

Gibson, E., & Pick, A. (2000). *An ecological approach to perceptual learning and development*. New York: Oxford Press.

Gilligan, C. (1982). *In a different voice*. Cambridge, MA: Harvard University Press.

Gilligan, C., Lyons, N., & Hanmer, T. (1990). *Making connections: The relational worlds of adolescent girls at Emma Willard School*. Cambridge, MA: Harvard University Press.

Gilliland, G., & Fleming, S. (1998, September). A comparison of spousal anticipatory grief and conventional grief. *Death Studies, 22* (6), 541–569.

Ginsburg, K. (2007). The importance of play in promoting healthy child development and maintaining strong parent-child bonds. *Pediatrics, 119* (1), 182–190.

Gittelsohn, J., Roche, K., Alexander, C., & Tassler, P. (2001). The social context of smoking among African American and white adolescents in Baltimore city. *Ethnicity & Health,* 6, 211–225.

Glaser, D. (2002). Child sexual abuse. In M. Rutter and E. Taylor (Eds.). *Child and adolescent psychiatry*. London: Blackwell.

Gleason, J. B. (1997). *The development of language*. Boston: Allyn & Bacon.

———. (2005). *The development of language*. Boston: Allyn & Bacon.

Gleick, J. (1992). *Genius: The life and science of Richard Feynman*. New York: Pantheon.

Gold, P. E., Jones, M. G., Korol, D. L., Manning, C. A., & Wilkniss, S. M. (1997). Age-related differences in an ecologically based study of rote learning. *Psychology and Aging, 12* (2), 372–375.

Goldberg, S., & DiVitto, B. (2002). Parenting children born preterm. In M. Bornstein (Ed.), *Handbook of parenting* (2nd edition). Mahwah, NJ: Erlbaum.

Goldman-Rakic, P. (1999). Working memory and the mind. The Editors of Scientific American, *The Scientific American Book of The Brain*. New York: The Lyons Press.

Goldsmith, M. F. (1988). Anencephalic organ donor program suspended; Loma Linda report expected to detail findings. *Journal of the American Medical Association, 260,* 1671–1672.

Goleman, D. (1995). *Emotional intelligence*. New York: Bantam.

———. (2006). *Social intelligence*. New York: Bantam.

Golinkoff, R., & Hirsh-Pasek, K. (2000). *How babies talk*. New York: Dutton.

Golombok, S., MacCallum, F., Goodman, E., & Rutter, M. (2002). *Child Development, 73* (3), 952–968.

Gomez, C., & Rosen, B. (2001). The leader-member exchange as a link between managerial trust and employee empowerment. *Group and Organization Management, 26* (1), 53–69.

Goode, E. (2000, June 27). Most ills are a matter of more than one gene. *The New York Times,* D1, D6.

Goodman, K. (1998). End-of-life algorithms. *Psychology, Public Policy, and Law, 4* (3), 719–727.

Gooren, L. (2006). The role of testosterone in erectile function and dysfunction. *Journal of Men's Health & Gender, 3* (3), 292–299.

Gopnik, A., Meltzoff, A. & Kuhl, P. (2000). *The scientist in the crib*. New York: Morrow.

Gordon, R., & Brill, D. (2001). The abuse and neglect of the elderly. *International Journal of Law & Psychiatry. Special Issue: Aging, 24,* 183–197.

Goreau, L. (1984). *Just Mahalia, baby*. New York: Pelican.

Gorski, P. (1999). Toilet training guidelines: Parents—The role of parents in toilet training. *Pediatrics, 103* (6), 1362–1363.

Gottlieb, G. (1997). *Synthesizing nature-nurture*. Mahwah, NJ: Erlbaum.

———. (2002). Developmental-behavioral initiation of evolutionary change. *Psychological Review, 109* (2), 211–218.

Gottlieb, G., Wahlsten, D., & Lickliter, R. (2006).The significance of biology for human development: A developmental psychobiological systems View. In W. Damon & R. Lerner (Series Eds.) & R. Lerner (Volume Ed.), *Handbook of child Psychology: Volume 1. Theoretical models of human development*. New York: John Wiley.

Gould, M. S., Greenberg, T., Velting, D. M., & Shaffer, D. (2003). Youth suicide risk and preventive interventions: A review of the past 10 years. *Journal of the American Academy of Child and Adolescent Psychiatry, 42,* 386–405.

Graber, J. A., & Brooks-Gunn, J. (1996). Transitions and turning points: Navigating the passage from childhood through adolescence. *Developmental Psychology, 32* (4), 768–776.

Graham-Rowe, D. (2002). Teen angst rooted in busy brain: A temporary growth spurt in the cortex triggers the tantrums of adolescence. *New Scientist, 176,* 16–23.

Granger, D., & Kivlighan, K. (2003). Integrating biological, behavioral, and social levels of analysis in early child development: Progress, problems, and prospects. *Child Development, 78* (4), 1058–1063.

Grant, D., & others. (1998). Substance abuse among African-American children: A developmental framework for identifying intervention strategies. *Journal of Human Behavior in the Social Environment. Special Issue: Human Behavior in the Social Environment from an African-American Perspective, 1,* 137–163.

Grant, J. (2000). Women managers and the gendered construction of personal relationships. *Journal of Family Issues, 21* (8), 963–985.

Grant, L. (1999). What sexual revolution? In R. Nye (Ed.), *Sexuality*. London: Oxford.

Gray, C. A., & Geron, S. M. (1995). The other sorrow of divorce: The effects on grandparents when their adult children divorce. *Journal of Gerontological Social Work, 23* (3/4), 139–159.

Green, F., Felstead, A., & Gallie, D. (2003). Computers and the changing skill-intensity of jobs. *Applied Economics, 35* (14), 1561–1577.

Greenberg, A. S., & Bailey, J. M. (1993). Do biological explanations of homosexuality have moral, legal, or policy implications? *Journal of Sex Research, 30* (3), 245–251.

Greenfield, J. (1999). Cultural change and human development. In E. Turiel (Ed.), *Development and cultural change: Reciprocal processes.* San Francisco: Jossey-Bass.

Greenfield, P., & Suzuki, L. (1998). Culture and human development: Implications for parenting, education, pediatrics, and mental health. In W. Damon (Series Ed.) & I. Sigel & K. Renninger (Volume Eds.), *Handbook of child psychology: Volume 4. Child psychology in practice.* New York: John Wiley.

Greenfield, P., Suzuki. L., & Rothstein-Fisch, C. (2006). Cultural pathways through human development. In W. Damon & R. Lerner (Series Eds.) & K. Ann Renninger & Irving Sigel (Volume Eds.), *Handbook of child psychology: Volume 4. Child psychology in practice.* New York: John Wiley.

Greenfield, S. (1997). *The human brain.* New York: Basic Books.

Greenhouse, L. (2000, June 6). Justices deny grandparents visiting rights. *New York Times,* 1, 15.

Greenspan, S. (2003). Child care research: A clinical perspective. *Child Development, 74* (4), 1064–1068.

Grilo, C. M., McGlashan, T. H., & Skodol, A. E. (2000). Stability and course of personality disorders: The need to consider comorbidities and continuities between axis I psychiatric disorders and axis II personality disorders. *Psychiatric Quarterly Special the Twelfth Annual New York State Office of Mental Health Research Conference, 71* (4), 291–307.

Grisso, T., & Tomkins, A. (1996). Communicating violence risk assessment. *American Psychologist, 51* (9), 928–930.

Grodner, M., Long, S., & DeYoung, S. (2004). *Foundations and clinical applications of nutrition.* Philadelphia: Mosby.

Grossman, J., & Kaufman, J. (2002). Evolutionary psychology: Promise and perils. In R. J. Sternberg, & J. C. Kaufman (Eds.), *The evolution of intelligence.* Mahwah, NJ: Erlbaum, 9–25.

Grotevant, H. (1998). Adolescent development in family contexts. In W. Damon (Series Ed.) & N. Eisenberg (Volume Ed.), *Handbook of child psychology: Volume 3. Social, emotional, and personality development.* New York: John Wiley.

Grusec, J., Goodnow, J., & Kucynski, L. (2000). New directions in analyses of parenting contributions to children's acquisition of values. *Child Development, 71* (1), 205–211.

Gruver, R. A. (2004). Current approaches to preventing osteoporosis: A healthy lifestyle helps protect against bone loss and includes diet, calcium supplementation, exercise, and avoidance of tobacco products and excessive alcohol consumption. Drug therapy can also be useful. *Journal of the American Academy of Physicians Assistants, 17* (11), 37–43.

Grych, J. H., & Clark, R. (1999). Maternal employment and development of the father-infant relationship in the first year. *Developmental Psychology, 35* (4), 893–903.

Guerra, N., Huesmann, L., & Spindler, A. (2003). Community violence exposure, social cognition, and aggression among urban elementary school children. *Child Development, 74* (5), 1561–1576.

Guia, D. M. (2003). Caregivers stress syndrome. Letters to the editor. *Townsend Letter for Doctors & Patients.*

Guttman, C. (2000). Older Americans 2000. *Geriatrics, 55,* 63–69.

Guyer, B., Hoyert, D., Martin, J., Ventura, S., MacDorman, M., & Strobino, D. (1999). Annual summary of vital statistics—1998. *Pediatrics, 104* (6), 1229–1246.

Haan, N. (1989). Personality at midlife. In S. Hunter & M. Sundel (Eds.), *Midlife myths.* Newbury Park, CA: Sage.

Haas, F. (2003). Bereavement care: Seeing the body. *Nursing Standards, 17,* 33–37.

Hagan, J., & Foster, H. (2003). S/He's a rebel: Toward a sequential stress theory of delinquency and gendered pathways to disadvantage in emerging adulthood. *Social Forces, 82*(1), 53–87.

Haggerty, R., Sherrod, L., Garmezy, N., & Rutter, M. (1996) *Stress, risk, and resilience in children and adolescents.* NY: Cambridge University Press.

Hahn, C., & DiPietro, J. A. (2001). In vitro fertilization and the family: Quality of parenting, family functioning, and child psychosocial adjustment. *Developmental Psychology, 37* (1), 37–48.

Haith, M., & Benson, J. (1998). Infant cognition. In W. Damon (Series Ed.) & D. Kuhn & R. Siegler (Volume Eds.), *Handbook of child psychology: Volume 2. Cognition, perception, and language.* New York: John Wiley.

Haley, W., LaMonde, L., Han, B., Narramore, S., & Schonwetter, R. (2001). Family caregiving in hospice: Effects on psychological and health functioning among spousal caregivers of hospice patients with lung cancer or dementia. *Hospice Journal, 15,* 1–18.

Haliburn, J. (2000). Reasons for adolescent suicide attempts. *Journal of the American Academy of Child & Adolescent Psychiatry, 39* (1), 13–14.

Hall, D., Eubanks, L., Meyyazhagan, S., Kenney, K., & Johnson, S. (2000). Education of overt surveillance in the diagnosis of Munchausen by proxy. *Pediatrics, 105* (6), 1305–1312.

Hall, G. S. (1904). *Adolescence.* (2 vols.) New York: Appleton-Century-Crofts.

Hallman, R. (1967). Techniques for creative teaching. *Journal of Creative Behavior, 1* (3), 325–330.

Halpern. C., & others. (2000). Adolescent males' willingness to report masturbation. *Journal of Sex Research, 37,* 327–332.

Hamby, S., & Sugarman, D. (1999). Acts of psychological aggression against a partner and their relation to physical assault and gender. *Journal of Marriage and the Family, 61* (2), 959–970.

Hamilton, C. (2000). Continuity and discontinuity of attachment from infancy through adolescence. *Child Development, 71* (3), 690–694.

Harding, J. (1998). *Sex acts: practices of femininity and masculinity.* London: Sage.

Harmon, A. (2004, August 26). Internet gives teenage bullies weapons to wound from afar. *The New York Times.*

Harper, J. (2004). Religion "very important" to most Americans. The Washington Times.

Harris, D. K., Changas, P. S., & Palmore, E. B. (1996). Palmore's first facts on aging quiz in a multiple-choice format. *Educational Gerontology, 22,* 575–589.

Harris, J., & Liebert, R. (1992). *Infant & child.* Englewood Cliffs, NJ: Prentice Hall.

Harris, P. (2006). Social cognition. In W. Damon & R. Lerner (Series Eds.) & D. Kuhn & R. Siegler (Volume Eds.), *Handbook of child psychology: Volume 2. Cognition, perception, and language.* New York: John Wiley.

Harrison, L. (2000). Why culture matters. In L. Harrison & S. Huntington (Eds.), *Culture matters.* New York: Basic Books.

Hart, C. (1998). 50% of fragile X patients lack telltale signs. *AAP News, 14* (6), 1, 16.

———. (2000). Genome project likely to bring new responsibilities to pediatricians. *AAP News, 16* (2), 1, 10.

Hart, D., Hofmann, V., Edelstein, W., & Keller, M. (1997). The relation of childhood personality types to adolescent behavior and development: A longitudinal study of Icelandic children. *Developmental Psychology, 33* (2), 195–205.

Hart, H., McAdams, D., Hirsch, B., & Baur, J. (2001). Generativity and social involvement among African Americans and white adults. *Journal of Research in Personality, 35,* 208–230.

Harter, S. (1993). Visions of self: Beyond the me in the mirror. In J. Jacobs (Ed.), *Developmental perspectives on motivation.* Lincoln: University of Nebraska Press.

———. (1998). The development of self-representations. In W. Damon (Series Ed.) & N. Eisenberg (Volume Ed.), *Handbook of child psychology: Volume 3. Child psychology in practice.* New York: John Wiley.

———. (1999). *The construction of the self.* New York: Guilford.

———. (2006). The self. In W. Damon & R. Lerner (Series Eds.) & N. Eisenberg (Volume Ed.), *Handbook of child psychology: Volume 3. Social, emotional, and personality development.* New York: John Wiley.

Hartl, D., & Jones, E. (2005). *Genetics: Analysis of genes and genomes.* Boston: Jones and Bartlett.

Harvard Health Letter. (1999a). *Driving licenses and the elderly.* Cambridge, MA: Harvard University Press.

———. (1999b). *Elderly licensing.* Cambridge, MA: Harvard University Medical School.

Harvard Men's Health Watch. (1997, October). Prudence and the prostate. *Harvard Men's Health Watch, 2* (3), 5–7.

———. (2004). Taste and smell: Your sensitive senses. Harvard Medical School, 8 (9), 1.

Harvey, E. (1999). Short-term and long-term effects of early parental employment on children of the National Longitudinal Survey of Youth. *Developmental Psychology, 35* (2), 445–459.

Hasan, H. (1998). Understanding the gang culture and how it relates to society and school. In L. H. Meyer, H. S. Park, M. Grenot-Scheyer, I. Schwartz, & B. Harry, (Eds.), *Making friends: The influences of culture and development. Children, youth & change: Sociocultural perspectives: Volume 3.* Baltimore: Brookes, 263–283.

Hastings, P., Zahn-Waxler, C., Robinson, J., Usher, B., & Bridges, D. (2000). The development of concern for others in children with behavior problems. *Developmental Psychology, 36* (5), 531–546.

Hauser-Cram, P. (2006). Young children with developmental disabilities and their families: Needs, policies, and services. In K. Thies & J. Travers, Eds.), *Handbook of human development for health care professionals.* Sudbury, MA: Jones & Bartlett.

Hauser-Cram, P., Pierson, D., Klein Walker, D., & Tivnan, T. (1991). *Early education in the public schools.* San Francisco: Jossey-Bass.

Havighurst, R., Neugarten, B., & Tobin, S. (1968). Disengagement and patterns of aging. In B. Neugarten (Ed.), *Middle age and aging.* Chicago: University of Chicago Press.

Hawkins, J. (2004). *On intelligence.* New York: Henry Holt.

Hays, K. (2004). Coping with college series: Tips for successful career planning for all four years of College. Illinois State Web site: http://www. counseling. ilstu.edu/DP/cope tips.html.

Heckert, D. A., Nowak, T. C., & Snyder, K. A. (1998). The impact of husbands' and wives' relative earnings on marital disruption. *Journal of Marriage and the Family, 60* (4), 690–703.

Heller, S., Larrieu, J., D'Imperio, R., & Boris, N. (1999). Research on resilience to child maltreatment: Empirical considerations. *Child Abuse & Neglect, 23* (4), 321–338.

Helzner, E. P., Cauley, J. A., Pratt, S. R., Wisniewski, S. R., Talbott, E. O., Zmuda, J. M., Harris, T. B., Rubin, S. M., Taaffe, D. R., Tylavsky, F. A., & Newman, A. B. (2005). Hearing sensitivity and bone mineral density in older adults: The Health, Aging, and Body Composition Study. *Osteoporosis International, 16* (12), 1675–1683.

Henden, H. (1999). Suicide, assisted suicide, and euthanasia. In D. G. Jacobs (Ed.), *The Harvard Medical School guide to suicide assessment and intervention.* San Francisco: Jossey-Bass, 540–560.

Henig, R. (2000) *The monk in the garden.* Boston: Houghton Mifflin.

Hennessey, B. A. (1995). Social, environmental, and developmental issues and creativity. Special Issue: Toward an educational psychology of creativity: I. *Educational Psychology Review, 7* (2), 163–183.

Henrich, C., Brown, J., & Aber, J. (2000). Evaluating the effectiveness of school-based violence prevention: Developmental approaches. *Social Policy Report, SRCD 13* (3).

Henry, B., Caspi, A., Moffit, T. E., & Silva, P. A. (1996). Temperamental and familial predictors of violent and nonviolent criminal convictions: Age 3 to age 18. *Developmental Psychology, 32* (4), 614–623.

Henry, D. (1999). Resilience in maltreated children: Implications for special needs adoption. *Child Welfare, 78* (5), 519– 540.

Herman-Giddens, M., Slora, E., Wasserman, R., Bourdony, C., Koch, G., & Hasemeier, C. (1997). Secondary sexual characteristics and menses in young girls in office practice: A study from the pediatric research office settings network. *Pediatrics, 99* (4), 505–518.

Hertzog, C. (1989). Influences of cognitive slowing on age differences in intelligence. *Developmental Psychology, 25,* 636–651.

Hertzog, C., Kidder, D. P., Mayhorn, C. B., Morrell, R. W., & Park, D. C. (1997). Effect of age on event-based and time-based prospective memory. *Psychology and Aging, 12* (2), 314–327.

Hess, D. W., Marwitz, J. H., & Kreutzer, J. S. (2003). Neuropsychological impairments after spinal cord injury: A comparative study with mild traumatic brain injury. *Rehabilitation Psychology, 48* (3), 151–156.

Hess, T., Auman, C., Colcombe, S., Rahhal, & Tamara, A. (2003). Memory performance.

Hetherington, E., & Kelly, J. (2002). *For better or for worse: Divorce reconsidered.* New York: Norton.

———— (2003). For better or for worse. divorce reconsidered. *Journal of Child Psychology & Psychiatry, 44* (3), 470–471.

Hetherington, M., & Stanley-Hagan, M. (1995). Parenting in divorced and remarried families. In M. H. Bornstein (Ed.), *Children and parenting: Volume 4.* Hillsdale, NJ: Erlbaum.

————. (2002). In M. Bornstein (Ed.), *Handbook of parenting* (2nd edition). Mahwah, NJ: Erlbaum.

Hetherington, E., Stanley-Hagan, M., & Anderson, E. (1989). Marital transitions: A child's perspective. *American Psychologist, 44,* 303–312.

Heyl, V., & Wahl, H. W. (2001, December). Psychosocial adaptation to age-related vision loss: A six-year perspective. *Journal of Visual Impairment & Blindness, 95* (12), 739–748.

Heywood, C. (2001). *A history of childhood.* Malden, MA: Blackwell.

Hiebert, E., & Raphael, T. (1996). Psychological perspectives on literacy and extensions to educational practice. In D. Berliner & R. Calfee (Eds.), *Handbook of educational psychology.* New York: Macmillan.

Hill, J. P. (1987). Central changes during adolescence. (Society for Research on Adolescence) Research on Adolescents and their families. In W. Damon (Ed.), *New directions in child psychology.* San Francisco: Jossey-Bass.

Hillman, J. L., & Stricker, G. (1996). Predictors of college students' knowledge of and attitudes toward elderly sexuality: The relevance of grandparental contact. *Educational Gerontology, 22,* 539–555.

Hinde, R. (1992). Developmental psychology in the context of other behavioral sciences. *Developmental Psychology, 28* (6), 1018–1029.

———— (1993). A comparative study of relationship structure. *British Journal of Social Psychology, 32* (3), 191–207.

Hindley, P., & van Gent, T. (2005) Psychiatric aspects of specific sensory impairments. In M. Rutter & E. Taylor (Eds.), *Child and adolescent psychiatry.* London: Blackwell.

Hines, A. M. (1997). Divorce-related transitions, adolescent development, and the role of the parent-child relationship: A review of the literature. *Journal of Marriage and the Family, 59* (2), 375–388.

Hingson, R. W., Heeren, T., Jamanka, A., & Howland, J. (2000). Age of drinking onset and unintentional injury involvement after drinking. *Journal of the American Medical Association, 284* (12), 1527–1533.

Ho, T., Leung, P., Hung, S., Lee, C., & Tang, C. (2000). The mental health of the peers of suicide completers and attempters. *Journal of Child Psychology and Psychiatry, 41,* 301–308.

Hobson, J. A. (2004). Freud returns? Like a bad dream. *Scientific American, 290* (5), 89.

Hodapp, R., & Dykens, E. (2006). Mental retardation. In W. Damon & R. Lerner (Series Eds.) & K. Renninger & I. Sigel (Volume Eds.), *Handbook of child psychology: Volume 4. Child psychology in practice.* New York: John Wiley.

Hoffman, M. (2000). *Empathy and moral development.* New York: Cambridge University Press.

Holinger, P. C., Offer, D., & Ostrov, E. (1987). Suicide and homicide in the United States: An epidemiologic study of violent death, population changes, and the potential for prediction. *American Journal of Psychiatry, 144* (2), 215–219.

Holmbeck, G., Paikoff, R., & Brooks-Gunn, J. (1995). Parenting adolescents. In M. Bornstein (Ed.), *Handbook of parenting: Volume 1. Children and parenting.* Mahwah, NJ: Erlbaum.

Honan, W. H. (1997, March 16). Drug arrests rise 18% on major college campuses, survey finds. *The New York Times,* p. 25.

Horn, J. L. (1975). *Psychometric studies of aging and intelligence.* New York: Raven Press.

————. (1978). Human ability systems. In P. B. Baltes (Ed.), *Life-span development and behavior: Volume 1.* New York: Academic Press.

Horn, J. L., Donaldson, G., & Engstrom, R. (1981). Apprehension, memory, and fluid intelligence decline in adulthood. *Research on Aging, 3* (3), 33–84.

Horowitz, F. D. (2000). Child development and the PITS: Simple questions, complex answers, and developmental theory. *Child Development, 71* (1), 1–10.

Horwitz, A., White, H., & Howell-White, S. (1996). Becoming married and mental health. *Journal of Marriage and the Family,* 58(4), pp. 895–907.

Household and Family Characteristics. (1999). *Married adults still in the majority.* Washington, D.C.: Office of the U.S. Census Bureau.

Howard, P. (2000). *The owner's manual for the brain.* Austin, TX: Bard Press.

Howe, P. (1997, October). Study of elders favors calcium, vitamin D. *The Boston Globe,* p. A12.

Hoy, A., Davis, H., & Pape. (2006). Teacher Knowledge and beliefs. In Patricia Alexander and Philip Winne (Eds.), *Handbook of educational psychology.* Mahwah, NJ: Lawrence Erlbaum.

Huang, B., Cornoni-Huntley, J., Hays, J., Huntley, R., Galanos, A., & Blazer, D. (2000). Impact of depressive symptoms on hospitalization risk in community-dwelling older persons. *Journal of American Geriatric Society, 48,* 1279–1284.

Huff, L. (2004). Where personality goes awry. *Monitor on Psychology, 35* (3), 42–44.

Hulit, L., & Howard, M. (1997). *Born to talk.* Needham Heights, MA: Allyn & Bacon.

Humes, L. E., & Floyd, S. S. (2005). Measures of working memory, sequence learning, and speech recognition in the elderly. *Journal of Speech, Language, and Hearing Research, 48* (1), 224–236.

Hunt, P. (Ed.). (1995). *Children's literature. An illustrated history.* New York: Oxford University Press.

Hunt, T., & Lindley, C. J. (1989). *Testing older adults.* Washington, D.C.: Center for Psychological Services.

Hunter, S., & Sundel, M. (1989). *Midlife myths.* Newbury Park, CA: Sage.

Hurwitz, A., Brady, D., Schaal, S., Samloff, I., Dedon, J., & Ruhl, C. (1997). *Gastric acidity in older adults, 278* (8): 659–662.

Hussey, J. M., Chang, J. J., & Kotch, J. B. (2006). Child maltreatment in the United States: Prevalence, risk factors, and adolescent health consequences. *Pediatrics, 118* (3), 933–943.

Huston, A., & Wright, J. (1998). Mass media and children's development. In W. Damon (Series Ed.) & I. Sigel & K. Renninger (Volume Eds.), *Handbook of child psychology: Volume 4. Child psychology in practice.* New York: John Wiley.

Huston, A., Wright, J., Marquis, J., & Green, S. (1999). How young children spend their time: Television and other activities. *Developmental Psychology, 35* (4), 912–925.

Hyman, S. (2001). Mental health in an aging population: The NIMH perspective. American *Journal of Geriatric Psychiatry, 9,* 330–339.

Isakson, K., & Jarvis, P. (1999). The adjustment of adolescents during the transition into high school: A short-term longitudinal study. *Journal of Youth and Adolescence, 28* (1), 1–16.

Isley, S., O'Neil, R., Clatfelter, D., & Parke, R. (1999). Parent and child expressed affect and children's social competence: Modeling direct and indirect pathways. *Developmental Psychology, 35* (2), 547–560.

Iwanir, S., & Ayal, H. (1991). Midlife divorce initiation. *Contemporary Family Therapy, 13* (6), 609–623.

Izard, C. (1982). *Measuring emotions in infants and young children.* New York: Cambridge University Press.

———. (1994). Intersystems connections. In Paul Ekman & Richard Davidson (Eds.), *The nature of emotion.* New York: Oxford University Press.

Izard, C., Fantauzzo, C., Castle, J., Haynes, O., Rayias, M., & Putnam, P. (1995). The ontogeny and significance of infants' facial expressions in the first 9 months of life. *Developmental Psychology, 31* (6), 997–1013.

Jackowitz, A., Nobvillo, D., & Tiehen, L. (2007). Special supplemental nutrition programs for women, infants, and children and infant feeding practices. *Pediatrics, 119* (2), 281–289.

Jackson, H., & Nuttall, R. (1997). *Childhood abuse: Effects on clinicians' personal and professional lives.* Thousand Oaks, CA: Sage.

Jackson, J. (1996). *Genetics and you.* Totowa, NJ: Humana Press.

Jacobs, J. A., & Gerson, K. (2001). Overworked individuals or overworked families? *Work and Occupations, 28* (1), 40–63.

Jackson, J. S., & Gibson, R. C. (1985). Work and retirement among the black elderly. In Z. S. Blou (Ed.), *Current perspectives on aging and the life cycle: Volume 1: Work, retirement, and social policy.* Greenwich, CT: JAI Press.

Jacobs, J., Lanza, S., Osgood, D., Eccles, J., & Wigfield, A. (2002). Changes in children's self-competence and values: Gender and domain differences across grades one through twelve. *Child Development, 73* (2), 509–527.

Jacobs, R., & Speckhardt, R. (2004). What do we do now that the sexual revolution is over? *The Humanist, 64* (6), 11–17.

Jacobvitz, D. B., & Bush, N. F. (1996). Reconstructions of family relationships: Parent-child alliances, personal distress, and self-esteem. *Developmental Psychology, 32* (4), 732–743.

James, L. E., Burke, D. M., Austin, A., & Hulme, E. (1998). Production and perception of "verbosity" in younger and older adults. *Psychology and Aging, 13* (3), 355–367.

James, W. (1890 [1981]). *Principles of psychology.* Cambridge, MA: Harvard University Press.

Jansen, B. *The Big6 in middle school.* Columbus, Ohio: Linworth Publishing.

Janus, S., & Janus, C. (1993). *The Janus report on sexual behavior.* New York: John Wiley.

Jaquish, G., & Ripple, R. E. (1990). Cognitive creative abilities across the adult life span. *Human Development, 34* (2), 143–152.

Jasper, M. (2000). Antepartum fetal assessment. In S. Mattson & J. Smith (Eds.), *Core curriculum for maternal-newborn nursing.* Philadelphia: W. B. Saunders.

Jeffreys, S. (1998). Behavior. In R. Nye (Ed.), *Sexuality.* London: Oxford.

Jefko, W. (1980). Redefining death. In E. Schneiderman (Ed.), *Death: Current perspectives.* Palo Alto, CA: Mayfield.

Jenkins, J., Simpson, A., Dunn, J., Rasbash, R., O'Connor, T. (2005). Mutual influence of marital conflict and children's behavior problems: Shared and non-shared family risks. *Child Development,* 76(1), 24–39.

Jenks, R. J., & Christiansen, L. (2002). A comparison of three catholic marital groups on sexual and gender issues. *Journal of Divorce & Remarriage, 38,* 157–165.

Jennings, J. R., Kamarck, T., Manuck, S., & Everson, S. A. (1997). Aging or disease? Cardiovascular reactivity in Finnish men over the middle years. *Psychology and Aging, 12* (2), 225–238.

Jeynes, W. H. (1999). Effects of remarriage following divorce on the academic achievement of children. *Journal of Youth & Adolescence, 28* (3), 385–393.

Jimerson, S., Pavelski, R., & Orliss, M. (2002). Helping children with eating disorders: Quintessential research on etiology, prevention, assessment, and treatment. In J. Sandoval (Ed.), *Handbook of crisis counseling, intervention, and prevention in the schools* (2nd edition). Mahwah, NJ: Erlbaum, 393–415.

Joensson, P., & Carlsson, I. (2000). Androgyny and creativity: A study of the relationship between a balanced sex-role and creative functioning. *Scandinavian Journal of Psychology, 41,* 269–274.

Jogerst, G., Dawson, J., Hartz, A., Ely, J., & Schweitzer, L. (2000). Community characteristics associated with elder abuse. *Journal of the American Geriatrics Society, 48,* 513–518.

Johnson, B. (2002). The intentional mentor: Strategies and guidelines for the practice of mentoring. *Professional Psychology: Research & Practice, 33,* 88–96.

Johnson, M. (1998). The neural basis of cognitive development. In W. Damon (Series Ed.) & D. Kuhn & R. Siegler (Volume Eds.), *Handbook of child psychology: Volume 4. Child psychology in practice.* New York: John Wiley.

———. (1999). *Developmental cognitive neuroscience.* London: Blackwell.

Johnson, R. (2002). The puzzle of later male retirement. *Economic Review (Kansas City) 87* (3), 5–28.

Johnston, L. D., O'Malley, P. M., Bachman, J. G., Schulenberg, J. E. (2005). *Monitoring the future national survey results on drug use, 1975–2004: Volume 2. College students and adults ages* (NIH Publication No. 05-5728). Bethesda, MD: National Institute on Drug Abuse.

Johnston, W. B. (1987). *Workforce 2000: Work and workers for the 21st century.* Indianapolis, IN: Hudson Institute.

Jones, S. (1993). *The language of genes.* New York: Anchor Books.

———. (1996). Imitation or exploration: Young infants' matching of adults' oral gestures. *Child Development, 67,* 1952–1969.

Jung, C. G. (1971a). *The portable Jung* (J. Campbell, Ed.). New York: Viking Press.

———. (1971b). *The spirit in man, art and literature.* New York: Princeton University Press.

———. (2001 [1927]). Psychology of the unconscious: A study of the transformations and symbolisms of the libido contribution to the history of the evolution of thought. (B. M. Hinkle, Trans.). Princeton: Princeton University Press.

Jung, C. G., & Hisamatsu, S. (1968). On the unconscious, the self and the therapy: A dialogue. *Psychologia: An International Journal of Psychology in the Orient, 11* (1–2), 25–32.

Kachru, Y. (2005). Teaching and learning of world englishes. In E. Hinkel (Ed.), *Handbook of research in second language teaching and learning.* Mahwah, NJ: Erlbaum.

Kacmar, K. M., & Ferris, G. R. (1989). Theoretical and methodological considerations in the age-job satisfaction relationship. *Journal of Applied Psychology, 74* (2), 201–207.

Kagan, J. (1984). *The nature of the child.* NY: Basic Books.

———. (1992). Yesterday's premises, tomorrow's promises. *Developmental Psychology, 28* (6), 990–997.

———. (1994). *Galen's prophecy. Temperament in human nature.* New York: Basic Books.

———. (1997). Temperament and the reactions to unfamiliarity. *Child Development, 68* (1), 139–143.

———. (1998a). Biology and the child. In W. Damon (Series Ed.) & N. Eisenberg (Volume Ed.), *Handbook of child psychology: Volume 3. Social, emotional, and personality development.* New York: John Wiley.

———. (1998b). *Three seductive ideas.* Cambridge, MA: Harvard University Press.

———. (2004). *The long shadow of temperament.* Cambridge, MA: Harvard University Press.

———. (2006). *An argument for mind.* New Haven: Yale University Press.

Kagan, J., & Fox, N. (2006). Biology, culture, and temperamental biases. In N. Eisenberg (Ed.), *Handbook of child psychology: Volume 3. Social, emotional, and personality development.* New York: John Wiley.

Kagan, J., & Snidman, N. (2004). *The long shadow of temperament.* Cambridge, MA: Harvard University Press.

Kahn, M. (2002). *Basic Freud.* New York: Basic Books.

Kakuchi, S. (1997, September 27). Graying of Japan. *The Boston Globe,* p. A3.

Kallman, F., & Jarvik, L. (1959). Individual differences in constitution and genetic background. In J. Birren (Ed.), *Handbook of aging and the individual.* Chicago: University of Chicago Press.

Kaltiala-Heino, R., Rimpelae, M., Rissanen, A., & Rantanen, P. (2001). Early puberty and early sexual activity are associated with bulimic-type eating pathology in middle adolescence. *Journal of Adolescent Health, 28,* 346–352.

Kamarck, T., Debski, T., & Manuck, S. (2000). Enhancing the laboratory-to-life generalizability of cardiovascular reactivity using multiple occasions of measurement. *Psychophysiology, 37,* 533–542.

Kandel, E. (2006). *In search of memory.* New York: Norton.

Kaneda, H., Maeshima, K., Goto, N., Kobayakawa, T., Ayabe-Kanamura, S., & Saito, S. (2000). Decline in taste and odor discrimination abilities with age, and relationship between gustation and olfaction. *Chemical Senses, 25,* 331–337.

Kaplowitz, P., & Oberfield, S. (2000). Re-examination of the age limit for defining when puberty is precocious in girls in the United States: Implications for evaluation and treatment. *Pediatrics, 104* (4), 936–941.

Kaslow, F. (2000). Families experiencing divorce. In W.C. Nichols, M. A. Pace-Nichols, et al. (Eds.), *Handbook of family development and intervention. Wiley series in couples and family dynamics and treatment.* New York: John Wiley, 341–368.

Kaslow, N., Webb Price, A., Wyckoff, S., Bender Grall, M., Sherry, A., Young, S., Scholl, L., Millington Upshaw, V., Rashid, A., Jackson, E., & Bethea, K. (2004). Person factors associated with suicidal behavior among African-American women and men. *Cultural Diversity & Ethnic Minority Psychology, 10* (1), 5–22.

Kassebaum, N. (1994). Head Start: Only the best for America's children. *American Psychologist, 49* (2), 123–126.

Katigbak, M., Church, A., Guanzon-Lapena, M., Carlota, A., del Pilar, G. (2002). Are indigenous personality dimensions culture specific? Philippine inventories and the five-factor model. *Journal of Personality & Social Psychology, 82,* 89–101.

Katzir, T., & Pare-Blagorv, J. (2006). Applying cognitive neuroscience research to education: The case of literacy. *Educational Psychologist, 41*(91), 53–74.

Kaufman, A., & Wang, J. (1992). Gender, race, and education differences on the K-BIT at ages 4 to 90 years. *Journal of Psychoeducational Assessment, 10* (3), 219–229.

Kaufman, A. S., & Ishikuma, T. (1993). Intellectual and achievement testing. In T. H. Ollendick, & M. Hersen (Eds.), *Handbook of child and adolescent assessment general psychology series: Volume 167.* Needham Heights, MA: Allyn & Bacon, 192–207.

Kaufman, A. S., Reynolds, C. R., & McLean, J. E. (1989). Age and WAIS-R intelligence in a national sample of adults in the 20- to 74-year age range: A gross-sectional analysis with education level controlled. *Intelligence, 13* (3), 235–253.

Kaufman, J. C., McLean, J. E., Kaufman, A. S., & Kaufman, N. L. (1994). White, black, and Hispanic differences on fluid and crystallized abilities by age across the 11- to 94-year range. *Psychological Reports, 75* (3), 1279–1288.

Kazdin, A. E. (Ed.). (1997). *Encyclopedia of psychology.* Washington, D.C.: American Psychological Association.

Keel, P., & others. (2001). Vulnerability to eating disorders in childhood and adolescence. In R. E. Ingram & J. M. Price (Eds.), *Vulnerability to psychopathology: Risk across the lifespan.* New York: Guilford, 389–411.

Kegan, R. (1994). *In over our heads.* Cambridge, MA: Harvard University Press.

Kellogg, B. (2000). *Fetal development.* In S. Mattson & J. Smith (Eds.), *Core curriculum for maternal-newborn nursing.* Philadelphia: W. B. Saunders.

Kellogg, N. (2007). Evaluation of suspected child physical abuse. *Pediatrics, 120* (1), 1232–1241.

Kellogg, R. (1967). *Understanding children's art.* Del Mar, CA: CRM Publishing.

——— (1970). *Analyzing children's art.* Palo Alto, CA: National Press Books.

——— (1979). *Children's drawings/children's minds.* New York: Avon.

Kelly, J. (2000). Children's adjustment in conflicted marriage and divorce: A decade review of research. *Journal of the American Academy of Child & Adolescent Psychiatry, 39,* 963–973.

Kelly, J., & Hansen, D. (1990). Social interactions and adjustment. In V. VanHasselt & M. Herson (Eds.), *Handbook of adolescent psychology.* New York: Pergamon Press, 131–146.

Kendall, J. (2003, October). *Fierce attachments.* Boston Globe, 3, 5.

Kendig, H., Hashimoto, A., & Coppard, L. (Eds.). (1992). *Family support for the elderly: The international experience.* Oxford: Oxford University Press.

Kensinger, E., Brierley, B., Medford, N., Growdon, J., & Corkin, S. (2004). Effects of normal aging and Alzheimer's disease on emotional memory. *Emotion, 2* (2), 118–134.

Kerns, K., Klepac, L., & Cole, A. (1996). Peer relationships and preadolescents' perceptions of security in the child-mother relationship. *Developmental Psychology, 32* (3), 457–466.

Kerns, K., Tomich, P., Aspelmeier, J., & Contreras, J. (2000). Attachment-based assessments of parent-child relationships in middle childhood. *Developmental Psychology, 36* (5), 614–626.

Kiernan, K. E., & Hobcraft, J. (1997). Parental divorce during childhood: Age at first intercourse, partnership and parenthood. *Population Studies, 51,* 41–55.

Killgore, W., & Oki, M. (2001). Sex-specific developmental changes in amygdala responses to affective faces. *Neuroreport: For Rapid Communication of Neuroscience Research, 12,* 427–433.

Kim, U. (1990). Indigenous psychology: Science and applications. In R. Brislin (Ed.), *Applied cross-cultural psychology.* Newbury Park, CA: Sage.

Kimmel, D. (1974). *Adulthood and aging.* New York: John Wiley.

Kindlon, D., & Thompson, M. (1999). *Raising Cain: Protecting the emotional life of boys.* New York: Ballantine Books.

King, I. (1914). *The high school age.* Indianapolis: Bobbs-Merrill.

King, K. (2000, February). Common teen suicide myths undermine prevention programs. *American Academy of Pediatrics News.* Elk Grove Village, IL: American Association of Pediatricians.

King, V., & Elder, G. H. (1998). Perceived self-efficacy and grandparenting. *Journal of Gerontology, 53* (5), 249–257.

Kinman, G., & Kinman, R. (2001). The role of motivation to learn in management education. *Journal of Workplace Learning, 13,* 132–144.

Kinnunen, U., & Pulkkinen, L. (2003). Childhood socio-emotional characteristics as antecedents of marital stability and quality. *European Psychologist, 8* (4), 223–237.

Kinsman, S., Romer, D., Furstenberg, F., & Schwarz, D. (1998). Early sexual initiation. *Pediatrics, 102* (5), 1185–1192.

Kitzmann, K. (2000). Effects of marital conflict on subsequent triadic family interactions and parenting. *Developmental Psychology, 36* (1), 3–13.

Klatsky, A. (1999). Moderate drinking and reduced risk of heart disease. *Alcohol Research & Health, 23* (1), 15–23.

———. (2001). *Alcohol in health and disease.* New York: Marcel Dekker.

Kling, K., Seltzer, M., & Ryff, C. (1997). Distinctive late-life challenges. *Psychology & Aging, 12* (2), 288–295.

Klonof-Cohen, H. (1997). Sleep position and sudden infant death in the United States. *Epidemiology, 3* (2), 327–329.

Knoester, C., & Booth, A. (2000). Barriers to divorce: When are they effective? *Journal of Family Issues, 21* (1), 78–99.

Knowles, M. (1989). *The adult learner: A neglected species.* Houston: Gulf.

Knox, D., Zusman, M., & Nieves, W. (1998). College students' homogamous preferences for a date and mate. *College Student Journal, 32* (4), 482–484.

Koch, H. (1960). The relation of certain formal attributes of siblings to attitudes held toward each other and toward their parents. *Monographs of the Society for Research in Child Development, 25* (4). Chicago: University of Chicago Press.

Kochanska, G. (2000). Mutually responsive orientation between mothers and their young children: Implications for early socialization. *Child Development, 68* (1), 94–11.

Kochenderfer-Ladd, B. (2003, October). Identification of aggressive and asocial victims and the stability of their peer victimization. *Merrill-Palmer Quarterly, 49* (4), 401–425.

Koenig, A., Cicchetti, D., & Rogosch, F. (2000). Child compliance/noncompliance and maternal contributors to internalization in maltreating and nonmaltreating dyads. *Child Development 71* (4), 1018–1032.

Koenig, H. G., Kvale, J. N., & Ferrell, C. (1988). Religion and well-being in later life. *The Gerontologist, 28* (1), 18–20.

Kohlberg, L. (1966). A cognitive-developmental analysis of children's sex-role concepts and attitudes. In E. Maccoby (Ed.), *The development of sex differences.* Palo Alto, CA: Stanford University Press.

———. (1975). The cognitive-developmental approach to moral education. *Phi Delta Kappan, 56,* 670–677.

———. (1981). *The philosophy of moral development.* New York: Harper & Row.

———. (1996). A cognitive-developmental analysis of children's sex-concepts and attitudes. In E. Maccoby (Ed.), *The development of sex differences.* Palo Alto, CA: Stanford University Press.

Kolata, G. (1990). *The baby doctors.* New York: Dell.

———. (1998). *Clone.* New York: Morrow.

Koplan, J., Thacker, S., & Lezin, N. (1999). Epidemiology in the 21st century: calculation, communication, and intervention. *American Journal of Public Health, 89* (8), 1153–1155.

Kopp, C. (1993). *Baby steps.* New York: Freeman.

Kosan, L. (2000, February). Young girls and their parents cope with an earlier onset of puberty. *The Boston Parents' Paper, 7.*

Kovas, M., Devlin, B., Pollock, M., Richards, C., & Mukerji, P. (1997). A controlled family history study of childhood-onset depressive disorder. *Archives of General Psychiatry, 54,* 613–623.

Kozol, J. (1991). *Savage inequalities.* New York: Crown.

Kramer, A., & Willis, S. (2004). Enhancing the cognitive vitality of older adults. In J. Lerner & A. Alberts (Eds.), *Current directions in developmental psychology.* New Jersey: Prentice Hall, 160–166.

Kramer, B., & Lambert, J. D. (Dec. 1999). Caregiving as a life course transition among older husbands: A prospective study. *Gerontologist, 39* (6), 658–667.

Kreeger, K.Y. (2002). Sex-based longevity: Societal and lifestyle issues—not biology—appear to have the greatest influences on whether men or women live longer. *The Scientist, 16* (10), 34–36.

Kres, J., & Elias, M. (2006). School-based social and emotional learning programs. In W. Damon & R. Lerner (Series Eds.) & K. Renninger & I. Sigel (Volume Eds.), *Handbook of child psychology: Volume 4. Child psychology in practice.* New York: John Wiley.

Krettenauer, T., Ullrich, M., Hofmann, V., & Edelstein, W. (2003). Behavioral problems in childhood and adolescence as predictors of ego-level attainment in early adulthood. *Merrill-Palmer Quarterly, 49,* 125–138.

Krogh, D. (2002). *Biology: A guide to the natural world.* Upper Saddle River, NJ: Prentice Hall.

Kübler-Ross, E. (1969). *On death and dying.* New York: Macmillan.

———. (1975). *Death: The final stage of growth.* Englewood Cliffs, NJ: Prentice Hall.

Kübler-Ross, E., & Warshaw, W. (1978). *To live until we say goodbye.* Englewood Cliffs, NJ: Prentice Hall.

Kuhn, D. (2000). Does memory development belong on an endangered topic list? *Child Development, 71* (1), 21–25.

———. (2004). Metacognitive Development. In J. Lerner & A. Alberts (Eds.), *Current directions in developmental psychology.* NJ: Prentice Hall, 55–60.

Kulik, L. (2001). Marital relations in late adulthood, throughout the retirement process. *Aging & Society, 21,* 447–456.

———. (2002). Marital equality and the quality of long-term marriage in later life. *Aging and Society, 22,* 459–468.

Kurdek, L. (1998). Relationship outcomes and their predictors: Longitudinal evidence from heterosexual married, gay cohabiting, and lesbian cohabiting couples. *Journal of Marriage and the Family, 60* (4), 553–568.

Kurpius, S. E., Foley Nicpon, M., & Maresh, S. M. (2001). Mood, marriage, and menopause. *Journal of Counseling Psychology, 48,* 77–84.

Kwong, E. W., & Kwan, A.Y. (2003). How older people manage stress: Enid Wai-yung Kwong and Alex Yiu-Huen Kwan studied older adults in Hong Kong in order to determine how they cope with stress and which stress management methods, if any, they choose to use. *Nursing Older People, 15* (3), 18–22.

Labouvie-Vief, G., & Lawrence, R. (1985). Object knowledge, personal knowledge, and processes of equilibration in adult cognition. *Human Development, 28,* 25–39.

LaBrie, J. W., Pedersen, E. R., & Tawalbeh, S. (Jan. 2007). Classifying risky-drinking college students: Another look at the two-week drinker-type categorization. *Journal of Studies on Alcohol, 68* (1), 86–91.

Ladd, G., & LeSieur, K. (1995). Parents and children's peer relationships. In M. Bornstein (Ed.), *Handbook of parenting: Volume 4. Applied and practical parenting.* Mahwah, NJ: Erlbaum.

Lamb, M. (1998). Nonparental child care: Context, quality, correlates, and consequences. In W. Damon (Series Ed.) & I. Sigel & K. A. Renninger (Volume Eds.), *Handbook of child psychology: Volume 4. Child psychology in practice.* New York: John Wiley.

Lamb, M., & Ahnert, L. (2006). Nonparental child care: Context, concepts, correlates, and consequences. In W. Damon & R. Lerner (Series Eds.) & K. Ann Renninger & Irving Sigel (Volume Eds.), *Handbook of child psychology: Volume 4. Child psychology in practice.* New York: John Wiley.

Lamb, M., Hwang, C., Ketterlinus, R., & Fracasso, M. (1999). Parent-child relationships. In M. Bornstein & M. Lamb (Eds.), *Developmental psychology: An advanced textbook.* Mahwah, NJ: Erlbaum.

Lambie, J., & Marcel, A. (2002). Consciousness and the varieties of emotion experience: A theoretical framework. *Psychological Review, 109* (2), 219–259.

Lang, F. (2001). Regulation of social relationships in later adulthood. *Journal of Gerontology, 56B,* P321–P326.

Langlois, J., & Liben, L. (2003). Child care research: An editorial perspective. *Child Development, 74* (4), 969–975.

Lantz, M. (2001). Suicide in late life: Identifying and managing at-risk older patients. *Geriatrics, 56,* 47–48.

Larivee, S., Normandeau, S., & Parent S. (2000). The French connection: Some contributions of French-language research in the post-Piagetian era. *Child Development, 71* (4), 823–839.

Larsson, M., Finkel, D., & Pedersen, N. (2000). Odor identification: Influences of age, gender, cognition, and personality. *Journals of Gerontology: Series B: Psychological Sciences & Social Sciences, 55B,* 304–310.

Lattal, K. (1992). B. F. Skinner and psychology. *American Psychologist, 47* (11), 1269–1272.

Lauber, M. O., Marshall, M. I., Meyers, J. (2005). Gangs. In S. W. Lee (Ed.), *Encyclopedia of School Psychology.* Thousand Oaks, CA: Sage.

Lawrence, R. H., Tennstedt, S. L., & Assmann, S. F. (1998). Quality of the caregiver-care recipient relationship: Does it offset negative consequences of caregiving for family caregivers? *Psychology & Aging, 13* (1), 150–158.

Lawson, D. M., & Brossart, D.F. (2004). The association between current intergenerational family relationships and sibling structure. *Journal of Counseling and Development, 82* (4), 472–483.

Leaper, C., Anderson, K., & Sanders, P. (1998). Moderators of gender effects on parents' talk to their children: A meta-analysis. *Developmental Psychology, 34* (1), 3–27.

Lee, G., DeMaris, A., Bavin, S., & Sullivan, R. (2001). Gender differences in the depressive effect of widowhood in later life. *Journal of Gerontology, 56B,* S56–S61.

Lee, G., Peek, C. W., & Coward, R. T. (1998). Race differences in filial responsibility expectations among older parents. *Journal of Marriage and the Family, 60* (3), 404–412.

Lee, J. M., Appugliese, D., Kaciroti, N., Corwyn, R. F., Bradley, R. H., & Lumeng, J. C. (2007). Weight status in young girls and the onset of puberty. Pediatrics, *119* (3), 593–595.

Legato, M. (1998). *Gender-specific aspects of human biology for the practising physician.* Armonk, NJ: Futura.

Lehman, H. C. (1953). *Age and achievement.* Princeton, NJ: Princeton University Press.

———. (1962). The creative production rates of present versus past generations of scientists. *Journal of Gerontology, 17,* 409–417.

———. (1964). The relationship between chronological age and high level research output in physics and chemistry. *Journal of Gerontology, 19,* 157–164.

Leibson, C., Garrard, J., Mitz, N., Waller, L., Indritz, M., Jackson, J., Rolnich, S., & Luepke, L. (1999). The role of depression in the association between self-rated physical health and clinically defined illness. *The Gerontologist, 39* (3), 291–298.

Leifer, G. (2003). *Introduction to maternity and pediatric nursing.* St. Louis, Mo: Saunders.

Leinonen, E., Korpisammal, L., Pulkkinen, L., & Pukuri, T. (2001). The comparison of burden between caregiving spouses of depressive and demented patients. *International Journal of Geriatric Psychiatry, 16,* 387–393.

Leland, J. (1998, June 16). The secret life of teens. *Newsweek,* p. 121.

Lemerise, E., & Arsenio, W. (2000). An integrated model of emotion processes and cognition in social information processing. *Child Development, 71* (1), 107–118.

Lenneberg, E. (1967). *Biological foundations language.* New York: Wiley.

Leon, I. (2002). Adoption losses: Naturally occurring or socially constructed? *Child Development, 73* (2), 652–653.

Lerner, J., & Ashman, O. (2006). Culture and lifespan development. In K. Theis & J. Travers (Eds.), *Handbook of human development for health care professionals.* Sudbury, MA: Jones & Bartlett.

Lerner, L., Petersen, A., and Brooks-Gunn, J. (Eds.) (1991). *The encyclopedia of adolescence.* London: Taylor & Francis.

Lerner, R. (1991). Changing organism—Context relations as the basic process of development: A developmental contextual perspective. *Developmental Psychology, 27* (1), 27–32.

———. (2002). *Concepts and theories of human development* (3rd edition). Mahwah, NJ: Erlbaum.

Lerner, R. M., & Simi, N. L. (1997). *A holistic, integrated model of risk and protection in adolescence: A developmental contextual perspective about research, programs, and policies.* Paper presented at a conference on "Developmental science and the holistic approach: A symposium followed up at the Royal Swedish Academy of Sciences," Wiks Castle, Sweden, May 24–27.

Lerner, R., Fisher, C., & Weinberg, R. (2000). Toward a science for and of the people: Promoting civil society through the application of developmental science. *Child Development, 71* (1), 11–20.

Lerner, R., & Galambos, N. (1998). Adolescent development: Challenges and opportunities for research, programs, and policies. In J. Spence, J. Darley, D. Foss (Editors), *Annual Review of Psychology.* Palo Alto, CA: Annual Reviews.

Lerner, R. M. (2000). Developing civil society through the promotion of positive youth development. *Journal of Developmental & Behavioral Pediatrics, 21* (1), 48–49.

Lerner, R. M. (Ed.). (1998). Theoretical models of human development. *Handbook of Child Psychology: Volume 1* (5th edition). New York: John Wiley.

Levinson, D. (1978). *The seasons of a man's life.* New York: Knopf.

———. (1986). A conception of adult development. *American Psychologist, 41* (1), 3–13.

———. (1990a). *Seasons of a woman's life.* Presented at the 98th annual convention of the American Psychological Association, Boston.

———. (1990b). A theory of life structure development in adulthood. In C. N. Alexander & E. J. Langer (Eds.), *Higher states of human development.* New York: Oxford University Press, 35–54.

Levitin, D. (2006). *This your brain on music.* New York: Dutton.

Levy, B. R., & Banaji, M. R. (2002). Implicit ageism. In T. D. Nelson (Ed.), Ageism: Stereotypes and prejudice against older persons. Cambridge, MA: MIT Press, 49–75.

Lewis, M., & Brooks-Gunn, J. (1979). *Social cognition and the acquisition of self.* New York: Plenum.

Lewis, M. (1997). *Altering fate: Why the past does not predict the future.* New York: Guilford.

———. (2000). The promise of dynamic systems approaches for an integrated account of human development. *Child Development, 71* (1), 36–43.

Lewis, M., Feiring, C., & Rosenthal, S. (2000). Attachment over time. *Child Development, 71* (3), 707–720.

Lewkowicz, D. (1996). Infants' response to the audible and visual properties of the face: 1. Role of lexical-syntactic content, temporal synchrony, gender, and manner of speech. *Developmental Psychology, 32* (2), 347–366.

Li, S. (2004). Connecting the many levels and facets of cognitive aging. In J. Lerner & A. Alberts (Eds.), *Current directions in developmental psychology.* NJ: Prentice Hall, 167–175.

Liben, L., Bigler, R., & Krogh, H. (2002). Language at work: Children's gendered interpretations of occupational titles. *Child Development, 73* (3), 810–828.

Liem, J., James, J., O'Toole, J., & Boudewyn, A. (1997). Assessing resilience in adults with histories of childhood sexual abuse. *American Journal of Orthopsychiatry, 67* (4), 594–605.

Lindenberger, U., & Baltes, P. B. (2000). *Life span psychology theory.* Washington, D.C., US: American Psychological Association; London, Oxford University Press. www.apa. org/books, from www.apa. org.proxy.bc.edu/books.

Lips, H. (2001). *Sex and gender.* Mountain View, CA: Mayfield.

Little, T., & Lopez, D. (1997). Regularities in the development of children's causality beliefs about school performance across six sociocultural contexts. *Developmental Psychology, 33* (1), 165–175.

Liu, R., & Gong, Y. (2001). Subjective well-being and stress level in elderly. *Chinese Mental Health Journal, 15,* 28–30.

Locke, J. (1904). *Some thoughts concerning education.* (Introduction and notes by R. H. Quick). New York: Macmillan.

Lockman, J., & Thelen, E. (1993). Introduction. *Child Development, 64* (4), 953–960.

Loeb, S., Fuller, B., Kagan, S., & Carrol, B. (2004). Child care in poor communities: Early learning effects of type, quality, and stability. *Child Development, 75* (1), 47–65.

Looby, E. (2001). The violence of sexual harassment: Physical, emotional and economic victimization. In D. S. Sandhu (Ed.), *Faces of violence: Psychological correlates, concepts, and intervention strategies.* Huntington, NY: Nova Science Publishers, 229–249.

Lord, C., & Bailey, A. (2006). Autism spectrum disorders. In M. Rutter & E. Taylor (Eds.), *Child and adolescent psychiatry.* London: Blackwell.

Love, J., Harrison, L., Sagi-Schwartz, A., van Ijzendoorn, M., Ross, C., Ungerer, J., Raikes, H., Brady-Smith, C., Boller, K., Brooks-Gunn, J., Constantine, J., Kisker, E., Pausell, D., & Chaan-Cohen, R. (2003). Child care quality matters: How conclusions may vary with context. *Child Development, 74* (4), 1021–1033.

Lovibond, D. (2004). No way to grieve: we have such an easy life that we don't know how to deal with death: David Lovibond mourns the passing of widow's weeds and black-edged notepaper. *Spectator, 295* (181), 16.

Luby, J. (200). *Depression.* In C. Zeanah, Ed.), Handbook of mental health. New York: Guilford.

Lumley, M., & Provenzano, K. (2003). Stress management through written emotional disclosure improves academic performance among college students with physical symptoms. *Journal of Educational Psychology, 95* (3), 641–649.

Luthar, S., & Cicchetti, D. (2000). The construct of resilience: Implications for interventions and social policies. *Development & Psychopathology, 12,* 857–885.

Lutz, C., & Przytulski, K. (1997). *Nutrition and diet therapy.* Philadelphia: F. A. Davis.

Lutz, D., & Sternberg, R. (1999). Cognitive development. In M. Bornstein & M. Lamb (Eds.), *Developmental psychology: An advanced textbook.* Mahwah, NJ: Erlbaum.

Lynch, S. (1998). Who supports whom? How age and gender affect the perceived quality of support from family and friends. *The Gerontologist, 38* (2), 231–238.

Lynskey, M., & Fergusson, D. (1997). Factors protecting against the development of adjustment difficulties in young adults exposed to childhood sexual abuse. *Child Abuse & Neglect, 21* (12), 1177–1190.

Lytton, H., & Gallagher, L. (2002). Parenting twins and the genetics of parenting. In M. Bornstein (Ed.), *Handbook of parenting: Volume 1* (2nd edition). Hillsdale, NJ: Erlbaum.

Lytton, H., Singh, J., & Gallagher, L. (1995). Parenting twins. In M. Bornstein (Ed.), *Handbook of parenting: Volume 1.* Hillsdale, NJ: Erlbaum.

Maccoby, E. (1998). *The two sexes: Growing up apart, growing up together.* Cambridge, MA: Belknap Press.

Maccoby, E., & Jacklin, C. (1974). *The psychology of sex differences.* Palo Alto, CA: Stanford University Press.

Maccoby, E., & Lewis, C. (2003). Less day care or different day care? *Child Development, 74* (4), 1069–1075.

Mack, J. E., & Hickler, H. (1982). *Vivienne: The life and suicide of an adolescent girl.* New York: New American Library.

Macmillan, R., McMorris, B., & Kruttschnitt, C. (2004). Linked lives: Stability and change in maternal circumstances and trajectories of antisocial behavior in children. *Child Development, 75* (1), 205–220.

Madaus, G. (1994). A technological and historical consideration of equity issues associated with proposals to change the nation's testing policy. *Harvard Educational Review, 64* (1), 76–95.

Maddox, B. (2006). *Freud's wizard.* Cambridge, MA: DaCapo Press.

Magid, K., & McKelvey, C. (1987). *High risk: Children without a conscience.* New York: Bantam.

Main, M. (1996). Introduction to the special section on attachment and psychopathology: Overview of the field of attachment. *Journal of Consulting and Clinical Psychology, 64* (2), 237–242.

Malcolm, M. L. (Oct 2006). "Shaking it off" and "toughing it out": Socialization to pain and injury in girls' softball. *Journal of Contemporary Ethnography.* 35(5), 495.

Malina, R. M., & others. (1998). Television viewing, physical activity and health-related fitness. *Journal of Adolescent Health, 23* (5), 318–325.

Malloy, L. C., Lyon, T. D., & Quas, J. A. (2007). Filial dependency and recantation of child sexual abuse allegations. *Journal of the American Academy of Child and Adolescent Psychiatry, 46* (2), 162–171.

Malloy, M., & Freeman, D. (2000). *Birth weight and gestational age.* Mahwah, NJ: Erlbaum.

Manning, C. (2002). Improving outcomes in depression: Integrated solutions should not be provided at the expense of reduced participation of statutory sector. *BMJ: British Medical Journal, 324* (7339), 737.

Manning, M., & Baruth, L. (2004). *Multicultural education of children and adolescents.* Needham Heights: Allyn & Bacon.

Mansfield, P. K., Koch, P. B., & Voda, A. M. (2000). Midlife women's attributions for their sexual response changes. *Health Care for Women International, 21,* 543–559.

Manuck, S., Jennings, R., Rabin, B., & Baum, A. (2000). *Behavior, health, and aging.* Mahwah, NJ: Erlbaum.

Marcia, J. (2002). Identity and psychosocial development in adulthood. *Identity, 2,* 7–28.

Marcus, L. (2002). *Ways of telling: Conversations on the art of the picture.* New York: Dutton Books.

Margolese, H. (2000). The male menopause and mood: Testosterone decline and depression in the aging male—Is there a link? *Journal of Geriatric Psychiatry & Neurology, 13,* 93–101.

Margolis, D. (2005). Gender. In K. Thies & J. Travers (Eds.). *Handbook of Human Development for Health Care Professionals.* Sudbury, MA: Jones & Bartlett.

Marks, N. F. (1996). Caregiving across the lifespan: National prevalence and predictors. Family Relations: *Journal of Applied Family & Child Studies, 45* (1), 27–36.

Marks, N. F., & Lambert, J.D. (1998). Marital status continuity and change among young and midlife adults: longitudinal effects on psychological well-being. *Journal of Family Issues, 19* (6), 652–687.

Marks, S., Huston, T., Johnson, E., & MacDermid, S. (2001). Role balance among white married couples. *Journal of Marriage and the Family, 63,* 1083–1098.

Marrs, R., Bloch, L., & Silverman, K. (1997). *Dr. Richard Marrs fertility book.* New York: Delacorte.

Marshall, J. R. (1994). The diagnosis and treatment of social phobia and alcohol abuse. *Bulletin of the Menninger Clinic, 58* (2A), A58–A66.

Marshall, N. L., Noonan, A. E., McCartney, K., Marx, F., & Keefe, N. (2001). It takes an urban village: Parenting networks of urban families. *Journal of Family Issues, 22* (2), 163–182.

Marshall, P. (2002). *Cultural diversity in our schools.* Belmont, CA: Wadsworth.

Marsiske, M., Delius, J., Maas, I., Lindenberger, U., Scherer, H., & Tesch- Römer, C. (1999). Sensory systems in old age. In P. B. Baltes & K. U. Mayer (Eds.), *The Berlin aging study: Aging from 70 to 100.* New York, NY: Cambridge University Press, 360–383.

Martikainen, P., & Valkonen, T. (1996). Mortality after the death of a spouse: Rates and causes of death in a large Finnish cohort. *American Journal of Public Health, 86* (8), 1087–1093.

Martin, J. (2004). *US infant mortality rate increases.* Washington, D.C.: Centers for Disease Control and Prevention.

Martocchio, J. J. (1989). Age-related differences in employee absenteeism: A meta-analysis. *Psychology and Aging, 4,* 409–414.

Maslow, A. (1987). *Motivation and personality.* (Revised by R. Frager, J. Fadiman, C. McReynolds, & R. Cox.) New York: Harper & Row.

Masten, A. (2001). Ordinary magic: Resiliency processes in development. *American Psychologist,* 56, 227–238.

Mattson, S. (2000). Ethnocultural considerations in the childbearing period. In S. Mattson & J. Smith (Eds.), *Core curriculum for maternal-newborn nursing.* Philadelphia: W. B. Saunders.

Matzo, M. L., Sherman, D. W., Lo, K., Egan, K. A., Grant, M., & Rhome, A. (2003). Strategies for teaching loss, grief, and bereavement. *Nursing Education,* 28, 71–76.

Mayer, P., & Ziaian, T. (2002). Indian suicide and marriage: A research note. *Journal of Comparative Family Studies, 33,* 297–308.

McAdams, D. P., de St. Aubin, E., & Logan, R. L. (1993). Generativity among young, midlife, and older adults. *Psychology and Aging, 8* (2), 221–230.

McAuley, W., & Travis, S. (2000). Factors influencing level of stress during the nursing home decision process. *Journal of Clinical Geropsychology, 6,* 269.

McCarthy, M. (2002). U.S. government releases nursing home report cards. (Policy And People). *The Lancet, 360* (9346), 1670.

McClintock, M., & Herdt, G. (1996). Rethinking puberty: The development of sexual attraction. *Current Directions in Psychological Science, 5,* 178–183.

McCool, J. P., Cameron, L. D., & Petrie, K. J. (2001). Adolescent perceptions of smoking imagery in film. *Social Science and Medicine, 52* (10), 1577–1587.

McCrae, R. (2001). Trait psychology and culture: Exploring intercultural comparisons. *Journal of Personality, 69,* 819–846.

McCrae, R., & Costa, P. T., Jr. (1984). *Emerging lives, enduring dispositions: Personality in adulthood.* Boston: Little, Brown.

———. (1990). *Personality in adulthood.* New York: Guilford Press.

———. (1995). Positive and negative valence within the five-factor model. *Journal of Research in Personality, 29* (4), 443–460.

———. (1996). Toward a new generation of personality theories: Theoretical contexts for the five-factor model. In J. S. Wiggins (Ed.), *The five-factor model of personality: Theoretical perspectives.* New York: Guilford Press, 51–87.

———. (1999). A five-factor theory of personality. In L. Pervin & O. John (Eds.). *Handbook of Personality: Theory and Research* (2nd edition). New York: Guilford Press, 139–154.

McCrae, R., Costa, P. T., Ostendorf, F., Angleitner, A., Caprara, G. V., Barbaranelli, C., et al. (1999). Age differences in personality across the adult life span: Parallels in five cultures. *Developmental Psychology, 35,* 466–482.

McCrae, R., Costa, P. T., Ostendorf, F., Angleitner, A., Hrebícková, M., & Avia, M. D., et al. (2000). Nature over nurture: Temperament, personality, and life span development. *Journal of Personality & Social Psychology, 78* (1), 173–186.

McElheny, V. (2003). *Watson and DNA.* Cambridge, MA: Perseus.

McEvoy, G. M., & Cascio, W. F. (1989). Cumulative evidence of the relationship between employee age and job performance. *Journal of Applied Psychology, 74,* 11–17.

McGhee, P. (1979). *Humor: Its origin and development.* San Francisco: Freeman.

———. (1988). The role of humor in enhancing children's development and adjustment. *Journal of Children in Contemporary Society, 20,* 249–274.

McGhee, P., & Panoutsopoulou, T. (1990). The role of cognitive factors in children's metaphor and humor comprehension. *International Journal of Humor Research, 3* (2), 119–146.

McGue, M., Slutske, W., & Iacono, W. (1999). Personality and substance use disorders. *Journal of Consulting & Clinical Psychology, 67* (3), 394–404.

McGuffin, P., & Rutter, M. (2006). Genetics of normal and abnormal development. In M. Rutter & E. Taylor (Eds.), *Child and adolescent psychiatry.* London: Blackwell.

McKelvey, M., & McKenry, P. (2000). The psychosocial well-being of black and white mothers following marital dissolution. *Psychology of Women Quarterly, 24,* 4–14.

McKnight, J., & Malcolm, J. (2000). Is male homosexuality maternally linked? *Psychology, Evolution & Gender, 2* (3), 229–239.

McLanahan, S., & Teitler, J. (1999). The consequences of father absence. In M. E. Lamb (Ed.), *Parenting and child development in "nontraditional" families.* Mahwah, NJ: Erlbaum, 83–102.

McLaughlin, S. (1998). *Introduction to language development.* San Diego: Singular.

McLoyd, V. (1998). Children in poverty: Development, public policy, and practice. In W. Damon (Series Ed.), D. Kuhn, & R. Siegler (Volume Eds.). *Handbook of child psychology: Volume 4. Child psychology in practice.* New York: Wiley.

McQuillan, G. (2000). *Implications of a national survey for STDs: Results from the NHANES survey.* Paper presented at the 2000 Infectious Disease Society of America Conference. September 7–10, New Orleans.

McVittie, C., Cavers, D., & Hepworth, J. (2005). Femininity, mental weakness, and Mead, M. (1972, April). *Long living in cross-sectional perspective.* Paper presented to the Gerontological Society, San Juan, Puerto Rico.

Meloy, J., Hempel, A., Mohandie, K., Shiva, A., & Gray, T. (2001). Offender and offense characteristics of nonrandom sample of adolescent mass murderers. *Journal of American Academy of Child and Adolescent Psychiatry, 40,* 719–728.

Meltz, B. (2004, April 15). *Early intervention can help a baby catch up to peers.* The Boston Globe, p. H6.

———. (2005). Laughing now might help your children. *Boston Globe,* August 4, 22, 25.

Merzenich, M. (1996). Cold Spring Harbor Symposium. *Quantitative Biology, 61,* 1–8.

Meschke, L., & others. (2000). Demographic, biological, psychological, and social predictors of the timing of first intercourse. *Journal of Research on Adolescence, 10,* 315–338.

Meshefedjian, G., McCusker, J., Bellavance, F., & Baumgarten, M. (1998). Factors associated with symptoms of depression among informal caregivers of demented elders in the community. *The Gerontologist, 38* (2), 247–253.

Michels, P. J., Johnson, N. P., Mallin, R., Thornhill, J. T., and others. (1999). Coping strategies of alcoholic women. *Substance Abuse,* 20 (4), 237–248.

Micklos, D., & Freyer, G. (2003). *DNA science.* New York: Cold Spring Harbor Laboratory Press.

Milbrath, C. (1998). *Patterns of artistic development in children.* Cambridge: Cambridge University Press.

Miller, B. (2001). Family relationships and adolescent pregnancy risk: A research synthesis. *Developmental Review, 21,* 1–38.

Miller, K. E., Barnes, G. M., Melnick, M., Sabo, D. F., & Farrell, M. P. (2002). Gender and racial/ethnic differences in predicting adolescent sexual risk: Athletic participation versus exercise. *The Journal of Health and Social Behavior, 43,* 436–450.

Miniño, A. M., Heron, M., Smith, B. L., & Kochanek, K. D. (2006) Deaths: Final data for 2004. *Health E-Stats.*

Mio, J. (2004). Asians on the edge: The reciprocity of allied behavior. *Cultural Diversity & Ethnic Minority Psychology, 10* (1), 90–94.

Mirchandani, K. (2000). "The best of both worlds" and "Cutting my own throat": Contradictory images of home-based work. *Qualitative Sociology, 23* (2), 159–182.

Mischel, H., & Mischel, W. (1983). The development of children's knowledge of self-control strategies. *Child Development, 54* (4), 603–619.

Mistry, R., Vandewater, E., Huston, A., & McLoyd, V. (2002). Economic well-being and children's social adjustment: The role of family process in an ethnically diverse low-income sample. *Child Development, 73* (3), 935–951.

Mitchell, C. M., O'Neil, T. D., Beals, J., Dick, R. W., Keane, E., & Manson, S. M. (1996). Dimensionality of alcohol use among American Indian adolescents: Latent structure, construct validity, and implications for developmental research. *Journal of Research on Adolescence, 6* (1), 151–180.

Moffett, S. (2006). *The three-pound enigma.* Chapel Hill, NC: Algonquin Press.

Mojet, J., Christ-Hazelhof, E., & Heidema, J. (2001). Taste perception with age: Generic or specific losses in threshold sensitivity to the five basic tastes? *Chemical Senses, 26,* 845–860.

Molina, B. S. G., & Chassin, L. (1996). The parent-adolescent relationship at puberty: Hispanic ethnicity and parent alcoholism as moderators. *Developmental Psychology, 32* (4), 675–686.

Montessori, M. (1967). *The absorbent mind.* New York: Dell.

———. (2003 [1912]). *The Montessori method.* New York: Barnes and Noble.

Moon, R., Patel, K., & Shaefer, S. (2000). Sudden infant death specific SIDS mortality: United States, 1991 versus 1995. *Pediatrics, 105* (66), 1227–1235.

Moore, D. (2002). *The dependent gene.* New York: Times Books.

Moore, G. (1983). *Developing and evaluating educational research.* Boston: Little, Brown.

Moore, K., & Persaud, T. (2003). *Before we are born: Essentials of embryology and birth defects.* Philadelphia: W. B. Saunders.

Moore, M. (1997). *Nutritional care.* St. Louis: Mosby.

Moran, B. (2000). Maternal infections. In S. Mattson & J. Smith (Eds.), *Core curriculum for maternal-newborn nursing.* Philadelphia: W. B. Saunders.

Moran, S., & Gardner, H. (2006). Extraordinary achievements: A developmental and systems analysis. In W. Damon & R. Lerner (Series Eds.) & D. Kuhn & R. Siegler (Volume Ed.), *Handbook of child Psychology: Volume 2. Theoretical models of human development.* New York: John Wiley.

Morris, J. (2006). An AARPer's life: Americans enter the brave new world of retirement with a lot of silly fantasies. And, says this writer, thank goodness for that. *The Wilson Quarterly, 30* (2), 70–75.

Morris, K., (2006). Genital mutilation and alternative practices. *Lancet,* 368, 64–67.

Mosher, C.E., & Danoff-Burg, S. (2004). Effects of gender and employment status on support provided to caregivers. *Sex Roles: A Journal of Research, 51,* 589–596.

Moshman, D. (1998). Cognitive development beyond childhood. In W. Damon (Ed.), *Handbook of child psychology.* New York: John Wiley.

Mui, A. (2001). Stress, coping and depression among elderly Korean immigrants. *Journal of Human Behavior in the Social Environment, 3,* 281–299.

Mullis, R., Hill, L., Wayne, E., & Readdick, C. (1999). Attachment and social support among adolescents. *Journal of Genetic Psychology, 160* (4), 500–502.

Munakata, Y. (2006). Information Processing approaches to development. In W. Damon & R. Lerner (Series Eds.) & R. Lerner (Volume Ed.), *Handbook of child psychology: Volume 1. Theoretical models of human development.* New York: John Wiley.

Munson, M. L., & Sutton, P. D. (2006). Births, marriages, divorces, and deaths: Provisional data for 2005. *National vital statistics reports*; 54 (20). Hyattsville, MD: National Center for Health Statistics.

Mupinga, E., Garrison, M., & Pierce, S. (2002). An exploratory study of the relationships between family functioning and parenting styles. *Family & Consumer Sciences Research Journal, 31* (1), 112–129.

Murphy, W., & others. (2001). An exploration of factors related to deviant sexual arousal among juvenile sex offenders. Sexual Abuse: *Journal of Research & Treatment, 13,* 91–103.

Murray, B. (1997a). Elderly people alter their social priorities as they age. *APA Monitor, 28* (10), 25.

——. (1997b). Our 20s appear to be the age we can't forget. *APA Monitor, 28* (10), 24.

——. (1997c). Psychologists help ease caregivers' stress. *APA Monitor, 28* (10), 26.

Murrell, A. J., Olson, J. E., & Frieze, I. H. (1995). Sexual harassment and gender discrimination: A longitudinal study of women managers. *Journal of Social Issues, 51* (1), 139–149.

Muscari, M. (1998). Prevention: Are we really reaching today's teens? *American Journal of Maternal/Child Nursing, 4* (2), 87–91.

Muse, D. (Ed.). (1997). *Multicultural resources for young readers*. New York: The New Press.

Mutcher, J., Burr., J., Massagli, M., & Pienta, A. (1999). Work transition and health in later life. *Journal of Gerontology, 54B*, S252–S261.

Muuss, R. E. (1996). *Theories of adolescence* (7th edition). New York: McGraw-Hill.

Nansel, T., Overpeck, M., Pilla, R., Ruan, W., Simons-Morton, B., & Scheidt, P. Bullying behaviors among U.S. youth. *Journal of the American Medical Association*, 285, 2094–2100.

Narvaez, D., Getz, I., Rest, J., & Thoma, S. (1999). Individual moral judgment and cultural ideologies. *Developmental Psychology, 35* (2), 478–488.

National Cancer Institute. (2000). Press release: *Questions and answers about hormone replacement therapy*. Bethesda, MD: National Institutes of Health.

National Coalition for Health Professional Education in Genetics. (2004) *Core competencies in genetics*. Lutherville, MD.

National Institute of Child Health and Human Development Early Child Care Research Network. (2003). Does amount of time spent in child care predict socioemotional adjustment during the transition to kindergarten? *Child Development, 74* (4), 1044–1049.

National Institute of Health. (2002, October). Facts about Postmenopausal Health. NIH Publication No. 02-5200. U.S. Department of Health and Human Services.

National Institute on Aging. (1999). *Progress report and Alzheimer's disease*. Washington, D.C.: United States

Department of Health and Human Services, NIH Publication No. 99-4664.

——. (2000). *Alzheimer's disease research update*. National Institute on Aging, ADEAR Center Email Address: ADEAR@ alzheimers.org.

National Institutes of Health. (2000). *Stem cells: A primer*. Bethesda, MD: NIH.

Nelson, C., Thomas, K., & de Haan, H. (2006). Neural basis of cognitive development. In D. Kuhn & R. Siegler (Eds.), *Handbook of child psychology*. New York: John Wiley.

Nelson, H., & others. (2000, August). Post menopausal hormone replacement therapy: Scientific review. *JAMA, The Journal of the American Medical Association, 288* (7), 872.

Nelson, W., Hughes, H., Katz, B., & Searight, R. (1999). Anorexic eating attitudes and behaviors of male and female college students. *Adolescence, 34* (135), 621–633.

Neugarten, B. (Ed.). (1968). *Middle age and aging*. Chicago: University of Chicago Press.

Neugarten, B., & Weinstein, K. K. (1964). The changing American grandparent. *Journal of Marriage and the Family, 26* (1), 199–206.

Neumann, I., Wigger, A., Torner, L., & Landgraf, R. (2000). Brain oxytocin inhibits basal and to stress-induced activity of the hypothalamo-pituitary-adrenal axis in male and female rats.

Ngai, S. S., Ngai, N., & Cheung, C. (2006). Environmental influences on risk taking among Hong Kong young dance partygoers. *Adolescence, 41* (164), 739–753.

NIA News. (2000). Scientists zero in on enzyme at work in Alzheimer's disease. Washington, D.C.: National Institute on Aging, www.alzheimers.org/nia.

NICHD Early Child Care Research. (1998). Early child care and self-control, compliance, and problem behavior at twenty-four and thirty-six months. *Child Development, 69*, 1145–1170.

——. (1999). Child care and mother-child interaction in the first 3 years of life. *Developmental Psychology, 35* (6), 1399–1413.

——. (2000). The relation of child care to cognitive and language development. *Child Development, 71* (4), 960–980.

——. (2001). Child-care and family predictors of preschool attachment and stability from infancy. *Developmental Psychology, 37* (6), 847–862.

——. (2004). Are child development outcomes related to before- and after-school arrangements? Results from the NICHD study of early child care. *Child Development, 75* (1), 280–295.

——. (2005a). Duration and developmental timing of poverty and children's cognitive and social development from birth through third grade. *Child Development, 76* (4), 795–810.

——. (2005b). Predicting individual differences in attention, memory, and planning in first graders from experiences at home, child care, and school. *Developmental Psychology, 41*(1), 99–114.

Nightingale, E. O., & Goodman, M. (1990). *Before birth*. Cambridge, MA: Harvard University Press.

NIH. (2000). *The estrogen-progesterone regimen*. Washington, D.C.: Author.

Niijhuis, J. (Ed.). (1992). *Fetal behavior: Developmental and perinatal aspects*. New York: Oxford University Press.

Nilsson, L., Furuhjelm, M., Ingleman-Sundberg, A., & Wirsen, C. (1993). *A child is born*. New York: Delacorte.

Nippold, M. A., Hesketh, L. J., Duthie, J. K., & Mansfield, T. C. (2005). Conversational versus expository discourse: A study of syntactic development in children, adolescents, and adults. *Journal of Speech, Language, and Hearing Research, 48* (5), 1048–1065. NJ: Erlbaum.

Noam, G. (1998). Clinical-developmental psychology: Toward developmentally differentiated interventions. In W. Damon (Series Ed.) & I. Sigel & K. Renninger (Volume Eds.), *Handbook of child psychology: Volume 4. Child psychology in practice*. New York: John Wiley.

Nordblom, K. (2004). Cohabitation and marriage in a risky world. *Review of Economics in the Household, 2* (3), 325–341.

Nugent, K., Lester, B., & Brazelton, B. (1995). *The cultural context of infancy*. Norwood, NJ: Ablex.

Nusslein-Volhard, C. (2006). *Coming to life*. Carlsbad, CA: Kales Press.

Nuttall, R., & Nuttall, E. (1980). *Family coping and disasters*. Boulder, CO: National Hazards Research Applications.

O'Dea, J. A., & Abraham, S. (1999). Onset of disordered eating attitudes and behaviors in early adolescence: Interplay of pubertal status, gender, weight, and age. *Adolescence, 34* (136), 671–679.

———. (2000). Improving the body image, eating attitudes, and behaviors of young male and female adolescents: A new educational approach that focuses on self-esteem. *International Journal of Eating Disorders, 28* (1), 43–57.

O'Hara, K. (2004). "Curb cuts" on the Information Highway: Older adults and the Internet. *Technical Communication Quarterly, 13,* 423–445.

Obeidallah, D. A., Brennan, R. T., Brooks-Gunn, J., Kindlon, D., & Earls, F. (2000). Socioeconomic status, race, and girls' pubertal maturation: Results form the Project on Human Development in Chicago Neighborhoods. *Journal of Research on Adolescence, 10* (4), 443–464.

Olds, S., London, M., & Ladewig, P. (1996). *Maternal-newborn nursing.* Reading, MA: Addison-Wesley.

Olweus, D. (1993). *Bullying at school: What we know and what we can do.* Cambridge, England: Oxford University Press.

———. (1995). Bullying or peer abuse at school: Facts and interventions. *Current Directions in Psychological Science, 4* (6), 196–200.

Olweus, D., & Limber, S. (2002). *Bullying prevention program.* Boulder, Colorado: University of Colorado at Boulder.

Ornstein, R., & Sobel, D. (1987). *The healing brain.* New York: Simon & Schuster.

Orpinas, P., & Horne, A. (2006). *Bullying prevention.* Washington, D.C.: American Psychological Association.

Ory, M., Hoffman, R. R., Yee, J. L., Tennstedt, S., & Schulz, R. (1999). Prevalence and impact of caregiving: A detailed comparison between dementia and nondementia caregivers. *The Gerontologist, 39* (2), 177–185.

Osofsky, J. (1995). The effects of exposure to violence on young children. *American Psychologist, 50* (9), 782–788.

Oswald, D. L., & Russell, B. L. (2006). Perceptions of sexual coercion in heterosexual dating relationships: The role of aggressor gender and tactics. *The Journal of Sex Research, 43* (1), 87–96.

Ovando, C., & Collier, V. (1998). *Bilingual and ESL classroom: Teaching in multicultural contexts.* New York: McGraw-Hill.

Overton, W. (1998). Developmental psychology: Philosophy, concepts, and methodology. In R. M. Lerner (Ed.), *Handbook of child psychology: Volume 1. Theoretical models of human development.* New York: John Wiley.

Owens, R. (1996). *Language development.* Boston: Allyn & Bacon.

Packer, A. (2000, Winter). *Teens and tobacco.* FCD Update. Needham, MA: FCD Educational Services.

Palfrey, J., Hauser-Cram, P., Bronson, M., Warfield, M., Sirin, S., & Chan, E. (2005). The Brookline Early Education Project: A 25 year follow-up study of a family-centered early health and development intervention. *Pediatrics, 116,* 144–152.

Palmore, E. B. (1985). How to live longer and like it. *Journal of Applied Gerontology, 4* (2), 1–8.

Palmore, E. B., Nowlin, J. B., & Wang, H. S. (1985). Predictors of function among the old-old: A 10-year follow-up. *Journal of Gerontology, 40* (2), 244–250.

Papalia, D., & Olds, S. (2004). *Human development.* New York: McGraw-Hill.

Papalia, D., Olds, S., & Feldman, R. (2004). *A child's world.* New York: McGraw-Hill.

Paris, S., & Cunningham, A. (1996). Children becoming students. In D. Berliner & R. Calfee (Eds.), *Handbook of educational psychology.* New York: Macmillan.

Paris, S., & Paris, A. (2006). Assessment of early reading. In W. Damon & R. Lerner (Series Eds.) & K. Renninger & I. Sigel (Volume Eds.), *Handbook of child psychology: Volume 4. Child psychology in practice.* New York: John Wiley.

Parke, R. (2002). Fathers and families. In M. Bornstein (Ed.), (2002). *Handbook of parenting* (2nd edition). Mahwah, NJ: Erlbaum.

Parke, R., & Brott, A. (1999). *Throwaway dads.* Boston: Houghton Mifflin.

Parke, R., & Buriel, R. (1998). Socialization in the family: Ethnic and ecological perspectives. In W. Damon (Series Ed.) & N. Eisenberg (Volume Ed.), *Handbook of child psychology: Volume 3. Child psychology in practice.* New York: John Wiley.

———. (2006). Socialization in the family. In W. Damon & R. Lerner (Series Eds.) & N. Eisenberg (Volume Ed.), *Handbook of child Psychology: Volume 3. Social, Emotional, and Personality/Development.* New York: John Wiley.

Parkhurst, H. B. (1999). Confusion, lack of consensus, and the definition of creativity as a construct. *Journal of Creative Behavior, 33* (1), 1–21.

Parten, M. (1932). Social participation among preschool children. *Journal of Abnormal Psychology, 27,* 243–269.

Patenaude, A., Guttmacher, A., & Collins, F. (2002). Genetic testing and psychology. *American Psychologist, 57* (4), 271–282.

Patton, W., & McMahon, M. (1999). *Career development and systems theory.* Pacific Grove, CA: Brooks/Cole.

Paul, R. W. (1987). Dialogical thinking. In J. B. Baron & R. J. Sternberg (Eds.), *Teaching thinking skills.* New York: Freeman.

Peake, P., Hebl, M., & Mischel, W. (2002). Strategic attention deployment for delay of gratification in working and waiting situations. *Developmental Psychology, 38* (2), 313–326.

Pearson, J., & Brown, G. (2000). Suicide prevention in late life: Direction for science and practice. *Clinical Psychology Review. Special Issue: Assessment and Treatment of Older Adults, 20,* 685–705.

Pelton, J., & Forehand, H. (2001). Discrepancy between mother and child perceptions of their relationship: I. Consequences for adolescents considered within the context of parental divorce. *Journal of Family Violence, 16,* 1–15.

Pennisi, E. (2001). A history of the Human Genome Project. *Science, 291* (5507), 1195–1207.

Peplau, L., Garnets, L., Spalding, L., Conley, T., & Veniegas, R. (1998). A critique of Bem's "exotic becomes erotic" theory of sexual orientation. *Psychological Review, 105,* 87–394.

Perkins, D. F., Luster, T., Villarruel, F., & Small, S. (1998). An ecological, risk-factor examination of adolescents' sexual activity in three ethnic groups. *Journal of Marriage and the Family, 60* (4), 660–673.

Perner, J., Lang, B., & Kloo, D. (2002). Theory of mind and self-control: More than a common problem of inhibition. *Child Development, 73* (3), 752–767.

Perodeau, G., Lauzon, S., Levesque, L., & Lachane, L. (2001). Mental health, stress correlates and psychotropic drug use or non-use among aged caregivers to elders with dementia. *Aging & Mental Health, 5,* 225–234.

Perozynski, L., & Kramer, L. (1999). Parental beliefs about managing sibling conflict. *Developmental Psychology, 35* (2), 489–499.

Perrone, K. M., & Worthington, E. L., Jr. (2001). Factors influencing ratings of marital quality by individuals within dual-career marriages: A conceptual model. *Journal of Counseling Psychology, 48* (1), 3–9.

Perry, W. (1968a). *Forms of intellectual and ethical development in the college years.* New York: Holt, Rinehart & Winston.

———. (1968b, April). *Patterns of development in thought and values of students in a liberal arts college: A validation of a scheme.* Washington, D. C.: U.S. Department of Health, Education, and Welfare, Office of Education, Bureau of Research. Final report.

———. (1981). Cognitive and ethical growth. In A. Chickering (Ed.), *The modern American college.* San Francisco: Jossey-Bass.

Peters, J. (1997). *When mothers work.* Reading, MA: Addison-Wesley.

Petersen, A. (1988). Adolescent Development. *Annual Review of Psychology, 39,* 583–607. Palo Alto, CA: Annual Reviews.

Pfaff, W. (1997). *The future of the U.S. as a great power.* Pittsburgh: Carnegie Council on Ethics and International Affairs.

Phillips, B. D. (2004). The future small business workforce: Will labor shortages exist? The available evidence is less than perfect. *Business Economics, 39* (4), 19–28.

Piaget, J. (1926). *The language and thought of the child.* New York: Harcourt, Brace, and World.

———. (1932). *The moral judgment of the child.* New York: Macmillan.

———. (1952a). *The origins of intelligence.* New York; Norton.

———. (1952b). *The origins of intelligence in children.* New York: International Universities Press.

———. (1966). *Psychology of intelligence.* Totowa, NJ: Littlefield, Adams, & Co.

———. (1967). *Six psychological studies.* New York: Random House.

———. (1973). *The child and reality.* New York: Viking.

Piaget, J., & Inhelder, B. (1969). *The psychology of the child.* New York: Basic Books.

Picard, C. L. (1999). The level of competition as a factor for the development of eating disorders in female collegiate athletes. *Journal of Youth and Adolescence, 28* (5), 583–594.

Pickett, M., Barg, F., & Lynch, M. (2001). Development of a home-based family caregiver cancer education program. *Hospice Journal, 15,* 19–40.

Pienta, A. M., Hayward, M. D., & Jenkins, K. R. (2000). Health consequences of marriage for the retirement years. *Journal of Family Issues, 21* (5), 559–586.

Pike, A., McGuire, S., Hetherington, E. M., Reiss, D., & Plomin, R. (1996). Family environment and adolescent depressive symptoms and antisocial behavior: A multivariate genetic analysis. *Developmental Psychology, 32* (4), 590–603.

Pines, A. (2004). Why are Israelis less burned out? *European Psychologist 9* (2), 69–77.

Pinker, S. (1994). *The language instinct.* New York: Morrow.

———. (1997). *How the mind works.* New York: Norton.

Pinquart, M., & Sorensen, S. (2001). Gender differences in self-concept and psychological well-being in old age: A meta-analysis. *The Journals of Gerontology, Series B, 56,* P195–205.

Pipp-Siegel, S., & Foltz, C. (1997). Toddlers' acquisition of self/other knowledge: Ecological and interpersonal aspects of self and other. *Child Development, 68* (1), 69–79.

Pisecco, S., Wristers, K., Swank, P., Silva, P. A., & Baker, D. B. (2001). The effect of academic self-concept on ADHD and antisocial behaviors in early adolescence. *Journal of Learning Disabilities, 34,* 450–458.

Pitkin, S., & Savage, L. (2004). Age-related vulnerability to diencephalic amnesia produced by thiamine deficiency: The role of time of insult. *Behavioural Brain Research 148* (1–2), 93–105.

Plomin, R., DeFries, J., McClearn, G., & Rutter, M. (1997). *Behavioral genetics: A primer* (3rd edition). New York: Freeman.

Plotkin, H. (1997). *Evolution in mind: An introduction to evolutionary psychology.* Cambridge, MA: Harvard University Press.

Plymale, M., Sloan, P., Johnson, M., Snapp, J., & LaFountain, P. (2001). Junior medical students' perceptions of an introductory hospice experience. *Hospice Journal, 15,* 41–51.

Polak, A., & Harris, P. (1999). Deception by young children following noncompliance. *Developmental Psychology, 35* (2), 561–568.

Pollak, S., Cicchetti, D., Hornung, K., & Reed, A. (2000). Recognizing emotion in faces: Developmental effects of child abuse and neglect. *Developmental Psychology, 35* (5), 679–688.

Pollack, W. (1998). *Real boys: Rescuing our sons from the myths of boyhood.* New York: Henry Holt.

Pomerantz, E., & Rudolph, K. (2003). What ensues from emotional distress? Implications for competence estimation. *Child Development, 74* (2), 329–345.

Popenoe, D. (1996). *Life without father.* New York: Martin Kessler Books.

Postman, N. (1982). *The disappearance of childhood.* New York: Dell.

Povinelli, D. & Giambrone, S. (2001). Reasoning about beliefs: A human specialization. *Child Development, 72* (3), 691–695.

Powell, C. (with Joseph Persico). (1995). *My American Journey.* New York: Random House.

Prencipe, A., & Helwig, C. (2002). The development of reasoning about the teaching of values in school and family contexts. *Child Development, 73* (3), 841–856.

Preyer, W. (1882). *The mind of the child.* New York: Appleton.

Pritham, U., & Sammaons, L. (1993). Korean's women's attitudes toward pregnancy and prenatal care. *Health Care, Women Int, 14,* 145.

Pruchno, R. (1999). Raising grandchildren: The experiences of black and white grandmothers. *The Gerontologist, 39* (2), 209–221.

Purugganan, O., Stein, R., Silver, E., & Benenson, B. (2000). Exposure to violence among urban school-aged children: Is it only on television? *Pediatrics, 106* (4), 949–953.

Purves, W., Sadava, D., Orians, G., & Heller, H. (2004). *Life: The science of biology.* New York: Freeman.

Putman, M. (2000). Risks associated with gestational age and birth weight. In S. Mattson & J. Smith (Eds.), *Core curriculum for maternal-newborn nursing.* Philadelphia: W. B. Saunders.

Putnam, S., Sanson, A., & Rothbart, M. (2002). Child temperament and parenting. In M. Bornstein (Ed.), *Handbook of parenting* (2nd edition). Mahwah, NJ: Erlbaum.

Putnam, S., & Stifter, C. (2005). Behavioral approach-inhibition in toddlers: Prediction from infancy, positive and negative affective components, and relations with behavior problems. *Child Development, 76* (1), 212–226.

Quality counts. (2004, January 8). *Education Week, 23.*

Qualls, S. H., Segal, D. L., Norman, S., Niederehe, G., & Gallagher-Thompson, D. (2002). Psychologists in practice with older adults: Current patterns, sources of training, and need for continued education. *Professional Psychology: Research & Practice, 33* (5), 435–442.

Range, L. M., & Stringer, T. A. (1996). Reasons for living and coping abilities among older adults. *International Journal of Aging and Human Development, 43* (1), 1–5.

Ratey, J. (2001). *A user's guide to the brain.* New York: Pantheon.

Ratner, P. A. (1998). Modeling acts of aggression and dominance as wife abuse and exploring their adverse health effects. *Journal of Marriage and the Family, 60,* 453–465.

Rawson, N. E., Gomez, G., Cowart, B., Restrepo, D., Meisami, E., & Mikhail, L., et al. (1998). Part XVII: Aging and the chemical senses. In C. Murphy (Ed.), *Olfaction and taste XII: An international symposium; Annals of the New York Academy of Sciences: Volume 855. International Symposium on Olfaction and Taste XII, 1997, San Diego, CA,*

US. New York: New York Academy of Sciences, 701–737.

Reed, K., Doty, D. H., & May, D. R. (2005). The impact of aging on self-efficacy and computer skill acquisition. *Journal of Managerial Issues, 17* (2), 212–229.

Reid, L., & Radhakrishnan, P. (2003). Race matters: The relation between race and general campus climate. *Cultural Diversity and Ethnic Minority Psychology, 9* (3), 236–275.

Reinke, B., Ellicott, A., Harris, R., & Hancock, E. (1985). Timing of psychosocial change in women's lives. *Human Development, 28* (2), 259–280.

Reisberg, L. (2000, January 28). Student stress is rising, especially among women. *The Chronicle of Higher Education,* A521.

Rensberger, B. (1996). *Life itself: Exploring the realm of the living cell.* New York: Oxford University Press.

Restak, R. (2001). *The secret life of the brain.* Washington, D.C.: The Dana Press & The Joseph Henry Press.

Reyes, B. (1997, October 13). More marrying outside of racial group, data show. *The Boston Globe,* p. A1.

Rich, M. (1999). Pediatricians should educate parents, youth about media's effects. *AAAP News, 13* (5), 28–29.

Richardson, R. (2006). *William James: In the maelstrom of American modernism.* Boston: Houghton Mifflin.)

Ridley, M. (2000). *Genome.* New York: HarperCollins.

Riedel, S. E., Fredman, L., & Langenberg, P. (1998). Associations among caregiving difficulties, burden, and rewards in caregivers to older post-rehabilitation patients. *Journal of Gerontology, 53B* (3), 165–174.

Roberts, L. J., & Leonard, K. E. (1998). An empirical typology of drinking partnerships and their relationship to marital functioning and drinking consequences. *Journal of Marriage and the Family, 60* (4), 515–526.

Robinson, J. D., & Cinciripini, P. M. (2006). The effects of stress and smoking on catecholaminergic and cardiovascular response. *Behavioral Medicine, 32* (1), 13–19.

Robinson, Kurpius, S. E., Nipcon, M. F., & Maresh, S. E. (2001). Mood, marriage and menopause. *Journal of Counseling Psychology, 48* (1), 77–84.

Rodkin, R. & Farmer, T. (2000). Heterogeneity of popular boys: Antisocial and prosocial configurations. *Developmental Psychology, 36* (1), 14–24.

Rodriguez, N., Mira, C., Myers, H., Morris, J., & Cardoza, D. (2003). Family or friends: Who plays a greater supportive role for Latino college students? *Cultural Diversity and Ethnic Minority Psychology, 9* (3), 236–250.

Roff, S. (2001). Suicide and the elderly: Issues for clinical practice. *Journal of Gerontological Social Work, 35* (2), 21–36.

Rogers, S. J., & White, L. (1998). Satisfaction with parenting: The role of marital happiness, family structure, and parents' gender. *Journal of Marriage and the Family, 60,* 293–308.

Rogoff, B. (1990). *Apprenticeship in thinking: Cognitive development in social context.* New York: Oxford University Press.

———. (2003). *The Cultural Nature of Human Development.* New York: Oxford University Press.

Ronge, L. (1998, October). Early fetal alcohol diagnosis helps patients over lifetime. *AAP News,* 14–16.

Rose, S. (2005). *The future of the brain.* NY: Oxford.

Roseman, M. (2007). Improving representation of divorcing parents and children. *American Journal of Family Law, 21* (1), 290–298.

Rosenbaum, J. (2004, Spring). It's time to tell the kids. *American Educator, 28,* 8–15, 41–42.

Rosenthal, S. (1996, July). Identifying risk-taking in teen girls. *Ob. Gyn. News,* 12.

Ross, R., Paganini-Hill, A., & Wan, P. (2000). Effective hormone replacement therapy on cancer risk. *Journal of the National Cancer Institute, 92,* 328–335.

Rosser, S. V. (2004). Using POWRE to ADVANCE: Institutional barriers identified by women scientists and engineers. *NWSA Journal,* 16(1), 50–79.

Rothbart, M. (1994). Emotional development: Changes in reactivity and self-regulation. In P. Ekman & R. Davidson (Eds.), *The nature of emotion.* Cambridge, England: Oxford University Press.

Rothbart, M., & Bates, J. (2006). Temperament. In W. Damon (Series Ed.) & N. Eisenberg (Volume Ed.), *Handbook of child psychology: Volume 3. Social, emotional, and personality development.* New York: John Wiley.

Rothbaum, F., Weisz, J., Pott, M., Miyake, M., & Morelli, G. (2000). Attachment and culture: Security in the United States and Japan. *American Psychologist, 55* (10), 1093–1104.

Rousseau, J. (1911). *Emile* (B. Foxley, Trans.). New York: Dutton.

Rowland, D. L., Greenleaf, W. J., Dorfman, L. J., & Davidson, J. M. (1993). Aging and sexual function in men. *Archives of Sexual Behavior, 22* (6), 545–557.

Roy, R., & Benenson, J. (2002). Sex and contextual effects on children's use of interference competition. *Developmental Psychology, 38* (2), 306–312.

Rubin, K. (2002). *The friendship factor.* New York: Viking.

Rubin, K., Bukowski, W., & Parker, J. (1998). Peer interactions, relationships, and groups. In W. Damon (Series Ed.) & N. Eisenberg (Volume Ed.), *Handbook of child psychology: Volume 4. Child psychology in practice.* New York: John Wiley.

———. (2006). Peer interactions, relationships, and groups. In W. Damon & R. Lerner (Series Eds.) & N. Eisenberg (Volume Ed.), *Handbook of child psychology: Volume 3. Social, emotional, and personality development.* New York: John Wiley

Rubin, K., Coplan, R., Nelson, L., Cheah, C., & Lagace-Sequin, D. (1999). Peer relationships in childhood. In M. Bornstein & M. Lamb (Eds.), *Developmental psychology: An advanced textbook.* Mahwah, NJ: Erlbaum.

Rubin, K., Fein, G., & Vandenberg, B. (1983). Play. In Paul Mussen (Series Ed.) and E. Mavis Hetherington, (Volume Ed.), *Handbook of child psychology: Volume 4. Socialization, personality, and social development.* New York: John Wiley.

Rubin, R. (1984). *Maternal identity and maternal experience.* New York: Springer.

Ruble, D., & Martin, C. (1998). Gender development. In W. Damon (Series Ed.) & N. Eisenberg (Volume Ed.), *Handbook of child psychology: Volume 3. Child psychology in practice.* New York: John Wiley.

Ruble, D., Martin, C., & Berenbaum, S. (2006). Gender development. In W. Damon & R. Lerner (Series Eds.) & N. Eisenberg (Volume Ed.), *Handbook of child psychology: Volume 3. Social, emotional, and personality development.* New York: John Wiley.

Ruffman, T., Slade, L., & Crowe, E. (2002). The relation between children's and mothers' mental state language and theory-of-mind understanding. *Child Development, 73* (3), 734–751.

Runions, K., & Keating, D. (2007). Young children's social information processing: Family antecedents and behavioral correlates. *Developmental Psychology, 43* (4), 838–849.

Rushton, J., & Ankney, C. D. (1997). Brain size and cognitive ability. *Psychonomic Bulletin and Review, 3* (1), 21–36.

Russell, C. H. (1989). *Good news about aging.* New York: John Wiley.

Rutter, M. (1983). School effects on pupil progress: Research findings and policy implications. *Child Development, 54* (1), 1–29.

———. (1995). Maternal deprivation. In M. Bornstein (Ed.), *Handbook of parenting: Volume 4. Applied and practical parenting.* Mahwah, NJ: Erlbaum.

———. (1997). Nature-nurture integration: The example of antisocial behavior. *American Psychologist, 52* (4), 390–398.

———. (2002a). Development and psychopathology. In M. Rutter and E. Taylor (Eds.). *Child and adolescent psychiatry.* London: Blackwell.

———. (2002b). Nature, nurture and development: From Evangelism through science toward policy and practice. *Child Development, 73* (1), 1–21.

———. (2006*). Genes and behavior.* Oxford: Blackwell.

Rutter, M., & Nikapota, A. (2006). Culture, ethnicity, society, and psychopathology. In M. Rutter and E. Taylor (Eds.), *Child and adolescent psychiatry.* London: Blackwell.

Rutter, M., & Rutter, M. (1993). *Developing minds.* New York: Basic.

Rutter, M., & Taylor, E. (Eds.). (2002). *Child and adolescent psychiatry.* London: Blackwell.

Rutter, V., & Schwartz, P. (2000). Gender, marriage, and diverse possibilities for cross-sex and same-sex pairs. In D. H. Demo, K. R. Allen, et al. (Eds.), *Handbook of family diversity* New York: Oxford University Press, 59–81.

Ryan, R. M. (1995). Psychological needs and the facilitation of integrative processes. *Journal of Personality, 63* (3), 397–427.

Rymer, R. (1993). Genie: *A scientific tragedy.* New York: Harper.

Saal, H. (1998). Alternative therapies for Down syndrome: Fact or false hope. *AAP News, 14* (5), 16.

Saarni, C., Campos, J., Camras, L., & Witherington, D. (2006). Emotional development: Action, communication, and understanding. In W. Damon & R. Lerner (Series Eds.) & N. Eisenberg (Volume Ed.), *Handbook of child psychology: Volume 3. Social, emotional, and personality/development.* New York: John Wiley.

Saarni, C., Mumme, D., & Campos, J. (1998). Emotional development: Action, communication, and understanding. In W. Damon (Series Ed.) & N. Eisenberg (Volume Ed.), *Handbook of child psychology: Volume 3. Social, emotional, and personality development.* New York: John Wiley.

Sadker, M., & Sadker, D. (1994). *Failing at fairness: How America's schools cheat girls.* New York: Scribner's.

Sadler, T. W. (1995). *Langman's medical embryology* (7th edition). Baltimore: Williams and Wilkins.

Sales, E. (1978). Women's adult development. In I. Fieze (Ed.), *Women and sex roles.* New York: Norton.

Salinger, J. D. (1945). *The catcher in the rye.* Boston: Little, Brown.

Salter, D., McMillan, D., Richards, M., Talbot, T. Hodges, J., Bentovim, A., Hastings, R., Stevenson, J., & Skuse, D. (2003). *The Lancet, 361* (9356), 471.

Saltus, R. (2000, July 4). *The man who fixes brains.* The Boston Globe, 1, 2.

Sameroff, A., & Haith, M. (Eds.), (1996). *The five to seven year shift: The age of reason and responsibility.* Chicago: University of Chicago Press.

Samuelson, L., & Smith, L. (2000). Grounding development in cognitive processes. *Child Development, 71* (1), 98–106.

Sansavini, A., Bertoncini, J., & Giovanelli, G. (1997). Newborns discriminate the rhythm of multisyllabic words. *Developmental Psychology, 33* (1), 3–11.

Santelli, J., Brener, N., Lowry, R., Bhatt, A., & Zabin, L. (1998). Multiple sexual partners among U.S. adolescents and young adults. *Family Planning Perspectives, 30* (6), 271–275.

Saul, J. (1997). Adult education and religion. *Adult Education Quarterly, 47* (3/4), 169.

Saunders, J. B. (1989). The efficacy of treatment for drinking problems. Special issue: Psychiatry and the addictions. *International Review of Psychiatry, 1* (1), 121–137. Saunders.

Savage, M. P., & Holcomb, D. R. (1999). Adolescent female athletes' sexual risk-taking behaviors. *Journal of Youth and Adolescence, 28,* 595–602.

Schacter, D. (1996). *Searching for memory.* New York: Basic Books.

Schaie, K. W. (1994). The course of adult intellectual development. *American Psychologist, 49* (4), 304–313.

Schaie, K. W., & Hertzog, C. (1983). Fourteen-year cohort-sequential analyses of adult intellectual development. *Developmental Psychology, 19* (4), 531–543.

Schairer, C., & others. (2000). Menopausal estrogen and estrogen-progestin replacement therapy and breast-cancer risk. *Journal of the American Medical Association, 283* (4), 485–491.

Schechter, M., & Roberge, L. (1976). Child sexual abuse. In *Child abuse and neglect: The family and the community,* (R. Helfer & C. Kempe, Eds.). Ballinger: Cambridge, MA.

Schieman, S. (2001). Age, education, and the sense of control. *Research on Aging, 23,* 153–162.

Schirrmacher, R. (1998). *Art and creative development for young children.* Albany, NY: Delmar.

Schmidt, H. G., Vermeulen, L., & Van der Molen, H. T. (2006). Long-term effects of problem-based learning: A comparison of competencies acquired by graduates of a problem-based and a conventional medical school. Medical *Education, 40* (6), 562–568.

Schneider, W., & Bjorklund, D. (1998). Memory. In D. Kuhn & R. Siegler (Volume Eds.), 1998. Cognitive, language, and perceptual development. In W. Damon (Series Ed.), *Handbook of child psychology.* New York: Wiley.

Schneider, W., & Pressley, M. (1997). *Memory development between two and twenty.* Mahwah, NJ: Erlbaum.

Schutz, P., & Lanehart, S. (Eds.). (2002). Emotions in education. *Educational Psychologist, 37* (2).

Schwartz, I. (2002). Sexual activity prior to coital interaction: A comparison between males and females. *Archives of Sexual Behavior, 28,* 63–69.

Scott, C. (2006). *Stem cell now.* NY: Pi Press.

Sebald, H. (1977). *Adolescence: A social psychological analysis* (2nd edition). Englewood Cliffs, NJ: Prentice Hall.

Segelken, R. (Dec 2005). Modifying our environment could slow or reverse obesity trend: changes in the home, workplace, school, community– even in clothing and dishware–could increase our level of physical activity and help us make better food choices. *Human Ecology, 33* (3), 6–10.

Seibert, S., & Kraimer, M. (2001). The five-factor model of personality and career success. J*ournal of Vocational Behavior, 58,* 1–21.

Seidman, S. (2000). *An educator's guide to adoption.* Silver Springs, MD: Celebrate Adoption.

Seifer, R., Schiller, M., & Sameroff, A. (1996). Attachment, maternal sensitivity, and infant temperament during the first year of life. *Developmental Psychology, 32* (1), 12–25.

Selman, R. (1980). *The growth of interpersonal understanding.* New York: Academic.

Seltz, J. (2000, May 28). Teen brains are different. *The Boston Globe,* E1, E5.

Selye, H. (1956). *The stress of life.* New York: McGraw-Hill.

———. (1975, October). Implications of stress concept. *New York State Journal of Medicine,* 2139–2145.

———. (1982). History and present status of the stress concept. In L. Goldberger & S. Breznitz (Eds.), *Handbook of stress: Theoretical and clinical aspects.* New York: The Free Press.

Senechal, M., & LeFevre, J. (2002). Parental involvement in the development of children's reading skill: A five-year longitudinal study. *Child Development, 73* (2), 445–460.

Seppa, N. (1996, August). Rwanda starts its long healing process. *APA Monitor,* p. 14.

Serbin, L., & Karp, J. (2004). Intergenerational studies of parenting and the transfer of risk from parent to child. In J. Lerner & A. Alberts (Eds.), *Current*

directions in developmental psychology. New Jersey: Prentice Hall, 71–77.

Shaffer, D., & Pfeffer, C. (2001). Practice parameter for assessment and treatment of children and adolescents with suicidal behavior. *Journal of the American Academy of Child and Adolescent Psychiatry, 40,* 24S–51S.

Shapiro, J. (2000). Euthanasia's home. *Annual Editions: Aging.* Sluice Dock, CT: Dushkin/McGraw-Hill.

Sharpe, P. S., Jackson, K. L., White, C., Vaca, V., Hickey, T., Gu, J., & Otterness, C. (1997). Effects of a one-year physical activity intervention for older adults at congregate nutrition sites. *The Gerontologist, 37* (2), 208–215.

Shavers, B. L., & Shavers, B. S. (2006). Racism and health inequity among Americans. *Journal of the National Medical Association, 98,* 386–396.

Sheldon, K., & Kasser, T. (2001). Getting older, getting better? Personal striving and psychological maturity across the life span. *Developmental Psychology, 37,* 491–501.

Shifrin, D. (1998). Three-year study documents nature of television violence. *AAP News, 14* (8), 23.

Shin, Y. (1999). The effects of a walking exercise program on physical function and emotional state of elderly Korean women. *Public Health Nursing, 16* (2), 146–154.

Shore, B. (1996). *Culture in mind: Cognition, culture, and the problem of meaning.* New York: Oxford University Press.

Shore, R. (1997). *Rethinking the brain: New insights into early development.* New York: Families and Work Institute.

Short, J. (2001). Youth collectivities and adolescent violence. In S. White (Ed.), *Handbook of youth and justice. The Plenum series in crime and justice.* New York: Kluwer/ Plenum, 237–264.

———. (2005). *The genome war.* New York: Ballantine

Shuey, D., Babishangire, B., Omiat, S., & Bagarukayo, H. (1999). Increased sexual abstinence among in-school adolescents as a result of school health education in Soroti district, Uganda. *Health Education Research, 14,* 411–419.

Siegler, R. (1996). *Emerging minds: The process of change in children's thinking.* New York: Oxford University Press.

———. (1998). *Children's thinking* (3rd edition). Upper Saddle River, NJ: Prentice Hall.

———. (2000). The rebirth of children's learning. *Child Development, 71* (1), 26–35.

Siegler, R., & Alibali, M. (2005). Children's thinking. Upper Saddle River, NJ: Prentice Hall.

Siegler, R, R., Deloache, J., & Eisenberg, N. (2006). *How children develop*. New York: Worth.

Simms, M., Dubowitz, H., & Szilagyi, M. (2000). Health care needs of children in the foster care system. *Pediatrics, 106* (4), 909–918.

Simons, R. L., Gordon, L. C., Conger, R. D., & Lorenx, F. O. (1999). Explaining the higher incidence of problems among children of divorce compared with those in two-parent families. *Journal of Marriage and the Family, 61* (1), 1020–1033.

Simonton, D. K. (1975). Age and literary creativity. *Journal of Cross-cultural Creativity, 6* (2), 259–277.

———. (1976). Biographical determinants of achieved eminence. *Journal of Personality and Social Psychology, 33* (2), 218–276.

———. (1977a). Creativity, age and stress. *Journal of Personality and Social Psychology, 35,* 791–804.

———. (1977b). Eminence, creativity and geographical marginality. *Journal of Personality and Social Psychology, 35,* 805–816.

———. (1993). Blind variation, chance configurations, and creative genius. *Psychological Inquiries, 4* (2), 225–228.

Simpson, J., Rholes, W., & Phillips, D. (1996). Conflict in close relationships: An attachment perspective. *Journal of Personality & Social Psychology, 71* (5), 899–914.

Simpson, M. J. (1996). Life as experienced in not-so-empty-nest households: A social constructionist inquiry. (Doctoral dissertation, //www.il.proquest.com/umi/]). *Dissertation Abstracts International: Section B: The Sciences & Engineering, 56* (10-B), 5839. (UMI Dissertation Order Number AAM9605730)

Singleton, J. (2000, Summer). Women caring for elderly family members: Shaping non-traditional work and family initiatives. *Journal of Comparative Family Studies, 31*(3), 367–375.

Skinner, B. F. (1938). *The behavior of organisms*. New York: Macmillan.

———. (1953). *Science and human nature*. New York: Macmillan.

———. (1957). *Verbal behavior*. New York: Appleton-Century-Crofts.

———. (1968). *The technology of teaching*. New York: Appleton-Century-Crofts.

———. (1971). *Beyond freedom and dignity*. New York: Knopf.

———. (1974). *About behaviorism*. New York: Knopf.

———. (1983). *A matter of consequences*. New York: Knopf.

Sleek, S. (1997). Weisel emphasizes need to thank elderly. *APA Monitor, 28* (10), 23.

Smith, D. (1997). Centenarians: Human longevity outliers. *The Gerontologist, 37* (2), 200–207.

———. (2002). The theory heard 'round the world. *Monitor on Psychology, 33* (9), 28–32.

Smith, D. B., & Moen, P. (1998). Spousal influence on retirement: His, her and their perceptions. *Journal of Marriage and the Family, 60,* 734–744.

Smith, G. (2005). *The genomics age*. New York: American Management Association.

Smith, J., & Baltes, P. (1999). Lifespan perspectives on development. In M. Bornstein & M. Lamb (Eds.), *Developmental psychology: An advanced textbook* Mahwah, NJ: Erlbaum, 47–73.

Smith, K. (2000). Normal childbirth. In S. Mattson & J. Smith (Eds.), *Core curriculum for maternal-newborn nursing*. Philadelphia: W. B. Saunders.

Smock, P., Manning, W., & Gupta, S. (1999). The effect of marriage and divorce on women's economic well-being. *American Sociological Review, 64,* 794–812.

Smotherman, W., & Robinson, S. (1996). The development of behavior before birth. *Developmental Psychology, 33* (3), 425–434.

Snowdon, D. (1997). Aging and Alzheimer's disease: Lessons from the nun study. *The Gerontologist, 37* (2), 150–156.

Snyder, H., Sickmund, M., & Poe-Yamagata, E. (1996). *Update on violence*. Washington, D.C.: Office of Justice.

Söderlund, H., Nyberg, L., Adolfsson, R., Nilsson, L., & Launer, L. J. (2003). High prevalence of white matter hyperintensities in normal aging: Relation to blood pressure and cognition. Cortex, *39* (4–5), 1093–1105.

Solm, M. (2004). Freud returns. *Scientific American, 290* (5), 82–89.

Spar, D. (2006). *The baby business*. Cambridge, MA: Harvard Business School Press.

Spira, E., Bracken, S., & Fischel, J. (2005). Predicting improvement after first-grade reading difficulties: The effects of oral language, emergent literacy, and behavior skills. *Developmental Psychology, 41* (1) 225–234.

Sprecher, S. (1999). "I love you more today than yesterday." *Journal of Personality and Social Psychology, 76* (1), 46–53.

Squire, L., & Kandel, E. (2000). *Memory: From mind to molecule*. New York: Scientific American Press.

Srivastava, A. (2003). Resilience and development of positive life adaptations. *Psychology & Developing Societies, 15* (1), 117–121.

Srivastava, S., John, O. P., Gosling, S. D., & Potter, J. (2003). Development of personality in early and middle adulthood: Set like plaster or persistent change? *Journal of Personality and Social Psychology, 84,* 104–116.

Sroufe, A. (1995). *Emotional development: The organization of emotional life in the early years*. New York: Cambridge University Press.

Statistical Abstract of the United States. (1995). *Gender and suicide*. Washington, D.C.: U.S. Government Printing Office.

Stein, A., & Barnes, J. (2002). Feeding and sleep disorders. In M. Rutter and E. Taylor (Eds.), *Child and adolescent psychiatry*. London: Blackwell.

Stepp, L. (2000). *Our last best shot*. New York: Riverhead.

Stern, D., Rahn, M. L., & Chung, Y. P. (1998). Design of work-based learning for students in the United States. *Youth & Society, 29* (4), 471–502.

Sternberg, R. (1988). *The triarchic mind: A new theory of human intelligence*. New York: Viking.

———. (1990). *Metaphors of mind: Conceptions of the nature of intelligence*. New York: Cambridge University Press.

———. (1996). *Successful intelligence.* New York: Simon & Schuster.

———. (1997). Construct validation of a triangular love scale. *European Journal of Social Psychology, 27,* 313–335.

———. (2000a). Cross-disciplinary verification of theories: The case of the triarchic theory. *History of Psychology, 3* (2), 177–179.

———. (2000b). What's your love story? *Psychology Today, 32* (4), 52–59.

———. (2002). *Why smart people can be so stupid.* New Haven, CT: Yale University Press.

———. (2003). *Cognitive psychology.* Belmont, CA: Wadsworth/Thompson.

———. (2004). Culture and intelligence. *American Psychologies, 59* (5), 325–338.

———. (2006). *Cognitive psychology.* Belmont, CA: Wadsworth.

Sternberg, R. (Ed.). (2000). *Handbook of intelligence.* New York: Cambridge University Press.

Sternberg, R., & Davidson, J. (1995). *The nature of insight.* Cambridge, MA: M.I.T. Press.

Sternberg, R., & Lubart, T. (1995). *Defying the crowd: Cultivating creativity in a culture of conformity.* New York: The Free Press.

Sterns, H. L., & Miklos, S. M. (1995). The aging worker in a changing environment: Organizational and individual issues. *Journal of Vocational Behavior, 47* (2), 248–268.

Stevens, J. C., & Cain, W. S. (1987). Old-age deficits in the sense of smell as gauged by thresholds, magnitude matching, and odor identification. *Psychology & Aging, 2,* 36–42.

Stevens-Simon, C., & Kaplan, D. (1998). Teen childbearing trends. *Pediatrics, 102* (5), 1205–1207.

Steward, E. (1995). *Beginning writers in the zone of proximal development.* Hillsdale, NJ: Erlbaum.

Stewart, A., & Ostrove, J. (1998). Women's personality in middle-age. *American Psychologist, 53* (11), 1185–1195.

Steyer, J. (2002). *The other parent.* New York: Atria Books.

Stice, E., Presenell, K., & Bearman, S. (2001). Relation of early menarche to depression, eating disorders, substance abuse, and comorbid psychopathology among adolescent girls. *Developmental Psychology, 37,* 608–619.

Stimmel, B. (1991). *The facts about drug use.* New York: Consumer Report Books.

Stipek, D., & Ryan, R. (1997). Economically disadvantaged preschoolers: Ready to learn but further to go. *Developmental Psychology, 33* (4), 711–723.

Stolberg, S. (2000, June 6). Despite ferment, gene therapy progresses. *The New York Times,* D1, D4.

Stossel, S. (1997). The man who counts the killings. *Atlantic Monthly, 279* (5), 86–104.

Strasburger, V., & Donnerstein, E. (1999). Children, adolescents, and the media. *Pediatrics, 103* (1), 129–149.

Stravynski, A., & Boyer, R. (2001). Loneliness in relation to suicide ideation and parasuicide: A population-wide study. *Suicide & Life-Threatening Behavior, 31,* 32–40.

Strough, J., Berg, C., & Sansone, C. (1996). Goals for solving everyday problems across the lifespan: Age and gender differences in the salience of interpersonal concerns. *Developmental Psychology, 32* (6), 1106–1115.

Sturdevant, M. S., & Spear, B. (2002). Adolescent psychosocial development. *Journal of the American Dietetic Association, 102,* S30–33.

Substance Abuse and Mental Health Services Administration. (1999). *Cigar smoking.* Washington, D.C.: Author.

Sudnow, D. (1967). *Passing on.* Englewood Cliffs, NJ: Prentice Hall.

Sugarman, L. (1986). *Lifespan development: Concepts, theories and interventions.* New York: Methuen.

Sullivan, J., Seem, D.L., & Chabalewski, F. (1999). Determining brain death. *Critical Care Nurse, 19* (2), 37–46.

Sun, Y. (2001). Family environment and adolescents' well-being before and after parents' marital disruption: A longitudinal analysis. *Journal of Marriage and the Family, 63,* 697–713.

Surjan, L., Devald, J., & Palfalvi, L. (1973). Epidemiology of hearing loss. *Audiology, 12,* pp. 396–410.

Suzuki, Y., Critchley, H. D., Suckling, J., Fukuda, R., Williams, S. C. R., & Andrew, C., et al. (2001). Functional magnetic resonance imaging of odor identification: The effect of aging. *Journals of Gerontology: Series A: Biological Sciences & Medical Sciences, 56* (12), M756–M760.

Swedo, S., Rettew, D., Kuppenheimer, M., Lum, D., Dolan, S., & Goldberger, E. (1991). Can adolescent suicide-attempters be distinguished from at-risk adolescents? *Pediatrics, 88* (5), 620–629.

Szechter, L., & Liben, L. (2007). Children's aesthetic understanding of photographic art and the quality of art-related parent-child interactions. *Child Development, 78* (3), 879–894.

Szkrybalo, J., & Ruble, D. (1999). "God made me a girl": Sex-category constancy judgments and explanations revisited. *Developmental Psychology, 35* (2), 392–402.

Szuchman, L., & Muscarella, F. (Eds.). (2000). *Psychological perspectives on human sexuality.* New York: John Wiley.

Tager-Flusberg, H. (1997). Putting words together: Morphology and syntax in the preschool years. In J. Gleason (Ed.), *The development of language.* Boston: Allyn & Bacon.

Talbot, M. (1998). Older widows' attitudes towards men and remarriage. *Journal of Aging Studies, 12* (4), 429–449.

Tamborlane, W. (1997). *The Yale guide to children's nutrition.* New Haven, CT: Yale University Press.

Tanner, J. (1990). *Fetus into man.* Cambridge, MA: Harvard University Press.

———. (1989). *Fetus into man.* Cambridge, MA: Harvard University Press.

Tapley, D., & Todd, W. D. (Eds.). (1988). *Complete guide to pregnancy.* New York: Crown.

Tardif, T., & Wellman, H. (2000). Acquisition of mental state language in Mandarin- and Cantonese-speaking children. *Developmental Psychology, 36* (1), 25–43.

Task Force on Sudden Infant Death Syndrome. (2005). The changing concept of sudden infant death syndrome. *Pediatrics, 116* (5), 1245–1255.

Taub, H. (1975). Effects of coding cues upon short-term memory. *Developmental Psychology, 11* (2), 254.

Taylor, M. (1996). The development of children's beliefs about social and biological aspects of gender. *Child Development, 67,* 1555–1571.

Taylor, N. (1995). Gay and lesbian youth. In T. DeCrescenzo. (Ed.), *Helping gay and lesbian youth.* New York: Haworth.

Terman, L. M. (1925). *Genetic studies of genius.* Palo Alto, CA: Stanford University Press.

The Harris Poll. (2005). *Majorities of U.S. adults favor euthanasia and physician-assisted suicide by more than two-to-one, #32.*

Thelen, E. (1995). Motor development: A new synthesis. *American Psychologist, 50* (2), 79–95.

Thelen, E., & Smith, L. (2006). Dynamic Systems theories. In W. Damon & R. Lerner (Series Eds.) & R. Lerner (Volume Ed.), *Handbook of child psychology: Volume 1. Theoretical models of human development.* New York: John Wiley.

Thiele, D. M., & Whelan, T.A. (2006). The nature and dimensions of the grandparent role (Author abstract). *Marriage & Family Review, 40* (1), 93–109.

Thies, K. (2006). Resiliency. In K. Theis & J. Travers (Eds.), *Handbook of human development for health care professionals.* Sudbury, MA: Jones & Bartlett.

Thies, K., & Travers, J. (2001). *Growth and development through the lifespan.* Thorofare, NJ: Slack.

Thoma, S., & Rest, J. (1999). The relationship between moral decision making and patterns of consolidation and transition in moral judgment development. *Developmental Psychology, 35* (2), 323–334.

Thomas, R. (1992). *Comparing theories of child development.* Belmont, CA: Wadsworth.

Thomasello, M. (2004). Culture and cognitive development. In J. Lerner & A. Alberts (Eds.), *Current directions in developmental psychology.* Englewood Cliffs, NJ: Prentice Hall, 49–54.

Thompson, J. (1998). Embryonic stem cell lines derived from human blastocysts. *Science, 282,* 1145–1147.

Thompson, J. A., & Bunderson, J. S. (2001). Work–nonwork conflict and the phenomenology of time. *Work and Occupations, 28* (1), 17–39.

Thompson, L., & Kelly-Vance, L. (2001). The impact of mentoring on academic achievement of at-risk youth. *Children & Youth Services Review, 23,* 227–242.

Thompson, P. (1998). Adolescents from families of divorce: Vulnerability to physiological and psychological disturbances. *Journal of Psychosocial Nursing, 36,* 34–41.

Thompson, R. (1998). Early sociopersonality development. In W. Damon (Series Ed.) & N. Eisenberg (Volume Ed.),

Handbook of child psychology: Volume 3. Social, emotional, and personality development. New York: John Wiley.

———. (1999). The individual child: Temperament, emotion, self, and personality. In M. Bornstein & M. Lamb (Eds.), *Developmental psychology: An advanced textbook.* Mahwah, NJ: Erlbaum.

———. (2000). The legacy of early attachments. *Child Development, 71* (1), 145–152.

———. (2006). The development of the person: Social understanding, relationships, conscience, self. In W. Damon & R. Lerner (Series Eds.) & N. Eisenberg (Volume Ed.), *Handbook of child psychology: Volume 3. Social, emotional, and personality development.* New York: John Wiley.

Tingus, K. D., Heger, A. H., Foy, D. W., & Leskin, G. A. (1996). Factors associated with entry into therapy in children evaluated for sexual abuse. *Child Abuse and Neglect, 20* (1), 63–68.

Tomada, G., & Schneider, B. (1997). Relational aggression, gender, and peer acceptance: Invariance across culture, stability over time, and concordance among informants. *Developmental Psychology, 33* (4), 601–609.

Tomasello, M. (2003). *Constructing a language.* Cambridge, MA: Harvard University Press.

Toussaint, L., & Webb, J.R. (2005). Gender differences in the relationship between empathy and forgiveness. *The Journal of Social Psychology, 145* (6), 673–686.

Toussaint, O. (2003). Normal brain aging: A commentary. *Neurobiology of Aging, 24* (Suppl. 1), S129–S130.

Townsend Letter for Doctors and Patients. (2003). *Caregiver stress syndrome. (Letters to the Editor),* 144–146.

Travers, B., & Travers, J. (2006). *Discovering children's literature in the 21st century.* Boston: Houghton Mifflin.

Travers, J., Elliott, S., & Kratochwill, T. (1993). *Educational psychology: Effective teaching, effective learning.* Dubuque, IA: Brown & Benchmark.

Treboux, D., Crowell, J., & Waters, E. (2004). When "new" meets "old": Configurations of adult attachment representations and their implications for marital functioning. *Developmental Psychology, 40* (2), 295–314.

Trelease, J. (2001). *Read-aloud handbook* (5th edition). New York: Penguin.

Tremblay, K., Piskosz, M., & Souza, P. (2003). Effects of age and age-related hearing loss on the neural representation of speech cues. *Clinical Neurophysiology, 114* (7), 1332–1343.

Tremblay, R., Hartup, W., & Archer, J. (2005). *Developmental origins of aggression.* NY: Guilford.

Tsaousis, I., & Nikolaou, I. (2001). The stability of the Five-Factor model of personality in personnel selection and assessment in Greece. *International Journal of Selection & Assessment, 9,* 290–301.

Tun, P. (1998). Fast noisy speech: Age difference in processing rapid speech with background noise. *Psychology & Aging, 13* (3), 424–434.

Turiel, E. (1998). The development of morality. In W. Damon (Series Ed.) & D. Kuhn & R. Siegler (Volume Eds.), *Handbook of child psychology: Volume 2. Cognition, perception, and language.* New York: John Wiley.

———. (2006). *Development and cultural change.* San Francisco: Jossey Bass.

Turner, J. S., & Helms, D. B. (1989). *Contemporary adulthood.* New York: Holt, Rinehart & Winston.

Turner, P., Runtz, M., & Galambos, N. (1999). Sexual abuse, pubertal timing, and subjective age in adolescent girls: A research note. *Journal of Reproductive & Infant Psychology, 17,* 111–118.

Tversky, A., & Kahneman, D. (1981). The framing of decisions and the psychology of choice. *Science, 211,* 453–458.

U.S. Census Bureau. (1996). *Statistical abstract of the United States.* Washington, D.C.: U.S. Government Printing Office.

———. (1999). *Vital statistics.* Washington, D.C.: U.S. Government Printing Office.

———. (2001). *Annual Report.* Washington, D.C.: U.S. Government Printing Office.

———. (2002a). Grandparents living with own grandchildren under 18 years and responsibility for own grandchildren: Table PCT015 of the Census 2001 Supplementary Survey. Retrieved November 12, 2002, from http://factfinder.census.gov/servlet/ BasicFactsServlet.

———. (2004). *Vital Statistics.* Washington, D.C.: U.S. Census Bureau.

U.S. Department of Agriculture. (2004). *Food imbalances.* U.S. Government Printing Office. Washington, D.C.

U.S. Department of Health, Education, and Welfare. (1972). Ch 1, p. 30

U.S. Department of Health and Human Services. (1996). *Suicide rates.* Washington, D.C.: U.S. Department of Health and Human Services.

———. (2004). *Overview of findings from the 2002 national survey on drug use and health.* Substance Abuse and Mental Health Services Administration: Washington, D.C..

———. (2001). *Youth violence: A report of the surgeon general.* Washington, D.C..

U.S. National Center for Health Statistics. (1986). *Advance data from vital and health statistics, No. 125.* DHHS Pub. No. (PHS) 86–1250. Hyattsville, MD: Public Health Service.

Umberson, D., Anderson, K., Glick, J., & Shapiro, A. (1998). Domestic violence, personal control, and gender. *Journal of Marriage and the Family, 60* (3), 442–452.

Unger, R., & Crawford, M. (1996). *Woman and gender: A feminist psychology.* New York: McGraw-Hill.

UNICEF. (2005). *The state of the world's children 2006: Excluded and invisible.* Washington, D.C.: UNICEF.

Uzgiris, U., & Raeff, C. (1995). Play in parent-child interactions. In M. Bornstein (Ed.), *Handbook of parenting.* Hillsdale, NJ: Erlbaum.

Valliant, G. (2002). *Aging well.* Boston: Little, Brown.

Vaillant, G., & Mukamal, K. (June 2001). Successful aging. *American Journal of Psychiatry, 158* (6), 839–847.

Valsiner, J. (1998). The development of the concept of development: Historical and epistemiological perspectives. In R. M. Lerner (Ed.), *Handbook of child psychology: Volume 1. Theoretical models of human development.* New York: John Wiley.

Van der Heide, A., Deliens, L., Faisst, K., Nilstun, T., Norup, M., & Paci, E., et al. (2003). End-of-life decision-making in six European countries: Descriptive study. *Lancet, 362* (9381), 345–350.

van Hoof, A. (2000). The identity status approach: In need of fundamental revision and qualitative change. *Developmental Review, 19* (4), 622–647.

van Ness, P. H., & Kasl, S. V. (2003). Religion and cognitive dysfunction in an elderly cohort. *The Journals of Gerontology Series B: Psychological Sciences and Social Sciences* (58), 521–529.

Vartanian, L., & Powlishta, K. (2001). Demand characteristics and self-report measures of imaginary audience sensitivity: Implications for interpreting age differences in adolescent egocentrism. *Journal of Genetic Psychology, 162,* 187–200.

Vigil, J. D. (1996). Street baptism: Chicano gang initiation. *Human Organization, 55,* 149–153.

Volling, B., McElwain, N., & Miller, A. (2002). Emotion regulation in context: The jealousy complex between young siblings and its relations with child and family characteristics. *Child Development, 73* (2), 581–600.

Von Eye, A., & Schuster, C. (2000). The odds of resilience. *Child Development, 71* (3), 563–566.

vonGunten, C., Ferris, F., & Emanuel, L. (2000). Ensuring competency in end-of-life care: Communication and relational skills. *Journal of the American Medical Association, 284,* 3051–3057.

Vygotsky, L. S. (1962). *Thought and language.* Cambridge, MA: M.I.T. Press.

———. (1978). *Mind in society.* Cambridge, MA: Harvard University Press.

Wachowiak, F., & Clements, R. (1997). *Emphasis art.* Reading, MA: Addison-Wesley.

Wade, N. (2007). Clinics hold more embryos than thought. *The New York Times,* January 24,

Wakschlag, L., Chase-Lansdale, P., & Brooks-Gunn, J. (1996). Not just "Ghosts in the Nursery": Contemporaneous intergenerational relationships and parenting in young African-American families. *Child Development, 67,* 2131–2147.

Wakschlag, L., & Hans, S. (1999). Relation of maternal responsiveness during infancy to the development of behavior problems in high-risk youths. *Developmental Psychology, 35* (2), 569–579.

Walker, L. (2000). Psychology and domestic violence around the world. *American Psychologist, 54* (1), 21–29.

Walker, L., Hennig, K., & Krettenauer, T. (2000). Parent and peer contexts for children's moral reasoning development. *Child Development, 71* (4), 1033–1048.

Walker-Barnes, C. J., & Mason, C. A. (2004). Delinquency and substance use among gang-involved youth: The moderating role of parenting practices. *American Journal of Community Psychology, 34* (3-4), 235–251.

Wallace, M. (2000). In sexuality and intimacy. *Textbook of Gerontological Nursing.* St. Louis, MO: Mosby Year Book.

Wallerstein, J., & Corbin, S. B. (1999). The child and the vicissitudes of divorce. In R. M. Galatszer-Levy, L. Kraus et al. (Eds.), *The scientific basis of child custody decisions* New York: John Wiley, 73–95.

Wallerstein, J., Lewis, J., & Blakeslee, S. (2002). *The unexpected legacy of divorce.* New York: Hyperion.

Warhol, J. (Ed.). (1998). *New perspectives in early emotional development.* Skillman, NJ: Johnson & Johnson Pediatric Institute.

Wasti, S., & Cortina, L. (2002). Coping in context: sociocultural determinants of responses to sexual harassment. *Journal of Personality & Social Psychology, 83* (2), 394–405.

Watamura, S., Donzella, B., Alwin, J., & Gunnar, M. (2003). Morning-to-afternoon increases in cortisol concentrations for infants and toddlers at child care. Age differences and behavioral correlates. *Child development, 74* (4), 1006–1024.

Waterman, A. (1999). Identity, the identity statuses, and identity status development: A contemporary statement. *Developmental Review, 19* (4), 591–621.

Waters, E., & Cummings, E. M. (2000). A secure base from which to explore close relationships. *Child Development, 71* (1), 164–172.

Waters, E., Hamilton, C., & Weinfield, N. (2000). The stability of attachment security from infancy to adolescence and early adulthood: General introduction. *Child Development, 71* (3), 678–683.

Waters, E., Kondo-Ikemura, K., Posada, G., & Richters, J. (1991). Learning to love: Mechanisms and milestones. In M. R. Gunnar & L. A. Sroufe (Eds.), *Minnesota Symposium in Child Psychology: Volume 23. Self-processes in development.* Hillsdale, NJ: Erlbaum, 217–255.

Waters, E., Merrick, S., Treboux, D., Crowell, J., & Albersheim, L. (2000). Attachment security in infancy and early adulthood: A twenty-year longitudinal study. *Child Development, 71* (3), 684–689.

Watson, J. (1930). *Behaviorism.* New York: Norton.

———. (1953). Lecture at Cold Spring Harbor.

———. (2003). *DNA: The secret of life.* New York: Knopf

Watson, M. (1995). The relation between anxiety and pretend play. In A. Slade & D. Wolf, (Eds.), *Children at play.* New York: Oxford University Press.

Wechsler, H. (1996). Alcohol and the American college campus: A report from the Harvard School of Public Health. *Change, 7/8,* 20–25, 60–62.

Wechsler, H., Davenport, A., Dowdall, G., Moeykens, B., & Castillo, S. (1994). Health and behavioral consequences of binge drinking in college: A national survey of students at 140 campuses. *JAMA, 272,* 1672–1677.

Wechsler, H., Molnar, B., Davenport, A., & Baer, J. (1999). College alcohol use: A full or empty glass? *Journal of American College Health, 47,* 247– 252.

Wechsler, H., Rigotti, N. A., Gledhill-Hoyt, J., & Lee, H. (1998). Increased levels of cigarette usage among college students: A cause for national concern. *Journal of the American Medical Association, 280* (19), 1673–1678.

Weigel, D., Devereux, P., Geoffrey, L., & Ballard-Reisch, D. (1998). A longitudinal study of adolescents' perceptions of support and stress: Stability and change. *Journal of Adolescent Research, 13* (2), 158–177.

Weinberg, N. (2004). Music and the brain. *Scientific American,* November, 89–95.

Weinfield, N., Sroufe, A., & Egeland, B. (2000). Attachment from infancy to early adulthood in a high-risk sample: Continuity, discontinuity, and their correlates. *Child Development, 71* (3), 695–702.

Weinraub, M., & Gringlas, M. (1995). Single parenthood. In M. Bornstein (Ed.), *Handbook of parenting: Volume 3.* Mahwah, NJ: Erlbaum.

Weinrich, J. D. (1987). A new socio-biological theory of homosexuality applicable to societies with universal marriage. *Ethology and Sociobiology, 8* (1), 37–47.

Weisner, T. (2000). Culture, childhood, and progress in sub-Saharan Africa. In L. Harrison & S. Huntington

(Eds.), *Culture matters.* New York: Basic Books.

Weissberg, R., & Greenberg, M. (1998). School and community competence-enhancement and prevention programs. In W. Damon (Series Ed.) & I. Sigel & K. Renninger (Volume Eds.), *Handbook of child psychology: Volume 4. Child psychology in practice.* New York: John Wiley.

Weissman, G. (2002). *The year of the genome.* New York: Times Books.

Weist, M., & Cooley-Quille, M. (2001). Advancing efforts to address youth violence involvement. *Journal of Clinical Child Psychology, 30,* 147–151.

Weksler, M. (1999). Obesity: Age-associated weight gain and the development of disease. *Geriatrics, 54,* 57–64.

Wellbery, C. (2005). IPT vs. CGT for the patient with complicated grief. *American Family Physician, 72* (11), 2338–2339.

Wellman, H., Cross, D., & Watson, J. (2001). Meta-analysis of theory-of-mind development: The truth about false belief. *Child Development, 72* (3), 655–684.

Werker, J., & Tees, R. (1999). Influences on infant speech processing: Toward a new synthesis. In J. Spence, J. Darley, & D. Foss (Eds.), *Annual review of psychology.* Palo Alto, CA: Annual Reviews.

Werner, E. (1995). Resilience in development. *Currents Directions in Psychological Science,* 4, 81–85.

Werner, E., & Smith, R. (1992). *Overcoming the odds: High-risk children from birth to adulthood.* Ithaca, NY: Cornell University Press.

———. (2001). *Journeys from childhood to midlife: Risk, resilience, and recovery.* NY: Cornell University Press.

Wertheimer, M. (1961). Psychomotor coordination of auditory-visual space at birth. *Science, 134,* 1692.

———. (1962). Psychomotor coordination of auditory-visual space at birth. *Science, 134,* 213–216.

Wertsch, J., & Tulviste, P. (1992). L. S. Vygotsky and contemporary developmental psychology. *Developmental Psychology, 28* (4), 548–557.

Westerhof, G., & others. (November 2001). Beyond life satisfaction: Lay conceptions of well-being among

middle-aged and elderly adults. *Social Indicators Research, 56* (2), 179–203.

Westin, D. Psychoanalytic theories. (2000). In A. Kazdin (Ed.), *Encyclopedia of psychology.* Washington, D.C.: American Psychological Association.

Whitaker, R., & Dietz, W. (1997). Predicting obesity in young adulthood from childhood and parental obesity. *New England Journal of Medicine, 337* (13), 869–873.

Whitbeck, L., Hoyt, D. R., & Huck, S. M. (1994). Early family relationships, intergenerational solidarity, and support provided to parents by their adult children. *Journal of Gerontology: Social Sciences, 49* (2), S85–S94.

Whitbeck, L., & others. (2001). Deviant behavior and victimization among homeless and runaway adolescents. *Journal of Interpersonal Violence, 16,* 1175–1204.

Whitbourne, S. (1999). Physical changes. In J. C. Cavanaugh & S. K. Whitbourne (Eds.), *Gerontology: An interdisciplinary perspective* New York: Oxford University Press, 91–122.

———. (2000). The normal aging process. In S. Krauss (Ed.), *Psychopathology in later adulthood: Wiley series on adulthood and aging* New York: John Wiley, 27–59.

———. (2001a). *Adult development & aging: Biopsychosocial perspectives.* New York: John Wiley.

———. (2001b). The physical aging process in midlife: Interactions with psychological and sociocultural factors. In M. E. Lachman (Ed.), *Handbook of midlife development. Wiley series on adulthood and aging.* New York: John Wiley, 109–155.

White, L. (1992). The effect of parental divorce and remarriage on parental support for adult children. *Journal of Family Issues, 13* (2), 234–250.

White, T. (2006). Code talk: Student discourse and participation with networked handhelds. *International Journal of Computer-Supported Collaborative Learning, 1* (3), 359.

Whitehurst, G., & Lonigan, C. (1998). Child development and emergent literacy. *Child Development, 69,* 848–872.

Whiting, W. L. IV, & Smith, A. D. (1997). Differential age-related processing limitations in recall and recognition tasks. *Psychology & Aging, 12* (2), 216–224.

Who's Who Special Report. (1997). *What parents of top teens don't know about their kids.* Lake Forest, IL: Educational Communications.

Wiederman, M. W., Pryor, T., & Morgan, C. D. (1996). The sexual experience of women diagnosed with anorexia nervosa or bulimia nervosa. *International Journal of Eating Disorders, 19* (2), 109–118.

Wiegman, O., & van Schie, E. (1998). Video game playing and its relations with aggressive and prosocial behaviour. *British Journal of Social Psychology, 37* (3), 367–378.

Wilbur, K., & McNeilly, D. (2001). Elder abuse and victimization. In J. E. Birren & K. W. Schaie (Eds.), *Handbook of the psychology of aging* (5th edition) San Diego: Academic Press, 569–591.

Wilgoren, J. (1999). Quality daycare, early, is tied to achievement as an adult. *The New York Times,* A16.

Wilkie, J. R., Ferree, M. M., & Ratcliff, K. S. (1998). Gender and fairness: Marital satisfaction in two-earner couples. *Journal of Marriage and the Family, 60,* 577–594.

Will, J., Self, P., & Data, N. (1976). Maternal behavior and perceived sex of infant. *American Journal of Orthopsychiatry, 46,* 135–139.

Willard, N. (2006). Flame Retardant, *School Library Journal, 52* (4), 55–57.

Willat, J. (2005). *Making sense of children's drawings.* Mahwah, NJ: Erlbaum.

Willemsen, E., Andrews, R., Karlin, B., & Willemsen, M. (2005). The ethics of the child custody process: Are the American Law Institute's guidelines the answer? *Child and Adolescent Work Journal, 22* (2), 183–202.

Williams, J., & Dunlop, L. (1999). Pubertal timing and self-reported delinquency among male adolescents. *Journal of Adolescence, 22,* 157–171.

Willmut, I., & Highfield, Roger. (2006). *After Dolly: The uses and misuses of human cloning.* New York: Norton.

Wilson, D., Gottfredson, D., & Najaka, S. (2001). School-based prevention of problem behaviors: A meta-analysis. *Journal of Quantitative Criminology, 17,* 247–272.

Wilson, J. (1993). *The moral sense.* New York: The Free Press.

Wilson, R., & Bennett, D. (2004). Cognitive activity and risk of Alzheimer's disease. In J. Lerner & A. Alberts (Eds.), *Current directions in developmental psychology.* Englewood Cliffs, NJ: Prentice Hall, 153–159.

Wise, P. M., Dubal, D. B., Wilson, M. E., Rau, S. W., & Liu, Y. (2001). Estrogens: Trophic and protective factors in the adult brain. *Frontiers in Neuroendocrinology, 22* (1), 33–66.

Wolf, R., & Pillemeer, K. (2000). Elder abuse and case outcome. *Journal of Applied Gerontology, 19,* 203–220.

Wolfinger, N. (1998). The effects of parental divorce on adult tobacco and alcohol consumption. *Journal of Health and Social Behavior, 39,* 254–269.

Wolford, B., McGee, T., Raque, T., & Coffey, O. D. (1996, August). Collaboration works for at-risk and delinquent youths. *Corrections Today,* 109–112.

Wolfson, M. (1989). *A review of the literature on feminist psychology.* Unpublished manuscript, Boston College, Chestnut Hill, MA.

Wolke, D., Skuse, D., & Reilly, S. (2007). The management of infant feeding problems. In P. Cooper & A. Stein (Eds.), *Feeding problems and eating disorders in children and adolescents.* Chur: Harwood Press.

Wong, S. (2006). *Dialogic approaches to TESOL.* Mahwah, NJ: Erlbaum.

Wong, T. Y. (2001). Effect of increasing age on cataract surgery outcomes in very elderly patients. *British Medical Journal, 322* (7294), 1104.

Woodruff-Pak, D. (1988). *Psychology and aging.* Englewood Cliffs, NJ: Prentice Hall.

Woodward, A., & Markman, E. (1998). Early word learning. In D. Kuhn & R. Siegler (Eds.), *Handbook of child psychology: Volume 2.* New York: John Wiley.

Woodward, K., & McCormick, J. (1996, November 25). The art of dying well (how Cardinal Joseph Bernardin set model for dying with grace). *Newsweek,* 22, 60.

Woodward, L. (2001). Life course outcomes of young people with anxiety disorders in adolescence. *Journal of the American Academy of Child & Adolescent Psychiatry, 40,* 1086–1093.

Woolfe, T., Want, S., & Siegal, M. (2002). Signposts to development: Theory of mind in deaf children. *Child Development, 73* (3), 768–778.

Wortman, C., & Boerner, K. (2007). Reactions to death of a loved one: Beyond the myths of coping with loss. In H. S. Friedman & R. C. Silver (Eds.), *Foundations of health Psychology.* New York: Oxford University Press.

Wortman, C., & Silver, R. (1989). The myths of coping with loss. *Journal of Consulting and Clinical Psychology, 57,* 349–357.

———. (2001). The myths of coping with loss revisited. In M. S. Stroebe, & R. O. Hansson (Eds.), *Handbook of bereavement research: Consequences, coping, and care.* Washington, D.C., 405–429. US: American Psychological Association; www.apa.org/books. From www.apa.org.proxy.bc.edu/books.

Wright, D. R., & Fitzpatrick, K. M. (2006). Violence and minority youth: The effects of risk and asset factors on fighting among African American children and adolescents. *Adolescence, 41* (162), 251–263.

Wright, J., Huston, A., Reitz, A., & Piemyat, S. (1994). Young children's perceptions of television reality: Determinants and developmental differences. *Developmental Psychology, 30* (2), 229–239.

Wright, P. J. (2006). PDE5 inhibitors compared. *Journal of Men's Health and Gender, 3* (4), 410.

Wright, V. (1999). Sleeping in adult beds risky for kids under 2. *AAP News, 15* (11), 32.

———. (2000, February). Knowledge, counseling can help prevent job injuries among teens. Elk Grove Village, IL.: American Association of Pediatrics News.

Wright, W. (1998). *Born that way: Genes, behavior, personality.* New York: Knopf.

Wyckoff, A. (1999). Consider religious, ethnic customs when diagnosing child abuse. *AAAP News, 13* (5), 18–19.

Yang, J., Dai, X., Yao, S., Cai, T., Gao, B., McCrae, R., Costa, P. (2002). Personality disorders and the five-factor model of personality in Chinese psychiatric patients. In P. T. Costa, Jr. & T. A. Widiger (Eds.), *Personality dis-orders and the five-factor model of personality*

(2nd edition). Washington, D.C.: American Psychological Association, 215–221.

Yeo, G., & Gallagher-Thompson, D. (Eds.). (2006). *Ethnicity and the dementias* (2nd edition). London: Routledge.

Yoder, K., & others. (2002). Event history analysis of antecedents to running away from home and being on the street. *American Behavioral Scientist. Special Issue: Advancing the Research Agenda on Homelessness: Politics and Realities, 45,* 51–65.

Young, R. A., Paseluikho, M. A., & Valach, L. (1997). The role of emotion in the construction of career in parent-adolescent conversations. *Journal of Counseling and Development, 76* (1), 36–44.

Youngblade, L. M., Theokas, C., Schulenberg, J., Curry, L., Huang, I., & Novak, M. (2007). Risk and promotive factors in families, schools, and communities. *Pediatrics, 119* (2), S47–54.

Yule, G. (1996). *The study of language.* Cambridge: Cambridge University Press.

Yunger, J., Carver, P., & Perry, D. (2004). Does gender identity influence children's psychological well-being? *Developmental Psychology, 40* (4), 572–582.

Yurgelun, T. (1998, November/December). Brain abnormalities in chronic schizophrenia. *Psychology Today,* 56–59.

Zarit, S., Stephens, M., Townsend, A., & Greene, R. (1998). Stress reduction for family caregivers: Effects of adult day care use. *Journal of Gerontology, 53B* (5), 267–277.

Zigler, E., & Finn-Stevenson, M. (1999). Applied developmental psychology. In M. Bornstein & M. Lamb, (Eds.), *Developmental psychology: An advanced textbook.* Mahwah, NJ: Erlbaum.

Zigler, E., & Hall, N. (2000). *Child development and social policy.* New York: McGraw-Hill.

Zigler, E., & Muenchow, S. (1992). *Head Start.* New York: Crown.

Zigler, E., & Styfco, S. (1994). *Head Start: Criticisms in a constructive context. American Psychologist, 49* (2), 127–132.

Zohar, A., & Bruno, R. (1997). Normative and pathological obsessive-compulsive behavior and ideation in childhood: A question of timing. *Journal of Child Psychology and Psychiatry and Allied Disciplines, 38,* 993–999.

Zucker, K. (2002). Gender identity disorder. In M. Rutter and E. Taylor (Eds.), *Child and adolescent psychiatry.* London: Blackwell.

Credits

Name Index

Subject Index